DA TIMES

DOG, OLD TRI

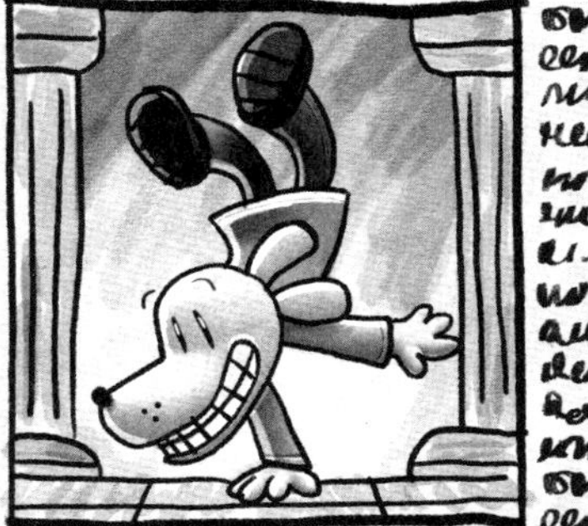

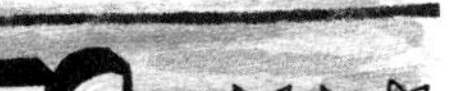

actually just fact

FIRST NO

SECOND ALSO NOT BEST

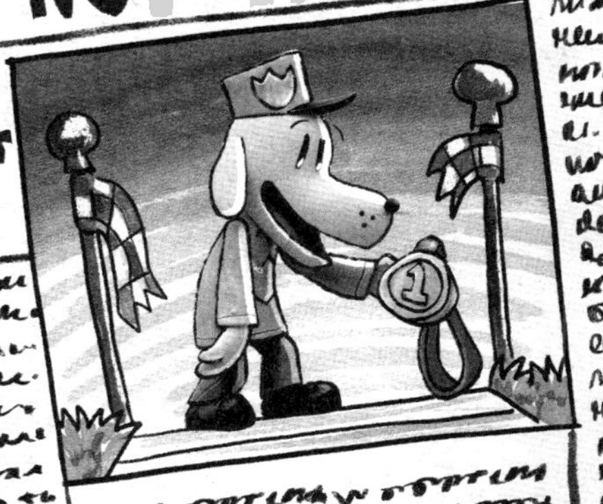

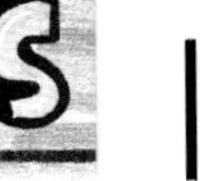

DA TIMES

ANOTHERDAY 11, 2024

DOG MAN GIVEN KEY TO

He deserves it and more.

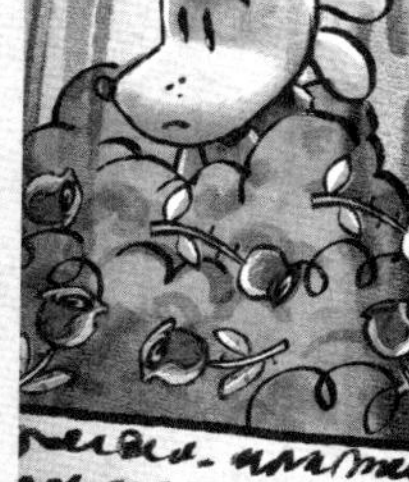

outlawed i

ANOTHERDAY 11, 2024

DA TIMES

LOSES POPULAR VOTE

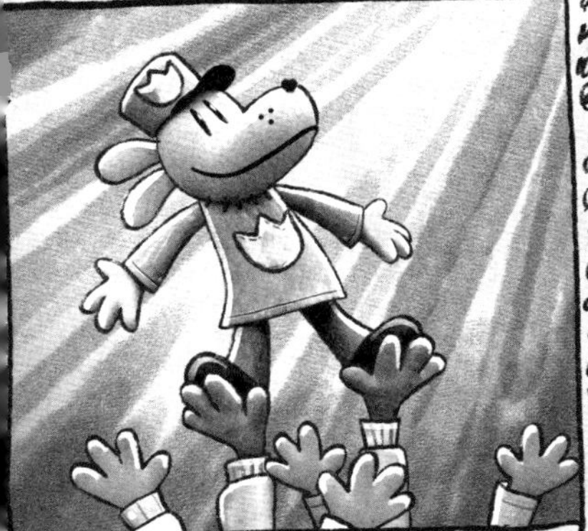

ACKS BETTER THAN MOM

3

OHKAY CITY

ANOTHERDAY 11, 2024

DA TIMES

Twice as much Awwww!?!

Get me some tissue.

We just can't even...

OHKAY CITY

DA TIMES

DOG MAN HAS HI

Dog treats awarded.

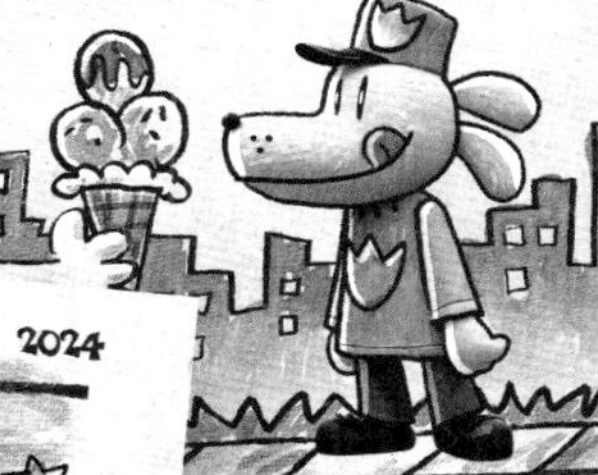

ANOTHERDAY 11, 2024

DA TIMES

AN FIXES EVERYTHING!

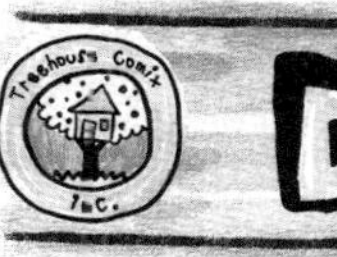

5-min late is offic

OHKAY CITY

DA TIME

TRIPLETS BARK 4 D

Babysitters walk out.

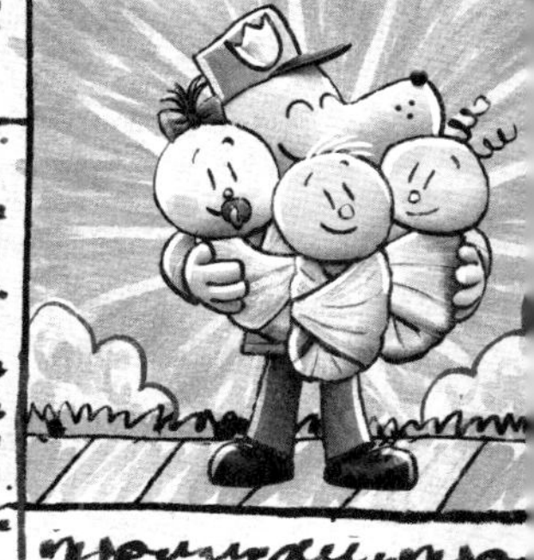

What's New Evil C

TIMES

Love DOG MAN

Pooch is cop of the month again.

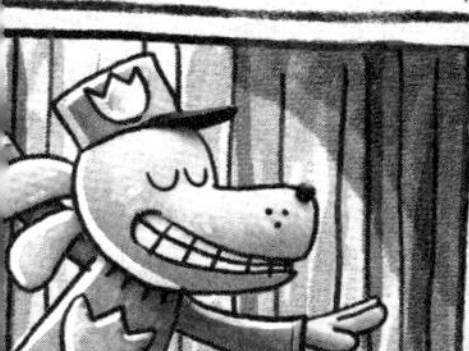

ANOTHERDAY 11, 2024

OHKAY CITY

DA TIMES

DOG COP HELPZ'EM ALL

Cross walks are supa safe now.

MUSH DOG MAN !!?!

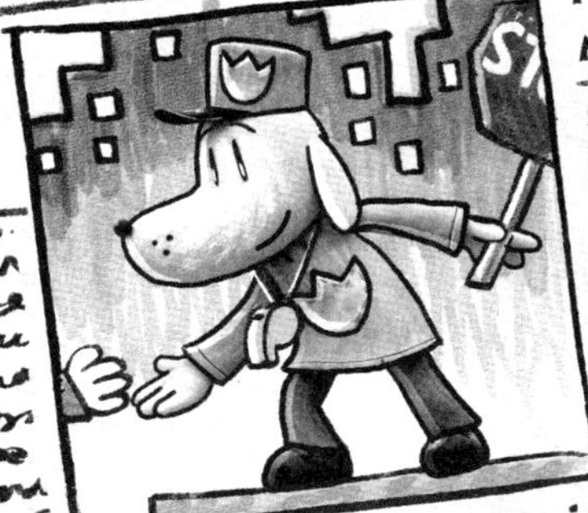

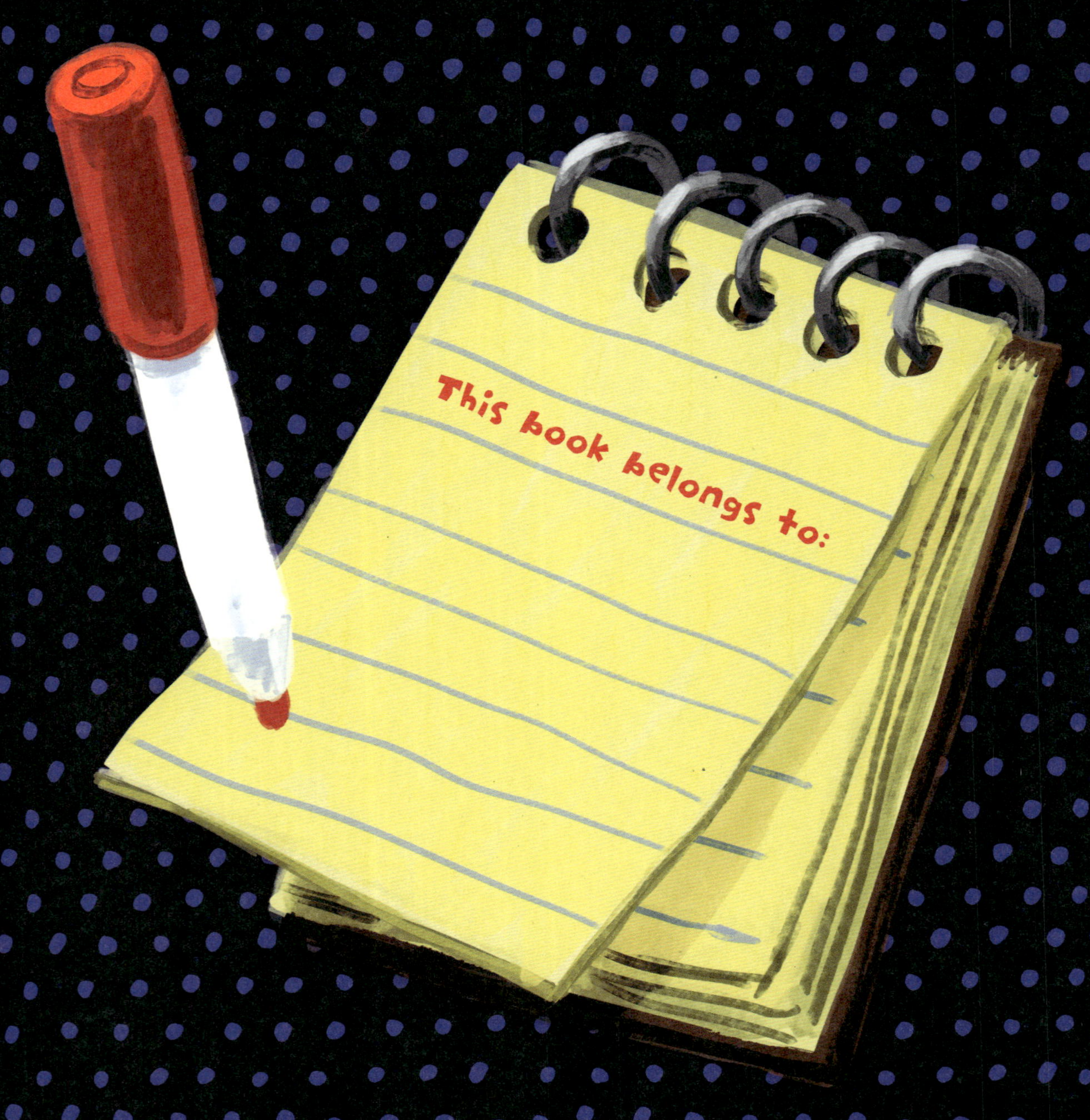
This book belongs to:

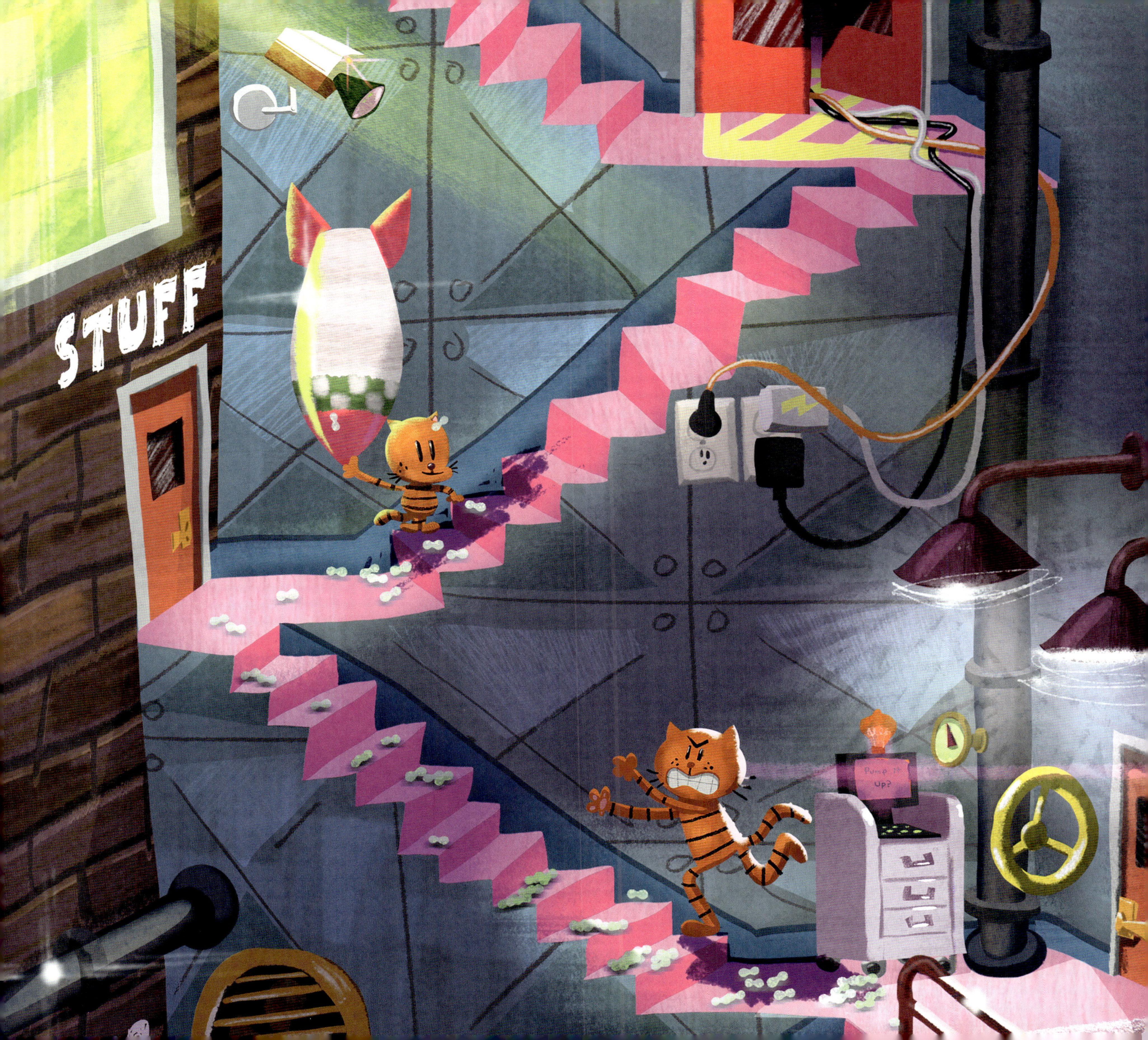
STUFF
Pump it
up?

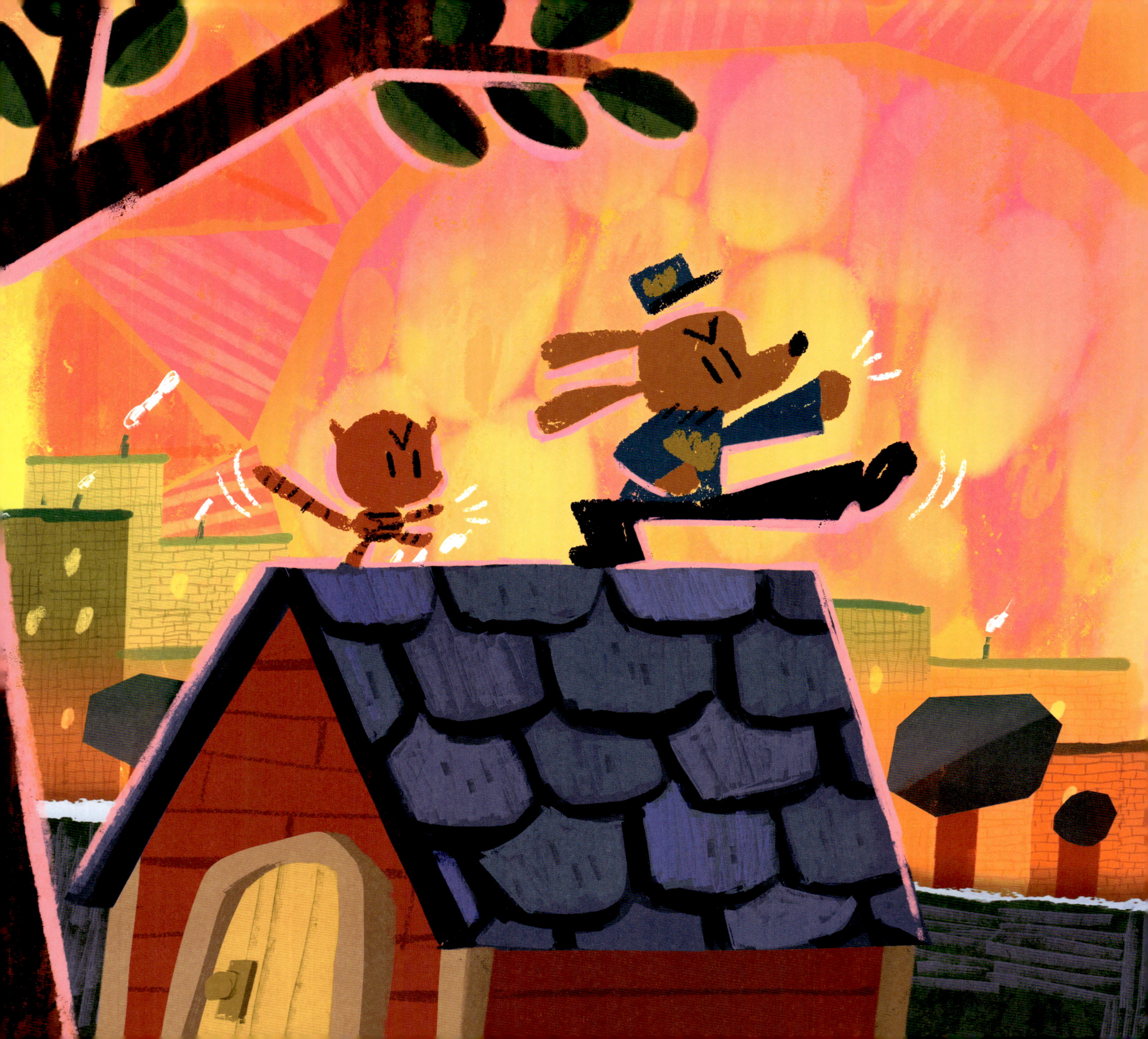

THE ART OF DREAMWORKS

DOG MAN

text by Ramin Zahed

foreword by Dav Pilkey
afterword by Peter Hastings

book design by iain R. Morris

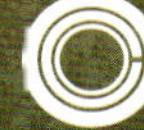

CAMERON + COMPANY
Petaluma, California

Contents

Page 1: Christopher Zibach; Pages 2–3: Lia Tin; This spread: Sébastien Piquet

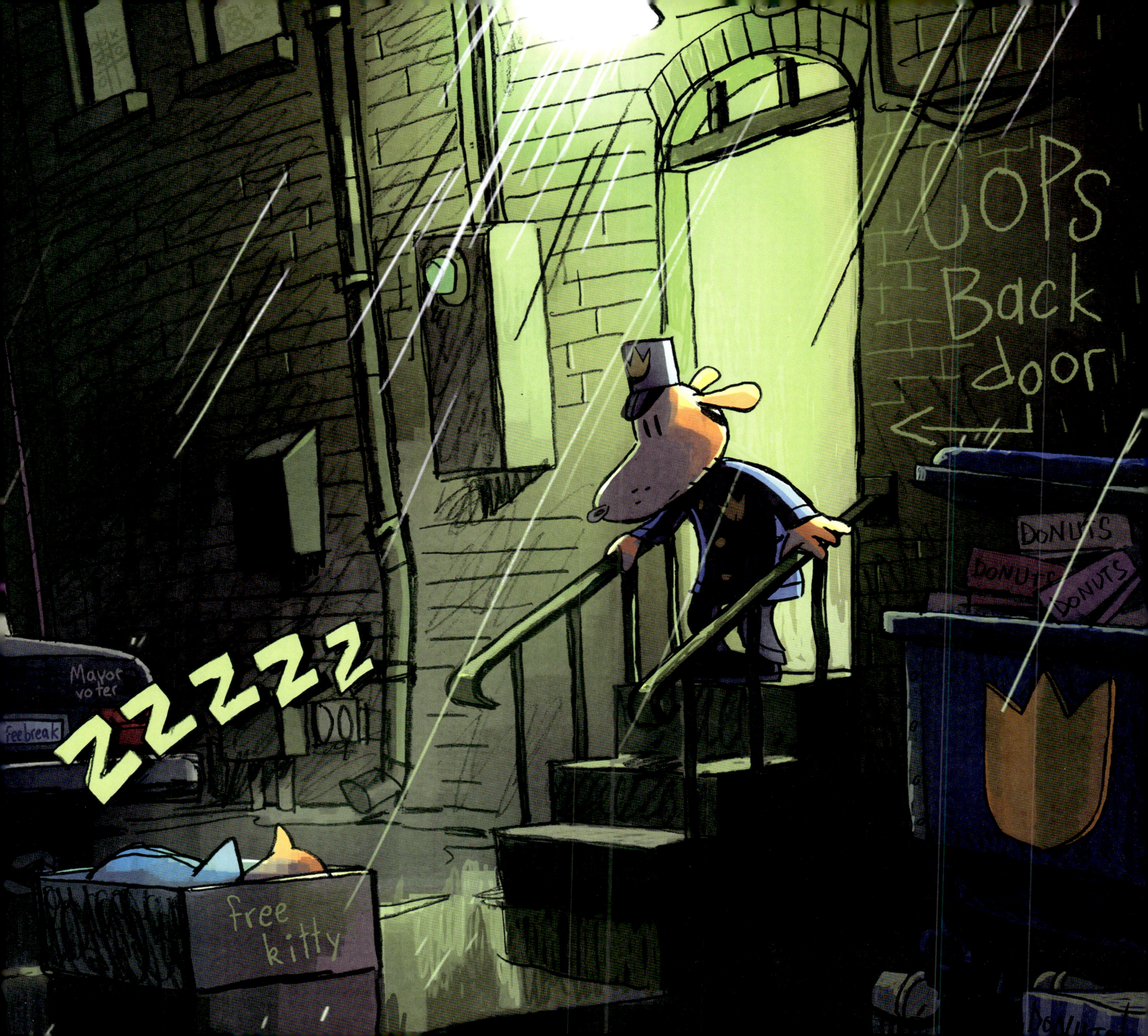
COPS
Back
door
DONUTS
DONUTS
DONUTS
Mayor
voter
feebreak
ZZZZZZ
free
kitty

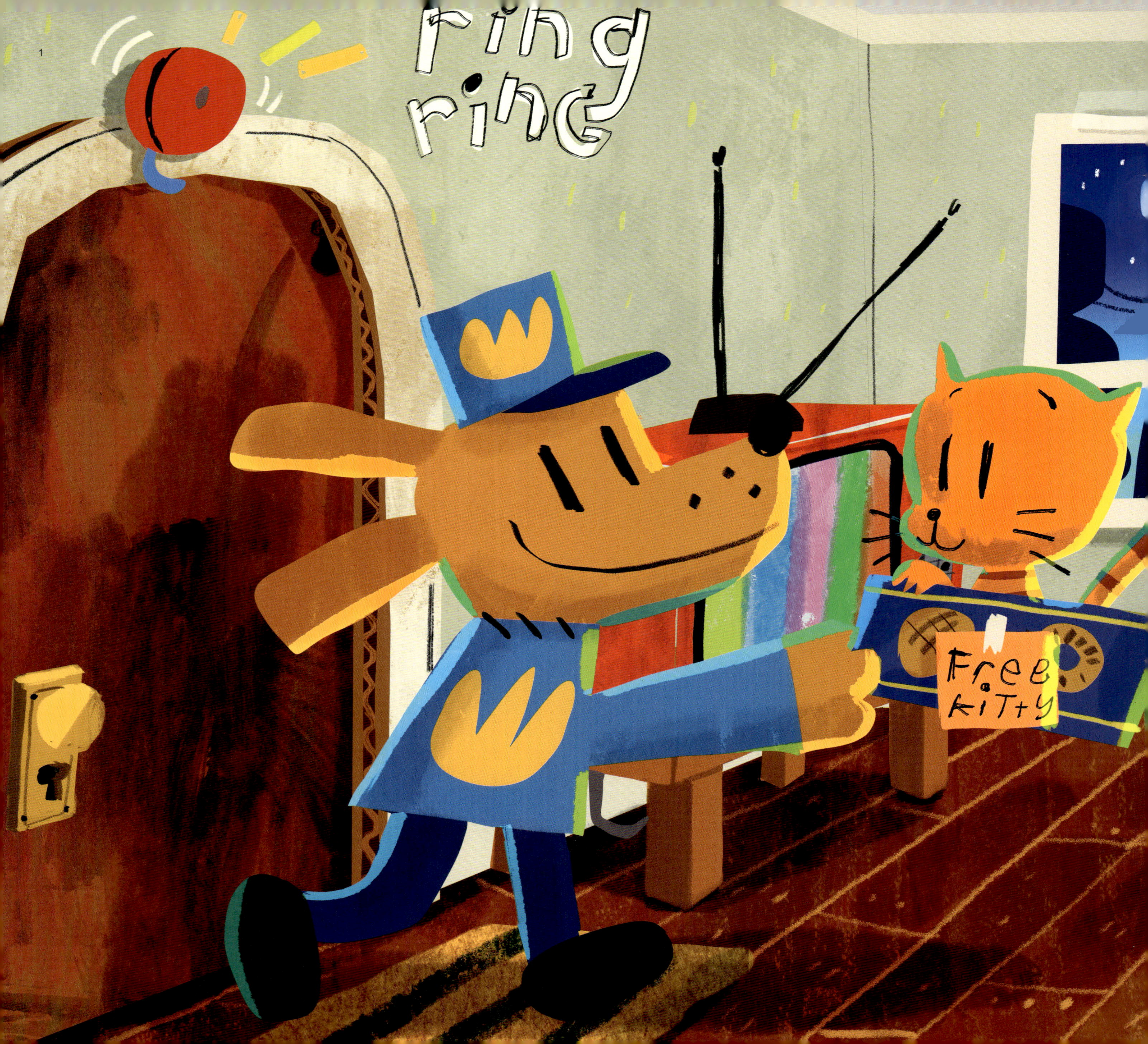
ring
ring
Free
kitty

foreword by Dav Pilkey

Dog Man began as a love story.

It was 1974, and I was eight years old. The Dog Man comics I made back then combined my love of dogs with my love of superheroes.

After nearly forty years of telling other stories, I began writing about Dog Man again.

He had changed over the years: different design . . . different characters . . . and different origin story.

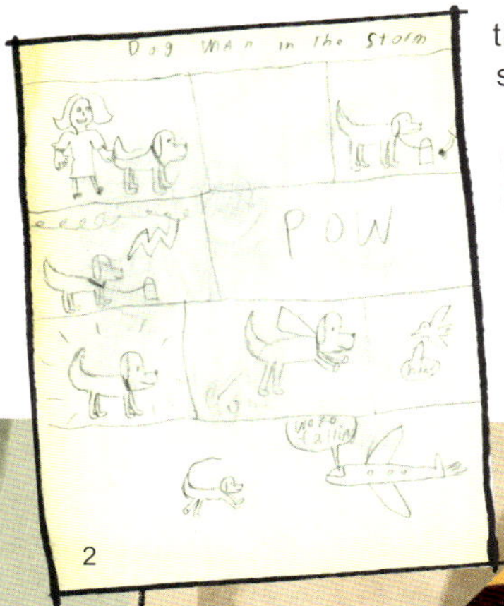

But one thing had remained the same: *Dog Man* was still a story about love.

Sometimes, children will point out to me that the Dog Man series isn't really about Dog Man. I tell them that the Captain Underpants series wasn't about Captain Underpants either.

That never helps.

Then I tell them that *Dog Man* is a story about love, and somehow they seem to understand.

For many of us, if we are very lucky, we have love stories of our own. We know that love, like all living things, grows when it is nurtured and cared for.

And so, it is with great love and appreciation that I give my deepest gratitude to the artists and dreamers who took my stories of love and added their own love. Because of this, the comics of an eight-year-old boy have grown into the film that this book celebrates.

Thank you, DreamWorks Animation and to everyone who filled every frame of this beautiful film with love.

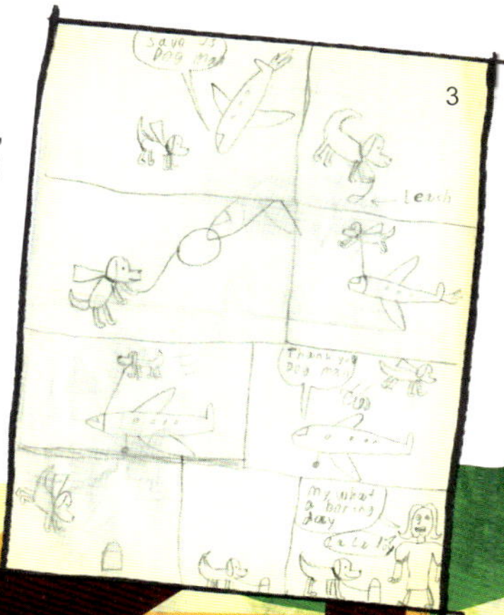

2

3

1: La Tin; 2 & 3: Dav Pilkey

introduction: A Canine Cop Wags His Tale

There are certain popular children's books that are simply perfect fits for animation, and Dav Pilkey's *Dog Man* sits high on that charmed pedestal. The zippy, imaginative, and hilarious world created by the *New York Times* bestselling author, who also penned the popular Captain Underpants book series, lends itself beautifully to the medium. Fortunately, Pilkey and DreamWorks Animation, which faithfully adapted Pilkey's *Captain Underpants* into a successful movie (*Captain Underpants: The First Epic Movie*, 2017) and a TV series (*The Epic Tales of Captain Underpants*, 2018–20) joined forces again to produce the *Dog Man* feature.

Dog Man, which was originally published in the fall of 2016, follows the delightfully insane adventures of a human-dog hybrid police officer who goes on a quest to arrest his sneaky feline archenemy, Petey the Cat. Complicating matters in this story is the arrival of Li'l Petey, Petey's adorable kitten clone with a heart of gold. A madcap series of inventions, plot twists, and high jinks keep the laughs coming in this visually inventive adaptation.

Dog Man's origins go back to the first Captain Underpants book, *The Adventures of Captain Underpants*, where he was the star of a comic book created by two friends, George and Harold. As Pilkey told *Publishers Weekly*, "By the ninth book, he was a character showing up in [their] comic. My fan mail started to change. Usually, kids would draw Captain Underpants. Starting with book number nine, they were all drawing Dog Man. That was one of the reasons I decided to break out and start a new series about Dog Man."

The new DreamWorks feature is directed by Emmy-winning animation veteran Peter Hastings, who also exec-produced the *Captain Underpants* TV series, and produced by Karen Foster (*Spirit Untamed*, *How to Train Your Dragon*). The film's production designer is Nate Wragg (*Puss in Boots: The Last Wish*), and the art director is Christopher Zibach (*Under the Boardwalk*)—both of whom are veterans of the *Captain Underpants* movie.

Hastings recalls being very excited about working on this new Pilkey project because he knew that he and the author were usually on the same wavelength. "It turned out that he really loved the *Captain Underpants* TV series," recalls the director. "Since we already had a track record of working together, he came on board. Things started to ramp up in 2021. It took a while, but I never had any doubts that we would be moving forward with this adventure. What made this experience so much fun was that our sensibilities completely aligned."

Hastings says one of the hardest aspects of the job was figuring out how much of the book series' tremendous amount of material they would use in the movie. "We ended up featuring storylines and characters from several of the books, specifically the first three volumes," he points out. "The third book, *A Tale of Two Kitties*, introduces some key characters—including Li'l Petey, 80-HD, and Flippy the Fish—and the emotional life of the series kicks up greatly there. There are also some bits from the seventh book, *For Whom the Ball Rolls*."

Producer Karen Foster recalls that Pilkey said yes to the project, provided that Hastings be on board as director. "Dav originally wanted the film to be done in stop-motion, but he loved what Peter had done in the TV series, so he wanted him to direct," she says. "We all wanted our movie to have a high-end, handmade, and toylike quality—things that come to life that don't feel like they're completely CG rendered. I'd describe it as a blend of CG and 2D, where things look a bit rough around the edges, as if they're elevated off the page."

As an example, she points to the simple design of Dog Man's head. "His head is rendered in CG, but you can still see the eyes and the mouth as line drawings," Foster points out. "The approach is quite different from anything else we have done at DreamWorks. Our approach was to maintain the hand of the creator, Dav."

"The world of Dog Man is quite multilayered, and Peter did such a great job of translating it," adds Foster. "Of course, the books are super funny, but parents who read them with their children are often surprised by how deeply heartfelt and intelligent they are. We were lucky because the movie is a real labor of love for all of us. Our director, Peter; production designer, Nate; and art director, Christopher, are all fathers. The editor is also a father who has read these books over and over with his kids. There's a lot of love that comes from the many artists who work on it because it's connected to their own experiences with their children."

Hastings agrees. "Dav has this amazing way of telling a very silly story and dropping in some big, personal-dynamic moments," notes the director. "There are some emotional beats that are so true to life and don't necessarily follow the norms of storytelling for kids. A lot of it is also because the Dog Man books are supposedly written by George and Harold from the Captain Underpants stories. There's an innocence to them, so they can do and say a lot of things that would sound weird coming from an adult, but they sound perfectly normal, funny, and silly from a kid. Our goal was not to reimagine or change Dav Pilkey's creation, but to expand on it."

"Dav's work is imbued with all the qualities we especially value at DreamWorks Animation: unexpected humor, memorable characters, unlikely and even improbable heroes, endless creativity, irreverence, heart, and a very, very specific sensibility," adds DreamWorks Animation president Margie Cohn. "Our development team had wanted to acquire the Dog Man book series for years and were thrilled when the stars aligned and we heard Dav was ready to make a *Dog Man* feature film. Dav also had studio talent he trusted in director Peter Hastings and production designer Nate Wragg, both of whom he knew from their work on the *Captain Underpants* projects."

"The great thing about this movie is that as funny and irreverent as it is, there is also a lot of heart," Cohn continues. "We want audiences to laugh with our characters, but there are also messages about love and family they can take home with them. In a Dav Pilkey world, anything can happen, and most things are over-the-top improbable, but his storytelling makes anything seem possible. A man and a dog can be combined into a 'Supa Cop,' and

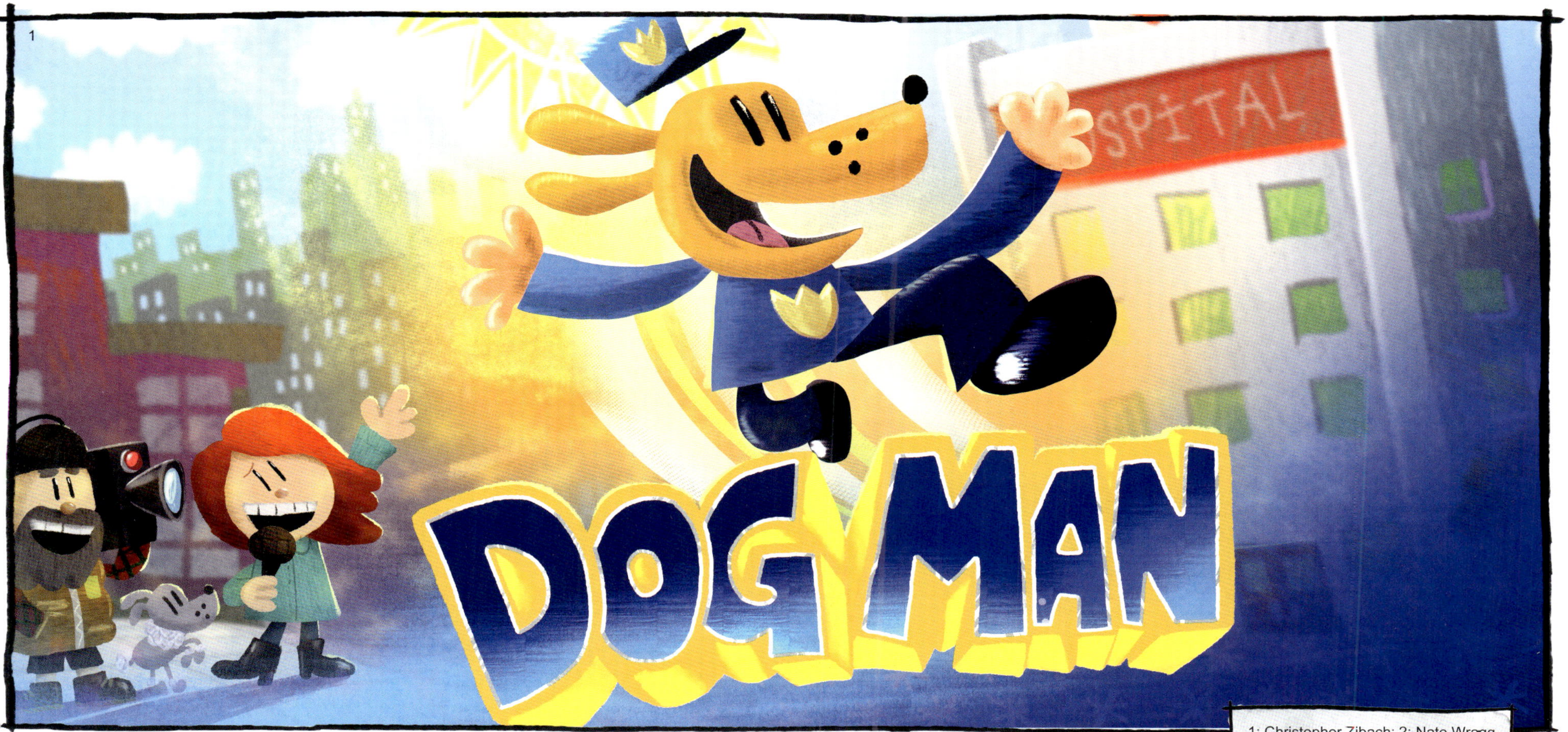

1

DOG MAN

SPITAL

1: Christopher Zibach; 2: Nate Wragg

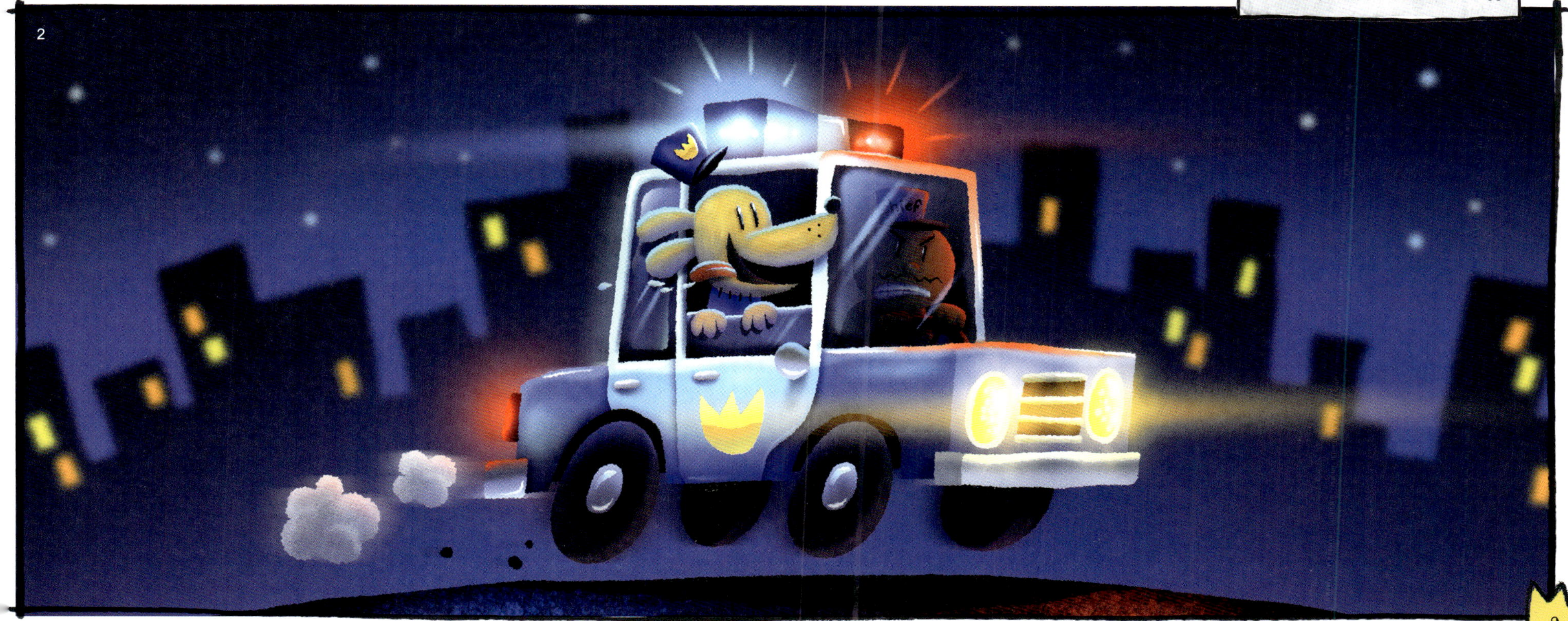

2

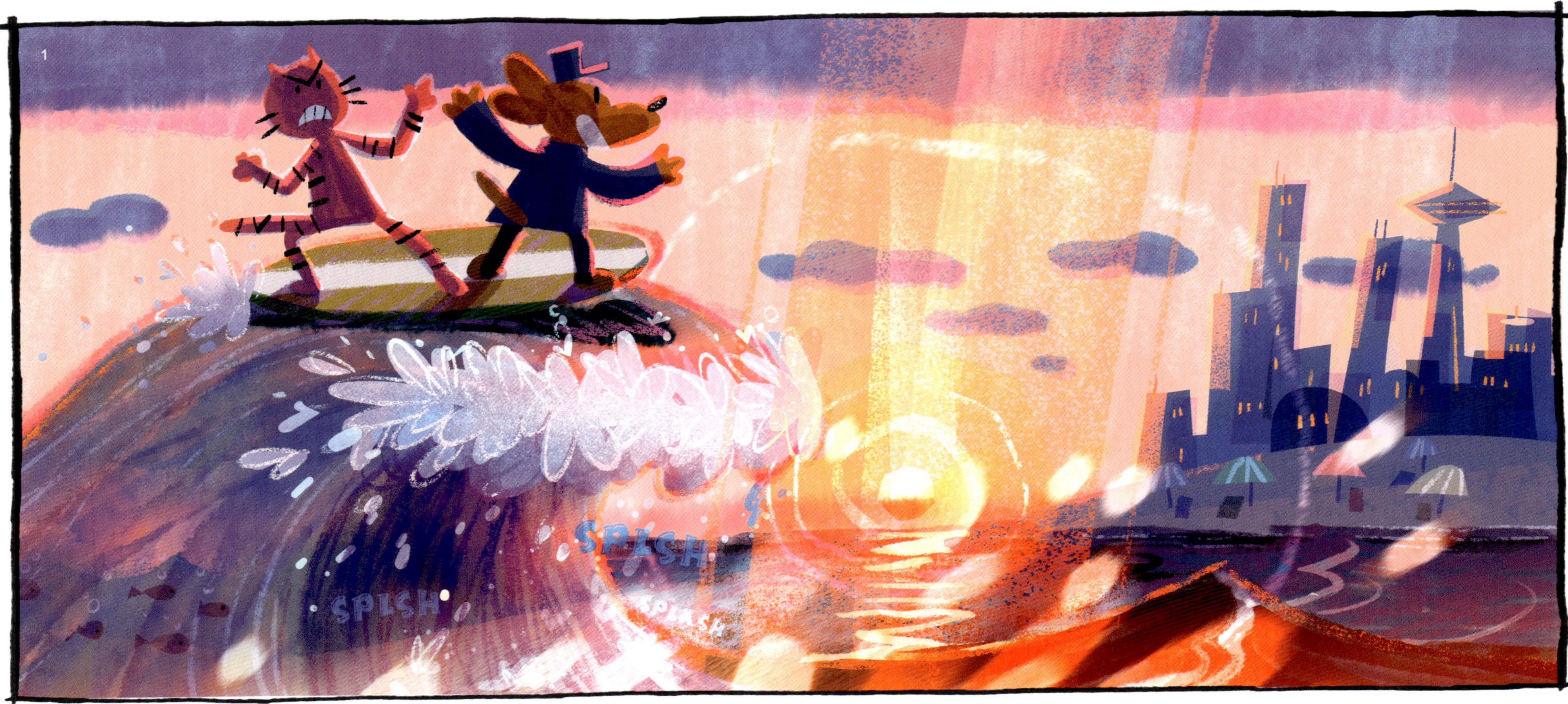

a dead psychokinetic evil fish can come alive after being covered in 'Living Spray.' This imaginative storytelling is tailor-made for what we do."

DreamWorks Animation chief creative officer Kristin Lowe is also a huge fan of the quirky look of Pilkey's graphic novels. "They seem like an obvious fit for animation, given their whimsical look and the simple fact that the main character is part dog, part man, all hero. That said, what Nate Wragg and this design team did with this material was a constant delight and surprise. The design was both wildly comic and entertaining but also incredibly sophisticated. I think we were also quite surprised when we found ourselves tearing up while listening to the pitch about Dog Man fighting a supervillain cat! Combining Peter's fantastic vision for the story with Nate's innovative and beautiful translation of the look was what won the day."

A High-End Handmade Style

The film's award-winning production designer, Nate Wragg, mentions that his team's visual approach took advantage of the growth in animation technology since *Captain Underpants* came out over eight years ago. "Although there are certain similarities because both are set in Pilkey's world, what's different is that we're going for that handmade, stylized approach," he explains. "While we made it in CG, we didn't want the audience to feel like it looked like any other CG movie they have seen. We're also not saying it's a 2D movie or a stop-motion movie. I would say it almost feels like a collage of artistic ideas. We leaned into a lot of artistic and illustrated materials and stylized treatments in a CG space, which helped us create this jewel of a movie."

Wragg is quick to point out that although the Dog Man world is seen through the lens of George and Harold's imagination, it's a living, breathing universe. "It's made by the hands of the kids, but we took the characters and their world seriously," says the acclaimed production designer. "The boys actually make an appearance or two in it, but we don't cut out wide and see that they're playing with a bunch of toys. This is a totally realized world that's highly stylized, and the characters are living in it seriously, even though it's a wildly silly world."

Dog Man's art director, Christopher Zibach, who is also a die-hard Pilkey fan, says the preposterous storylines of the series allowed them to push the visual medium as far as they could. "We could be as crazy and flat-out ridiculous as possible because that's what the books do as well," he says. "I remember the first visuals that Nate showed us were already delivering on that promise. The shape design was already silly, and it had fun-for-fun's-sake written all over it."

Zibach also mentions that Pilkey's books served as the ultimate guide for understanding the amount of details and realism they were allowed to bring into their designs. "We had the ability to play in that world and try to represent something that's both somewhat realistic but also totally following cartoon logic. For example, when depicting trees or buildings or cars, we wanted to go with the bare necessities in terms of details, so you know that they are the objects you think they are. Less was definitely more here."

Clean, primary colors also play a big role in the look of the movie. "The comics are so flat, punchy, and saturated," notes Zibach. "So, we were tasked with looking at highly stylized movies like *Dick Tracy*. We wanted the reds, greens, and blues to be pure and to deliver a really strong statement. We followed a certain logic in designing the different sets; for example, Dog Man's home needed to be happier and cozier because our hero is beloved by everyone. But for Petey's domain, since he is the evilest cat in the world, we leaned into different genres to get that classic 'mad scientist' vibe. We couldn't

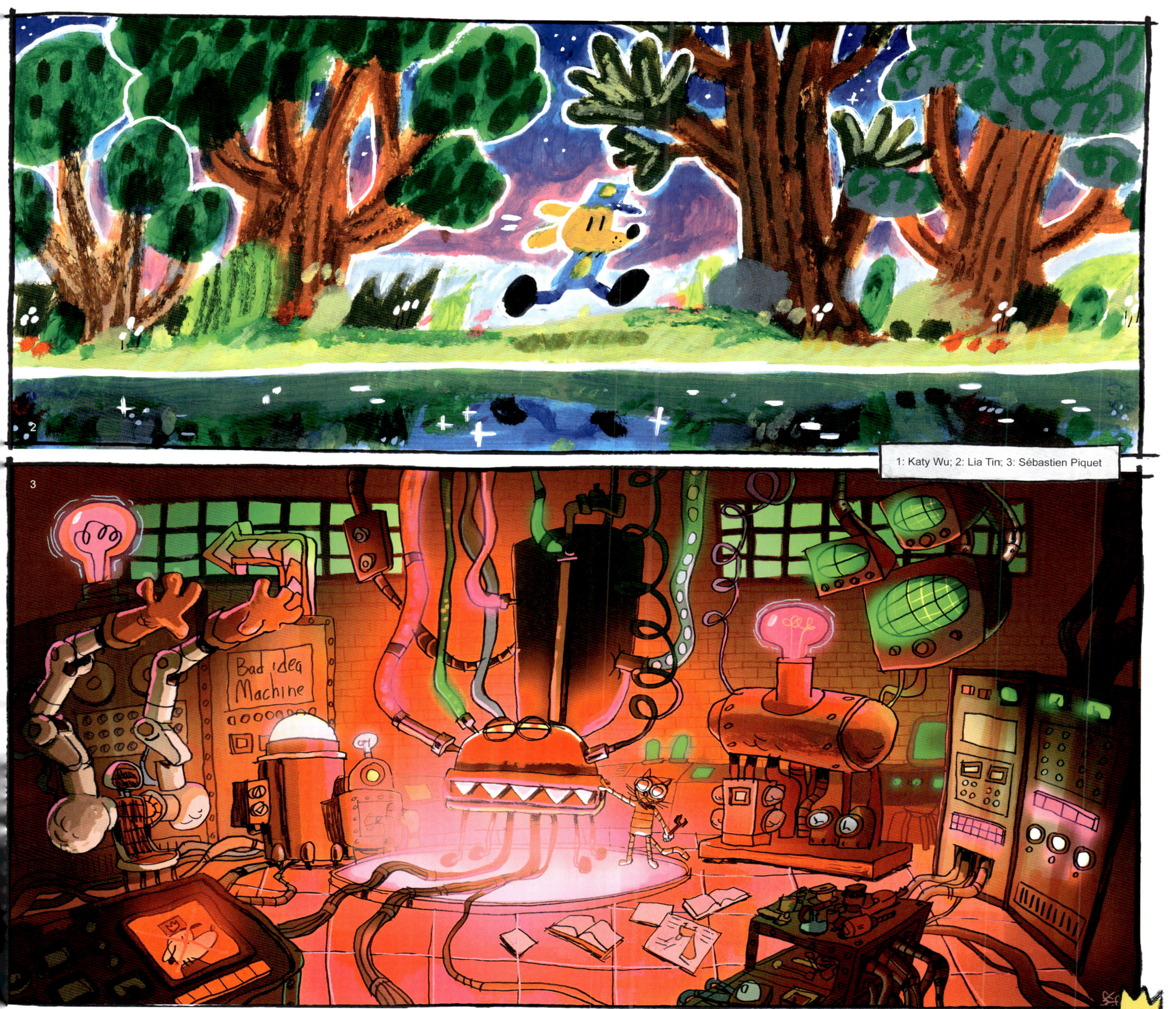

1: Katy Wu; 2: Lia Tin; 3: Sébastien Piquet

1

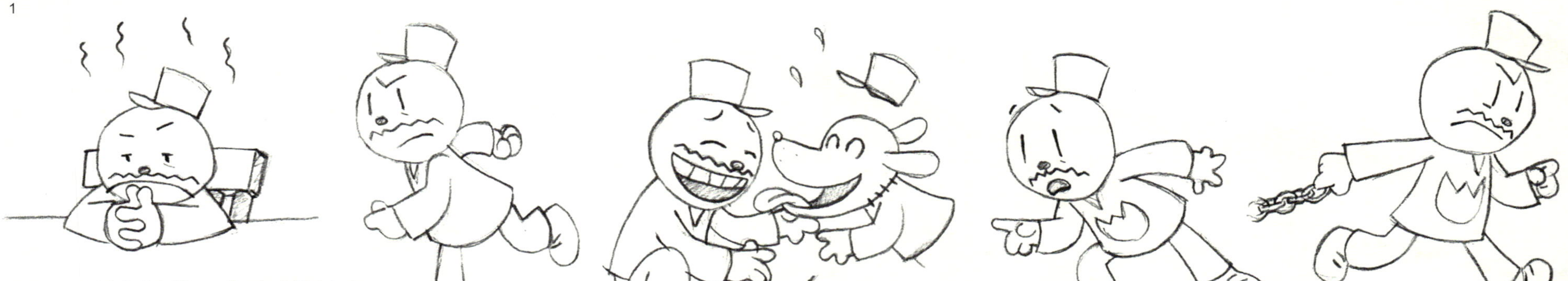

1: John Hill; 2 & 3: Nate Wragg; Overleaf: Christopher Zibach; color script contributors: Lia Tin, Sebastien Piquet, Katy Wu, Nate Wragg, Vahe Yefremian

2

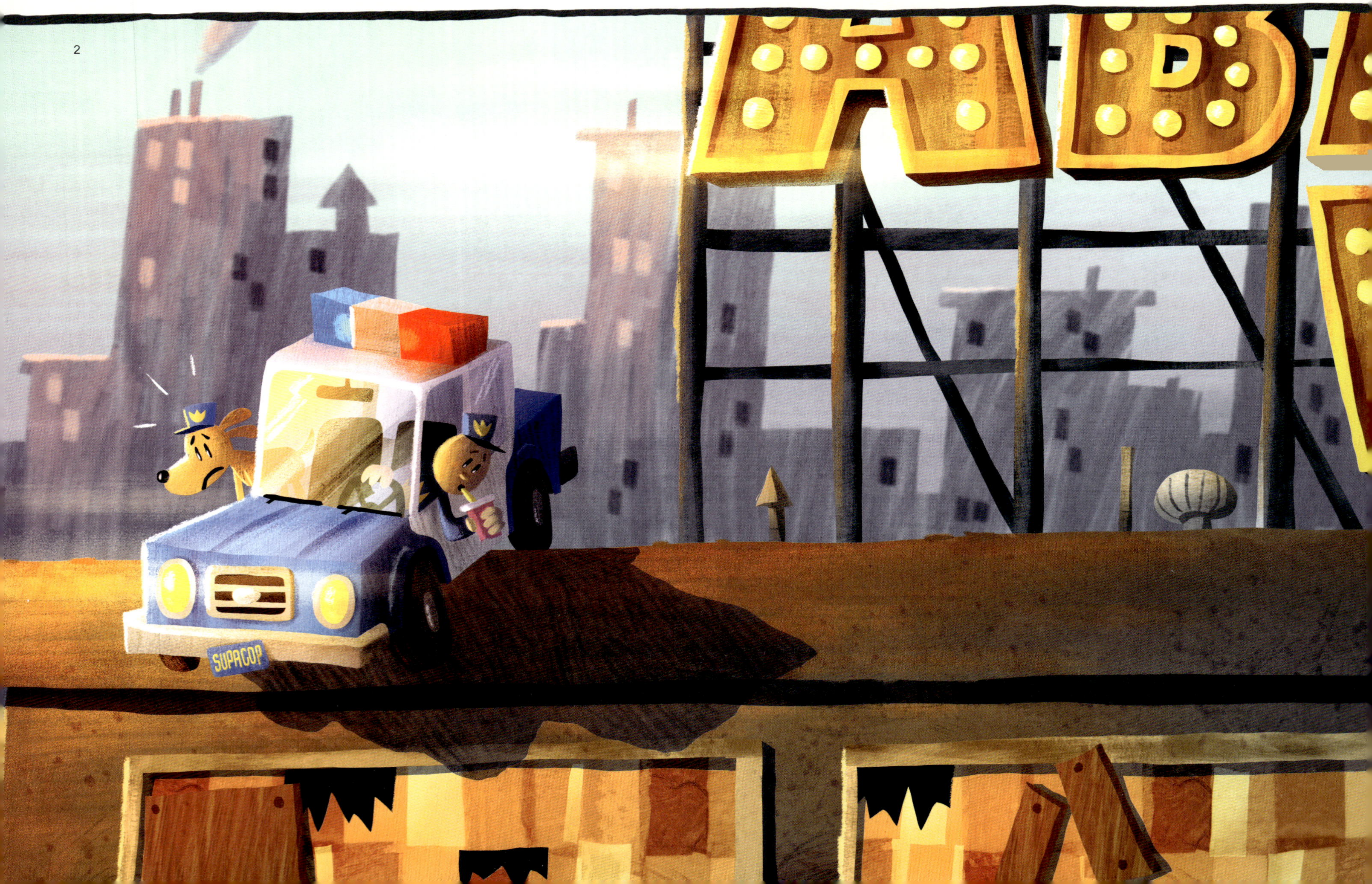

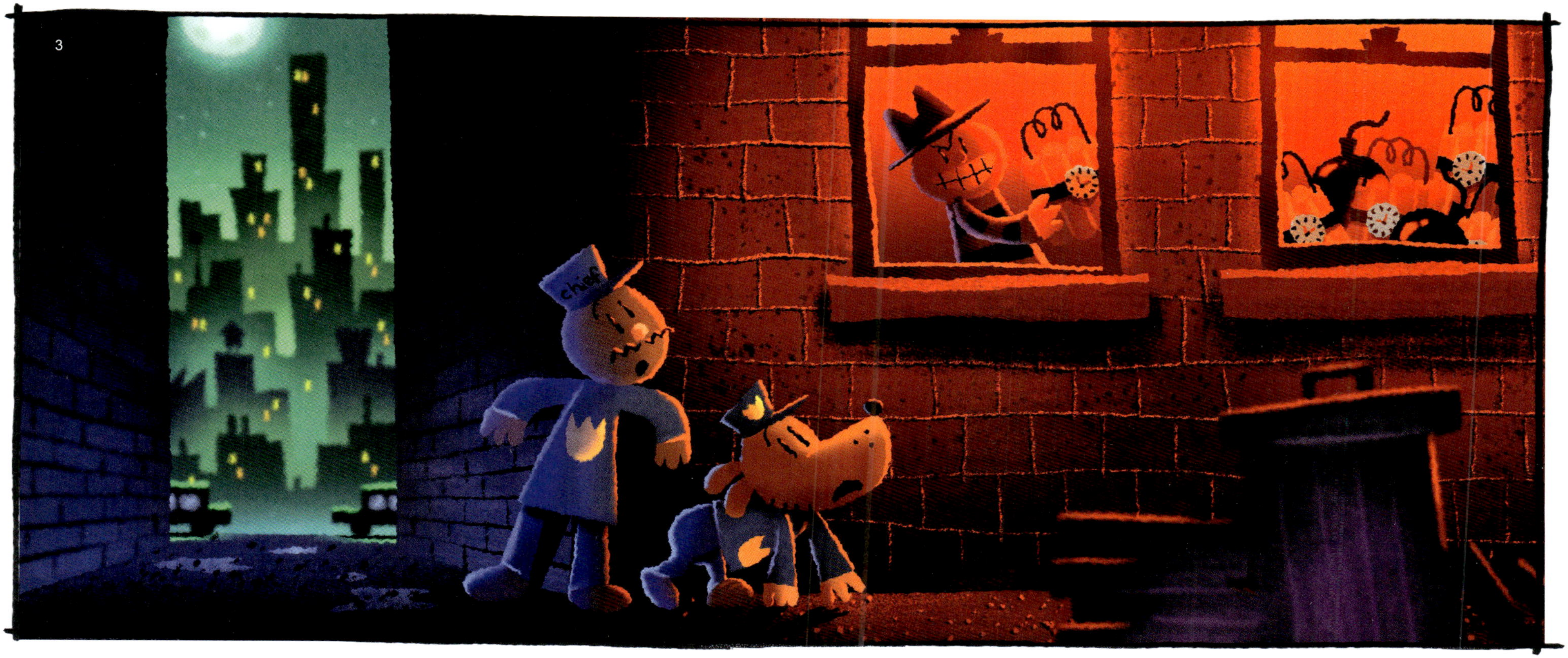

represent everything a mad scientist might need in his lab, but we get away with blinky lights, Tesla coils, and cartoony icons that even kids under seven recognize as science."

Popping with Personality and Texture

For head of character animation John Hill, who has had a colorful career working on 2D-animated features such as *The Land Before Time* and *Spirit: Stallion of the Cimarron* and popular CG-animated hits such as *Shrek Forever After*, *Puss in Boots*, *Trolls*, and *The Croods: A New Age*, the movie promised an opportunity to blend his expertise in both fields. "The first thing I did was buy the complete series of Dog Man books and devour them all," he recalls. "Then, they showed me some of the artwork that our production designer Nate and art director Christopher had created, and I just knew that this was going to be a unique and fun project. They were able to figure out a style of animation that fit this handmade world, where you can see the crayon colors, textures, and collage work on the buildings."

Hill adds, "We had worked out each of the specific characters' personalities and backstories with our director, so the character animation reflects that. For example, Dog Man moves in a way that's correct for his background and makeup as a character, which is quite different from the Chief, who has a different weight and personality. Of course, Petey and Li'l Petey all have unique movements as well, but they all have to match the style of this Pilkey world."

Hill mentions that the team at DreamWorks was able to create a special style that combined the best of 2D, CG, and stop-motion. "The characters look very similar to what they do in the book, but we are moving them around in a 3D world," he adds. "In addition, the buildings, the cars, and the gadgets all have unique textures; you rarely see flat colors. If someone is wearing a denim shirt, you can actually see the brushstrokes on it. We had to nail down how a sweater would look in this world and how it would live in the backgrounds that are created for each scene."

Head of layout and cinematography Scott Cullen (*The Bad Guys*; *Puss in Boots: The Last Wish*) helped develop the special camera language for the movie. "This unique style was pretty new for DreamWorks," he explains. "It's more layered and sophisticated than the *Captain Underpants* movie. I love all the intricate details and the layering of the textures, which result in a hand-painted look. You could pause any frame in the movie and get all these different combinations of 2D, CG, and stop-motion. For the cinematography, we used cutout sets that remind you of something you'd see in a Wes Anderson movie. We shot through walls and craned up through the ceilings to reveal characters on different floors of a building. We've never done anything like that before."

Dog Man's visual effects supervisor Louis Flores says the film's third act, which features the buildings coming to life, as well as a giant robot battle, offered him and his team at Jellyfish Pictures many great chances to push the visual fireworks. "We had a lot of visual development on these scenes because the books are very stylized, so they are not going to have the typical VFX elements. Our city doesn't look like a traditional one; the buildings don't have every window in the model. They're kind of offset and quirky, and they're missing certain things. The texture that's applied to them is artistically handled, so that every building takes on its own character. Everything is designed to embrace the Pilkey style in a 3D fashion."

He adds, "It was so exciting to see everything coming together. I remember how much my son loved these books when he was younger, so for us, it's really about the kids and all the fans loving how the whole team brought this world from 2D to 3D and making sure they will be happy with how we brought these charming books to animated life."

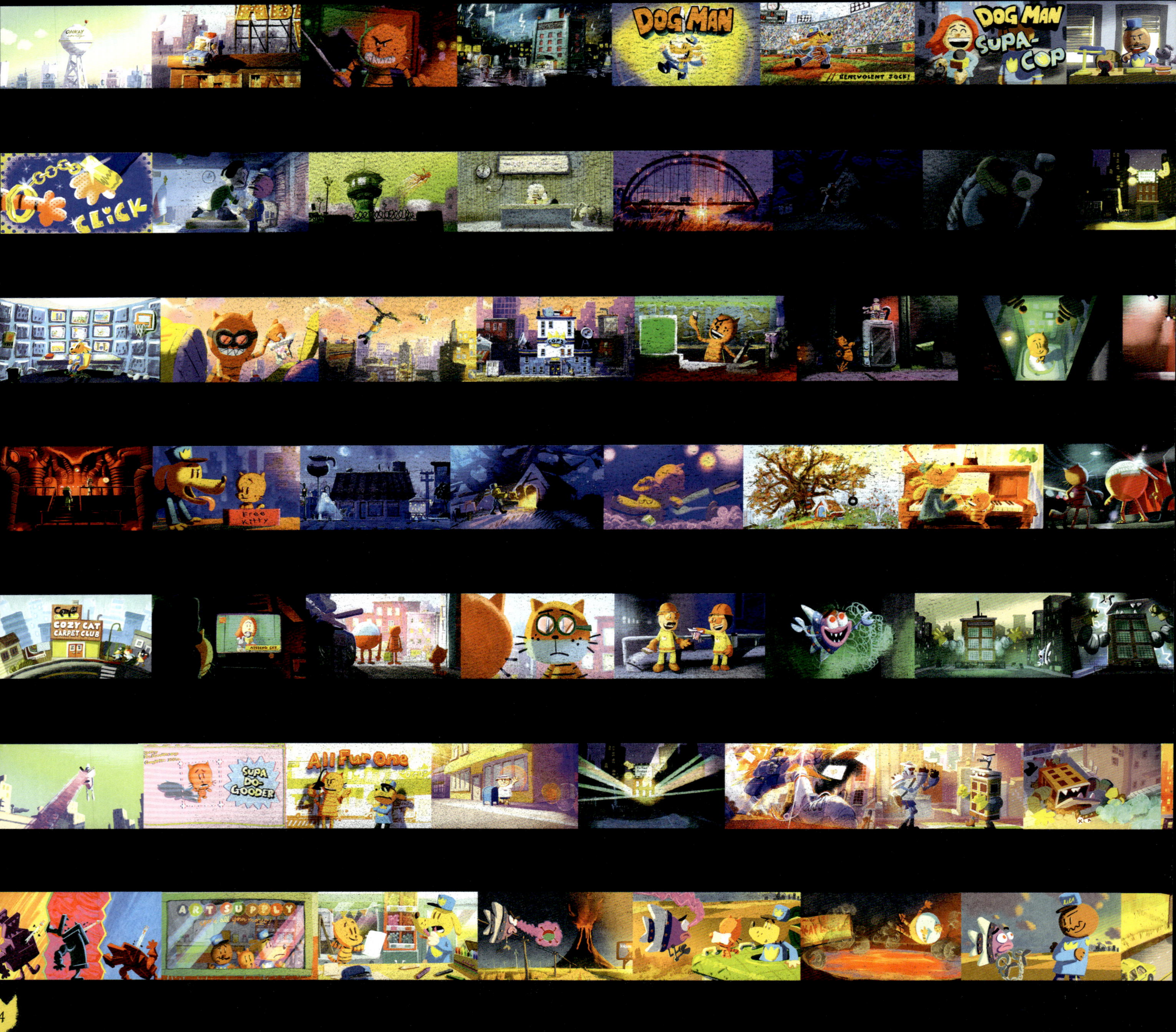

DOG MAN
DOG MAN
SUPA-COP
CLICK
COZY CAT CARPET CLUB
Free Kitty
SUPA DO-GOODER
All Fur One
ART SUPPLY

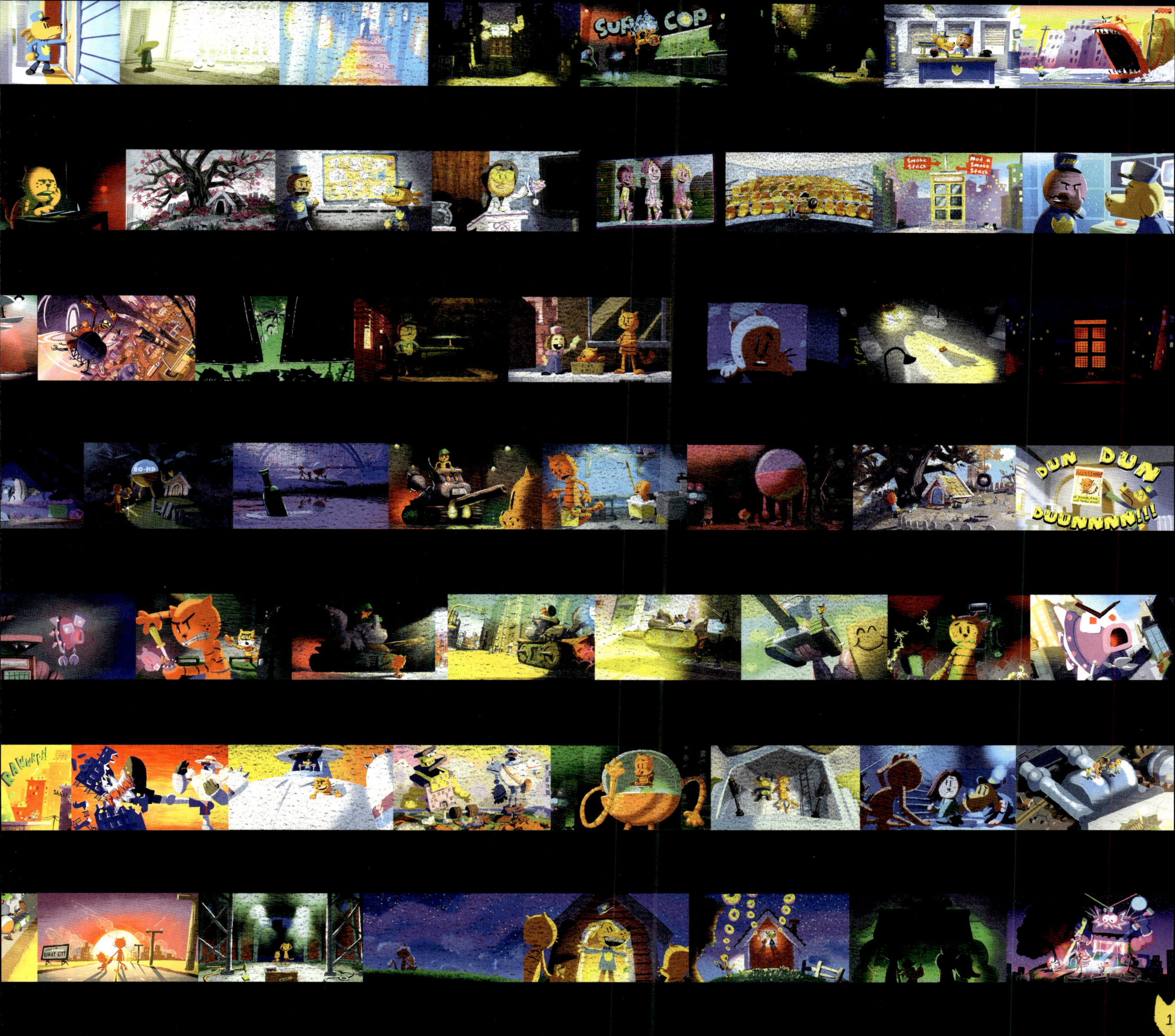
COP
Smoke Stack
Not a Smoke Stack
DUN DUN DUUNNNN!!!
MISSING!
RAWWRR!!
Shhh!

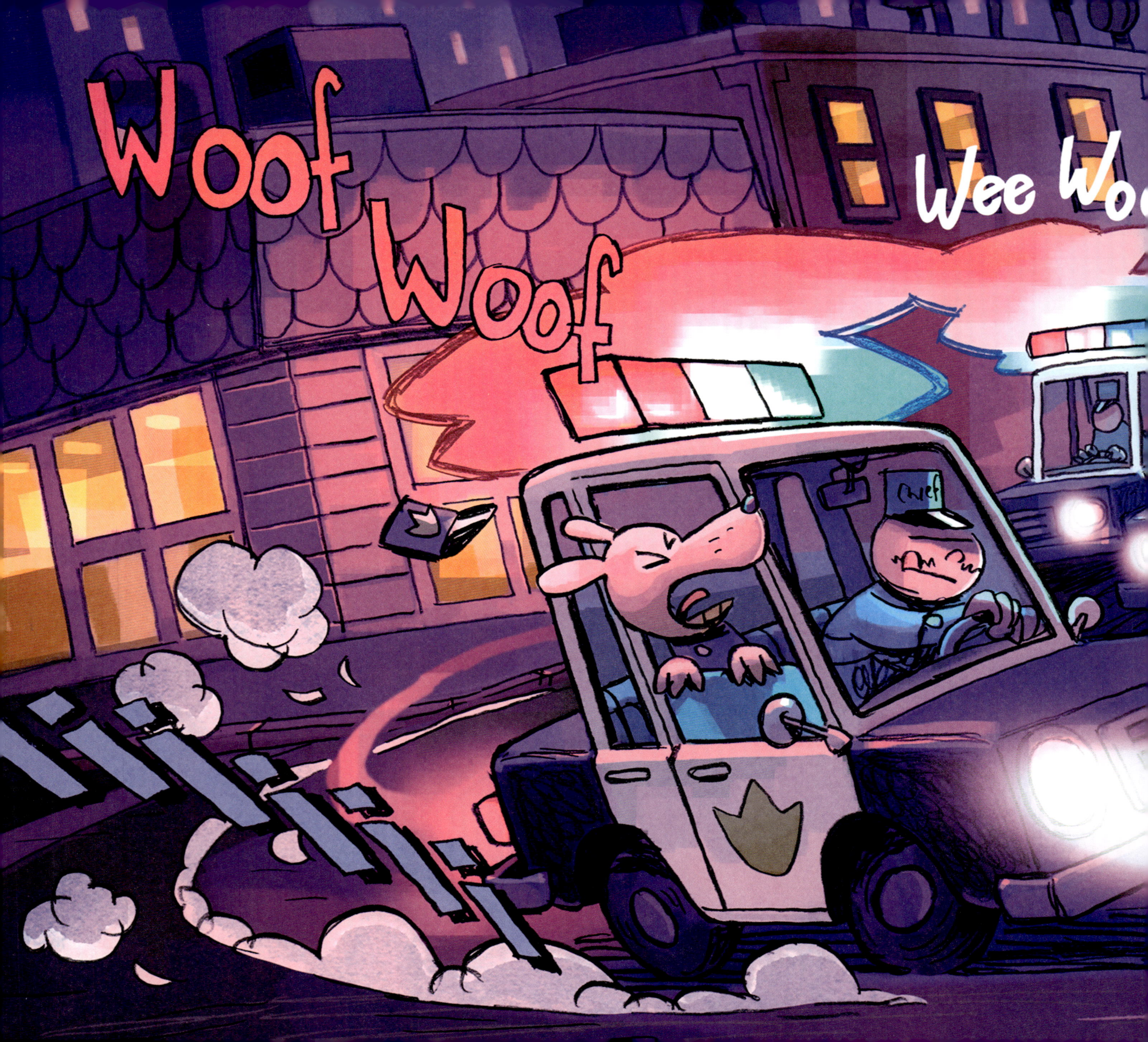

Woof
Woof
Wee Wo
Chief

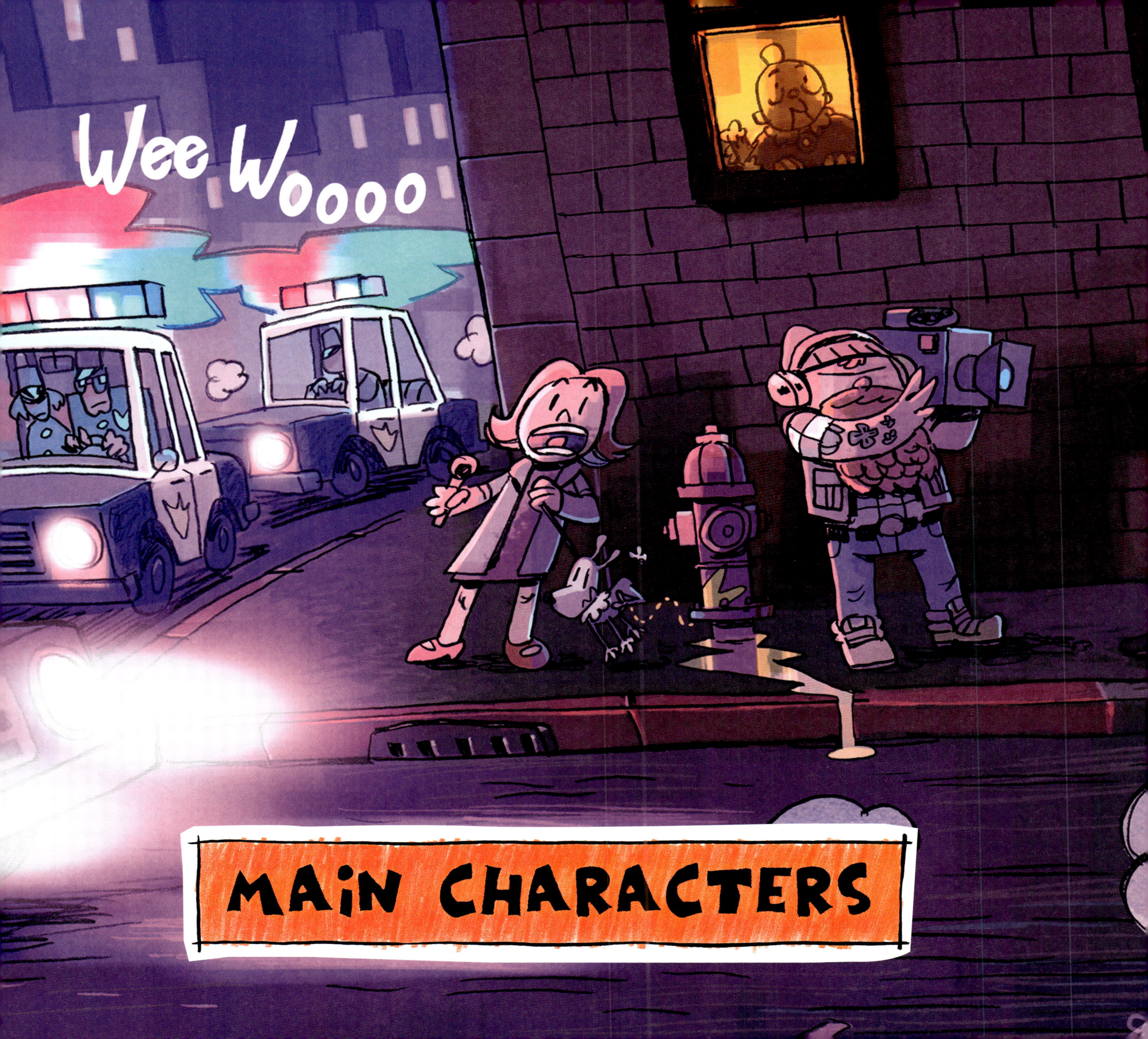
Wee Woooo
MAIN CHARACTERS

Officer Knight and Greg the dog

Officer Knight makes an early appearance both in the first Dog Man book and the movie. Our first introduction to Knight (voiced by Peter Hastings) comes from master villain Petey the Cat, who points out, "Officer Knight is a tough cop with kung fu skills, but he's got no brains. And Greg the Dog is smart, but his body is his weakness. These guys are nothing!"

Knight is not too bright, but he's deeply devoted to fighting crime and protecting the world from Petey's evil schemes. He also has a deep bond with his loyal, smart, and playful canine companion, Greg. Sadly, as a result of a bomb explosion planned by Petey, both Officer Knight and his faithful dog are horribly injured. After being rushed to the hospital, the tending doctor tells the officer that the dog's body is dying, and a nurse comes up with the brilliant idea to fuse Greg's head onto Knight's body. The result is a wonderful new police officer who is part dog, part man, all hero. As described by Pilkey in the first Dog Man book, "The doctor cut off Greg's head and sewed it onto a cop's body, and soon, a brand-new crime-fighting sensation was unleashed."

The film's production designer, Nate Wragg, explains that Knight was imagined as a handsome goof, a hunky cop who's a bit dopey. "He's kind of reminiscent of Channing Tatum in *21 Jump Street*. We opened the movie with Officer Knight and Greg the Dog in pursuit of Petey, the world's most evil cat. Knight is good at what he does, but he's also kind of a buffoon. We can see that Greg is clearly the brains of the operation. He is a bit more aware of impending danger and better at problem-solving. It's a fun dynamic to watch as Office Knight has to be rescued by his dog. He would have probably met his demise quite some time ago if it hadn't been for Greg!"

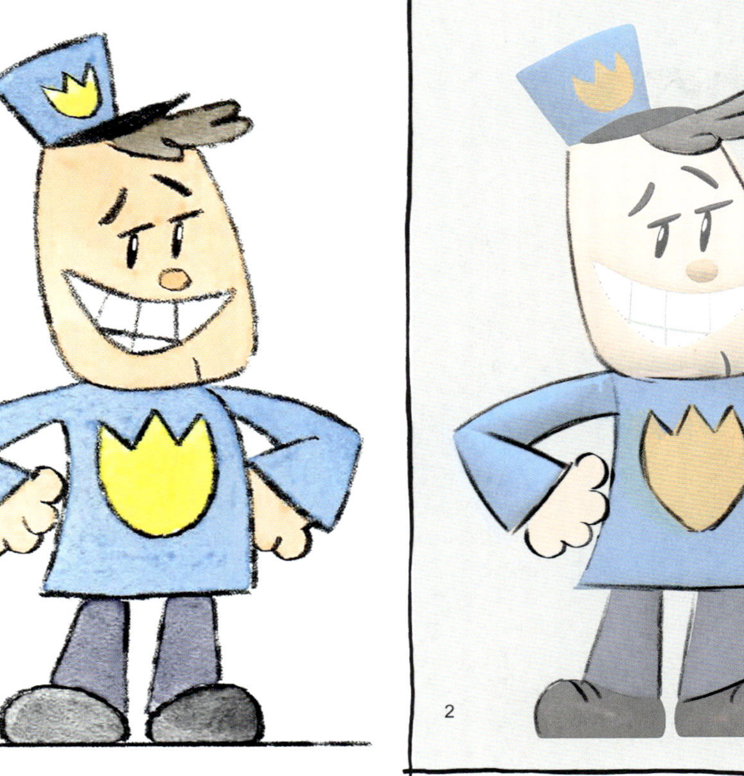

1

2

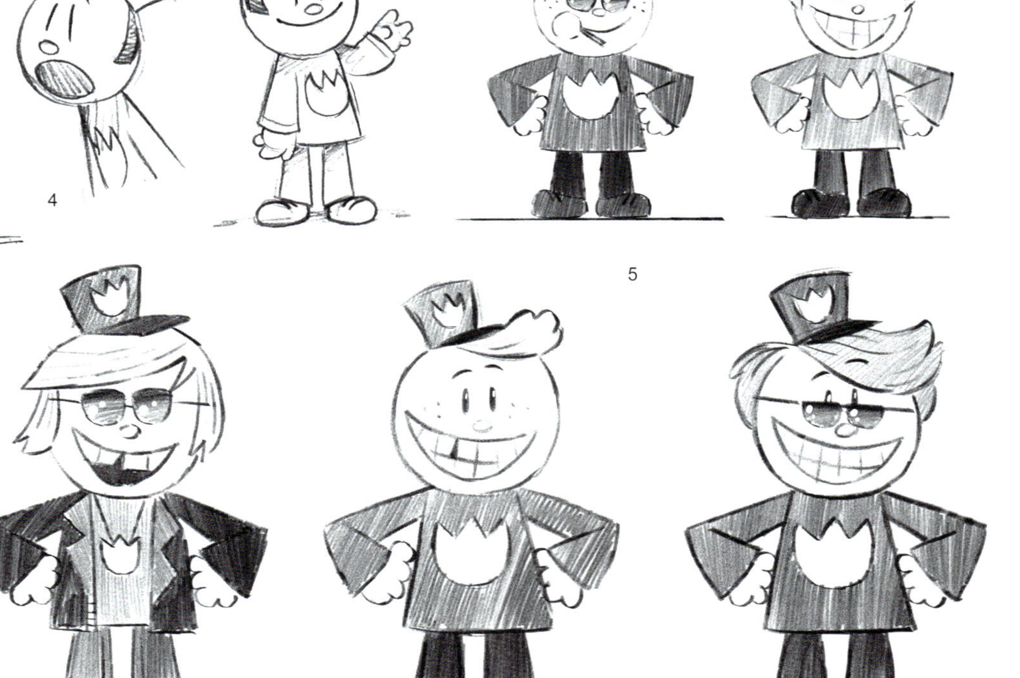

3

4

5

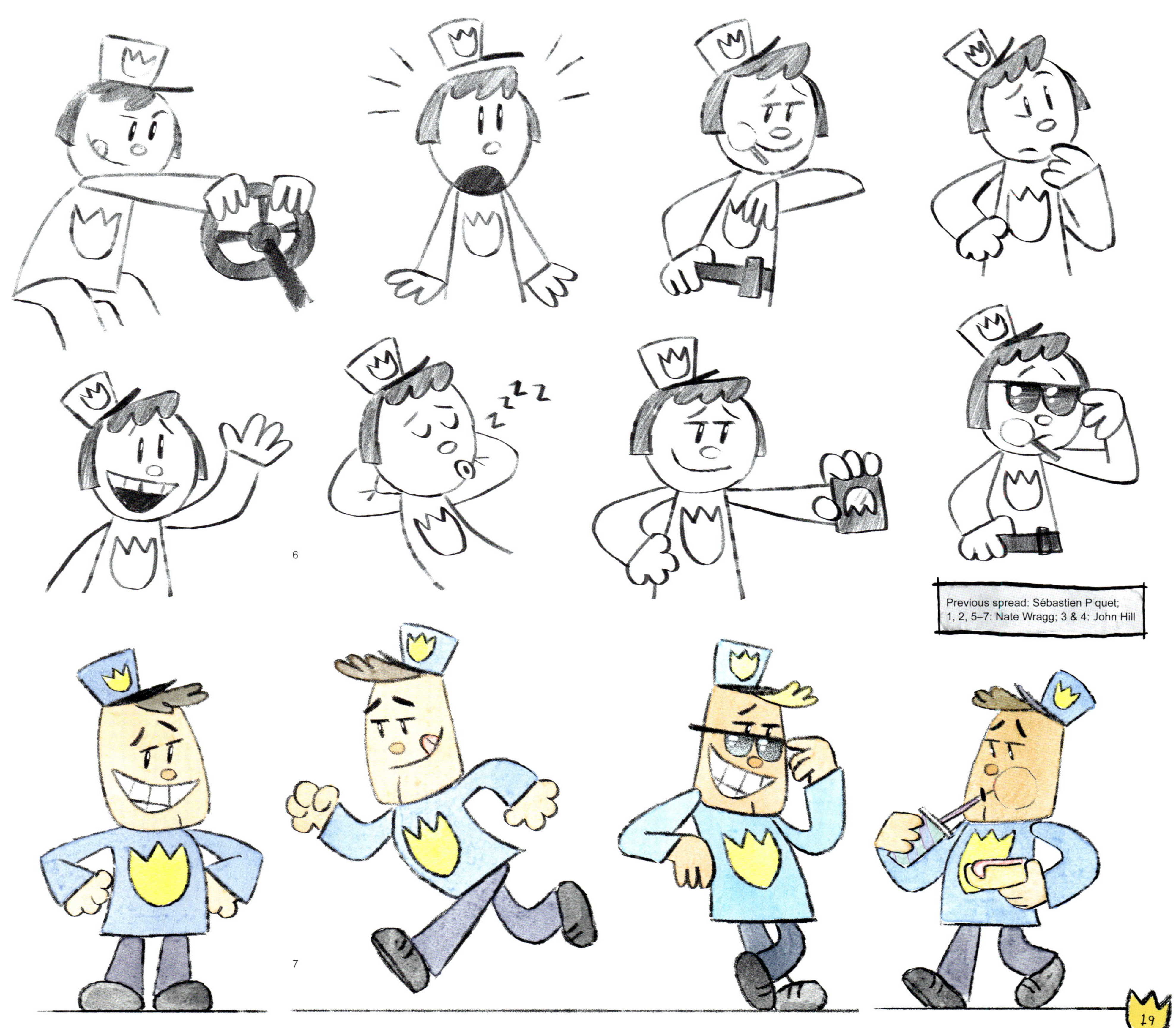

6

7

Previous spread: Sébastien P quet;
1, 2, 5–7: Nate Wragg; 3 & 4: John Hill

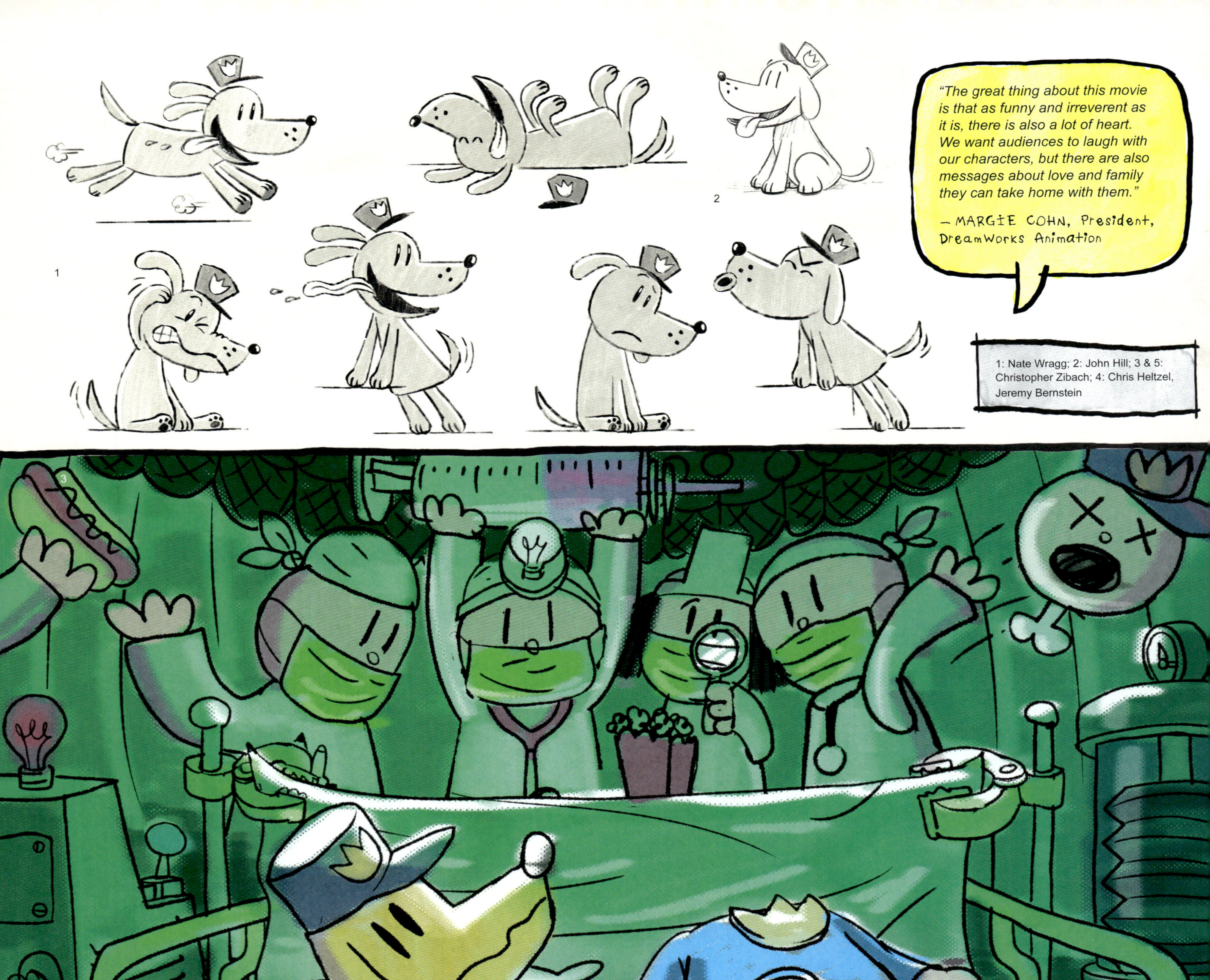

"The great thing about this movie is that as funny and irreverent as it is, there is also a lot of heart. We want audiences to laugh with our characters, but there are also messages about love and family they can take home with them."

—MARGIE COHN, President, DreamWorks Animation

1: Nate Wragg; 2: John Hill; 3 & 5: Christopher Zibach; 4: Chris Heltzel, Jeremy Bernstein

4

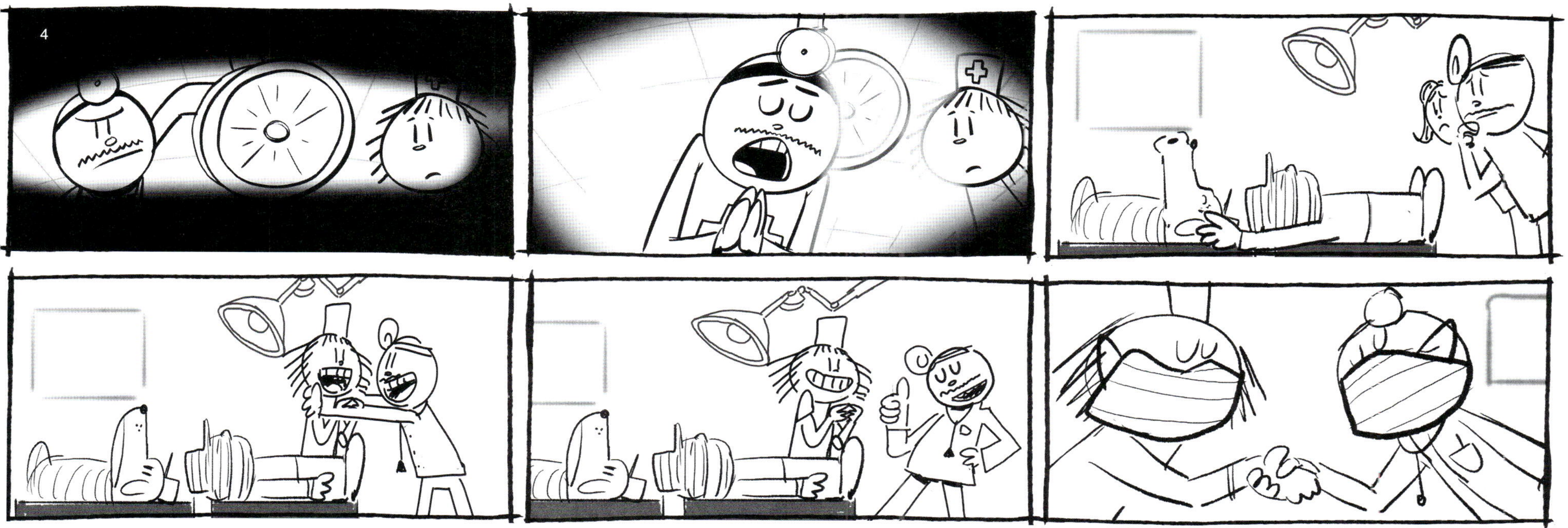

5

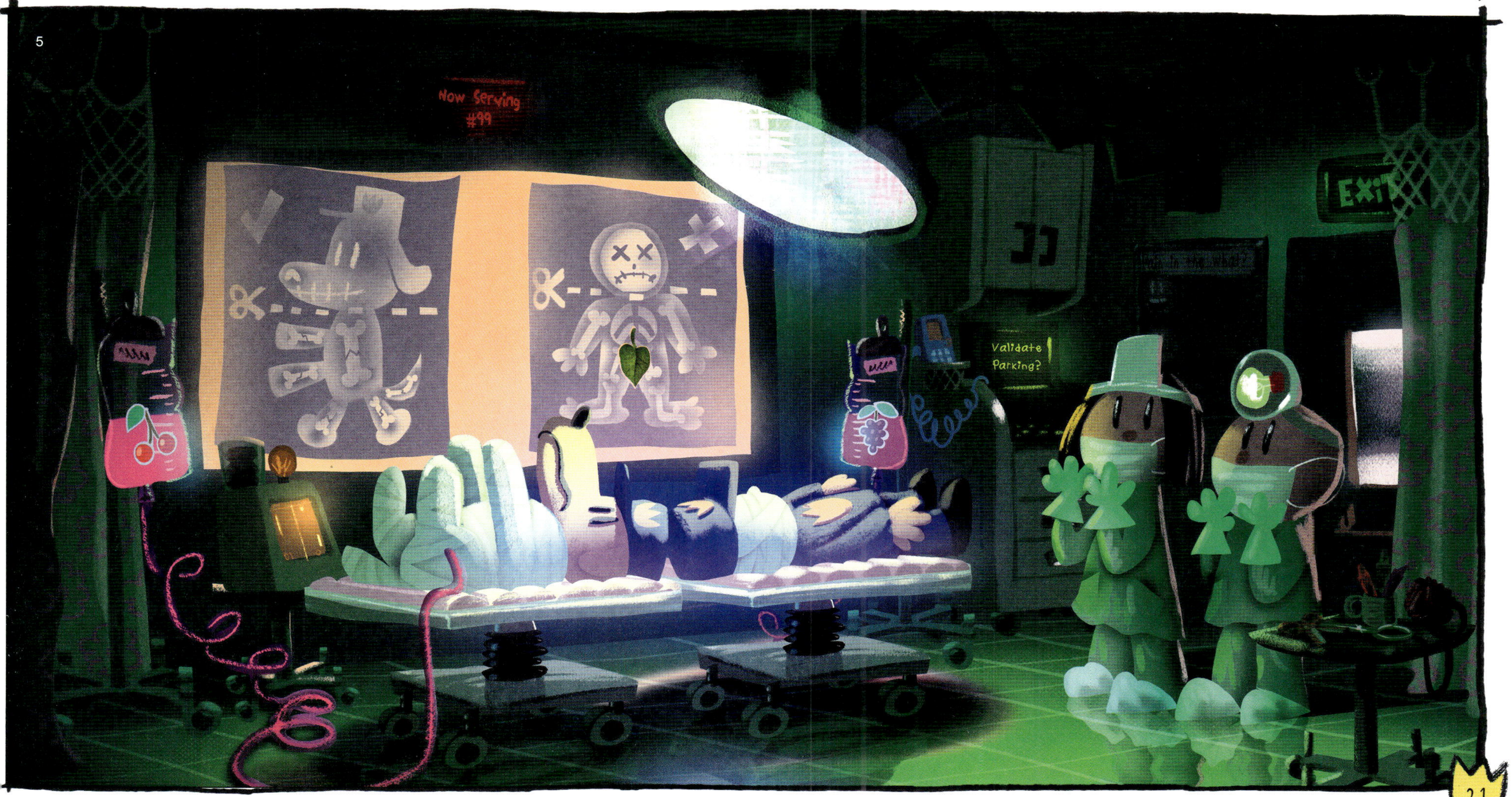

Dog Man

"The beginning of the movie offers the origin story of Dog Man, which makes him a more lovable character as he leans into his dog side," says director Peter Hastings. "We had so much fun engaging him in all the behavioral traits of a dog, such as loyalty and caring, as well as silly fundamental things like having to bark at squirrels or chase balls. But our dog has responsibilities as a policeman as well. We got to play with both sides of this character and just generally ignore the fact that he has these big stitches on his neck."

Obviously, the look of Dog Man in the movie owes a lot to Pilkey's original drawings for the books. As production designer Nate Wragg mentions, "We also wanted to bring to the film a kind of wacky artistry and zaniness so that the overall visual feeling is a playful kids' creation come to life. We adjusted our approach to a traditional CG model to work in tandem with animation to always favor Dog Man's classic profile. We are controlling where the camera goes on him so that, just like the original illustrations, he always has that profile. In the early stages of development, we were treating him too much like a fully functioning 3D vinyl toy. Then, we realized that we had lost the inherent silliness of how he looks. So, in the final version, he even has the triangle-shaped body, silly hat, and dots for eyes."

This approach was also used in the choice of fur on Dog Man's head. "To deliver that desired illustrative approach, we did not just source a library of realistic material. We used scribbles and crayons that convey a feeling of fur," says Wragg.

Head of character animation John Hill admits that Dog Man's mouth created some of the biggest challenges. "In the books, he simply has a black line as his mouth," he explains. "But we had to figure out quite a range of shapes. We kept a black line when he smiled, but then, there are times when you can't see a mouth at all. That was one of the interesting discoveries we made: You become more involved with the character when there's no mouth. He's just kind of staring at you, and it really draws you into the character. Or you could have a huge, wide-open mouth displaying his sharp teeth."

The animation team had to figure out what to do with Dog Man's ears, which are always sticking out in silhouettes. "We managed to do that and also have them lie on the side of his head like a regular dog, which is a good way to transition between the two," adds Hill. "Keeping him in three-quarter profile helped a lot. He can turn his head, but we don't keep any shots where he's looking straight at the camera. Most of the characters have round balloon heads, with black lines for mouths, a circle for a nose, and black lines again for the pupils. So, we basically had to rearrange all those things to convey a wide range of emotions."

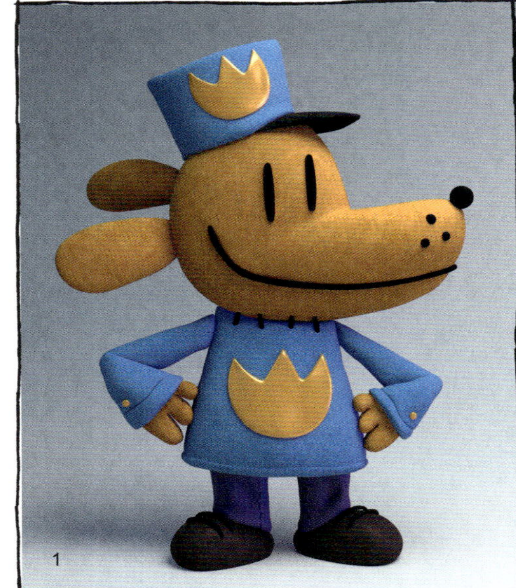
1

"When Dog Man opens his mouth, you suddenly see his teeth appear. When he closes it, you just see a line again, and sometimes that line disappears as well. You simply accept the rules of Pilkey's world."

—KAREN FOSTER, Producer

2

1: Paul Schoeni; 2: Katy Wu; 3: John Hill; 4: Nate Wragg

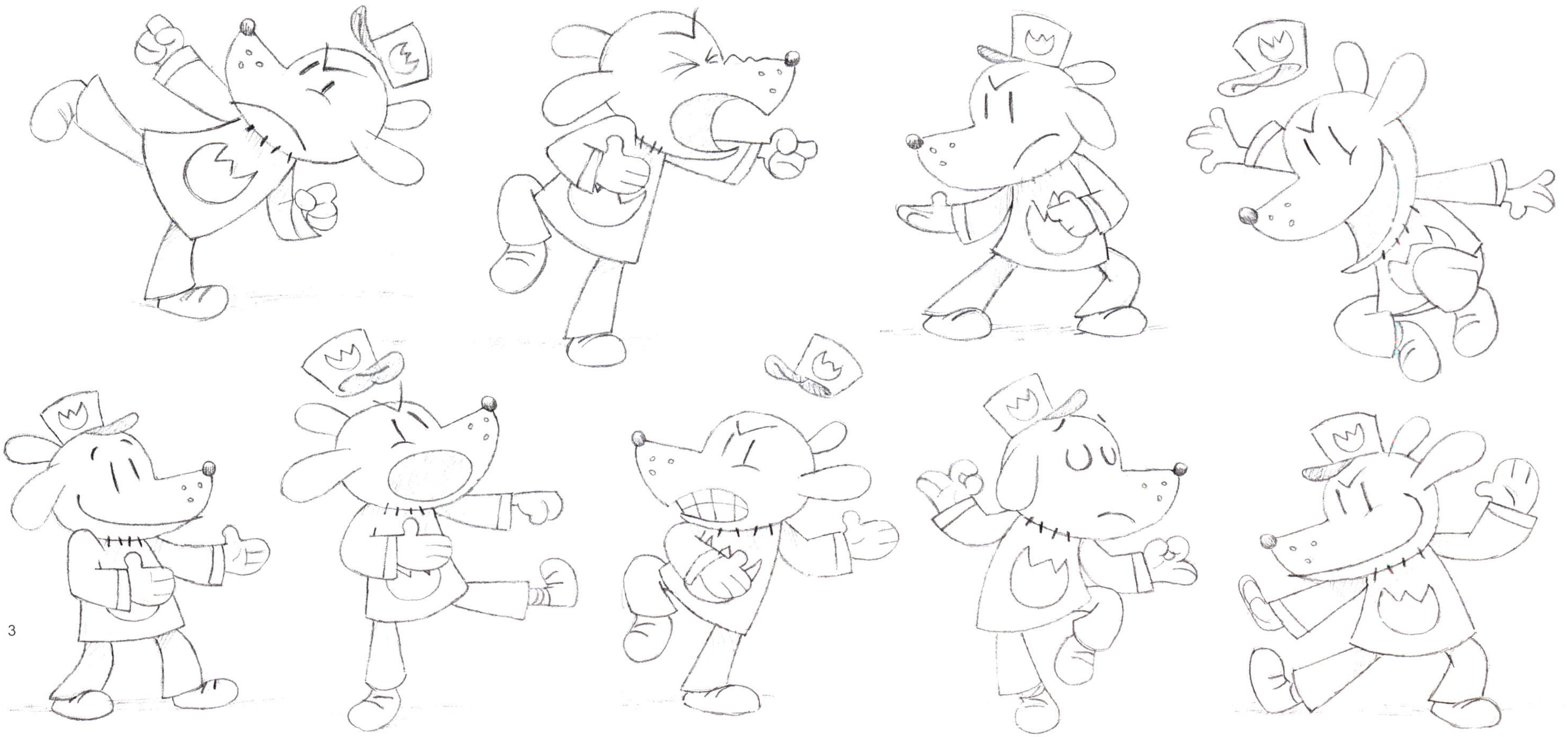

3

4

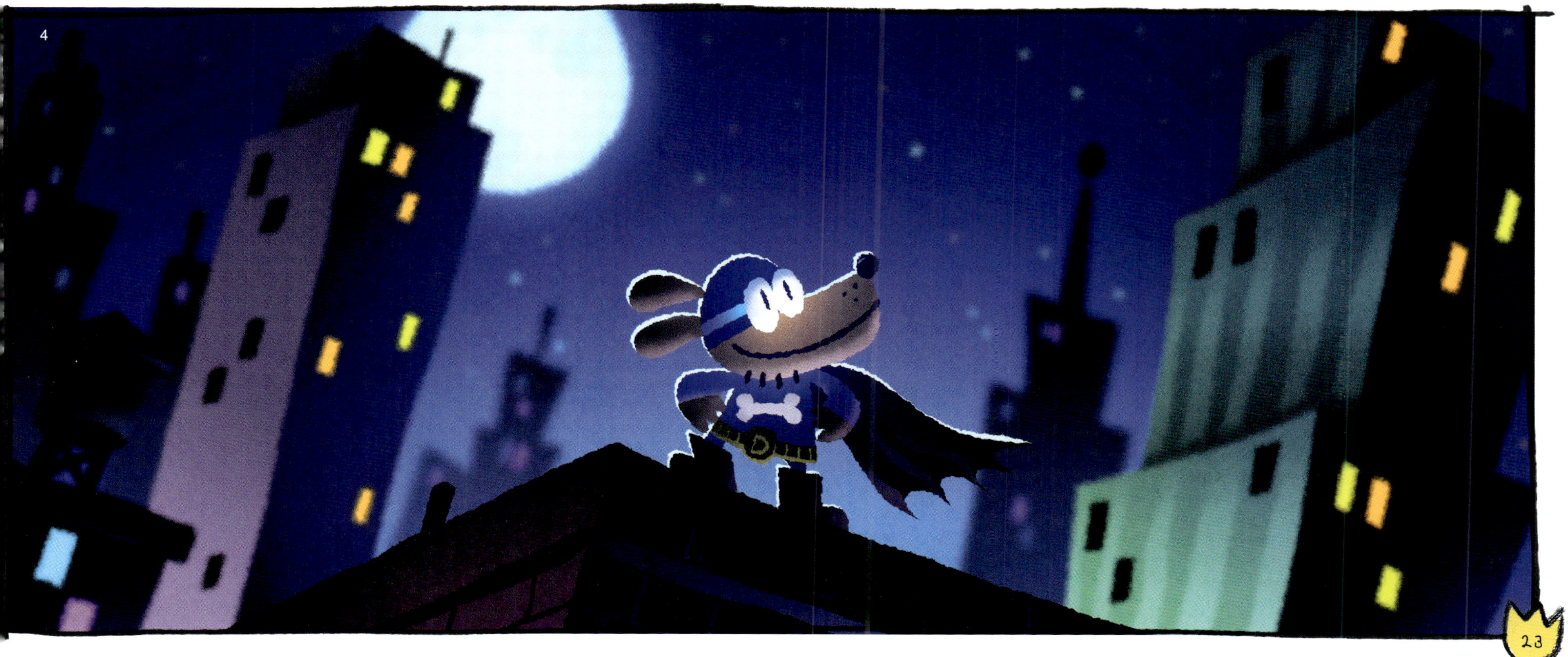

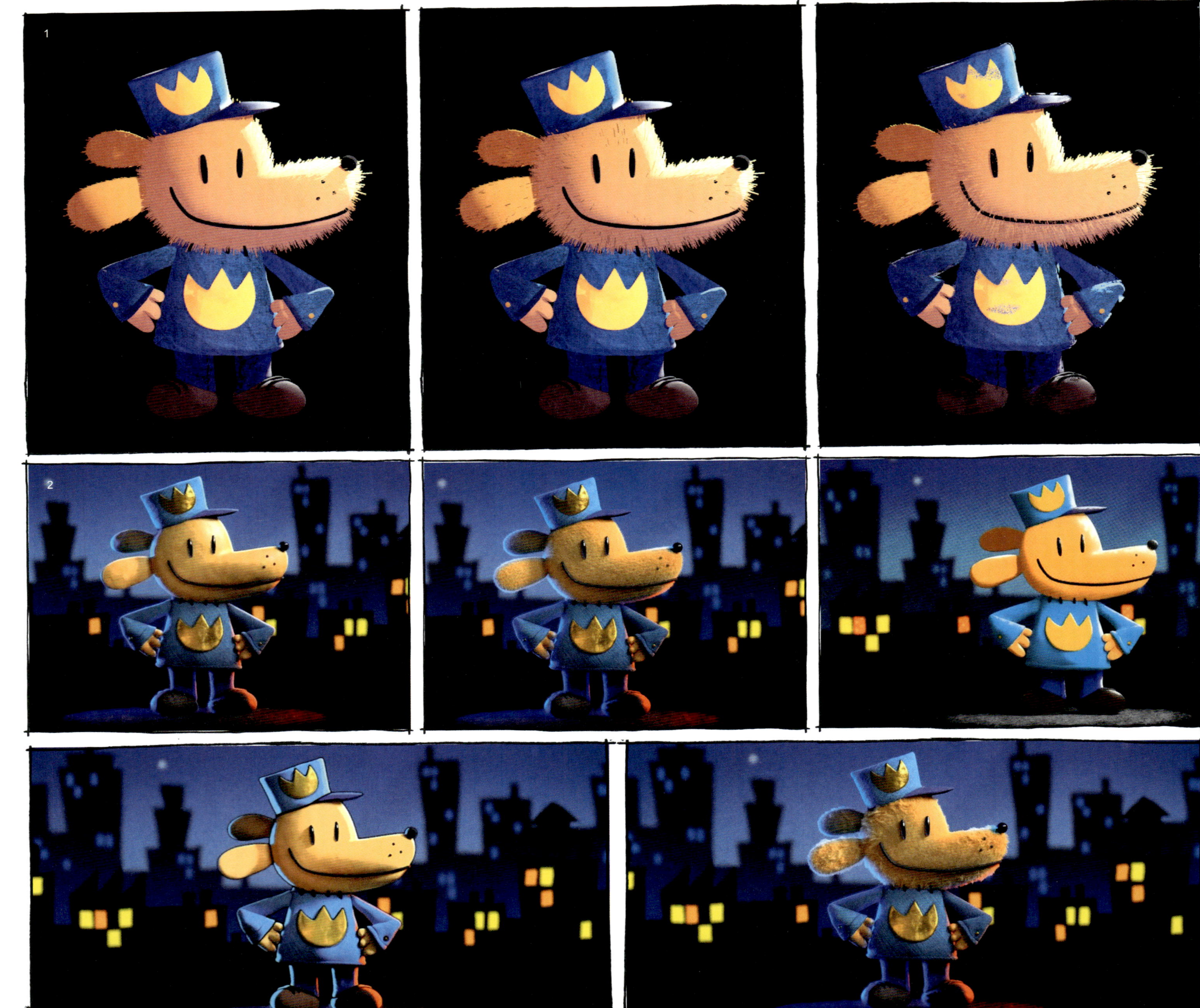
1
2

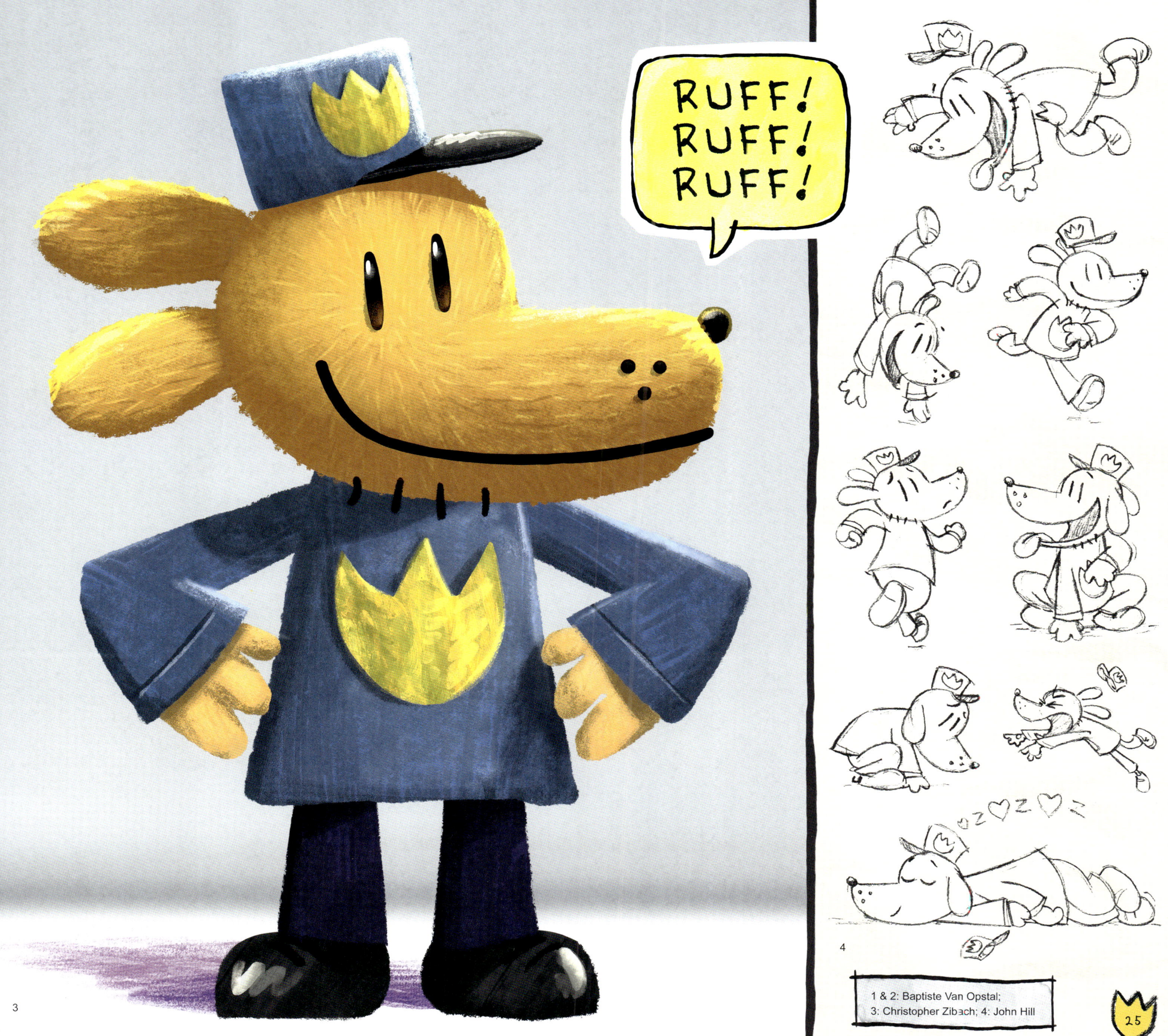

1 & 2: Baptiste Van Opstal;
3: Christopher Zibach; 4: John Hill

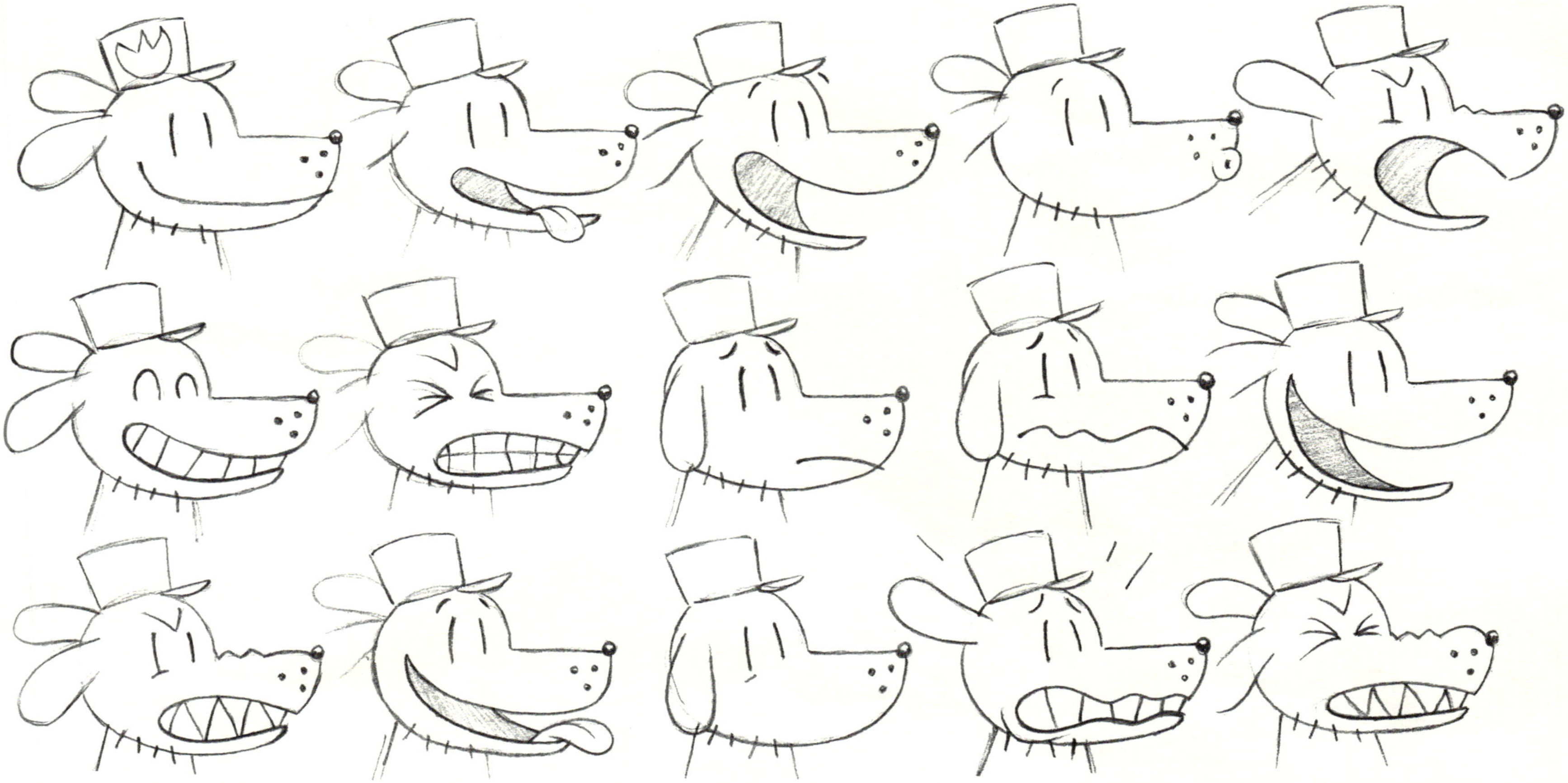

1

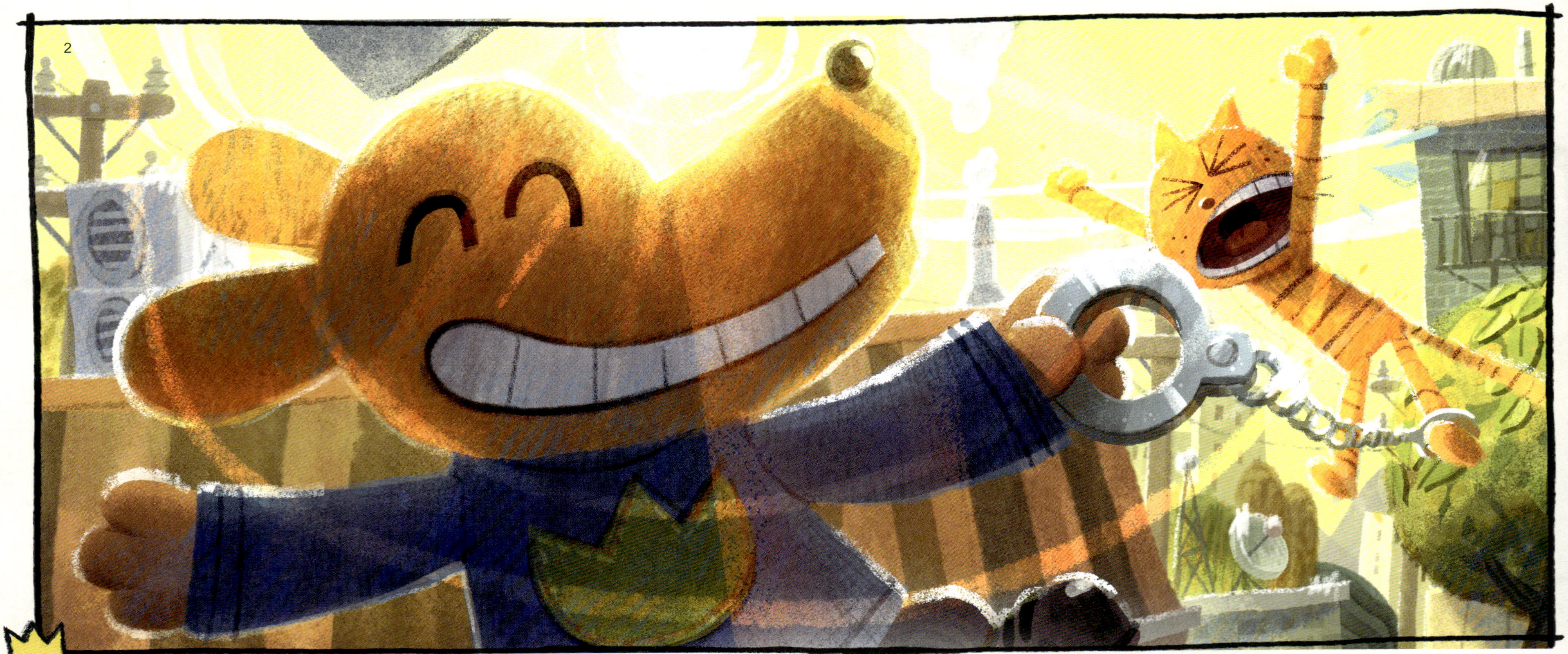

2

3

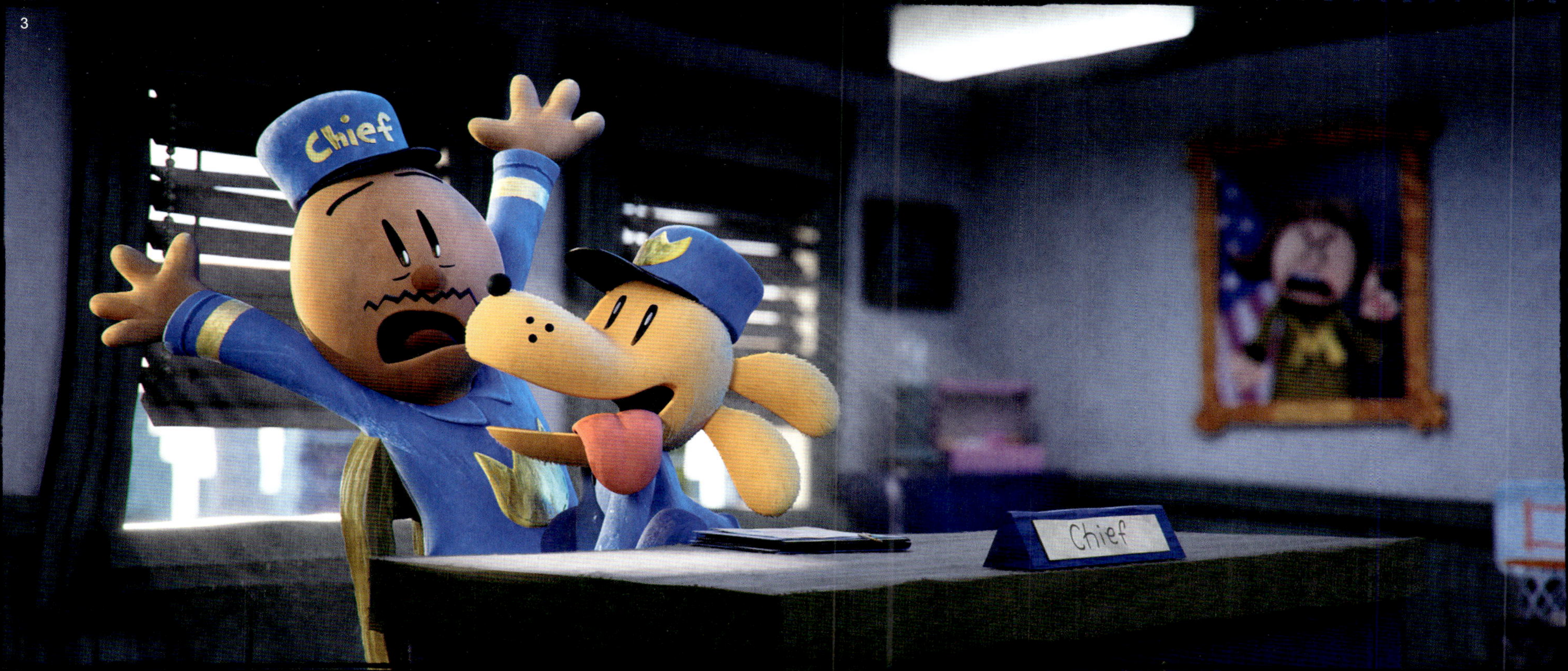

4

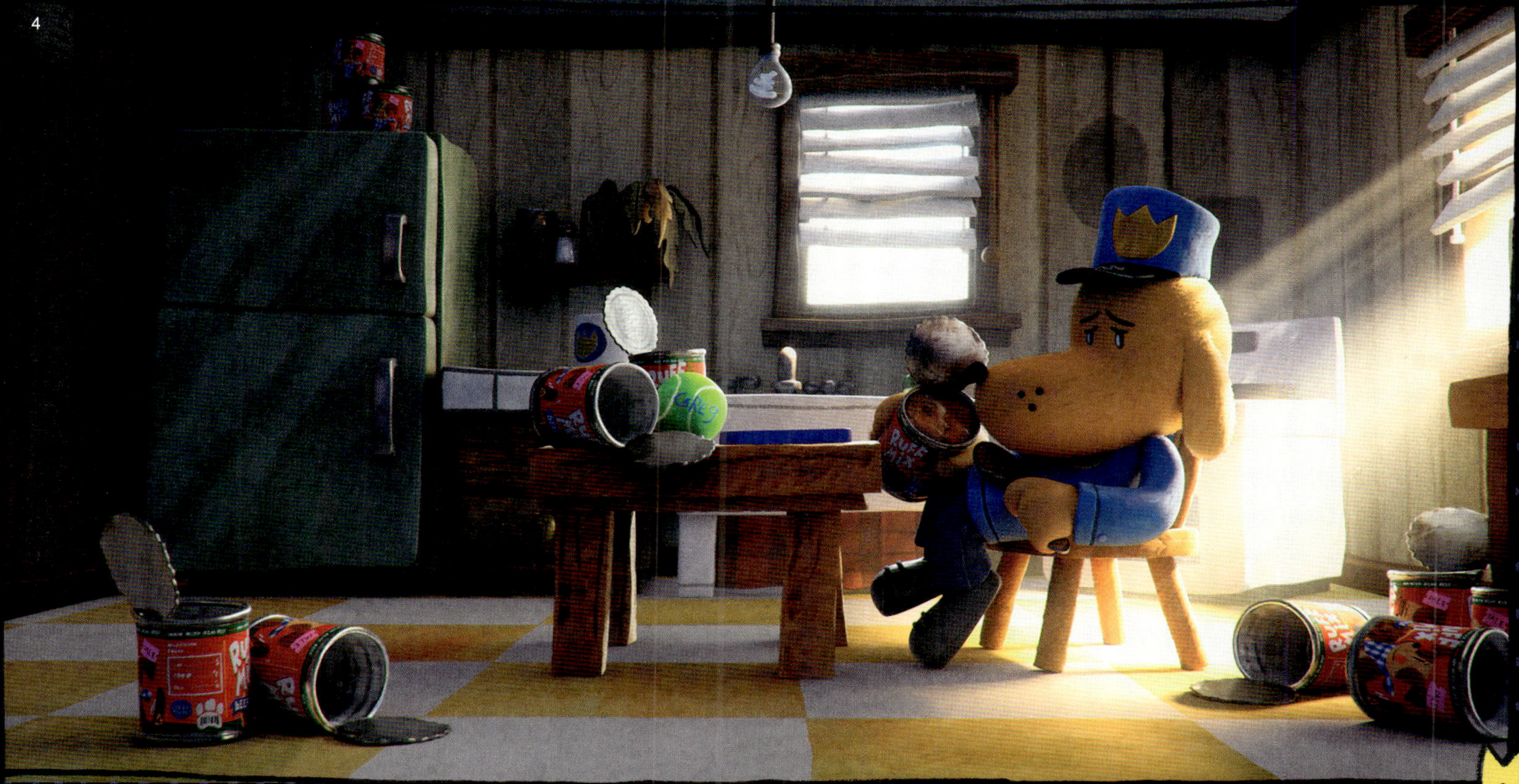

1: John Hill; 2: Katy Wu

3: ***Animation:*** Nicholas Georgeou, Ricky Honmong; ***Lighting:*** Saul Barreto

4: ***Rigging:*** Alessandro Boschian-Pest, Xavier Roca Crespo, Joan Valdivielso, Èlia Garcia Amores, Roger Bosque, Asier Lizaso Zelaia, Samuel Pinhorne, Rémi Colcombe; ***Rough Layout:*** Nicholas Manfredi; ***Animation:*** Oz Durose; ***Lighting:*** Jamie Tremelling

Petey the Cat

Every good story needs a clever and complicated villain, and *Dog Man* gives us Petey, the World's Most Evilest Cat, an orange cat with horizontal black stripes on his body and a flat tail. Voiced to perfection by Pete Davidson, he has a very complicated history with his father and eventually becomes Dog Man's friend (in the fifth book of the series, *Lord of the Fleas*). As Petey tells his good-hearted clone/son Li'l Petey, "If you only knew the horrible things I've done . . . the awful, unforgivable things! I'm just evil through and through!"

"Petey is a classic villain and the kind of character who can never catch a break," says director Peter Hastings. "Yes, he can be mean and evil, but he is also a great foil for Dog Man. He represents someone who is fighting against their true nature. Once Li'l Petey enters the picture, he becomes the truth mirror, and he helps Petey confront his own prejudices. When Petey meets his estranged father, he realizes that he doesn't want to be like him. Petey's reality, goals, and needs are all challenged by the arrival of this little kid, who is literally a tiny version of him."

Production designer Nate Wragg says Petey is a wonderful villain whom you love to hate at first, but then you end up loving him anyway. "I like the fact that he has all these outrageous invention ideas that try to take Dog Man down, but they always end up being more annoying than functional," he says. "I think Petey's crazy ideas for taking over the world or defeating Dog Man are actually the kind of comically silly ideas born in a ten-year-old's mind, and that makes sense because the whole world is created by George and Harold."

Head of character animation John Hill mentions that even the way Petey moves and acts evolves when Li'l Petey enters his life. "We all know that he's this evil, crazy cat with some major issues, but once Li'l Petey comes along, it kind of softens him. He is originally a kind of explosive and very emotional character, but his son makes a big impact and calms him down eventually."

1

2

3

1 & 5: Nate Wragg; 2, 3, 6 & Overleaf: Lia Tin; 4: John Hill

4

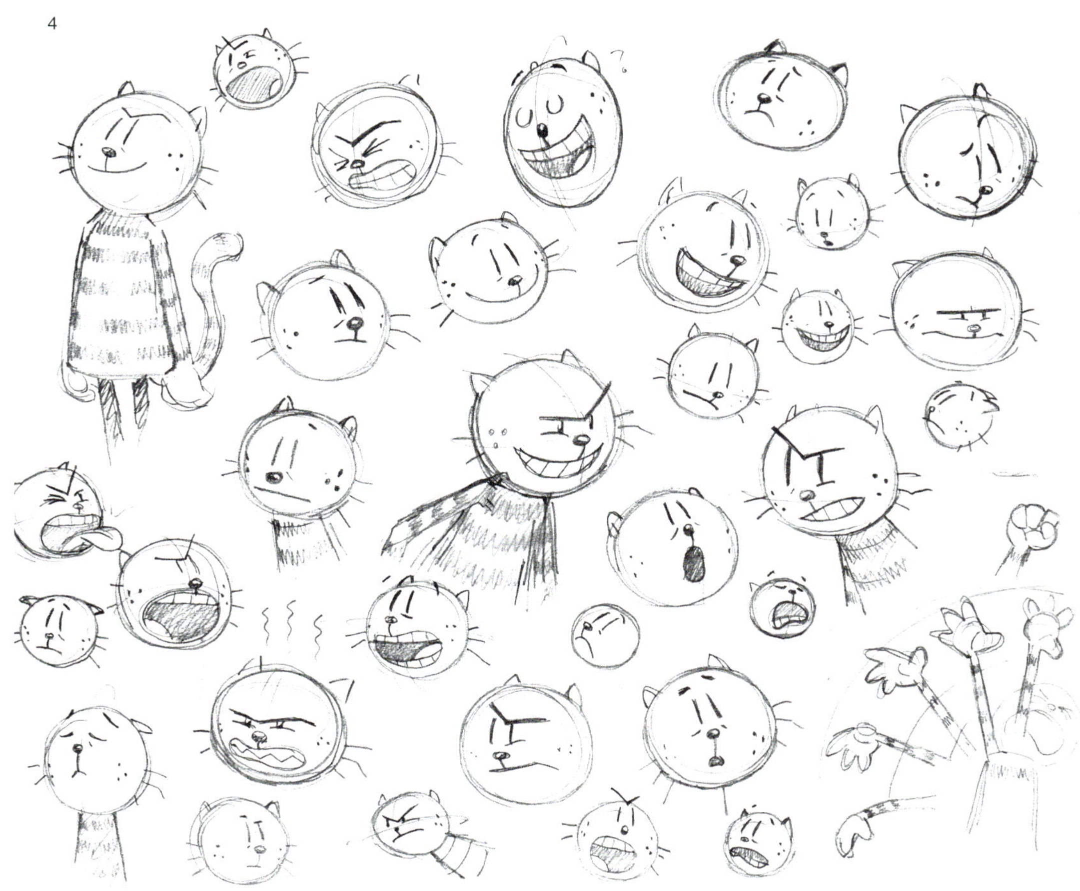

5

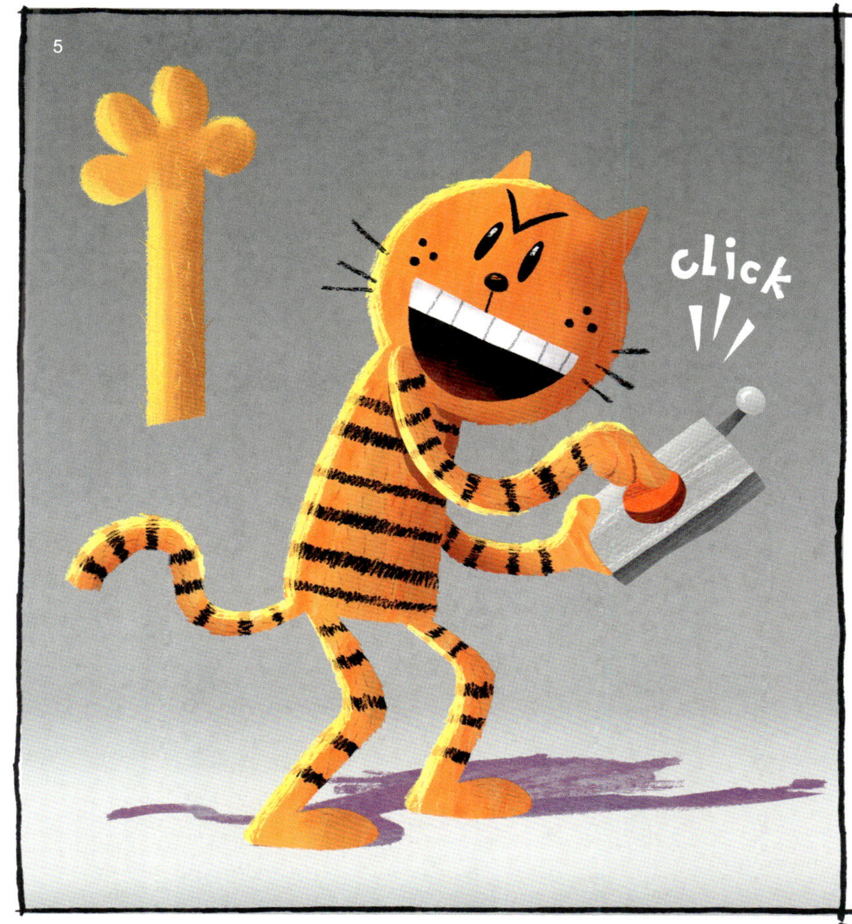

6

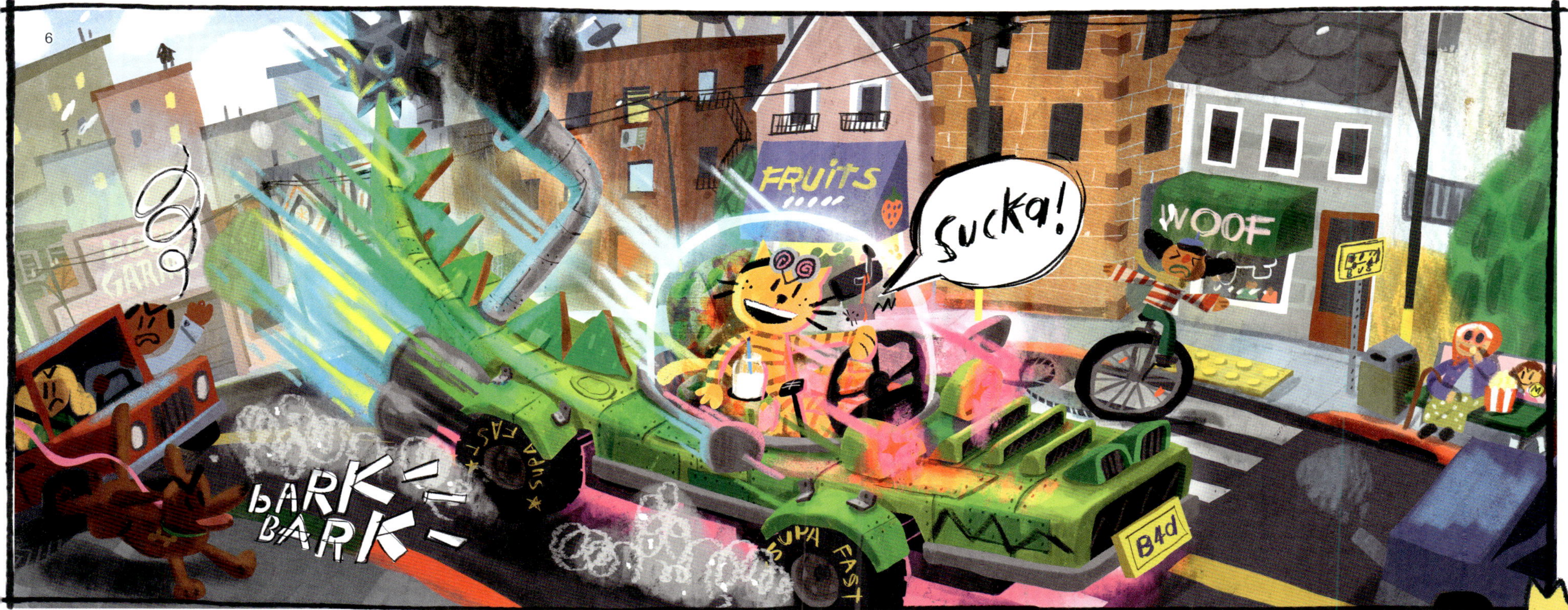

Sucka!

FRUITS

WOOF

bARK-
BARK-

SUPA FAST

B4d

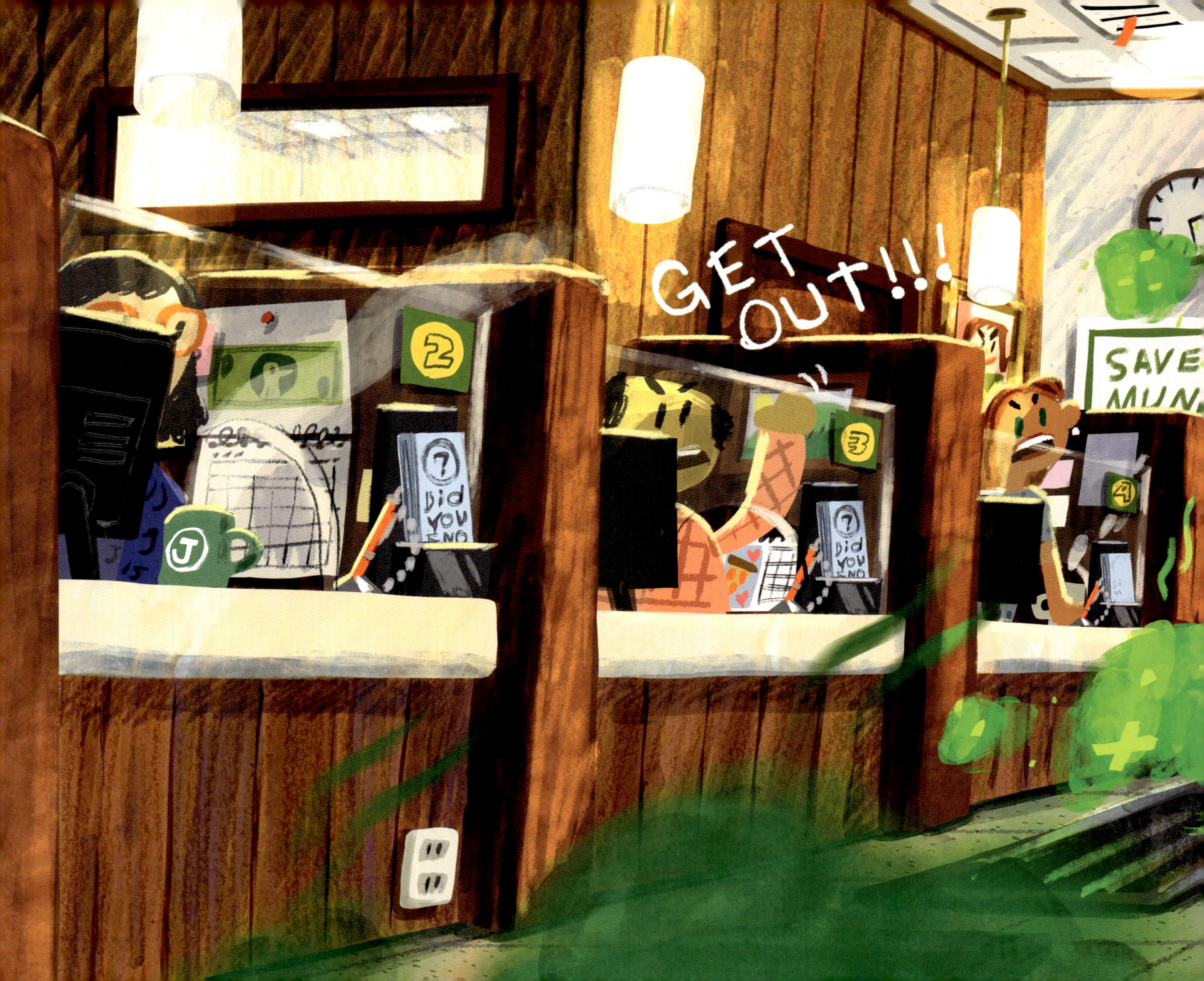
GET OUT!!!
SAVE

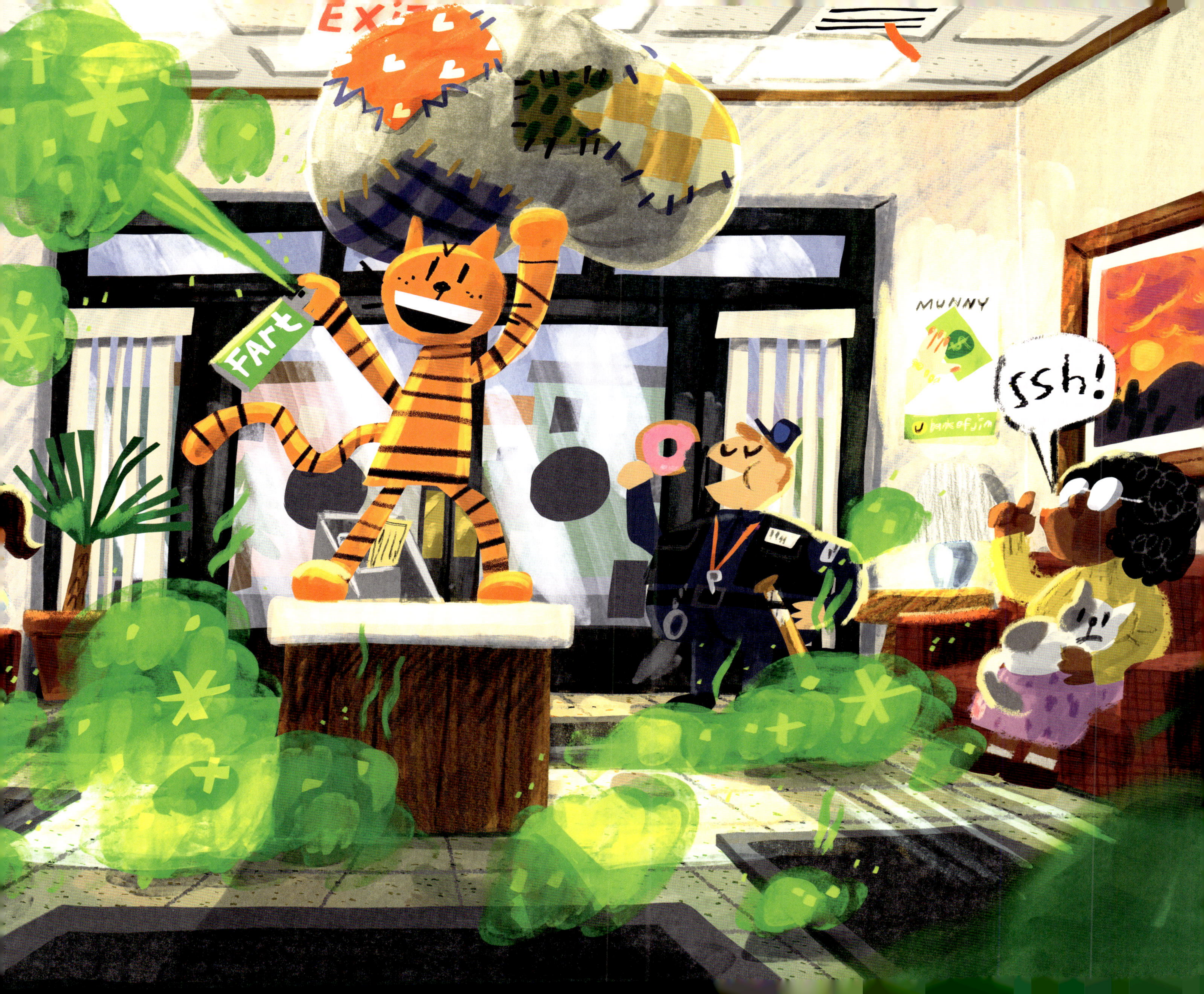
FART
MUNNY
ssh!

1

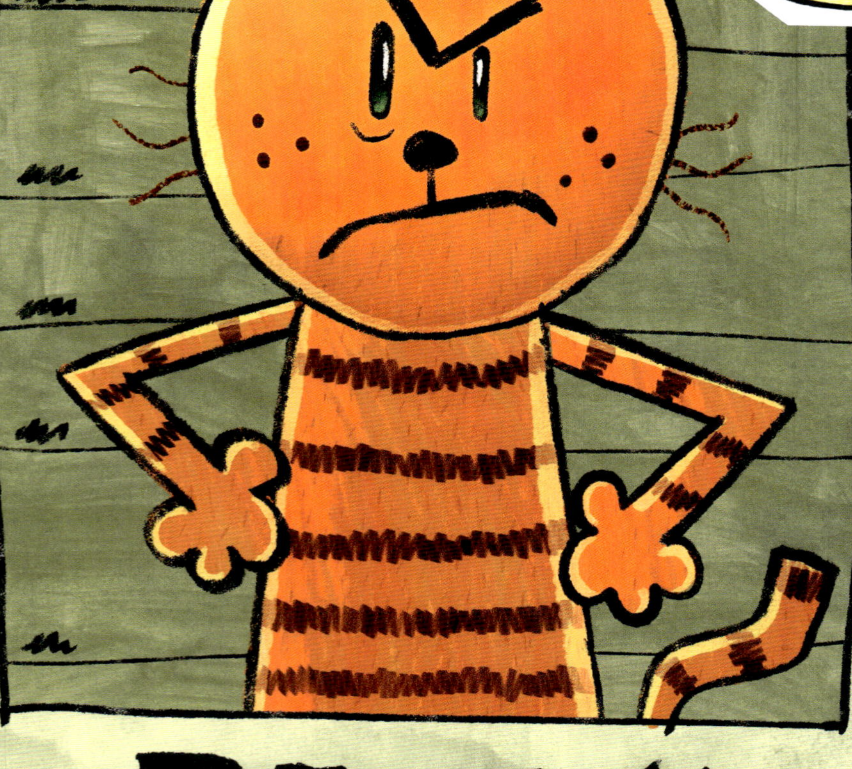

2

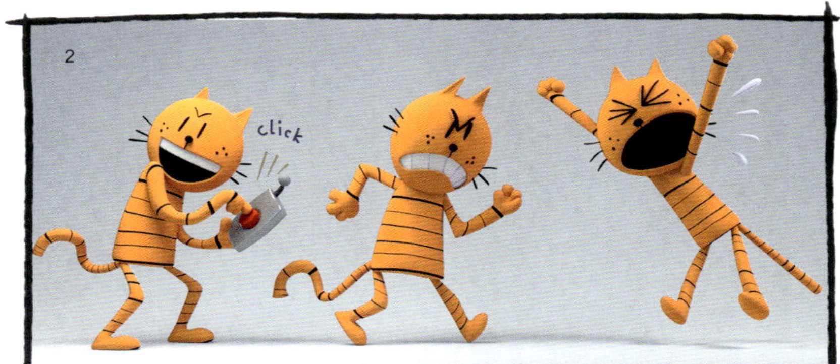

"Petey is supposed to be our evil cat. But once Li'l Petey comes along, he changes, and his anger softens. His movements also change as a result."

—JOHN HILL, Head of Character Animation

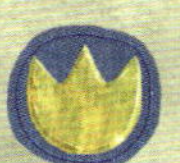

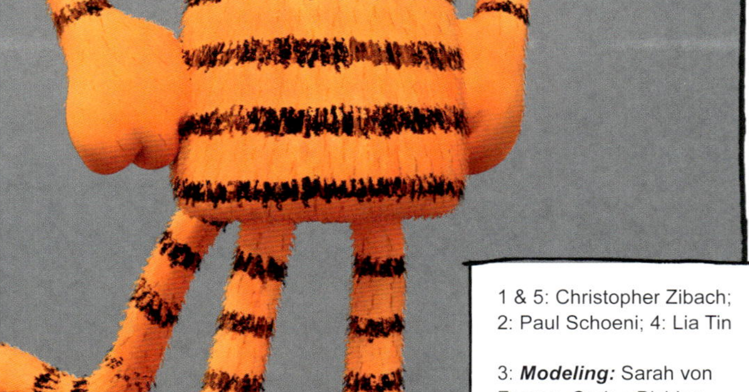

3

1 & 5: Christopher Zibach; 2: Paul Schoeni; 4: Lia Tin

3: ***Modeling:*** Sarah von Fersen, Carina Bichler; ***Surfacing:*** Hannah Wong, Suzanne Lokker, Salvatore Sorvillo, Daniele La Mura

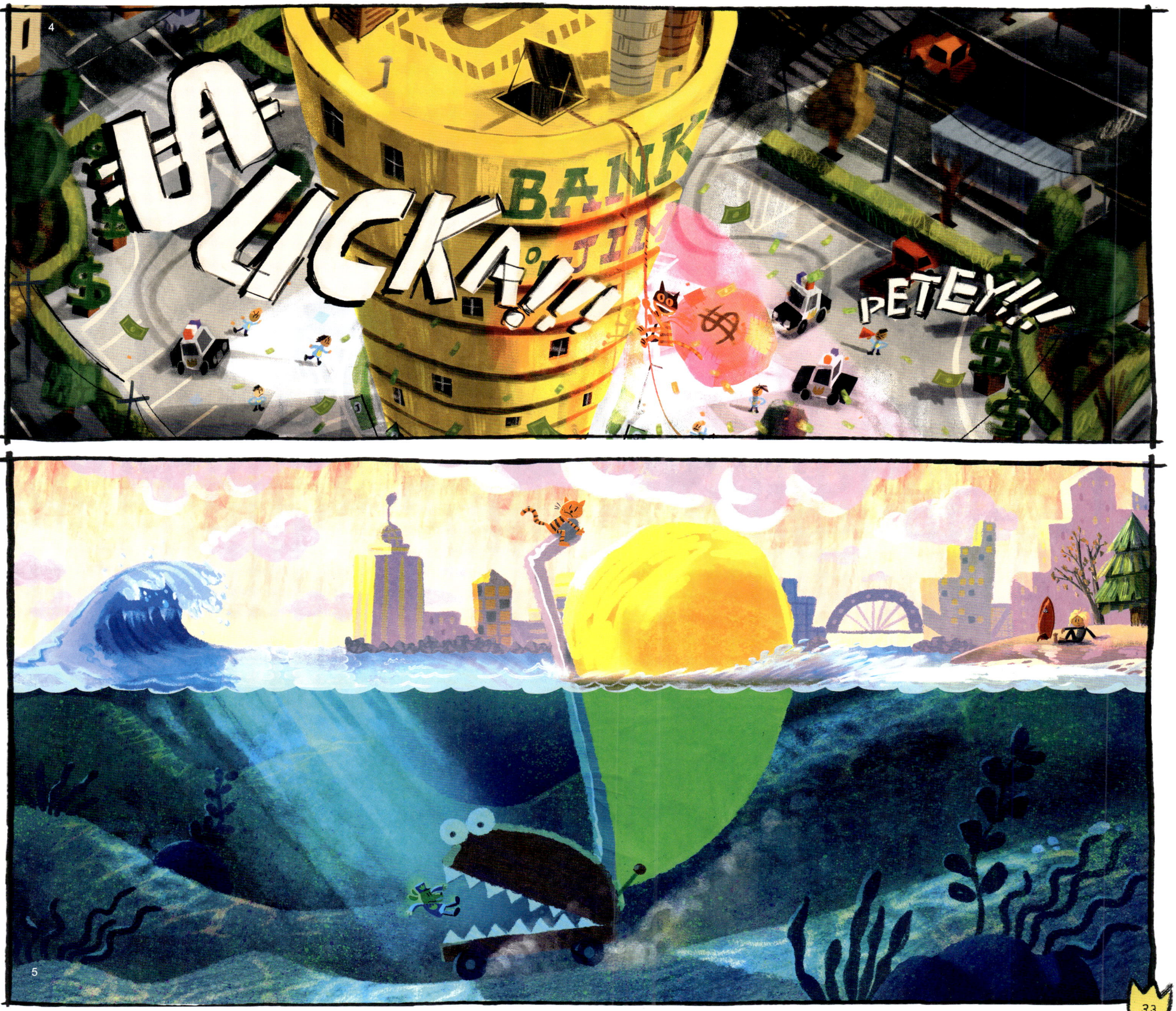

4

SLICKA!!!

BANK

PETEY!!!

5

Li'l Petey

Petey's son, who is literally his clone, is another anthropomorphic orange tabby cat with black stripes on his body and tail. Often described as pure-hearted and a force for good, Li'l Petey (voiced by Lucas Hopkins) eventually ends up living with Petey during the week and with Dog Man on weekends. He refers to Petey as "Papa" and loves making comics and telling jokes. He made his first appearance in the third Dog Man book, *A Tale of Two Kitties*.

"He is the voice of truth and innocence without being precocious," says director Peter Hastings. "We found it was so much fun to have Dog Man and Petey start out having this adversarial relationship, and then have them both develop separate relationships with Li'l Petey. When the little one gets into trouble, they must work together to save him. In a way, Dog Man starts out as someone who doesn't have a family but wants one, while Petey repeatedly gets a family and doesn't want it. But they are all brought together thanks to Li'l Petey and the power of sharing and caring."

"Li'l Petey ends up being the character who brings out the best in everybody and creates this somewhat contemporary shared-custody exchange between Dog Man and Petey," says production designer Nate Wragg. "It's a unique and cool storytelling dynamic to have between hero and villain."

Wragg mentions that because the design team stayed very faithful to Dav Pilkey's original illustration, Li'l Petey also resembles the simple drawings in the books. "We knew that he could skew very young, but I think that because of who he is and what he brings out in others, we have a very universal character who appeals to everyone. Our vision was that we wanted the original Dog Man fans to immediately recognize all these characters. So our CG-animated Petey, Li'l Petey, and Dog Man were not a reimagining—they were just brought to a new medium. We have the creative license to push this world into spaces that they haven't been before, but everything is done through the lens of Pilkey's vision."

Producer Karen Foster recalls the scene where Petey is walking home after leaving Li'l Petey with Dog Man to stay for a while. "He now sees the world through different eyes, thanks to his son. He sees weeds as flowers and notices the beautiful stars in the sky. We present this idea that we can change our perspectives and break the cycle of abuse. We all recognize the unconditional love of a pet—unless it's a cat!—and how it can transform your heart, and Li'l Petey brings that to both Dog Man and Petey."

1

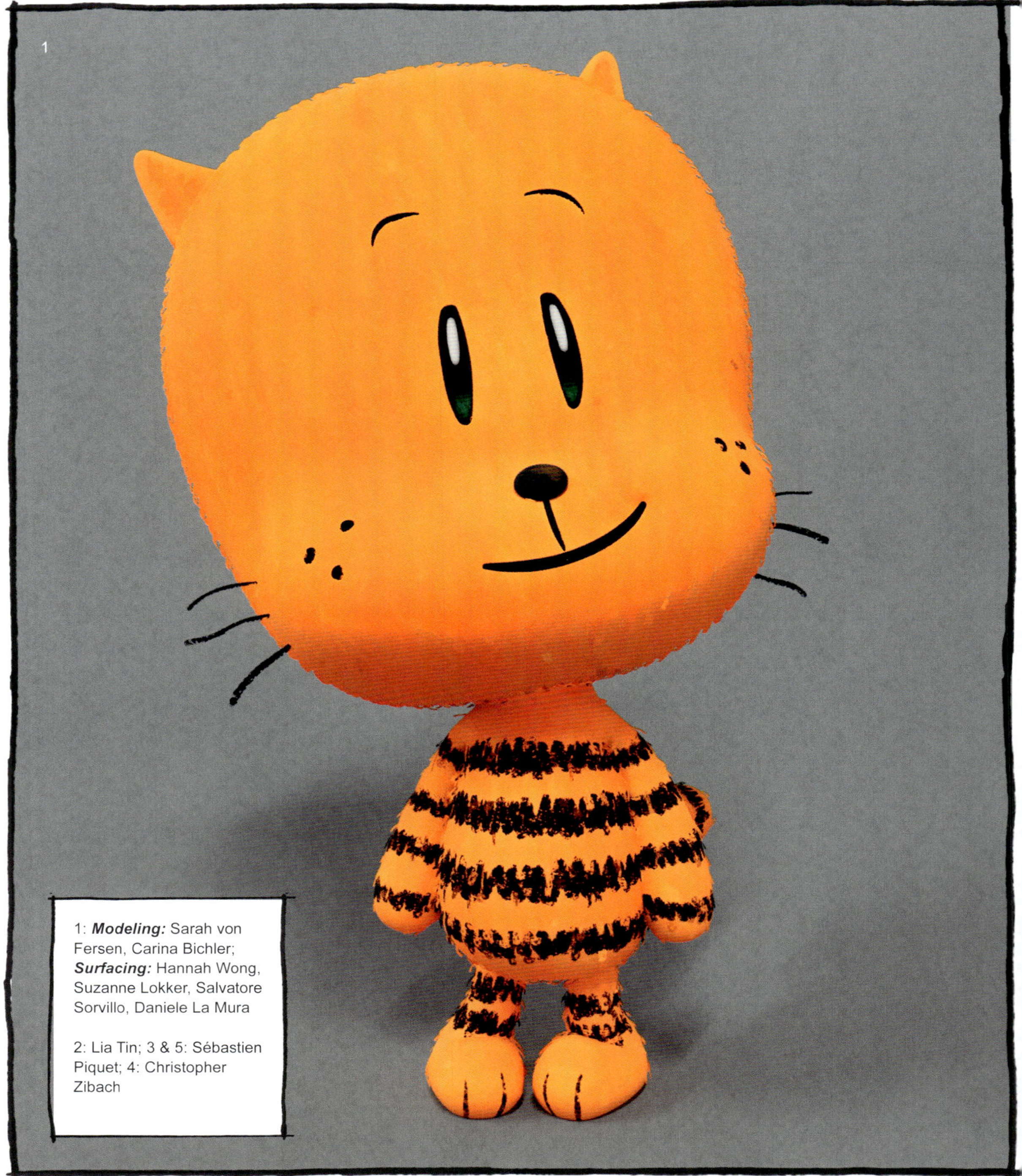

1: ***Modeling:*** Sarah von Fersen, Carina Bichler; ***Surfacing:*** Hannah Wong, Suzanne Lokker, Salvatore Sorvillo, Daniele La Mura

2: Lia Tin; 3 & 5: Sébastien Piquet; 4: Christopher Zibach

2

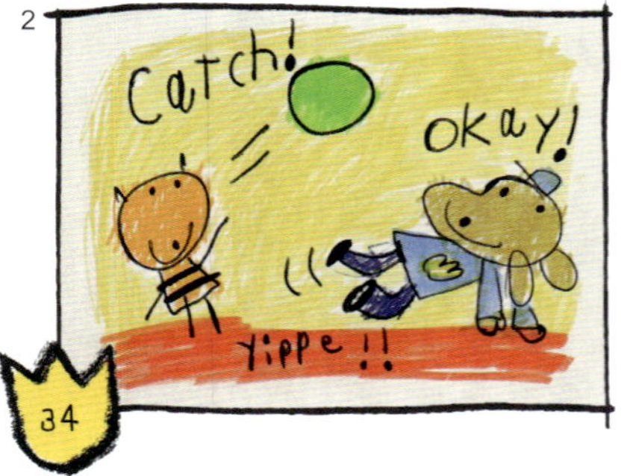

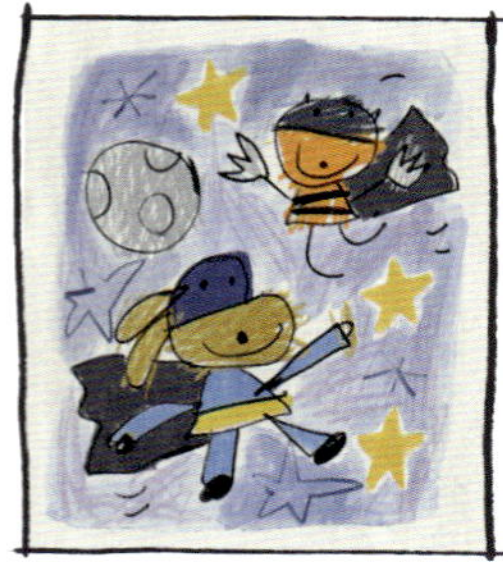

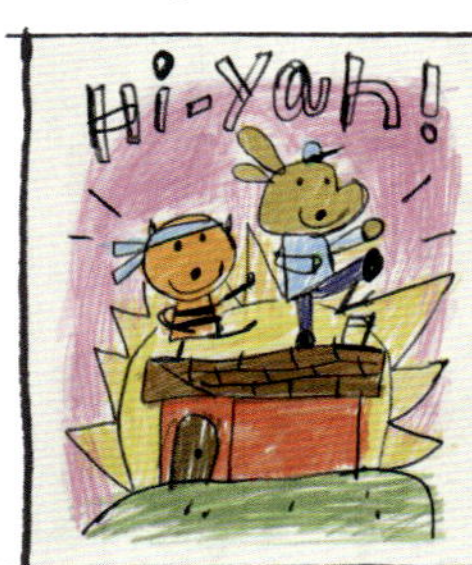

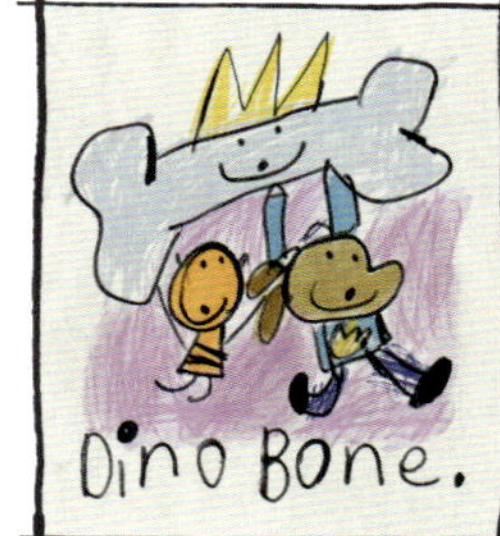

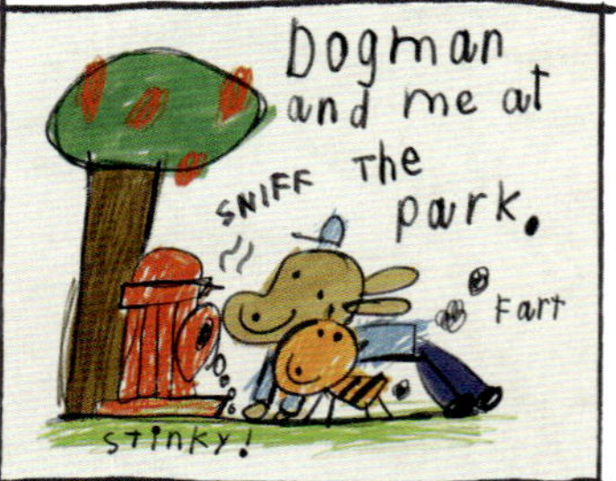

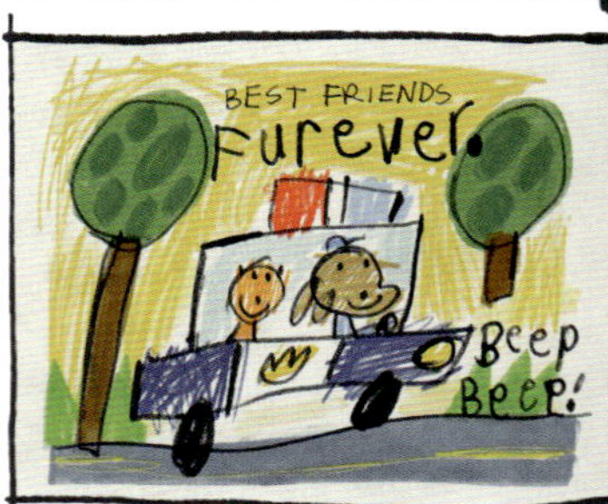

Lonely in the world
Alone?
Sad?
Call 0732

3

4

5

COPS
to Protect from the rain

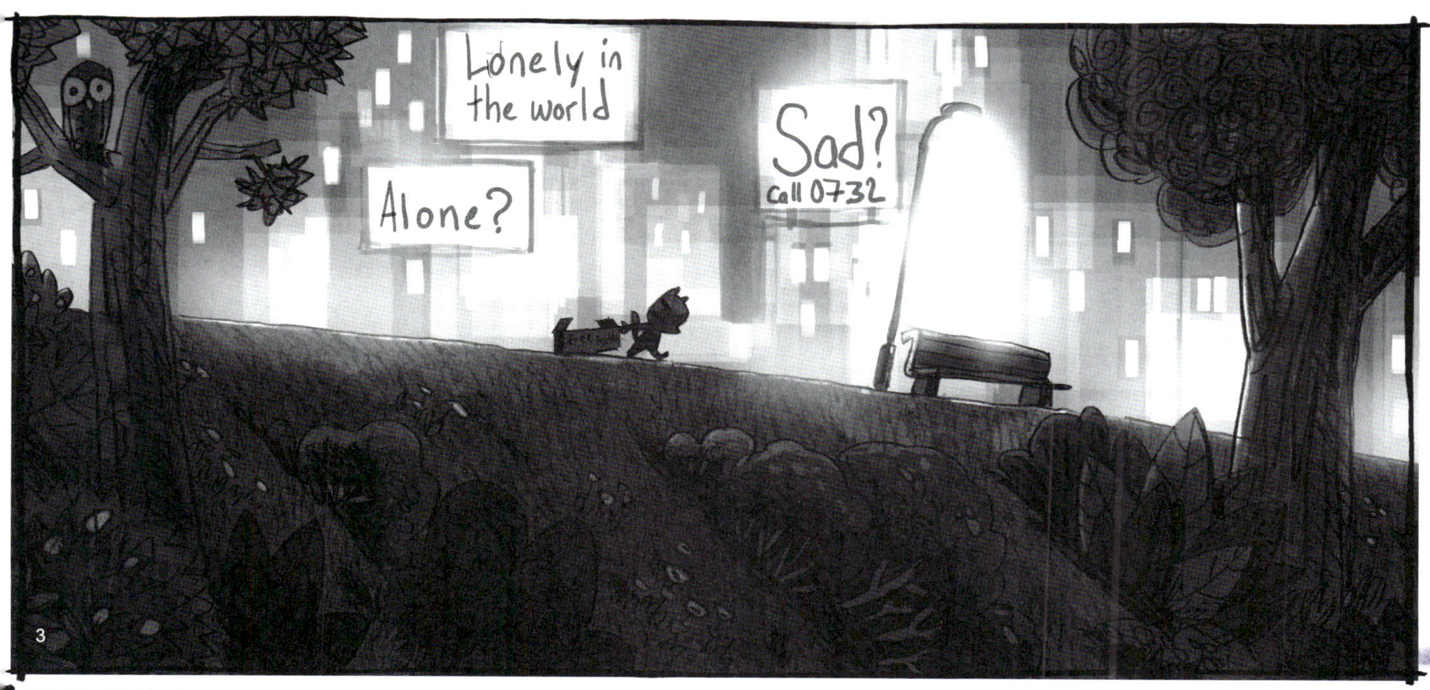

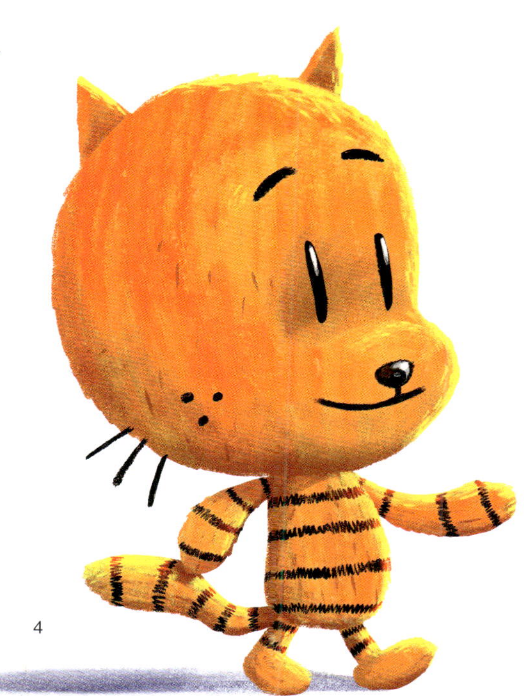

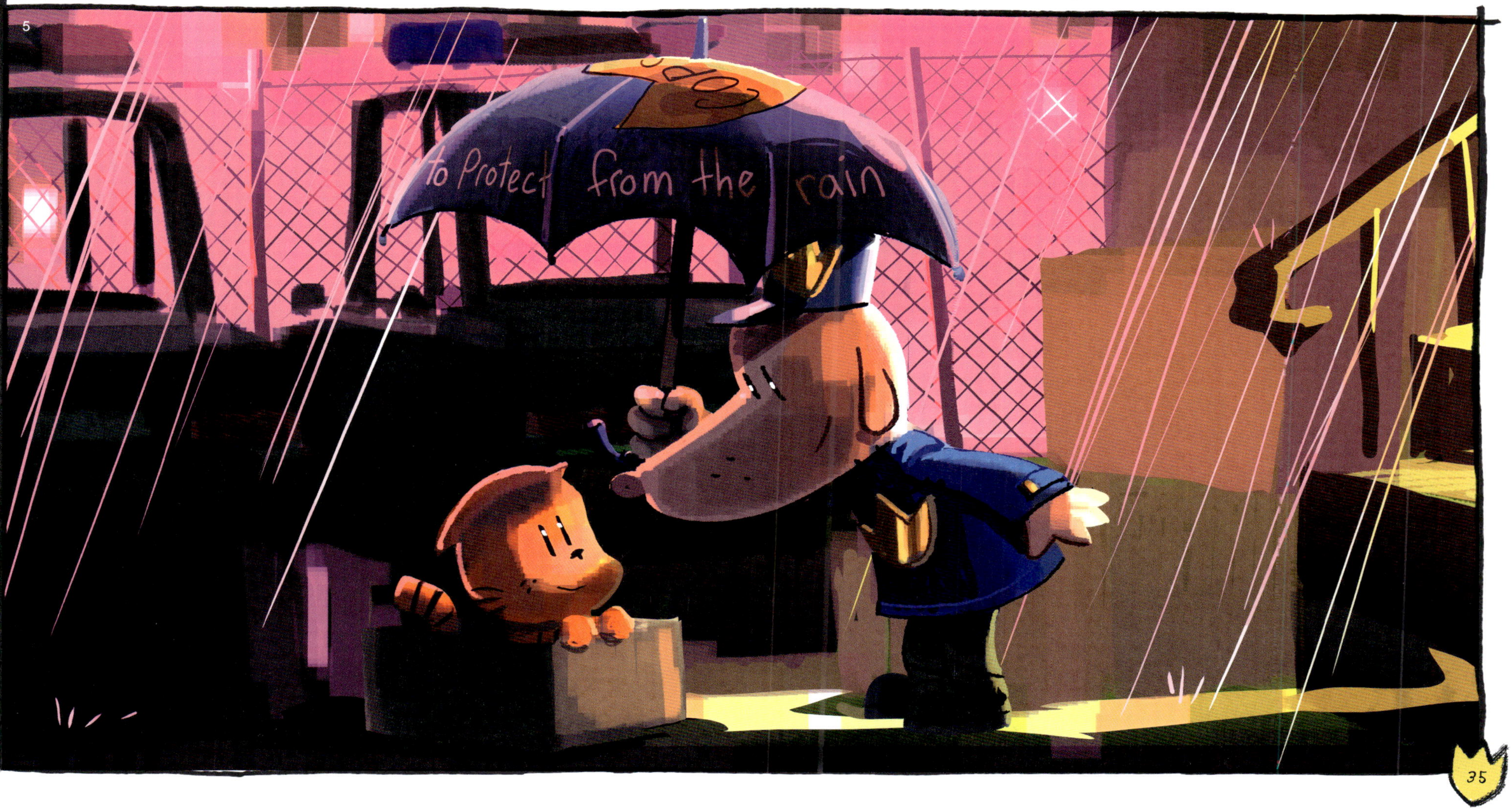

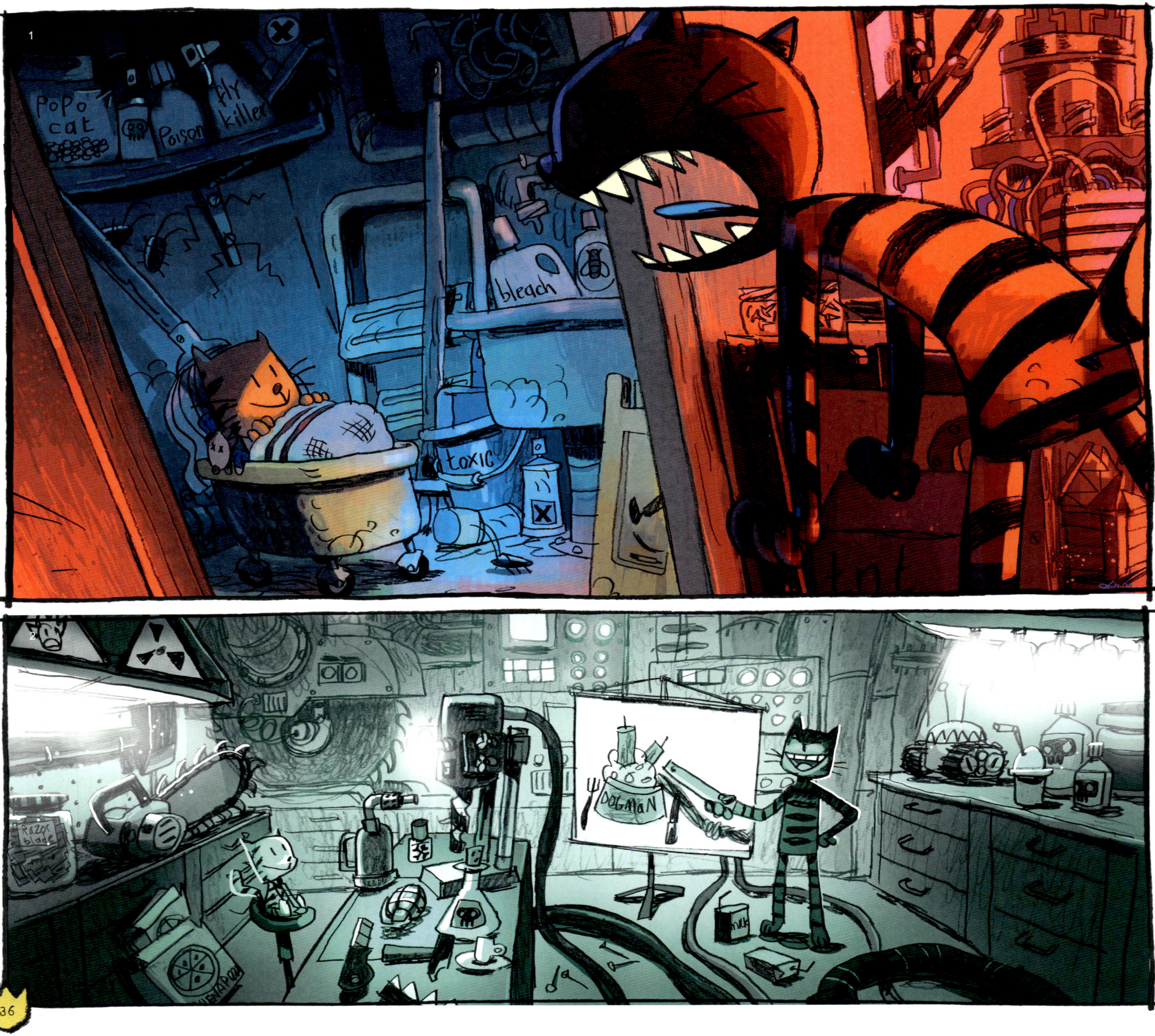

Popo cat
Poison
fly killer
bleach
toxic

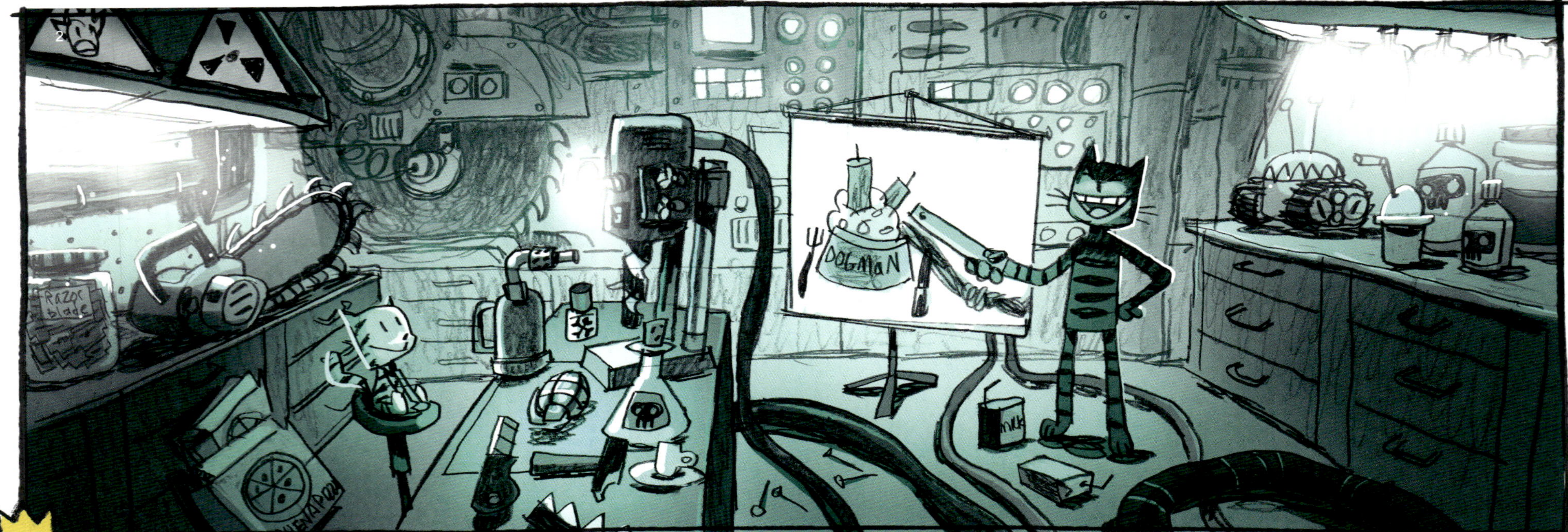
DOGMAN
Razor blade
milk

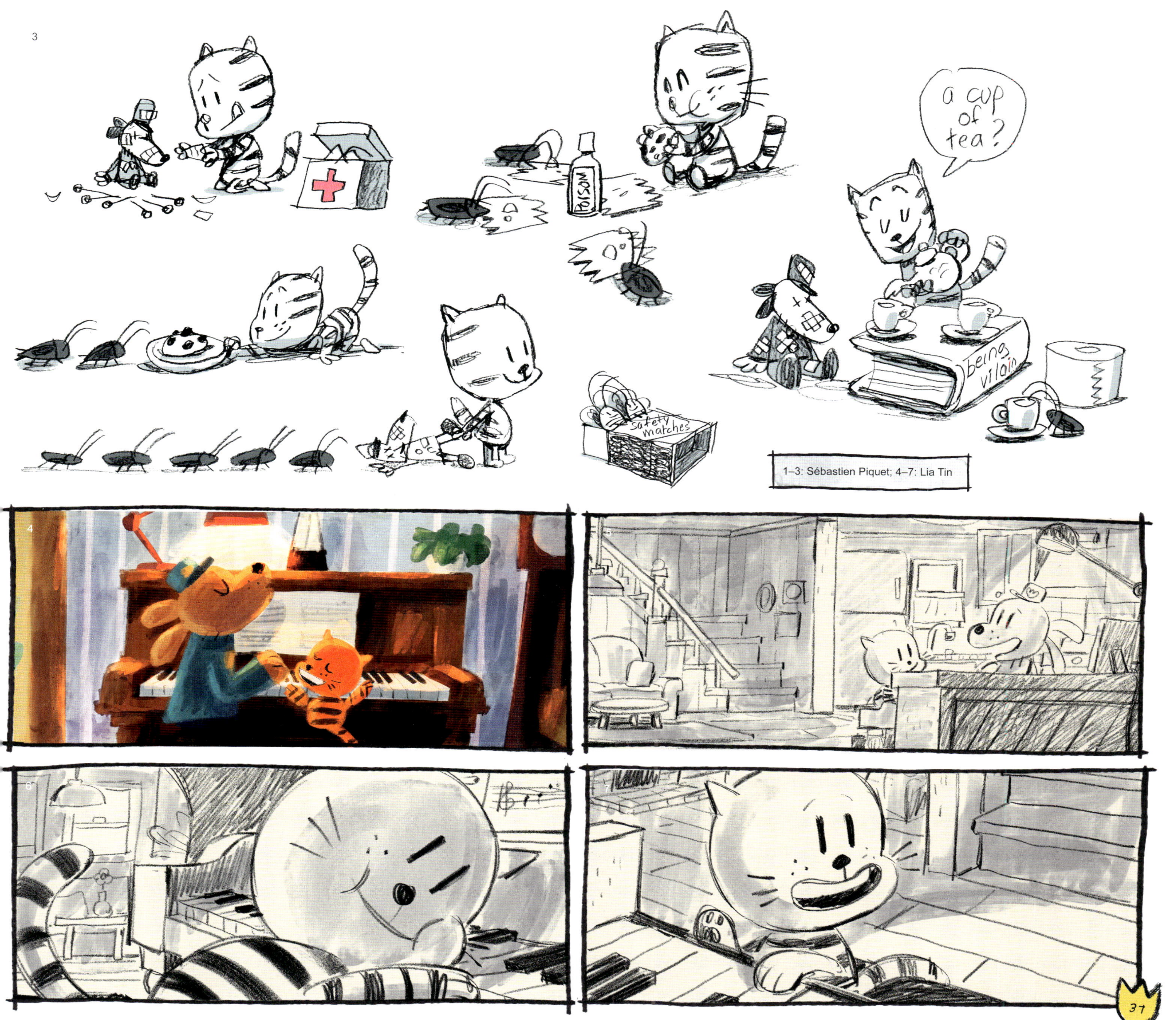

1–3: Sébastien Piquet; 4–7: Lia Tin

Chief

The head of the police department, Chief (voiced by Lil Rel Howery) is Dog Man's boss, whose uniform consists of a blue shirt with a yellow badge and hat that says "Chief." He has a black zigzag mustache and a round nose. He can be bossy, forgetful, and impulsive, but he's generally a good guy.

"He interacts with Dog Man a lot, and he's always sort of overlooked because Dog Man is the hero, after all," says production designer Nate Wragg. "He is emotionally a bit insecure, and he's annoyed by all the mayhem that Petey and Dog Man can create. He loves his job and wears his heart on his sleeve, and of course, he has a crush on Sarah Hatoff."

Producer Karen Foster says she loves all the different layers in Chief's personality. "I find him particularly charming. He's funny and gruff, and his character came to life with Lil Rel Howery's lively performance," she says. "You can tell he really cares, even when he's yelling at Dog Man. He also doesn't want to reveal his secret love for Sarah, and he holds it in, but it's irrepressible."

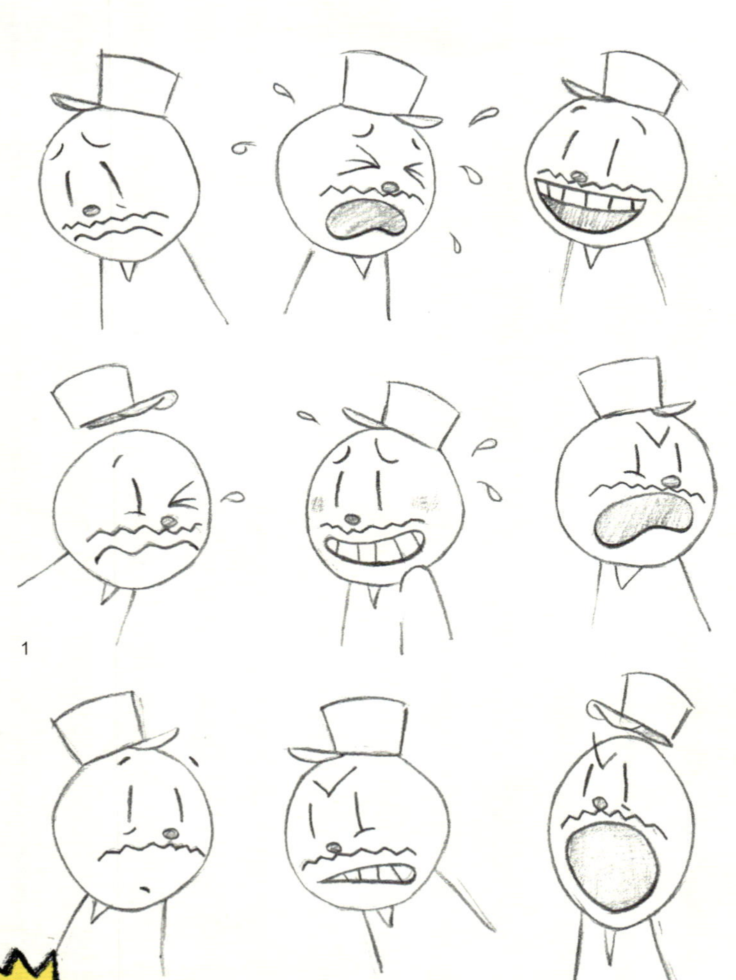

1

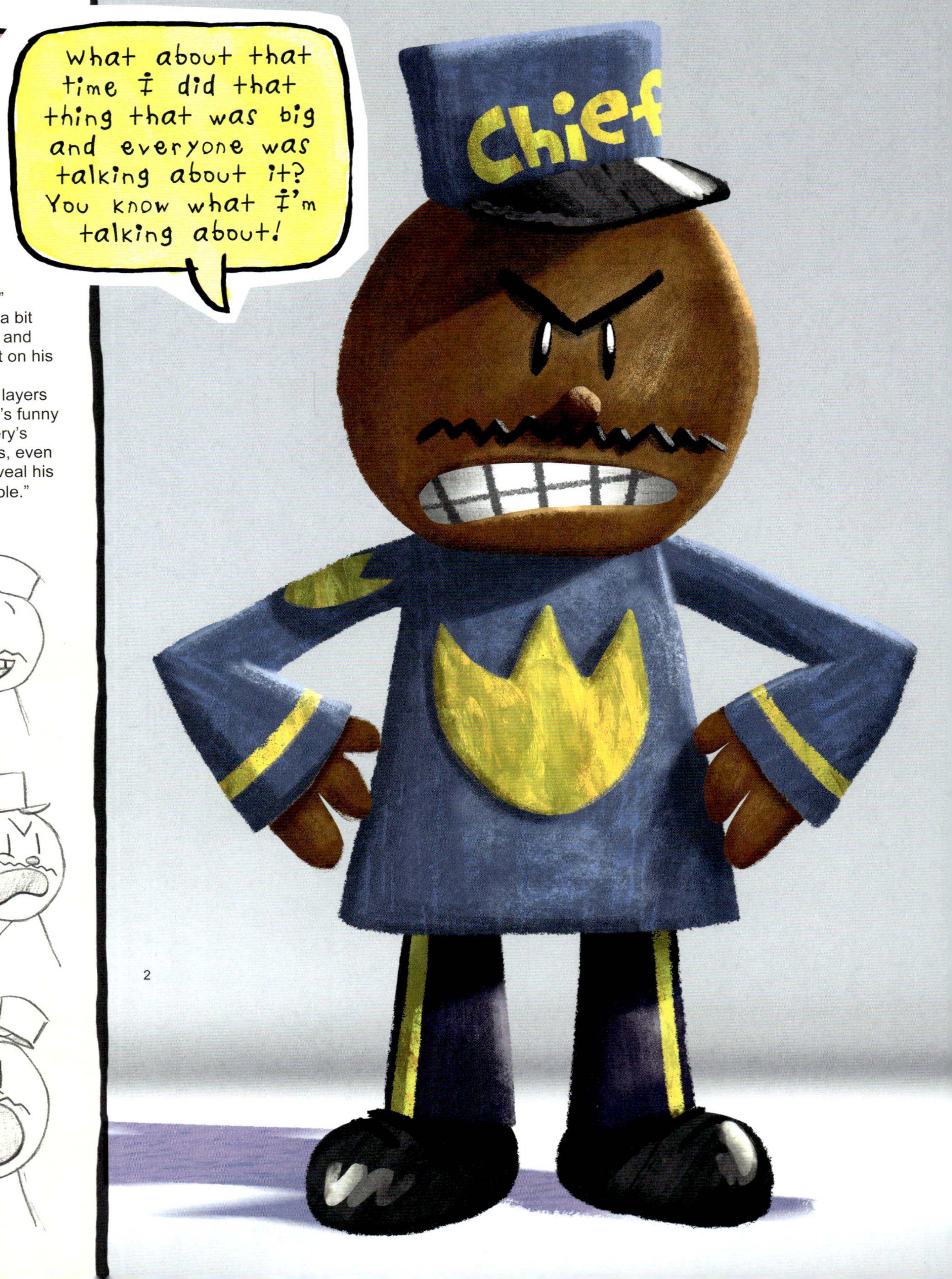

What about that time I did that thing that was big and everyone was talking about it? You know what I'm talking about!

Chief

2

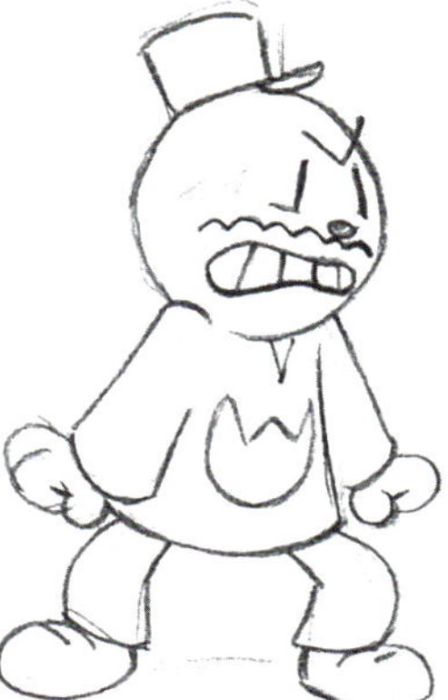

4

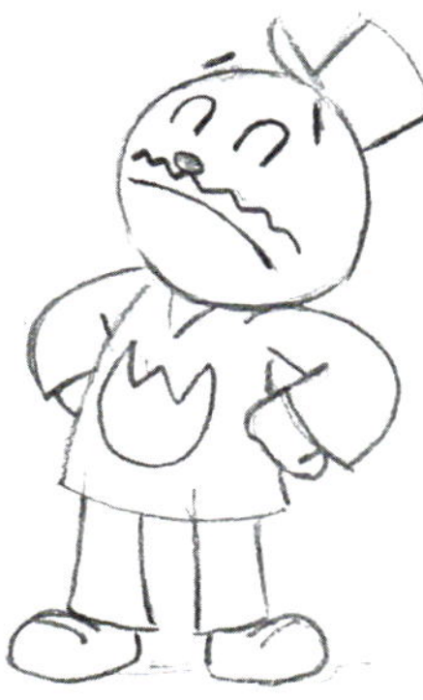

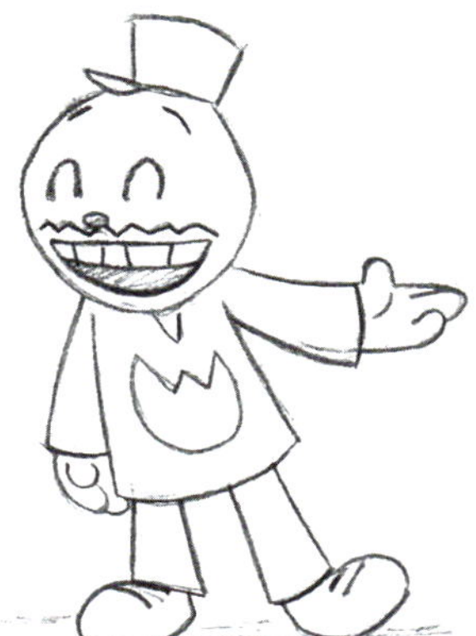

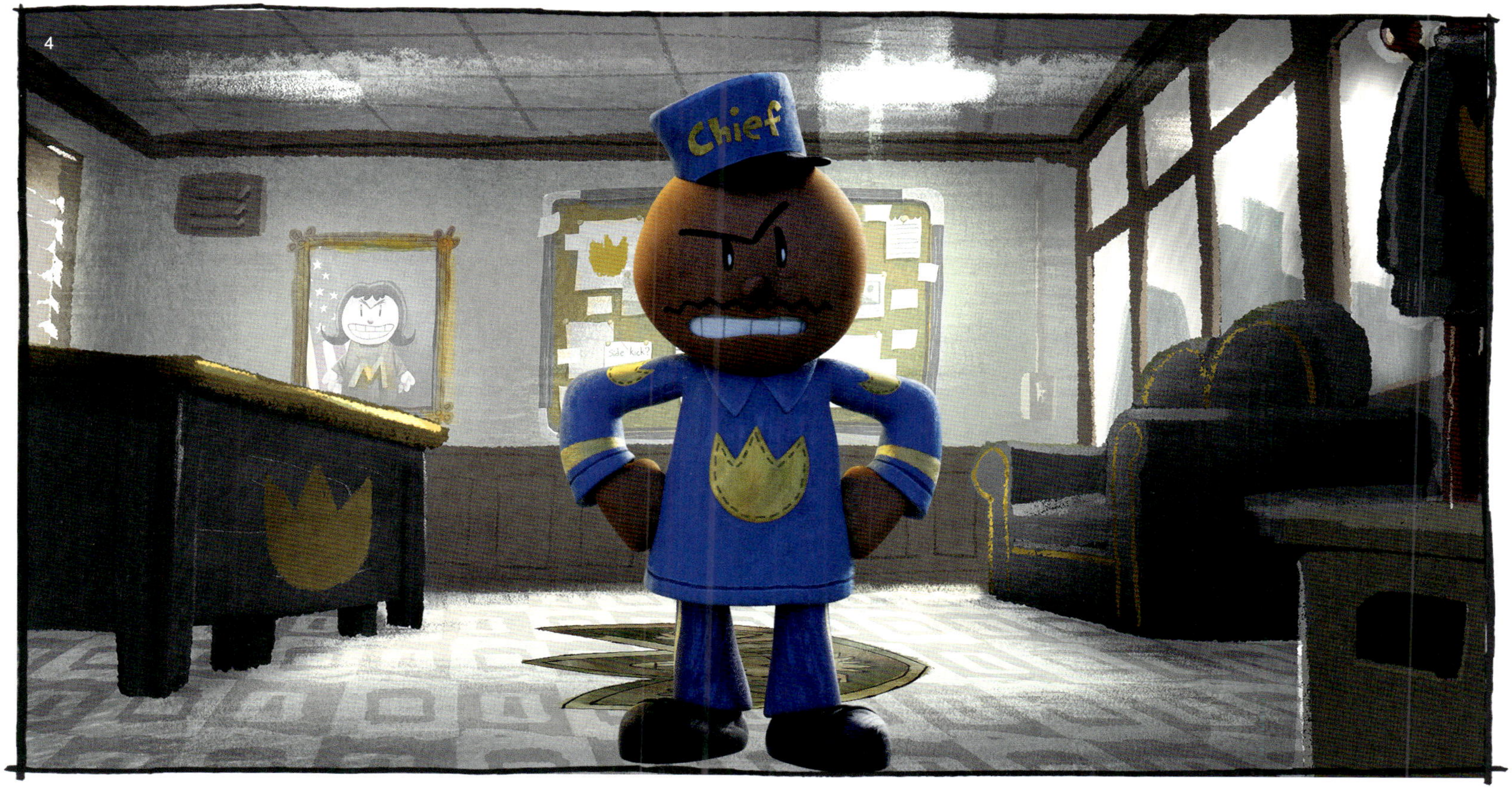

3

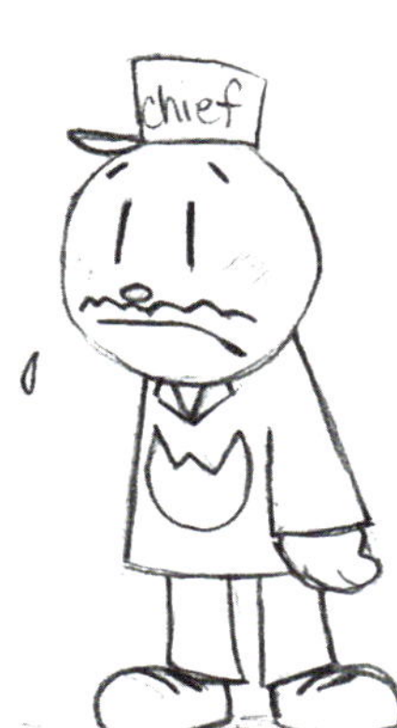

5

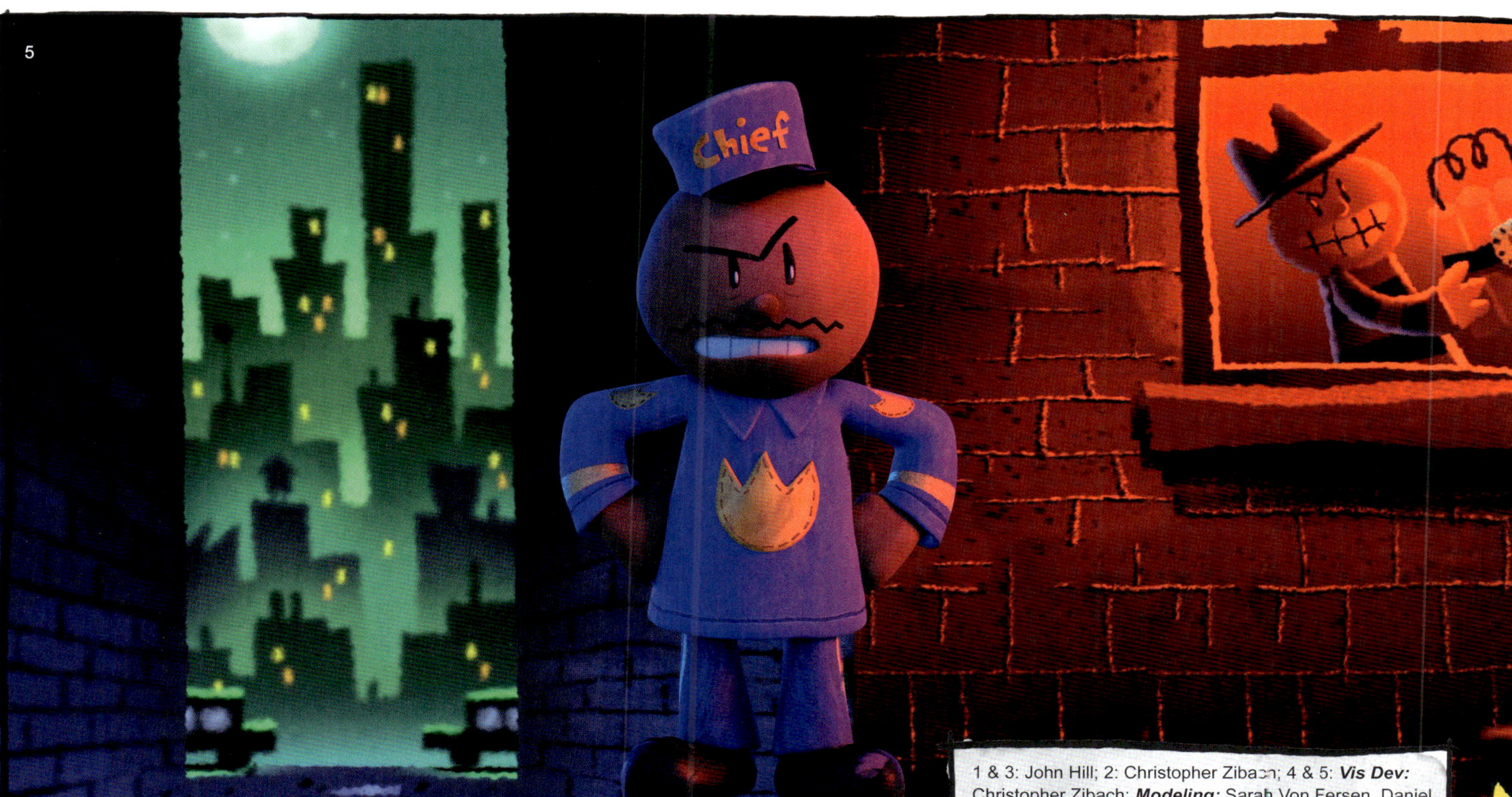

1 & 3: John Hill; 2: Christopher Zibach; 4 & 5: ***Vis Dev:*** Christopher Zibach; ***Modeling:*** Sarah Von Fersen, Daniel Olah; ***Surfacing:*** Hannah Wong, Daniele La Mura

"We imagined having a table full of different art supplies so we could create a 3D collage of illustrated art rather than photo-real images. We then created characters that share the same properties with the backgrounds, and soon we felt like we had brought an illustrated children's book to life."

— NATE WRAGG, Production Designer

1

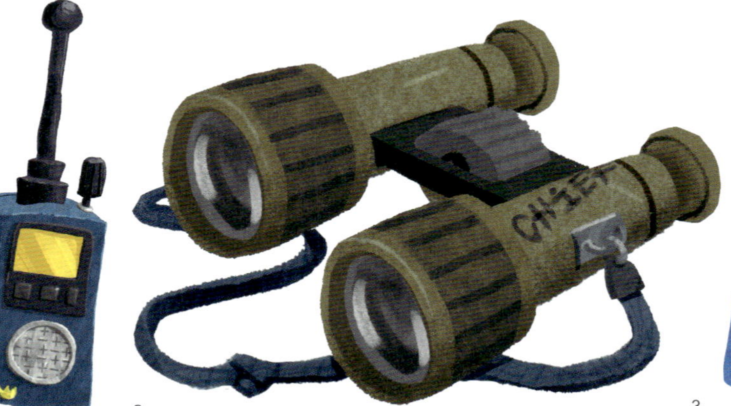

2

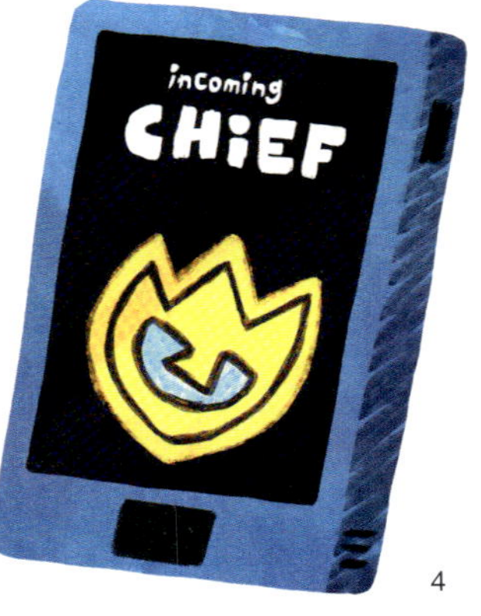

3

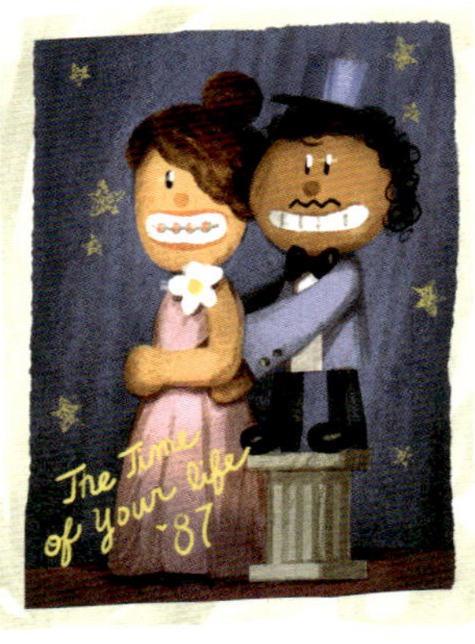

4

5

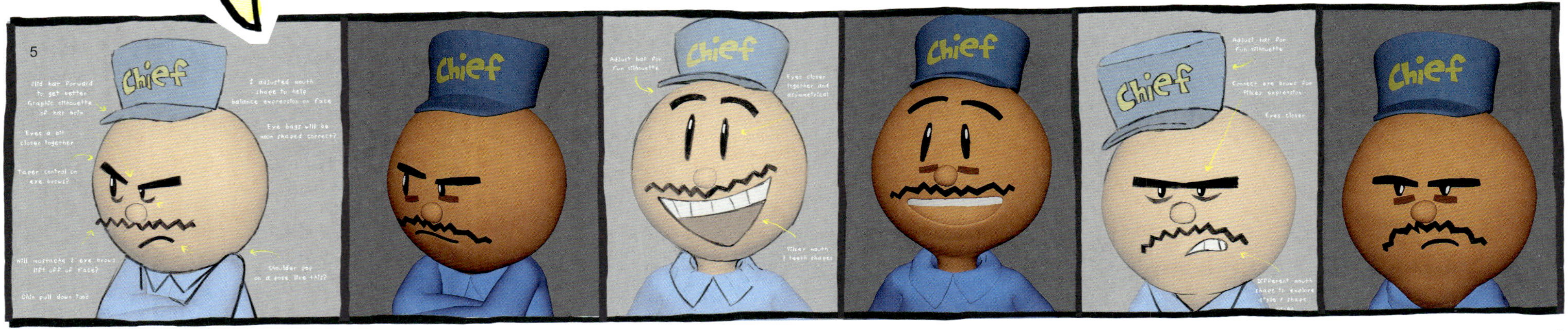

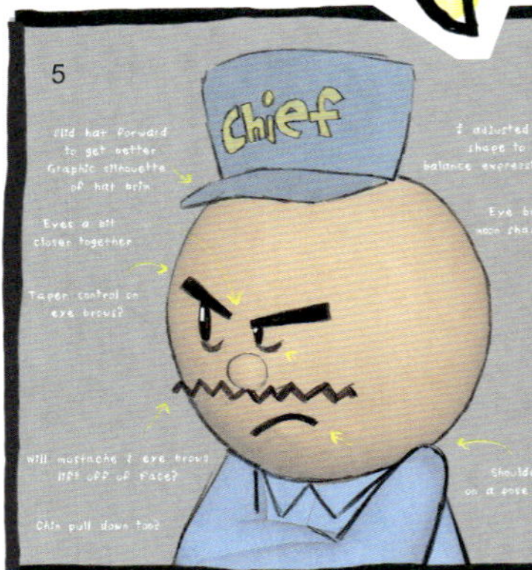

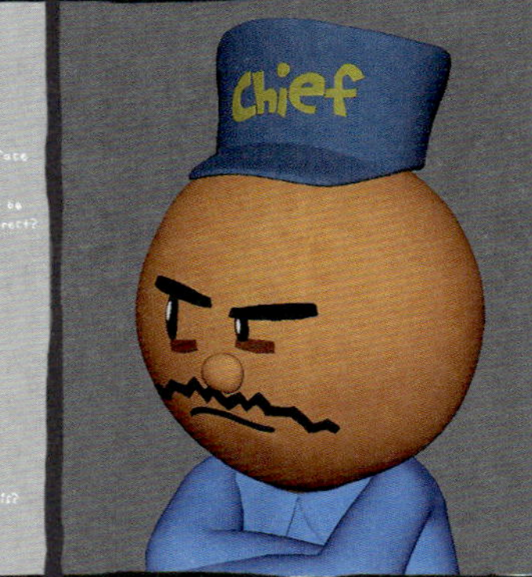

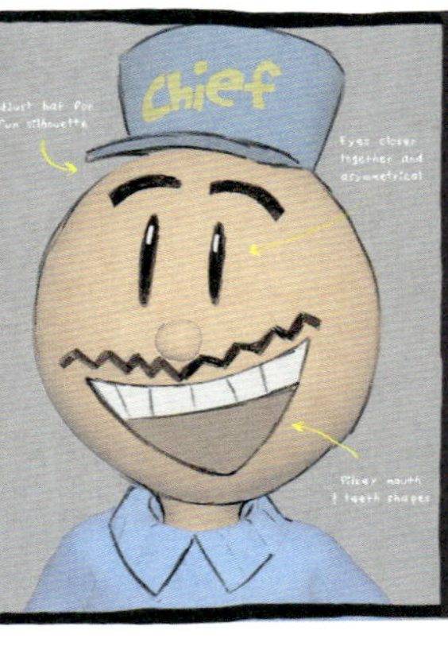

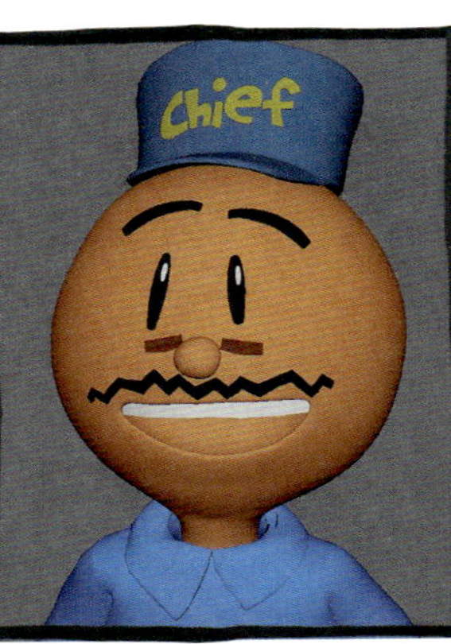

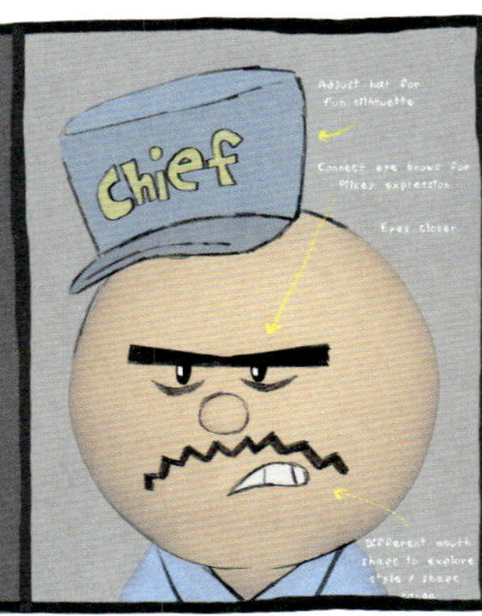

6

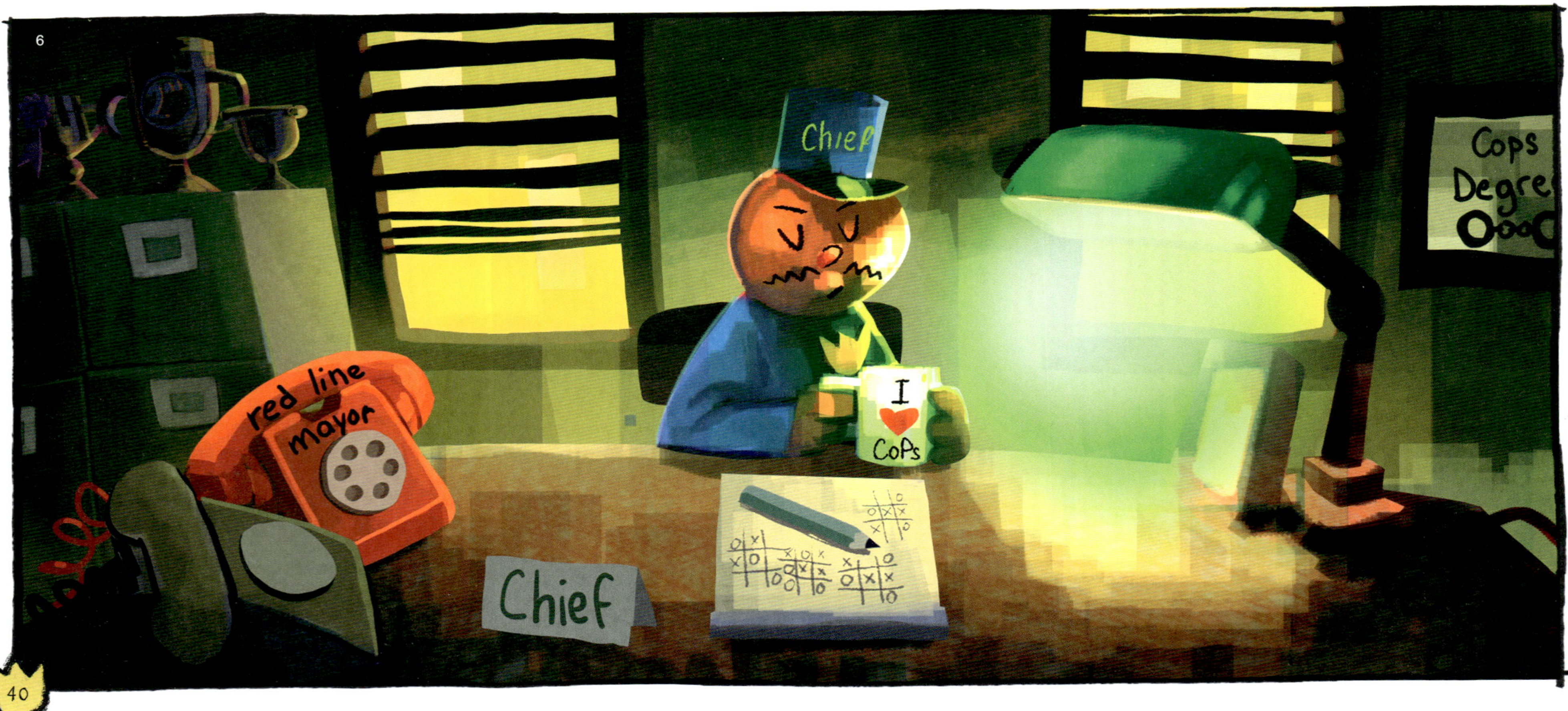

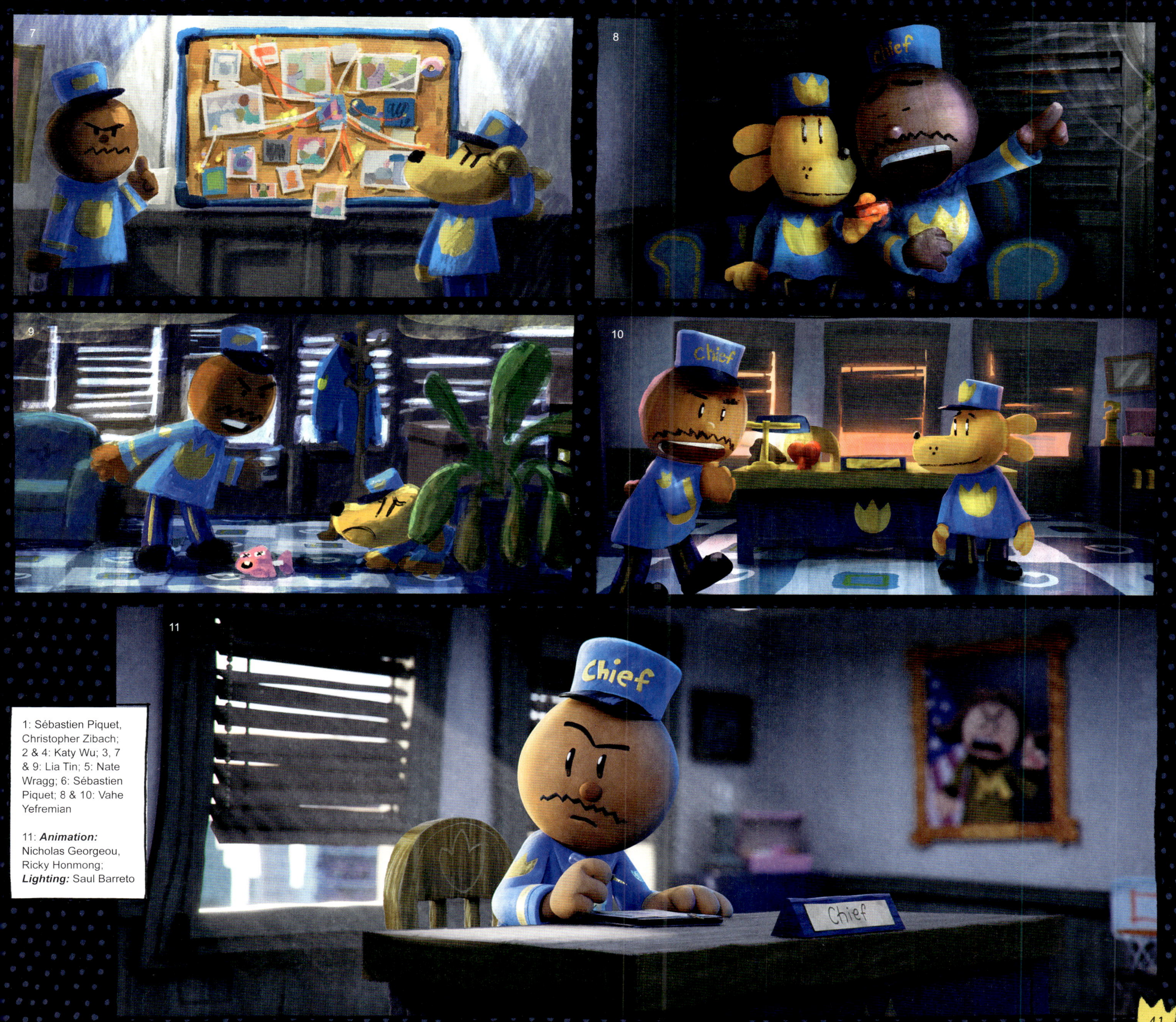

1: Sébastien Piquet, Christopher Zibach; 2 & 4: Katy Wu; 3, 7 & 9: Lia Tin; 5: Nate Wragg; 6: Sébastien Piquet; 8 & 10: Vahe Yefremian

11: ***Animation:*** Nicholas Georgeou, Ricky Honmong; ***Lighting:*** Saul Barreto

Sarah Hatoff

The female lead in the movie is none other than the clever and resourceful on-the-street reporter Sarah Hatoff (voiced by Isla Fisher), who works for the TV news program, *Live Breaking News Live*. She is the first to report on Knight's accident and the birth of Dog Man, Supa Cop.

"Sarah is the kind of ace street reporter who's always looking to get the scoop, and there's a fun dynamic going on between her and Chief," says production designer Nate Wragg. "She is our window to how the general public is seeing the news and the wild events that are happening in the city. She's a strong lead and doesn't let anyone push her around, and she's a fun, charming, and appealing character. Sarah is a great contrast to Chief."

"The thing about Sarah is that she's a strong and ambitious reporter, but she will focus her attention on caring for somebody when she has to," says director Peter Hastings. "She befriends Dog Man and Li'l Petey, and she also keeps the audience informed about what is happening in the city."

Sarah's dog, Zuzu, doesn't have a huge role, but she's always around. In the books, she's described by Pilkey as "a feisty poodle who bites first and asks questions later. Actually, she doesn't really ask questions. She's a dog!" Her design in the movie follows the original look from the book series.

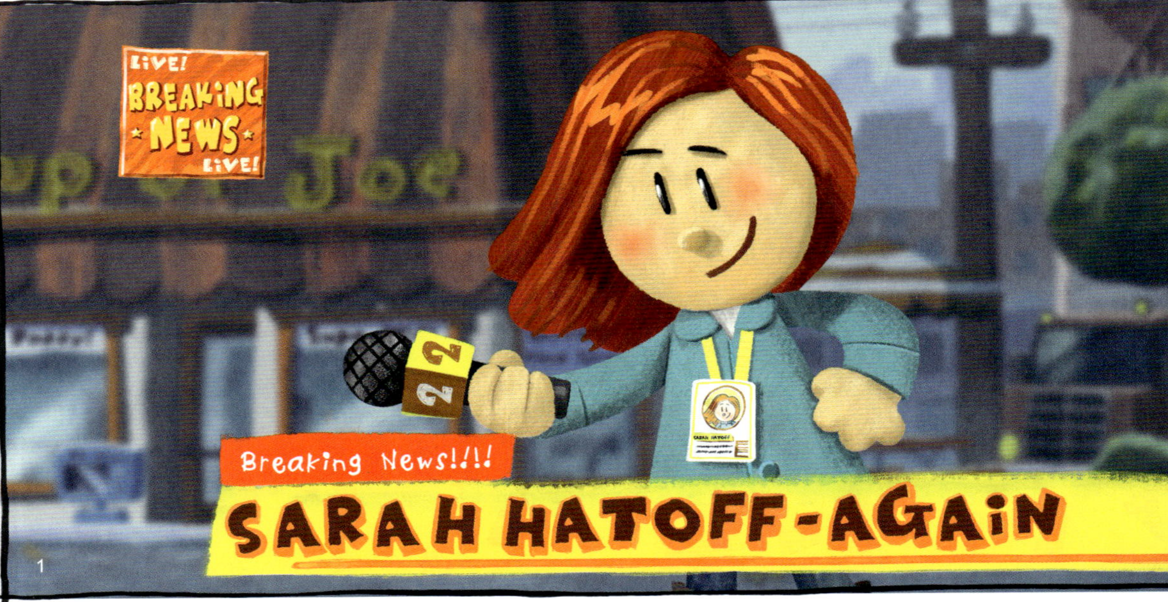

1

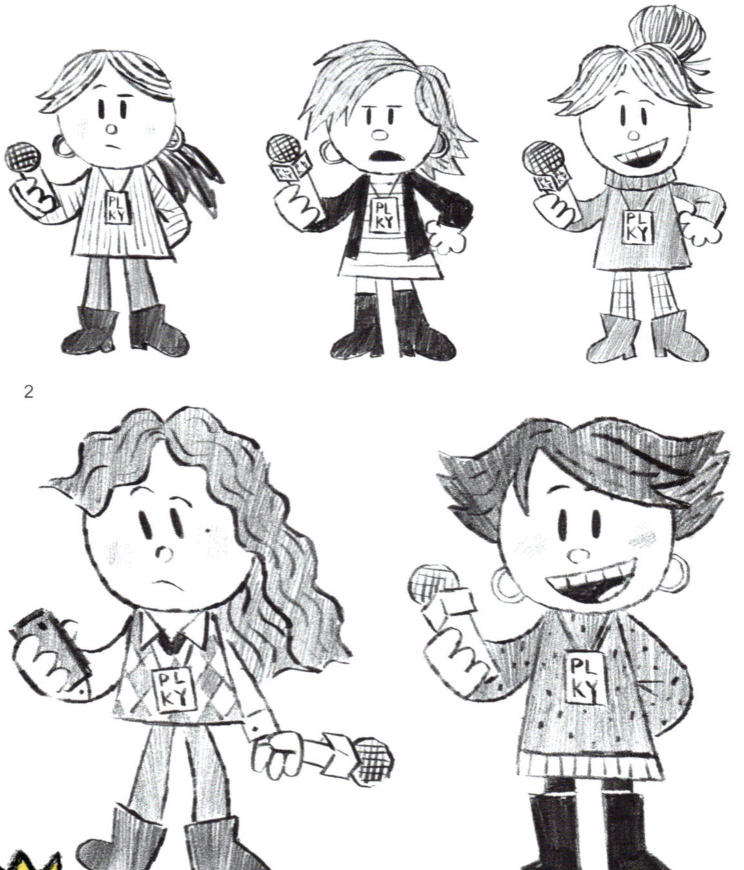

2

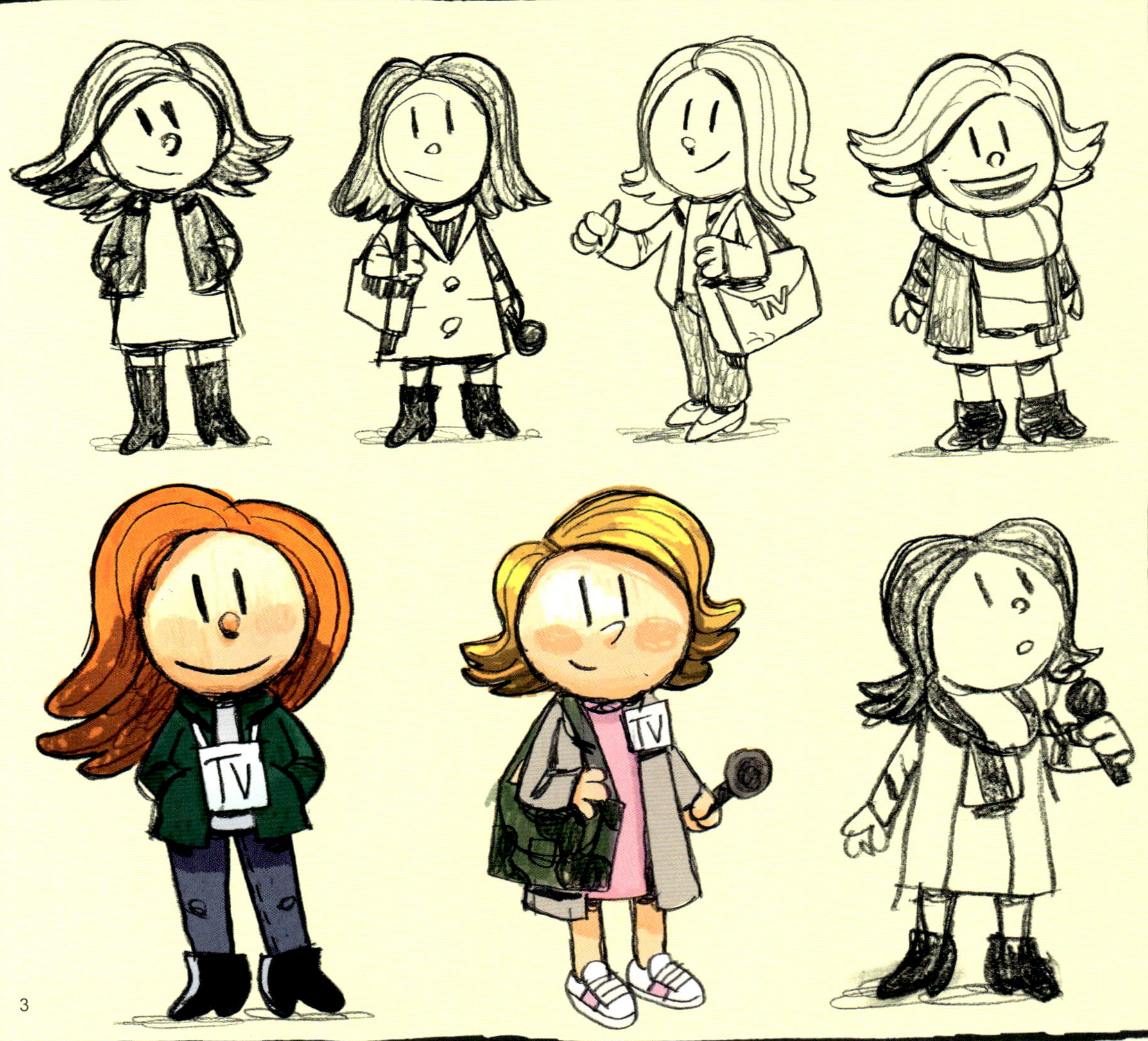

3

"Although the characters are very close to what they look like in the books, we are moving them in a 3D world. But we also have some unique textures on the characters themselves. They are not just flat colors. You can see the strokes of colors on the characters and their clothes."

—JOHN HILL, Head of Character Animation

This is Sarah Hatoff, reporting live from the Major Hospital in Town. This just in—it stopped raining!

1: Christopher Zibach; 2: Nate Wragg; 3: Sébastien Piquet

4: ***Modeling:*** Sarah von Fersen, Aceysele Madorran Armas, Daniel Olah, Maddalena Delvecchio; ***Surfacing:*** Hannah Wong, Benjamin Murray, Leopoldine Perdrix

1, 6 & Overleaf: Lia Tin; 2 & 3: Nate Wragg; 4: Sébastien Piquet

5: ***Layout:*** Angel Cano, Bernadi Matas Bergas; ***Animation:*** Sam Webster; ***Lighting:*** Saul Barreto

Opportunity for a pun...
Sarah Hat-ON??

lil hat to match

Maybe a more square jaw? Everyone in the film has rounded faces.

1

rolled up sleeves, maybe flats so she can run, etc. hair is short.

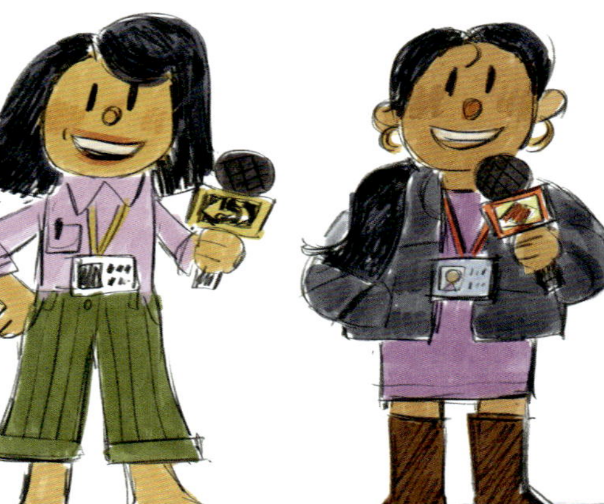

I also think Sarah would be dressed a bit smart, but still functional as well.

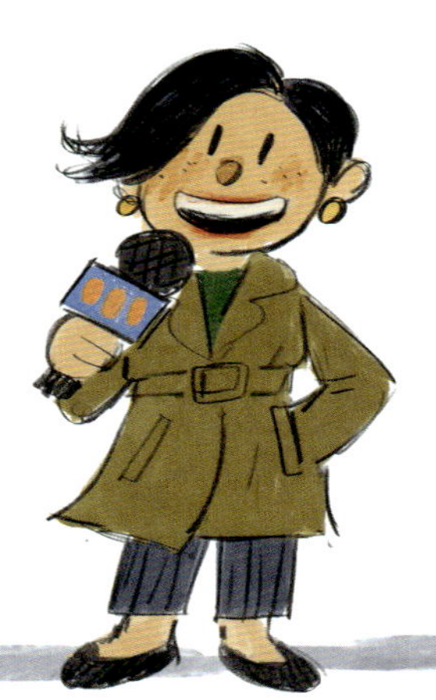

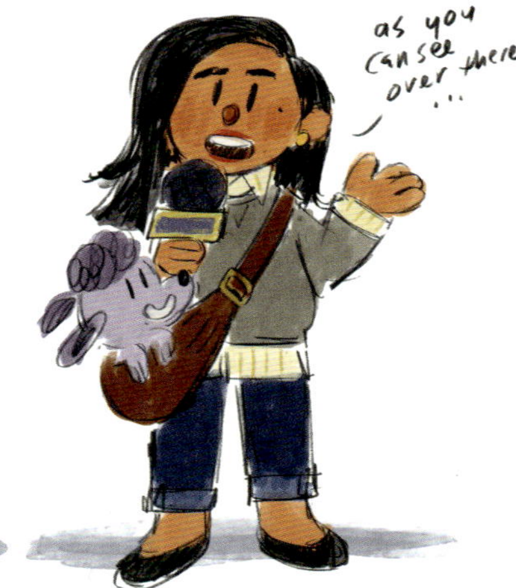

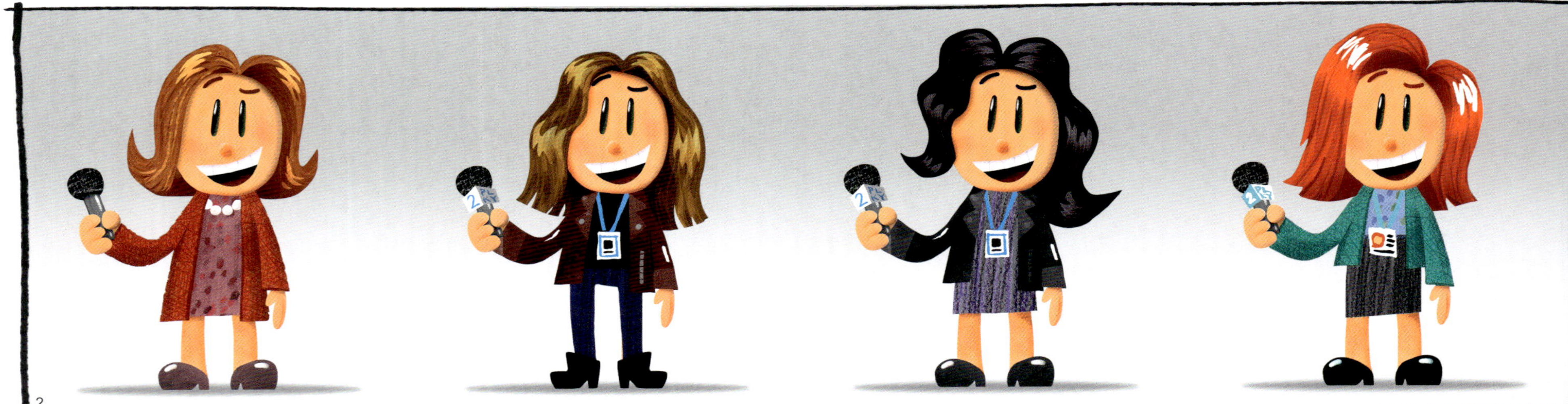

2

3

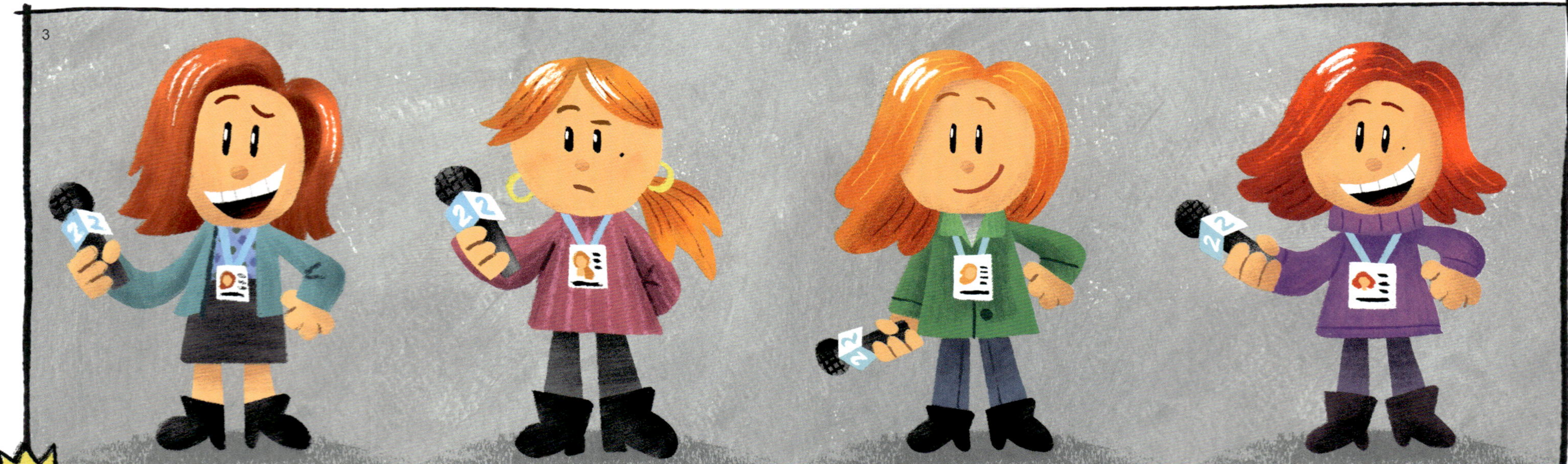

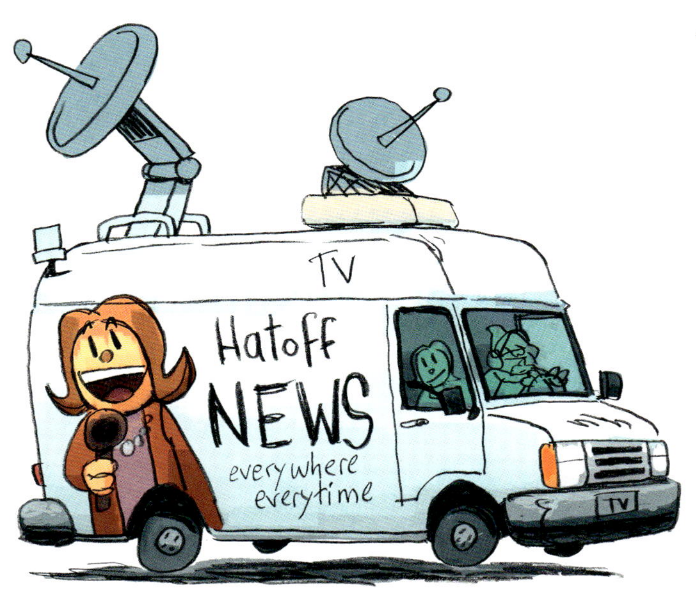

4

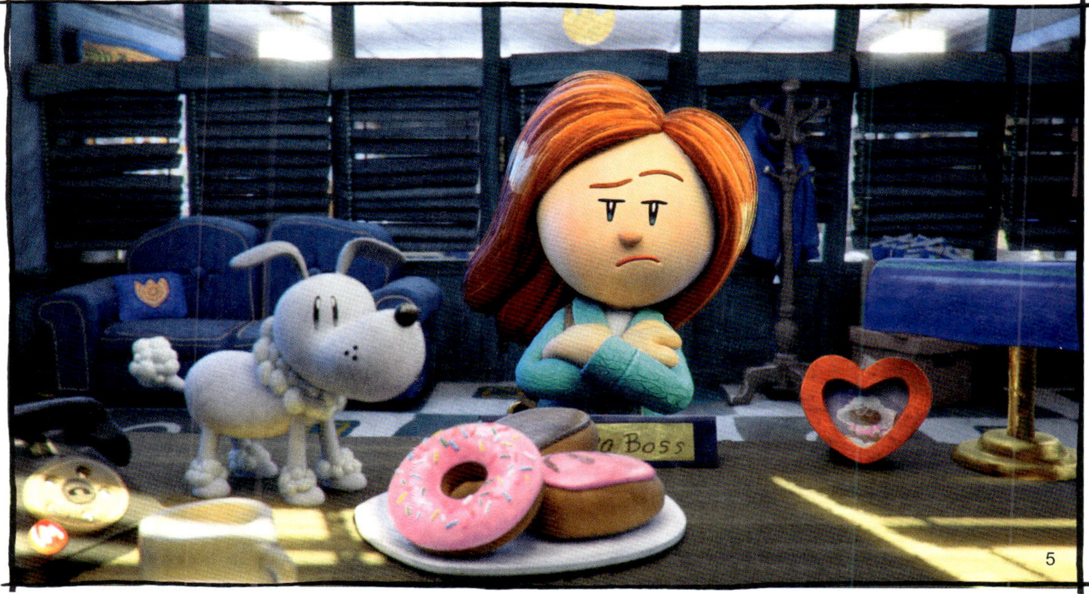

5

6

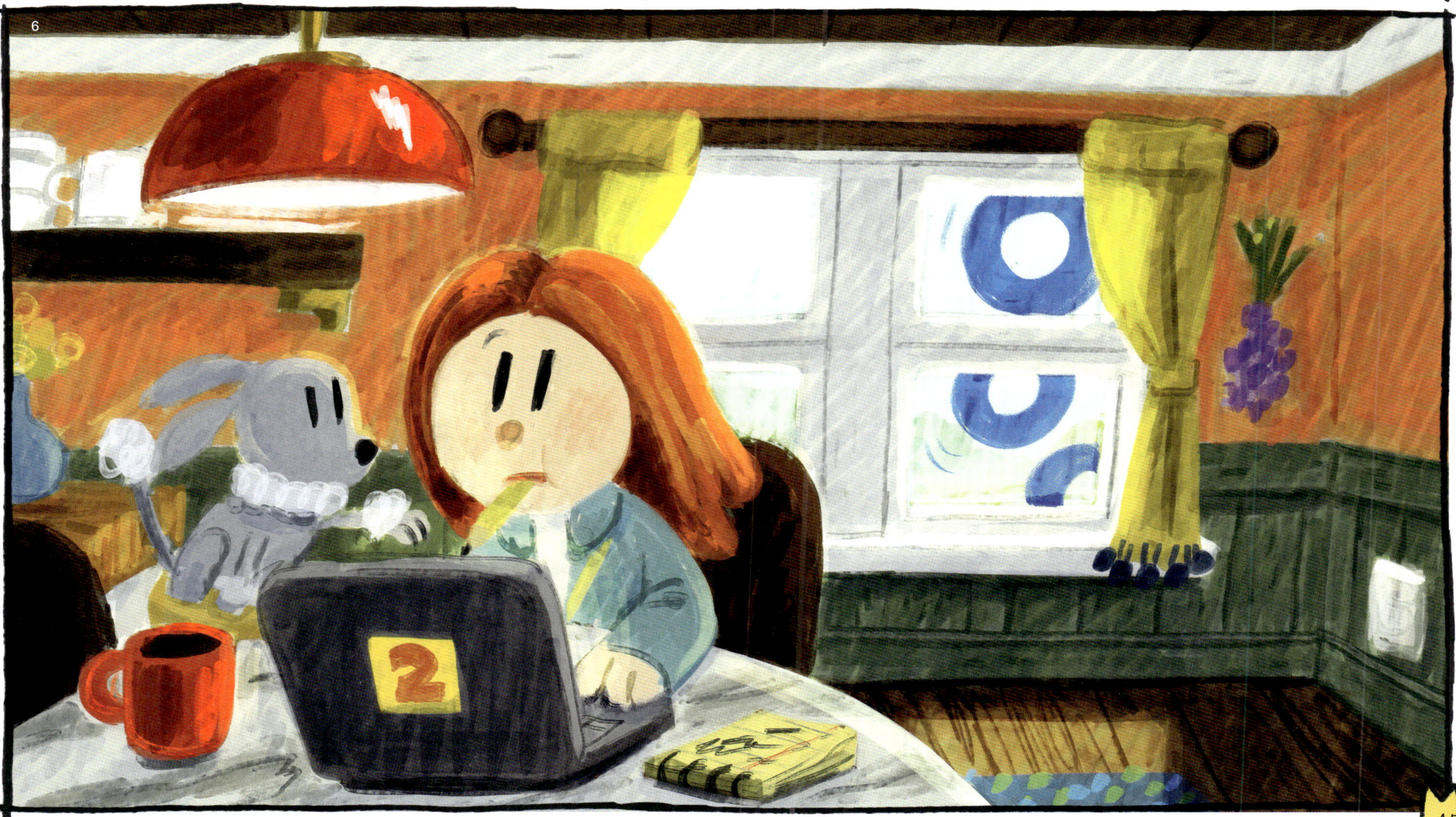

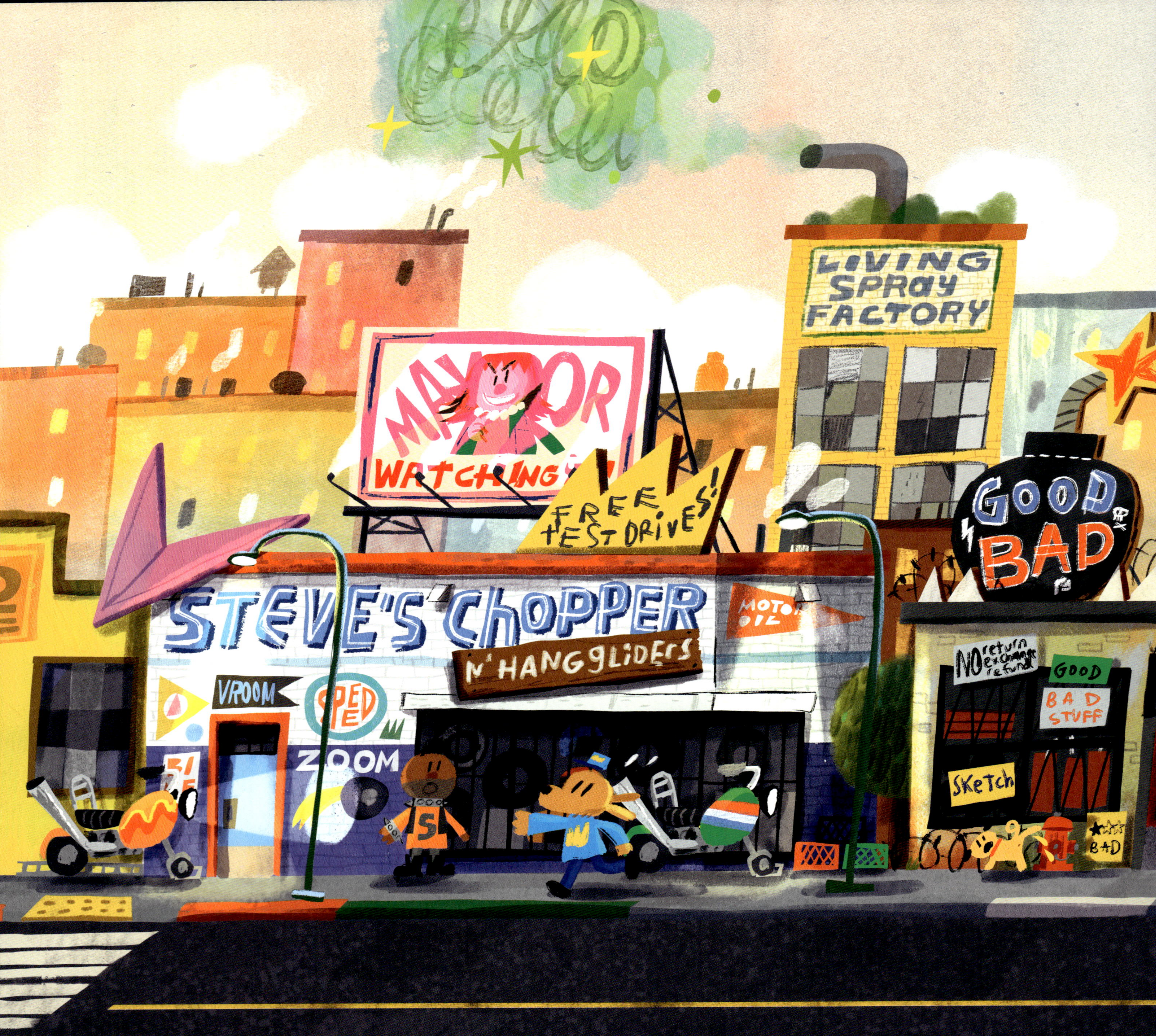

LIVING SPRAY FACTORY
MAYOR
WATCHING
FREE TEST DRIVES!
STEVE'S CHOPPER
N' HANGGLIDERS
VROOM
SPEED
ZOOM
GOOD BAD
NO return NO exchange refund
GOOD
BAD STUFF
SKETCH
BAD

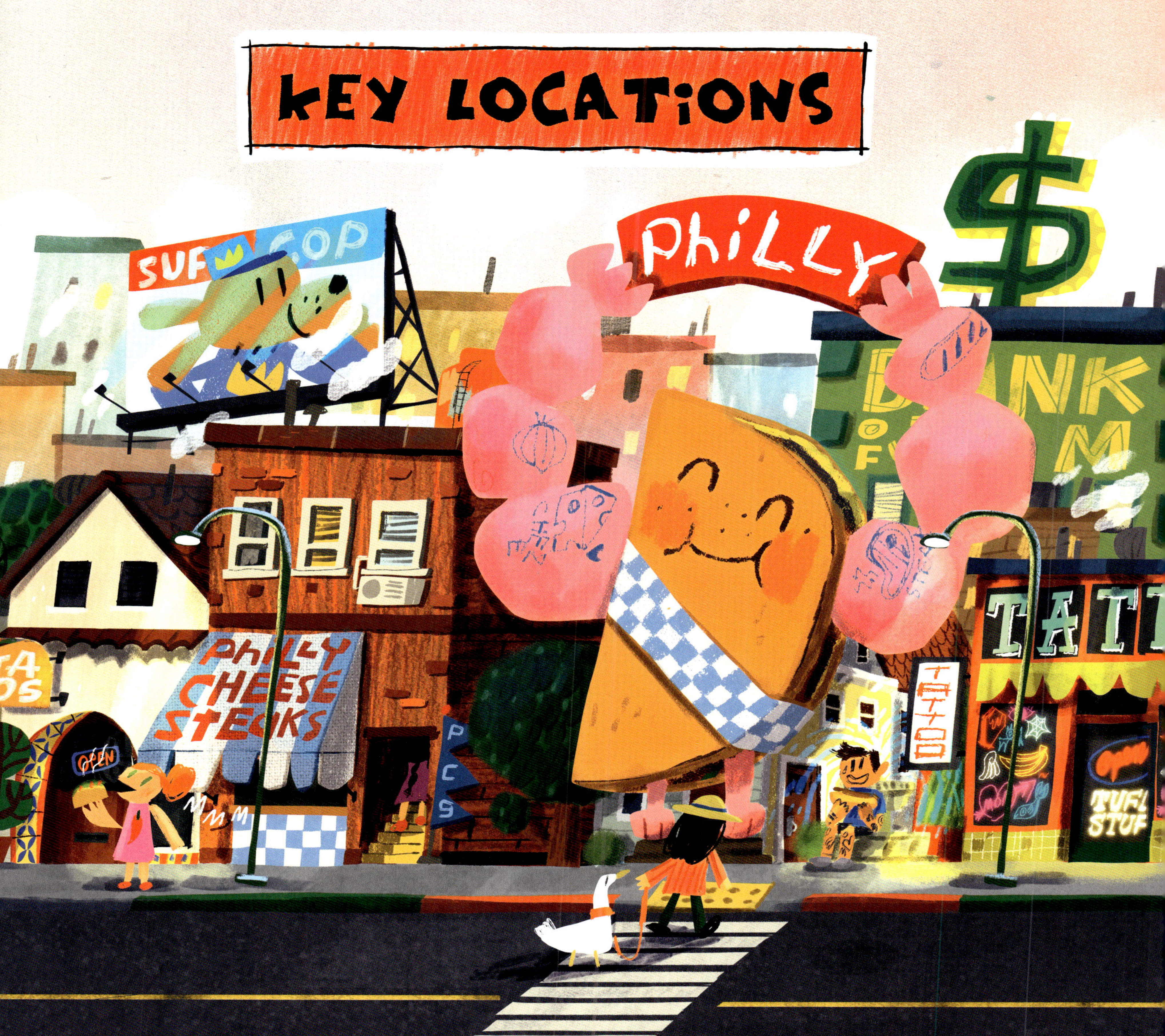
KEY LOCATIONS
PHILLY
PHILLY CHEESE STEAKS
MMM
OPEN
PCS
TATTOO

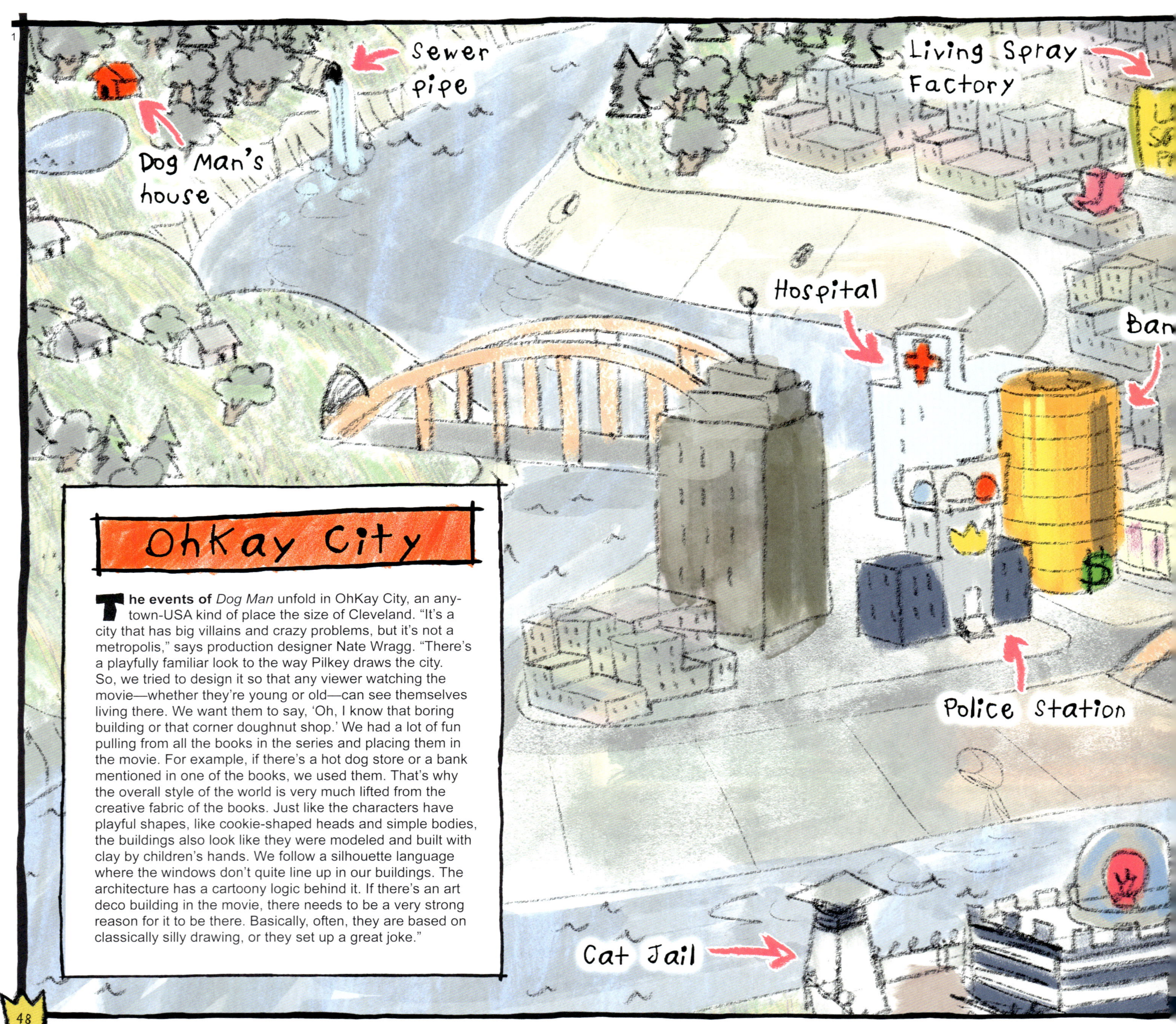

OhKay City

The events of *Dog Man* unfold in OhKay City, an any-town-USA kind of place the size of Cleveland. "It's a city that has big villains and crazy problems, but it's not a metropolis," says production designer Nate Wragg. "There's a playfully familiar look to the way Pilkey draws the city. So, we tried to design it so that any viewer watching the movie—whether they're young or old—can see themselves living there. We want them to say, 'Oh, I know that boring building or that corner doughnut shop.' We had a lot of fun pulling from all the books in the series and placing them in the movie. For example, if there's a hot dog store or a bank mentioned in one of the books, we used them. That's why the overall style of the world is very much lifted from the creative fabric of the books. Just like the characters have playful shapes, like cookie-shaped heads and simple bodies, the buildings also look like they were modeled and built with clay by children's hands. We follow a silhouette language where the windows don't quite line up in our buildings. The architecture has a cartoony logic behind it. If there's an art deco building in the movie, there needs to be a very strong reason for it to be there. Basically, often, they are based on classically silly drawing, or they set up a great joke."

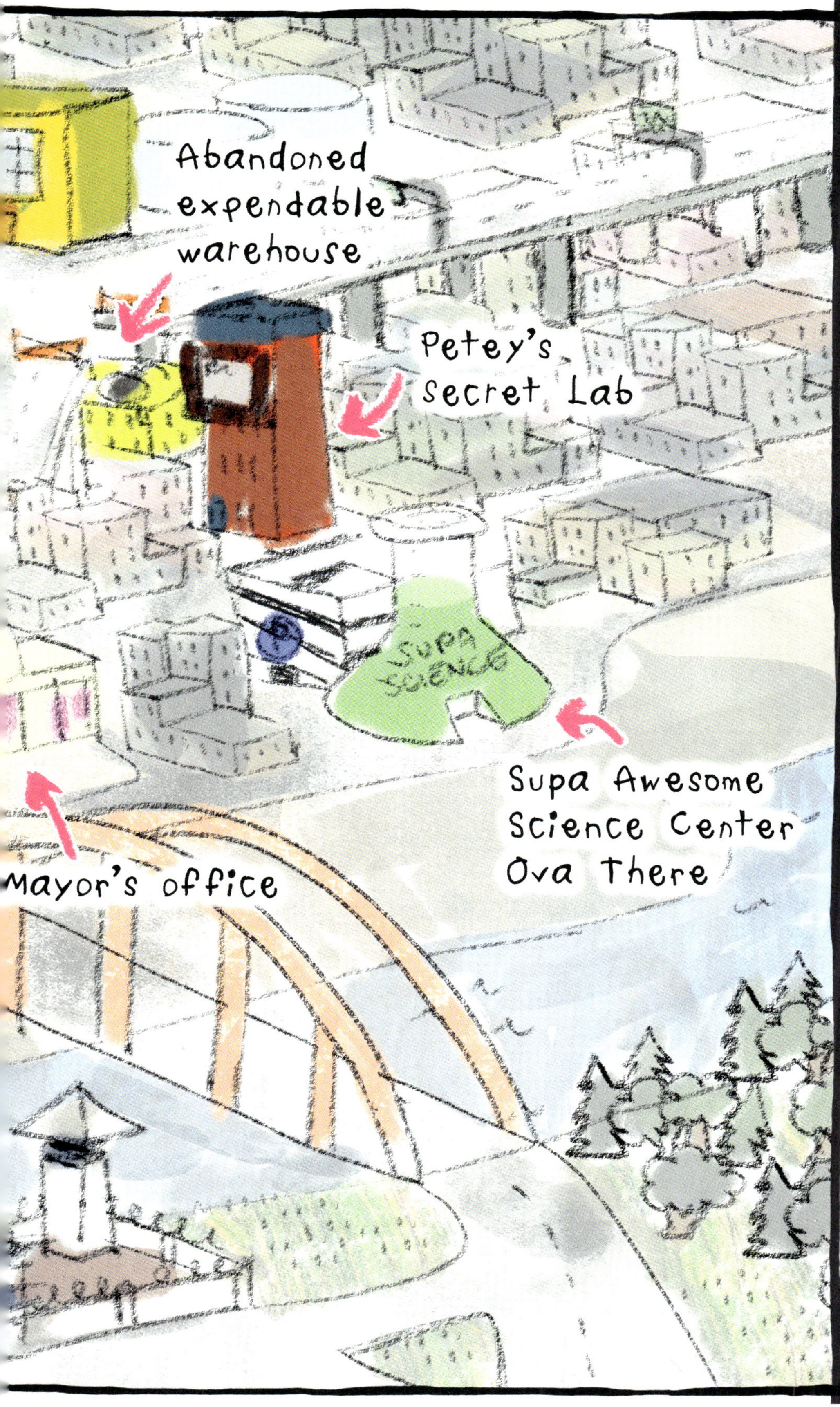

Abandoned expendable warehouse

Petey's secret Lab

Supa Awesome Science Center Ova There

Mayor's office

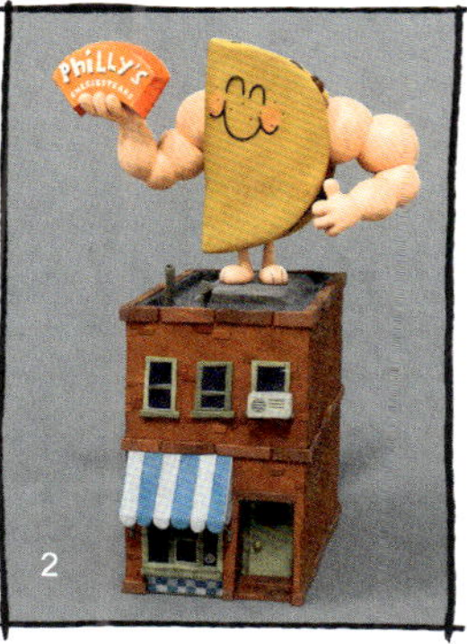
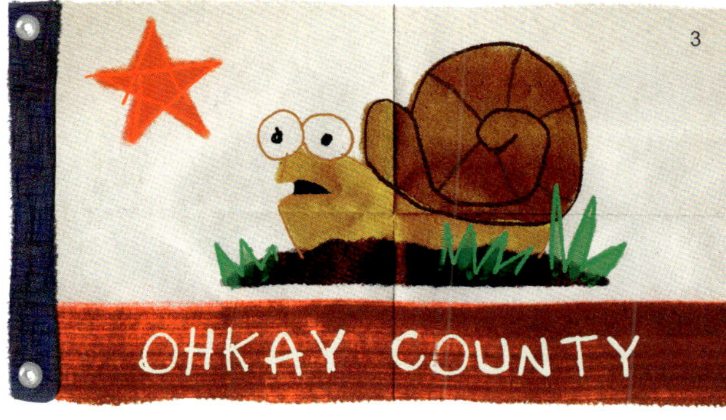

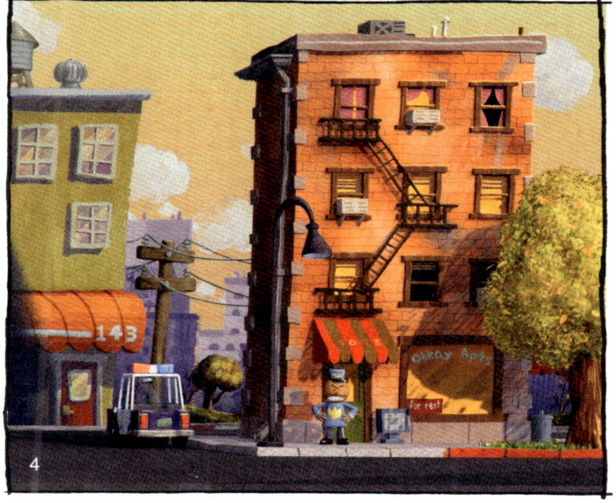

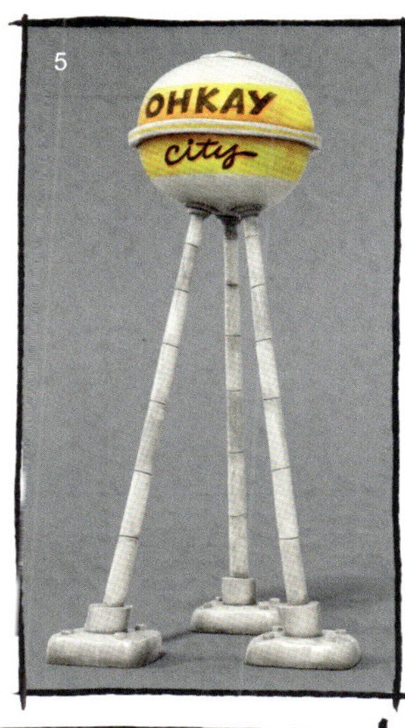

1 & 3: Christopher Zibach

2: ***Vis Dev:*** Lia Tin; ***Modeling:*** Fran Lara, Divyasa Mishra, Marta Macedo; ***Surfacing:*** Hannah Wong, Peter Hargan

4: ***Vis Dev:*** Lia Tin; ***Modeling:*** Fran Lara, Divyasa Mishra, Marta Macedo; ***Surfacing:*** Hannah Wong, Peter Hargan

5: ***Vis Dev:*** Lia Tin; ***Modeling:*** Fran Lara, Divyasa Mishra, Marta Macedo; ***Surfacing:*** Hannah Wong, Peter Hargan

6: ***Vis Dev:*** Lia Tin, Sebastien Piquet; ***Modeling:*** Fran Lara, Divyasa Mishra, Marta Macedo; ***Surfacing:*** Hannah Wong, Peter Hargan

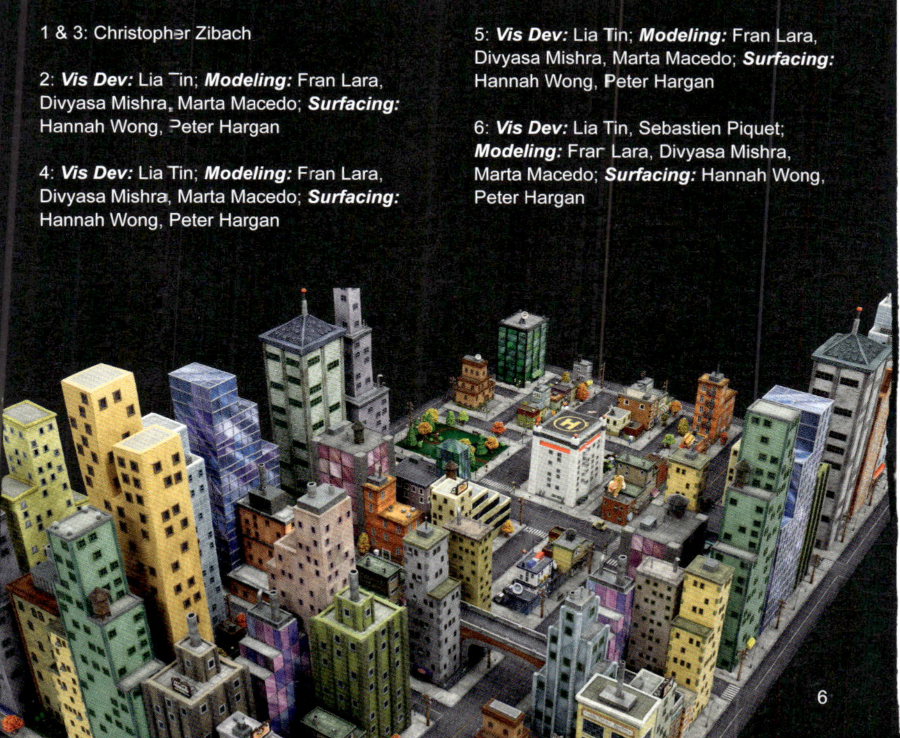

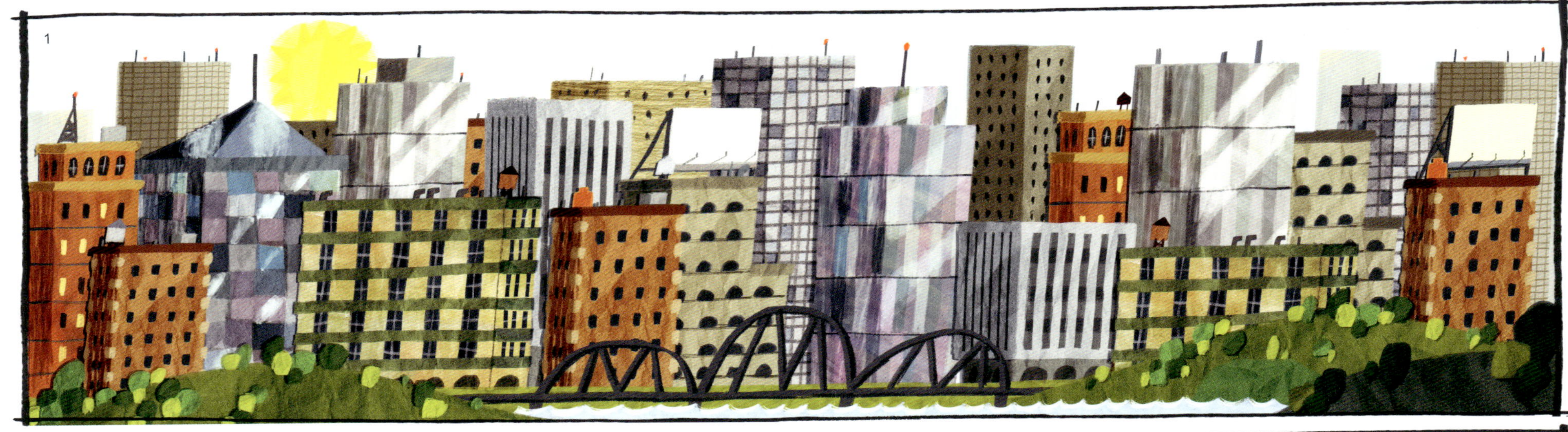

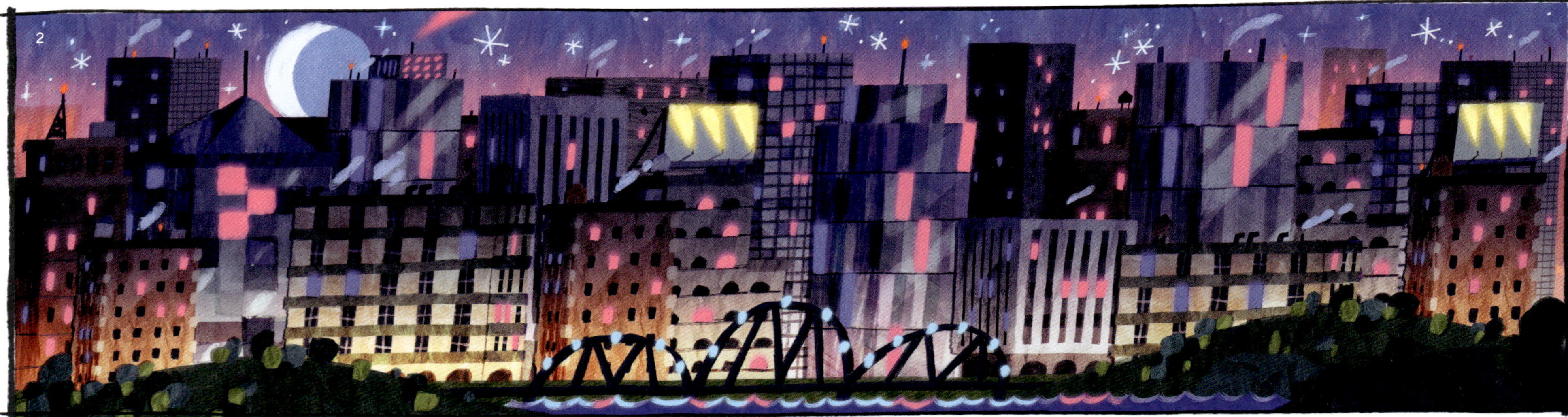

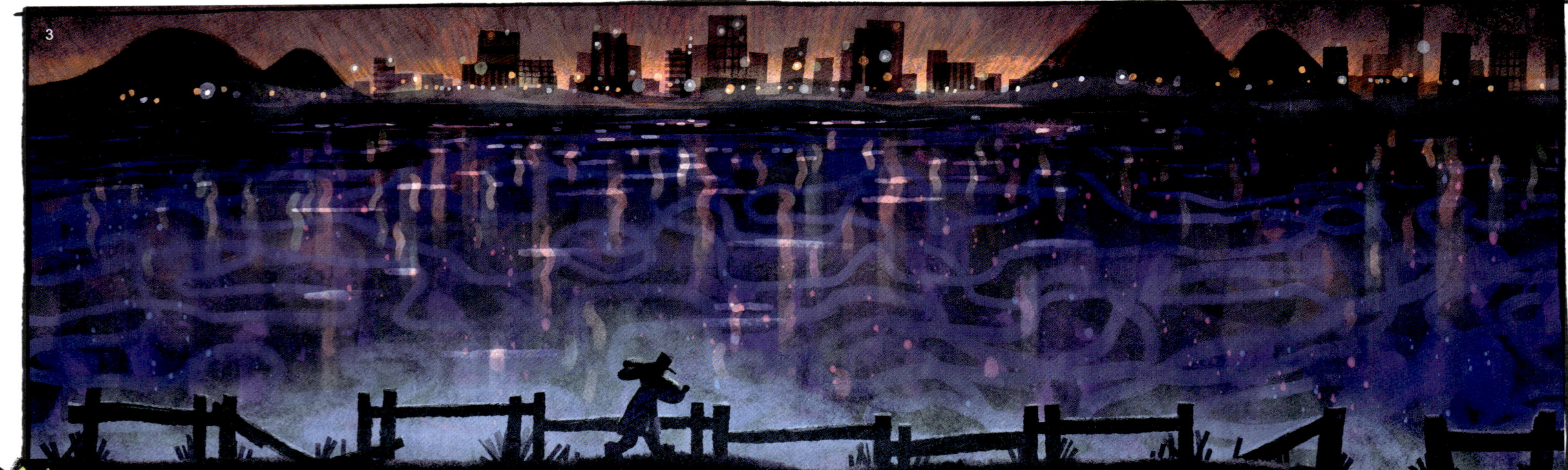

1, 2 & 4: Lia Tin; 3: Katy Wu

5: ***Modeling:*** Fran Lara, Erica Eguia, Nathan Brown, Raúl Gómez Díez; ***Surfacing:*** Hannah Wong, Callum Harwood

4

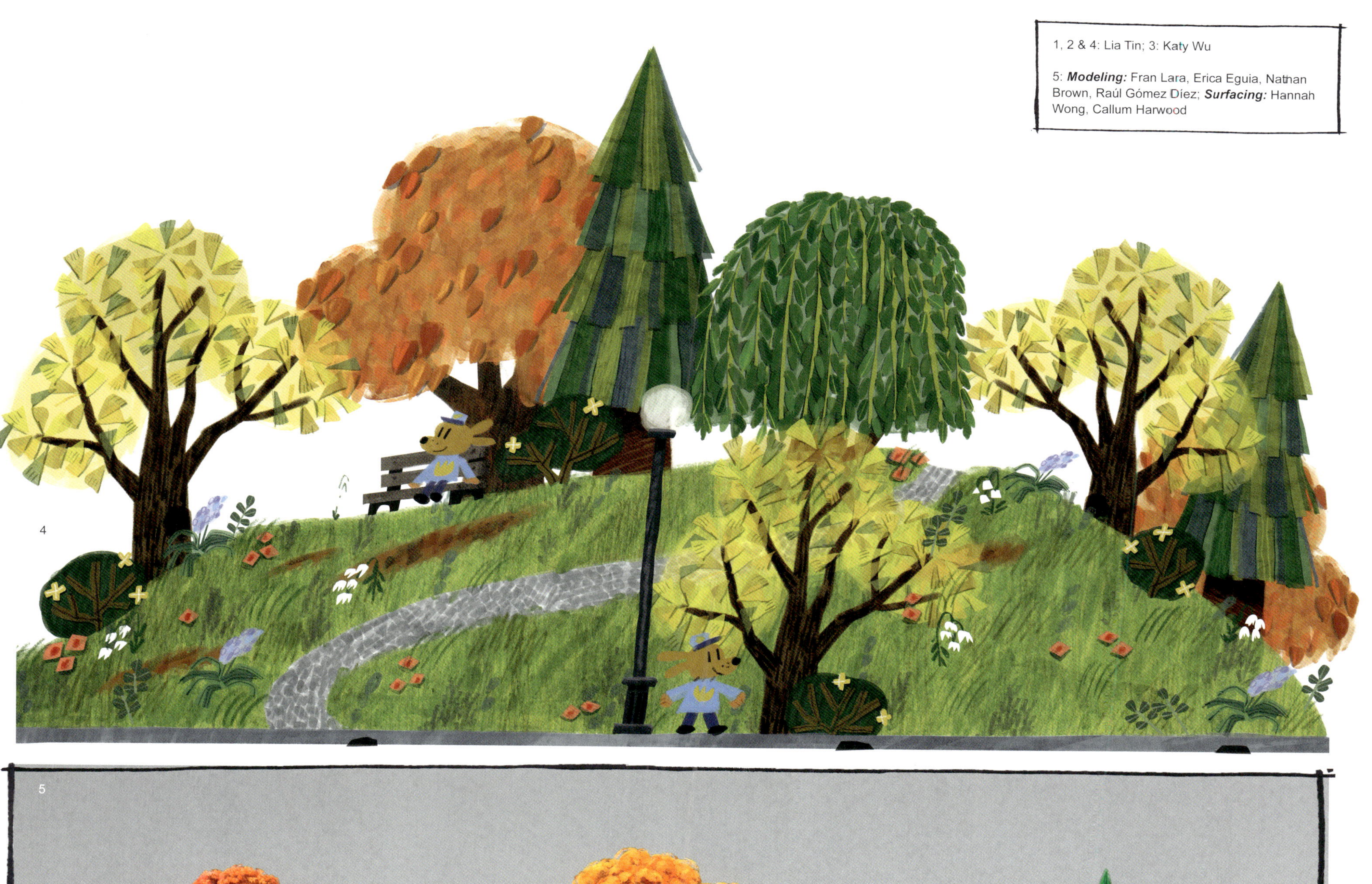

5

1

yarn & stuff

yarn n STUFF

MEH
The Indifferent Store

2

order here
DRINKS
NEW
Dippy's
Tips
Kash
HOT!!
DiPPY'S
DONUTS

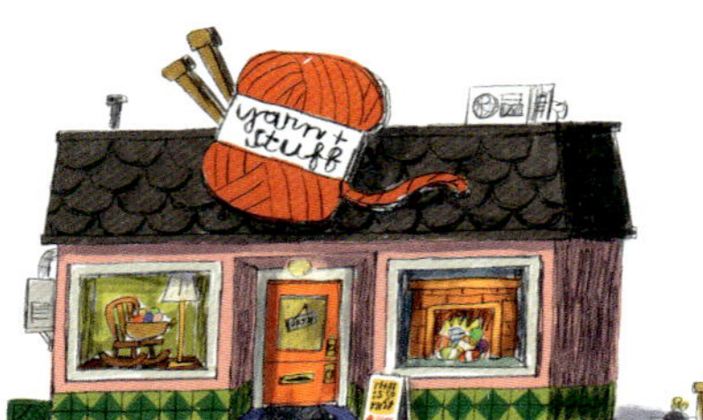

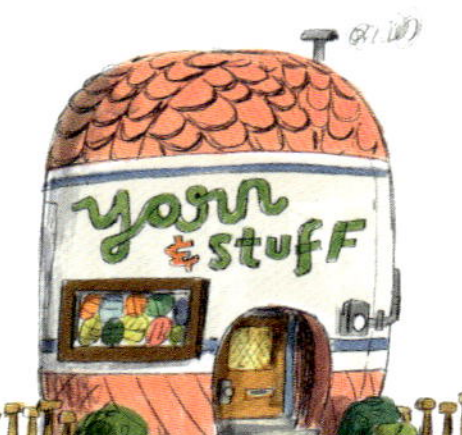

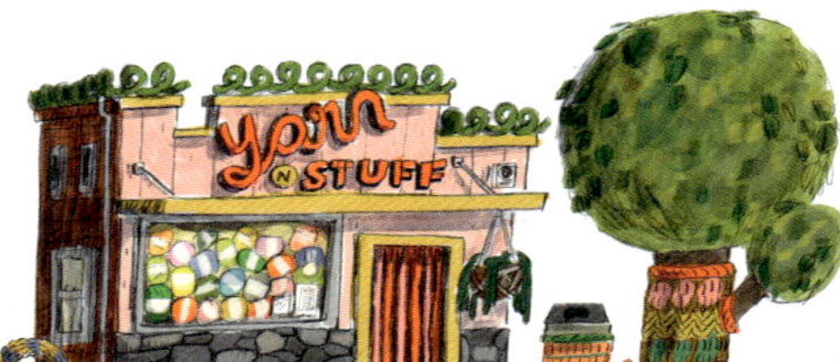

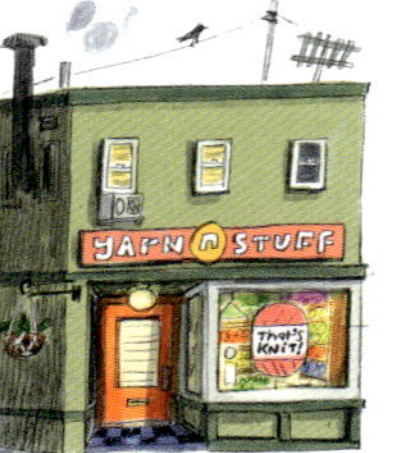

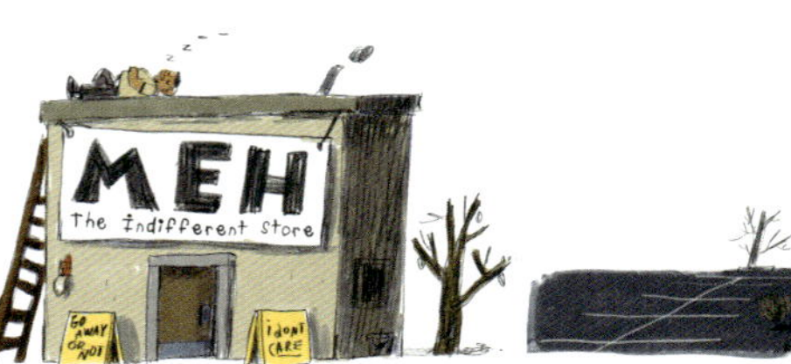

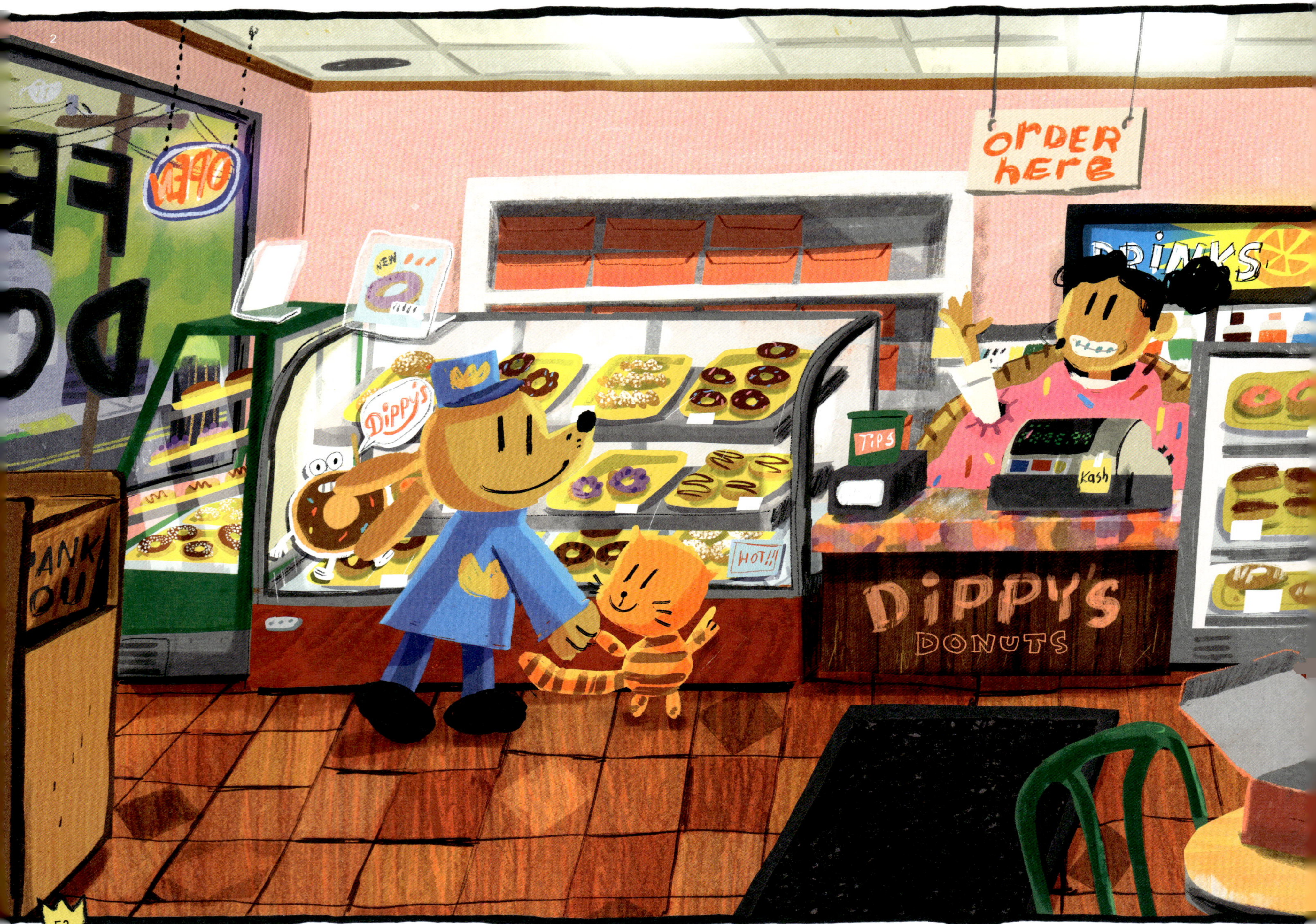

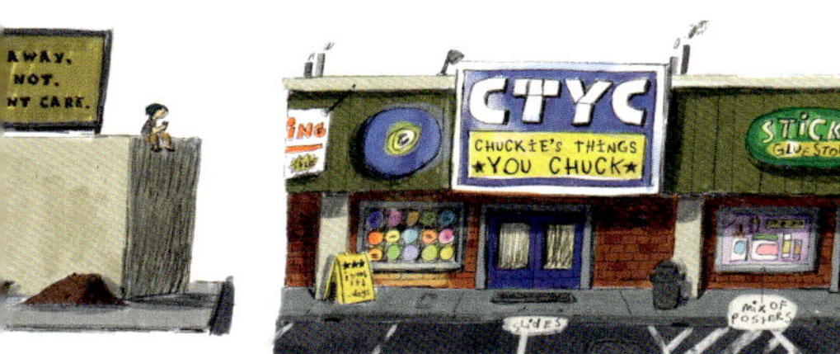

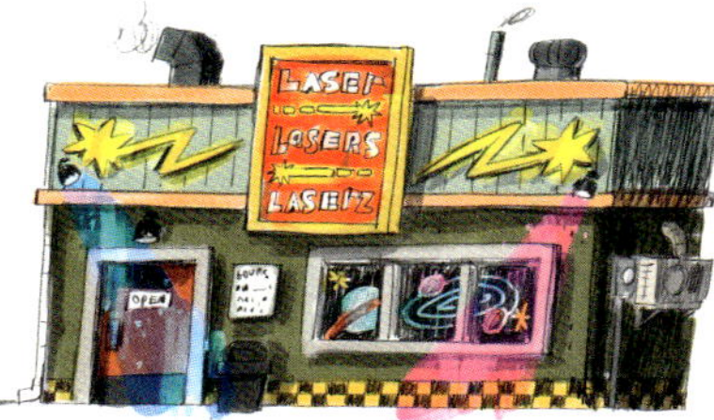

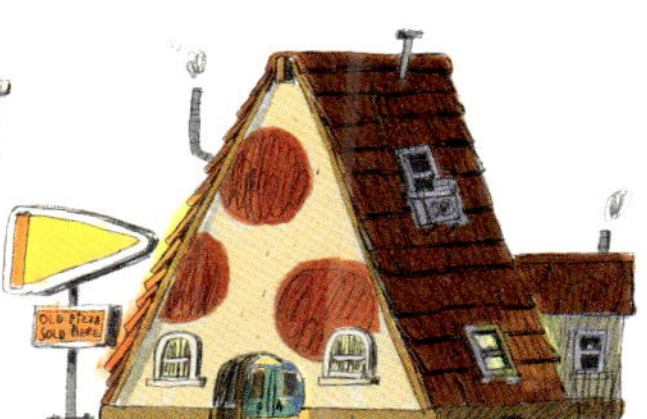

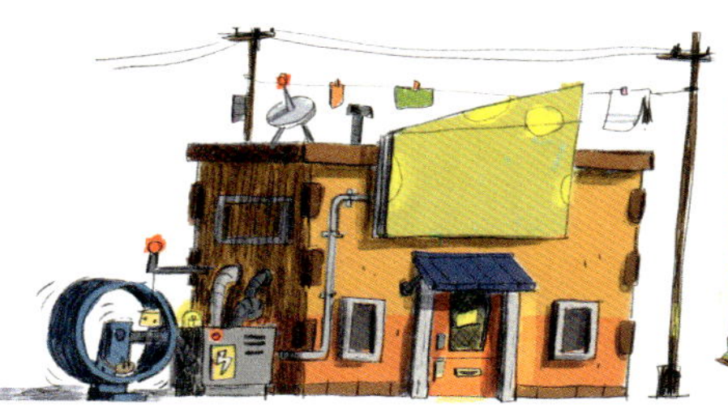

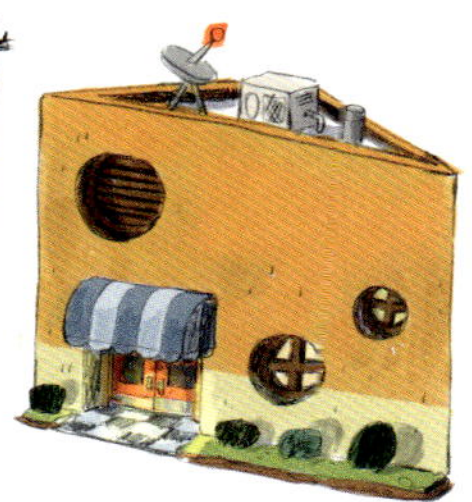

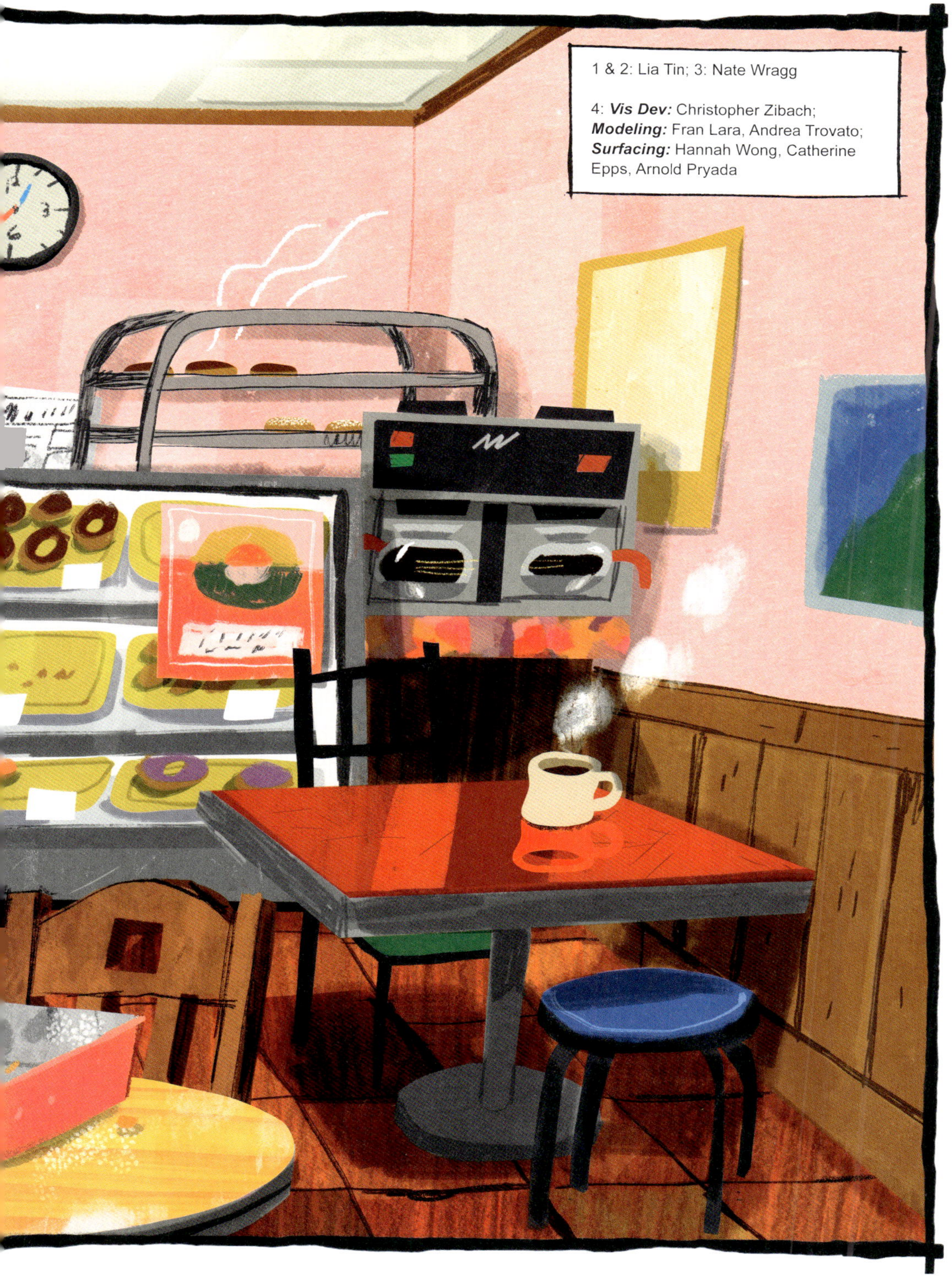

1 & 2: Lia Tin; 3: Nate Wragg

4: ***Vis Dev:*** Christopher Zibach; ***Modeling:*** Fran Lara, Andrea Trovato; ***Surfacing:*** Hannah Wong, Catherine Epps, Arnold Pryada

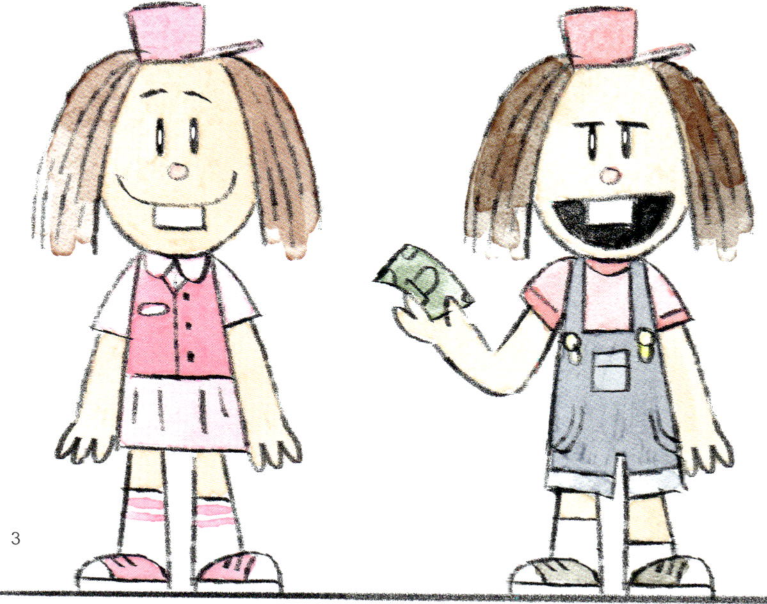

3

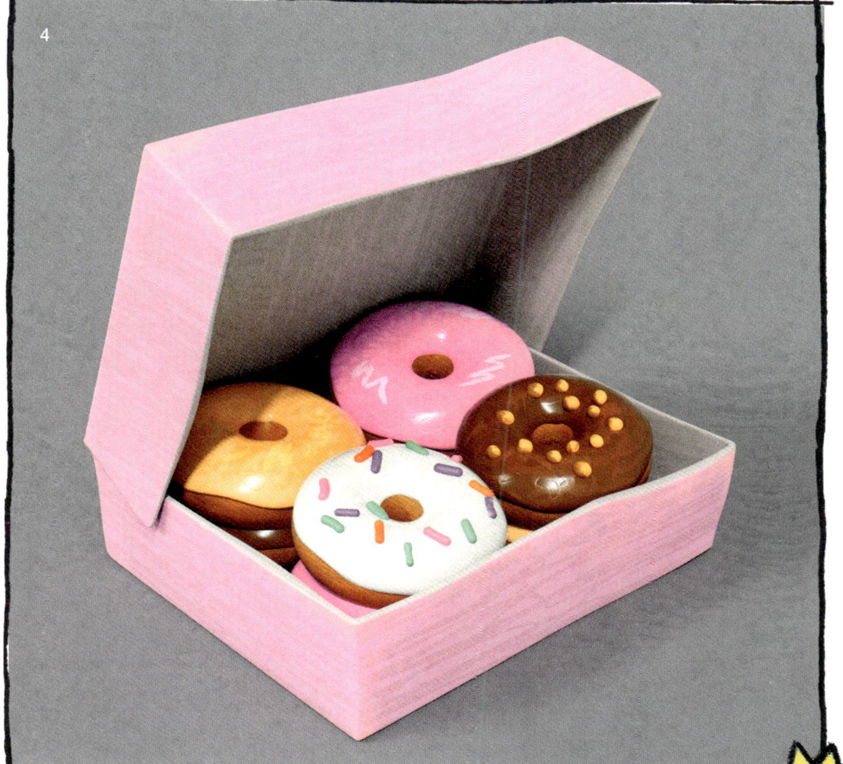

4

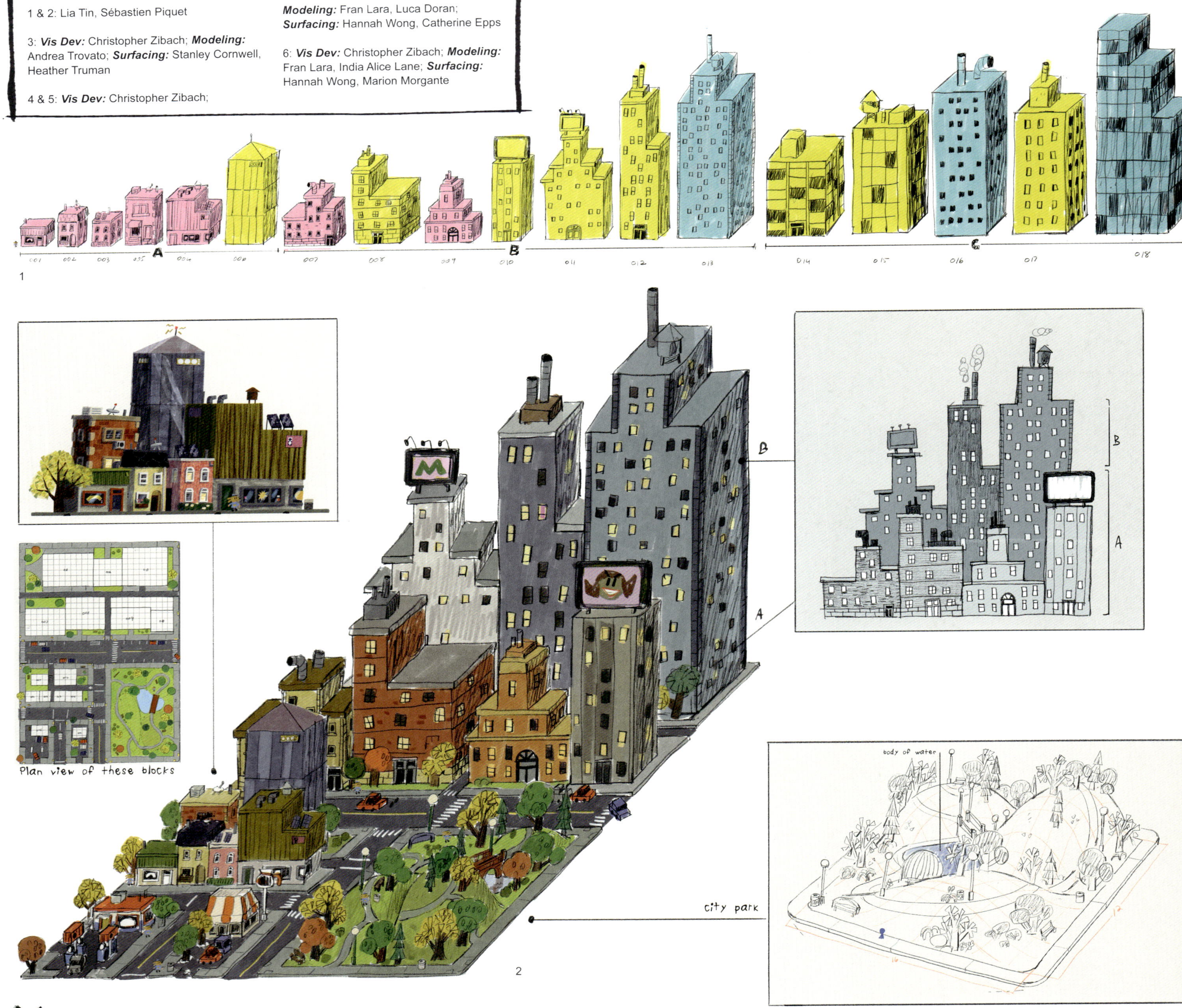

1 & 2: Lia Tin, Sébastien Piquet

3: ***Vis Dev:*** Christopher Zibach; ***Modeling:*** Andrea Trovato; ***Surfacing:*** Stanley Cornwell, Heather Truman

4 & 5: ***Vis Dev:*** Christopher Zibach; ***Modeling:*** Fran Lara, Luca Doran; ***Surfacing:*** Hannah Wong, Catherine Epps

6: ***Vis Dev:*** Christopher Zibach; ***Modeling:*** Fran Lara, India Alice Lane; ***Surfacing:*** Hannah Wong, Marion Morgante

FRÄNKZ
Hot Dogs
Exit
FRÄNKZ
Hot Dogs
Drive-Thru ova there
kinda good!
kinda tasty!

3

FRÄNKZ
Hot Dogs

4

FRÄNKZ
Hot Dogs

5

Joe'z
Cup of Joe
No Potty!
Supa Wifi
Caffinate Then Scram
Open

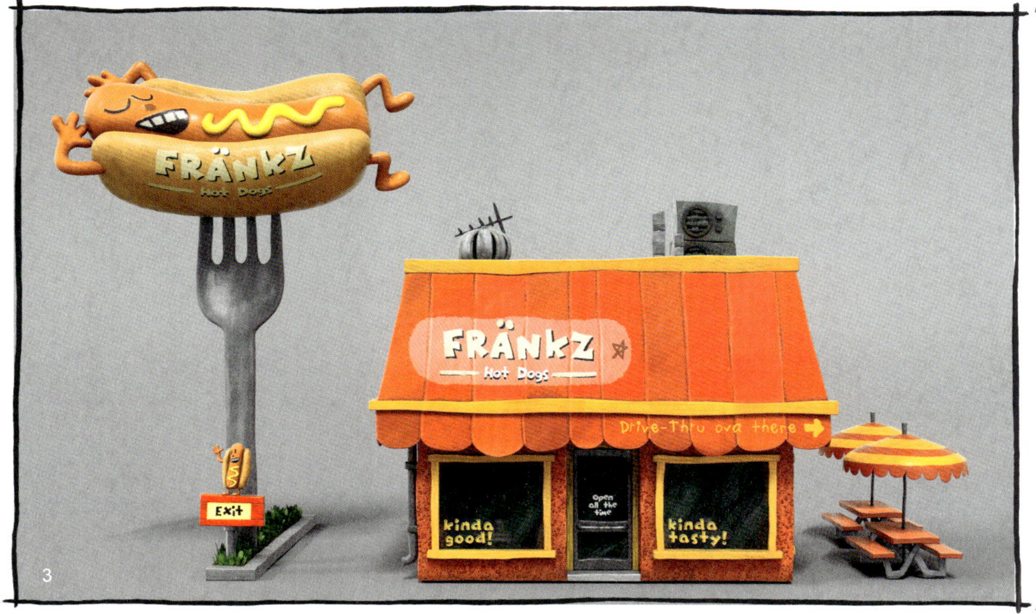

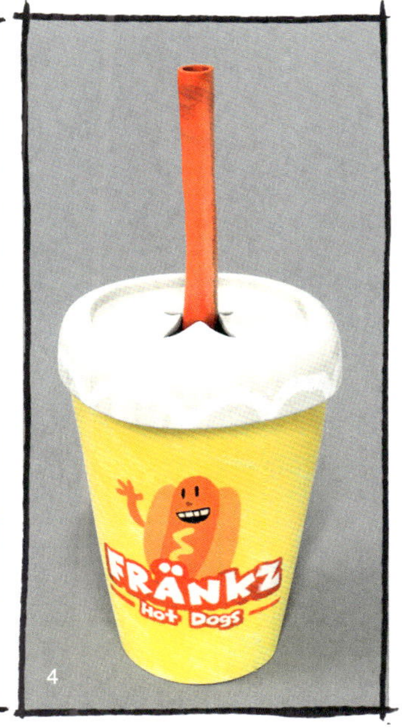

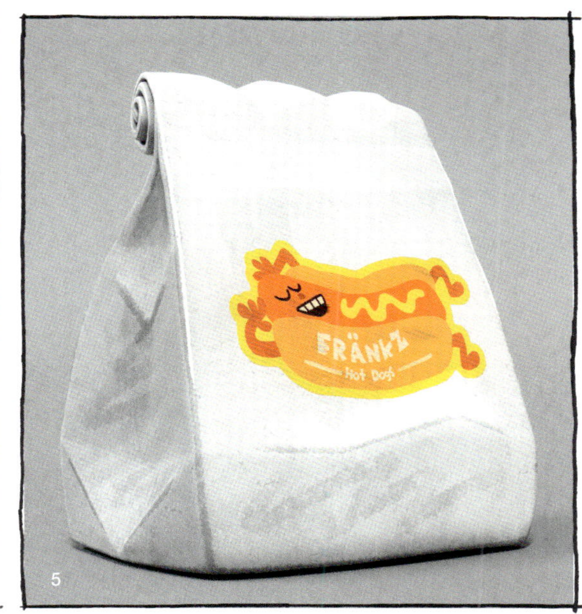

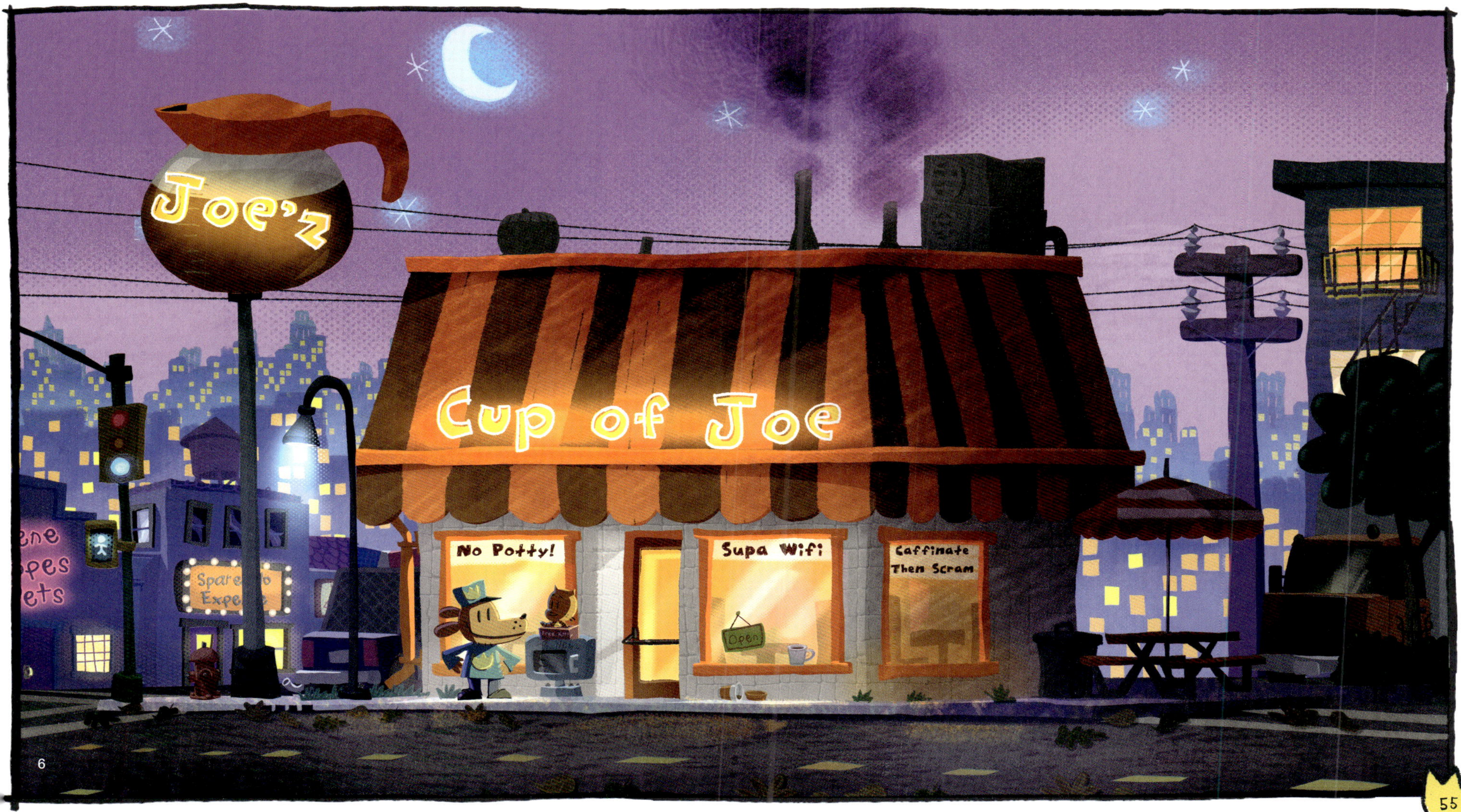

6

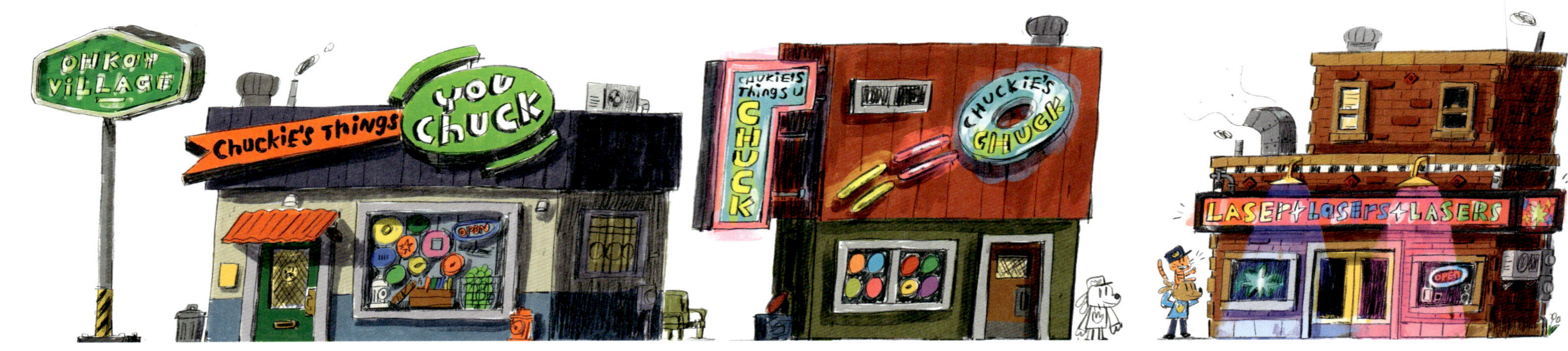
OHKAY VILLAGE
Chuckie's Things
YOU CHUCK
OPEN
CHUCKIE'S Things U CHUCK
CHUCKIE'S CHUCK
LASERS LOSERS LASERS
OPEN

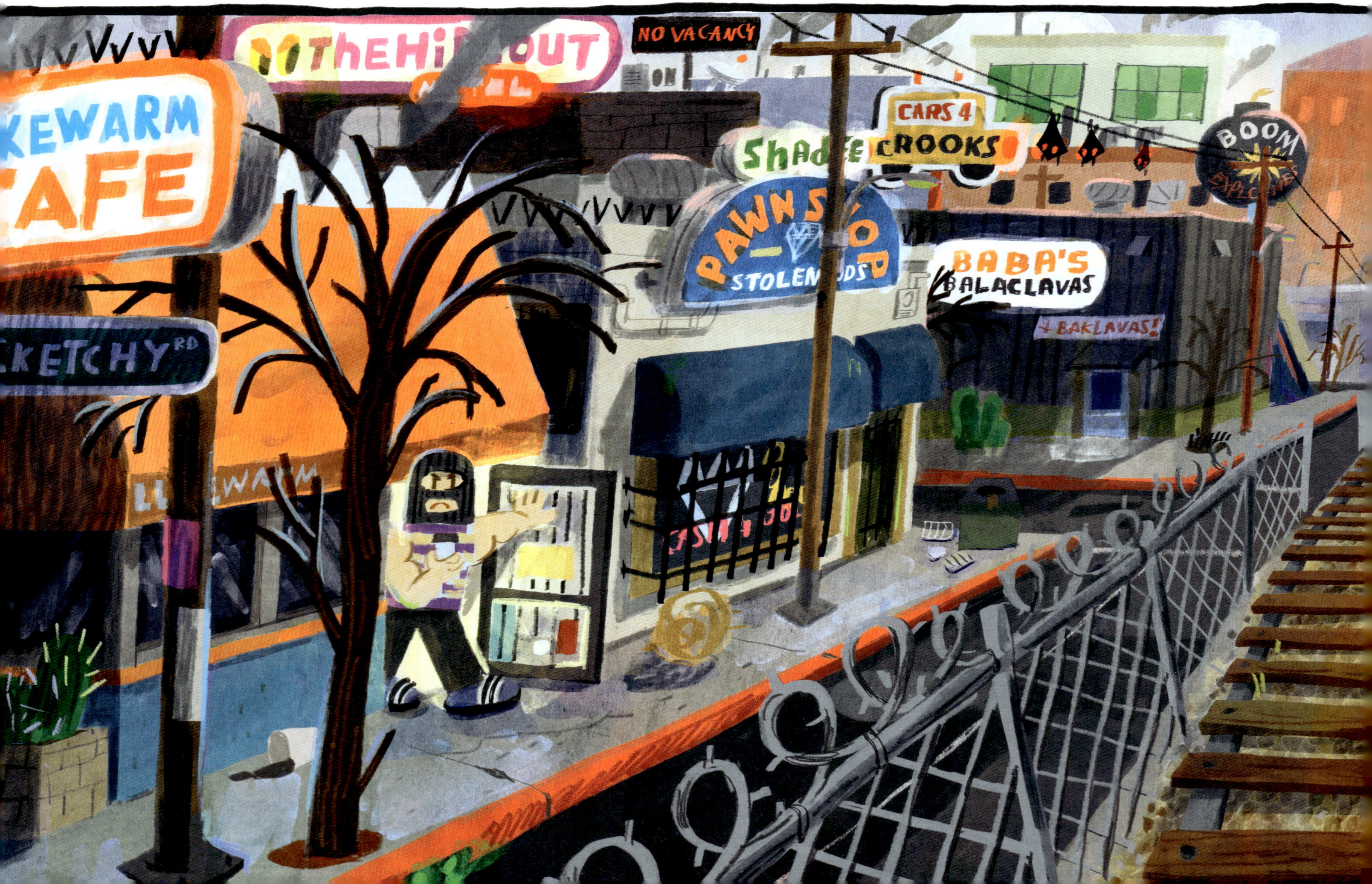

THE HIDEOUT
NO VACANCY
LUKEWARM CAFE
SKETCHY RD
SHADY
CARS 4 CROOKS
BOOM EXPLOSIVES
PAWN SHOP
STOLEN GOODS
BABA'S BALACLAVAS
+ BAKLAVAS!
LUKEWARM

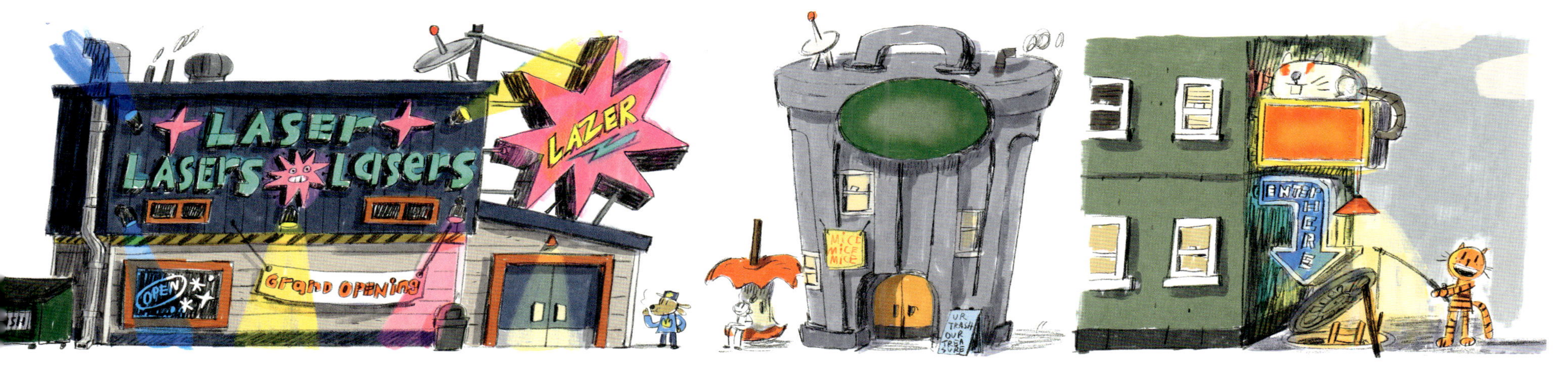

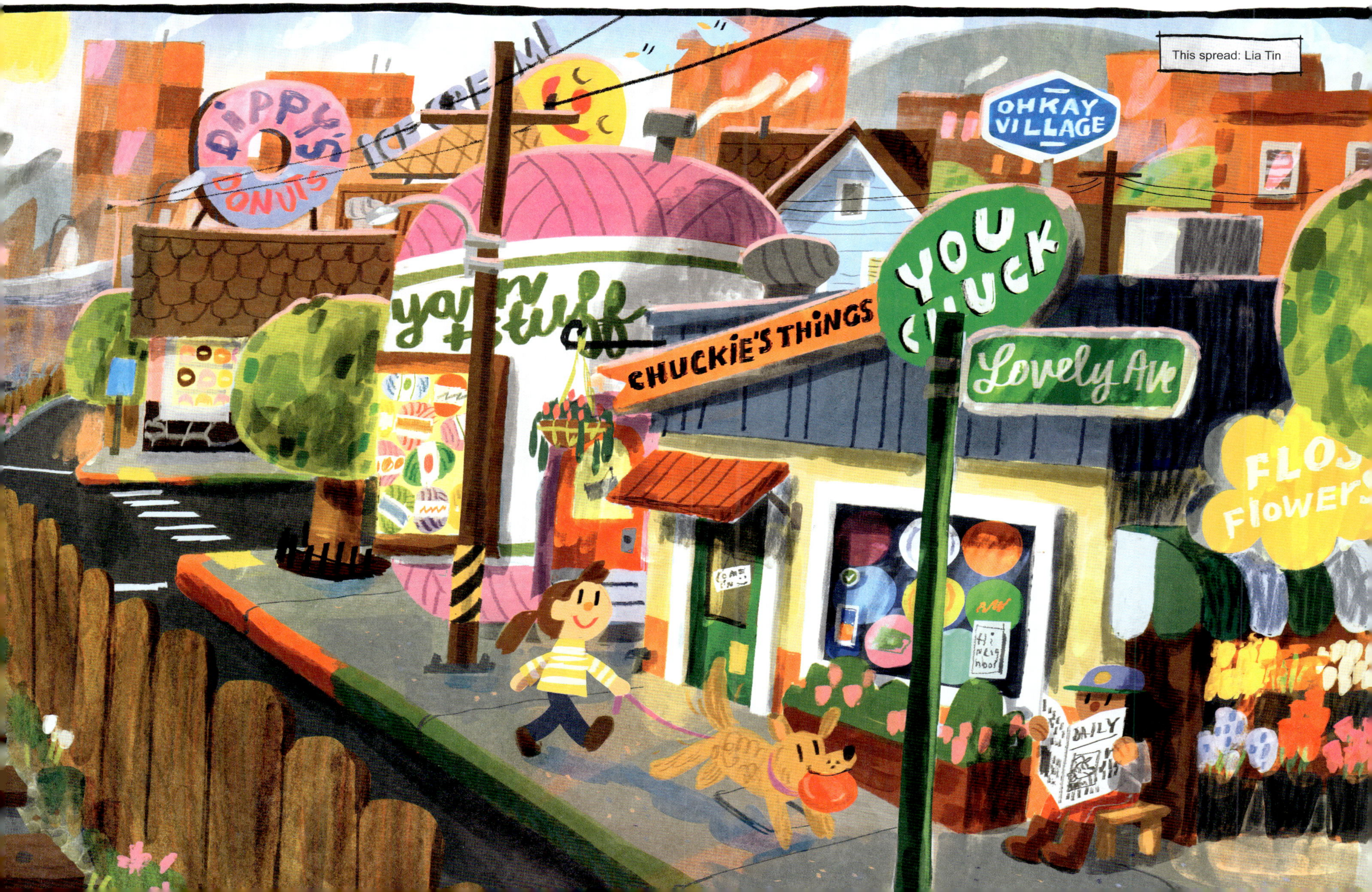

This spread: Lia Tin

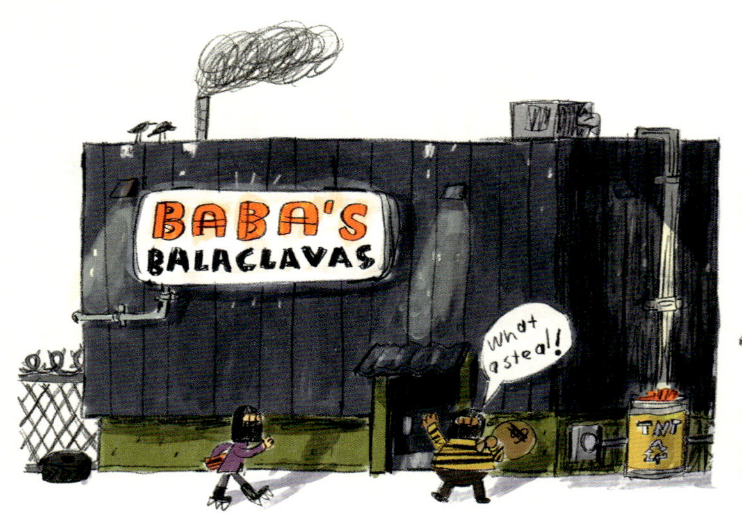
BABA'S
BALACLAVAS
What a steal!
TNT

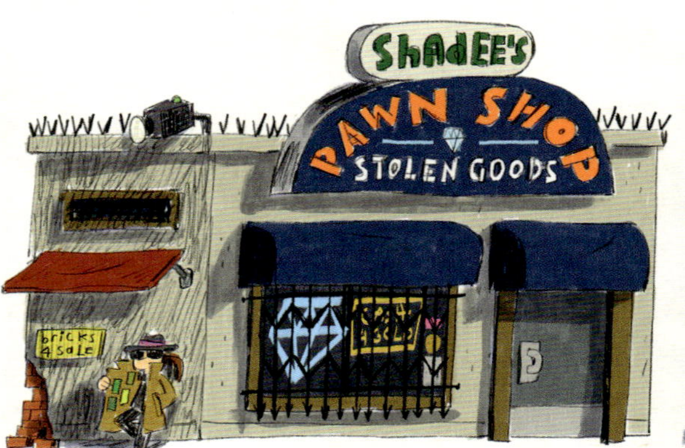
ShadEE's
PAWN SHOP
STOLEN GOODS
bricks 4 sale

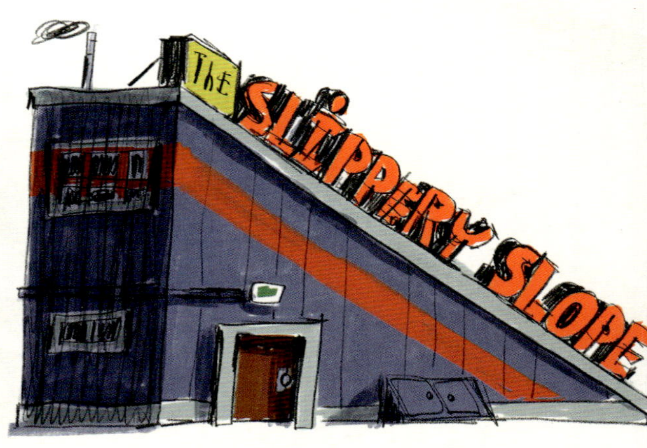
The SLIPPERY SLOPE

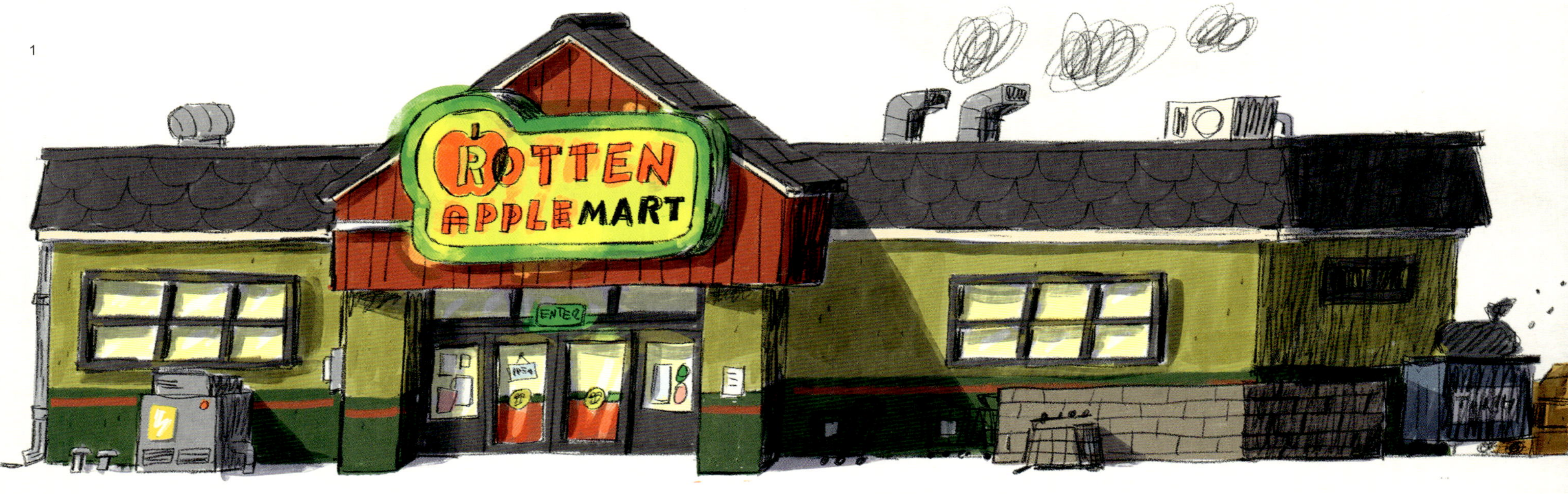
ROTTEN APPLE MART
ENTER

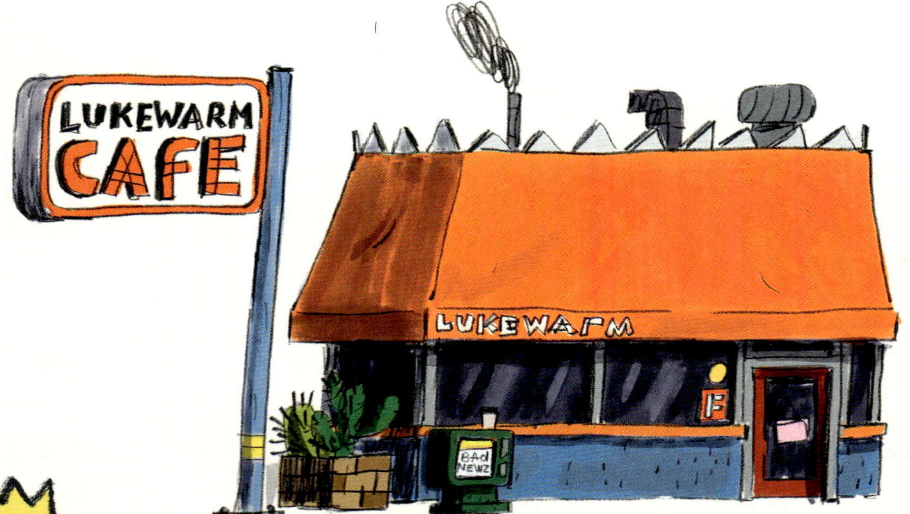
LUKEWARM
CAFE
LUKEWARM
BAD NEWZ

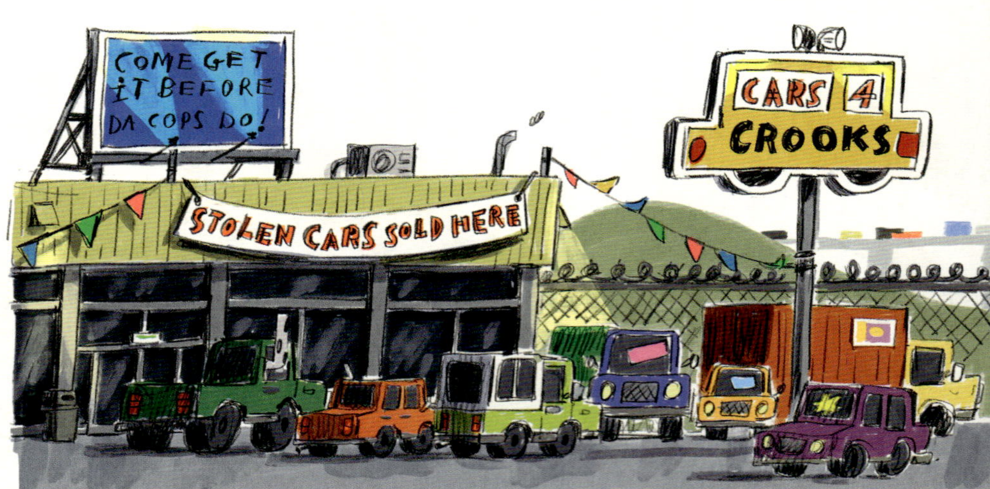
COME GET IT BEFORE DA COPS DO!
STOLEN CARS SOLD HERE
CARS 4 CROOKS

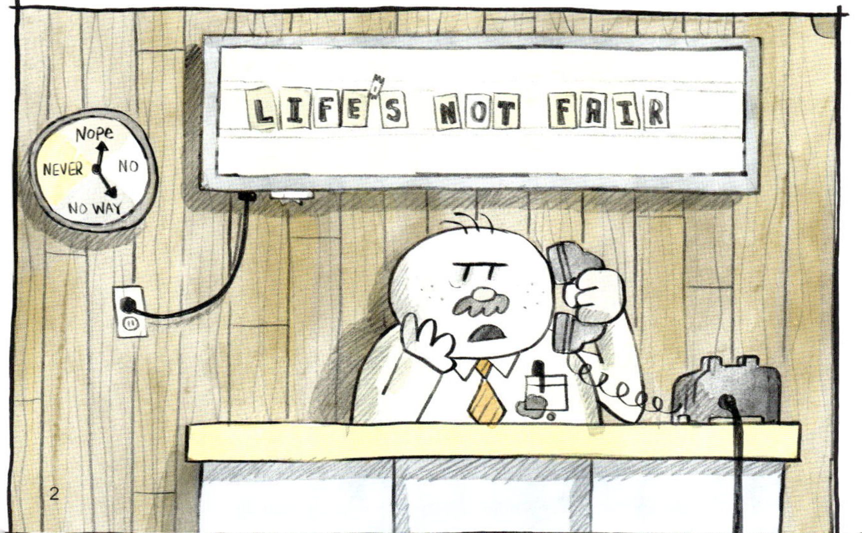

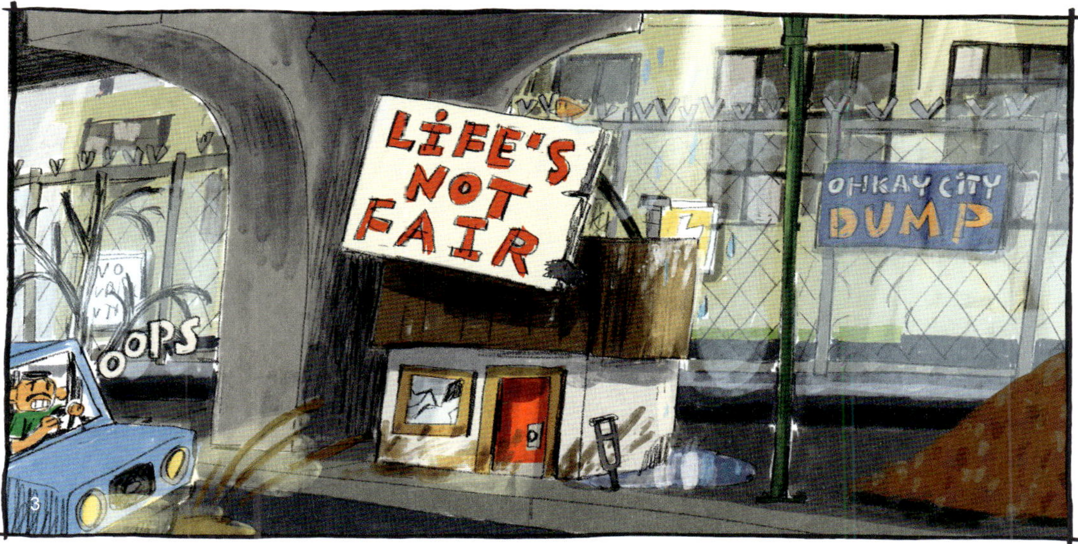

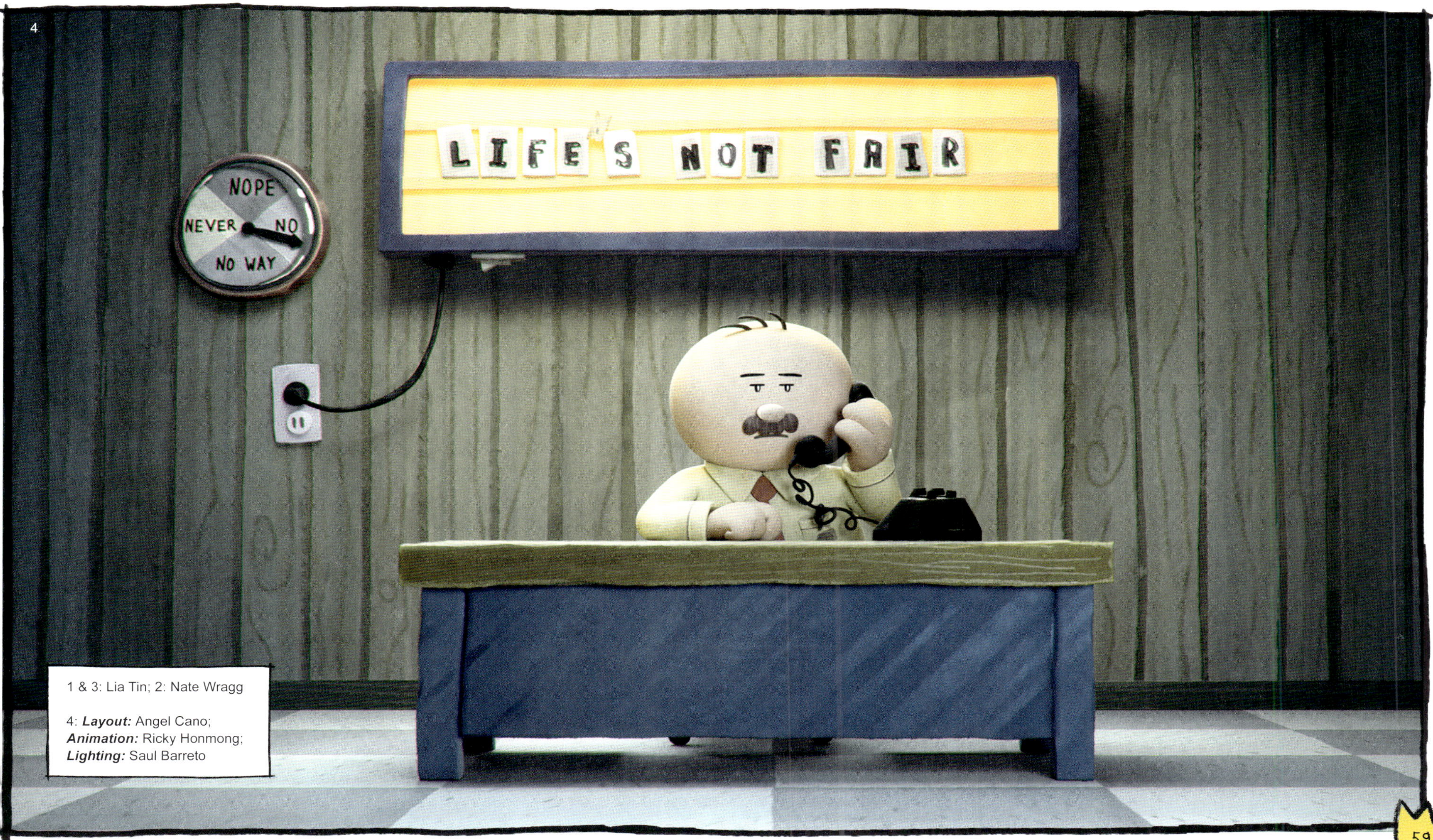

4

1 & 3: Lia Tin; 2: Nate Wragg

4: ***Layout:*** Angel Cano; ***Animation:*** Ricky Honmong; ***Lighting:*** Saul Barreto

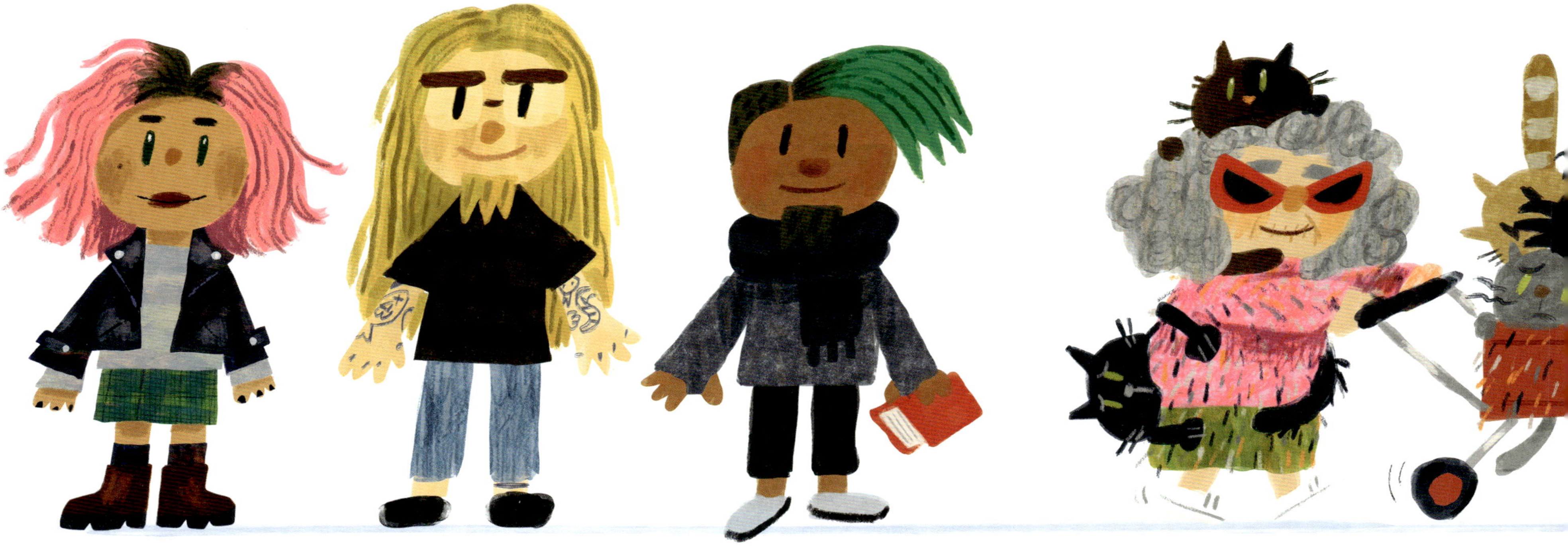

hipsters

cat lady

cats

This spread: Lia Tin

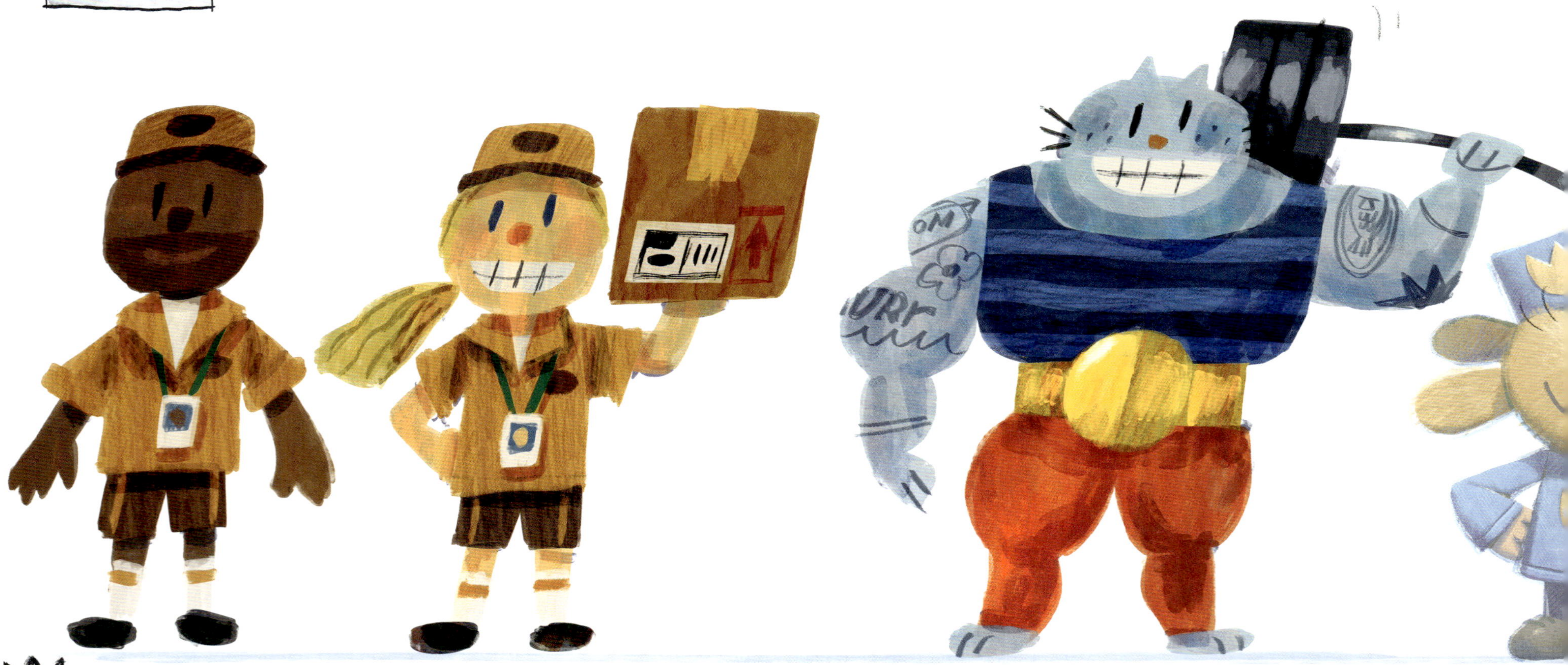

delivery people

mr. whiskers

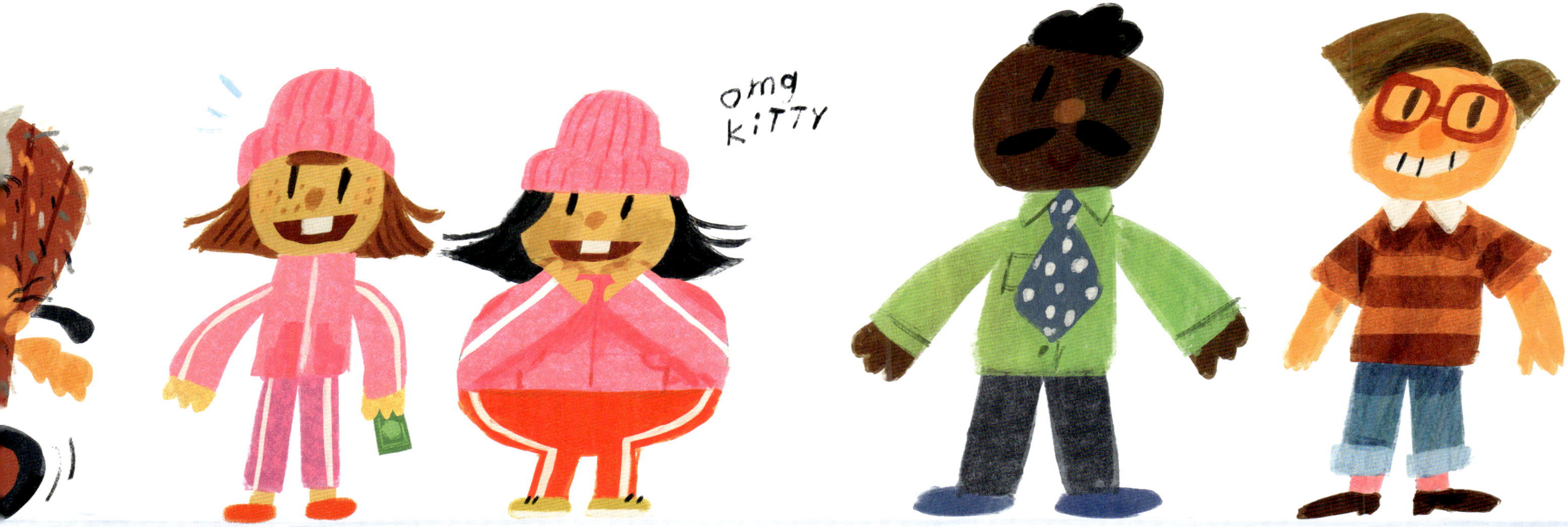

omg
kitty

eager cat girl

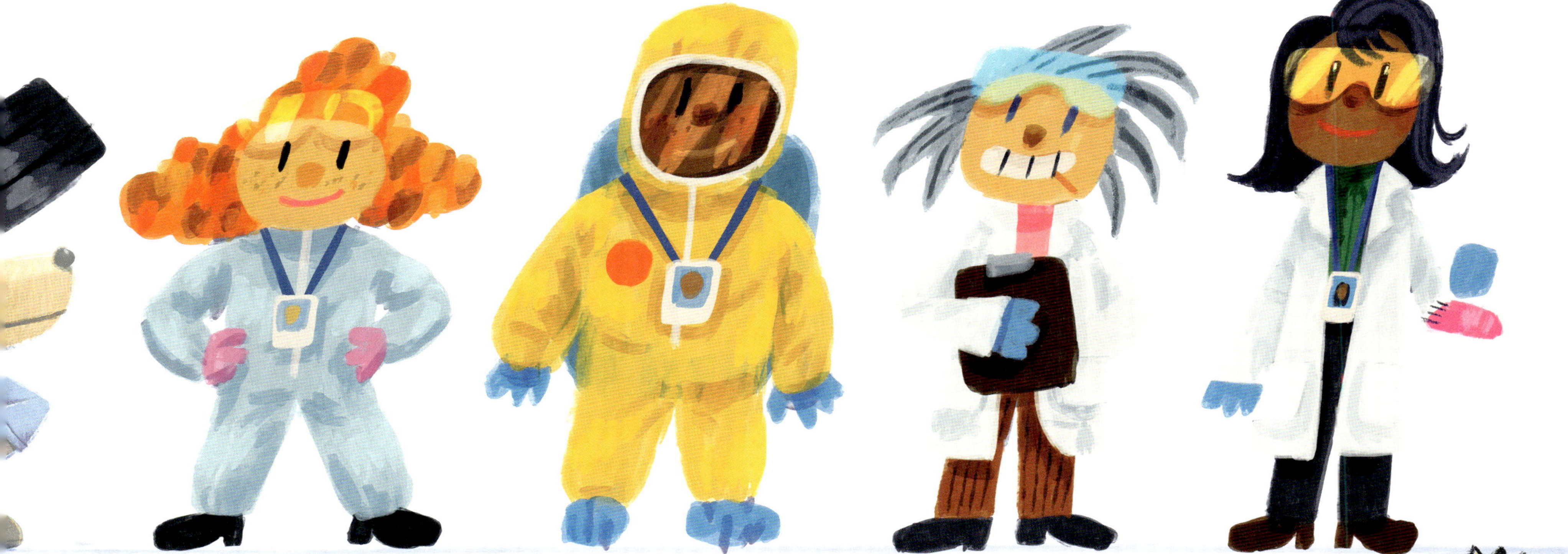

scientists

1

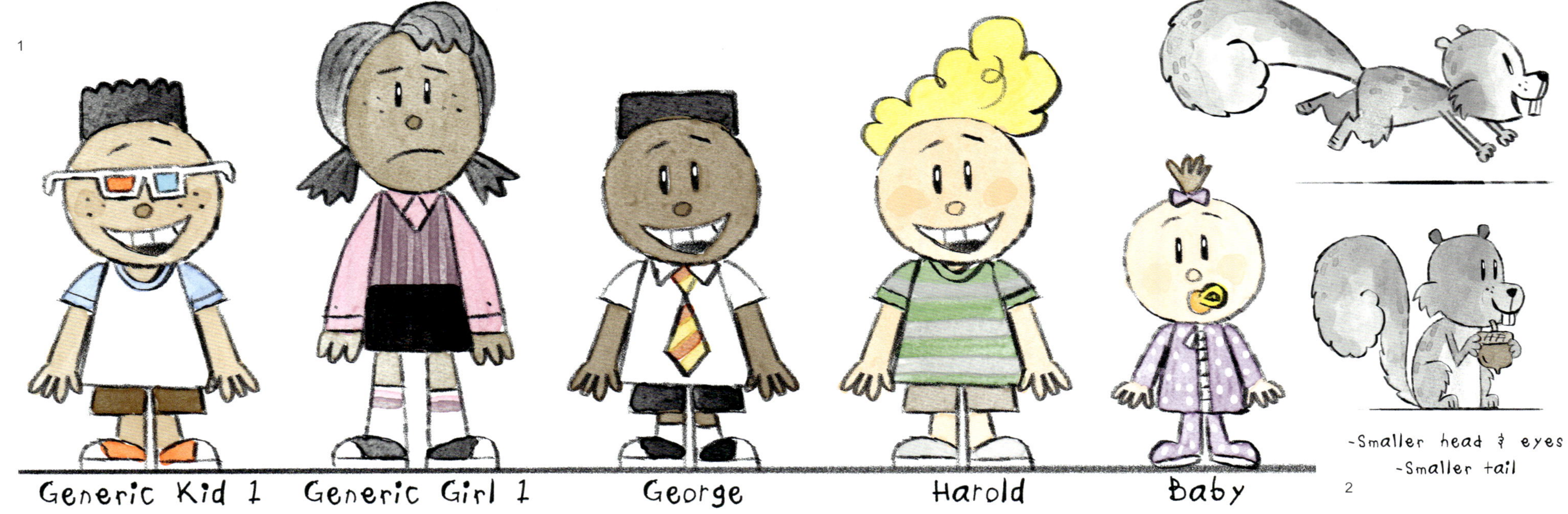

2

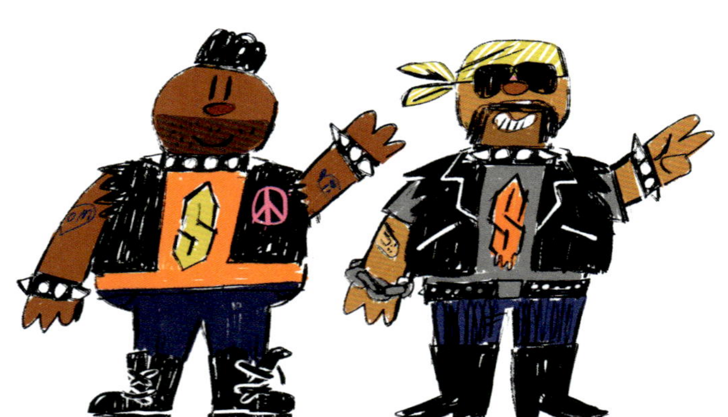

3

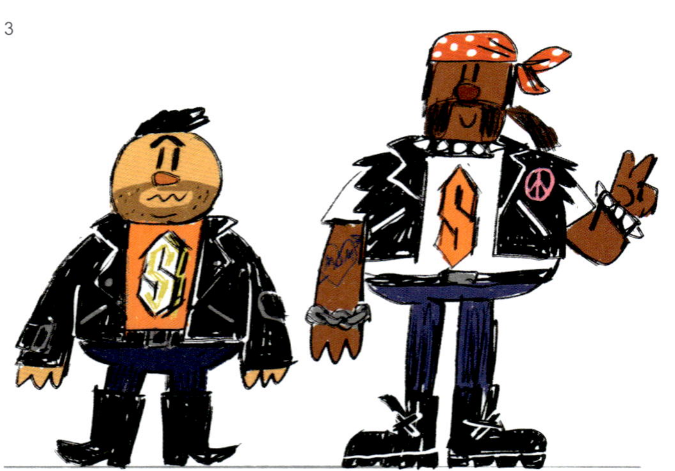

1, 2 & 5: Nate Wragg;
3: Lia Tin

4: ***Modeling:*** Sarah von Fersen, Maddalena Delvecchio, Zoe Arabella Lane; ***Surfacing:*** Hannah Wong, Greta Levickyte

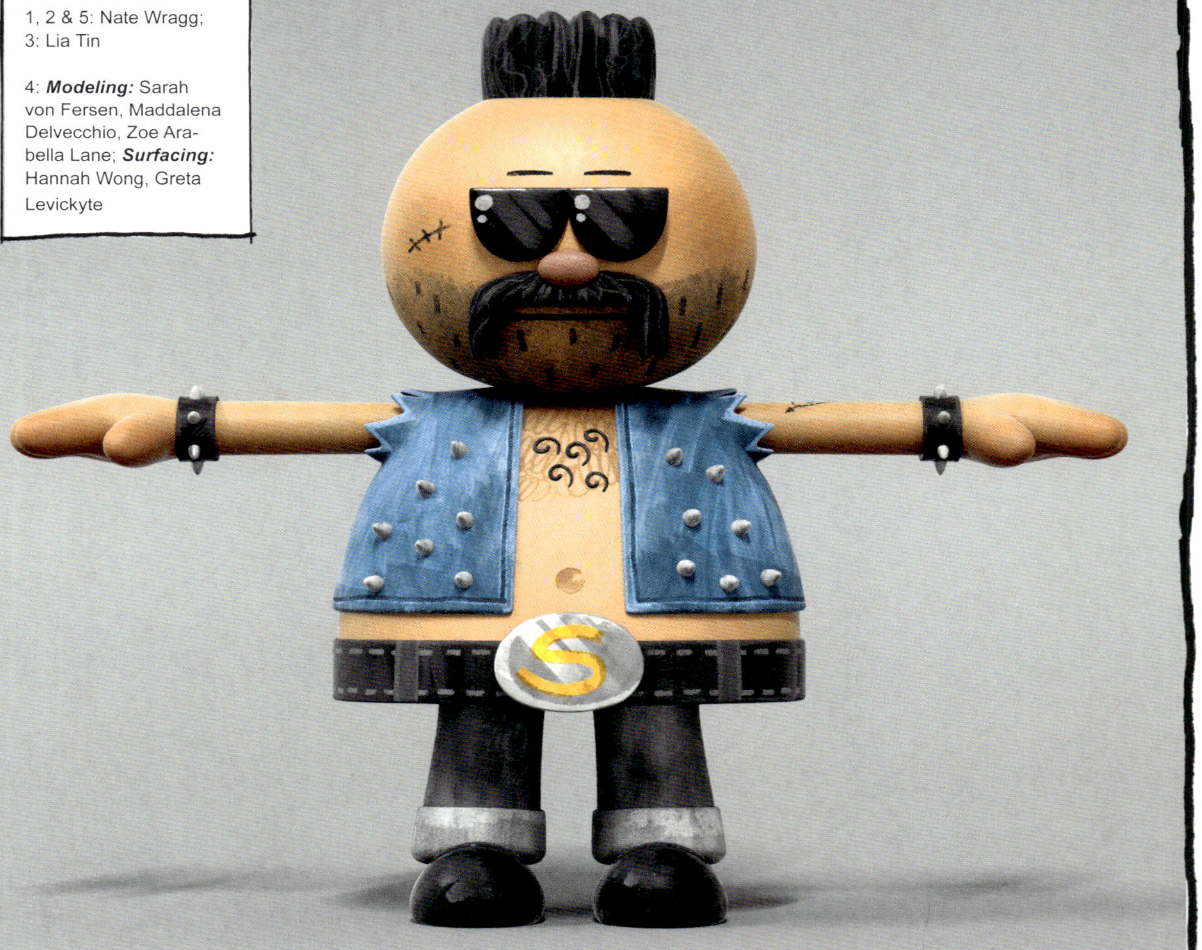

4

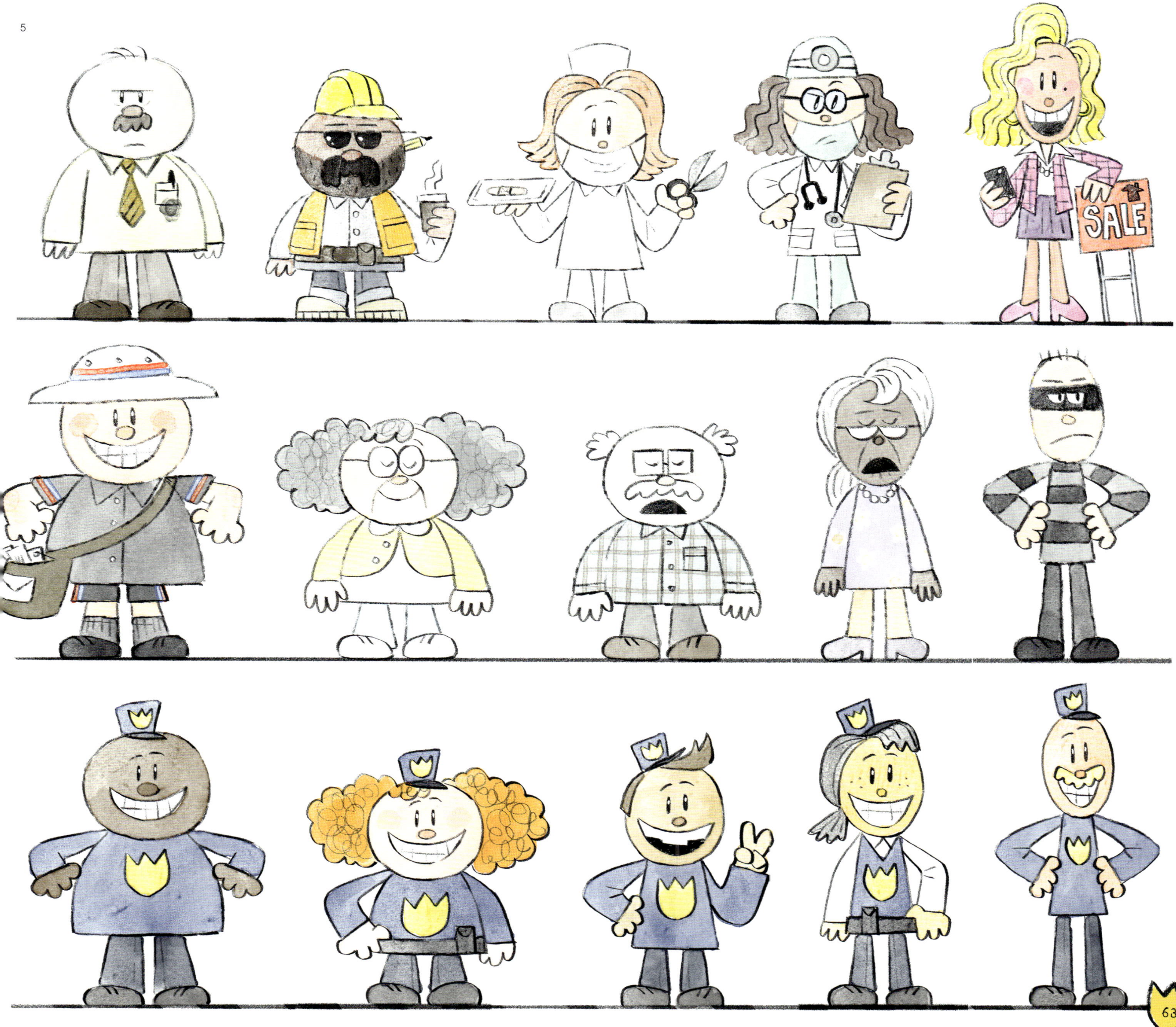

5

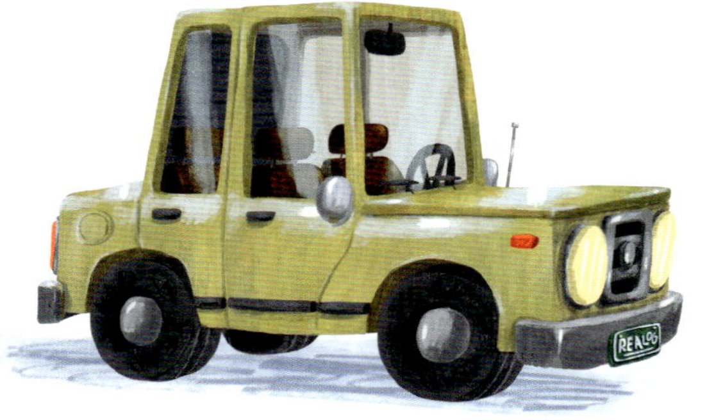

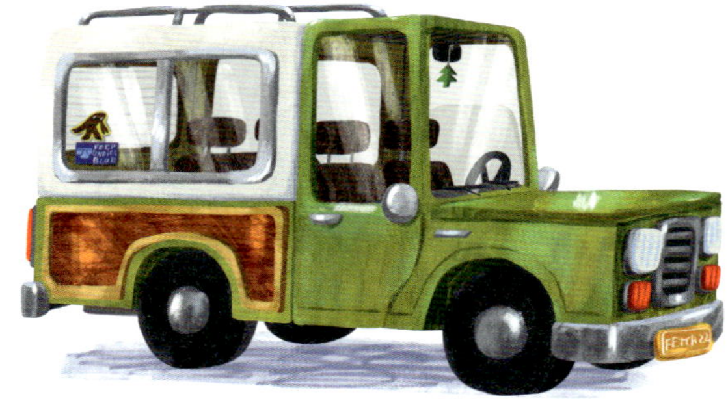

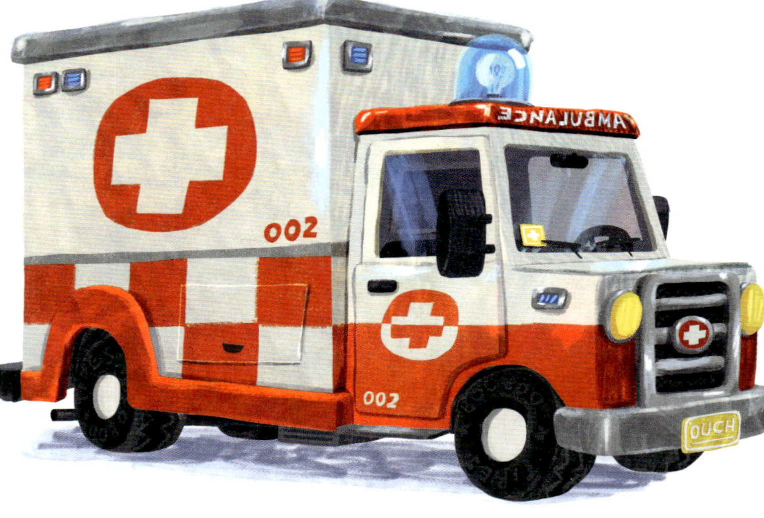

1

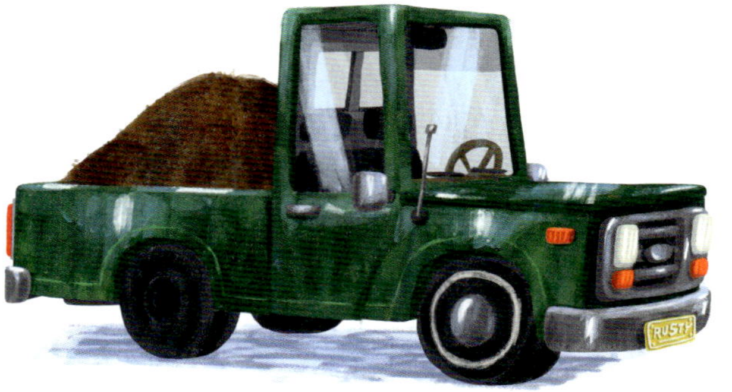

1–4: Lia Tin; 5: Katy Wu

2

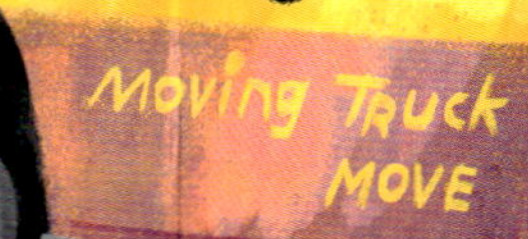

jello-like sirens

windows slightly tinted?

watercolor bounce light & crayon highlight

"cops" is painted on

slight emboss on letters

3 increased the size of hubcaps

4

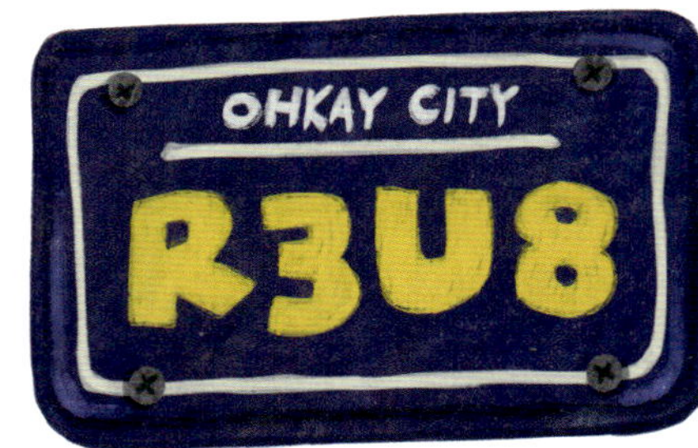

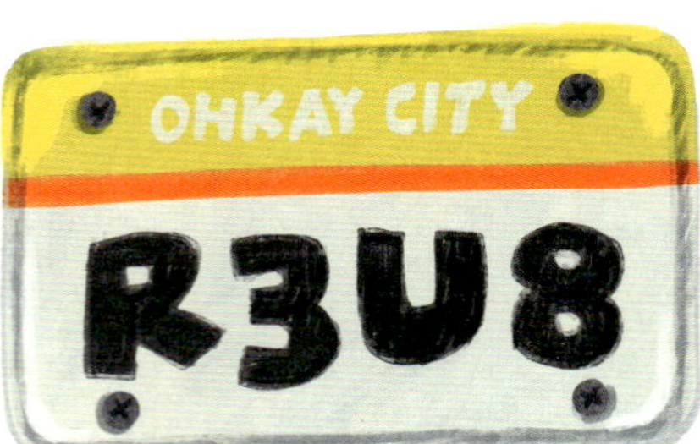

5

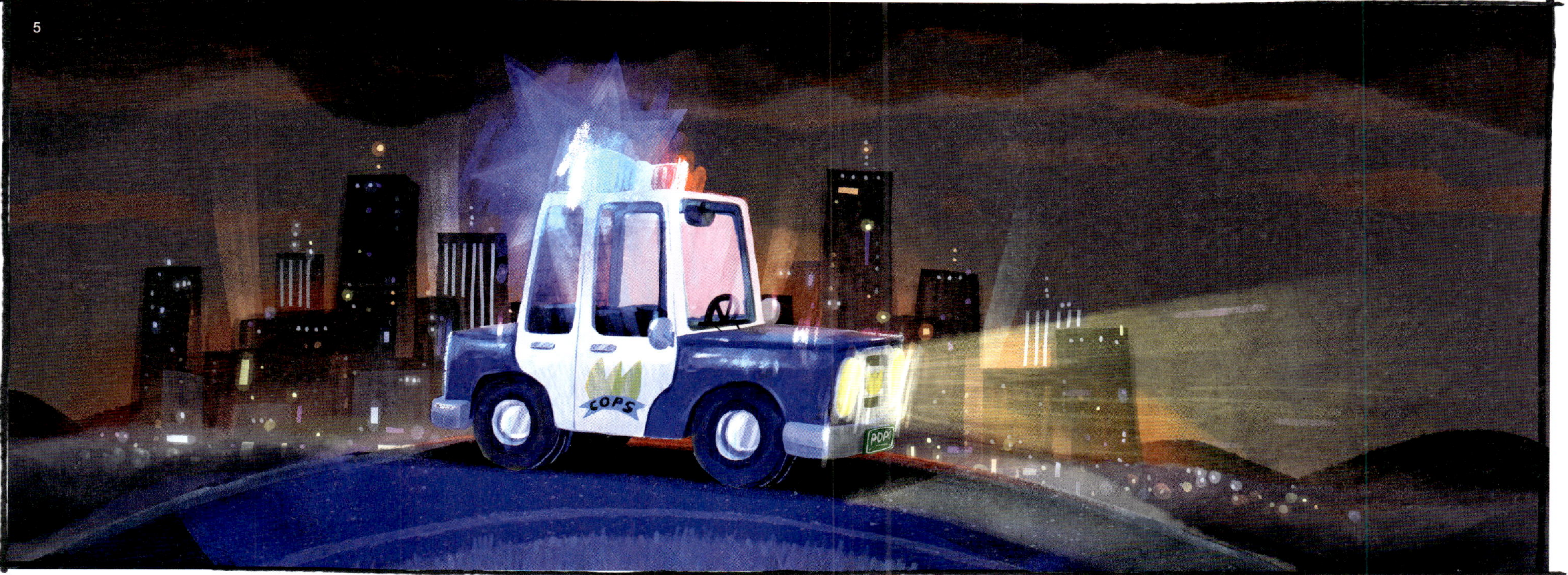

6: ***Modeling:*** Fran Lara, Catherine Epps, Andrea Trovato, Marta Macedo, Athanasios Zagkliveris, Ryan Narvaez, Luca Doran

Surfacing: Hannah Wong, Stanley Cornwell, Arnold Pryada, Leopoldine Perdrix, Lucía Álvarez Cisneros, Samir Necib

6

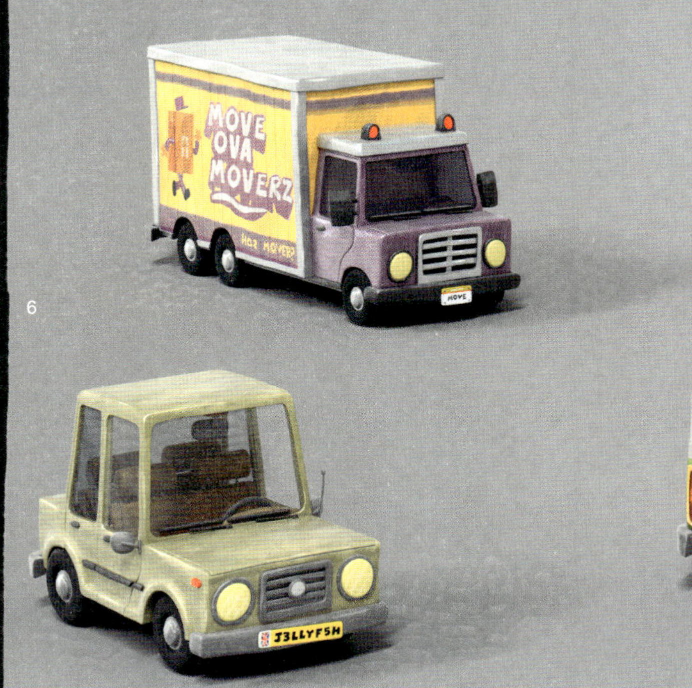

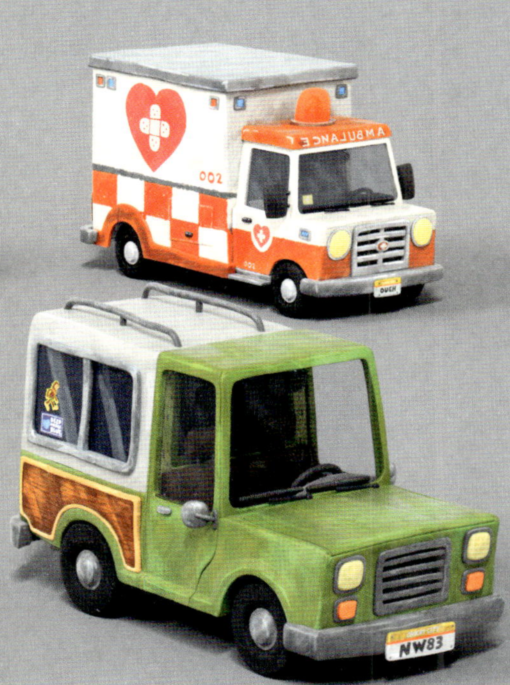

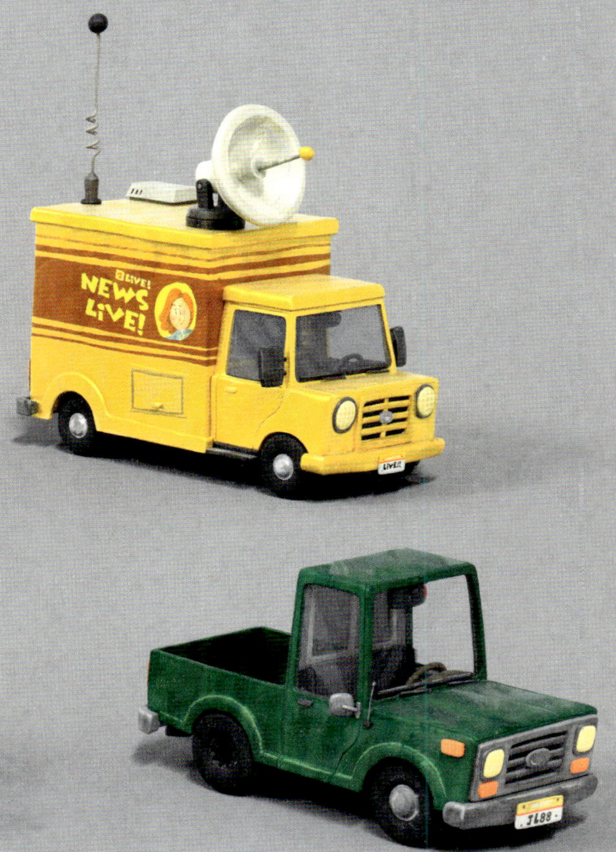

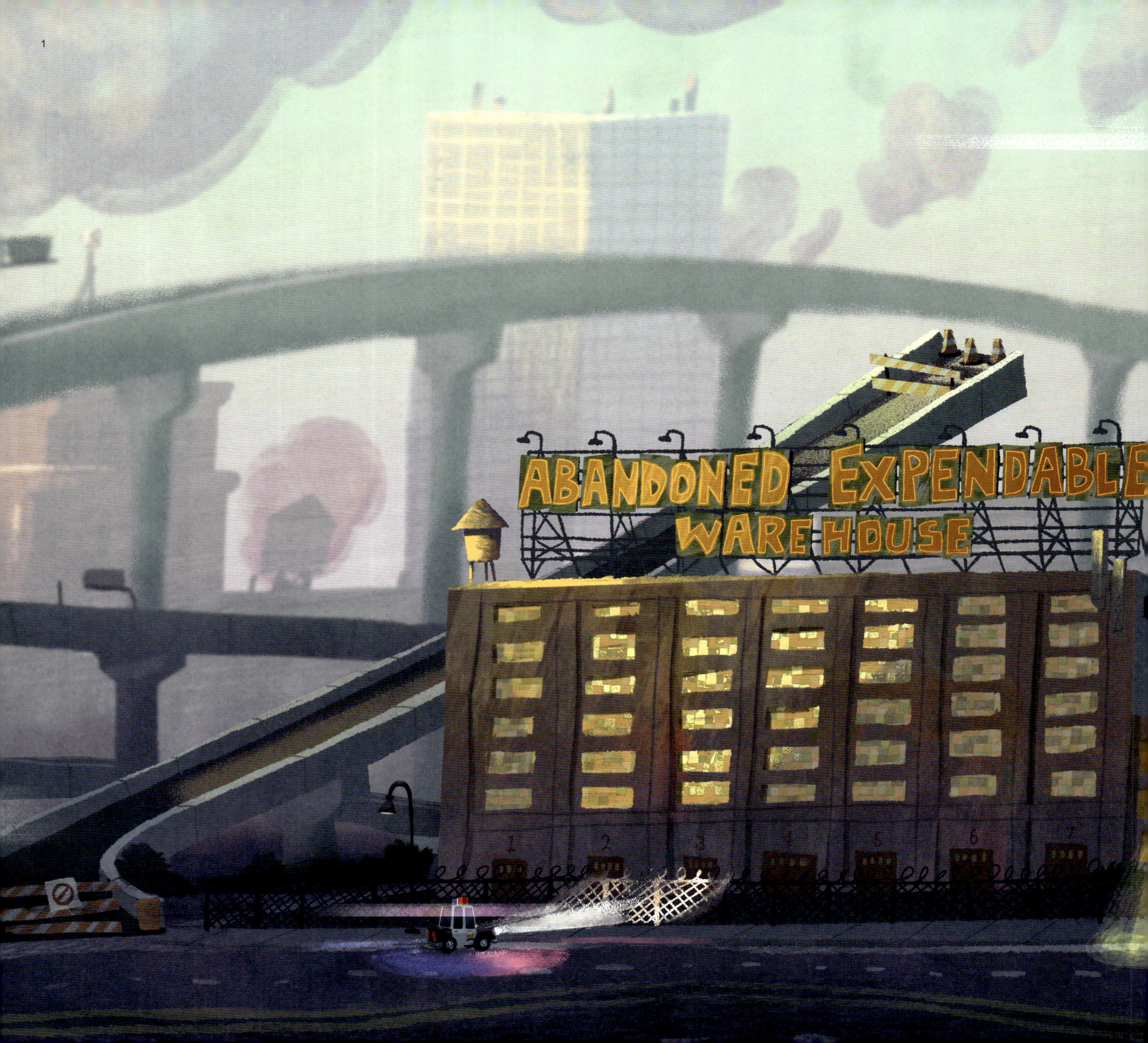
ABANDONED EXPENDABLE
WAREHOUSE

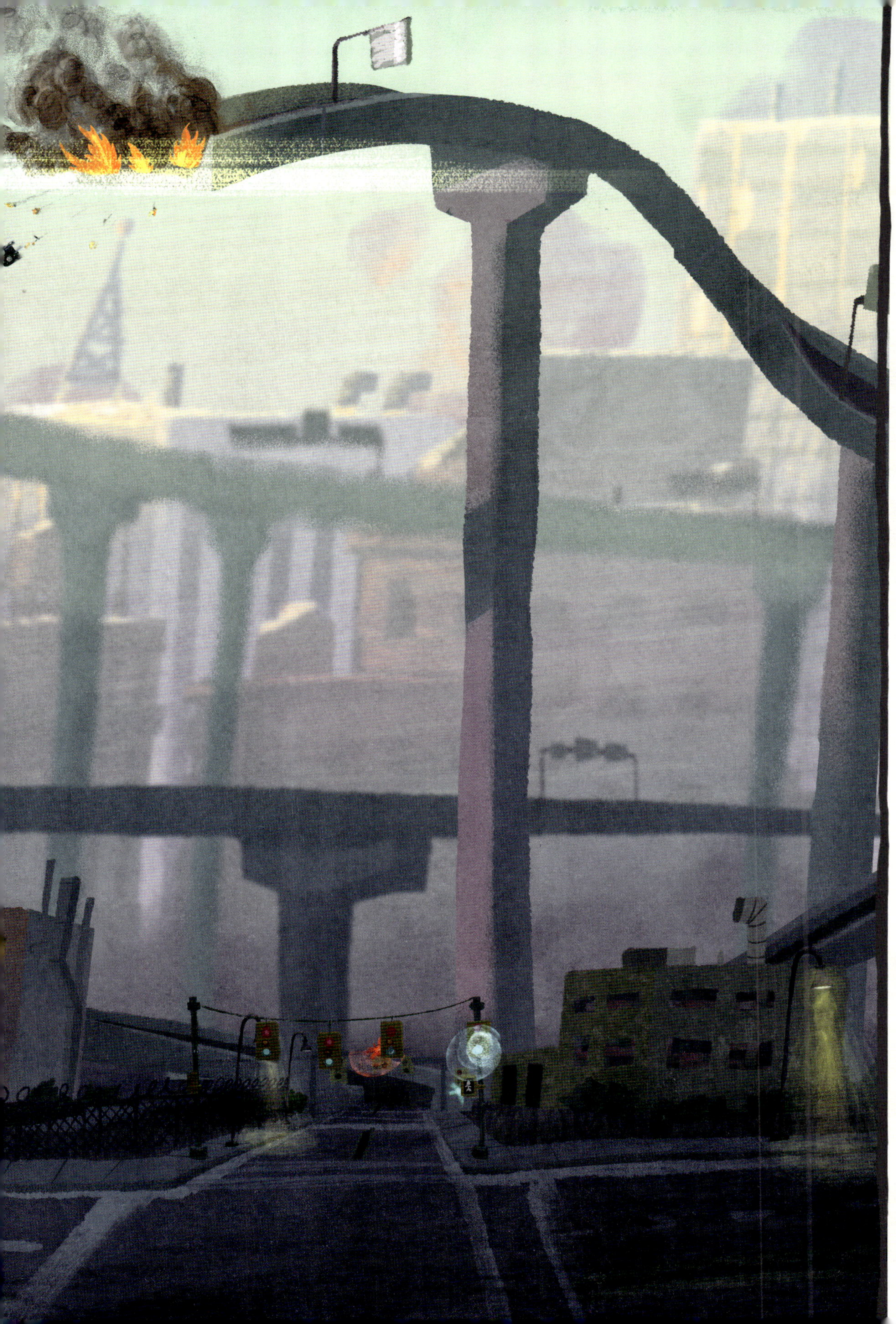

Abandoned Expendable Warehouse

Some of the buildings were lifted from the books, but inspired many more created for the movie. For example, in the opening of the movie, Officer Knight and his dog land on top of the Abandoned Expendable Warehouse to defuse a bomb thrown by Petey. Knight yells at Chief to get everybody out of the building as soon as possible, but Chief tells him, "There's nobody there because it's an abandoned building!"

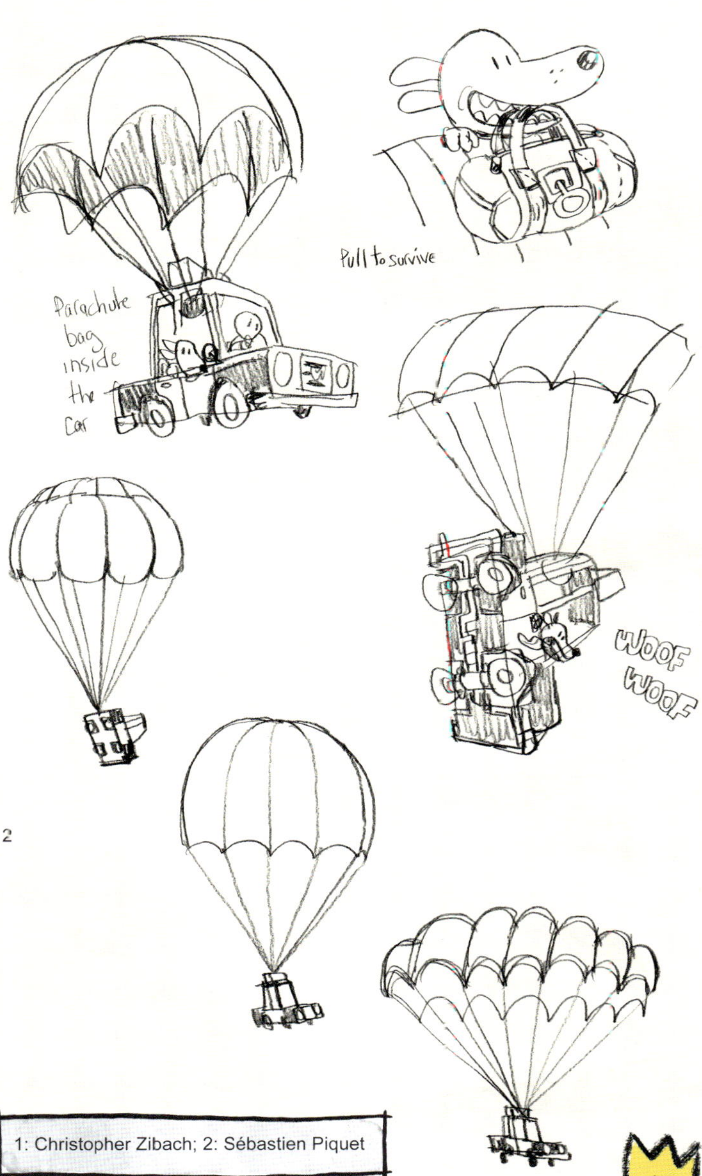

2

1: Christopher Zibach; 2: Sébastien Piquet

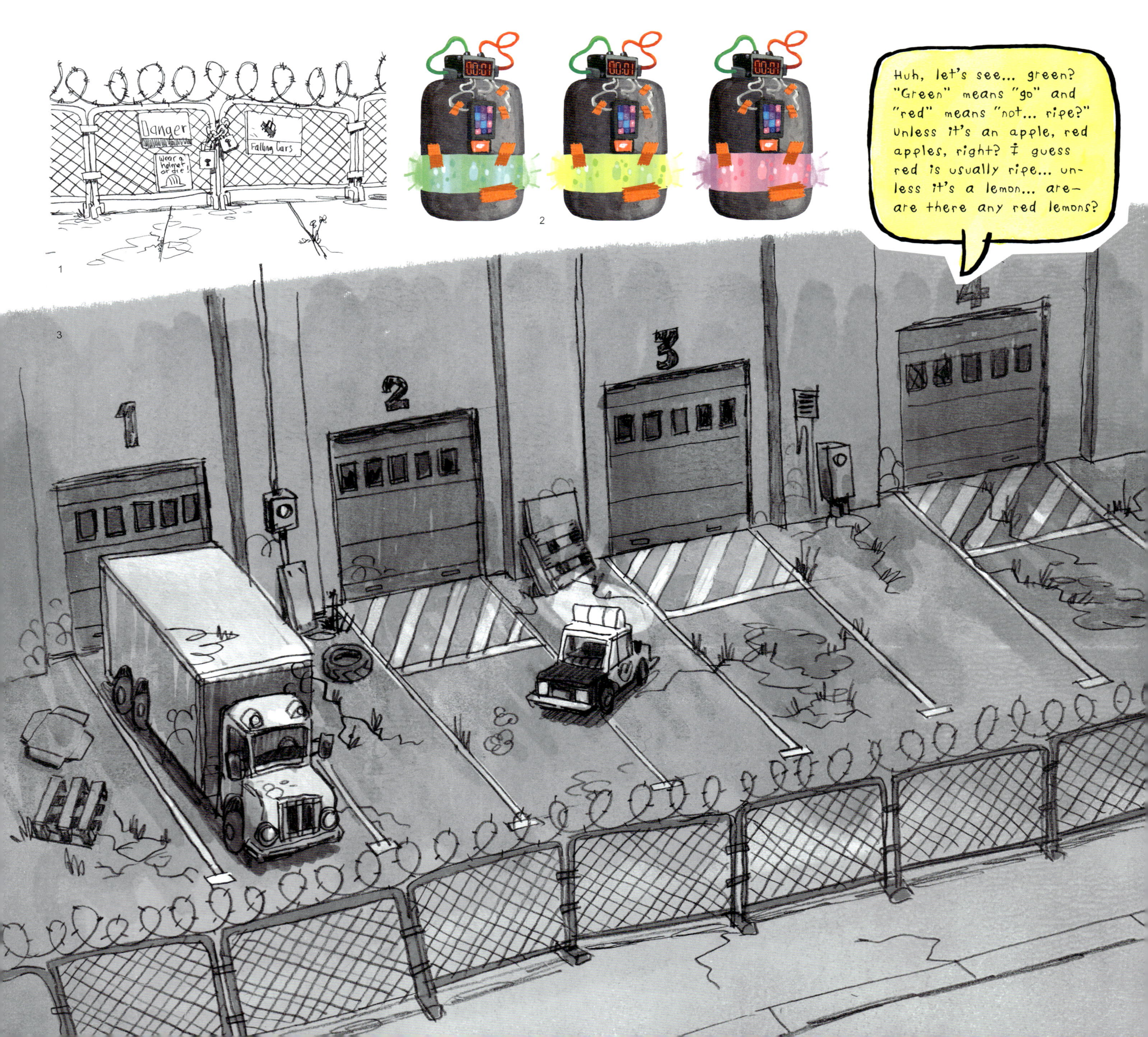
Danger
Wear a helmet or die!
Falling Cars
Huh, let's see... green? "Green" means "go" and "red" means "not... ripe?" Unless it's an apple, red apples, right? I guess red is usually ripe... unless it's a lemon... are- are there any red lemons?
1
2
3
4
1
2
3

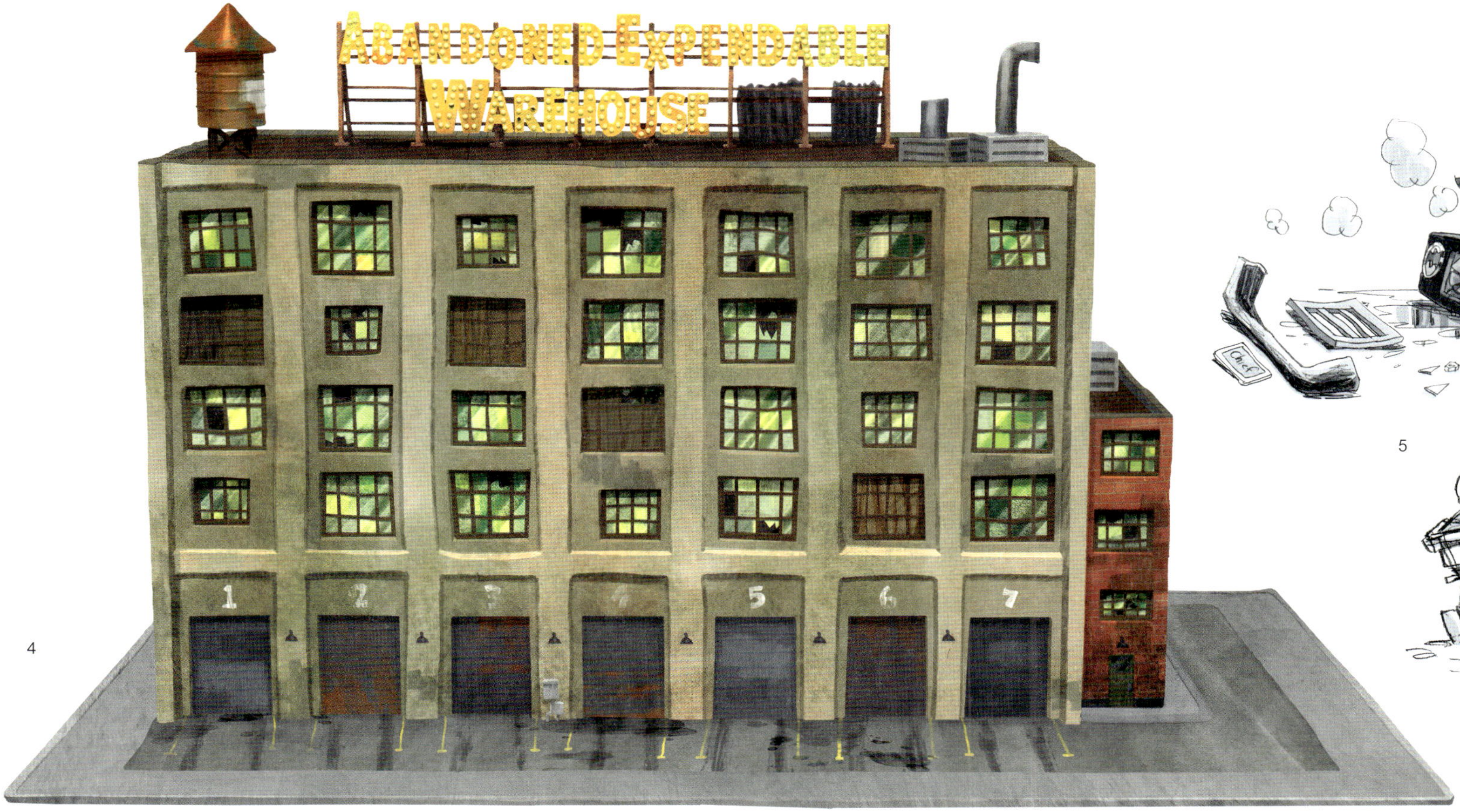

4

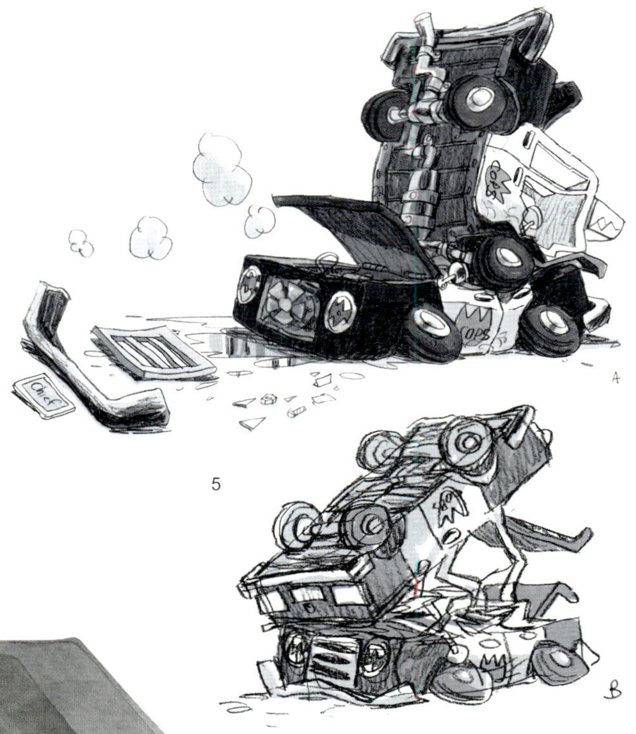

5

A

B

1–3, 5 & 6: Sébastien Picuet;
4: Vahe Yefremian

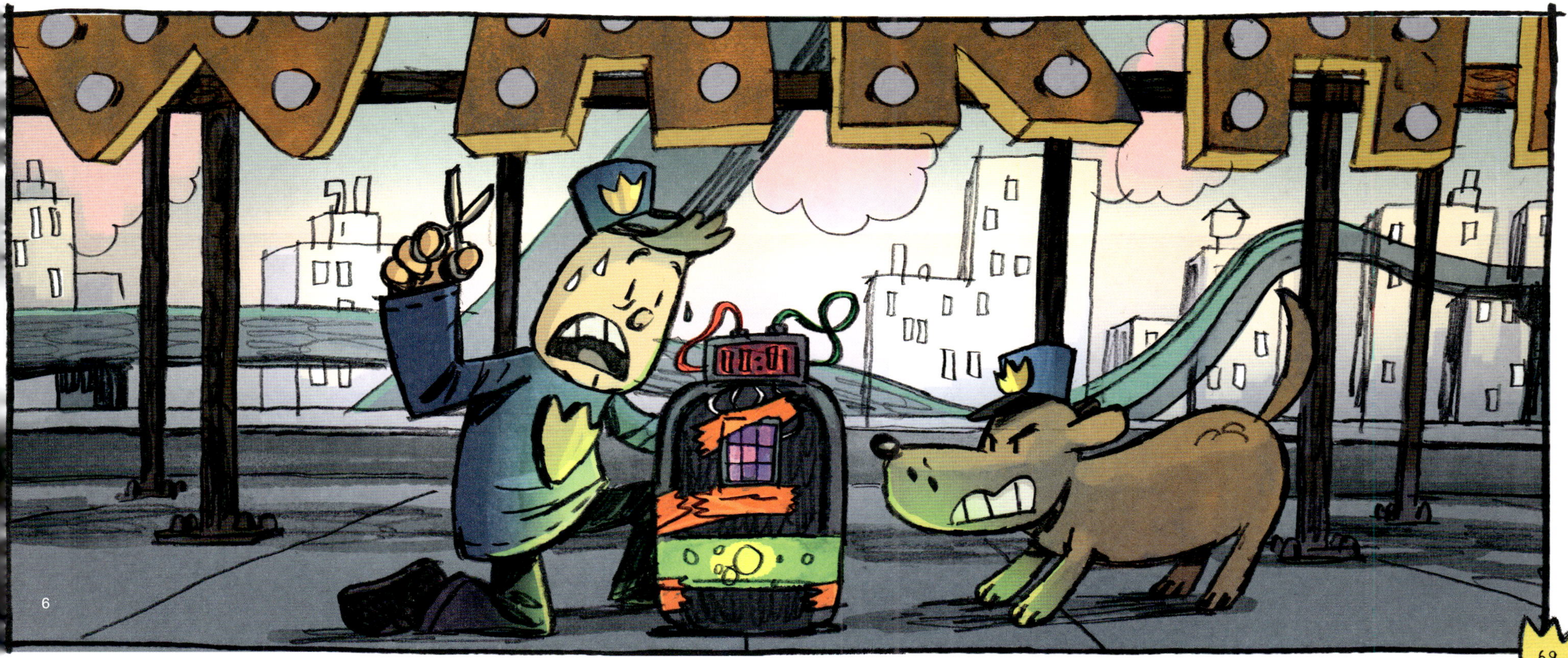

6

Hospital

Among the first locations in the movie is the hospital, where Officer Knight and his dog, Greg, are taken after a bomb explodes in the film's opener. This is where a nurse comes up with the brilliant idea to stitch Greg the Dog's head onto Officer Knight's body to save them both after their terrible accident.

1

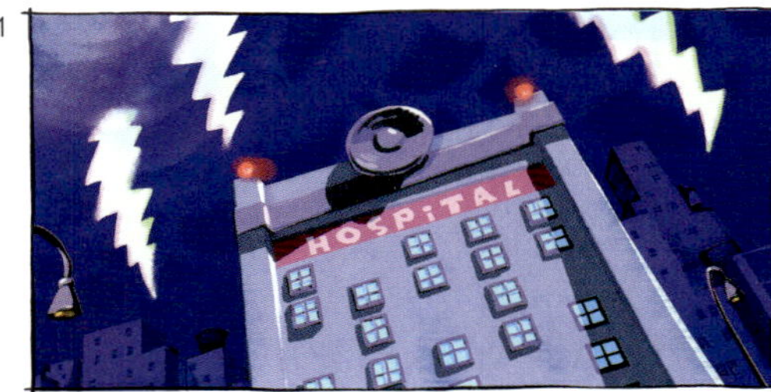

2

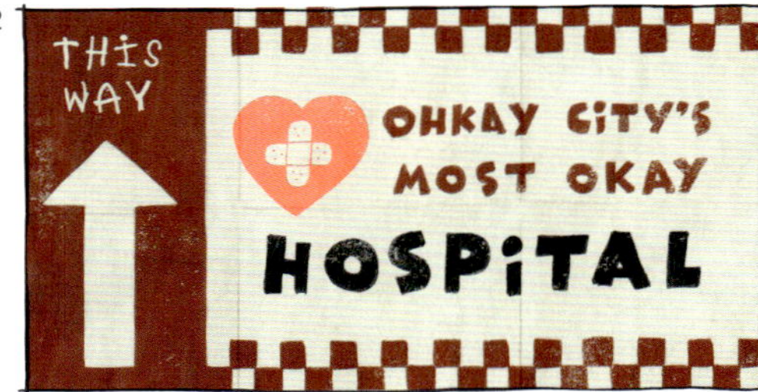

3

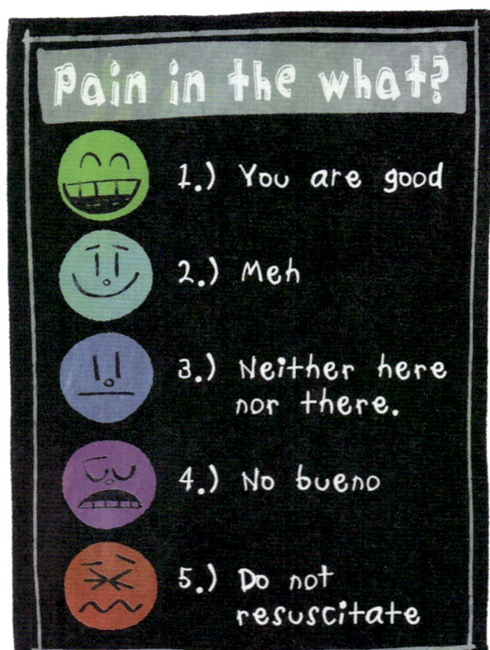

4

1, 3 & 4: Christopher Zibach; 2: Lia Tin

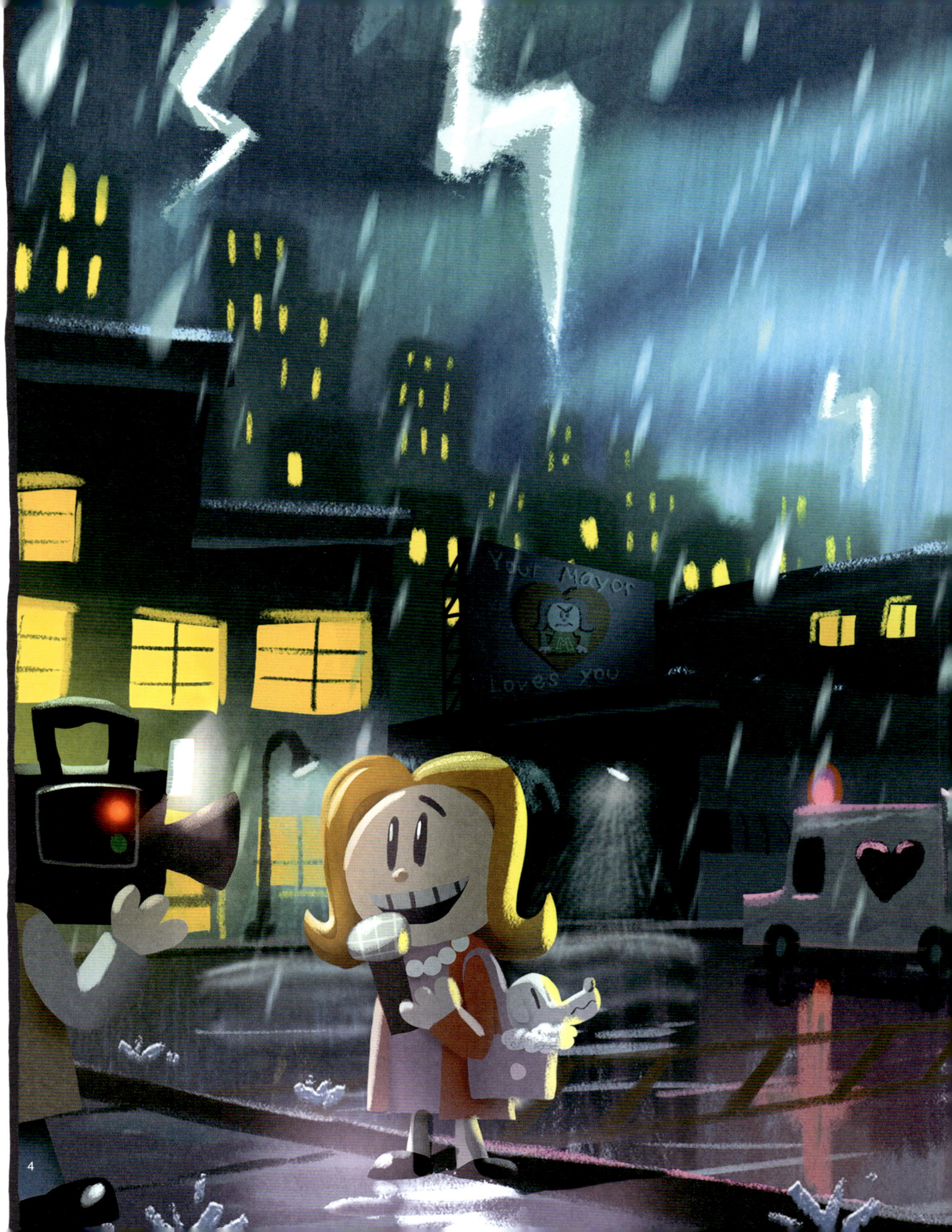

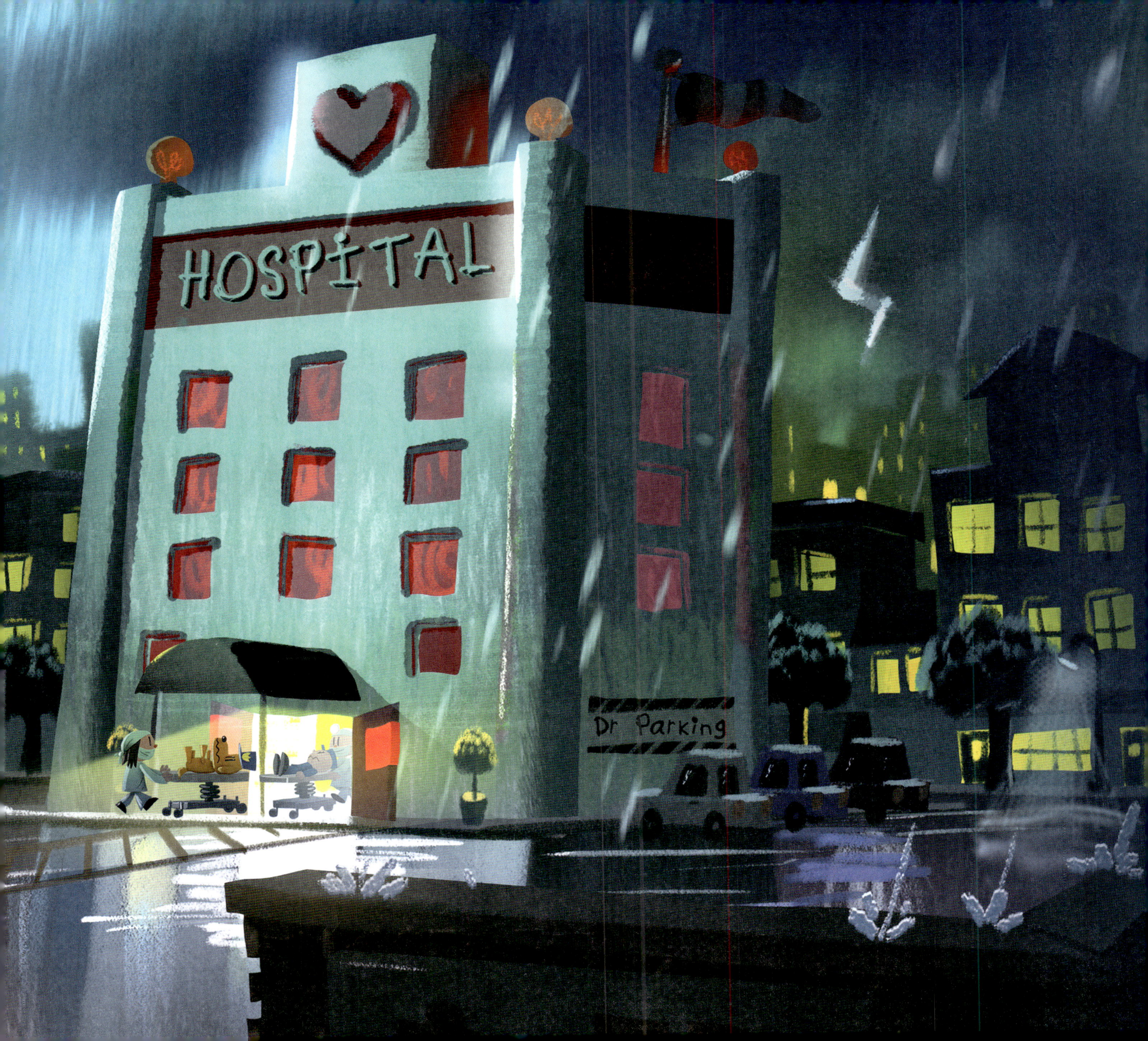
HOSPITAL
Dr Parking

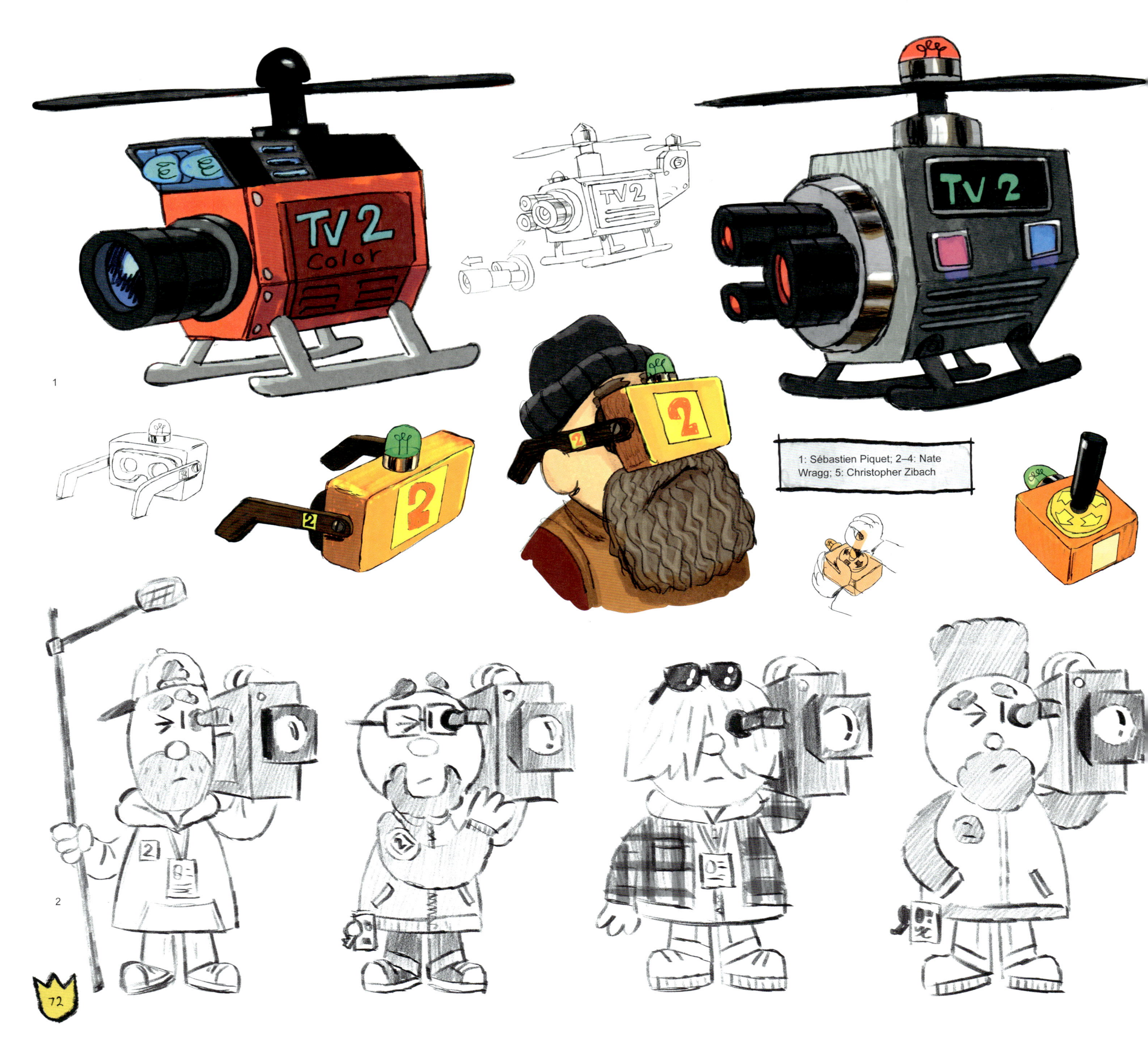

1: Sébastien Piquet; 2–4: Nate Wragg; 5: Christopher Zibach

Seamus

A down-to-earth cameraman who is always at Sarah Hatoff's side, Seamus (voiced by Billy Boyd) is usually at the ready to help those in need. He insists on wearing shorts even in the dead of winter, because that's just the kind of guy he is.

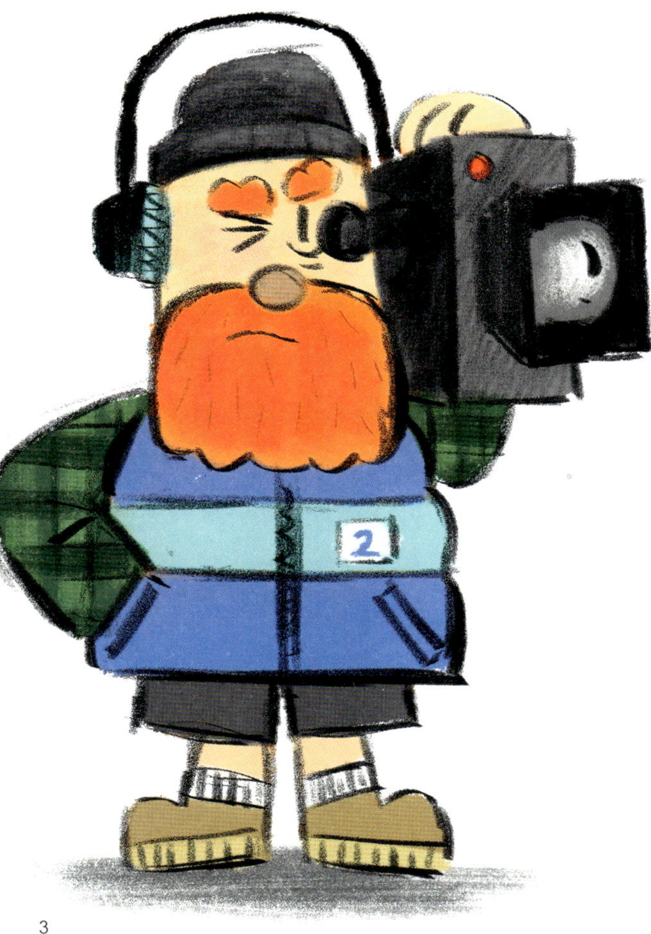

3

4

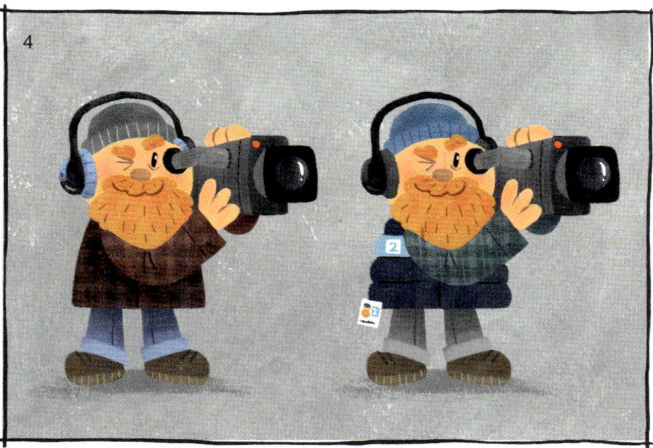

5

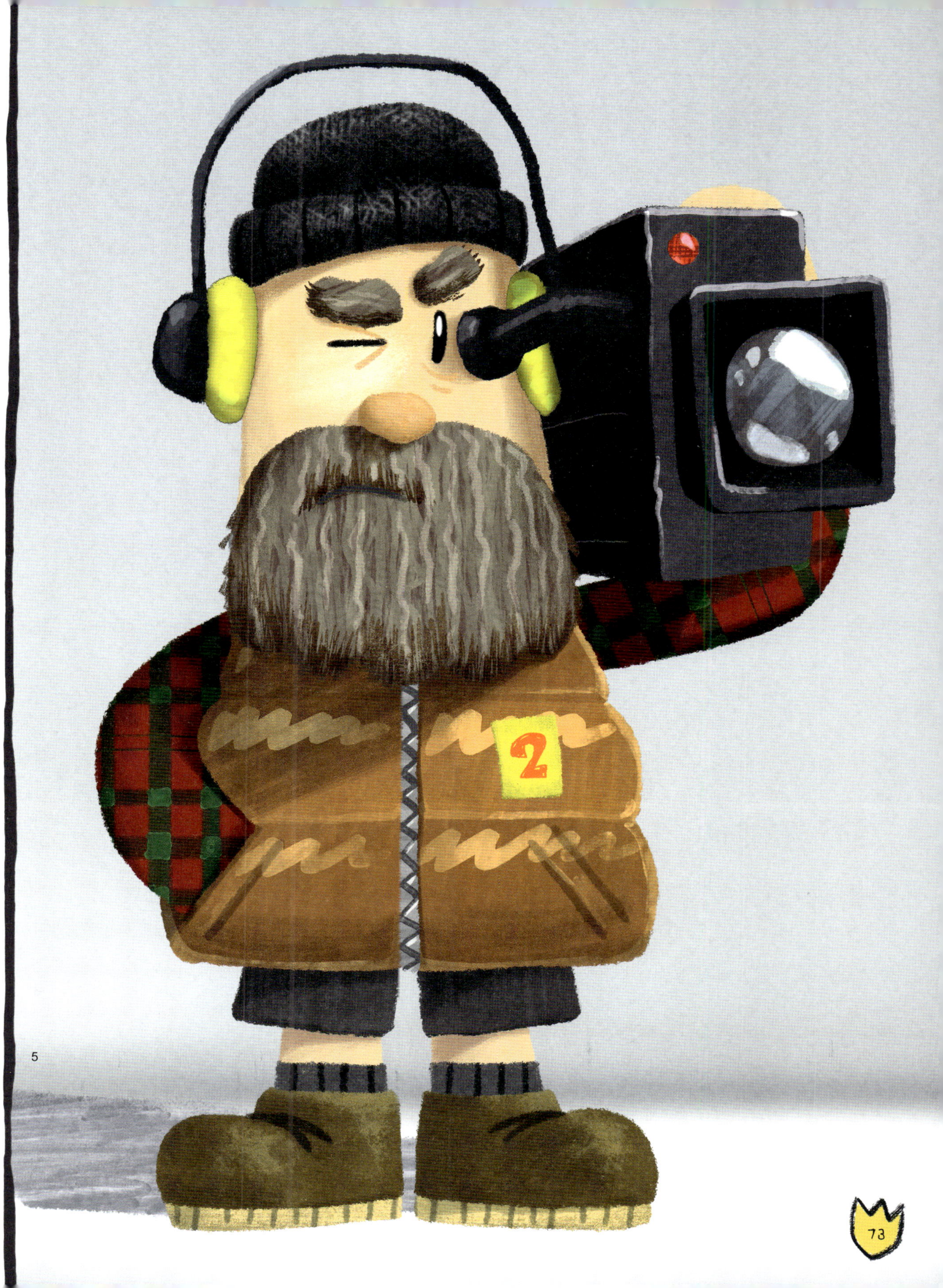

Police Station

For the police station, which is the Chief's home base, the creative team opted for a children's comic-book noir feeling. "You are supposed to feel like you're in the quintessential gumshoe movie police station," explains production designer Nate Wragg. "It has a mix of old-timey elements and some contemporary things. We looked at some heavily art-directed movies like *Dick Tracy*, which was also inspired by vintage comics. I really liked that they celebrated iconic elements of cities, and we wanted to do the same thing with our police station."

Art director Christopher Zibach adds, "The police station is a set that we return to often because Chief is constantly trying to run things while also trying to control Dog Man's actions. We needed the Chief's office to have character and a unique quality in and of itself. As we explored that with our team, we thought it would be fun to have the cops buying all their material from a catalog. So, their badges, phones, couch cushions, lamps, and computers all follow the same blue and gold palette. So, if you look closely, the potted plant that Dog Man hides behind has a police badge on it. There's even a cop siren and a megaphone on the roof of the building."

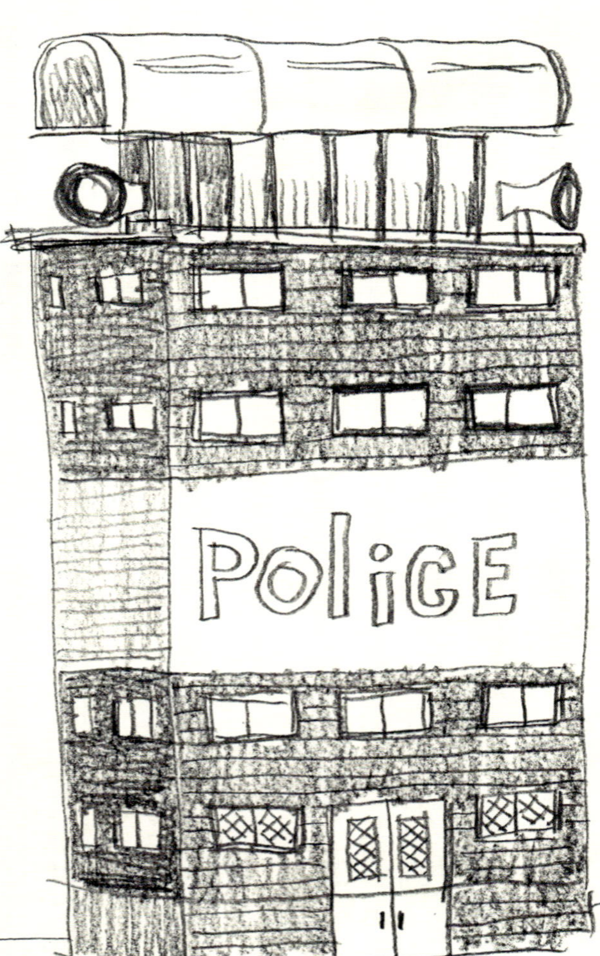

1

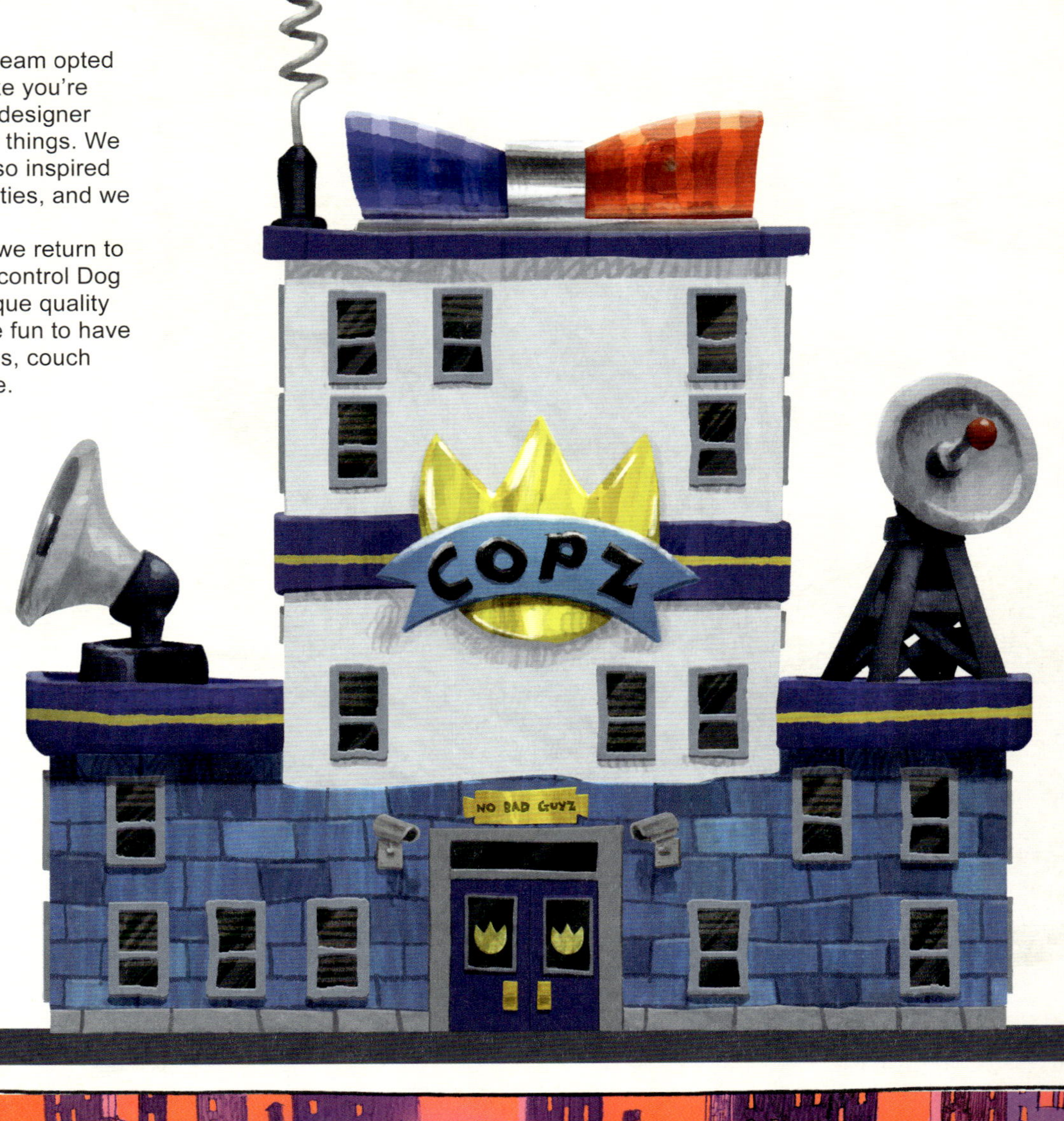

2

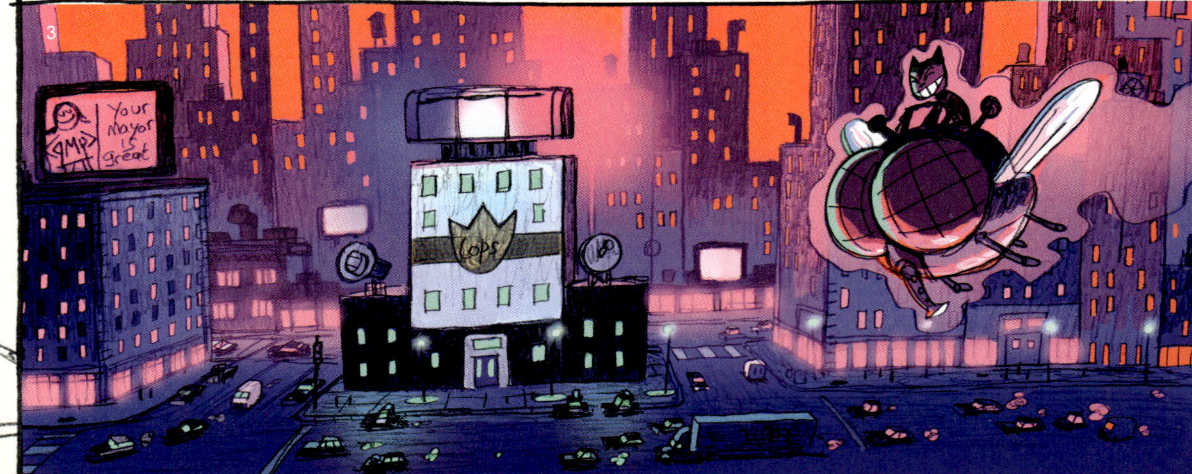

3

1 & 3: Sébastien Piquet;
2: Vahe Yefremian

4: ***Modeling:*** Fran Lara, Bianca Florina Bancila, Divyasa Mishra; ***Surfacing:*** Hannah Wong, Samir Necib, Suzanne Lokker

"Every building is designed to have its own personality and character. The same is true for the vegetation. They are all designed to embrace the Pilkey style in a 3D fashion."

—LOUIS FLORES, Visual Effects Supervisor

4

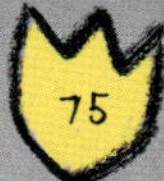

1, 3, 6 & 7: Christopher Zibach; 2: Katy Wu; 4, 5 & 8: Sébastien Piquet

1

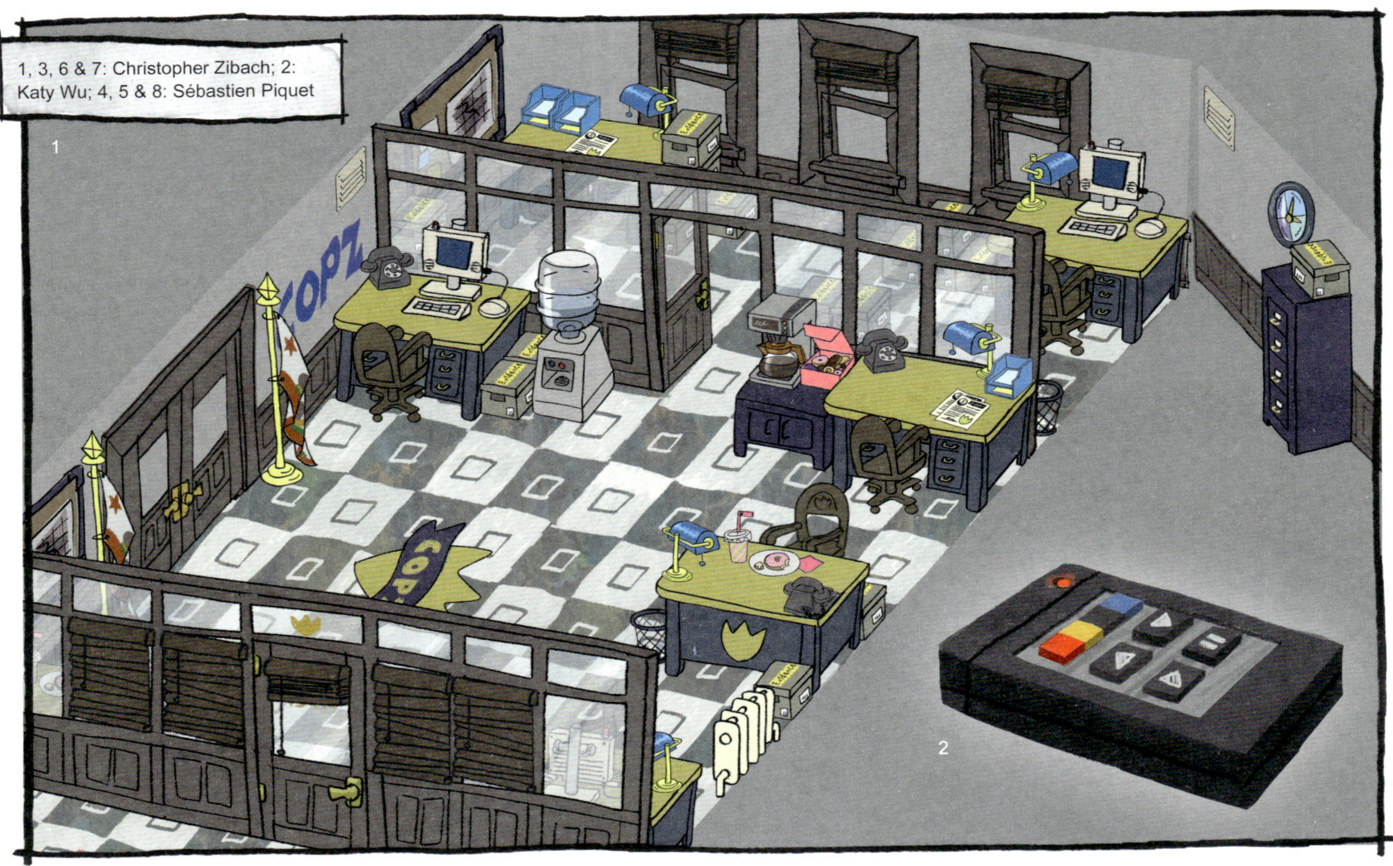

2

3

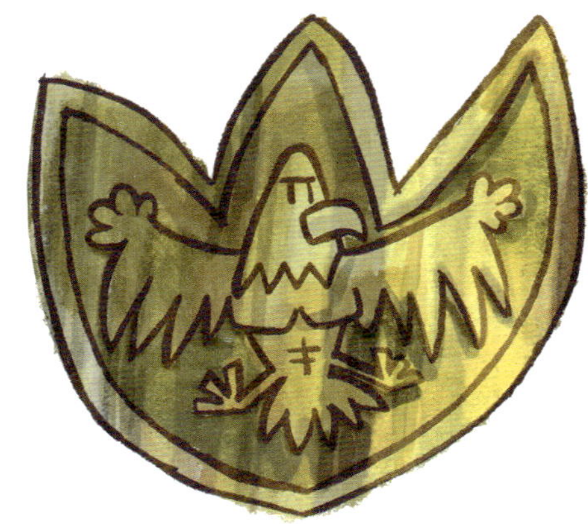

4

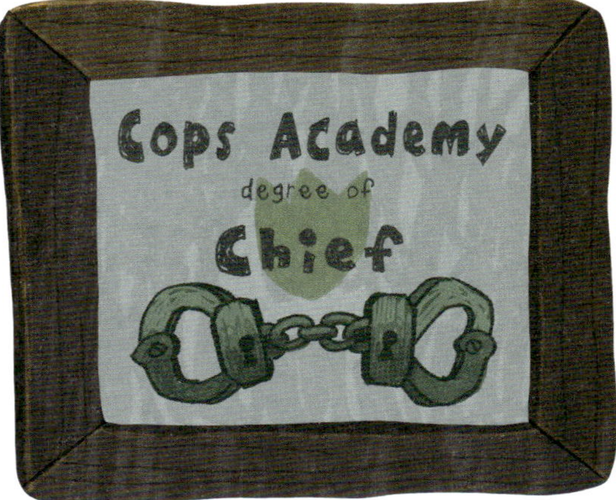

5

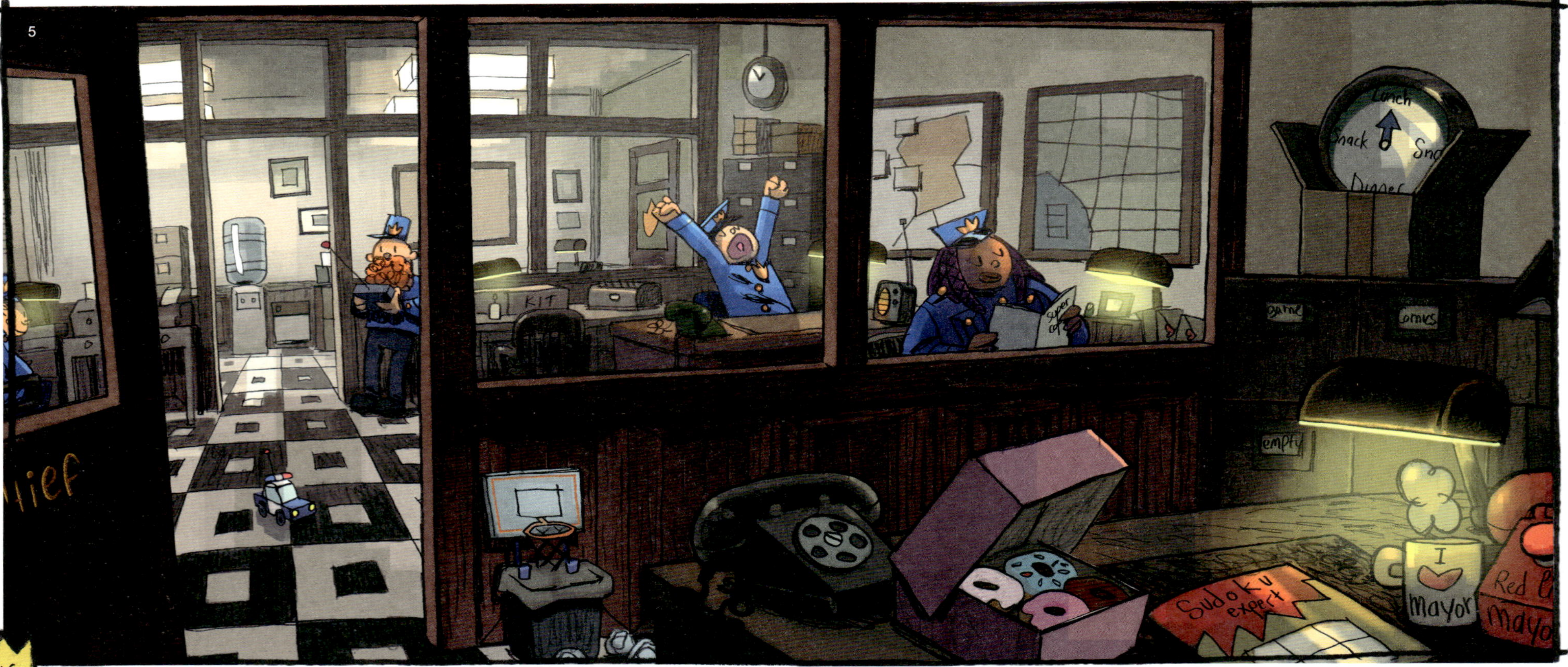

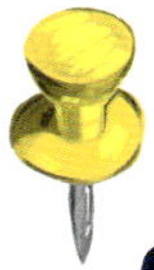

Push pin modeling and string from previous version of bulletin board can be reused

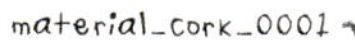

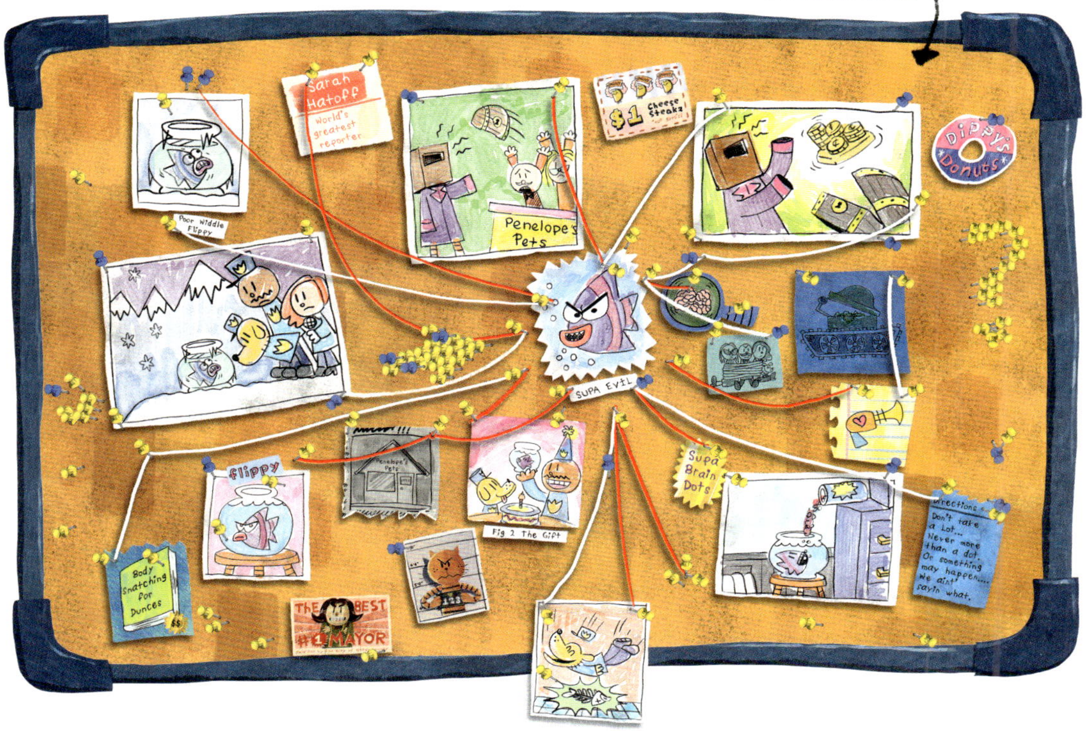

6

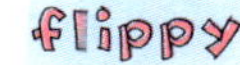

1-FlippyTitleCard

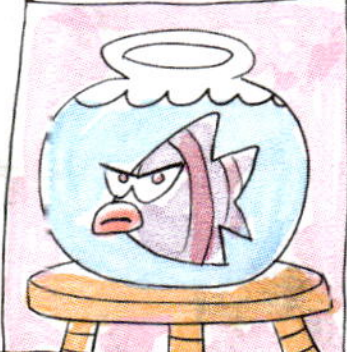

Fig 2 The Gift

2-Chiefs-BDay

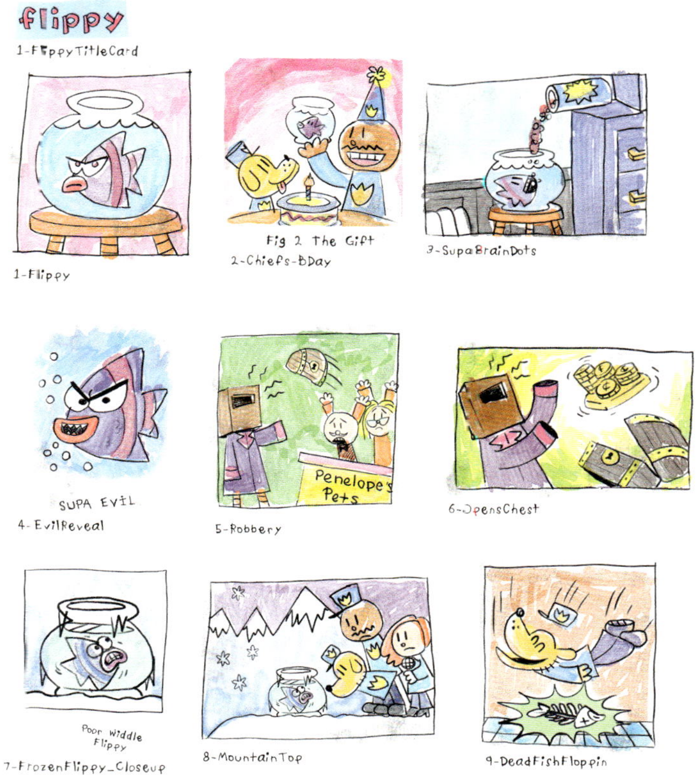

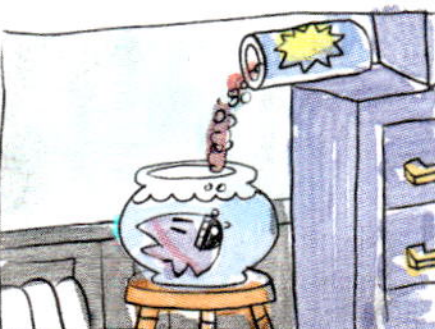

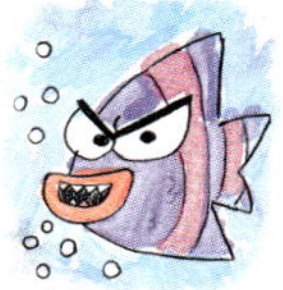

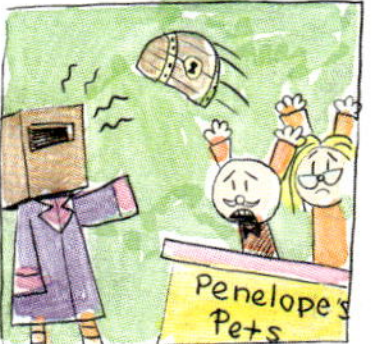

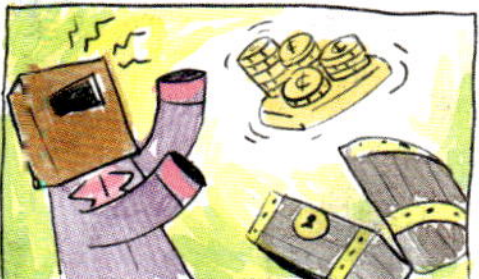

7

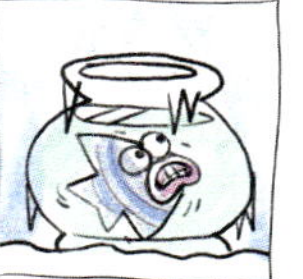

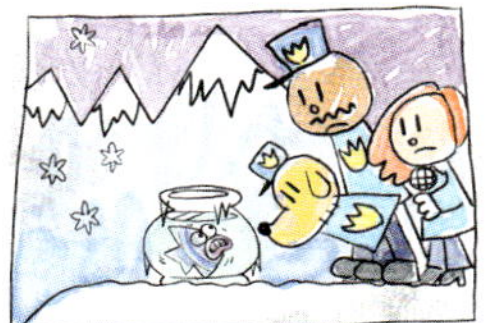

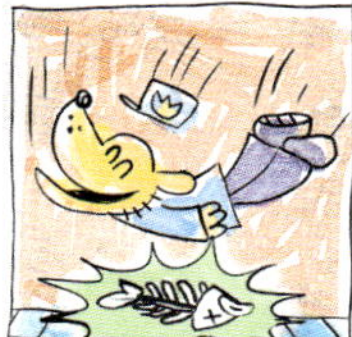

8

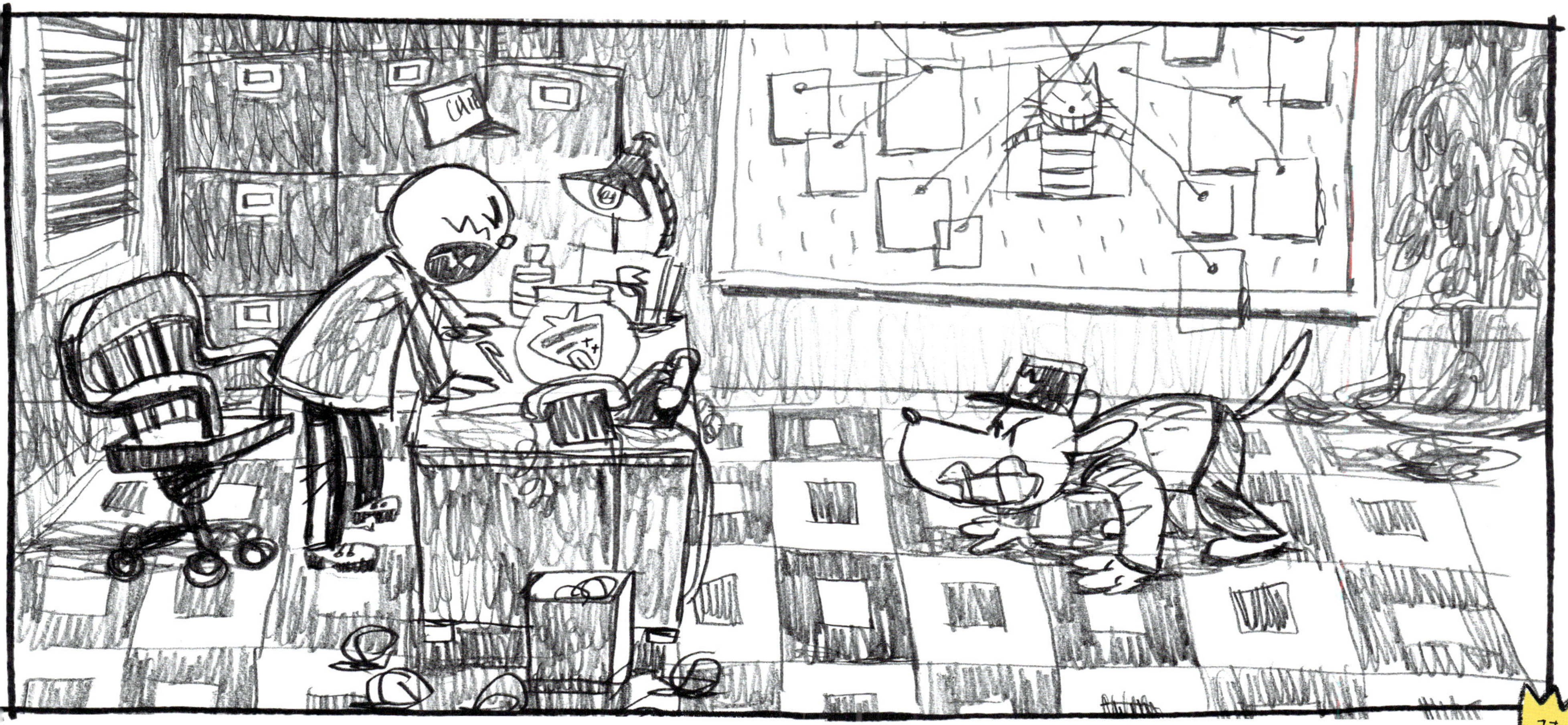

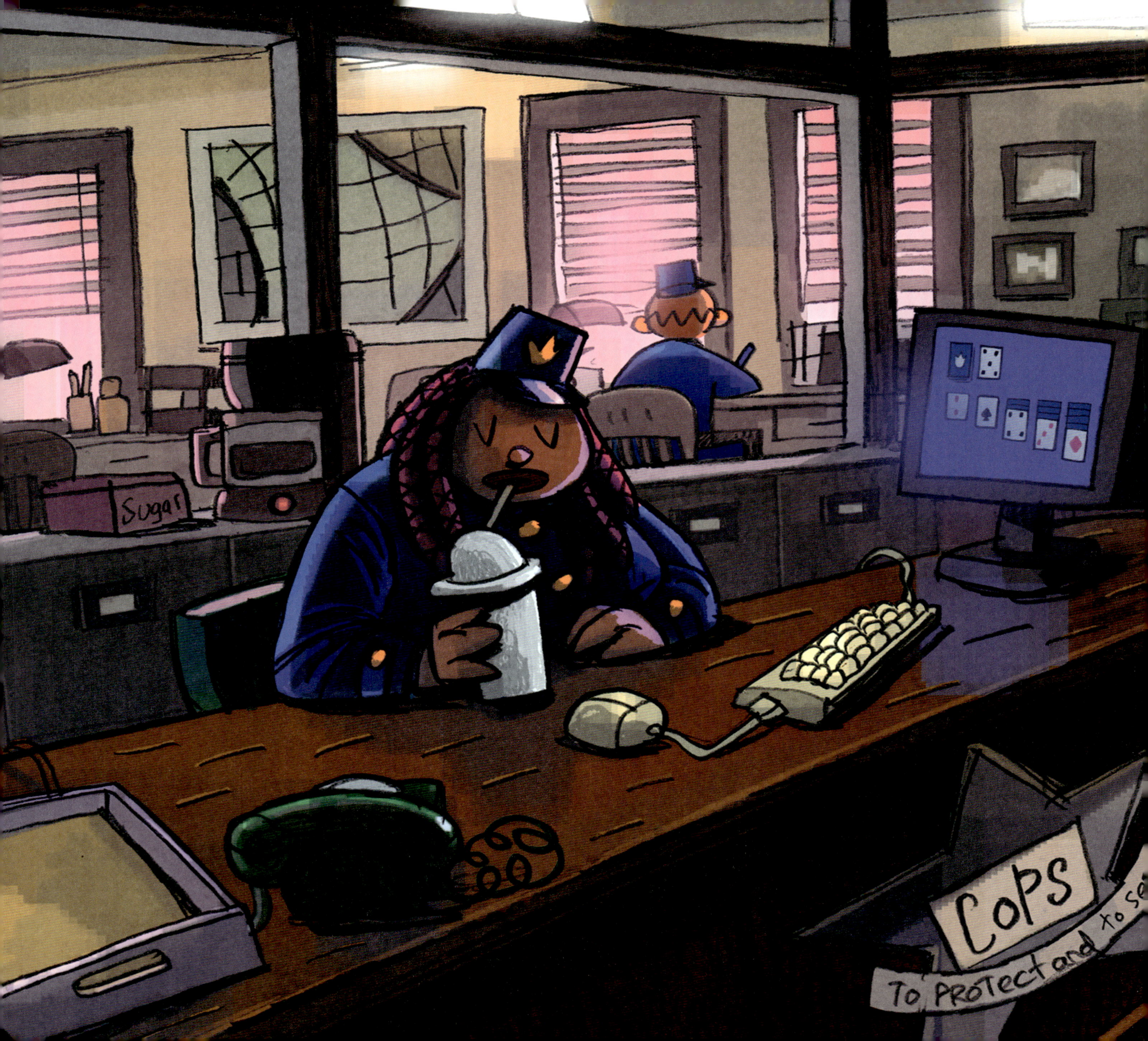
Sugar
CoPS
To PROTECT and to se

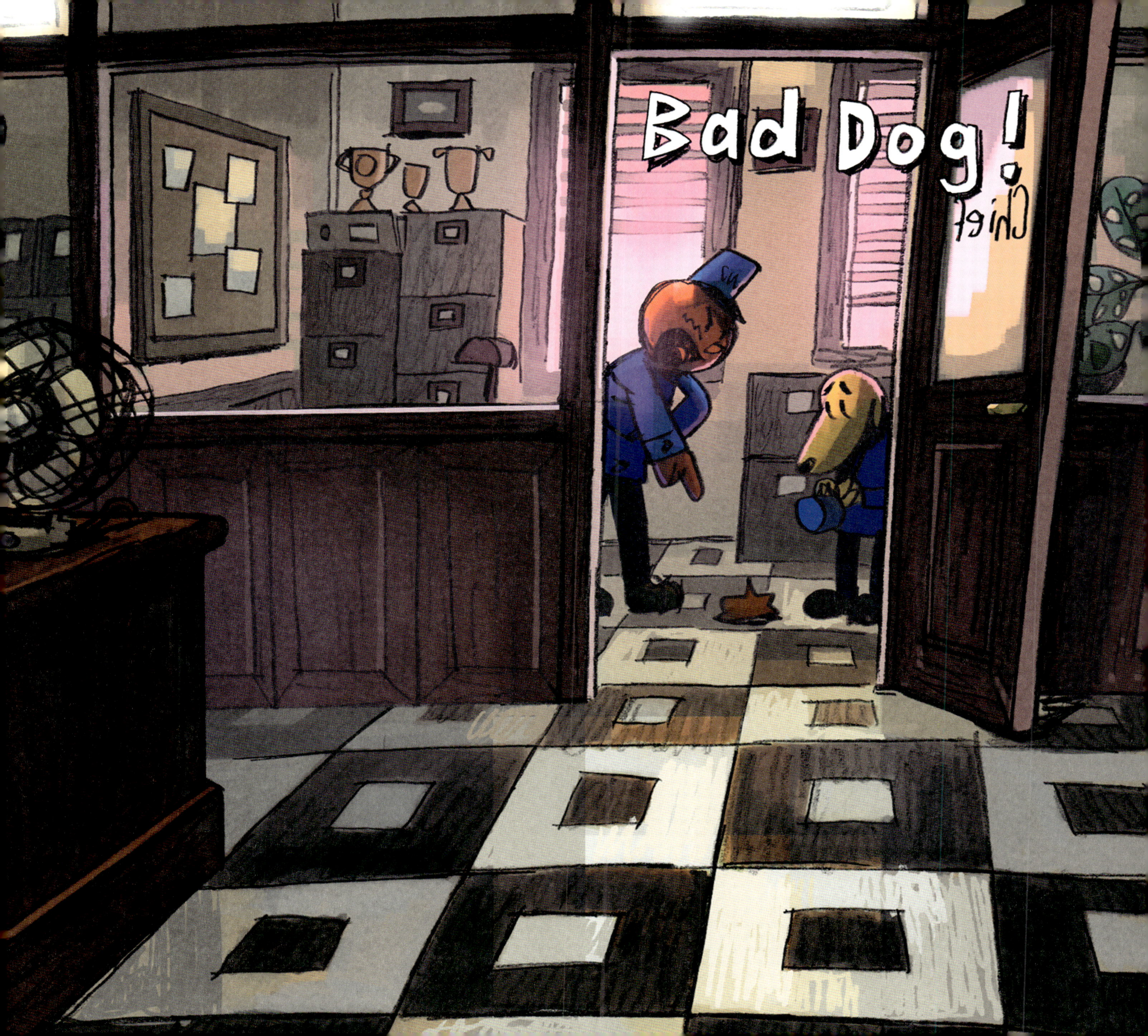

Bad Dog!
Chief

Shhhh... if you're going to catch that cat, you're going to need my special gear...

1

Material_Brickwall_003
Add some dirt smudges on it.

Lamp shape is a flat silhouette.

material_wallTiles_auditorium

Add some dirt smudges on it and missing tiles.

sketchy lines on stairs, ceiling and wall silhouettes.

Pipes are a silhouette

Entrance to Vault Room is a cheated 3D entryway.

2

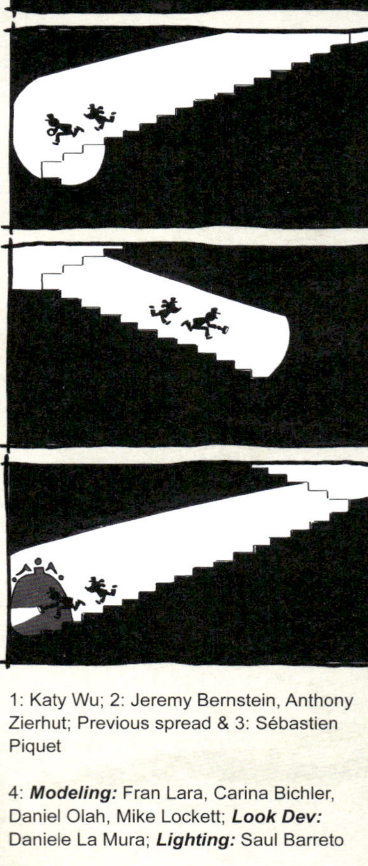

1: Katy Wu; 2: Jeremy Bernstein, Anthony Zierhut; Previous spread & 3: Sébastien Piquet

4: ***Modeling:*** Fran Lara, Carina Bichler, Daniel Olah, Mike Lockett; ***Look Dev:*** Daniele La Mura; ***Lighting:*** Saul Barreto

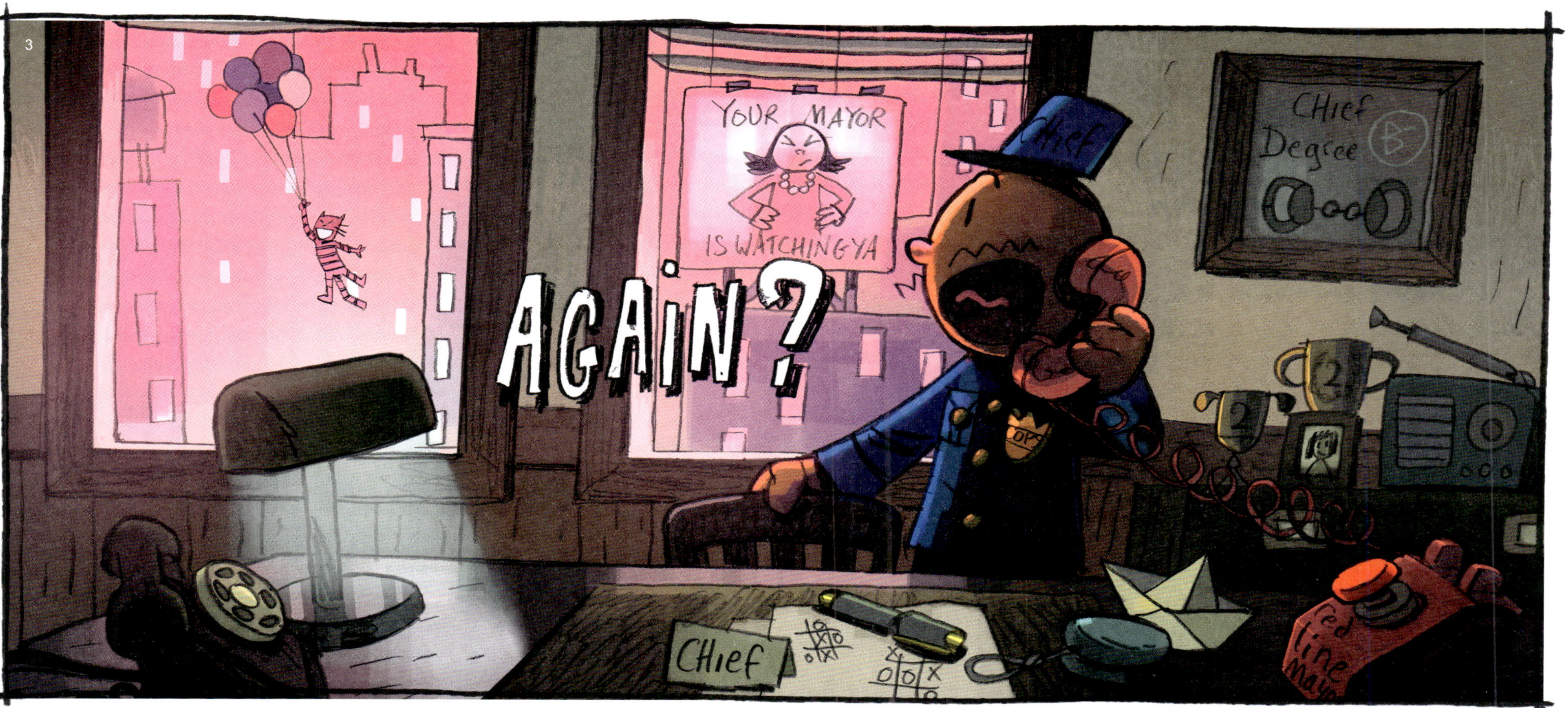

3

YOUR MAYOR
IS WATCHING YA

Chief

Chief
Degree

AGAIN?

Chief

4

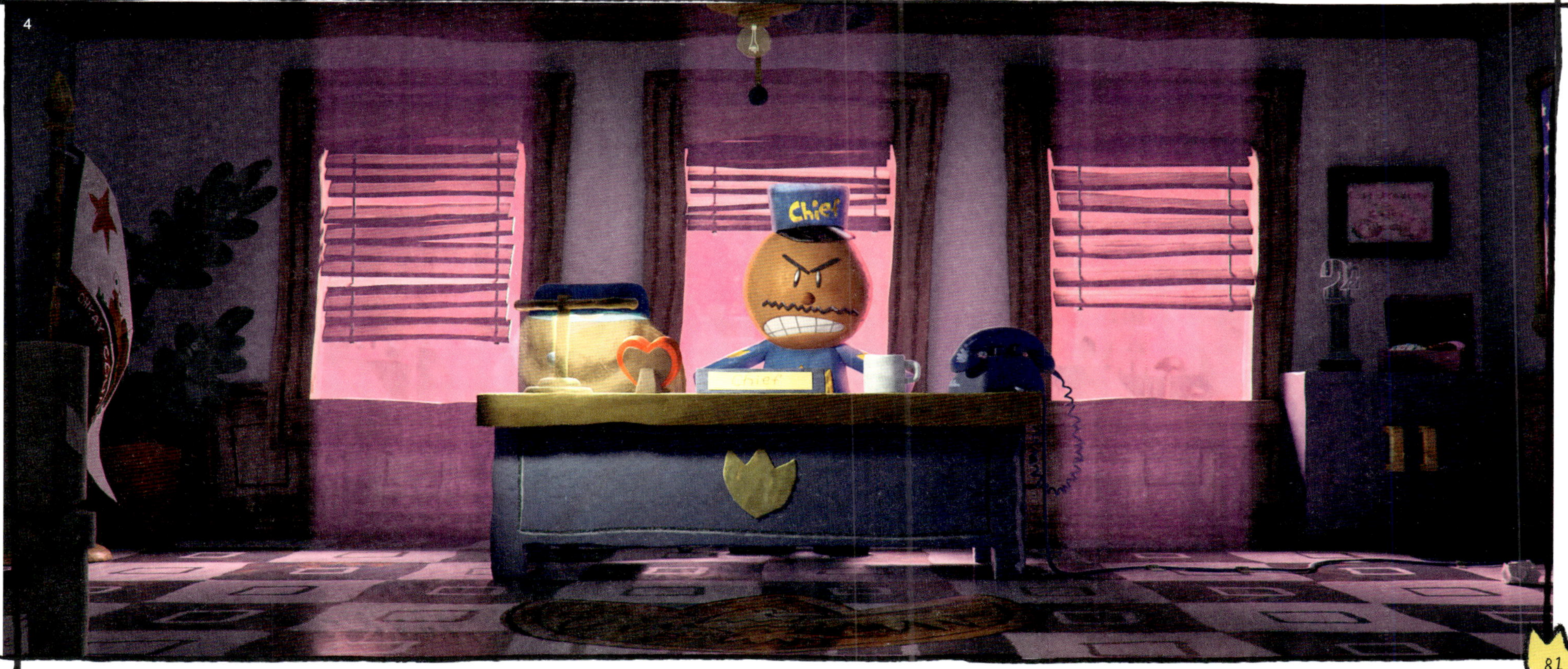

Chief

1

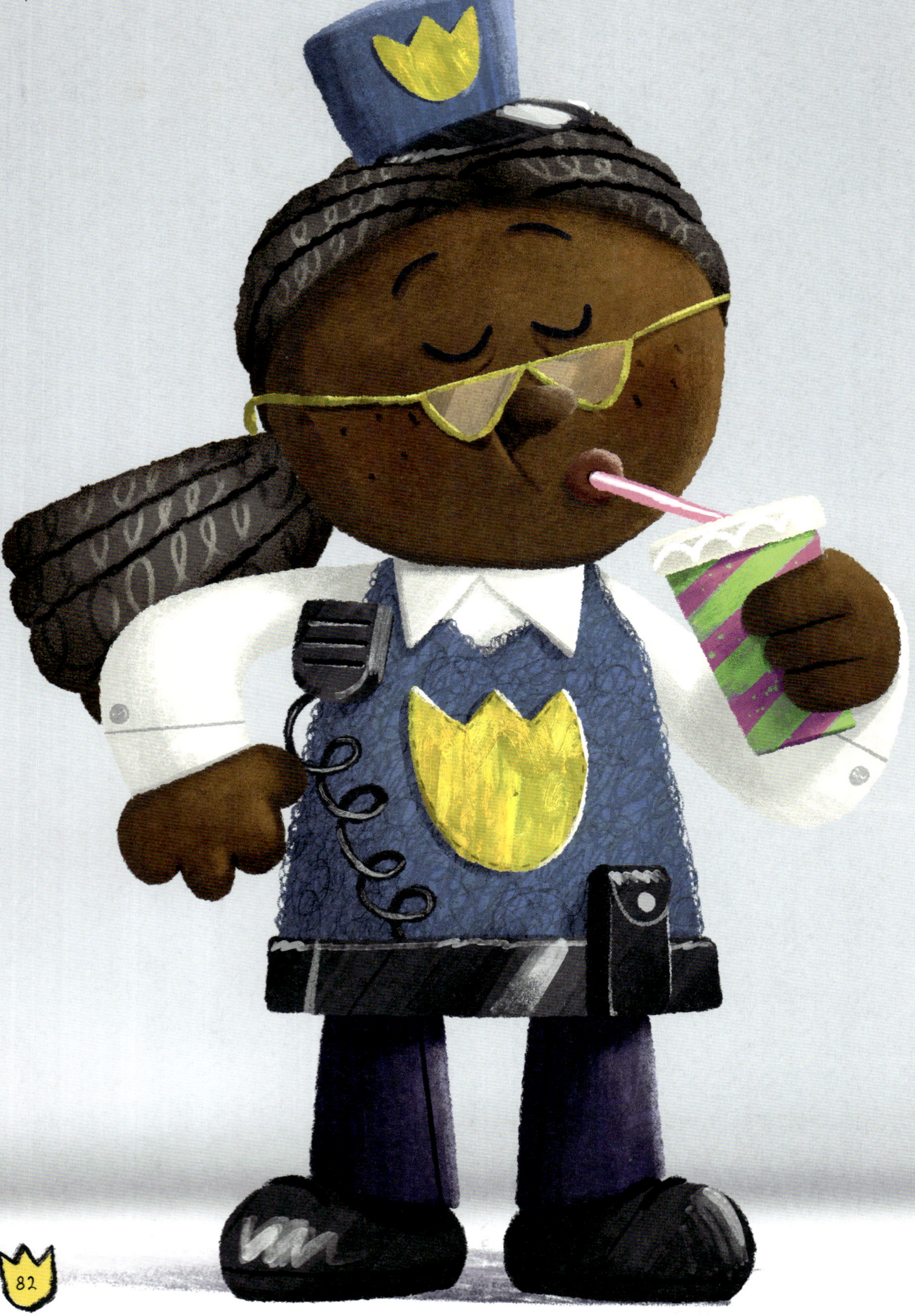

Millie

Millie (voiced by Luenell) is a new take on a character first introduced in the book *Dog Man: Unleashed*. She was imagined as an older female on the city's police force by the film's artists. "We all kind of fell in love with her," says production designer Nate Wragg. "She's super funny, very sarcastic, and quite quirky. She's probably older than some of the furniture in the building, and she knows her way around the place and is everybody's friend. We love her sense of humor."

2

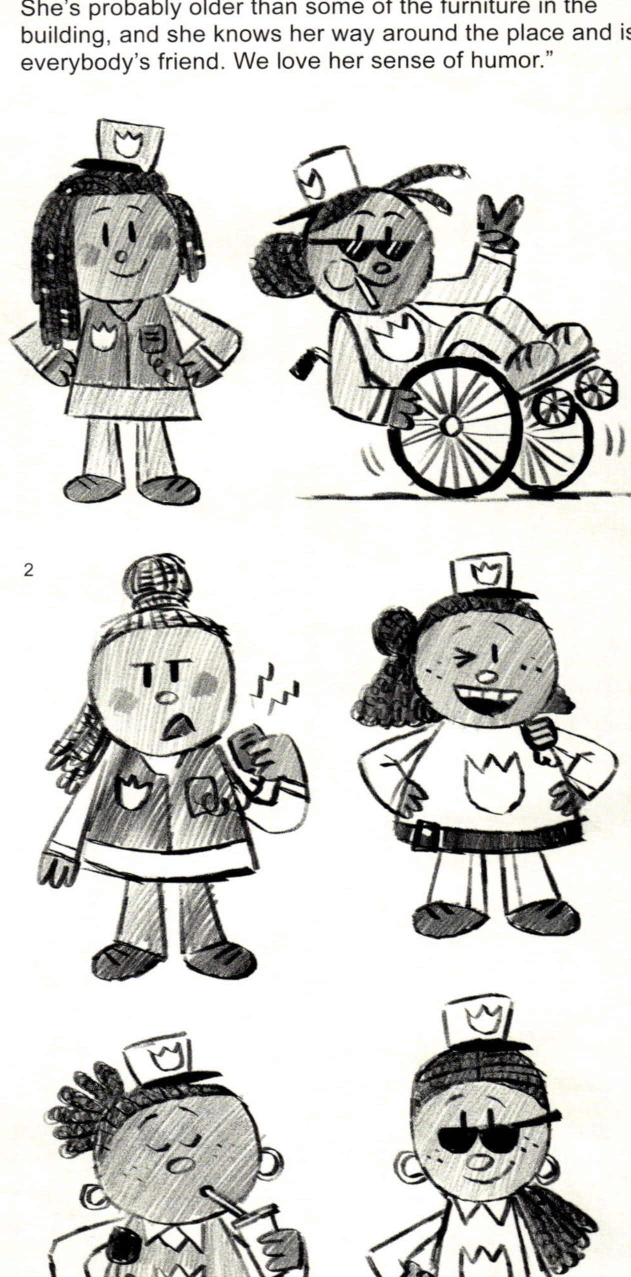

3

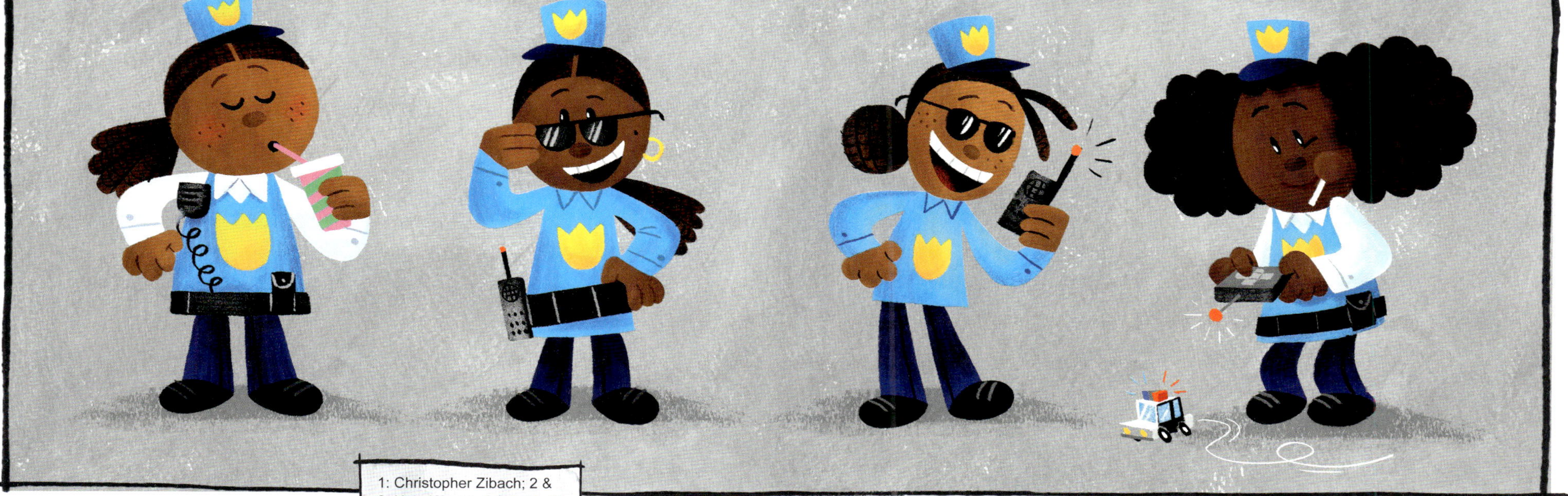

1: Christopher Zibach; 2 &
3: Nate Wragg; 4 & 5: Lia Tin

4

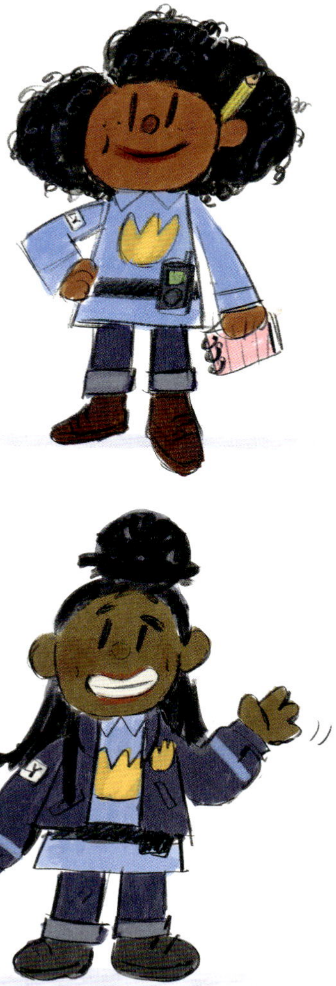

5

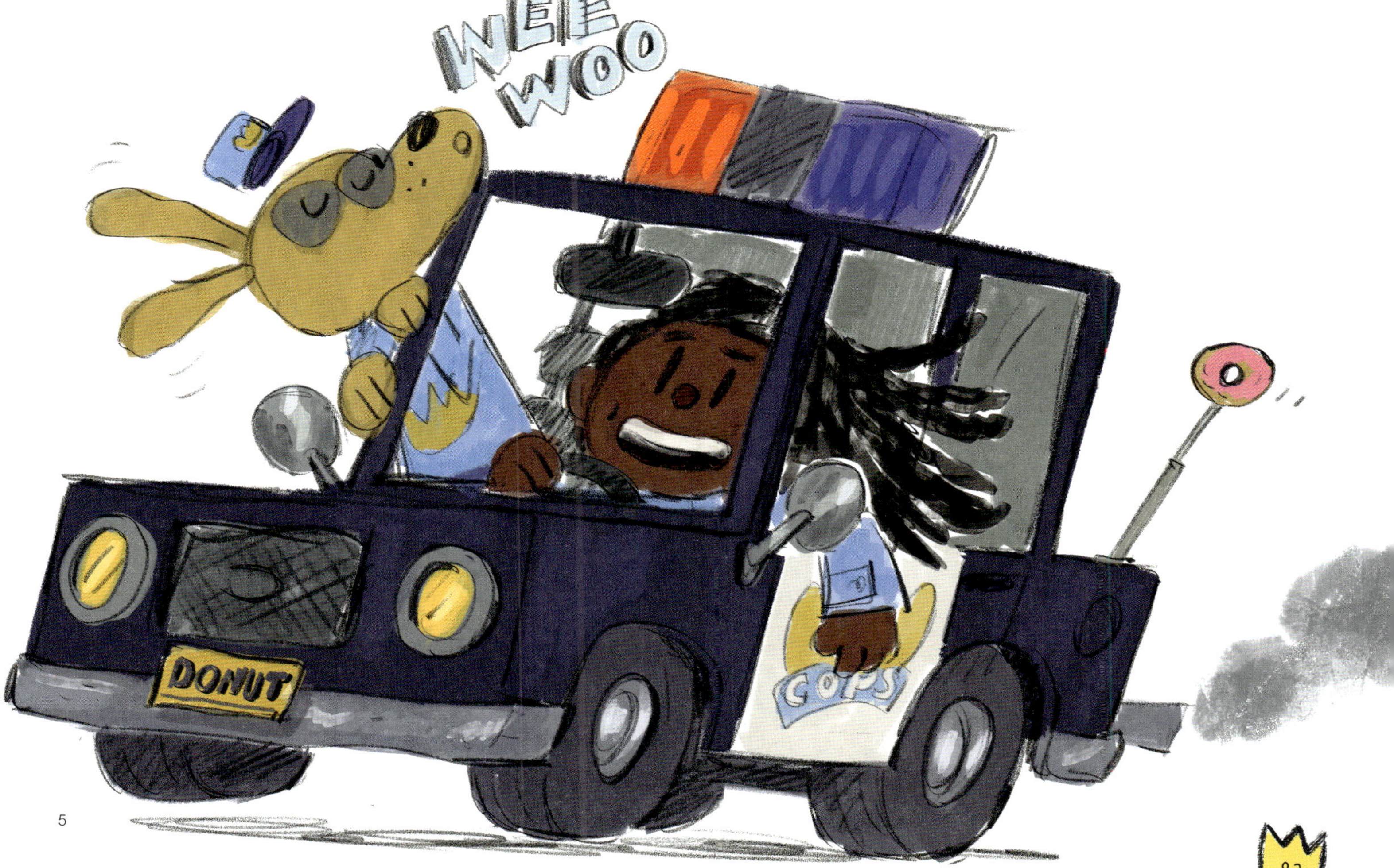

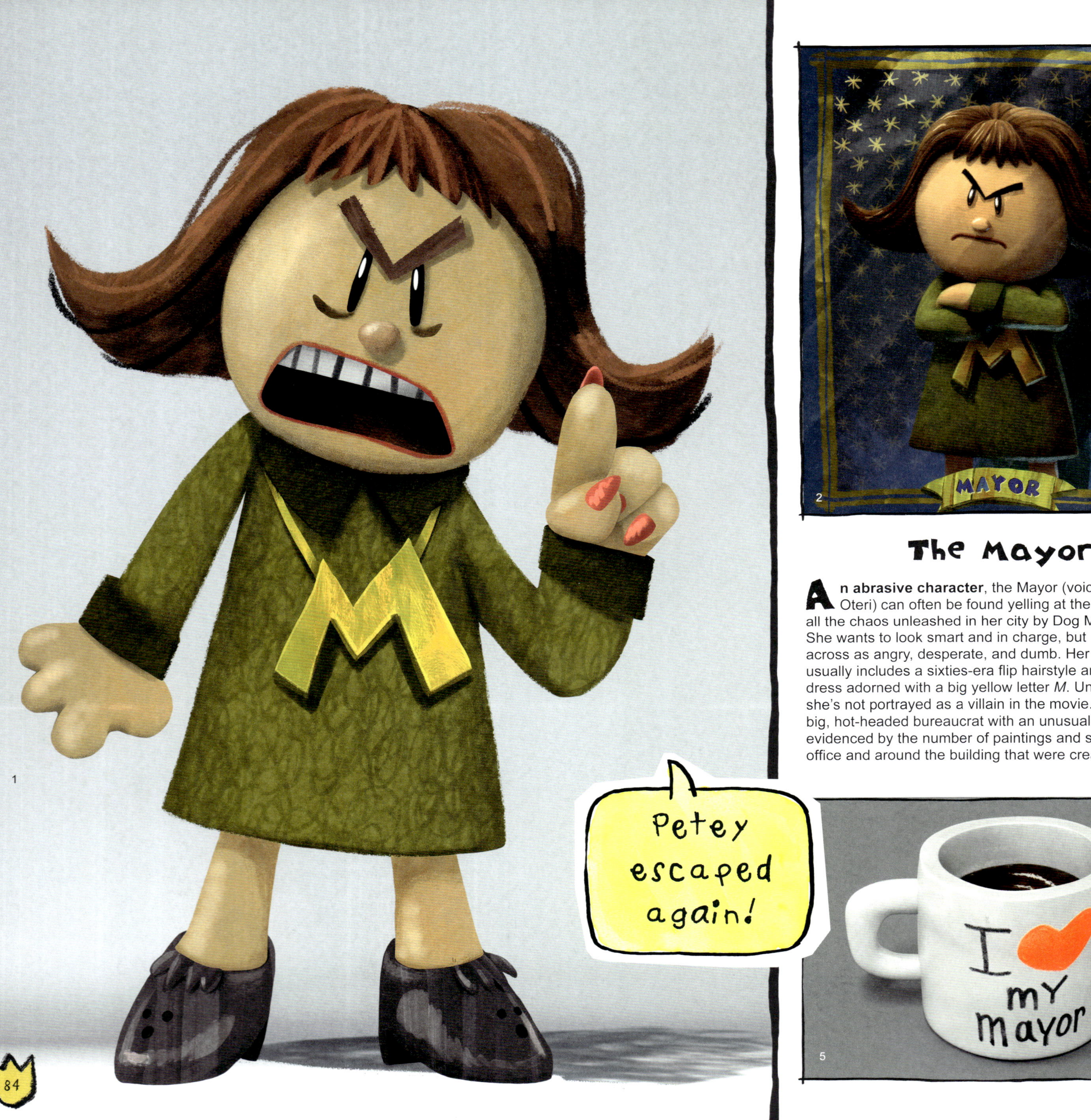

1

2

The Mayor

An abrasive character, the Mayor (voiced by Cheri Oteri) can often be found yelling at the Chief, due to all the chaos unleashed in her city by Dog Man and Petey. She wants to look smart and in charge, but she often comes across as angry, desperate, and dumb. Her signature look usually includes a sixties-era flip hairstyle and a dark green dress adorned with a big yellow letter *M*. Unlike the books, she's not portrayed as a villain in the movie. She is simply a big, hot-headed bureaucrat with an unusually large ego—as evidenced by the number of paintings and statues in her office and around the building that were created in her hono

5

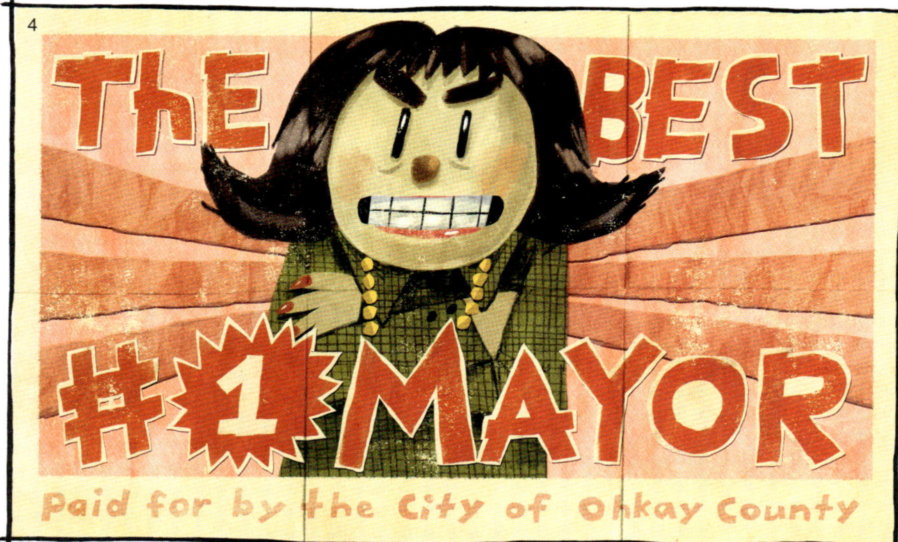

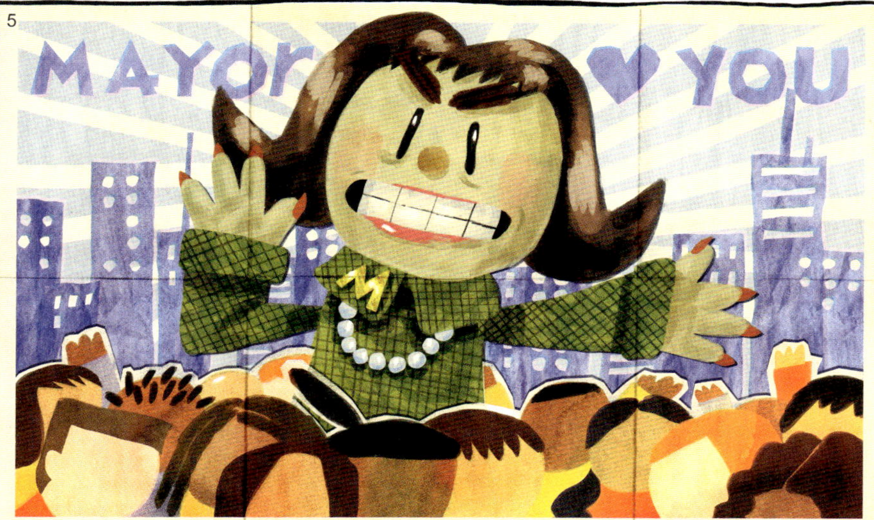

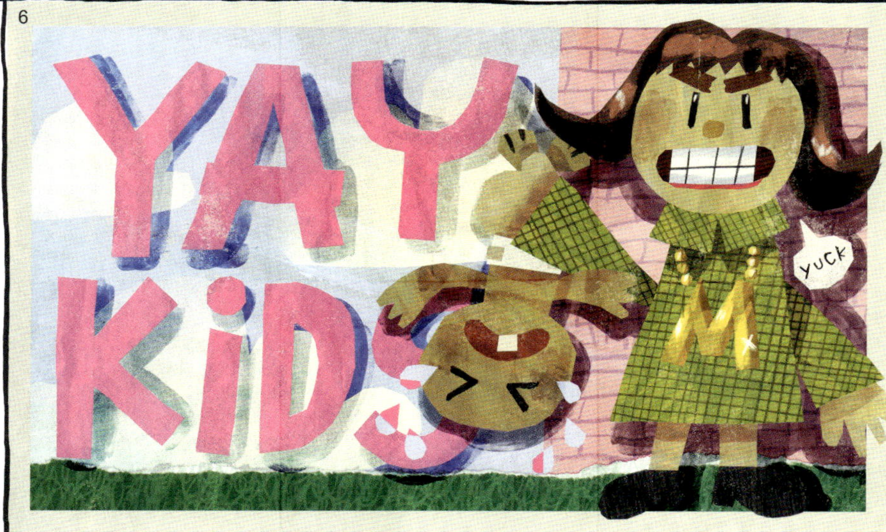

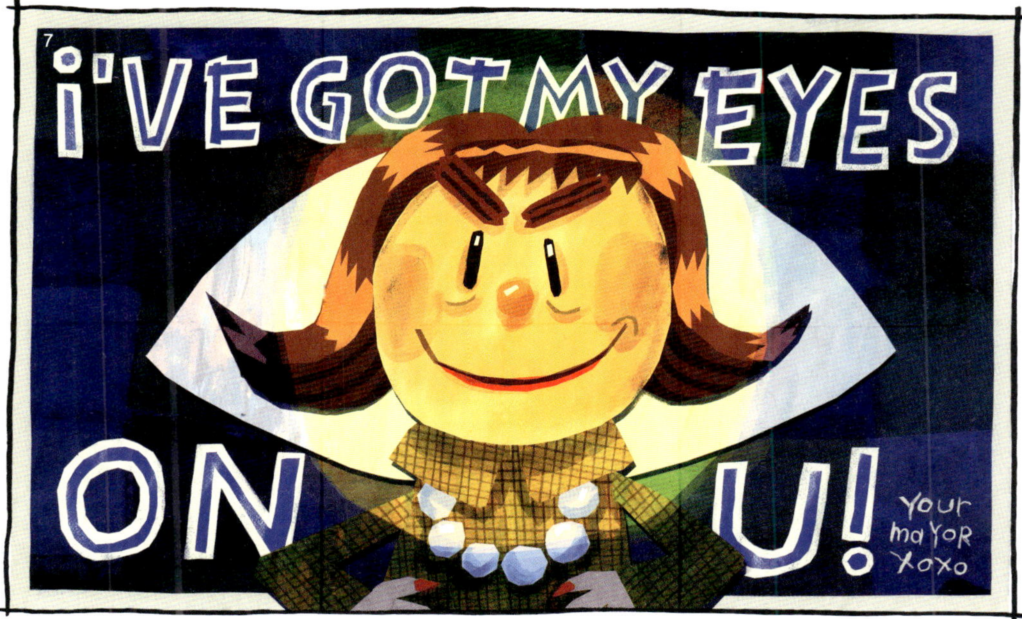

1 & 2: Christopher Zibach

3: ***Vis Dev:*** Christopher Zibach; ***Modeling:*** Fran Lara; ***Surfacing:*** Arnold Pryada, Peter Hargen

4–7: Lia Tin;

8: ***Layout:*** Sunil Dutta; ***Animation:*** Aziz Koçanaoğulları; ***Digital Matte Painter:*** Anh Cao, Jon Kiefert; ***Lighting:*** Elisa Sanguin

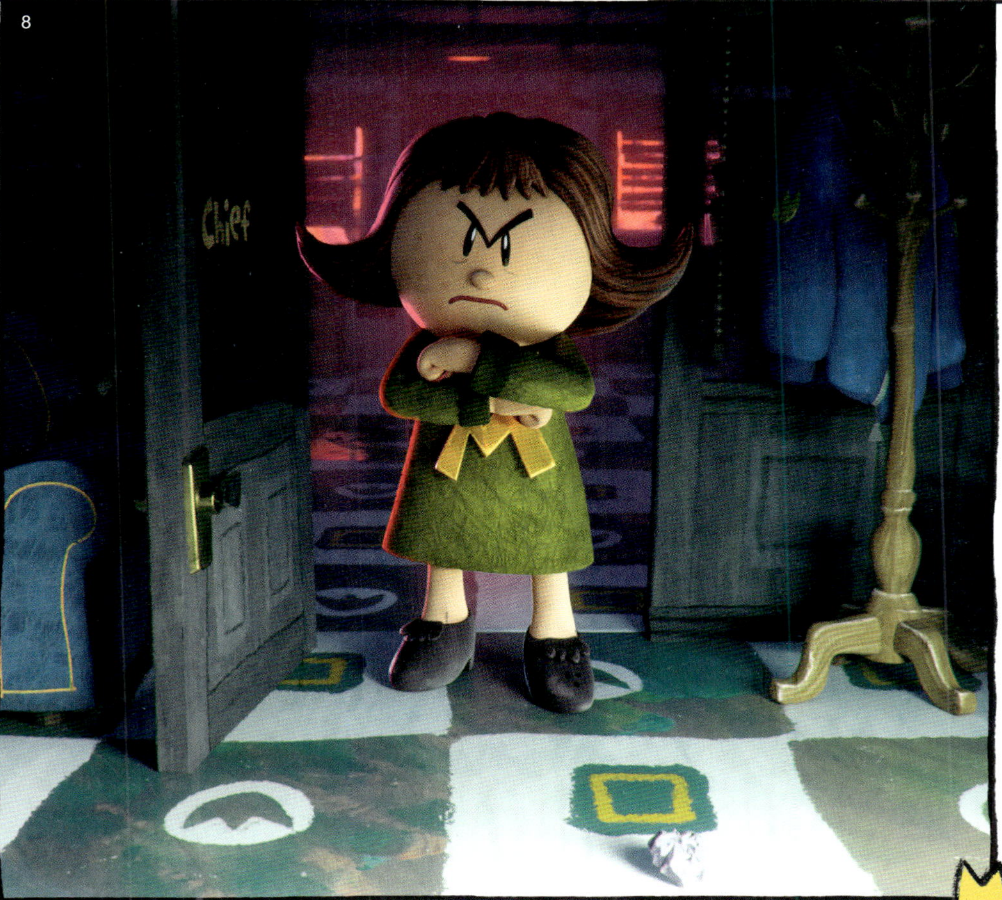

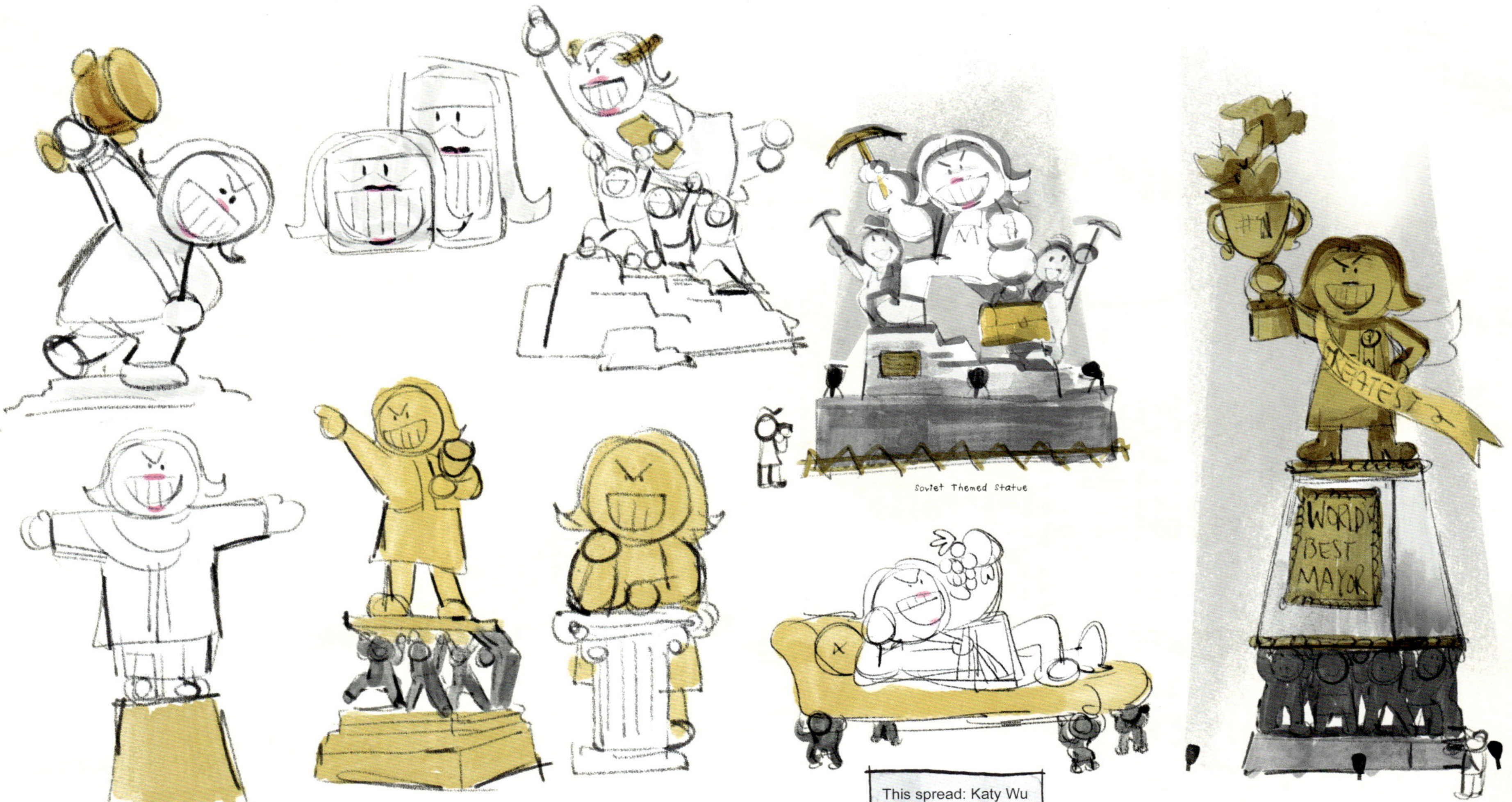

Soviet Themed Statue

This spread: Katy Wu

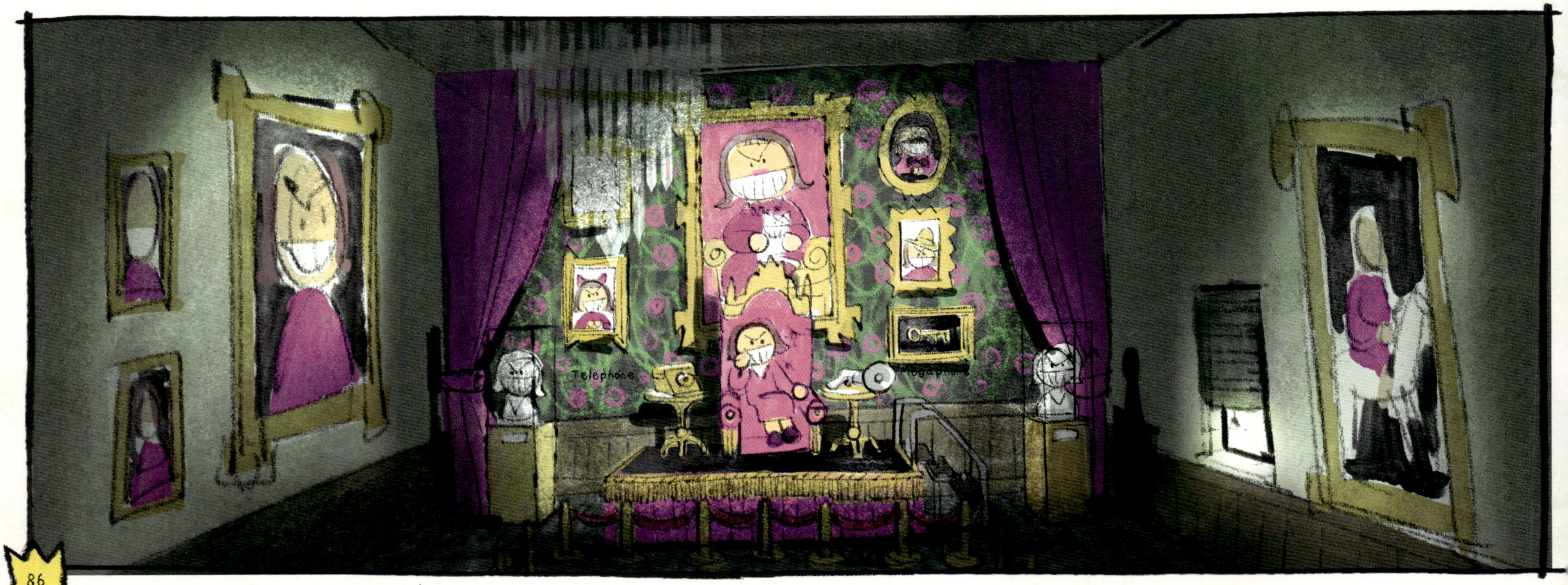

Telephone

Megaphone

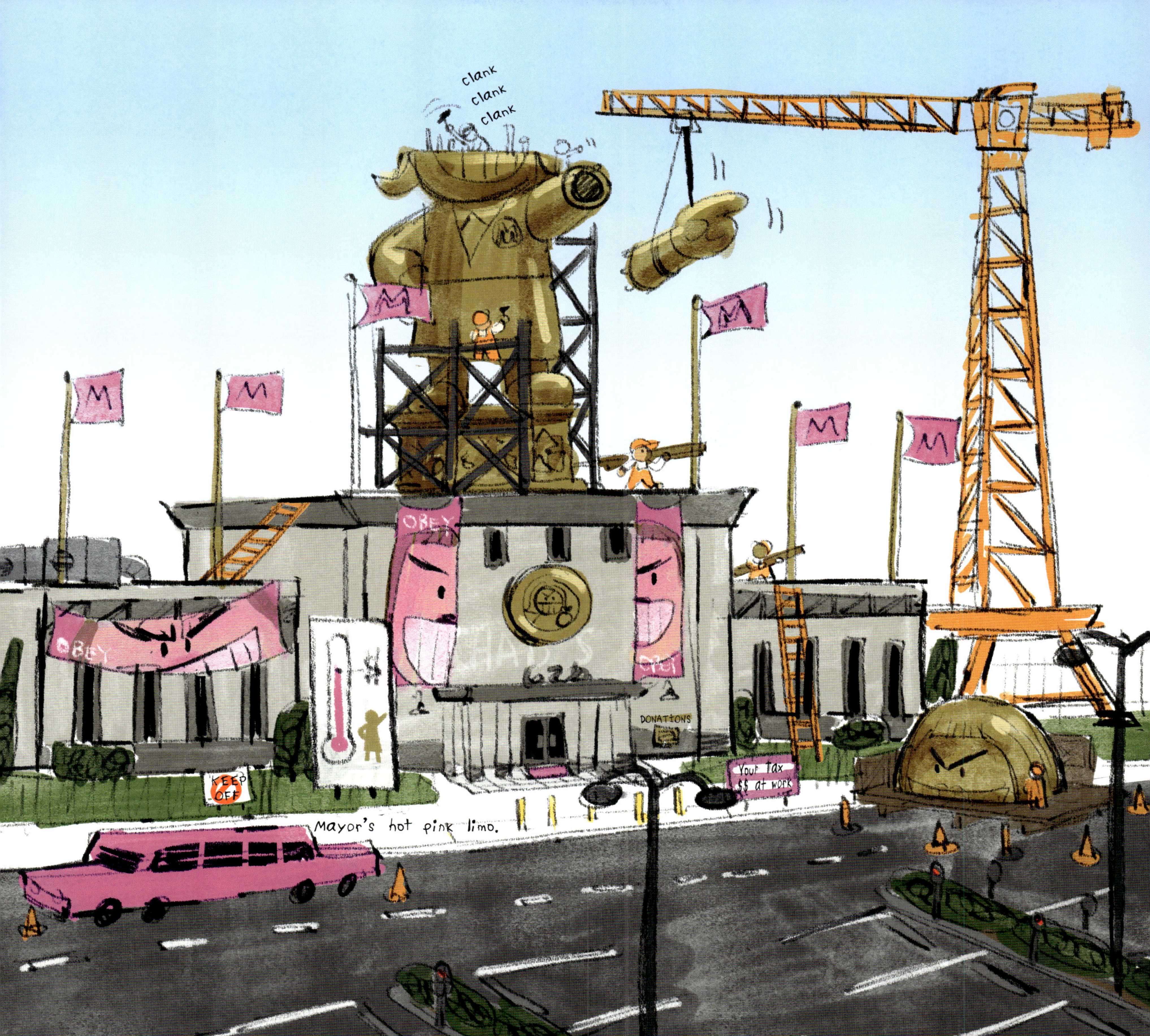

clank
clank
clank
OBEY
OBEY
OBEY
DONATIONS
KEEP OFF
Your tax $$ at work
Mayor's hot pink limo.

Petey's Secret Lab

When you're a classic cartoon villain, you need a secret lab to create your diabolically clever inventions, and Petey is no exception. This wacky testing ground is where he puts together the robot 80-HD, as well as cool vehicles and gadgets like a sewer croc car, a cage vehicle, The Make No Bones 2000, The Butt Sniffer 2000, and The Squirrel Shooter 2000.

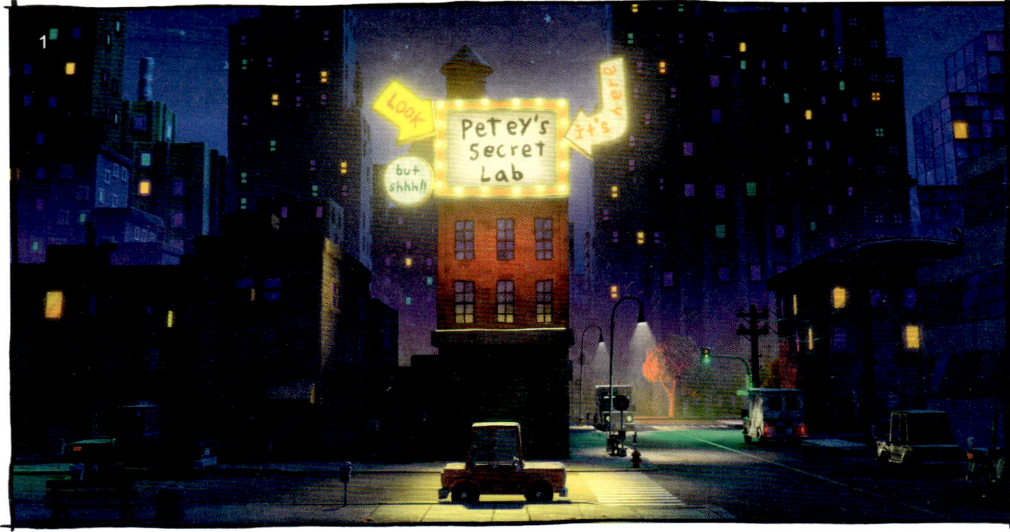

1: ***Animation:*** Claire Louise Hodges; ***Digital matte painter:*** Aymeric Arnaud; ***Lighting:*** Jamie Tremelling

2–4: Sébastien Piquet

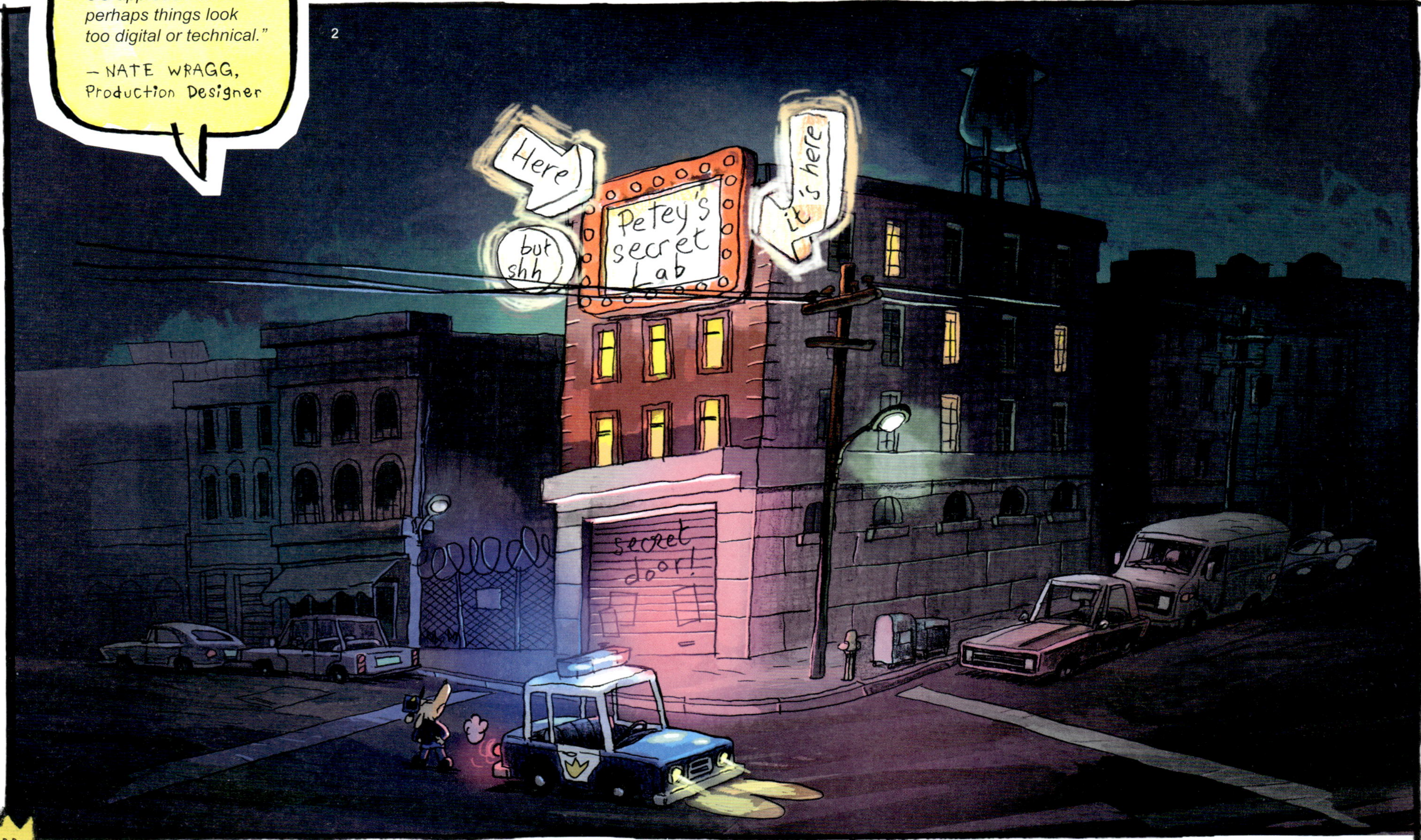

"Throughout the movie, we made a big effort to avoid drifting into an unintentional CG approach where perhaps things look too digital or technical."

—NATE WRAGG, Production Designer

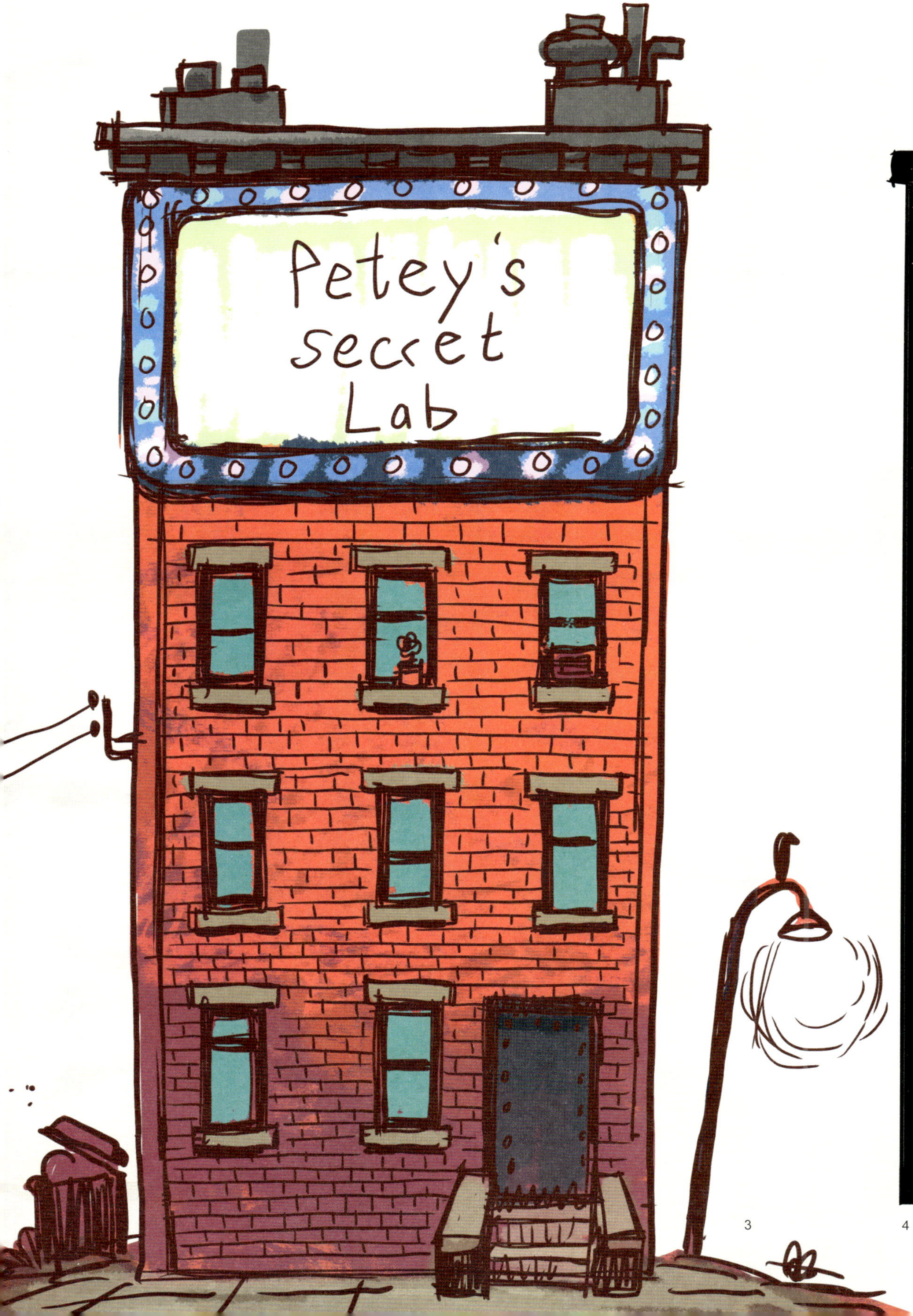

Petey's secret Lab

Bed

WELCOME

3

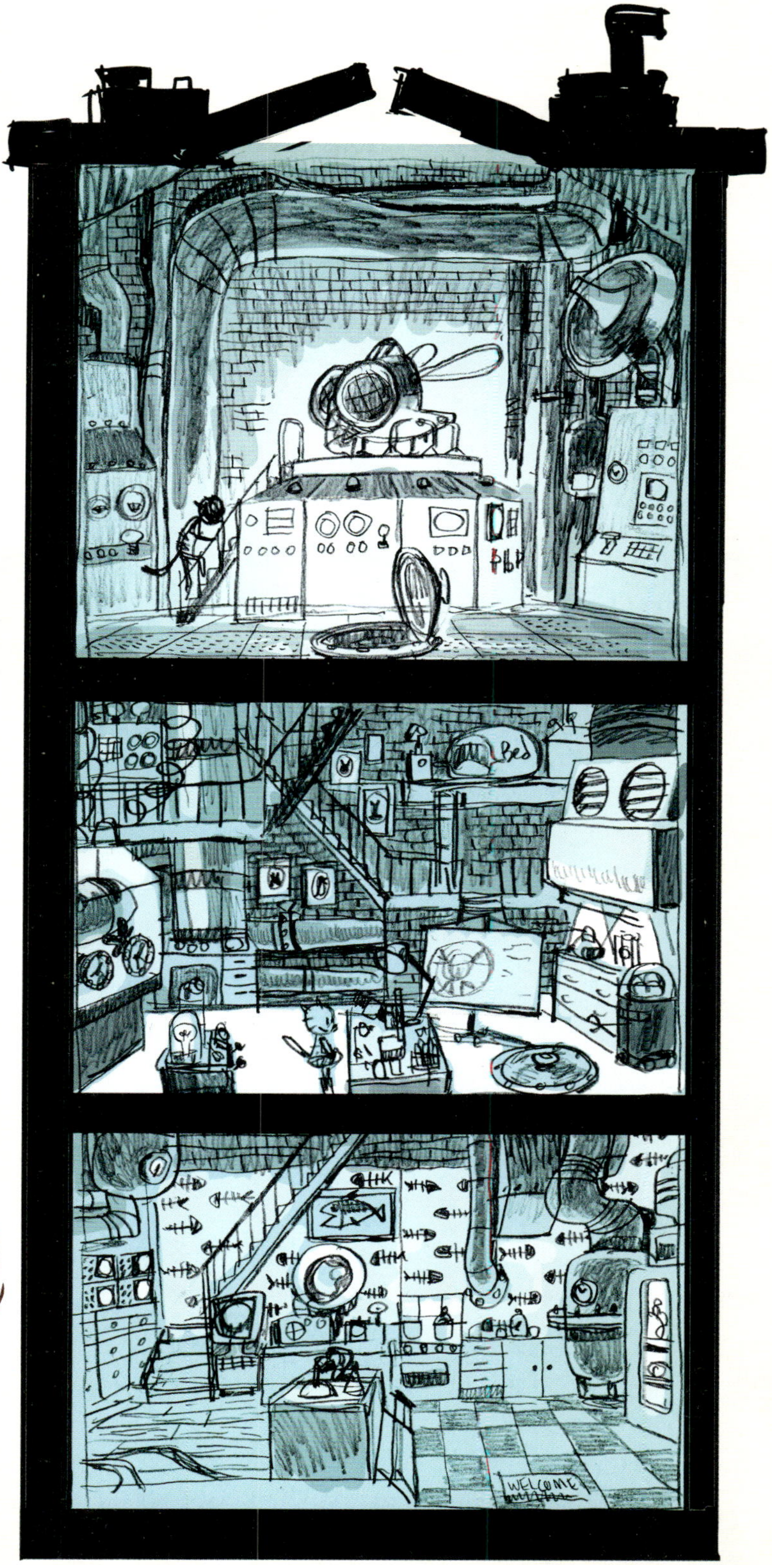

4

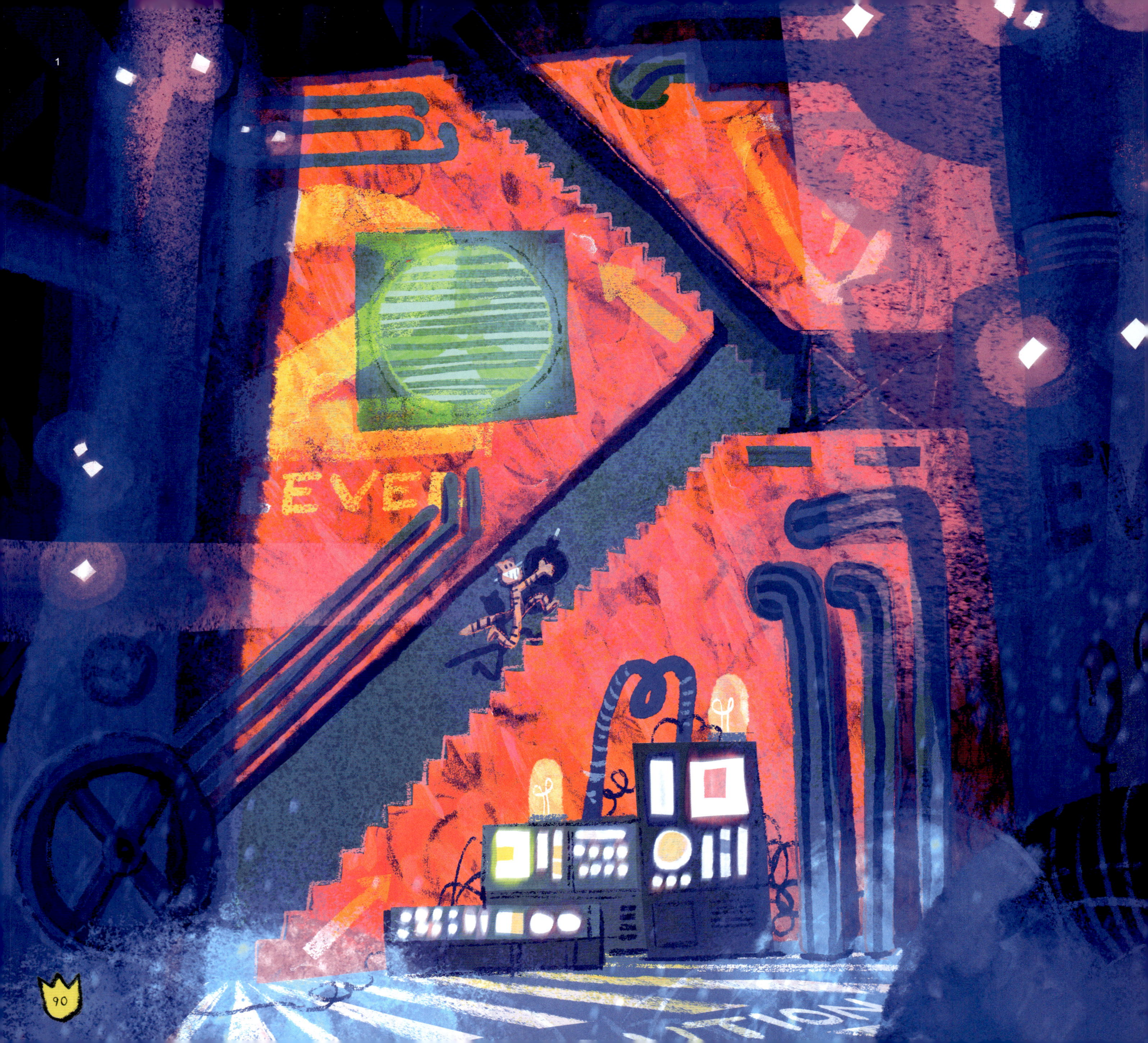

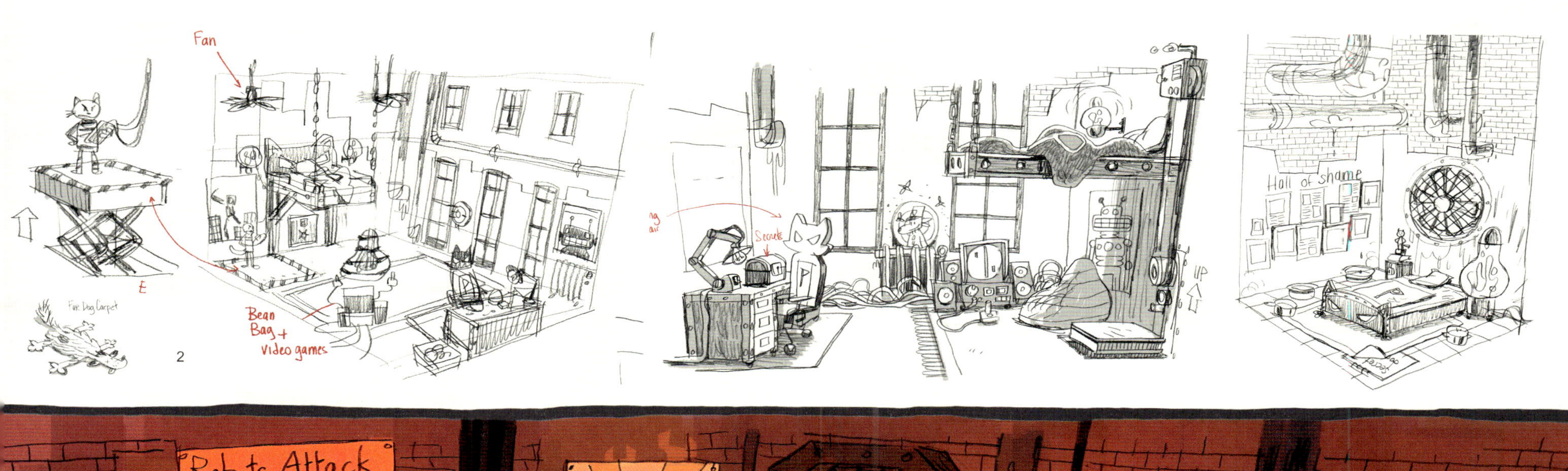

2

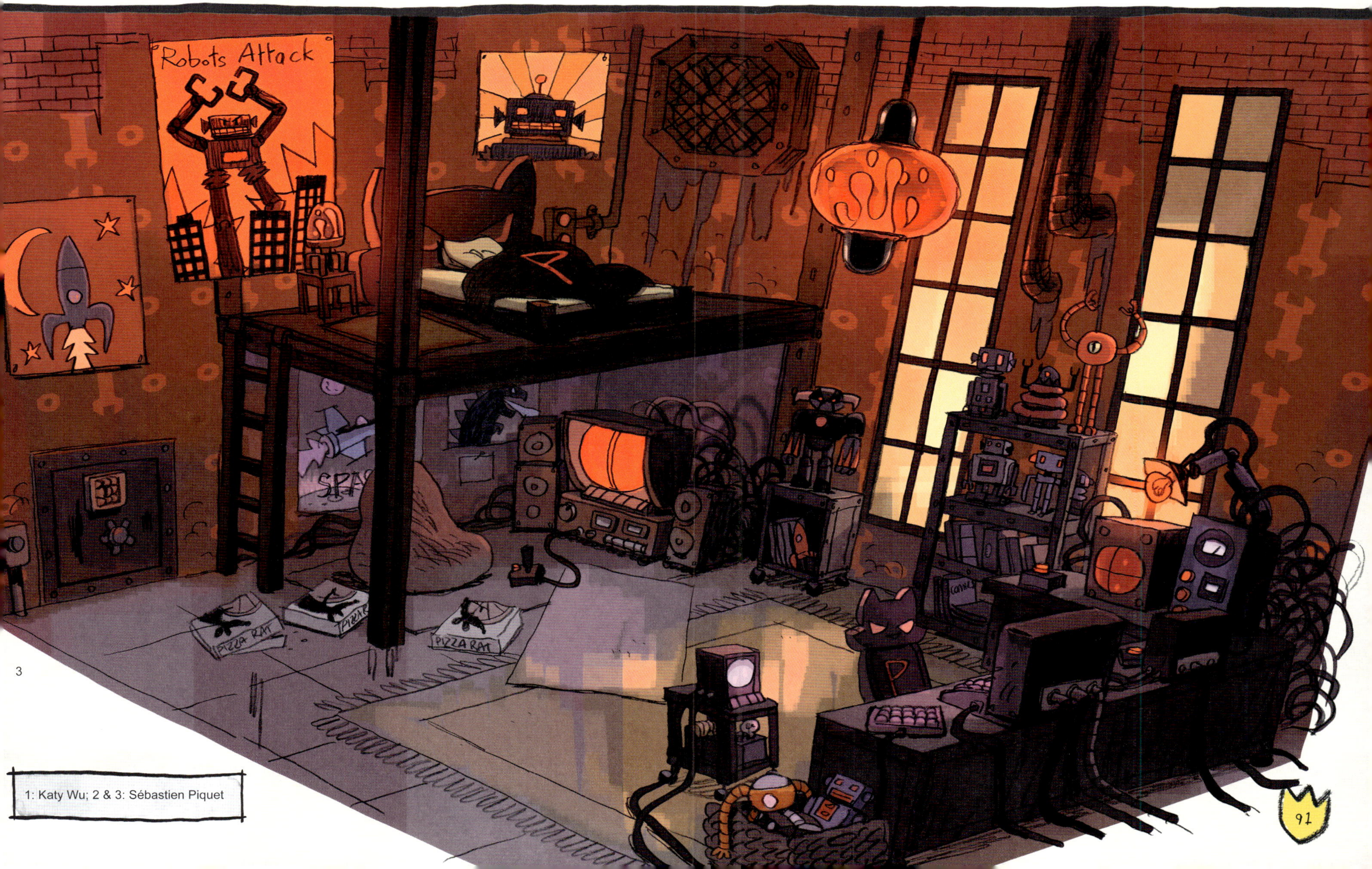

3

1: Katy Wu; 2 & 3: Sébastien Piquet

1

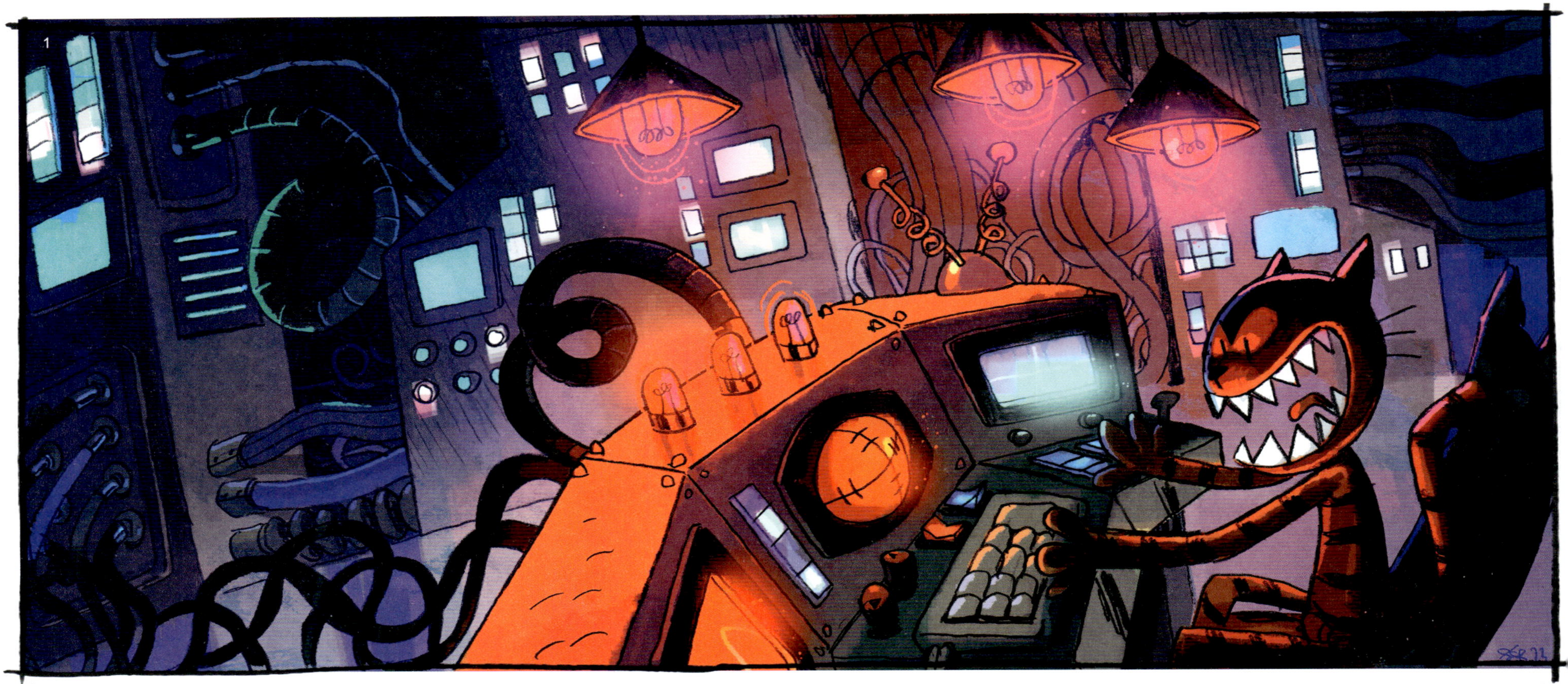

2

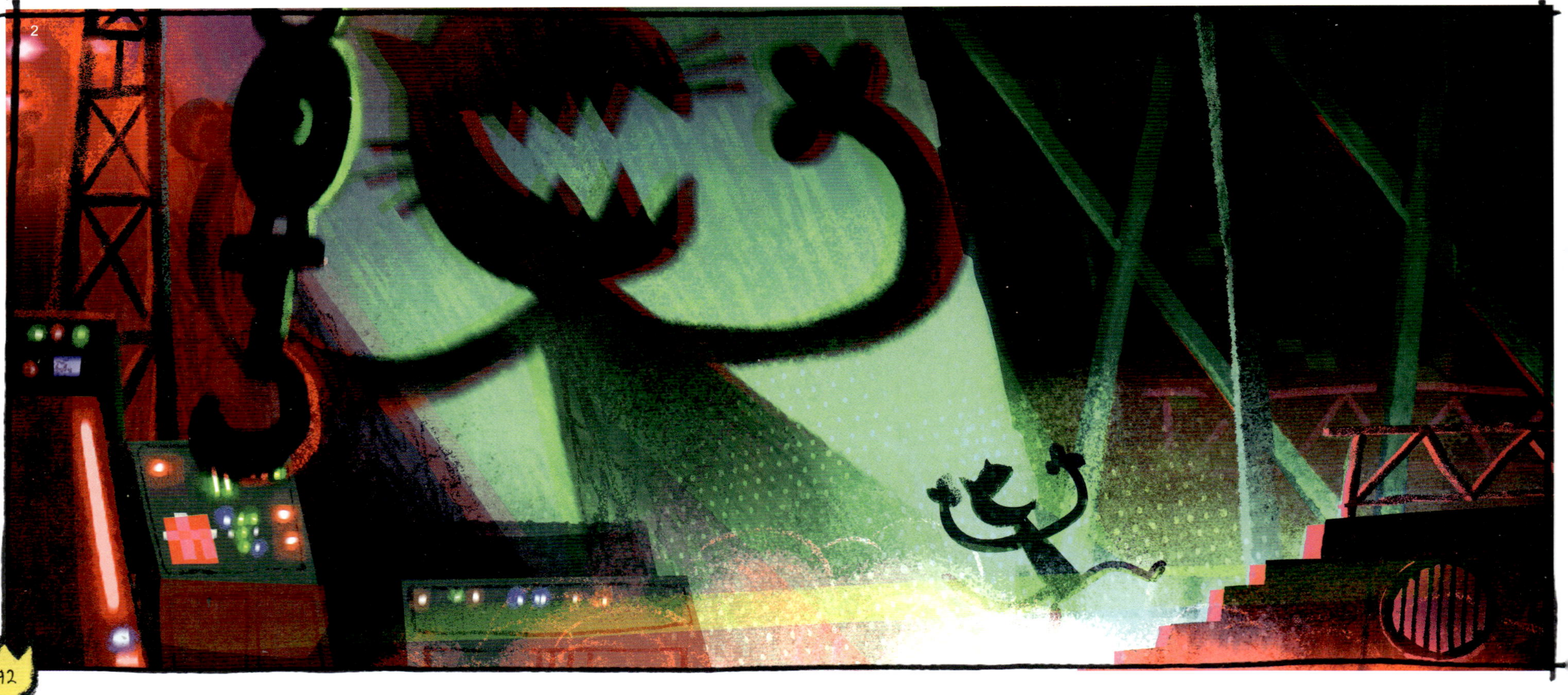

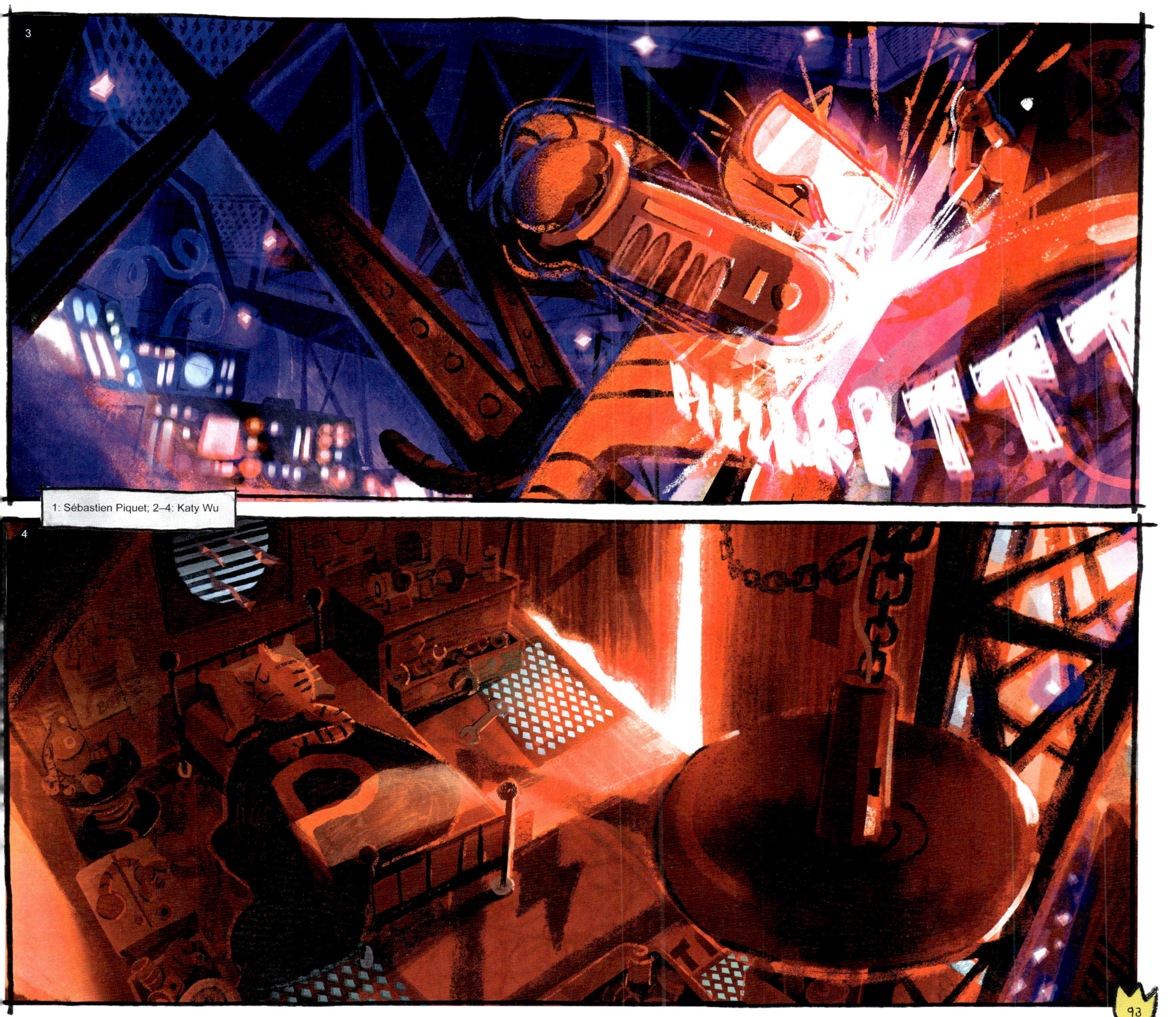

1: Sébastien Piquet; 2–4: Katy Wu

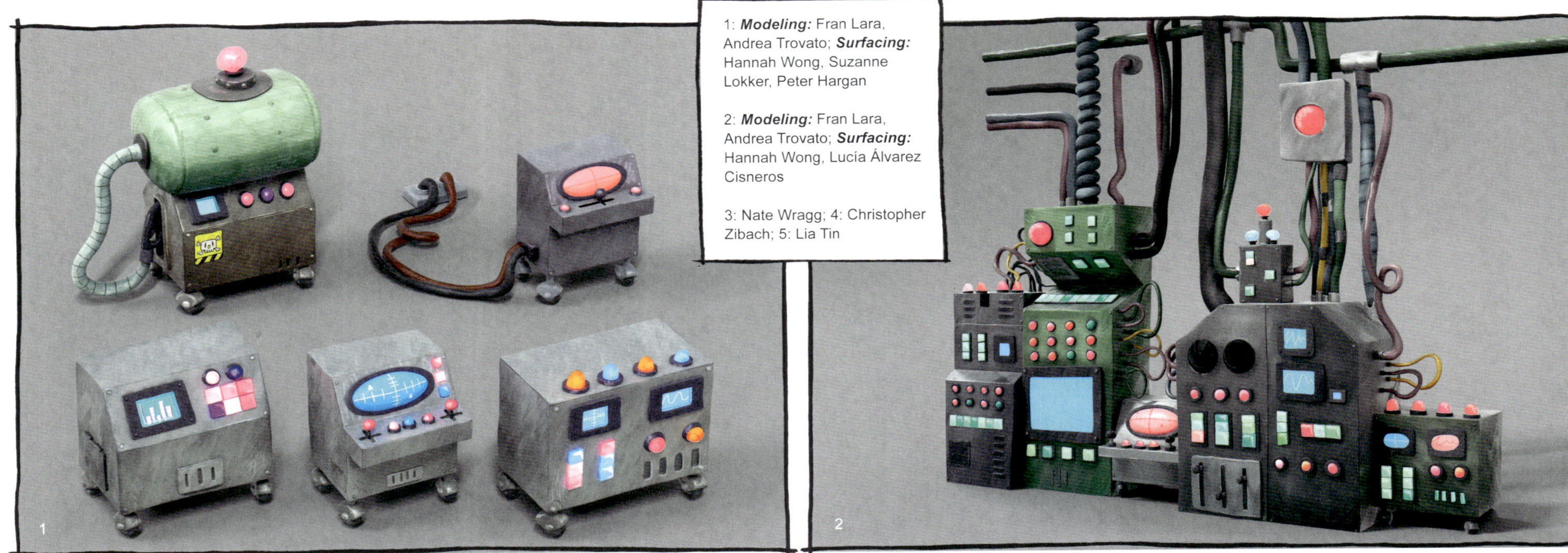

1: ***Modeling:*** Fran Lara, Andrea Trovato; ***Surfacing:*** Hannah Wong, Suzanne Lokker, Peter Hargan

2: ***Modeling:*** Fran Lara, Andrea Trovato; ***Surfacing:*** Hannah Wong, Lucía Álvarez Cisneros

3: Nate Wragg; 4: Christopher Zibach; 5: Lia Tin

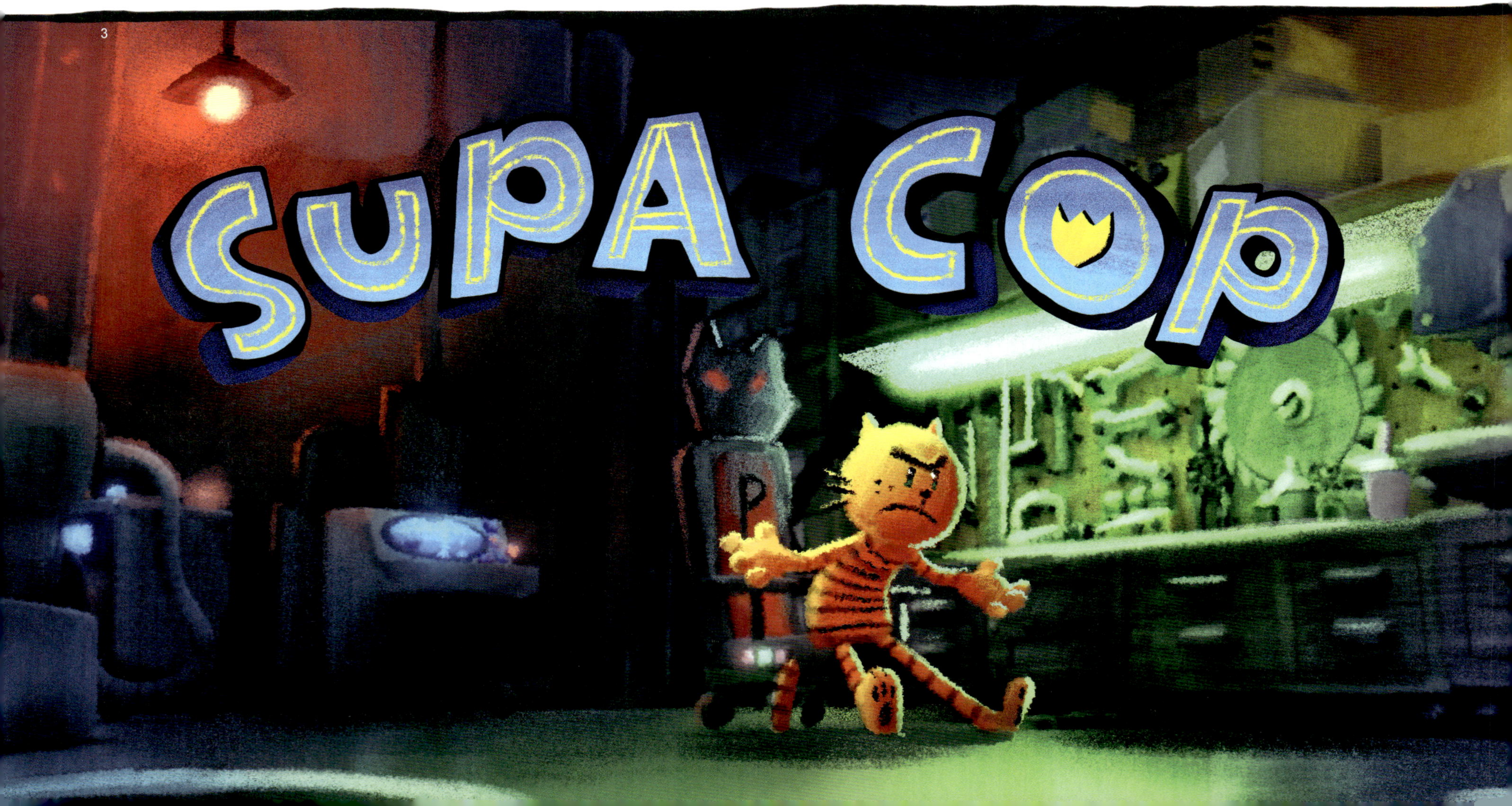

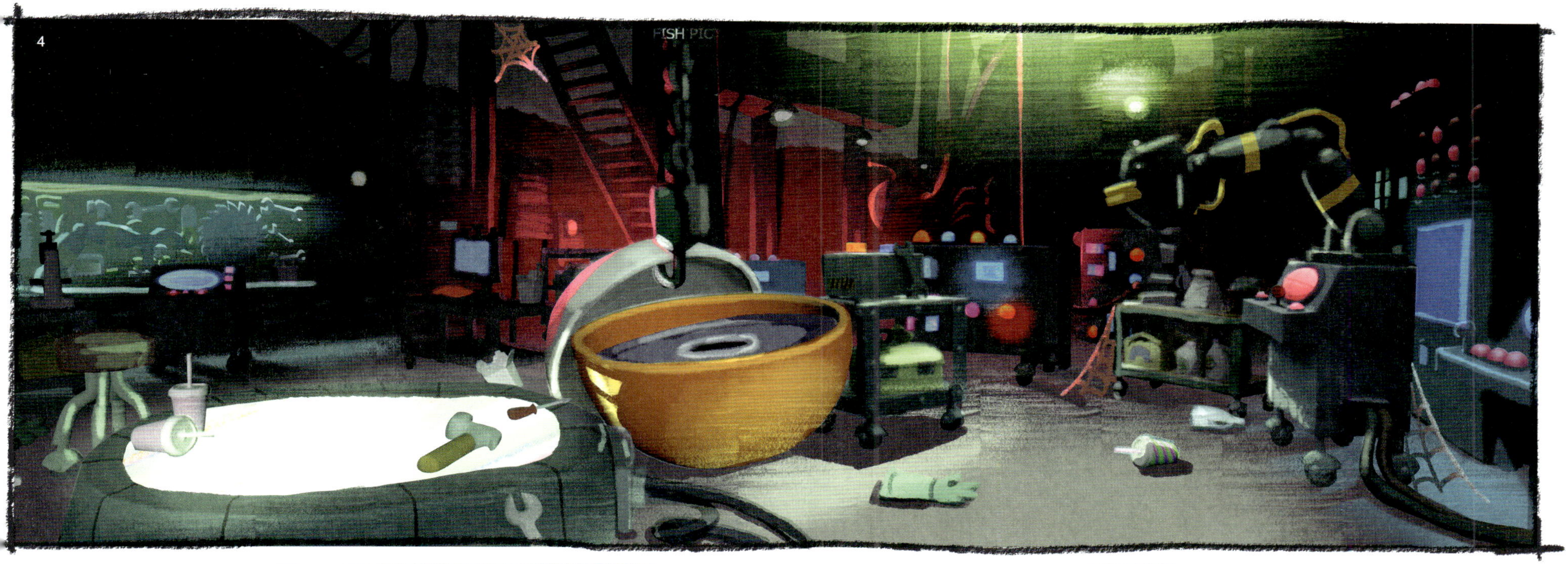

4

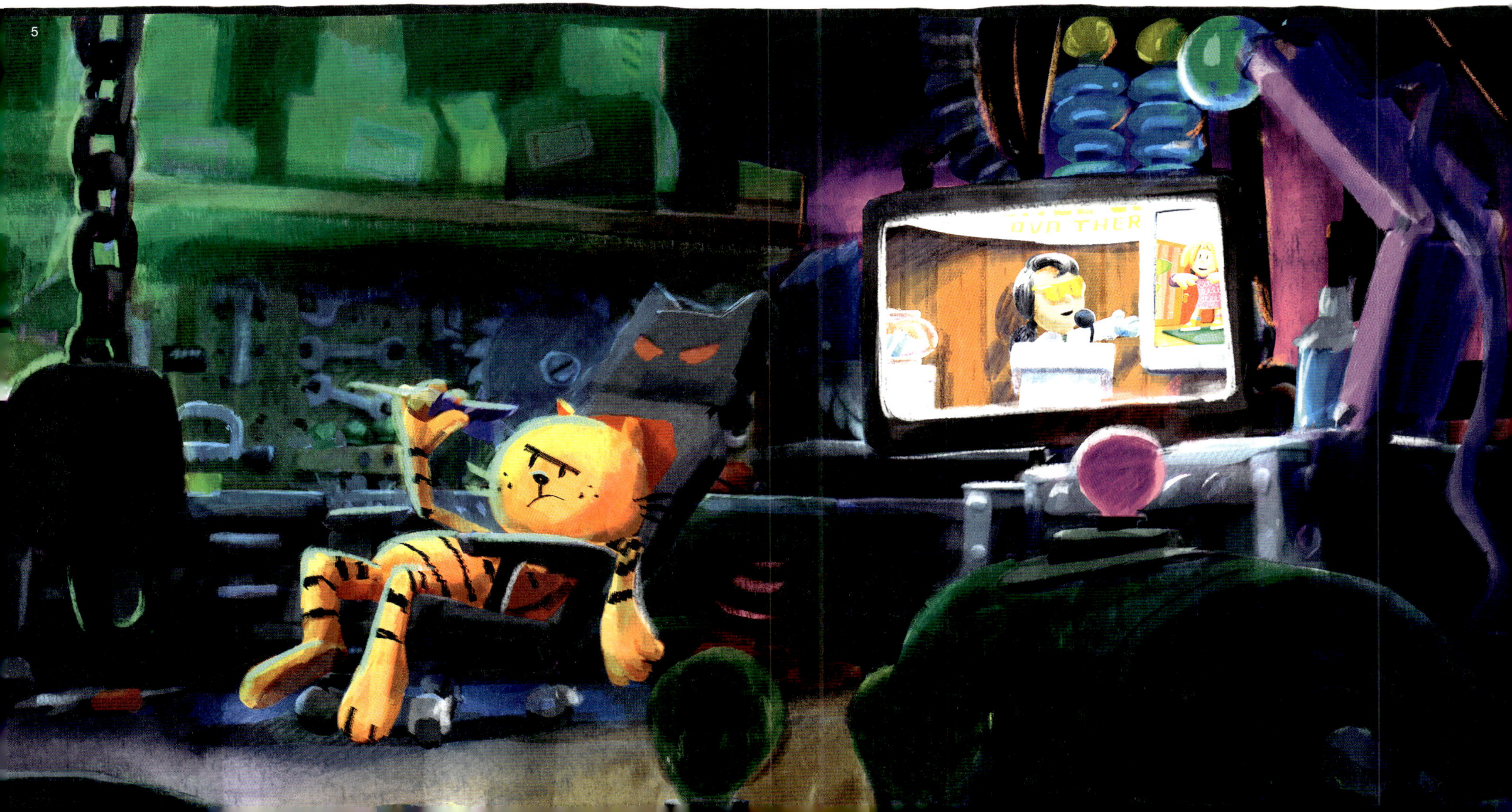

5

1

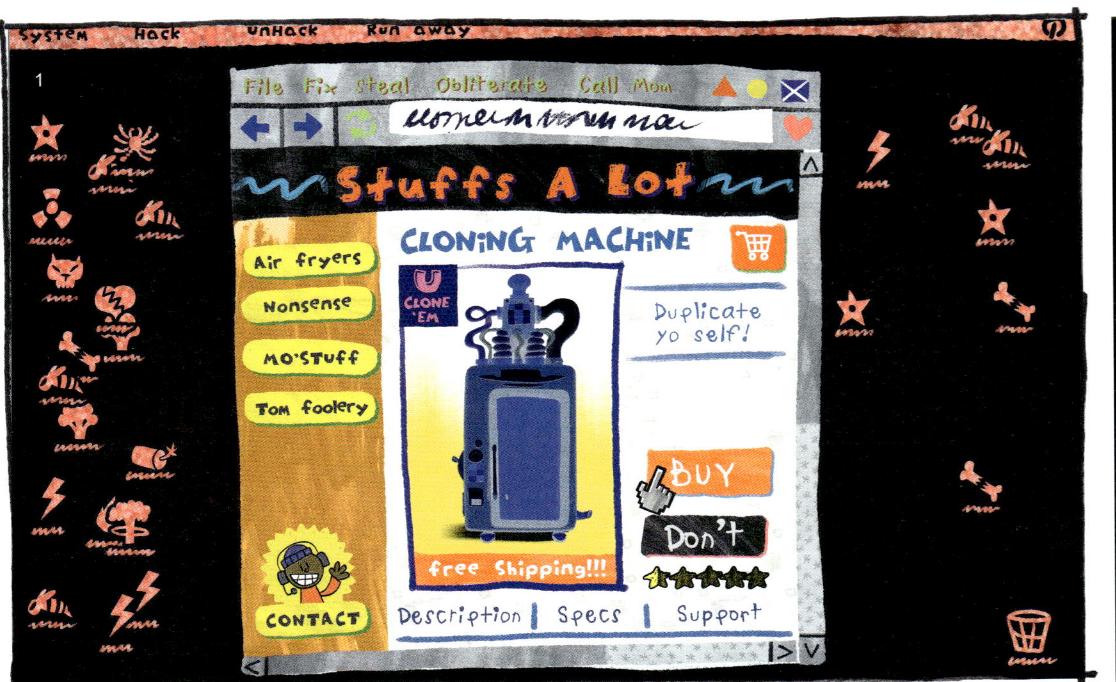

2

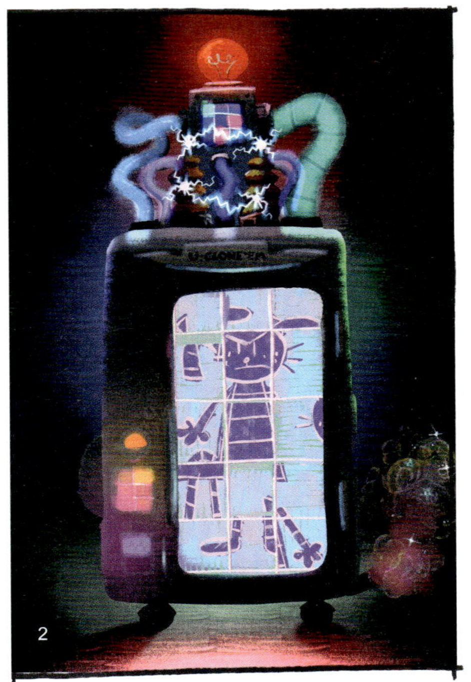

Cloning Machine

When Petey's butler tells him that the only person who could work for him is himself, Petey gets the brilliant idea to order a cloning machine online. "The machine is a silly contraption that is delivered to his lab," explains production designer Nate Wragg. "It looks like a giant vintage fridge with a bunch of blinky lights and buttons." The simple cloning process begins when Petey inserts one of his whiskers into the gadget. Of course, the machine spits out Li'l Petey instead of a full-grown adult Petey—and that's when the fun starts.

3

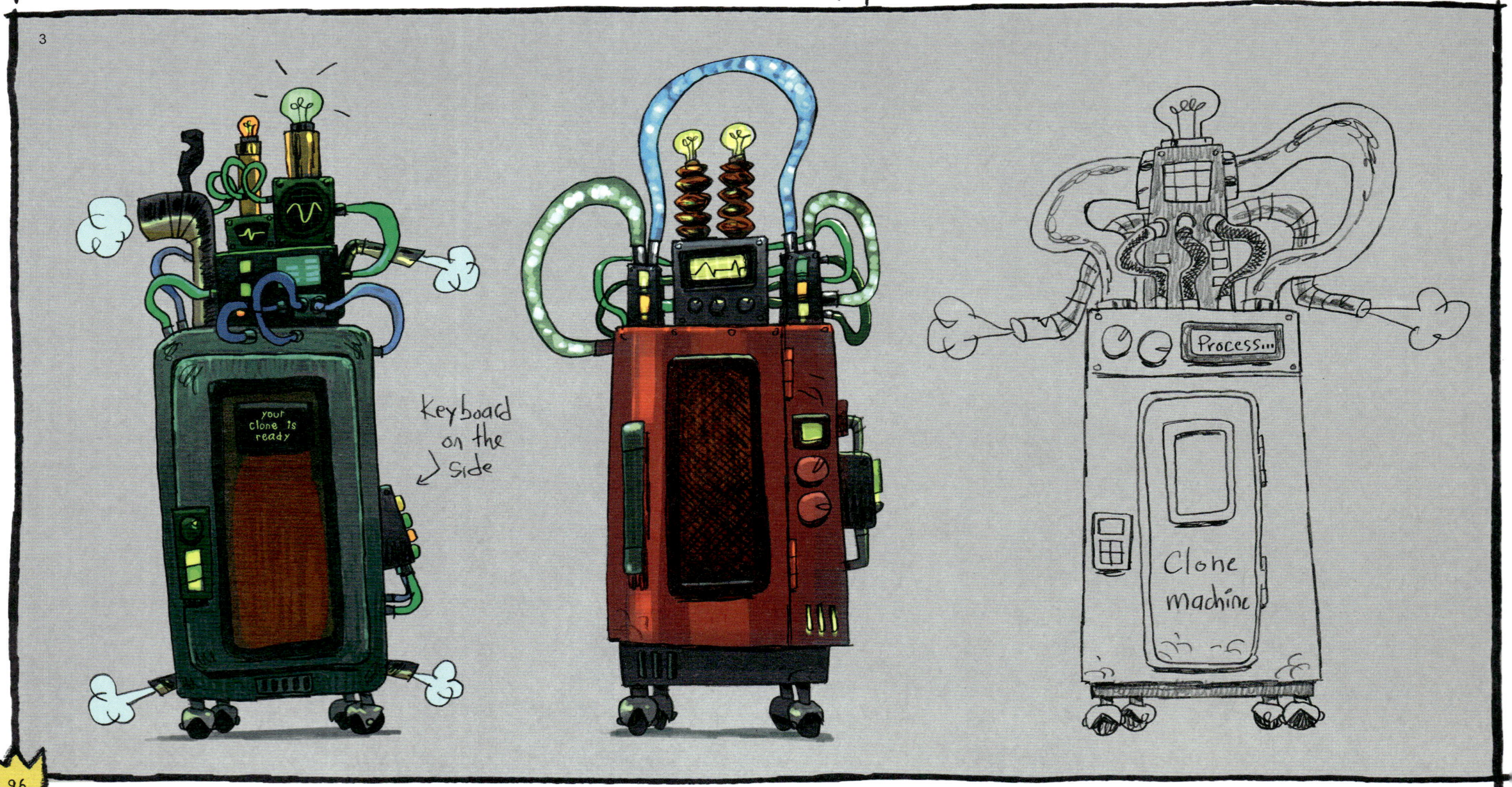

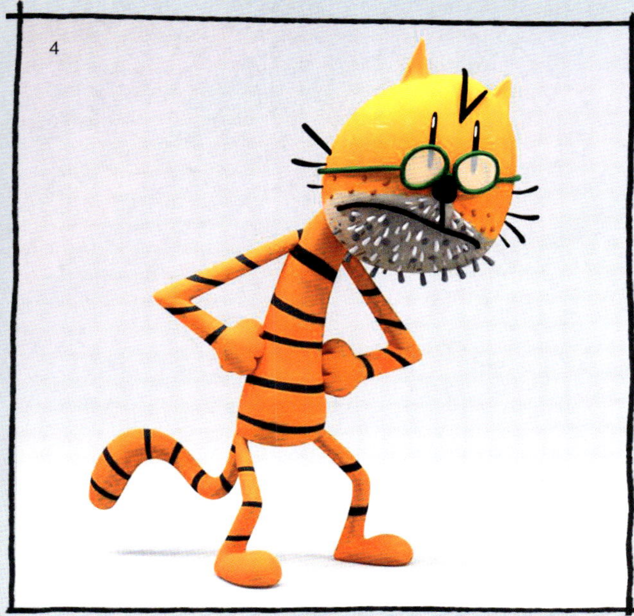

Grampa

One of the most complicated and surprising characters in the movie, Grampa (voiced by Stephen Root) is Petey's awful father who abandoned him and his family. Li'l Petey invites him in with open arms, thinking that he will make everything fine and help Petey's wounds. "Grampa is neither a good father nor grandfather," says production designer Nate Wragg. "He is grouchy, inconsiderate, and absolutely self-serving. On the surface, he is used as a good source of comic opportunities, but I think adults and even kids will see a deeper pattern of behavior going on underneath it all. His presence in the movie makes everything a bit more meaningful and reflective of the real world at large."

1, 2 & 5: Christopher Zibach; 3: Sébastien Piquet; 4: ***Modeling:*** Paul Schoeni

5

"Grampa is just a flat-out jerk, and that is a surprise both in the book and in the movie. They are not going to change him. Dav [Pilkey] told me that he was never going to redeem that character because that is just what happens in real life."

—PETER HASTINGS, Director

80-HD

Petey invents the robot known as 80-HD (full name: 80-HEXOTRON DROIDFORMIGON) to protect Li'l Petey. Originally created by Petey to create mayhem, it ends up fighting for good instead of evil under the direction of Li'l Petey. In the books, Li'l Petey replaces 80-HD's original missiles with solar panels to help the environment.

80-HD is an original creation by Pilkey, and its name is a play on words because the author/illustrator suffered from ADHD and dyslexia as a young boy. "It's simply a pun because the robot doesn't really have attention deficit hyperactivity disorder. It ends up being a heroic character," says production designer Nate Wragg. "I love its great design, which is kind of a robot version of Petey himself, with a big barrel cylinder and cartoony arms and legs, as things have in Pilkey's world."

1

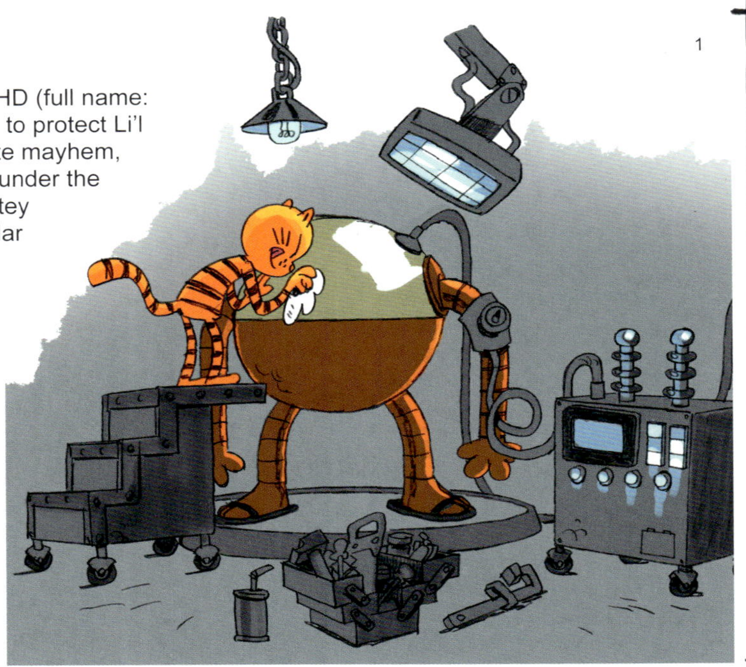

2

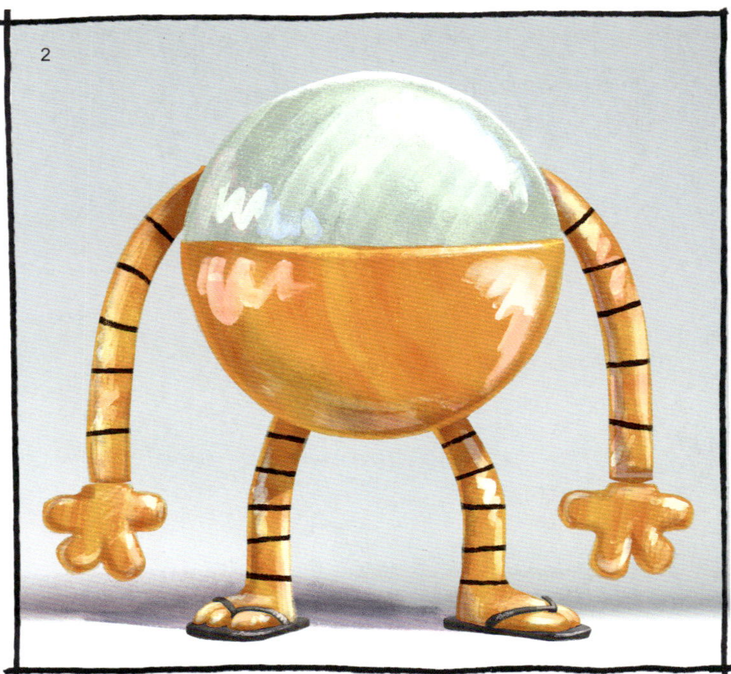

3

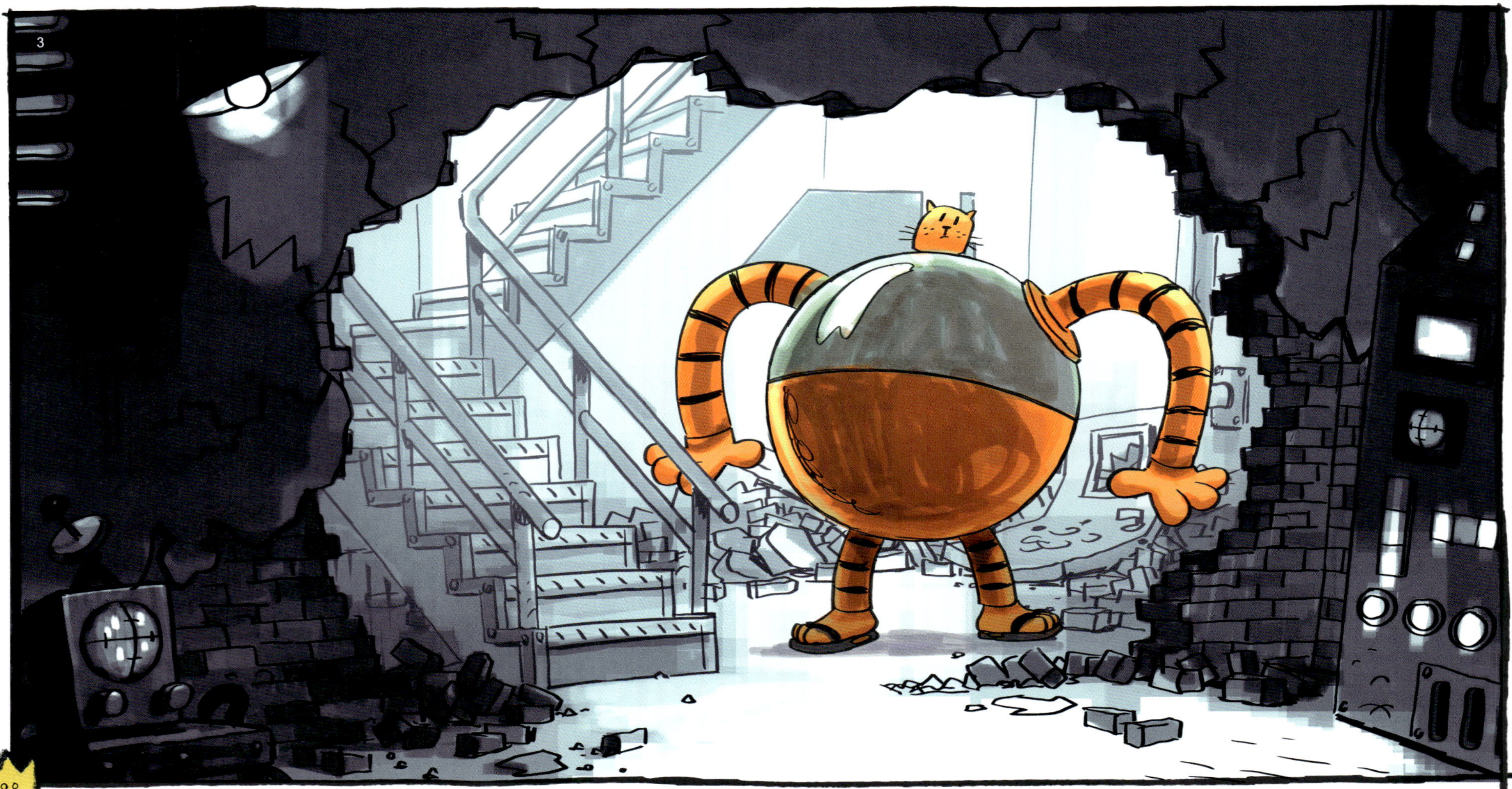

4

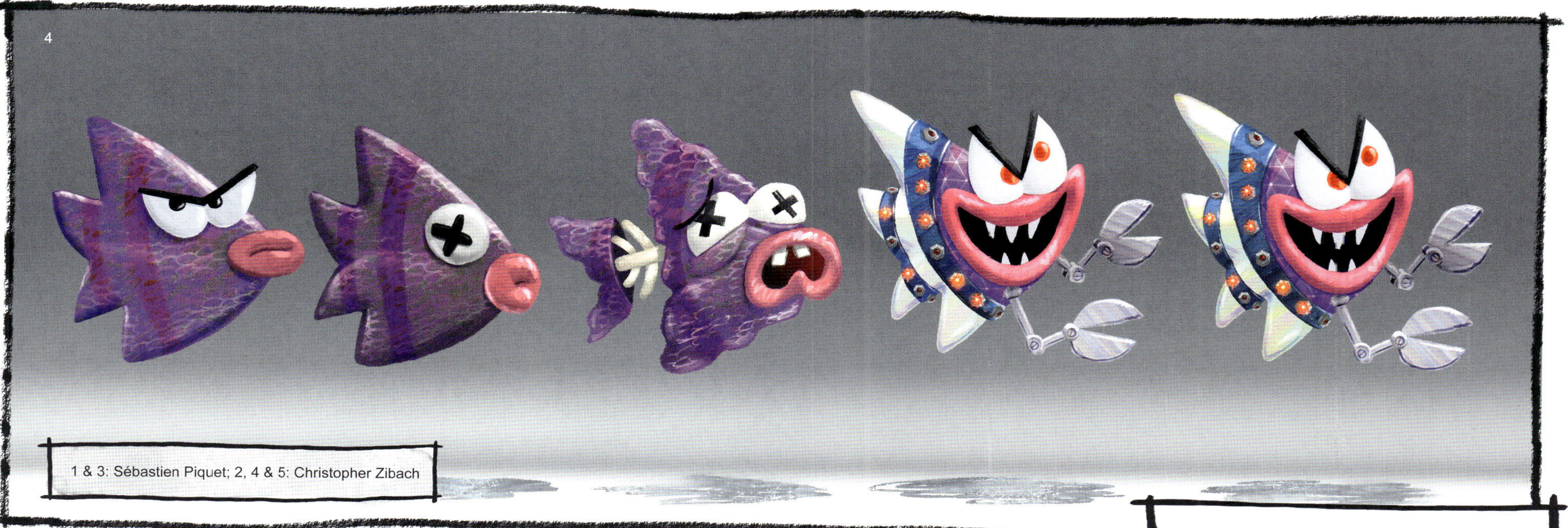

1 & 3: Sébastien Piquet; 2, 4 & 5: Christopher Zibach

5

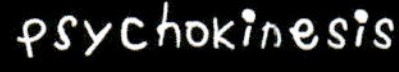

flippy the fish

Possibly one of the first dead fish villains in the history of cinema, Flippy is brought to life by exposure to some potent Living Spray from The Living Spray Factory. His goal is to get rid of all do-gooders and to control everything. As he confesses to Li'l Petey in the movie, he wants to destroy the world because nobody likes him and because he was bullied in school and called "Fatty Fish Face." "He slides into the playfully classic villain trope," says production designer Nate Wragg. "But everything about him is clearly seen from the perspective of imaginative ten-year-old boys."

Petey's vehicles

Being the villainous mastermind that he is, Petey enjoys coming up with new ways to torment and destroy his enemies. Elaborate machines and gadgets are used to scare or lure Dog Man: conveyances like vacuum and cage vehicles, The Make No Bones 2000, Love It Or Leash It 2000, The Butt Sniffer 2000, and The Squirrel Shooter 2000.

"To frighten Dog Man, Petey invents a giant dog crate with big teeth on wheels and a huge vacuum with mechanical eyes and an oversized chomping mouth," explains production designer Nate Wragg. "They're not really useful inventions. They all come across as silly and absurd and not necessarily practical. A sewer croc car that he drives around in the beginning of the movie is as ridiculous as it sounds. It's based on what a ten-year-old would think is a cool racing car."

The rest of the vehicles in the town are also playful and familiar. "They are not shiny, brand-new cars," adds Wragg. "The audience may recognize them as cars from the '80s or '90s."

The Butt Sniffer 2000

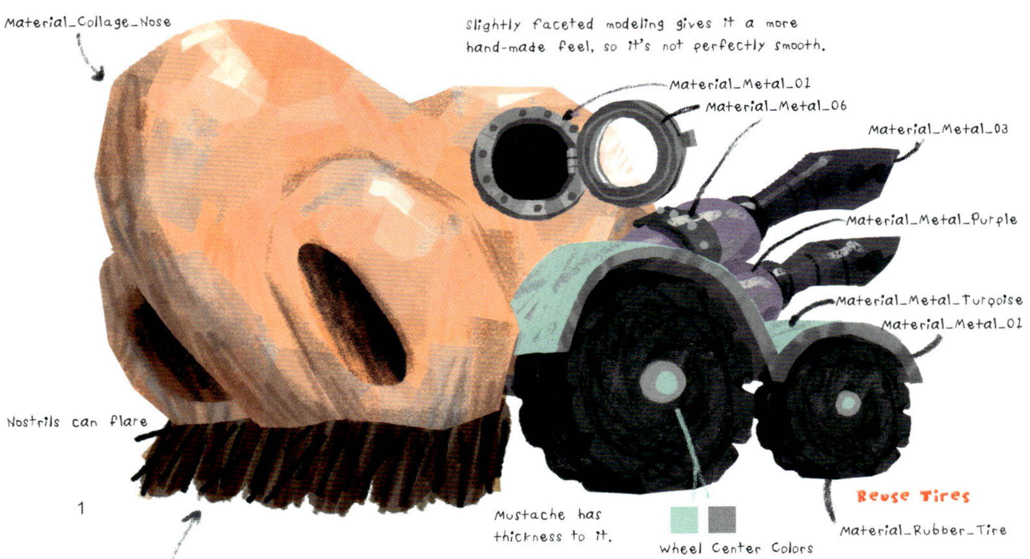

1

bee plane

POSSIBILITY TO OPEN & CLOSE THE EYES

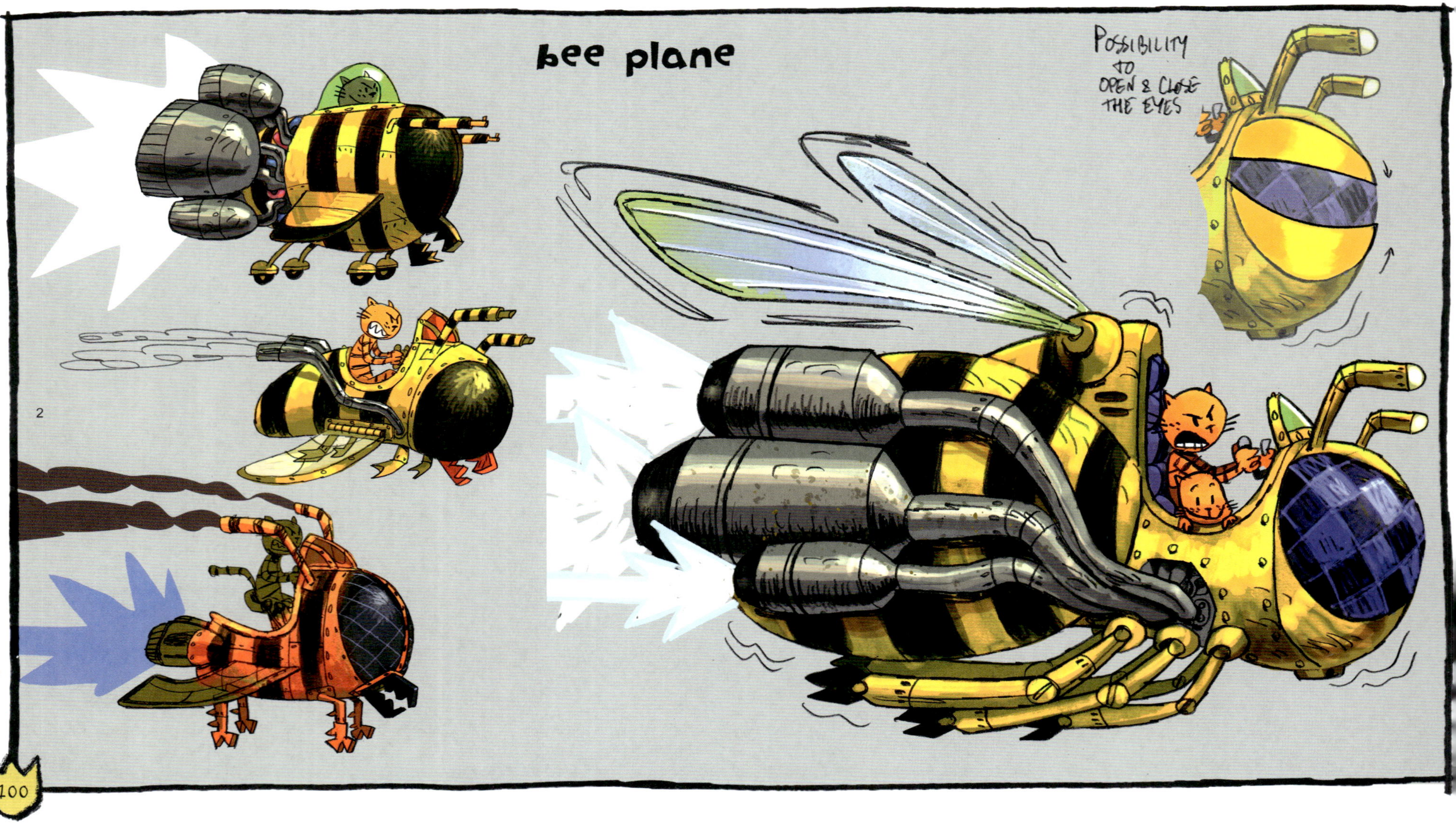

2

cage vehicle

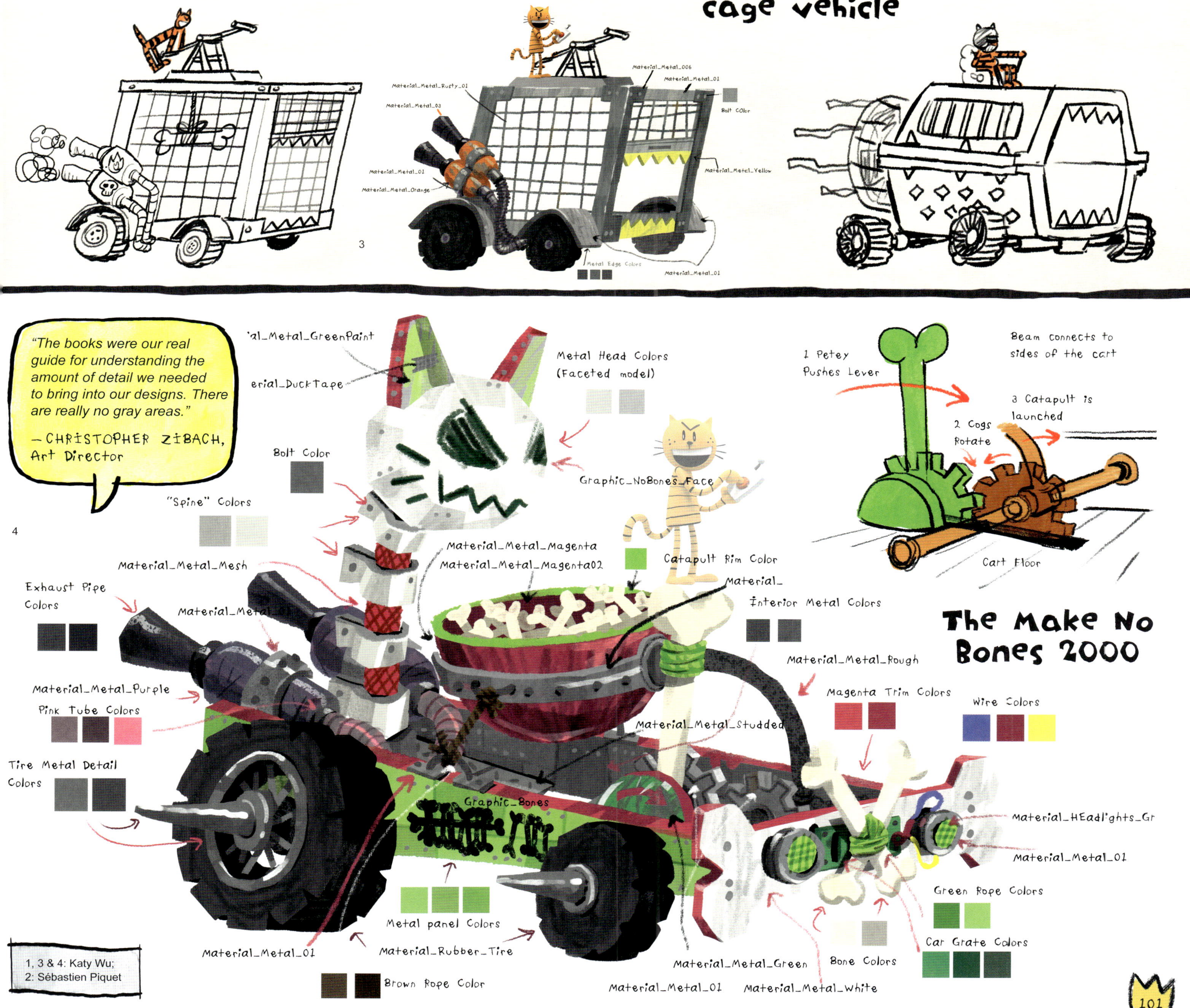

"The books were our real guide for understanding the amount of detail we needed to bring into our designs. There are really no gray areas."

—CHRISTOPHER ZIBACH, Art Director

The Make No Bones 2000

1, 3 & 4: Katy Wu;
2: Sébastien Piquet

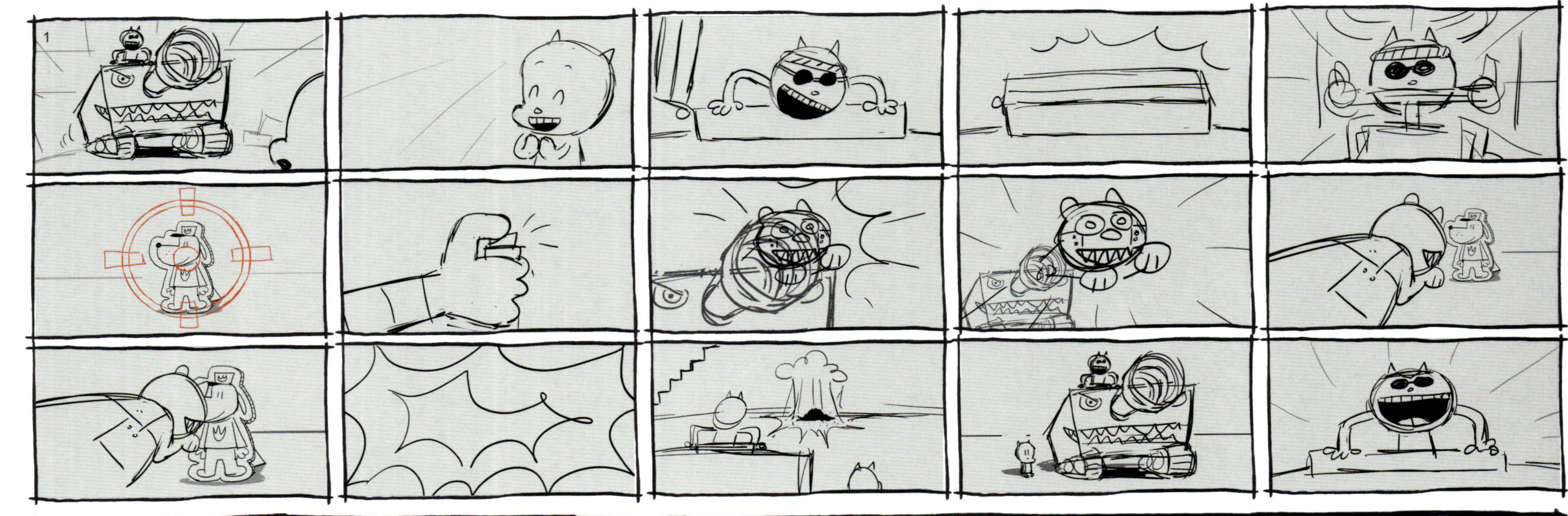

2

The Squirrel Shooter 2000

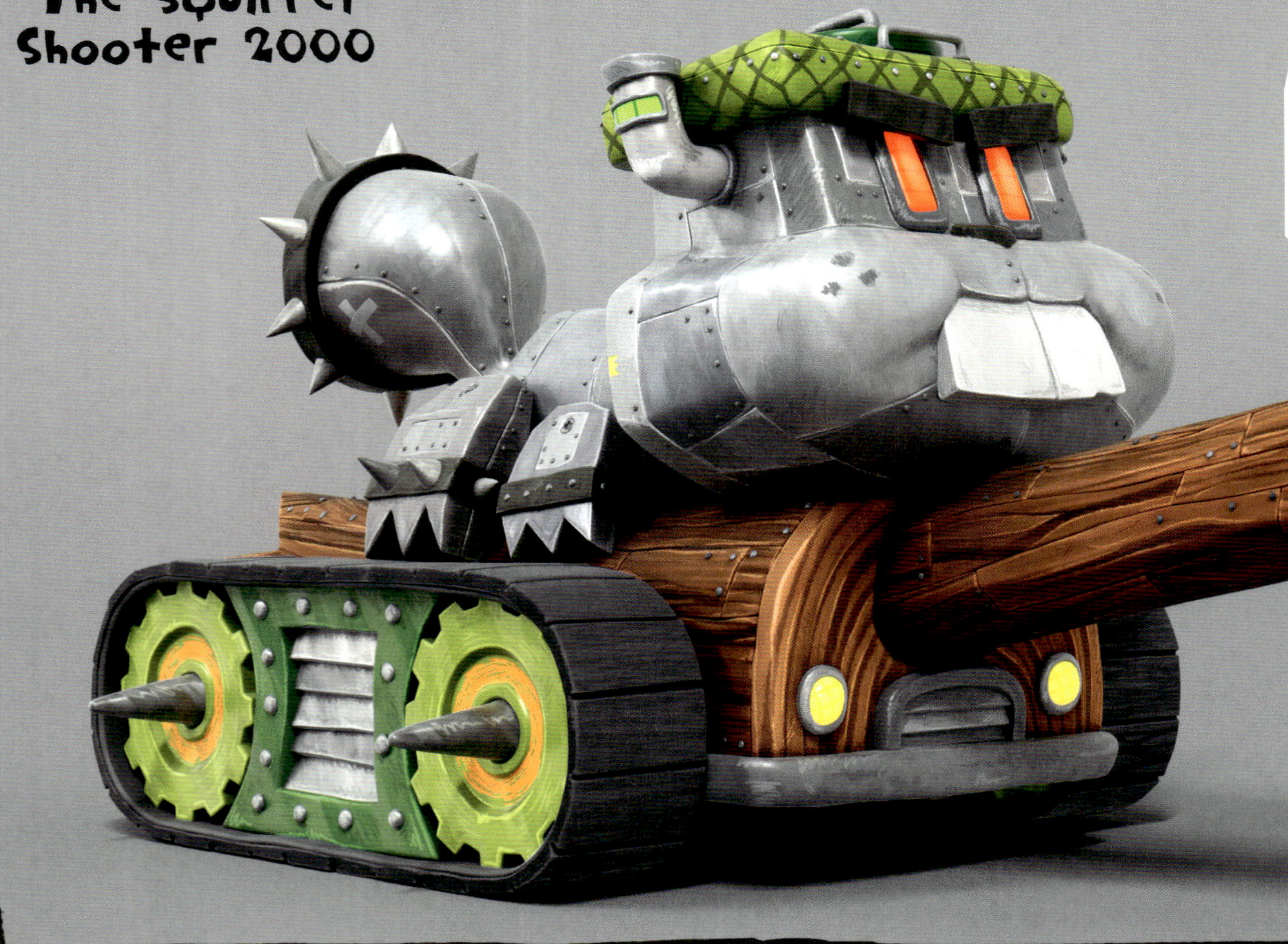

"To me, the movie is going to stand out thanks to its sophisticated camera language and the advanced level of texture, cinematography, surfacing, and look development."

—SCOTT CULLEN, Head of Layout and Cinematography

1: Hanna Kim

2: ***Vis Dev:*** Lia Tin; ***Modeling:*** Fran Lara, Erica Eguia; ***Surfacing:*** Hannah Wong, Leopoldine Perdrix

3–5: Lia Tin

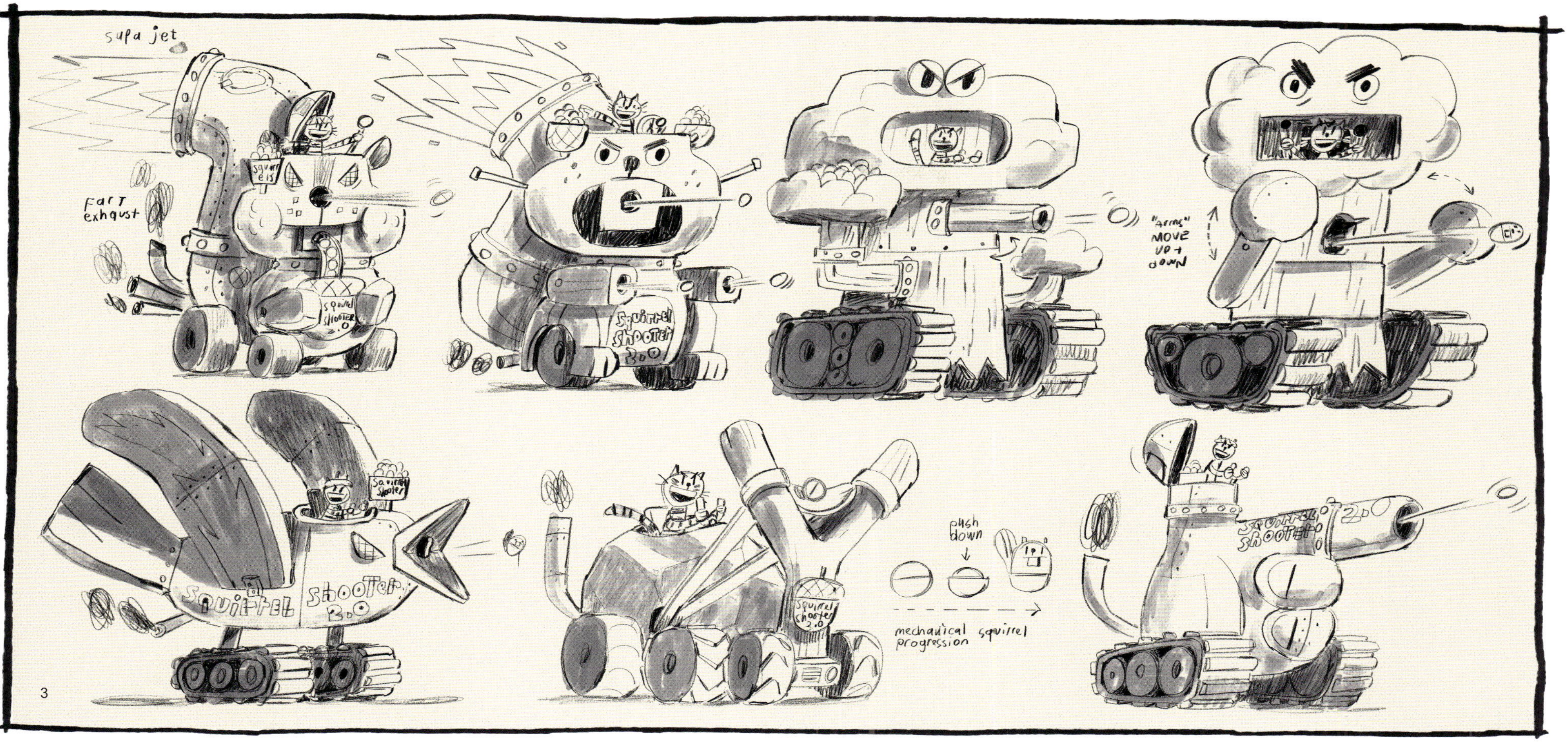

supa jet

fart exhaust

Squirrel Shooter 2.0

"arms" move up + down

push down

mechanical squirrel progression

3

4

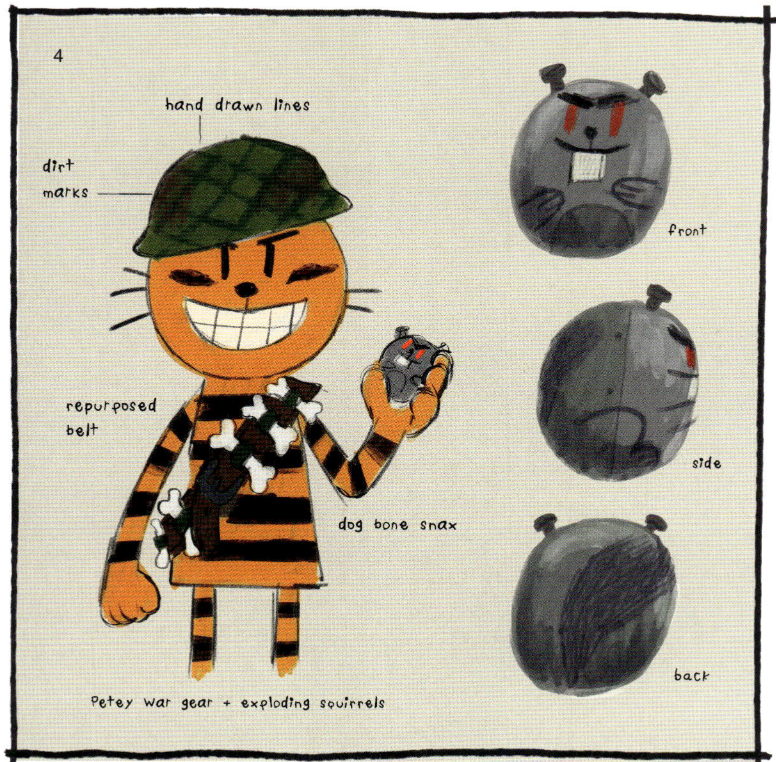

5

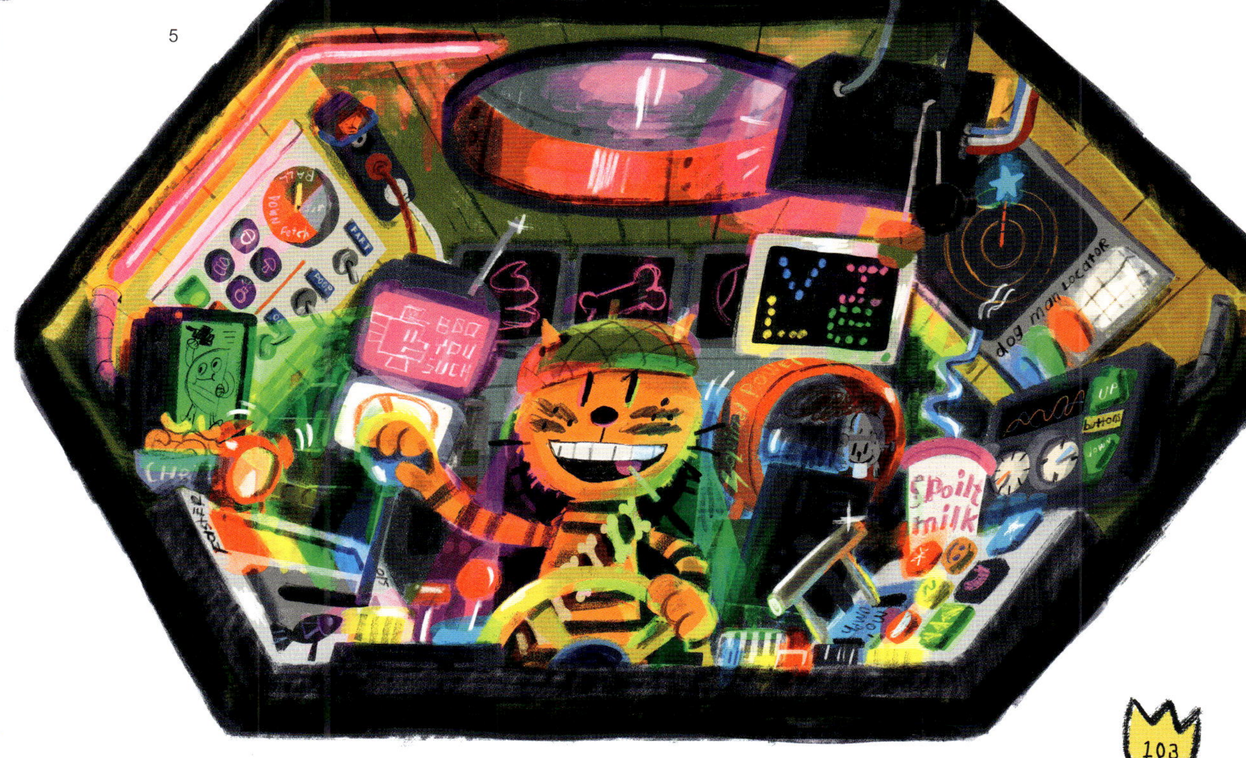

1

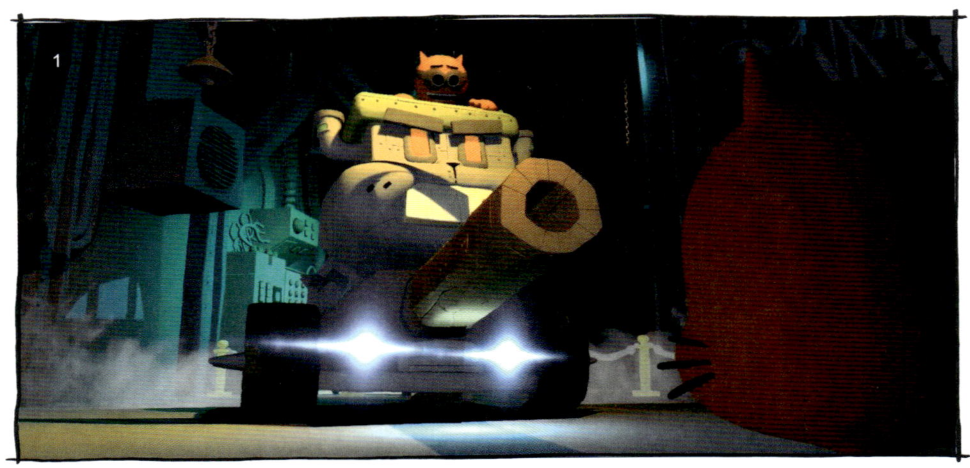

2

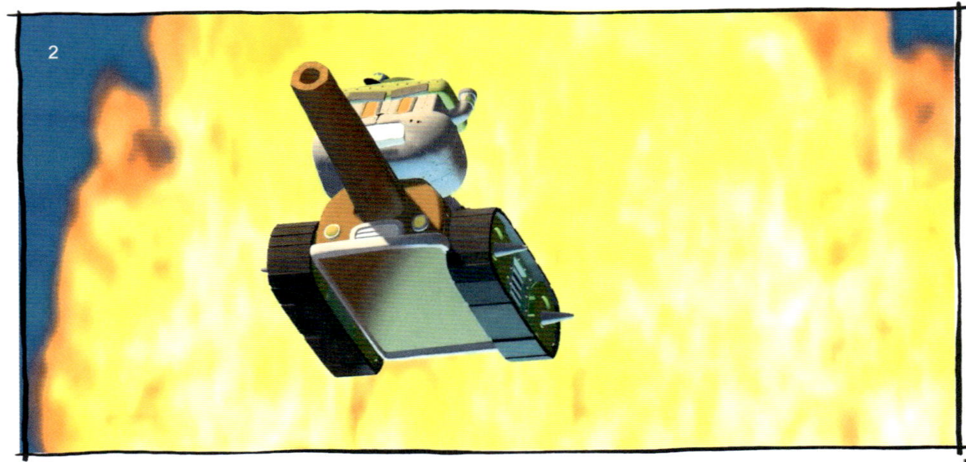

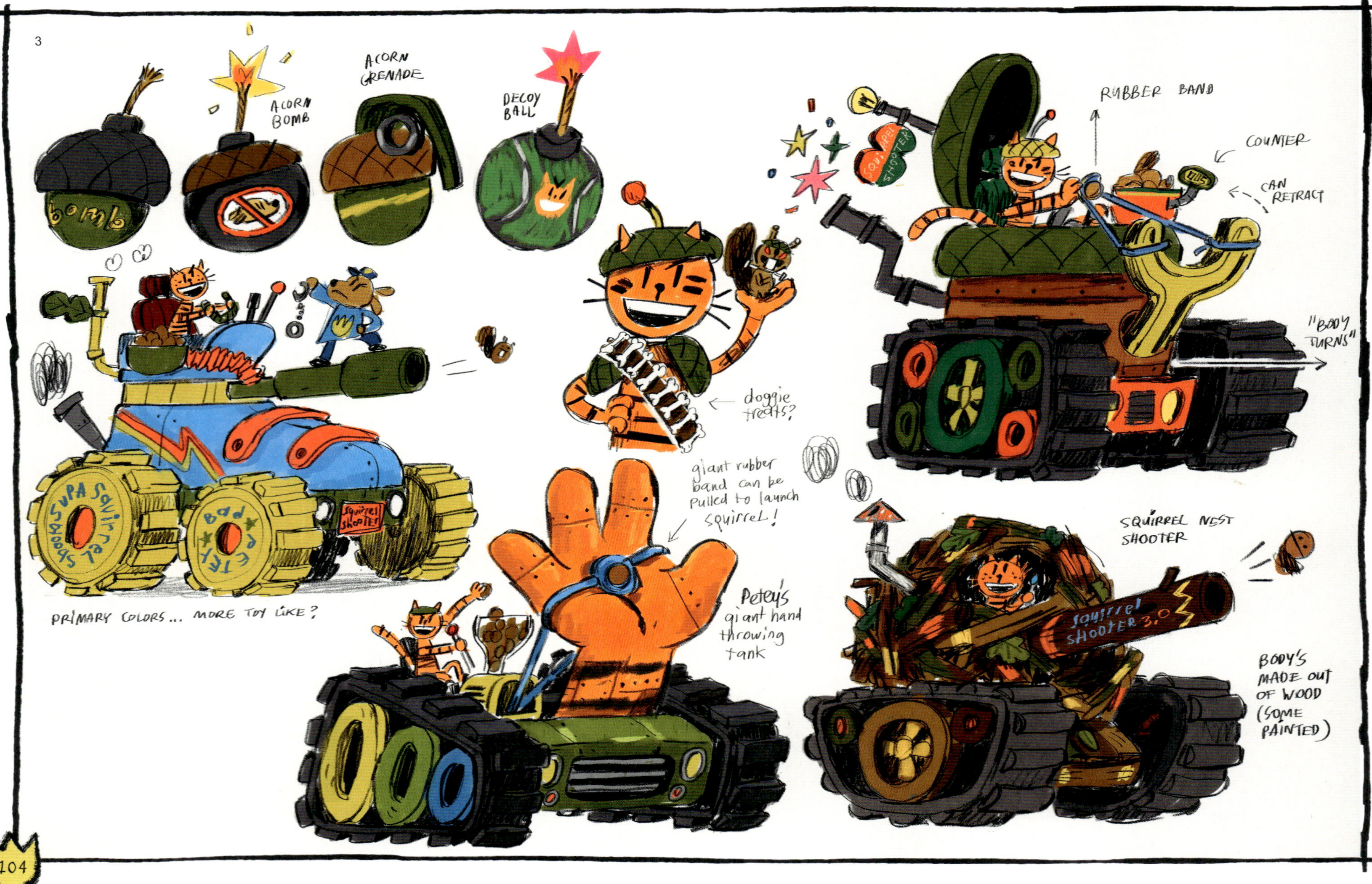

3

ACORN BOMB

ACORN GRENADE

DECOY BALL

bomb

RUBBER BAND

COUNTER

CAN RETRACT

"BODY TURNS"

SQUIRREL SHOOTER

doggie treats?

SUPA Squirrel Shoots

Bad PETEY

Squirrel Shooter

PRIMARY COLORS... MORE TOY LIKE?

giant rubber band can be pulled to launch squirrel!

Petey's giant hand throwing tank

SQUIRREL NEST SHOOTER

Squirrel Shooter 3.0

BODY'S MADE OUT OF WOOD (SOME PAINTED)

The Love it Or Leash it 2000

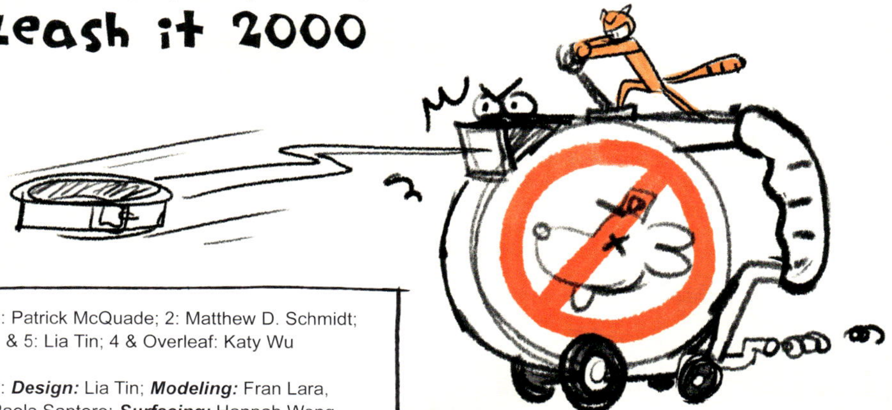

1: Patrick McQuade; 2: Matthew D. Schmidt; 3 & 5: Lia Tin; 4 & Overleaf: Katy Wu

6: ***Design:*** Lia Tin; ***Modeling:*** Fran Lara, Paola Santoro; ***Surfacing:*** Hannah Wong, Leopoldine Perdrix, Arnold Pryada

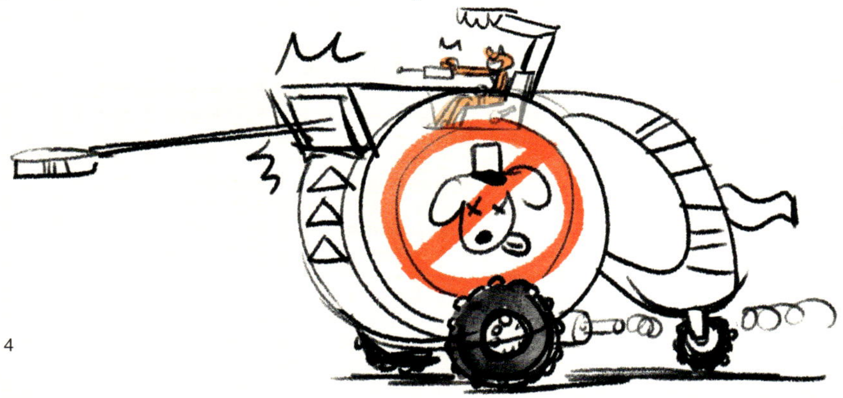

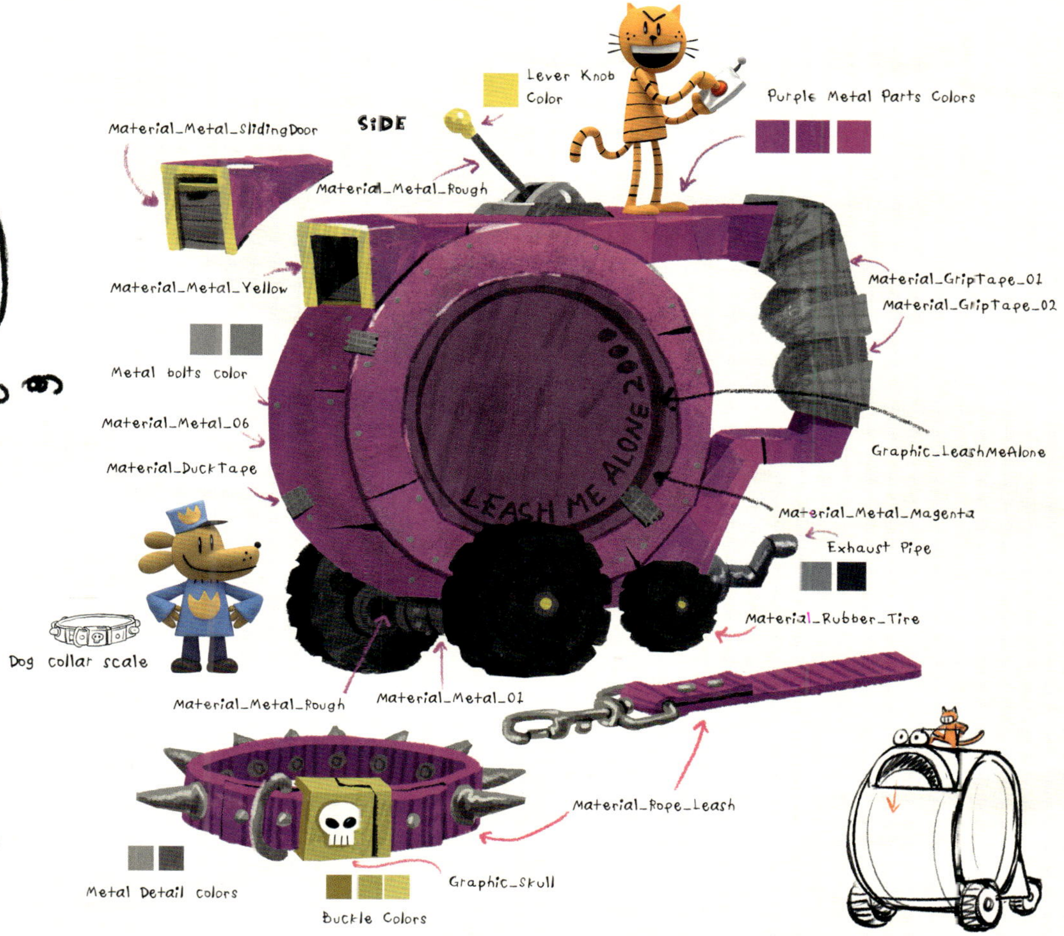

4

SIDE

Lever Knob Color

Purple Metal Parts Colors

Material_Metal_SlidingDoor

Material_Metal_Rough

Material_Metal_Yellow

Material_GripTape_01

Material_GripTape_02

Metal bolts color

Material_Metal_06

Material_DuckTape

Graphic_LeashMeAlone

Material_Metal_Magenta

Exhaust Pipe

Material_Rubber_Tire

Dog collar scale

Material_Metal_Rough

Material_Metal_01

Material_Rope_Leash

Graphic_Skull

Metal Detail colors

Buckle Colors

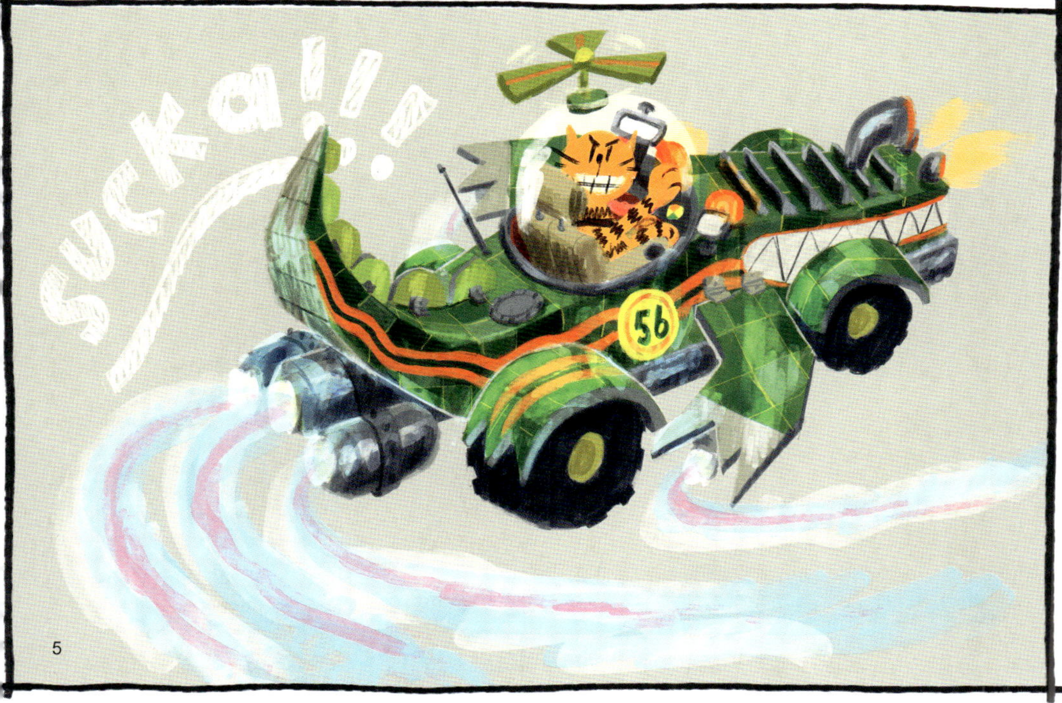

5

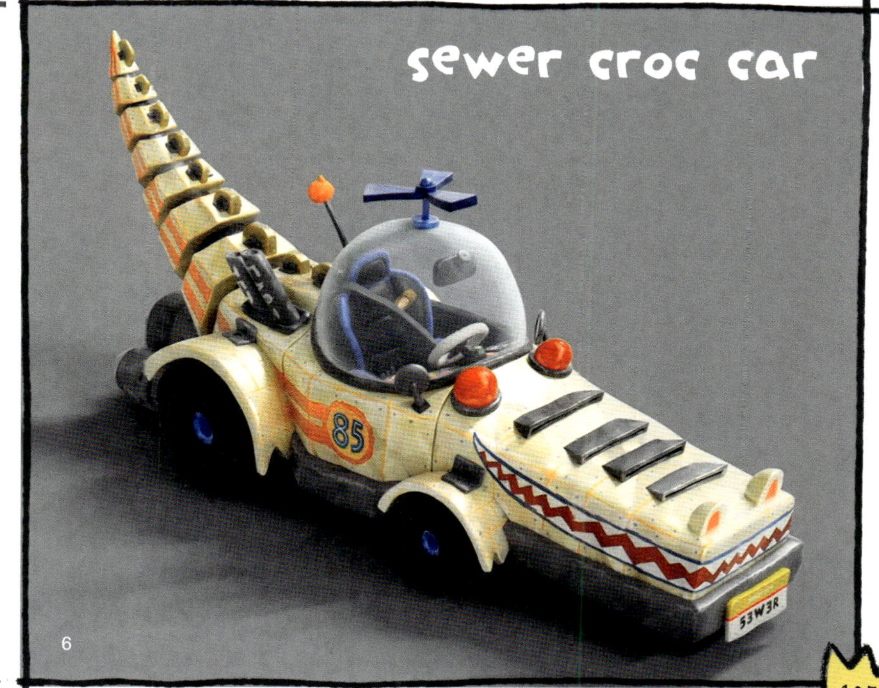

6

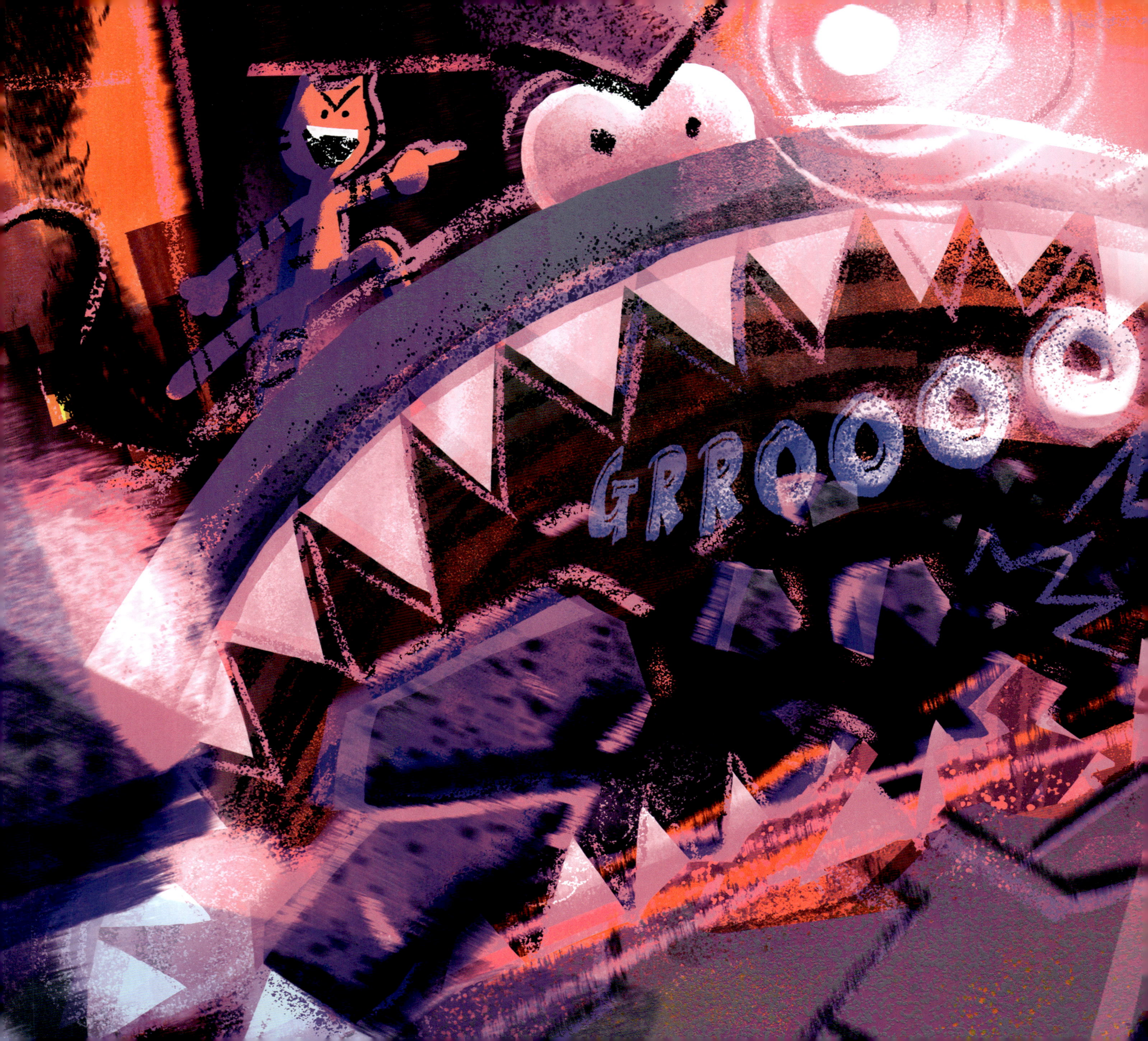
GRROOOO

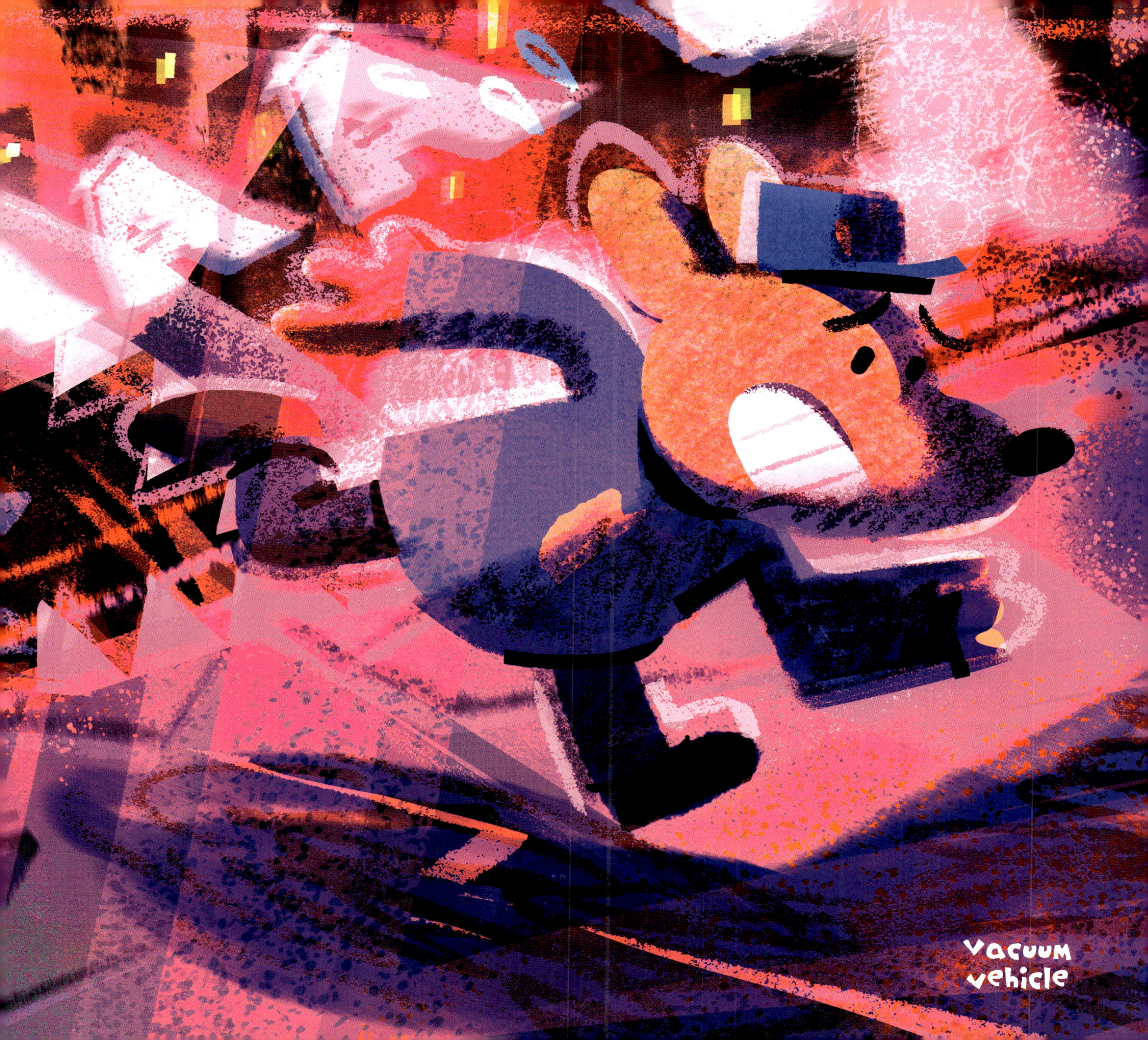
vacuum
vehicle

Butler

Petey's sarcastic assistant, Butler (voiced by Poppy Liu), provides a lot of comic relief and deadpan remarks in the mad scientist's world. She is not afraid of hiding her feelings and always speaks her mind, often rolling her eyes in the process. For example, when Petey says, "I've got to build a giant, dog-eating vacuum cleaner," she immediately responds with, "You could also buy a five-dollar firecracker because it scares dogs just the same."

"She's a really fun character who is very different from the original, more traditional butler from the books," says production designer Nate Wragg. "In the movie, she's like a twenty-one-year-old intern or someone who doesn't care about her job."

1

2

3

4

1 & 4: Christopher Zibach; 2: Lia Tin;
3: Nate Wragg; 5: Marceline Tanguay;
6: Christopher Zibach, Nate Wragg

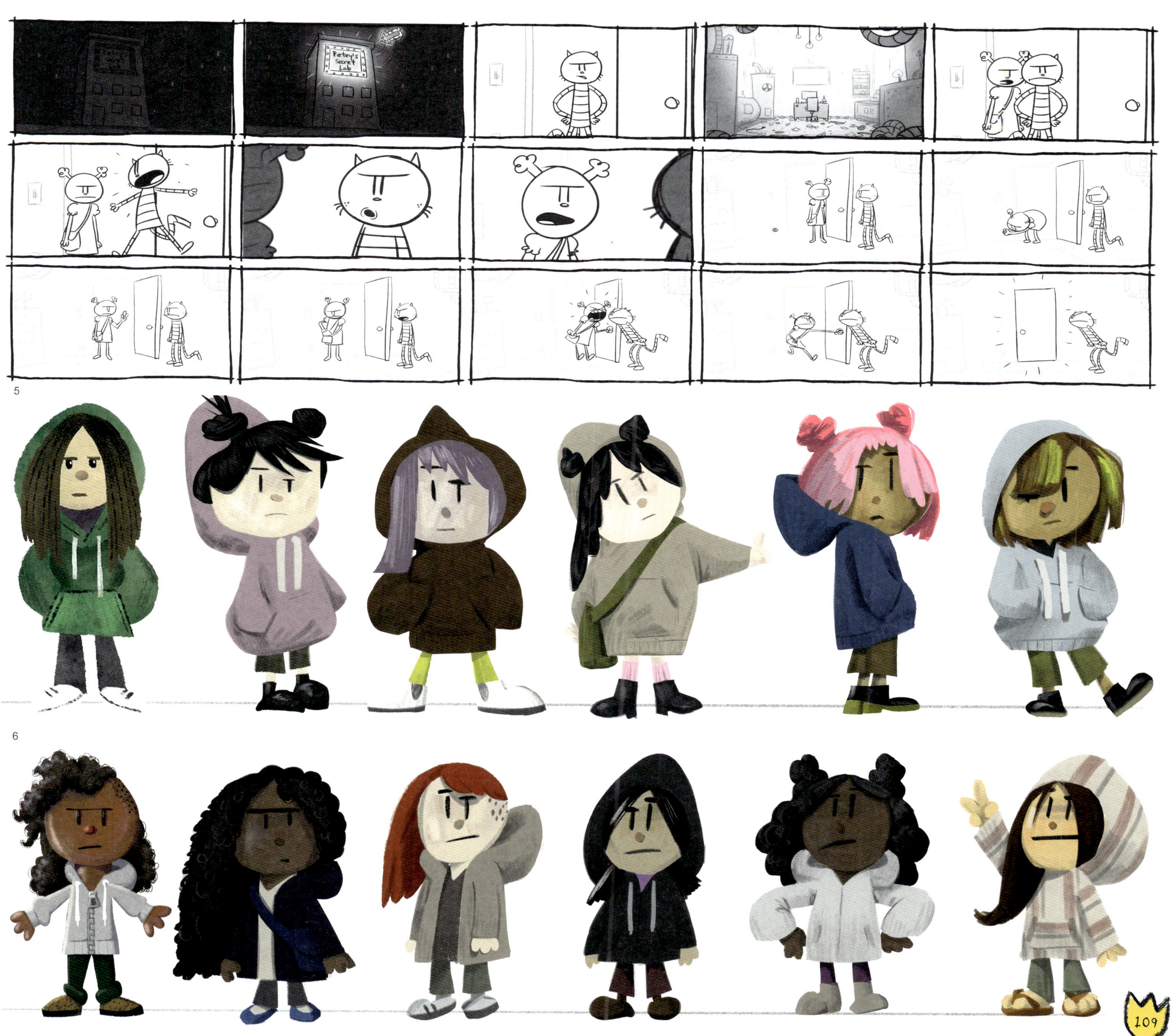

5

6

Officer Knight's house

When **Dog Man** returns to his old home, he comes to the realization that his life is no longer what it used to be before his accident. Officer Knight's fickle girlfriend, Alice, has left him, and their house is being repainted and sold. The real estate agent has finished painting it and is holding an open house for buyers. According to production designer Nate Wragg, "It's definitely not a fancy, extravagant neighborhood, even though all those homes would cost way too much by today's standards. The house has some charm and character, and it's located in a lived-in neighborhood."

"In this scene, Dog Man takes a moment to remember their good times together and is feeling this sense of loss because those days are gone forever," Wragg continues. "Although there's some comedy in there, it actually cuts deep because the scene has a strong emotional pull."

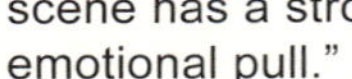

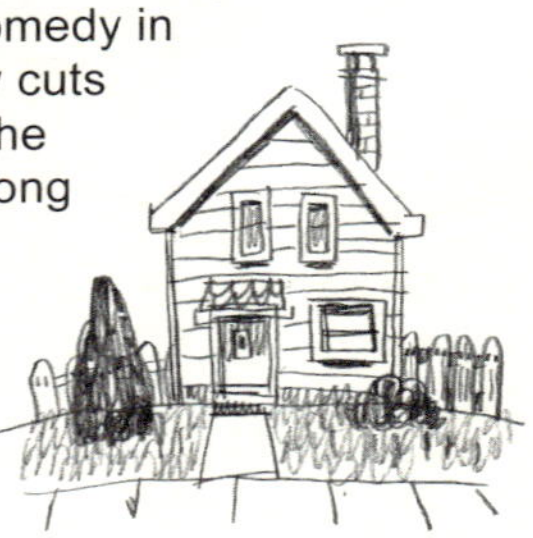

1

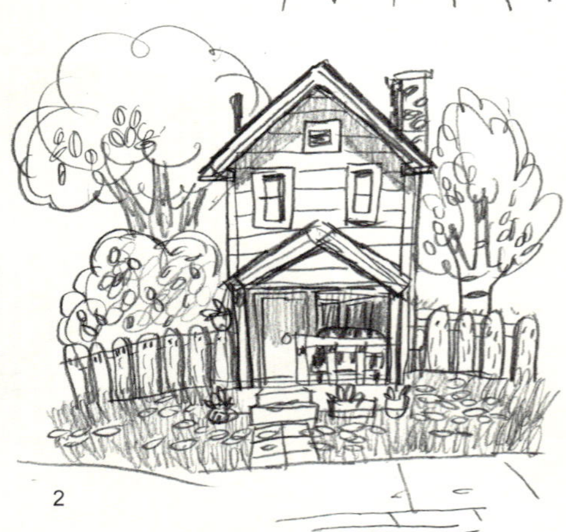

2

3

1 & 2: Sébastien Piquet; 3: Katy Wu

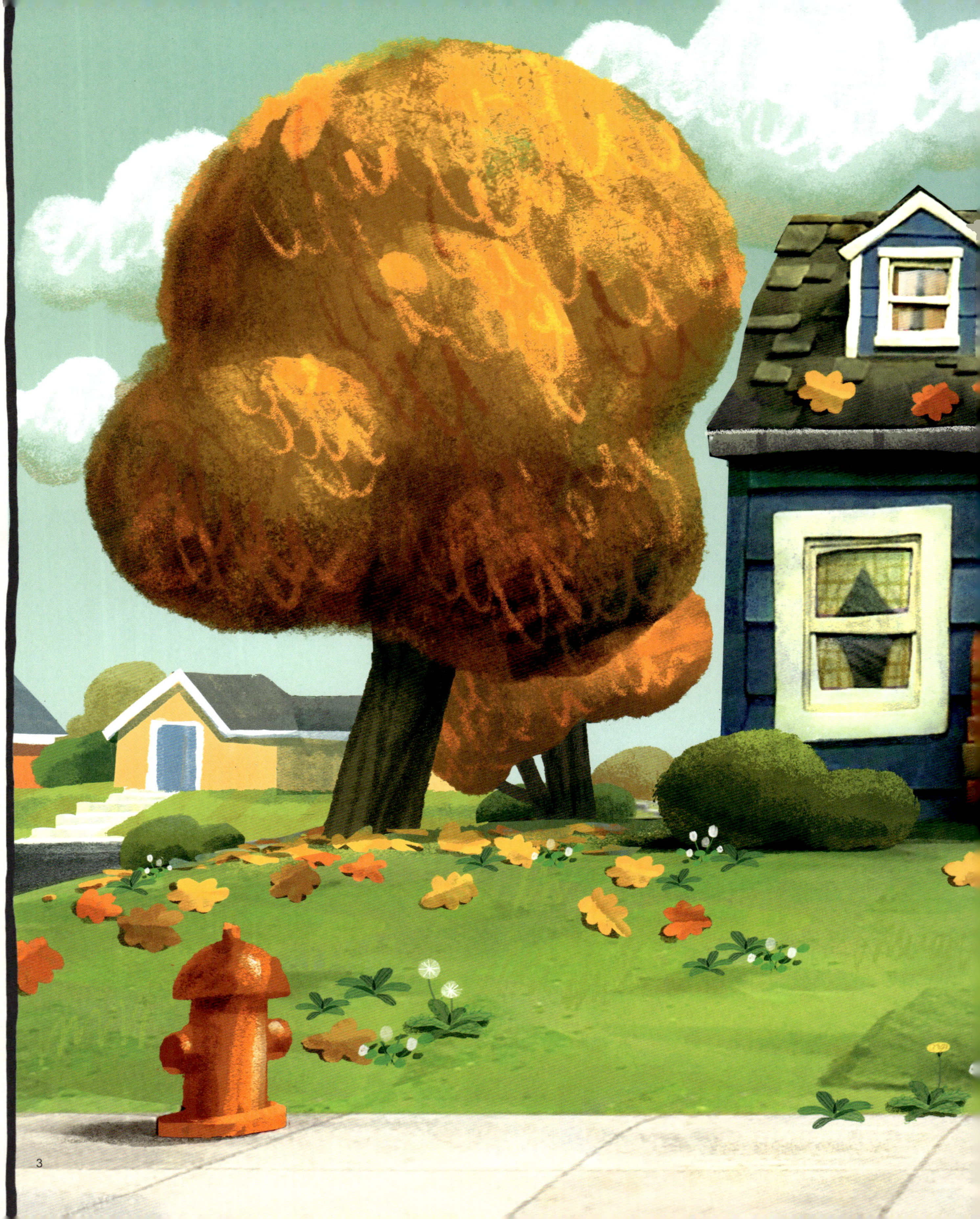

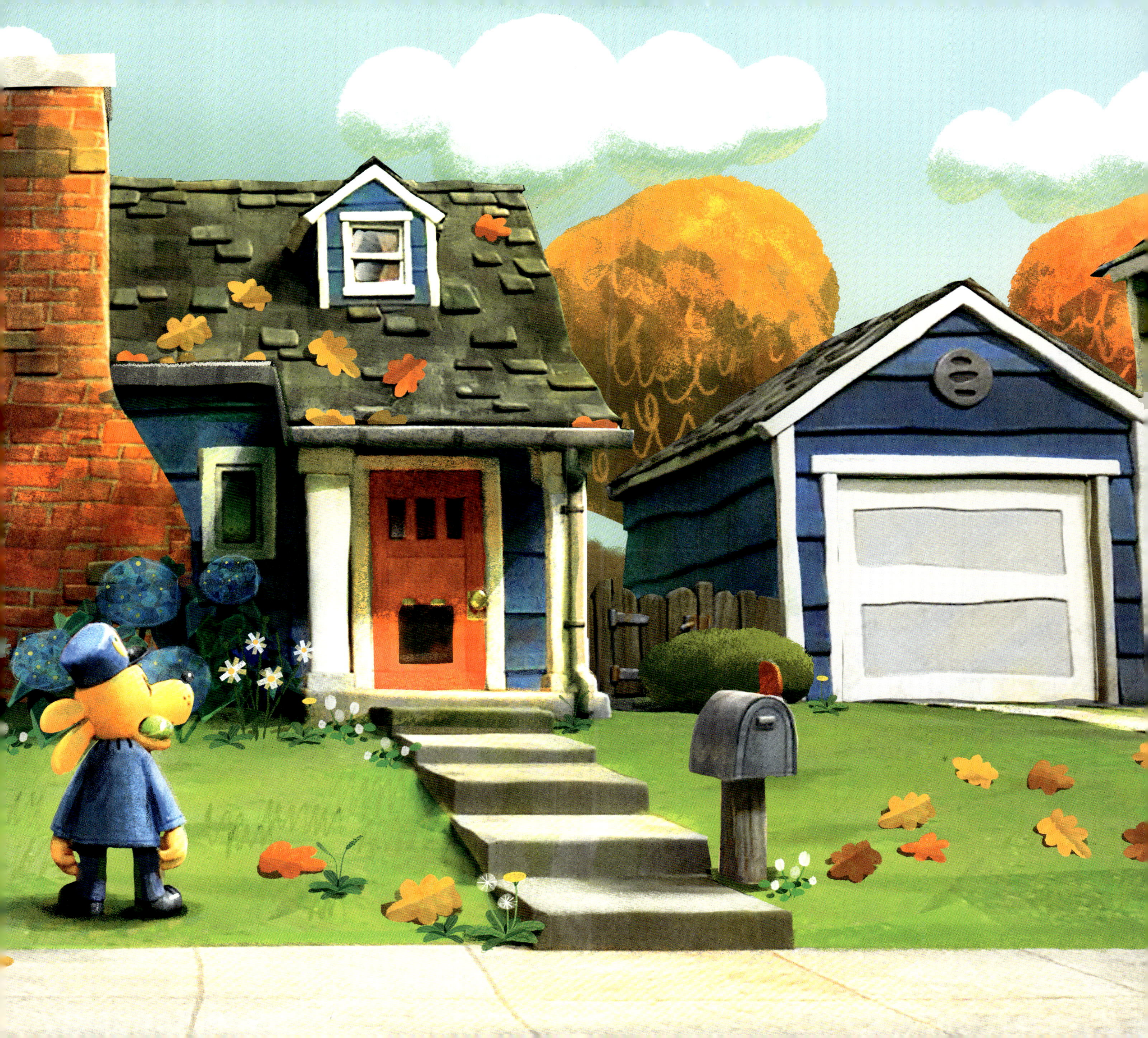

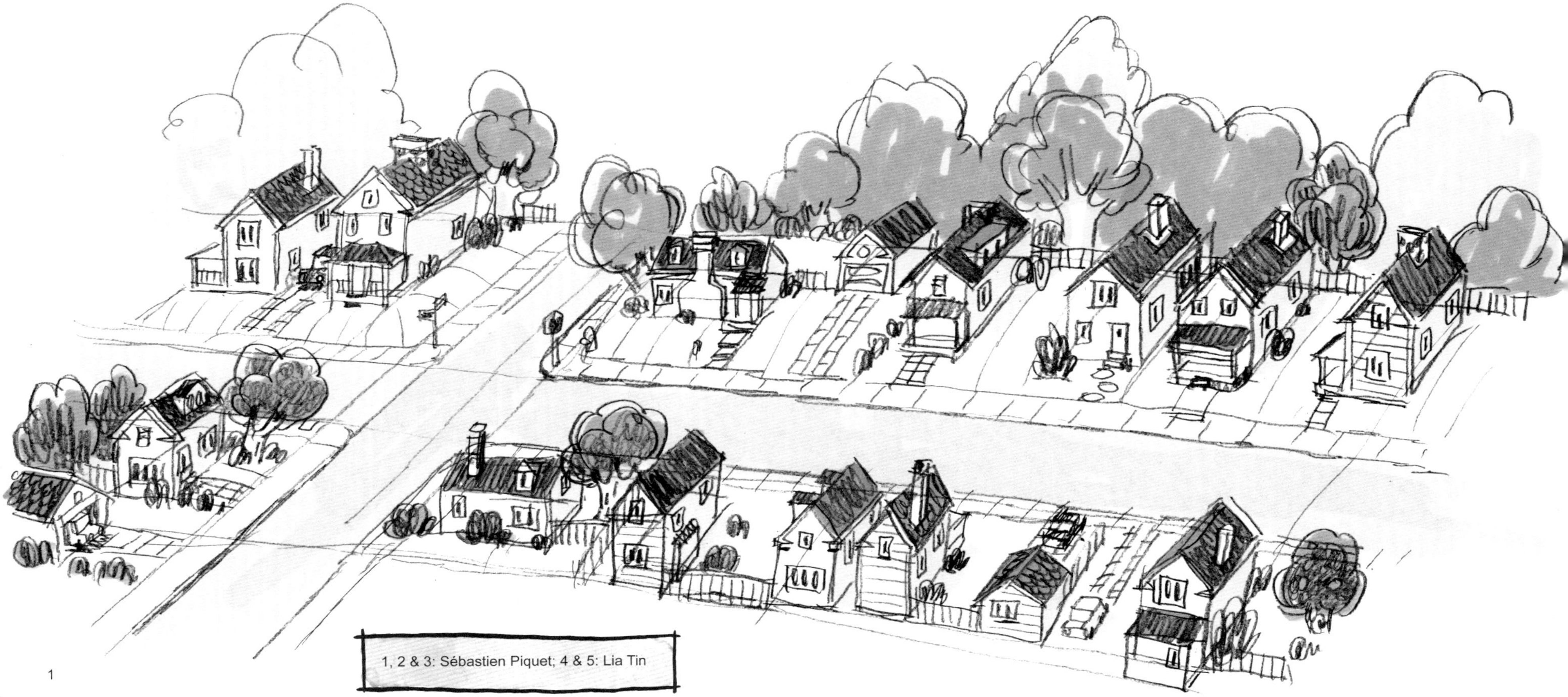

1

1, 2 & 3: Sébastien Piquet; 4 & 5: Lia Tin

2

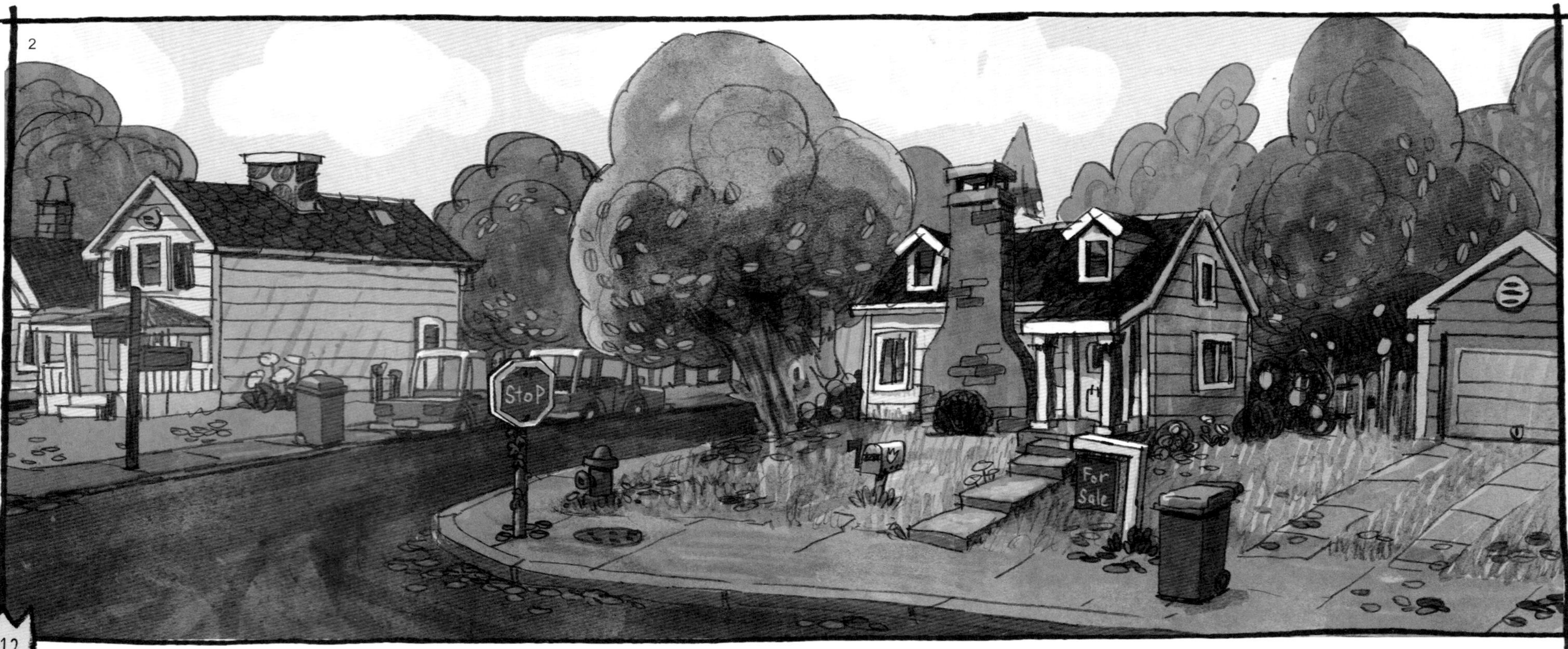

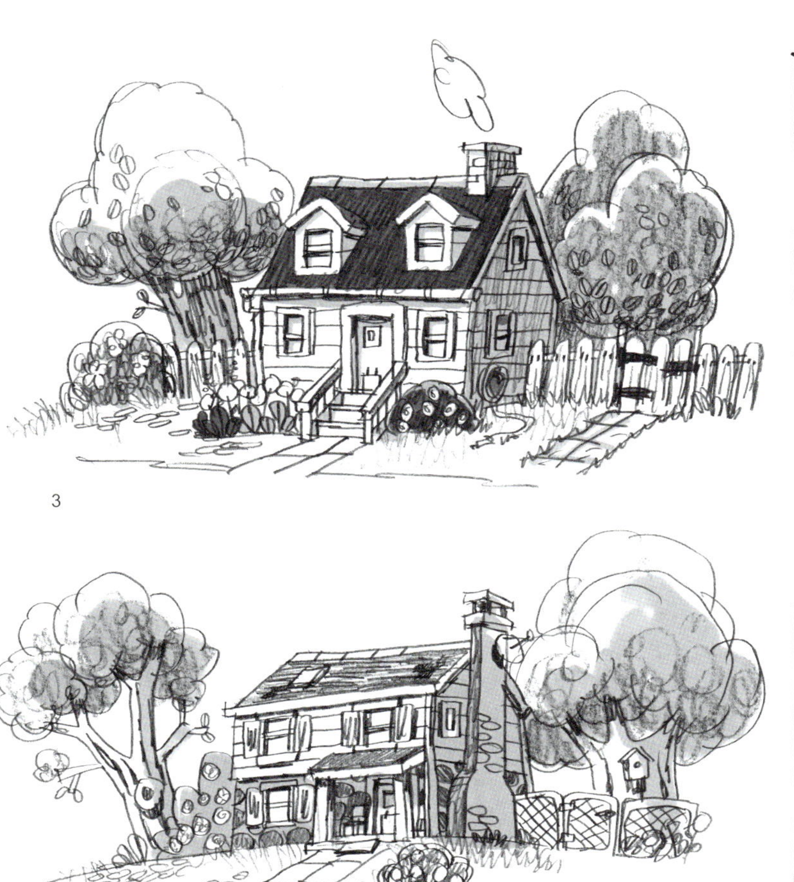

3

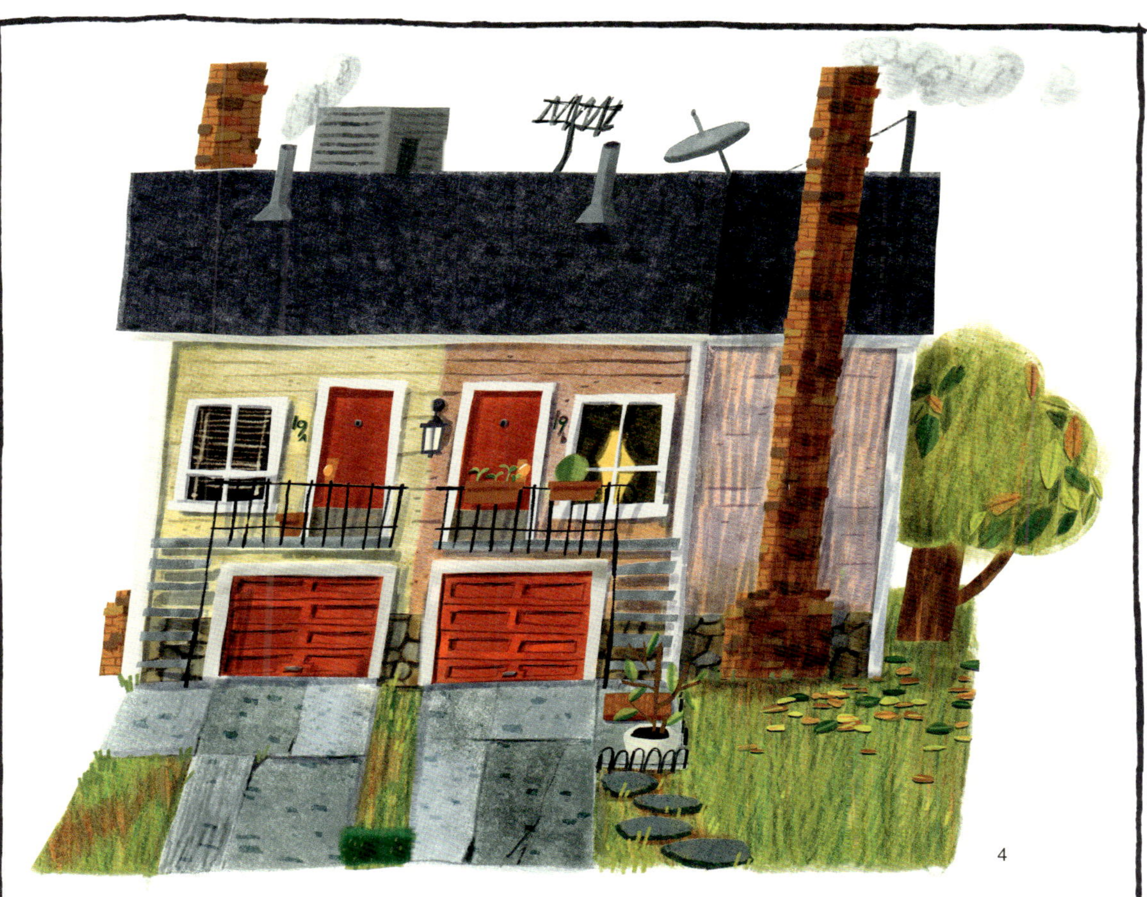

4

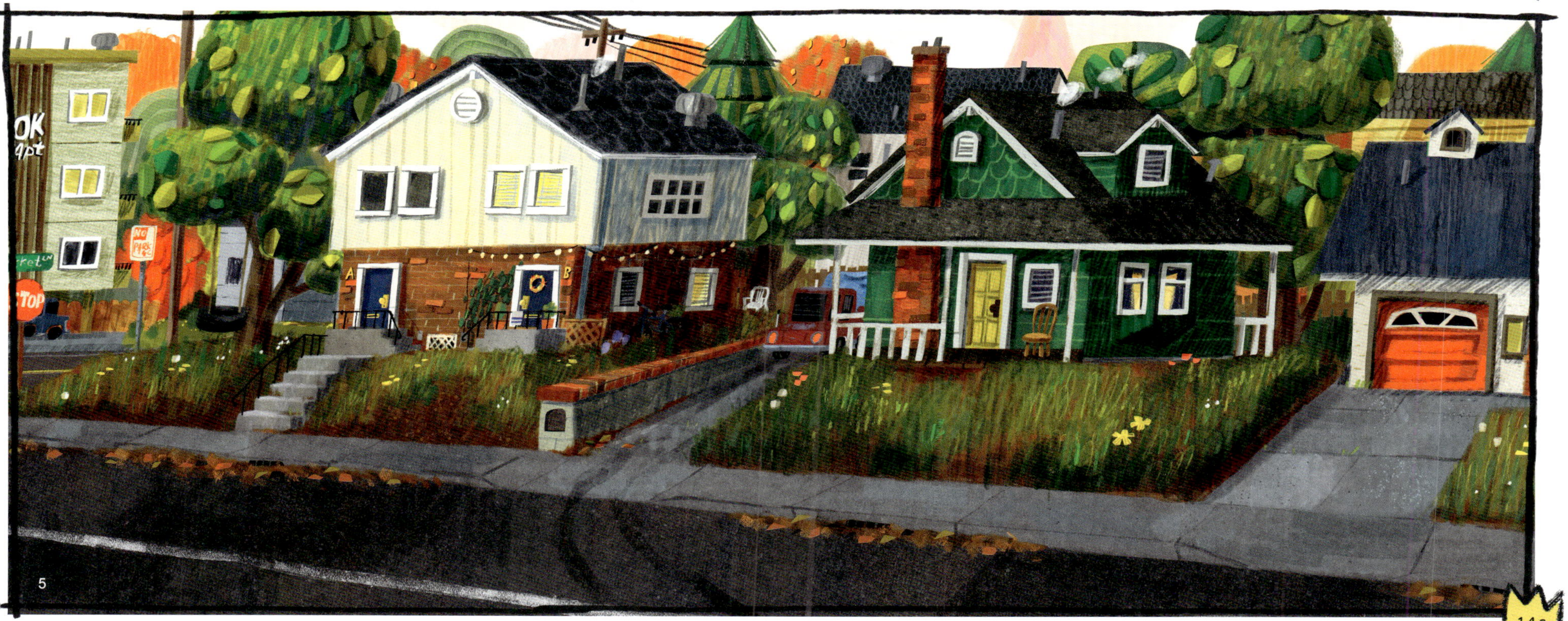

5

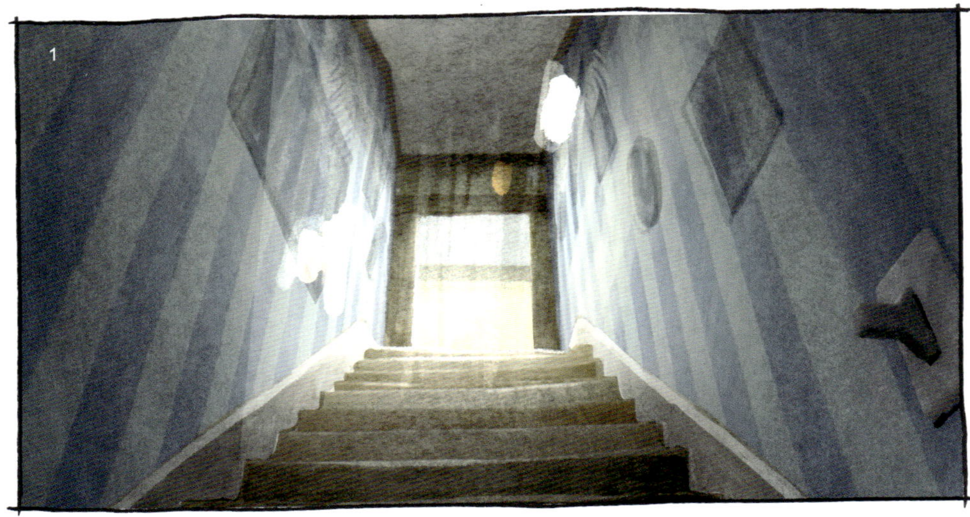
1

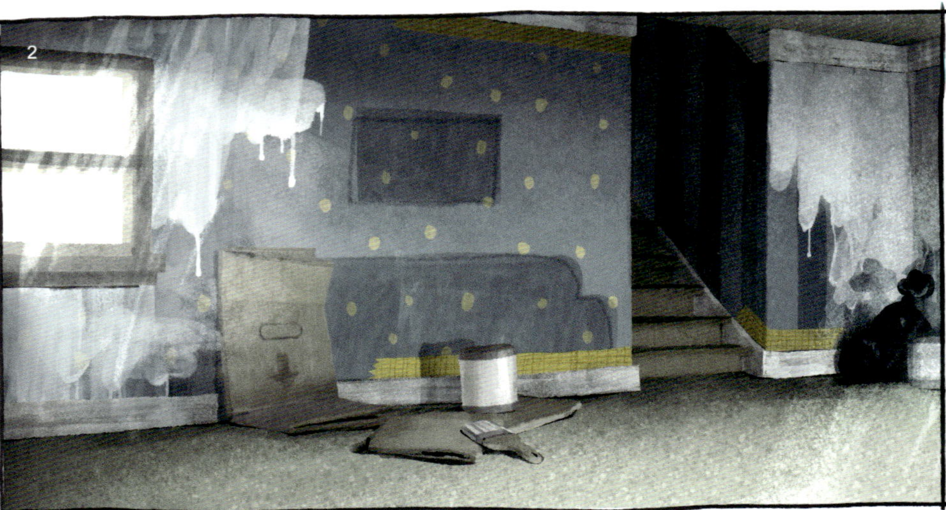
2

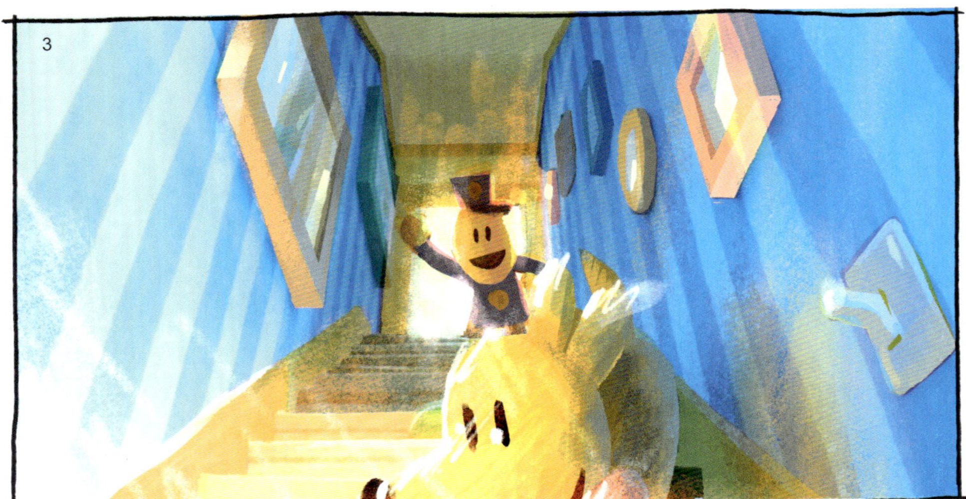
3

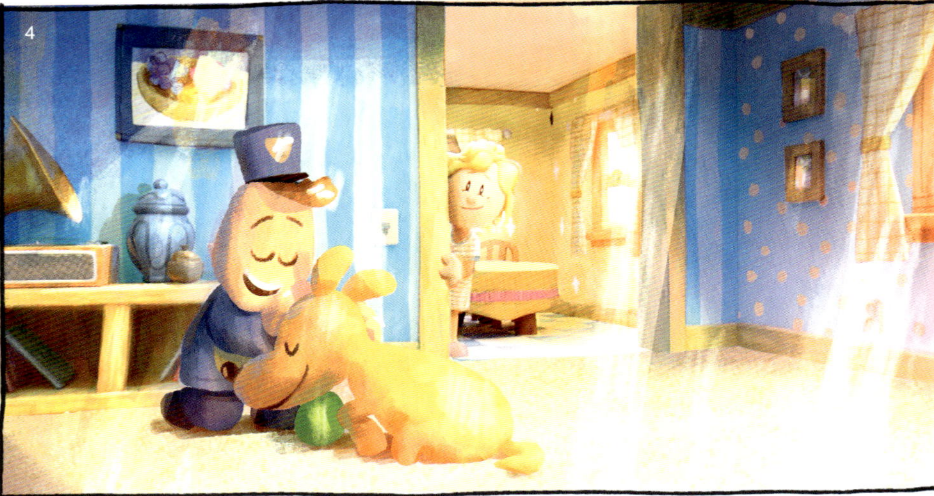
4

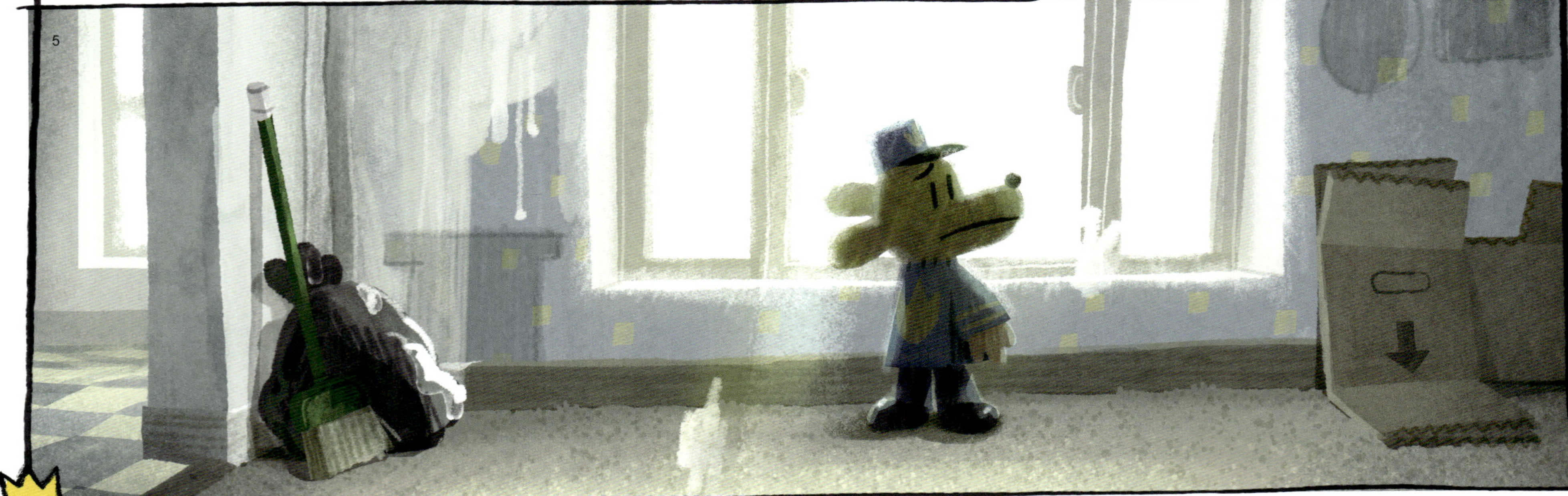
5

Alice

Alice is Officer Knight's ex-girlfriend, who leaves him when she realizes he is now part dog, part man, all hero. We only see her in Dog Man's flashbacks as he reminisces about their happy days together.

1–5: Katy Wu; 6, 9 & 10: Nate Wragg

7: ***Modeling:*** Fran Lara, Samuel Pinhorne, Andrea Trovato; ***Surfacing:*** Hannah Wong, Greta Levickyte

8: Lia Tin

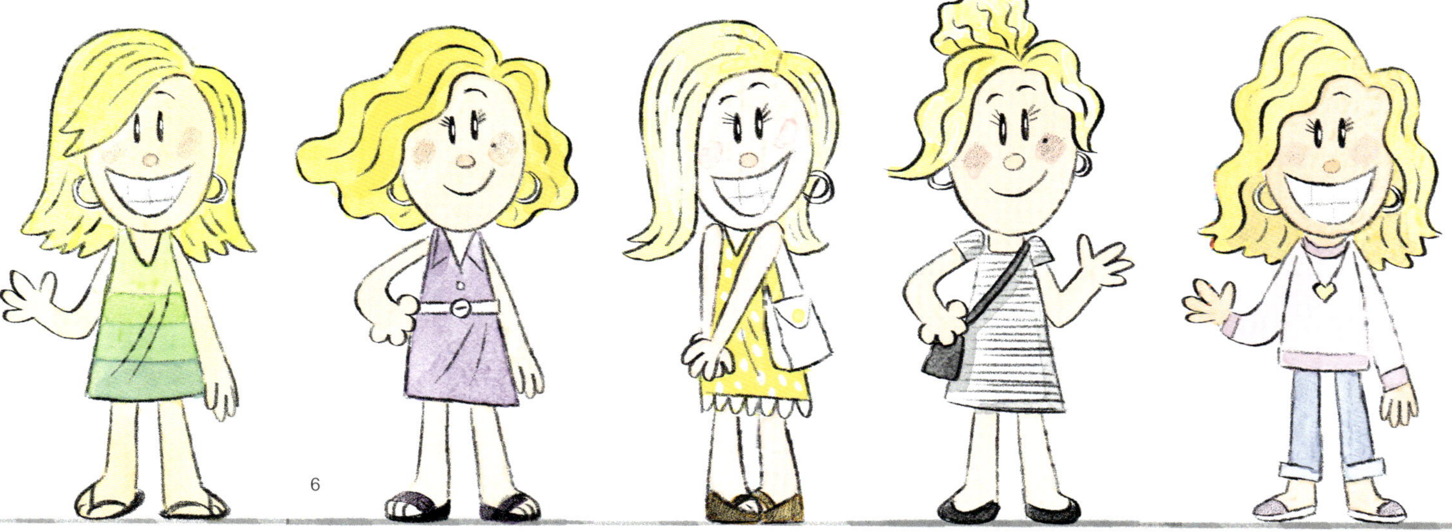

6

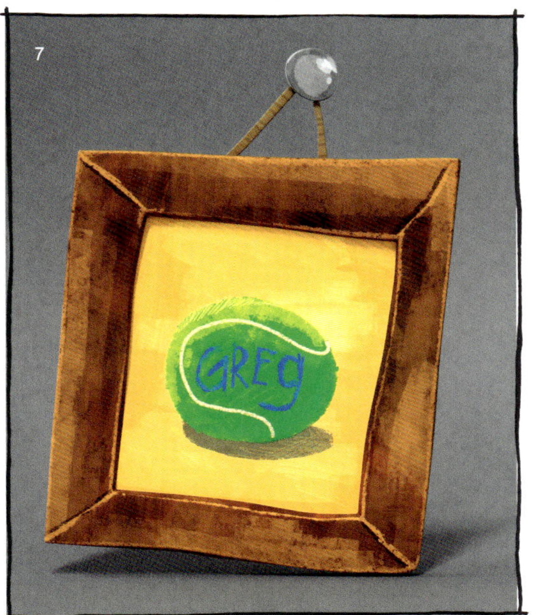

7

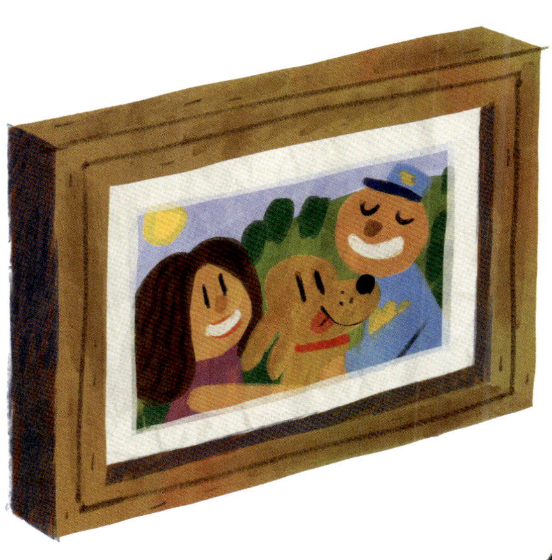

8

Real Estate Agent

An absent-minded, silly character, the agent tells Dog Man that she's selling the house because Knight's girlfriend has left him. She spills the beans about the split without any consideration for Dog Man, who is deeply affected by this turn of events.

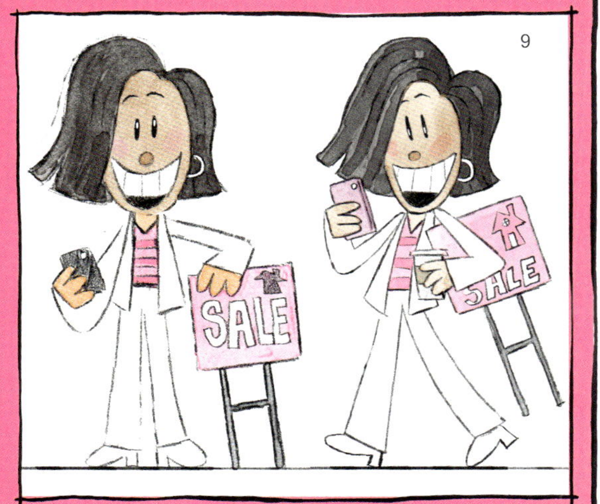

9

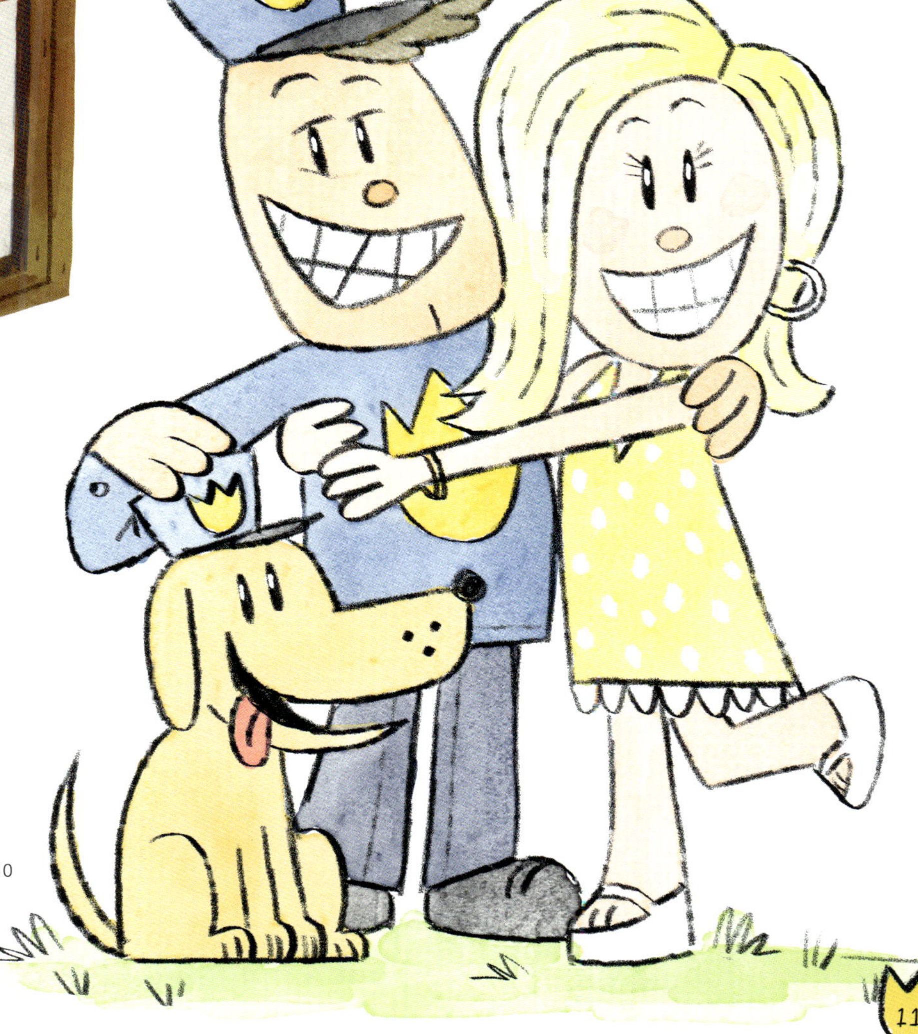

10

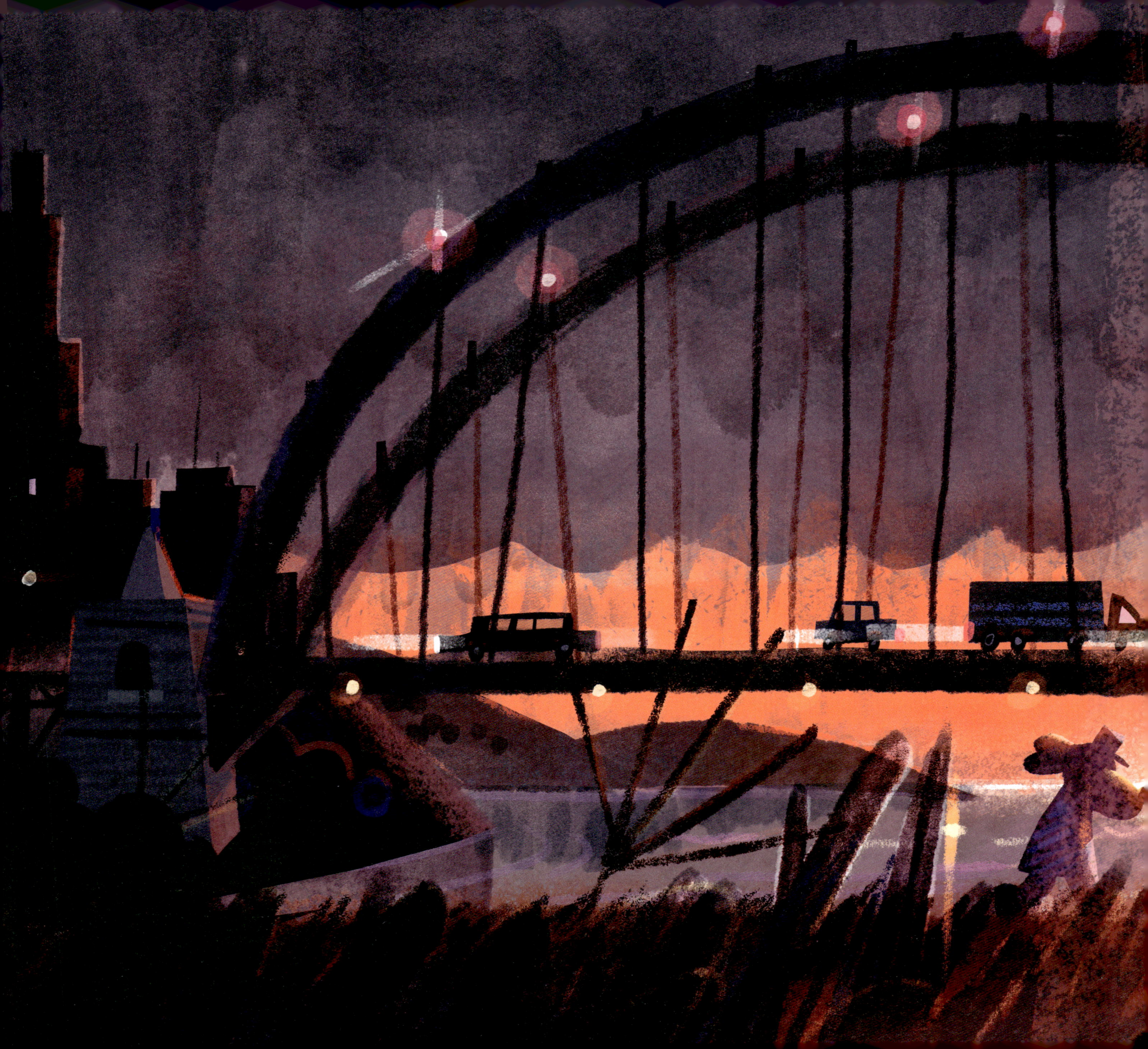

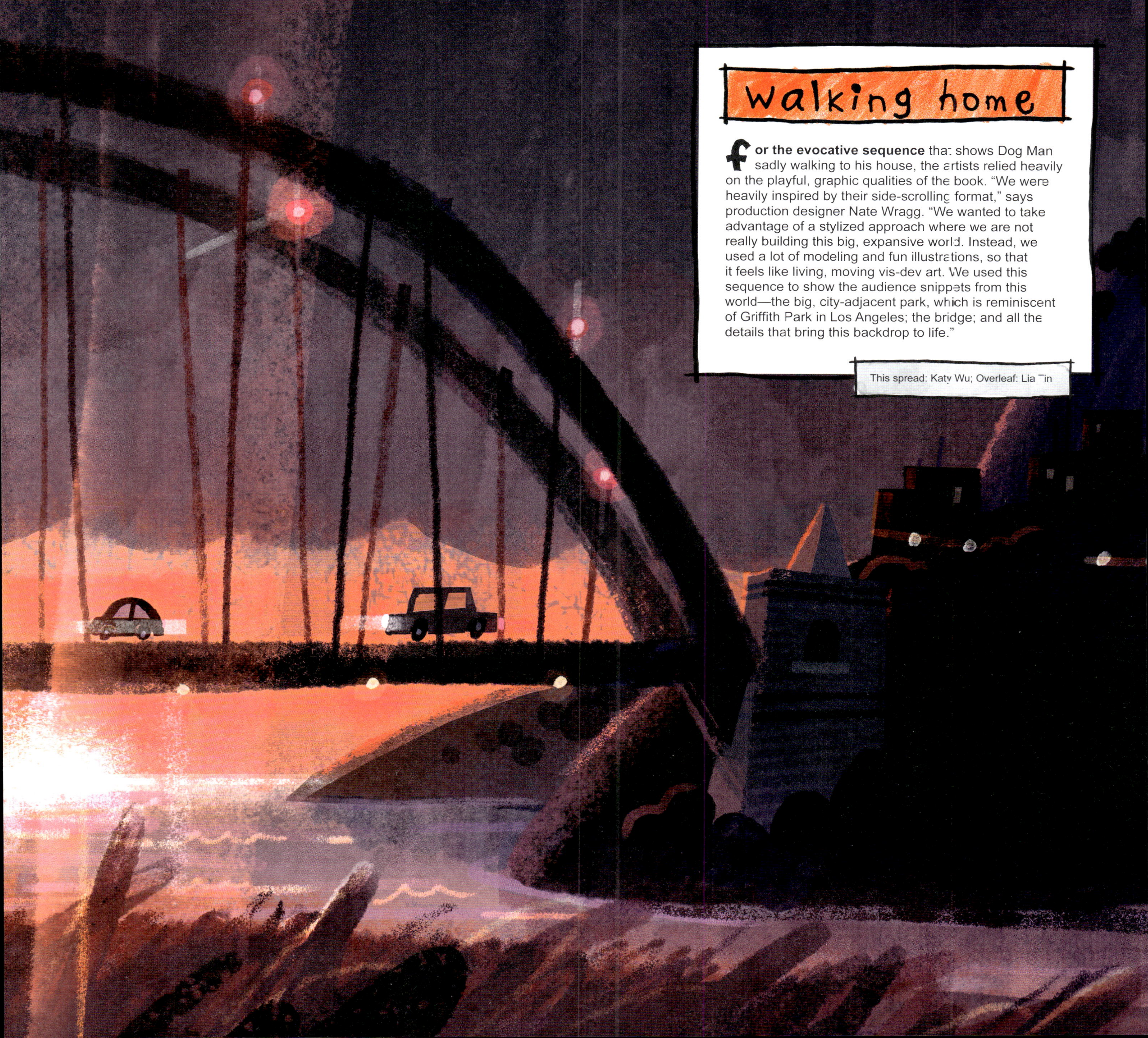

walking home

For the evocative sequence that shows Dog Man sadly walking to his house, the artists relied heavily on the playful, graphic qualities of the book. “We were heavily inspired by their side-scrolling format,” says production designer Nate Wragg. “We wanted to take advantage of a stylized approach where we are not really building this big, expansive world. Instead, we used a lot of modeling and fun illustrations, so that it feels like living, moving vis-dev art. We used this sequence to show the audience snippets from this world—the big, city-adjacent park, which is reminiscent of Griffith Park in Los Angeles; the bridge; and all the details that bring this backdrop to life.”

This spread: Katy Wu; Overleaf: Lia Tin

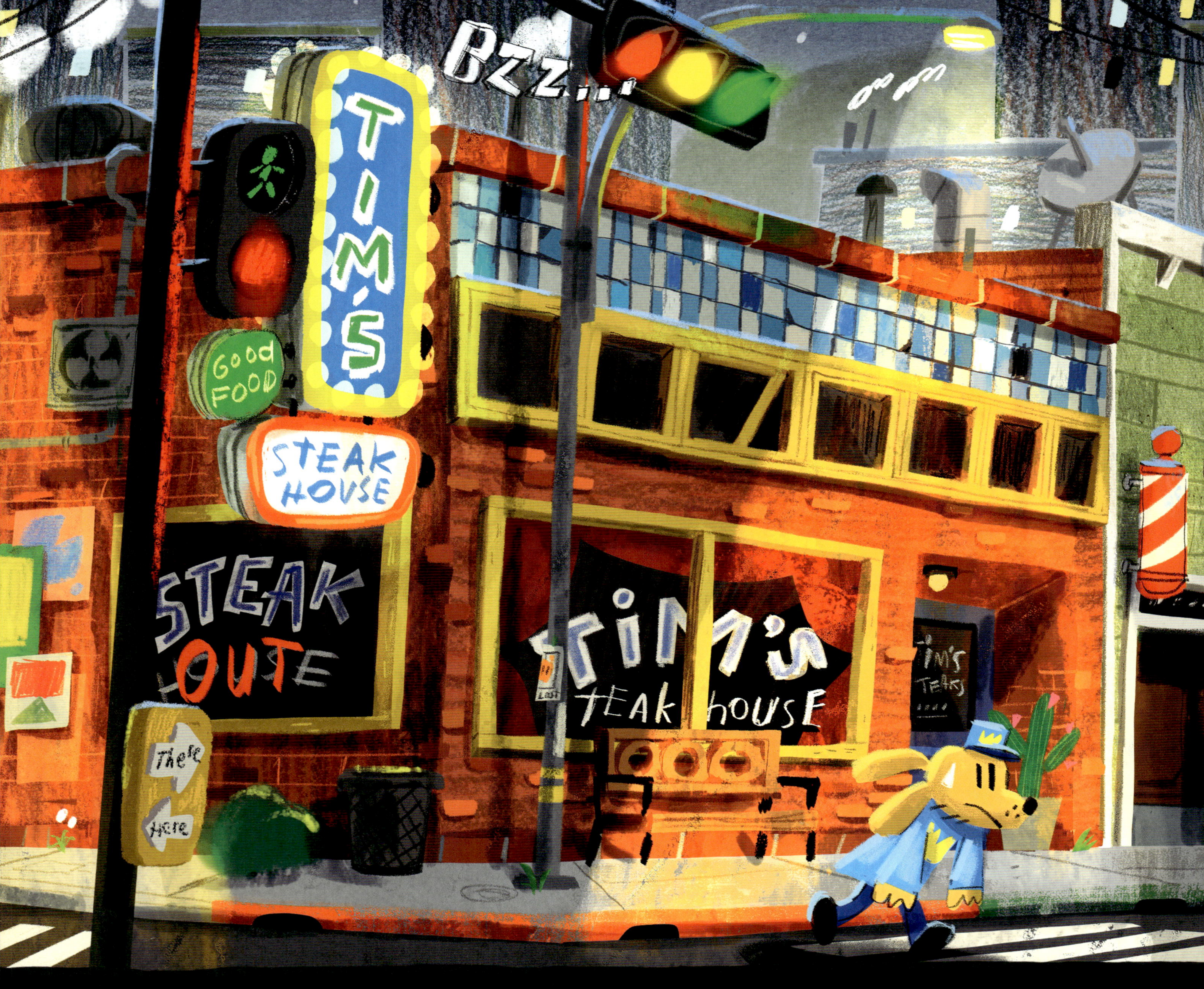

Bzz...
TIM'S
Good FOOD
STEAK HOUSE
STEAK
There
Here
TEAK HOUSE

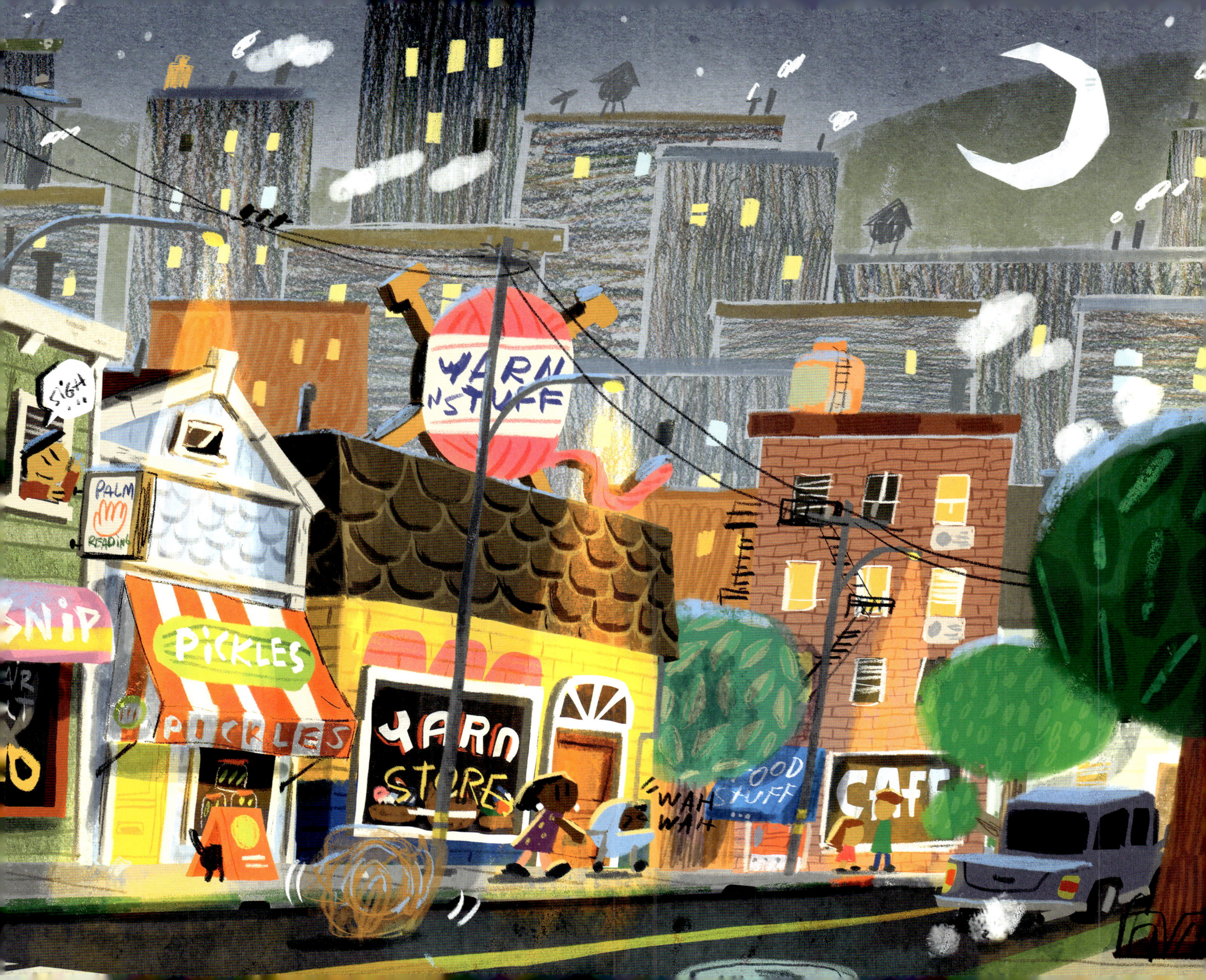
SIGH...
PALM READING
SNIP
PICKLES
PICKLES
YARN 'N STUFF
YARN STORE
WAH WAH
OOD STUFF
CAFE

Dog Man's house

Dog Man's house is designed to follow a fun cartoon logic. From the outside, it looks like it's just the size of a small doghouse. But when you enter his new house, there's a grandfather clock, a big couch, and a nice kitchen. "We wanted it to look just like the house Dav Pilkey draws in his books," says production designer Nate Wragg. "It sits on a cartoony little hill and is nicely silhouetted next to the hill. It feels a bit run-down, but when Li'l Petey moves in, he infuses all this happiness into the home, decorating it with his drawings and comics and creating a warm and inviting place. Even though Dog Man has a shared custody arrangement with Petey, he actually feels more like a big brother to Li'l Petey, so their living arrangement almost feels like how a kid would imagine a sleepover with a friend," adds Wragg. "They are making crafts and drawing comics, and we wanted to show how much fun they are having together around the house."

1

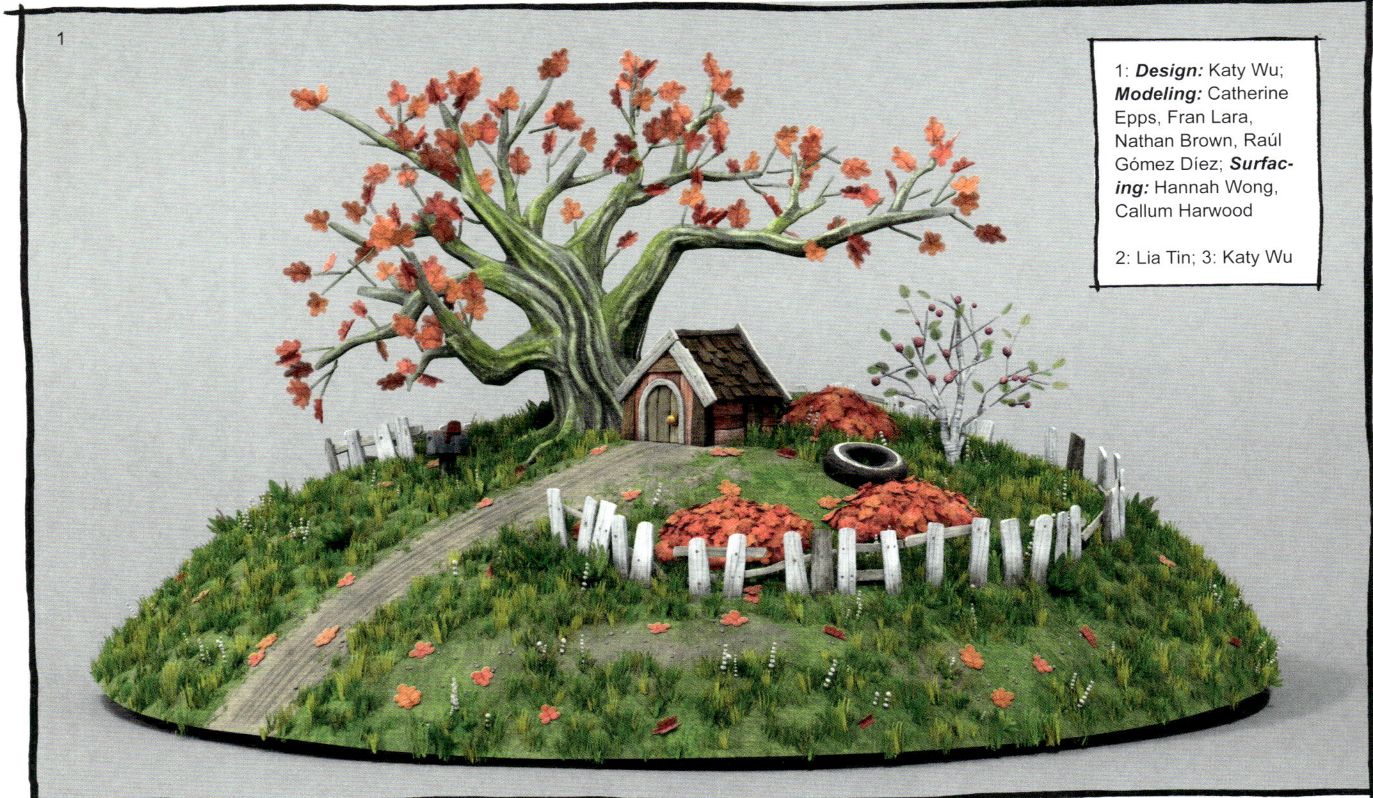

1: ***Design:*** Katy Wu; ***Modeling:*** Catherine Epps, Fran Lara, Nathan Brown, Raúl Gómez Díez; ***Surfacing:*** Hannah Wong, Callum Harwood

2: Lia Tin; 3: Katy Wu

2

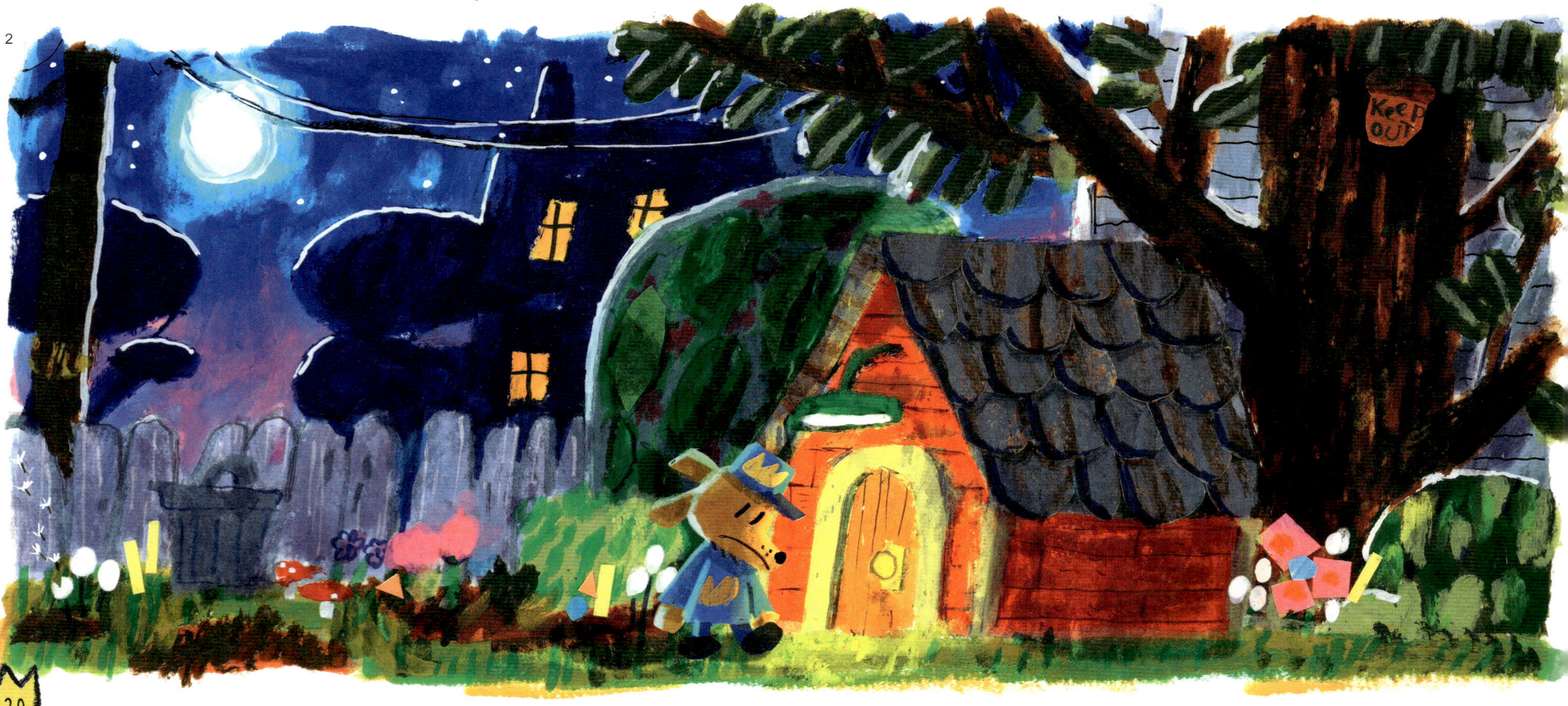

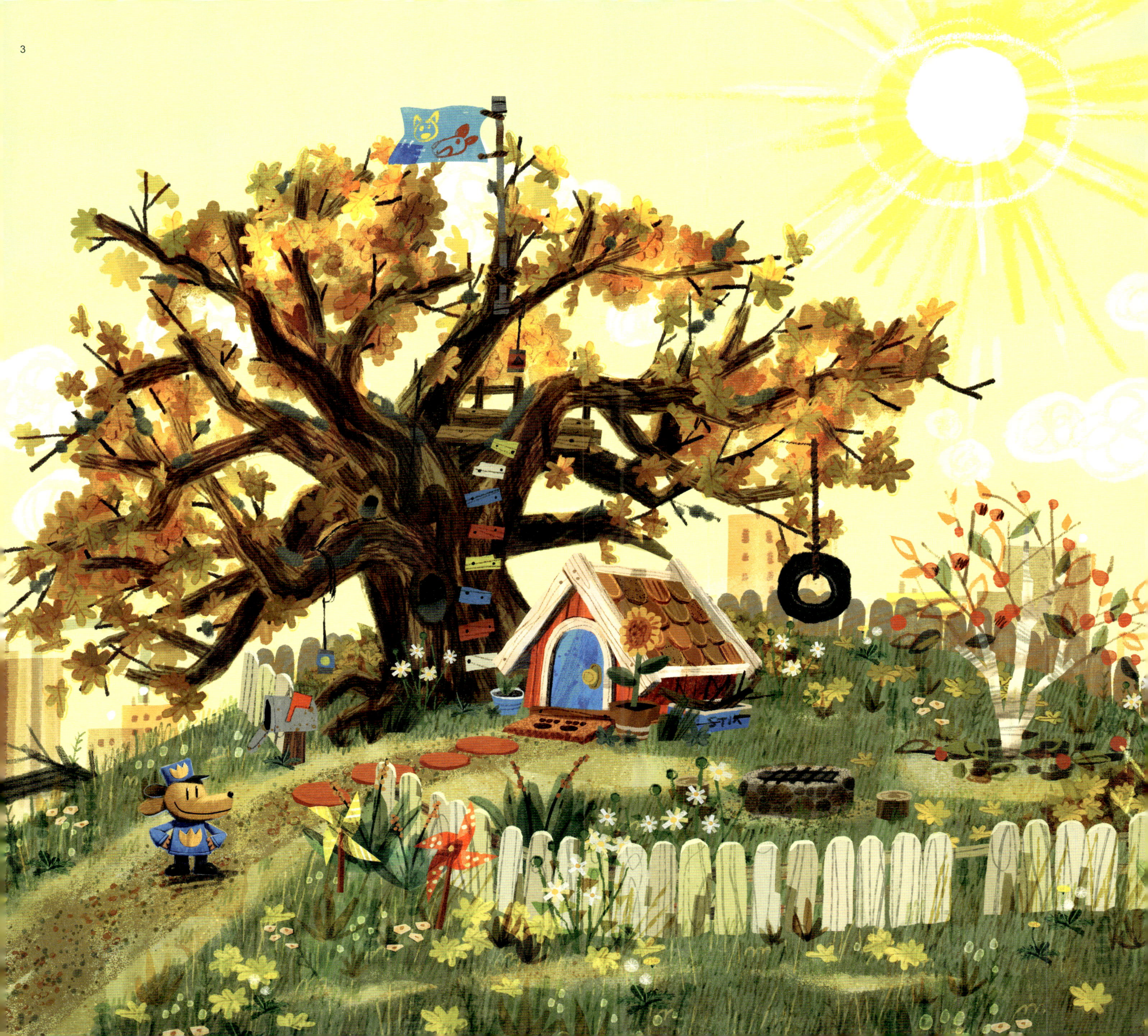
STIK

Sequence 750: Dog Man Supa Losa

One of the film's pivotal scenes, which is a great example of how the filmmakers balance moments of deeply felt emotion with great visuals and humor, is sequence 750, the "Supa Losa" interlude. It depicts one of our hero's lowest emotional moments: Dog Man has been unjustly taken off the case to find and capture Petey the Cat and demoted to a security guard detail, guarding the dead Flippy the Fish. Once he gets home, he plays the song "I'm So Lonesome I Could Cry," which aptly reflects his sorrows.

Looking back at the sequence, production designer Nate Wragg explains that parts of it were set up to closely match how they were drawn in the books. "We designed the sets and the camerawork to feel very flat and graphic to enhance the style of not only this sequence but the look and feel of our movie," he recalls. "Parts of the end of this sequence are also shot in a flat and graphic way but designed to give the audience the feeling that Dog Man's house is a bit toylike, almost as if it were a dollhouse cut in half."

Eventually, the sequence ended up being a mix of 3D (CG) models, digital matte painting (DMP), and After Effects. "Our character is a 3D element, walking on 3D sets, but our set extensions were all done with DMP and After Effects to give the world a more illustrated look and feel as it expands out," explains Wragg. "Our biggest challenge was finding a balance between the 3D sets and the 2D set extensions. We had to make sure that the audience couldn't feel the separation or seams where the two parts connected. We wanted them to get lost in this illustrated 3D world and not be able to see how we did it."

"This scene is a great example of 'sad/funny,'" says the film's head of story, Anthony Zierhut (*Puss in Boots: The Last Wish*; *The Croods: A New Age*). "Yes, Dog Man is very sad and lonely, but his choice of listening to a very old country song by the legendary Hank Williams is kind of random and over-the-top. Dog Man reverts, in his emotional state, to his dog nature and howls along with the music. As he passes a photo of his old life as Greg the Dog and Officer Knight with his girlfriend, Alice, posing happily in front of their now-sold home, Dog Man is again overcome with emotion and embraces the photo. This is funny because he's already walked away from it, but unexpectedly comes back and howls even louder."

"The main challenge was keeping it true to the honest human emotion of sadness, loss, and loneliness, yet giving it the twist of having him react as a dog would," adds Zierhut. "This shows the dichotomy of Dog Man's existence: part dog, part man. And it shows it in a very funny way.

This spread: Lia Tin

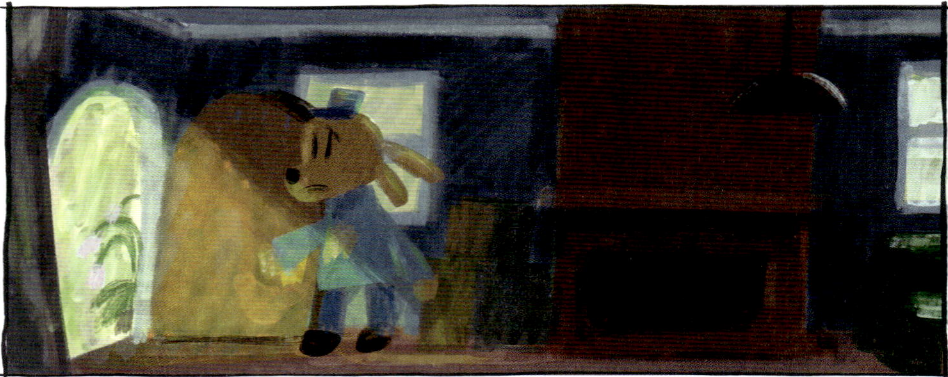

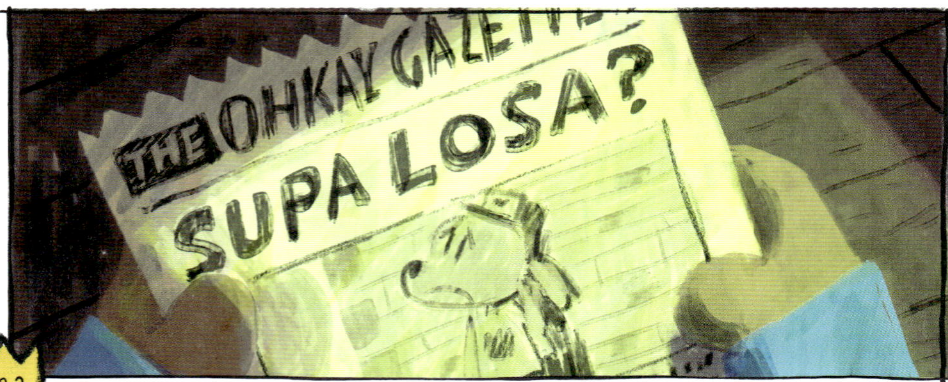

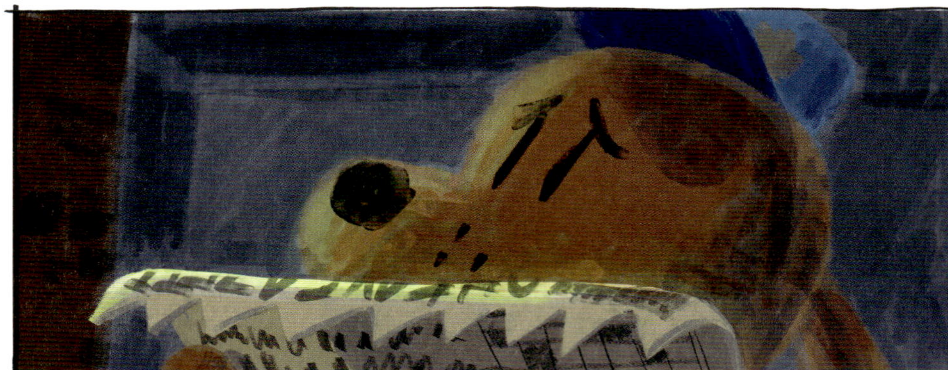

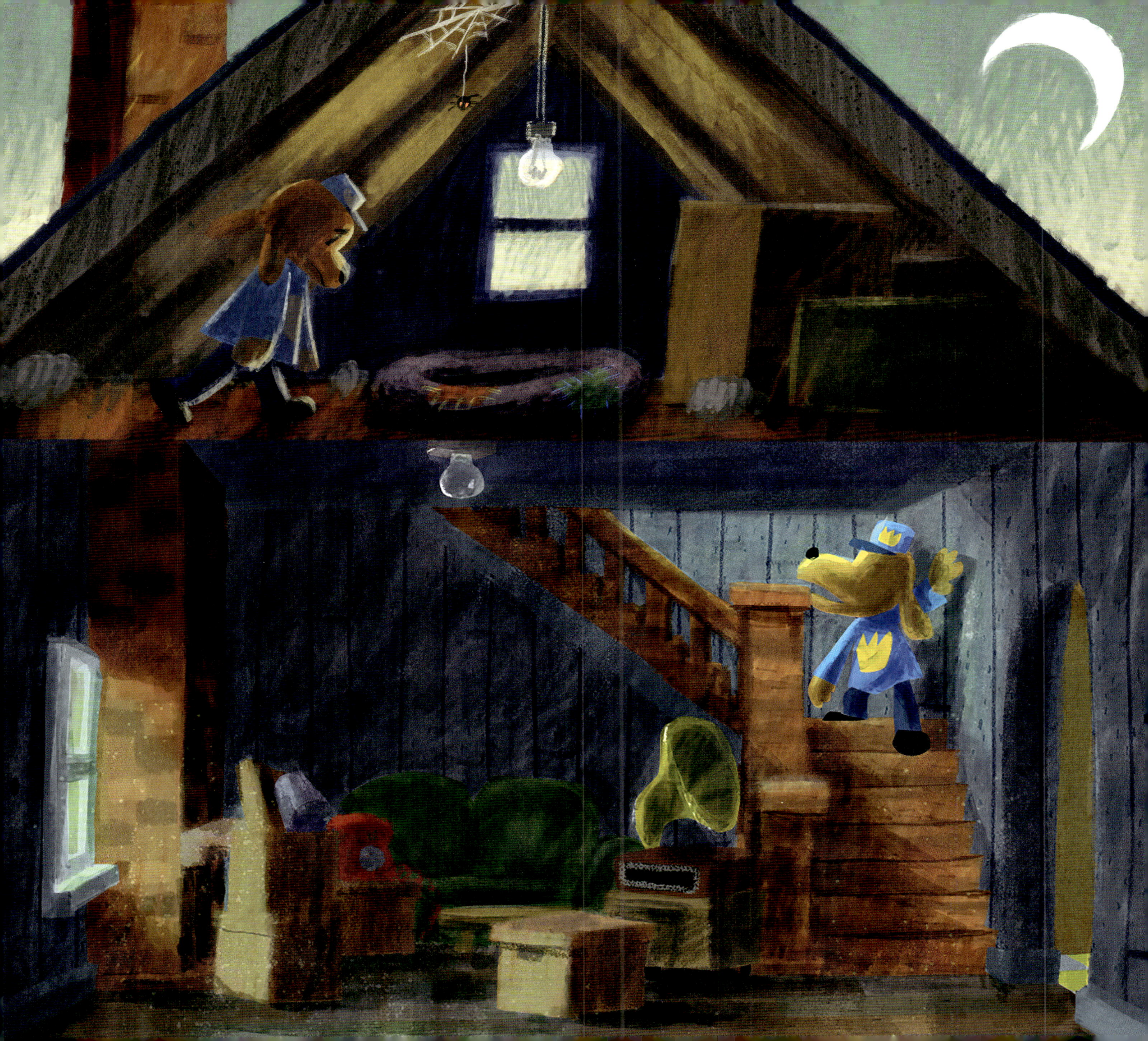

I love Marceline Tanguay's storyboards for the scene. They perfectly captured the sad/funny mood. Her acting in the storyboards made us all laugh in the editing room and translated well to the finished scene."

Head of layout Scott Cullen recalls that this sequence was the first of a group of different travel sequences in the movie, so he and his team wanted to shoot it in a unique and recognizable way. "We used long lenses and linear camera moves to achieve a similar stylized look from the art," he points out. "Technically, we wanted it to feel like one long, continuous shot of Dog Man walking across different sets without doing something simple like cross dissolves. There were many different variations that we tried, such as where the background swaps over a single frame and using different foreground elements to wipe the different backgrounds on. Ultimately, we ended up going with Dog Man walking continuously in the foreground with the different sets and backgrounds dissolving behind him, which we then revisited in the same way throughout the other travel sequences across the film."

Head of character animation John Hill mentions that it's not often that one character is featured in a completely nonspeaking sequence in an animated movie. "It was a challenge to convey all the emotion and colors of Dog Man with our limited designed character facial features," he says. "This attempt to allow the humor to come from him reacting to the situation also had to be true to his character."

Hill also points out that stylistically, the movie's character animation was done mostly on twos (one image per two frames) and only occasionally on ones (one image per frame). "This crafted a subtle handmade feel to the motion of the characters in this world. As our face designs are similar to the books, they are simple and economical, but they need to convey a complex range of emotions. Our mantra throughout the film was 'less is more.'"

One challenge was animating Dog Man's unique design from unwanted angles. "His iconic ears required some unique posing from animation and special treatment when rendered to feel perfectly natural for him," explains Hill. "In profile, Dog Man's ears are on the far side of his head, with movable points that connect to his head that aren't seen by the audience. This look is straight from Dav Pilkey's books. It also gets tricky when we move from that kind of profile ear pose to another where they hang from the sides of his head. We generally use that pose when he is feeling low or downcast. Transitioning between the two types of ear designs was done through careful animation from the team and not lingering in the transitions."

Dog Man's mouth introduced its own set of challenges. As Hill points out, "We wanted a range of design shapes that required some R & D to get something working for our director. Jellyfish Pictures created a small team led by Tim Gibson to develop a workable mouth rig and robust controls. In the end, we found success with a simplistic look for his mouth shapes, but it required some complicated controls to be developed. His mouth is by far the most complex in our cast of characters."

"All said, working on the production's knowns and unknowns with good people is key to keeping one's artistic soul alive," concludes Hill. "More important, that's how a good movie can become great!"

1: Katy Wu; 2 & 3: Marceline Tanguay

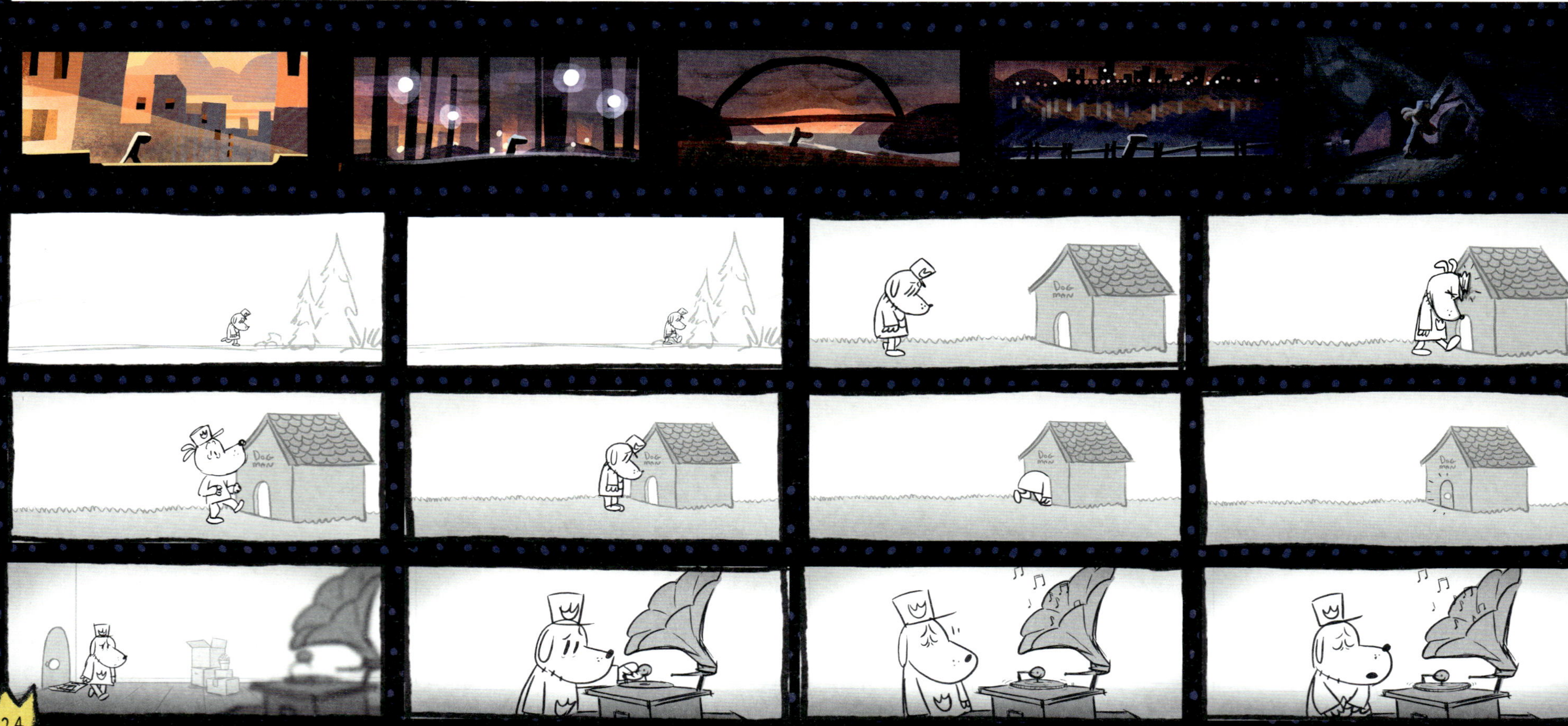

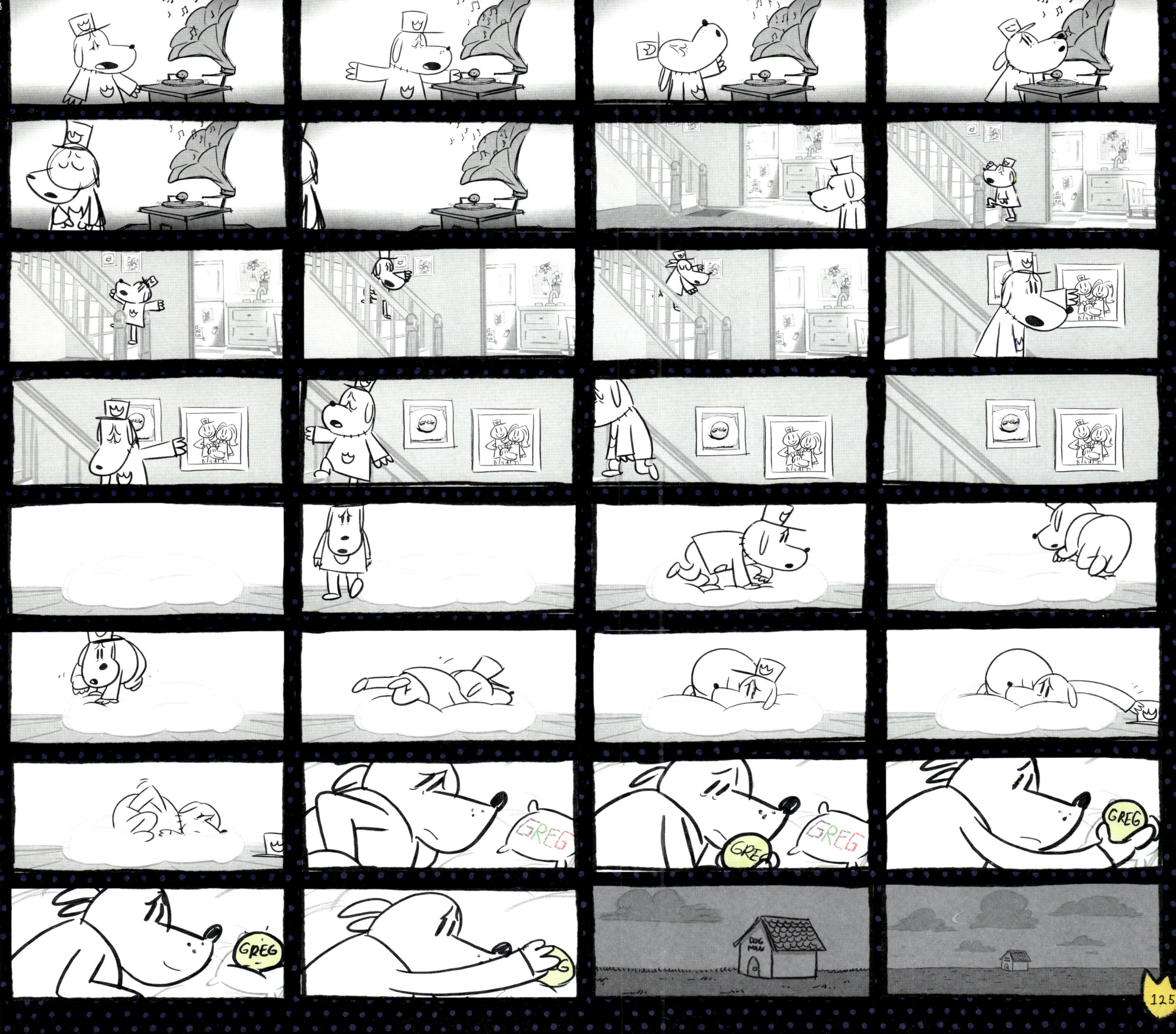
GREG
GREG
GREG
GREG
GREG

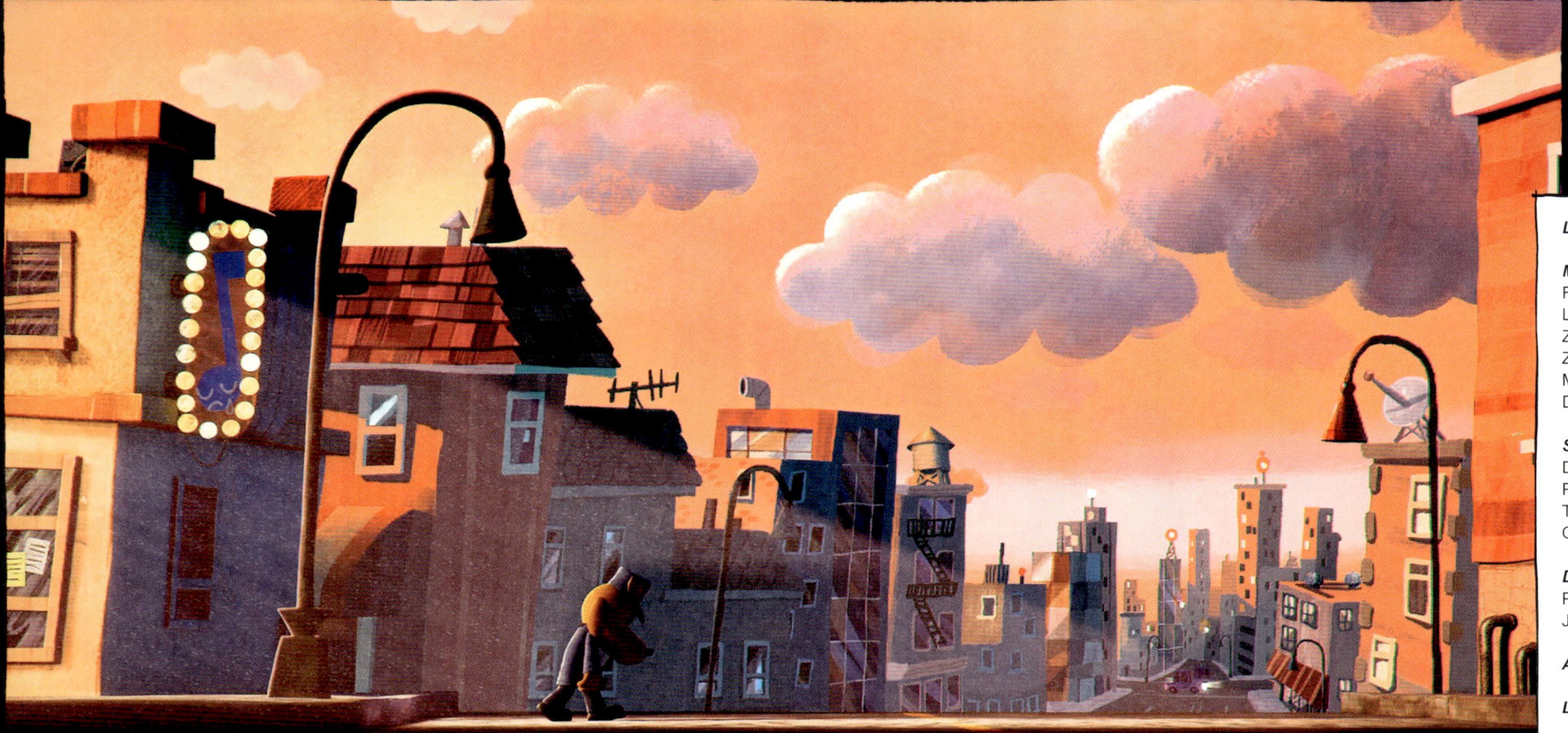

Layout: Tom Bruno

Modeling: Sarah von Fersen, Fran Lara, Luca Doran, Athanasios Zagkliveris, Carina Bichler, Zoe Arabella Lane, Maddalena Delvecchio, Daniel Olah

Surfacing: Hannah Wong, Daniele La Mura, Peter Hargan, Heather Truman, Virginia Daniele, Catherine Epps

Digital Matte Painting: Paul Phippen, Anh Cao, Jon Kiefert

Animation: Daniel Escobar

Lighting: Saul Barreto

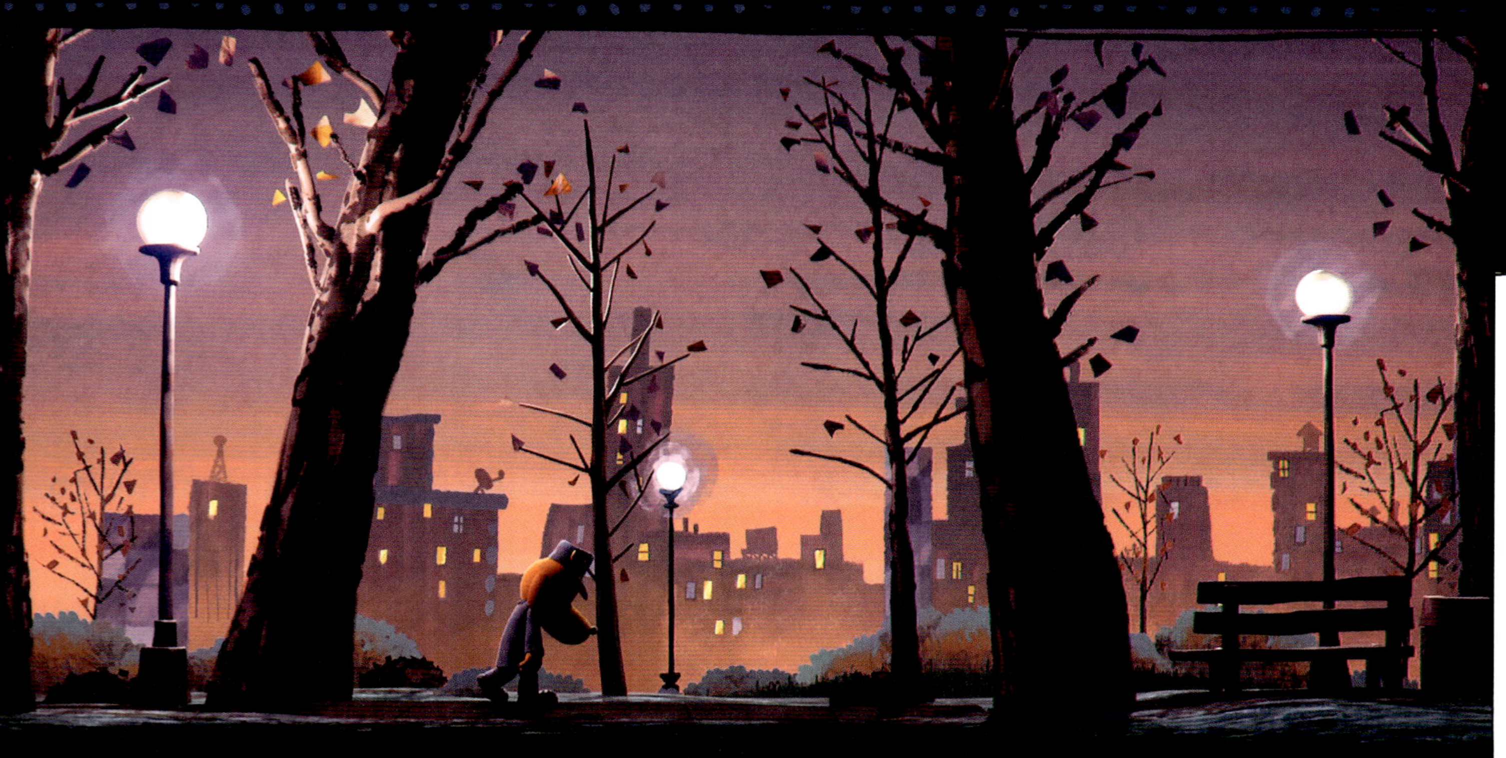

Layout: Tom Bruno

Modeling: Sarah von Fersen, Fran Lara, Catherine Epps, Romain Bivar Segurado, Alberto de la Guía Marín, Carina Bichler, Zoe Arabella Lane, Daniel Olah, Maddalena Delvecchio

Surfacing: Hannah Wong, Daniele La Mura, Stanley Cornwell, Leopoldine Perdrix

Digital Matte Painting: Paul Phippen, Anh Cao, Jon Kiefert

Animation: Daniel Escobar

Lighting: Saul Barreto

This spread: Katy Wu, Christopher Zibach, Nate Wragg

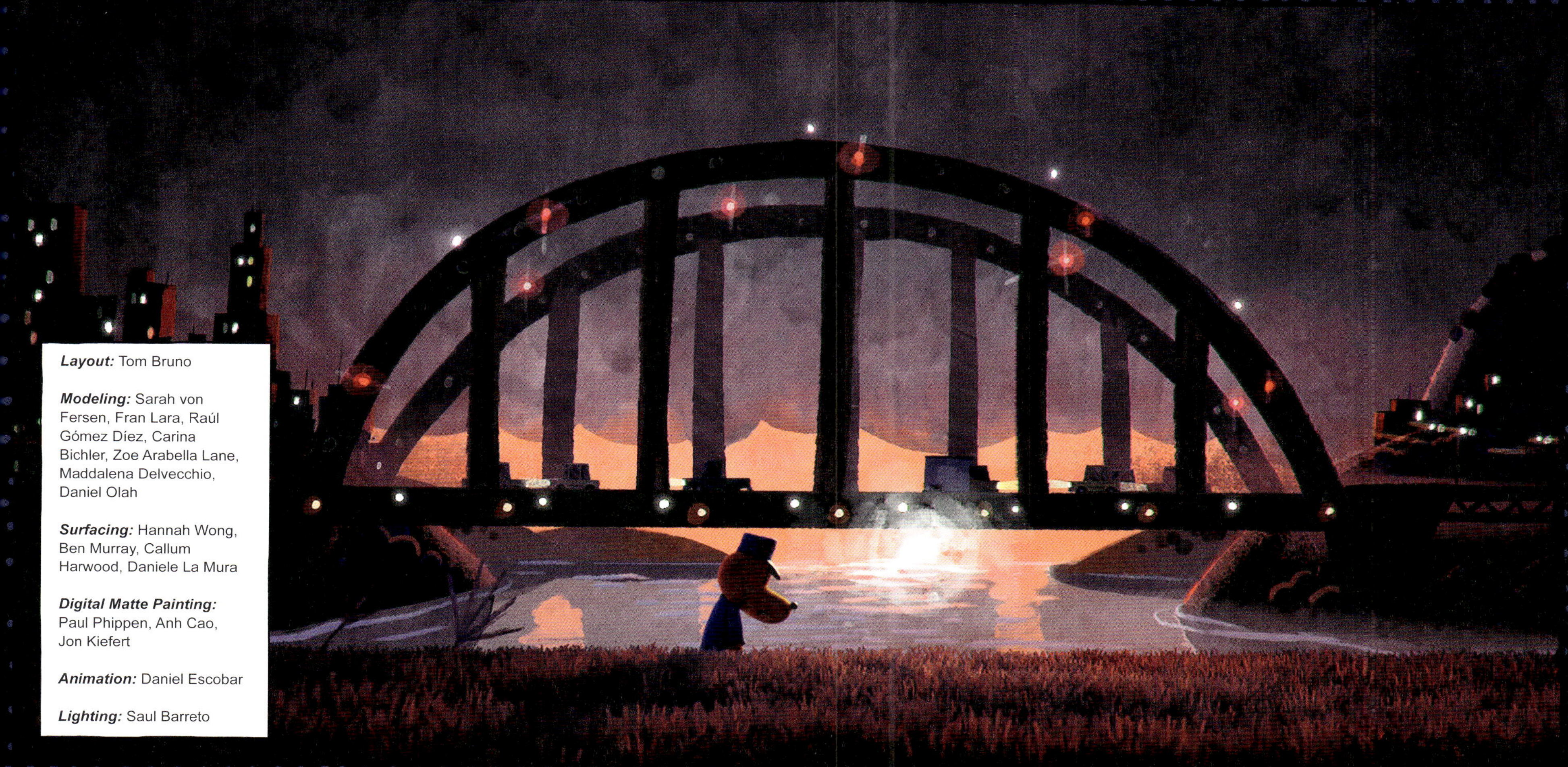

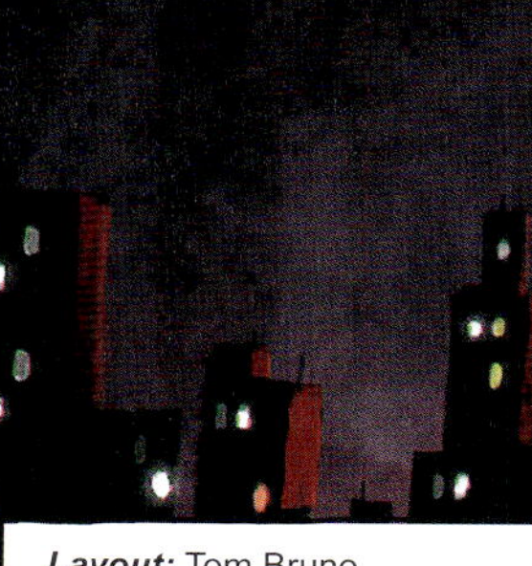

Layout: Tom Bruno

Modeling: Sarah von Fersen, Fran Lara, Raúl Gómez Díez, Carina Bichler, Zoe Arabella Lane, Maddalena Delvecchio, Daniel Olah

Surfacing: Hannah Wong, Ben Murray, Callum Harwood, Daniele La Mura

Digital Matte Painting: Paul Phippen, Anh Cao, Jon Kiefert

Animation: Daniel Escobar

Lighting: Saul Barreto

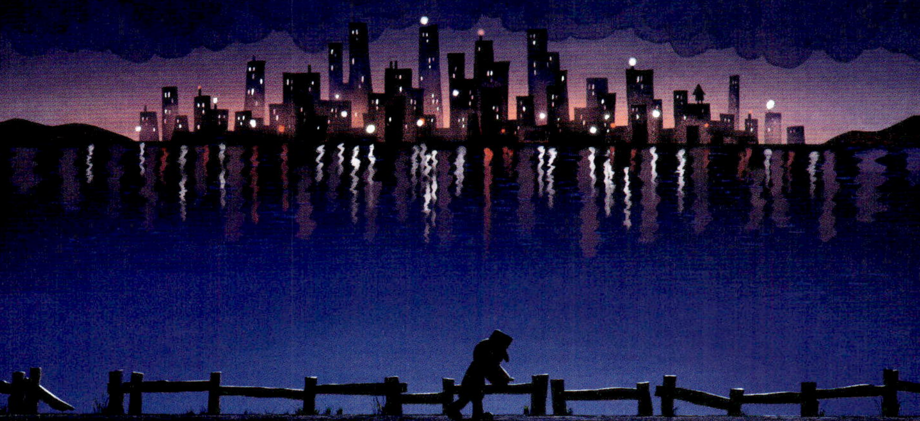

Layout: Tom Bruno

Modeling: Sarah von Fersen, Fran Lara, Raúl Gómez Díez, Catherine Epps, Carina Bichler, Zoe Arabella Lane, Maddalena Delvecchio, Daniel Olah

Surfacing: Hannah Wong, Daniele La Mura, Callum Harwood, Suzanne Lokker, Greta Levickyte, Marion Morgante, Catherine Epps, Virginia Daniele

Digital Matte Painting: Paul Phippen, Anh Cao, Jon Kiefert

Animation: Daniel Escobar

Lighting: Saul Barreto

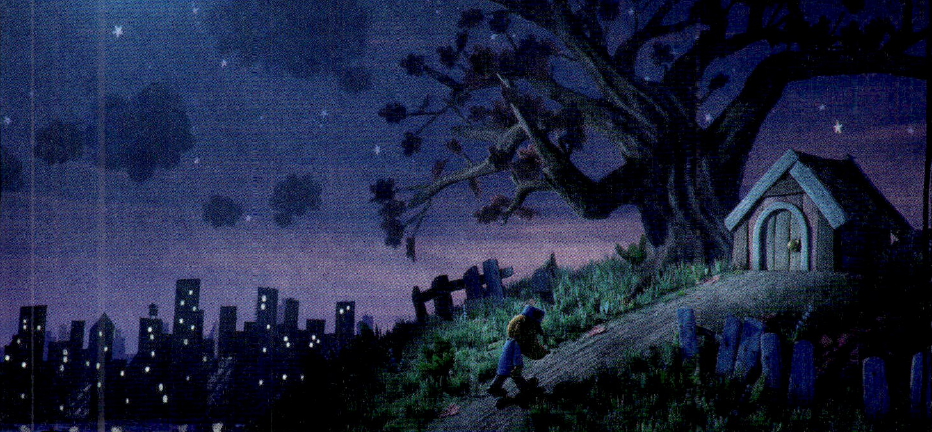

Layout: Tom Bruno

Modeling: Sarah von Fersen, Fran Lara, Raúl Gómez Díez, Catherine Epps, Carina Bichler, Zoe Arabella Lane, Maddalena Delvecchio, Daniel Olah

Surfacing: Hannah Wong, Daniele La Mura, Callum Harwood, Suzanne Lokker, Greta Levickyte, Marion Morgante, Catherine Epps, Virginia Daniele

Digital Matte Painting: Paul Phippen, Anh Cao, Jon Kiefert

Animation: Daniel Escobar

Lighting: Saul Barreto

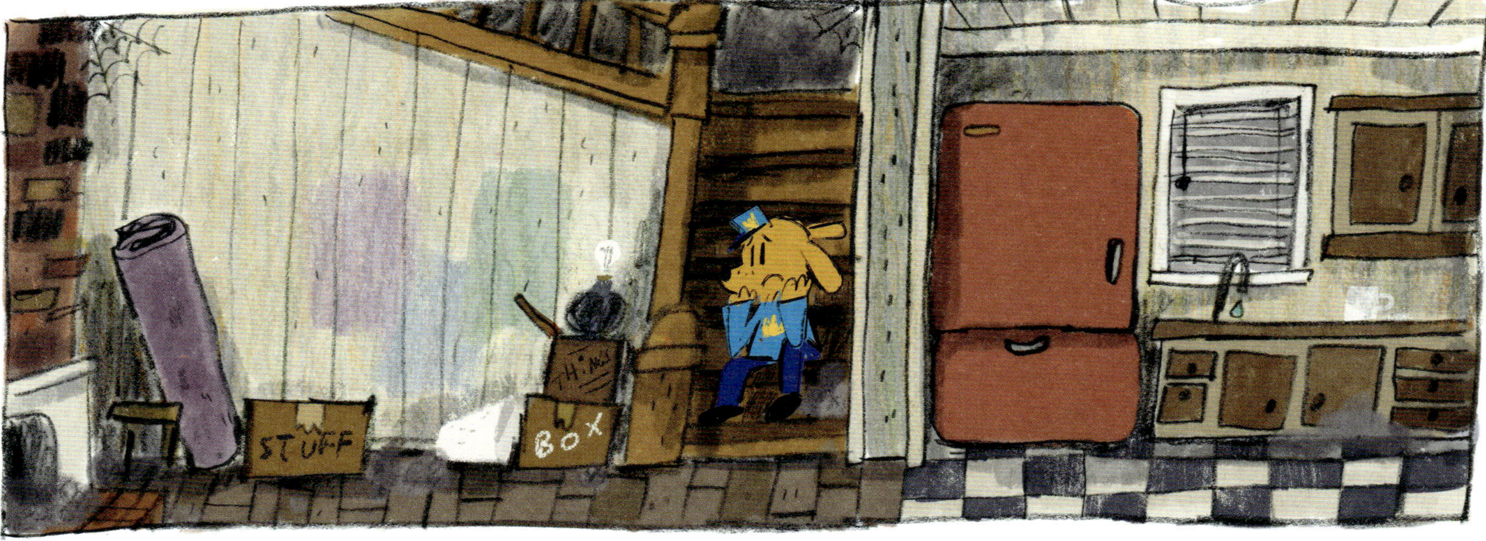

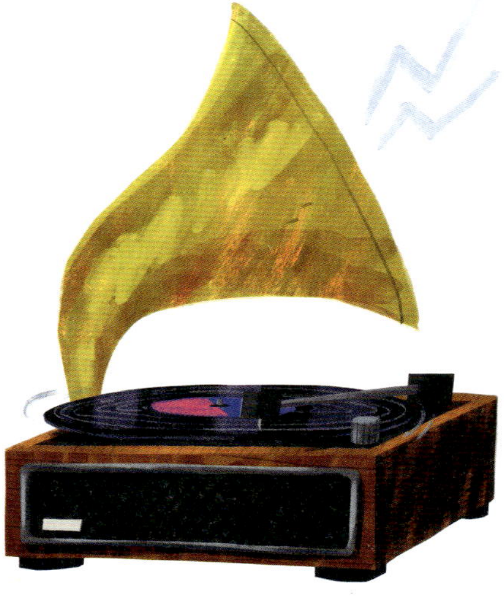

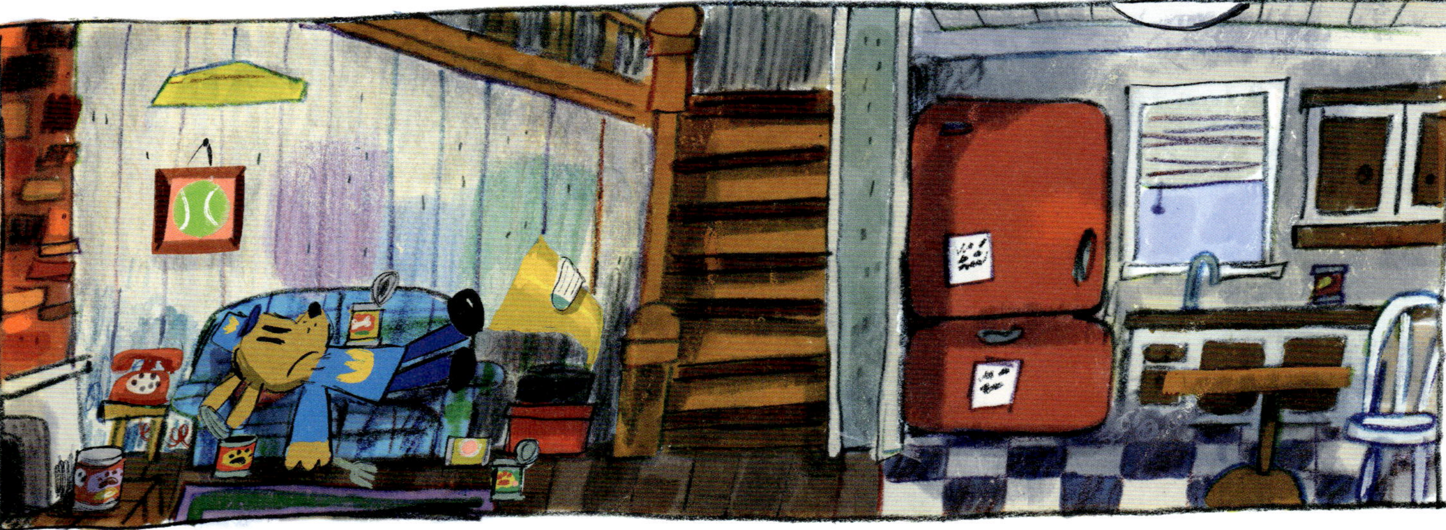

This spread: Lia Tin

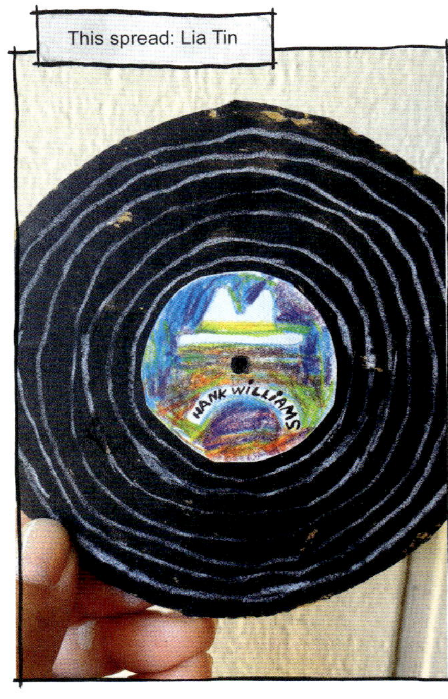

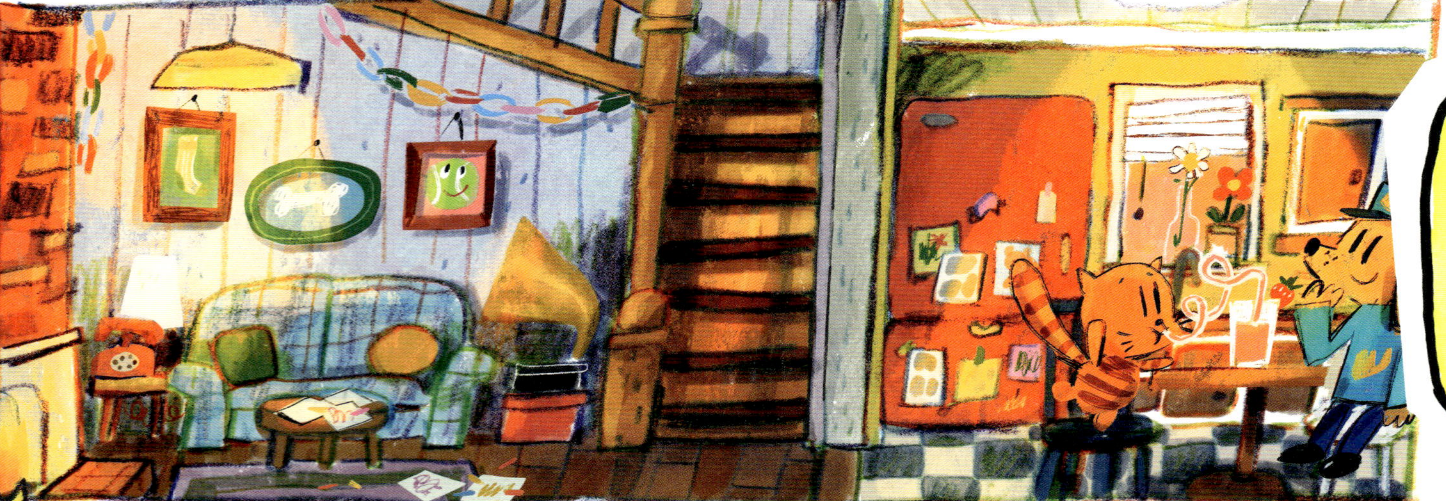

"For Dog Man's house, we looked at various diorama-like constructions because we wanted it to feel like a playful toy set. We used simple shapes, added a tree, and put it on top of a hill. The house goes through various stages as it transforms from a drab, lonely place to a warm, welcoming home when it has all the characters in it."

—CHRISTOPHER ZIBACH, Art Director

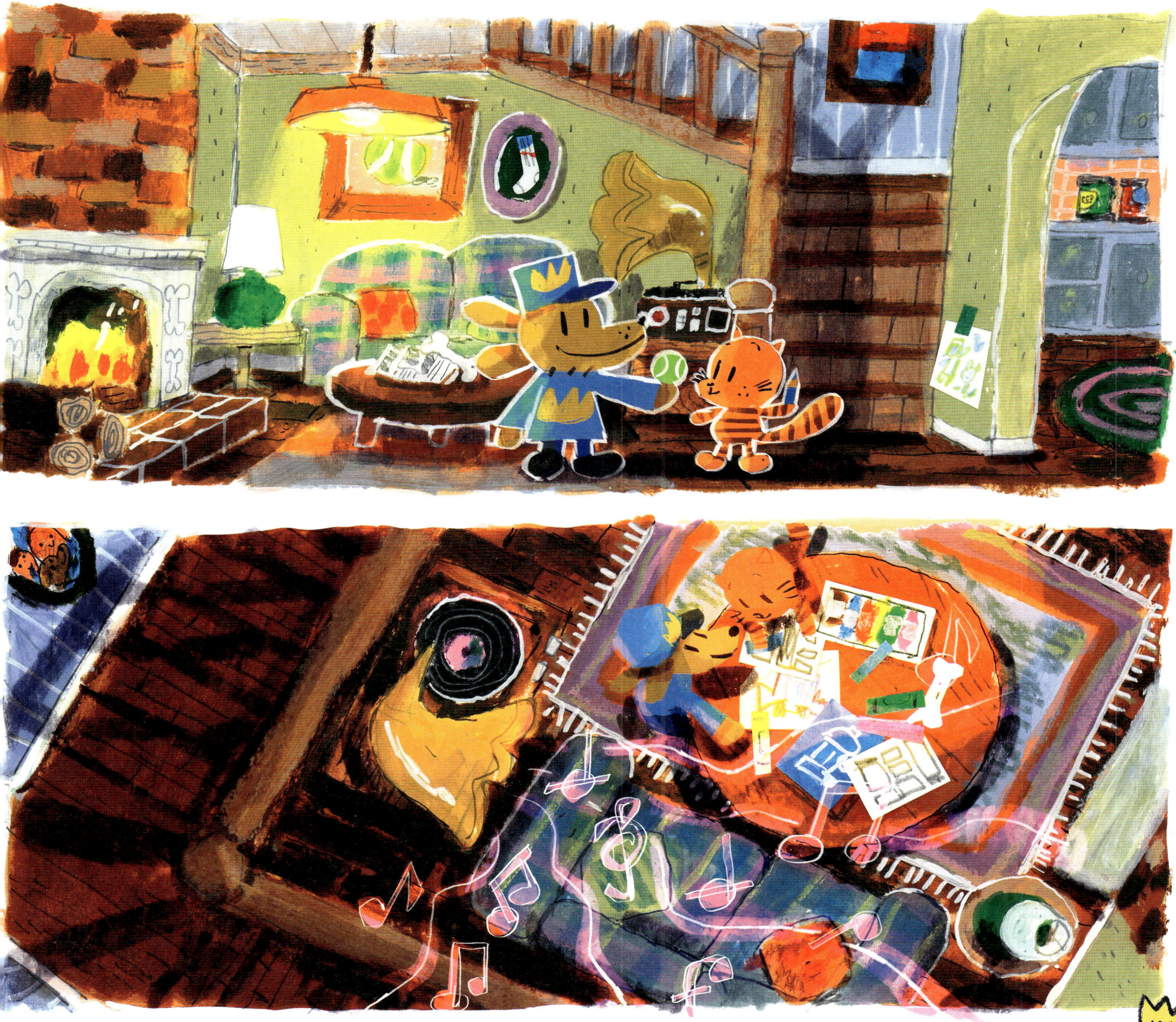

1

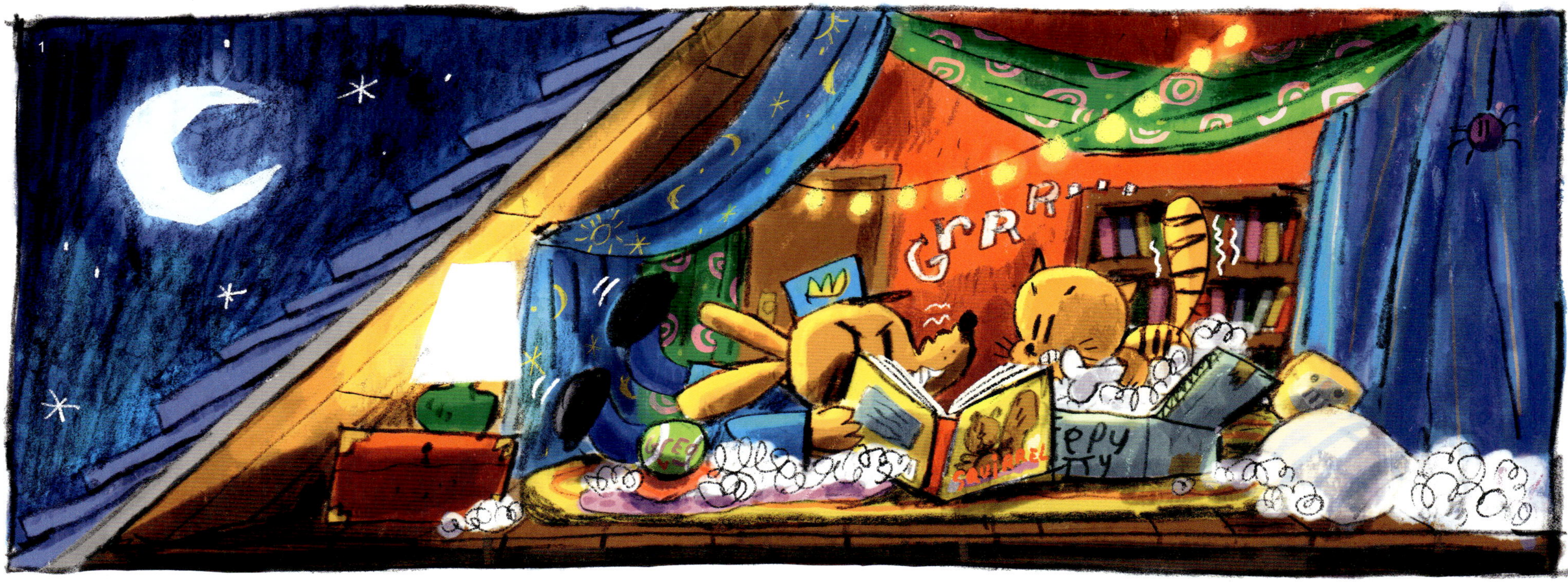

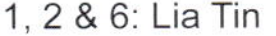

1, 2 & 6: Lia Tin

3: ***Modeling:*** Fran Lara, Samuel Pinhorne, Andrea Trovato; ***Surfacing:*** Hannah Wong, Greta Levickyte

4: ***Modeling:*** Fran Lara; ***Surfacing:*** Hannah Wong, Heather Truman

5: ***Modeling:*** Fran Lara; ***Surfacing:*** Stanley Cornwell

7: John Hill; 8–10: Scott Cullen, Samantha Wade, Danny D. Clark; 11: Katy Wu

2

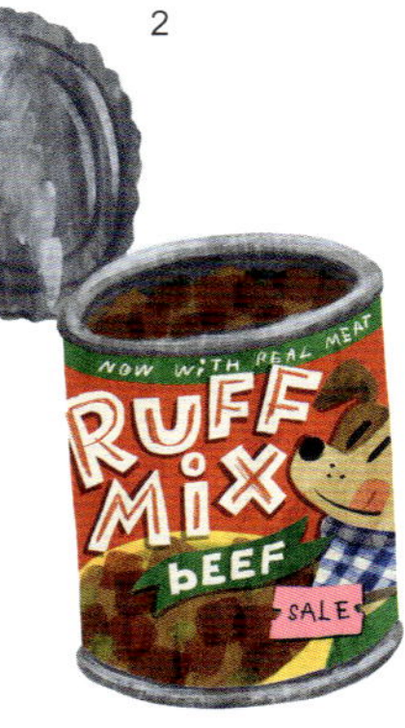

3

4

5

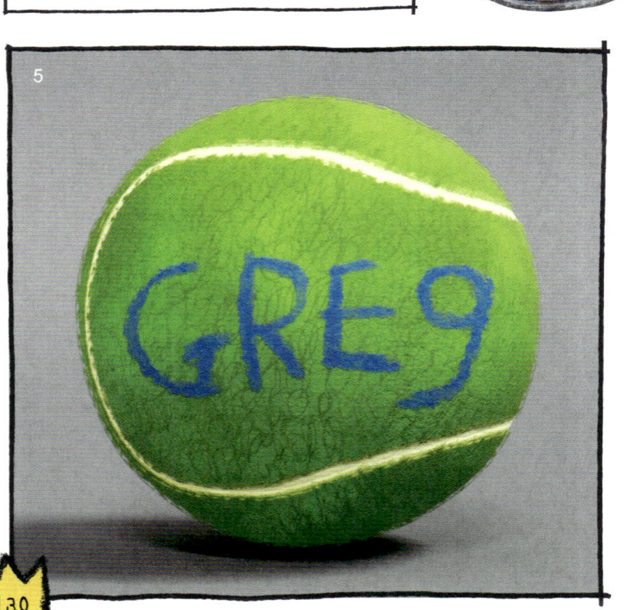

6

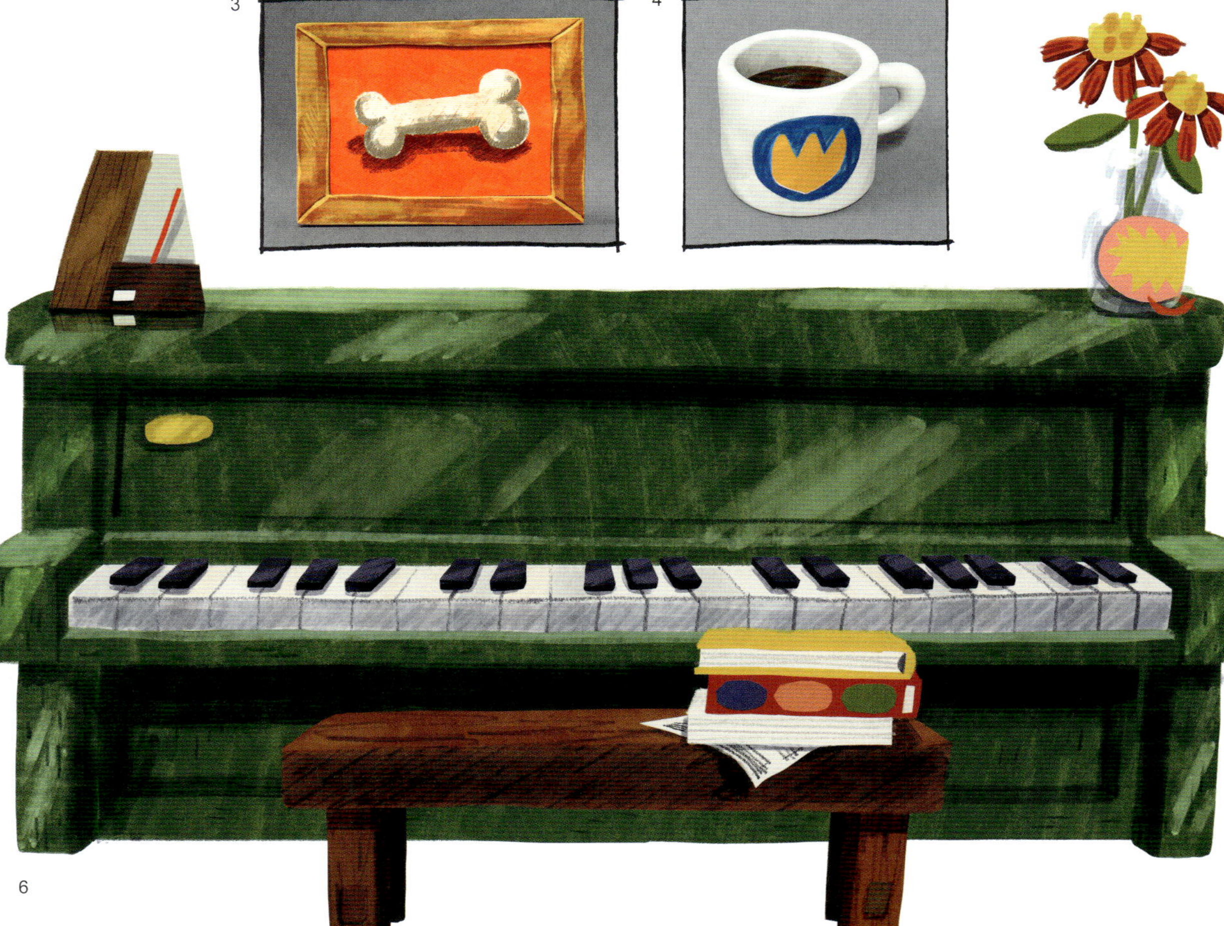

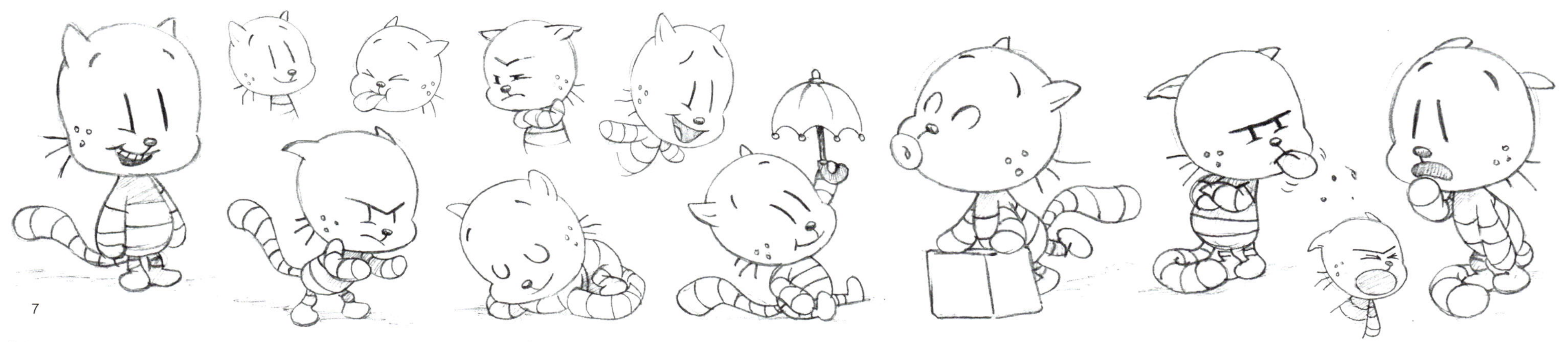

7

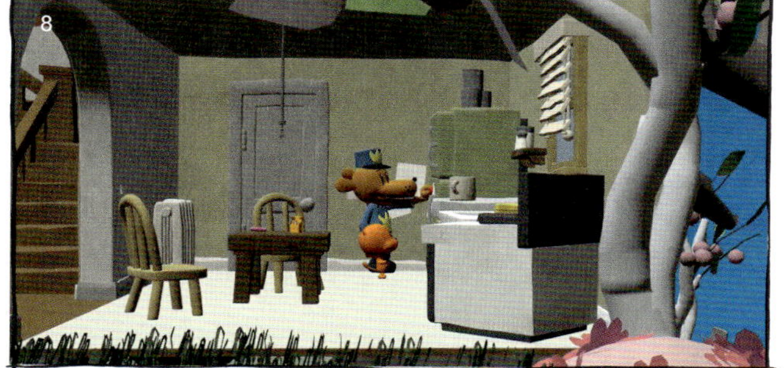

8

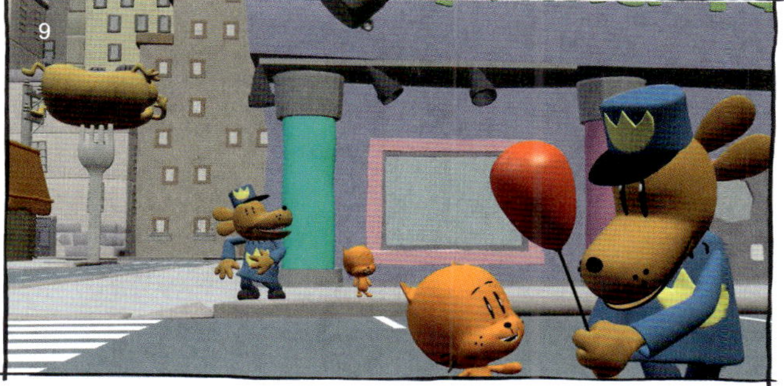

9

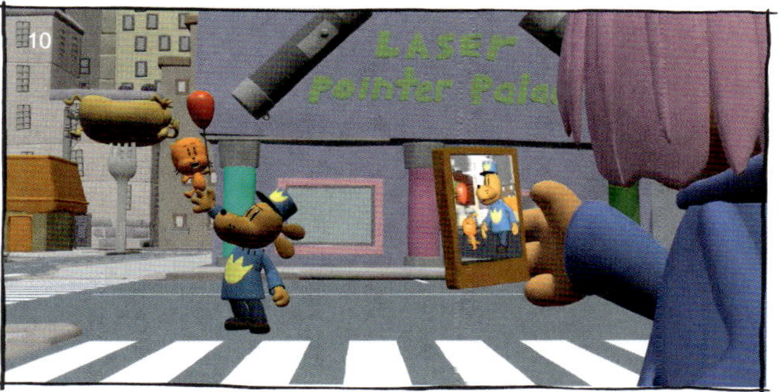

10

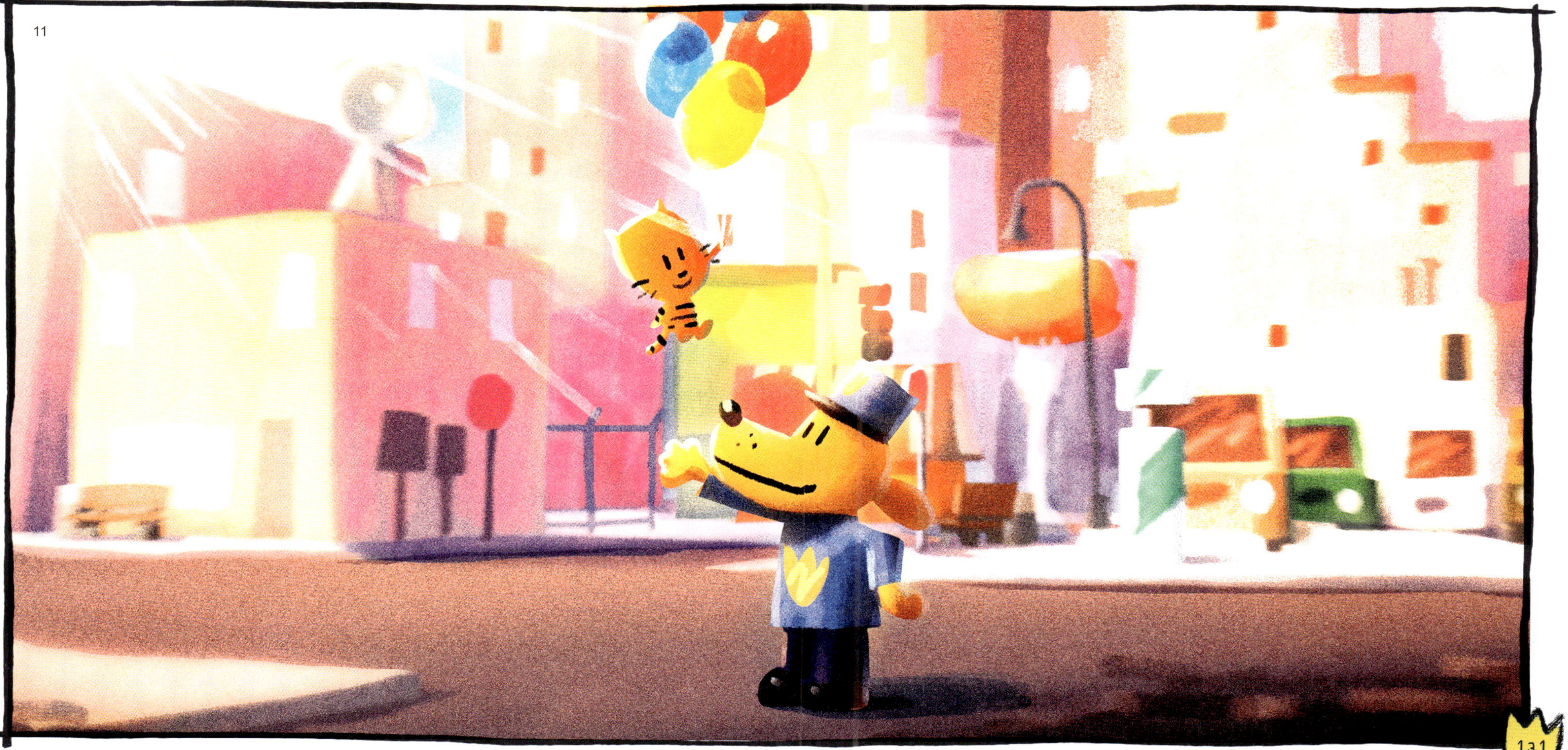

11

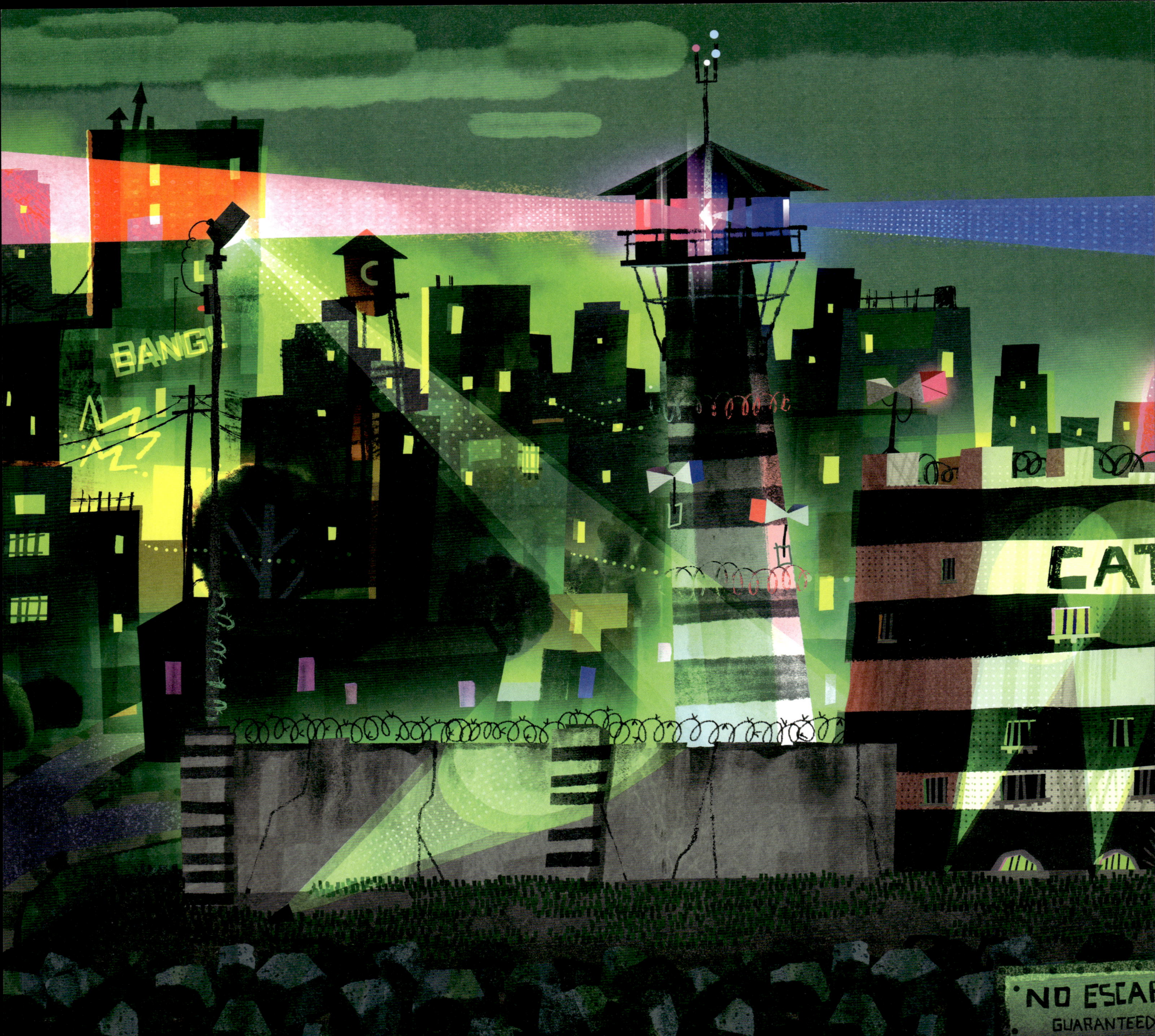
BANG!
CAT
NO ESCAP
GUARANTEED

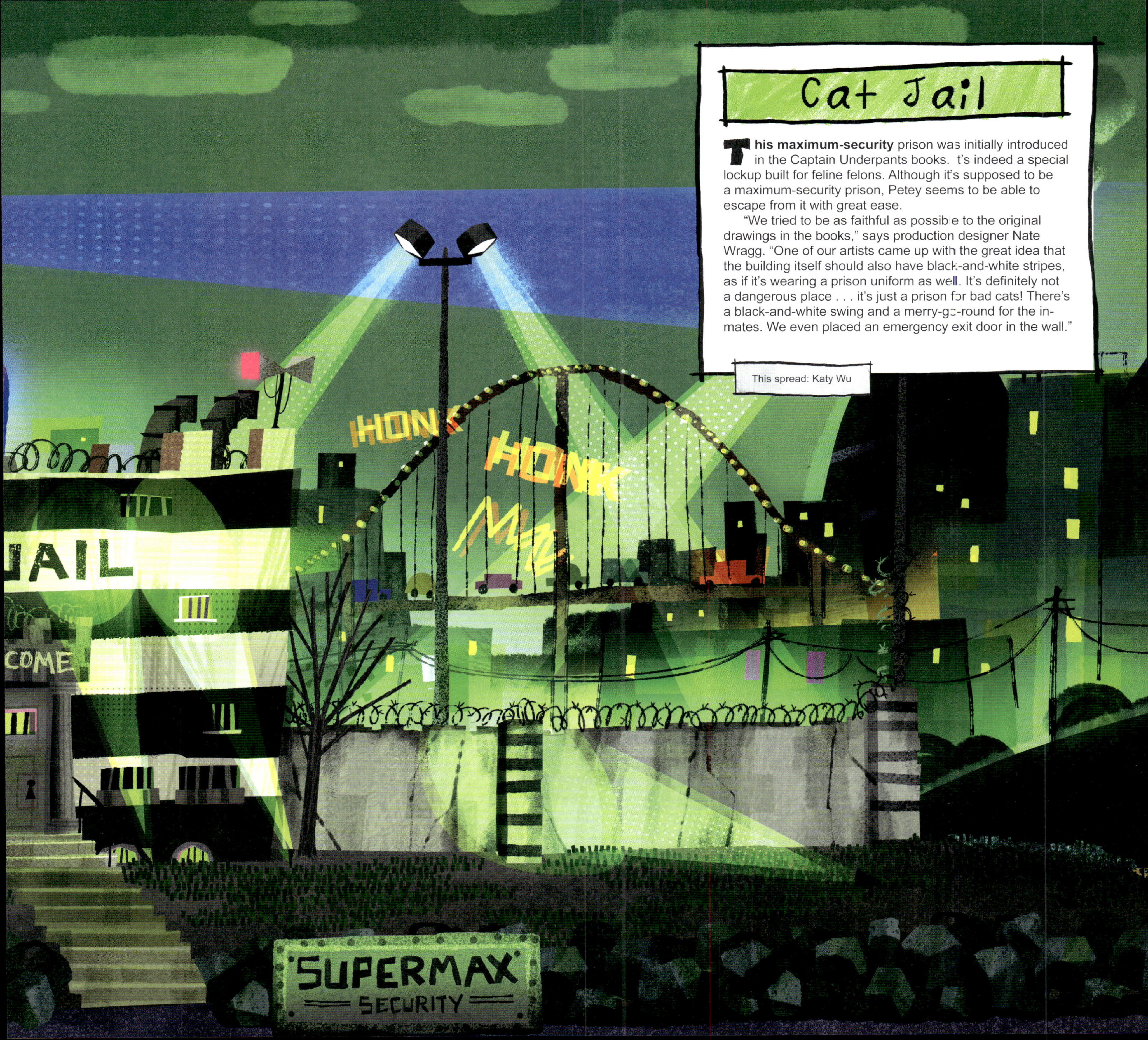

Cat Jail

This maximum-security prison was initially introduced in the Captain Underpants books. It's indeed a special lockup built for feline felons. Although it's supposed to be a maximum-security prison, Petey seems to be able to escape from it with great ease.

"We tried to be as faithful as possible to the original drawings in the books," says production designer Nate Wragg. "One of our artists came up with the great idea that the building itself should also have black-and-white stripes, as if it's wearing a prison uniform as well. It's definitely not a dangerous place . . . it's just a prison for bad cats! There's a black-and-white swing and a merry-go-round for the inmates. We even placed an emergency exit door in the wall."

This spread: Katy Wu

1

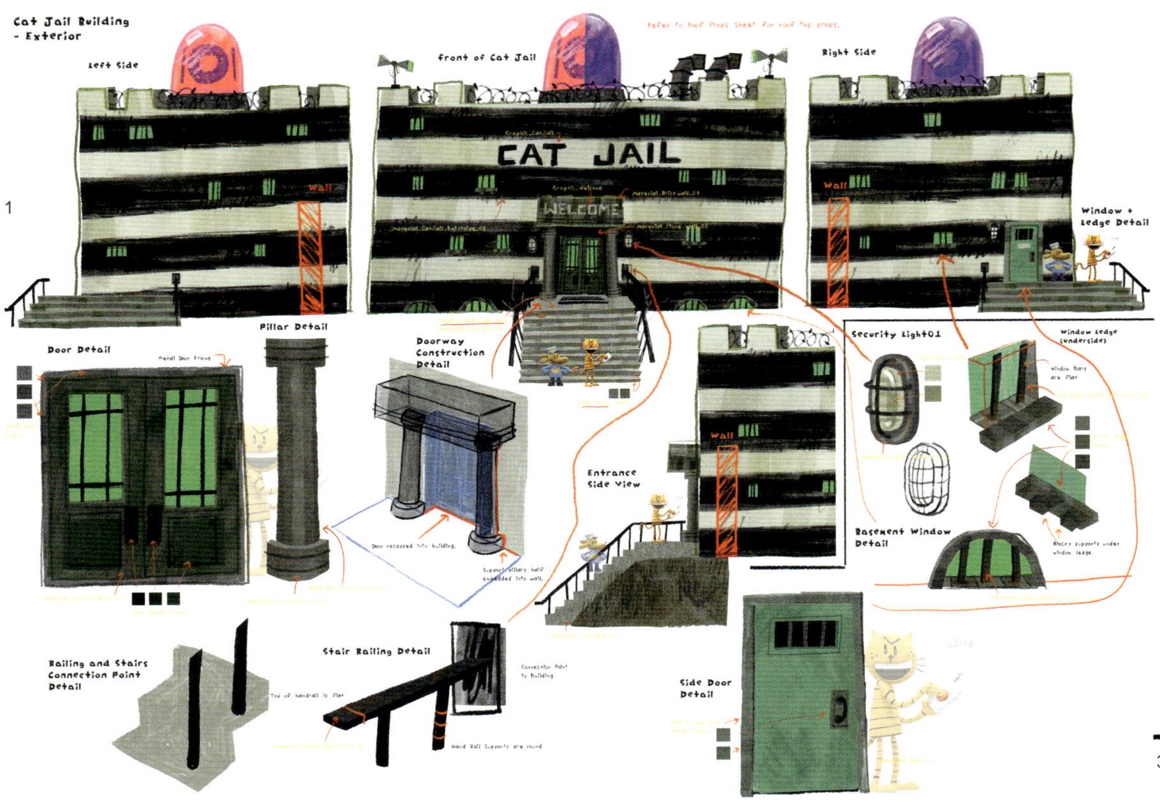

Cat Jail Building - Exterior

Left Side

Front of Cat Jail

Right Side

CAT JAIL

WELCOME

Wall

Window + Ledge Detail

Door Detail

Pillar Detail

Doorway Construction Detail

Security Light01

Window Ledge (underside)

Entrance Side View

Basement Window Detail

Railing and Stairs Connection Point Detail

Stair Railing Detail

Side Door Detail

3

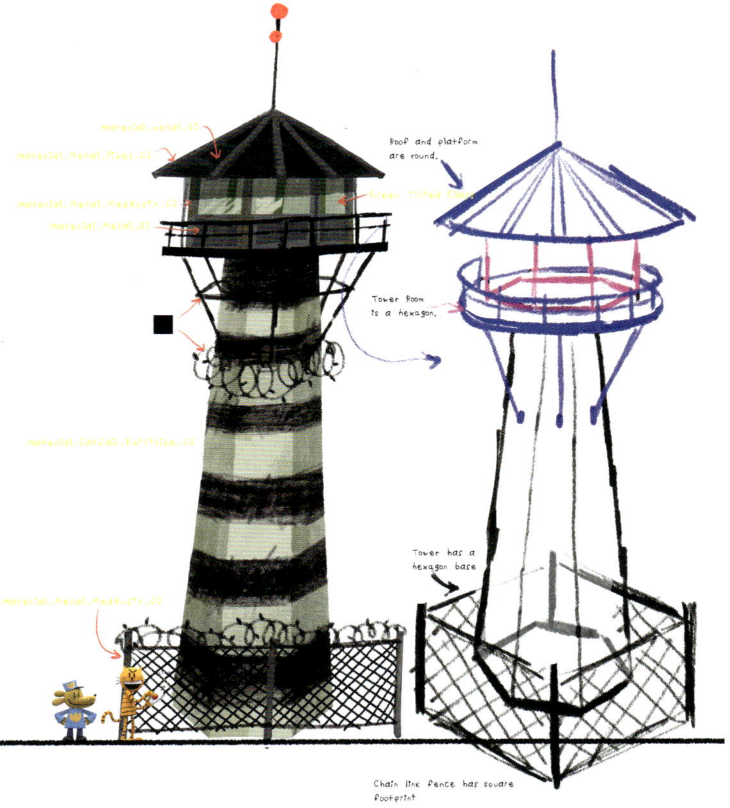

Roof and platform are round.

Tower Room is a hexagon.

Tower has a hexagon base

Chain link fence has square footprint

2

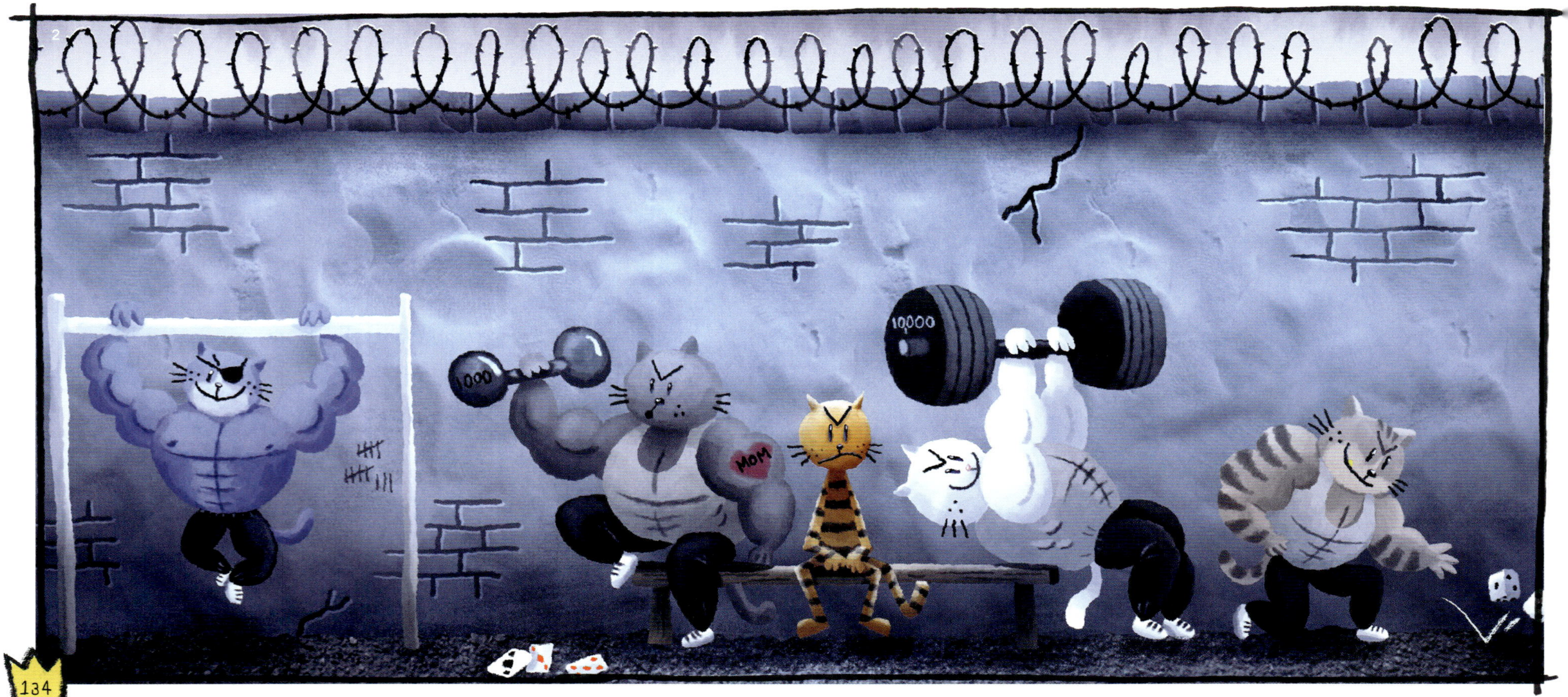

1000

10,000

MOM

4

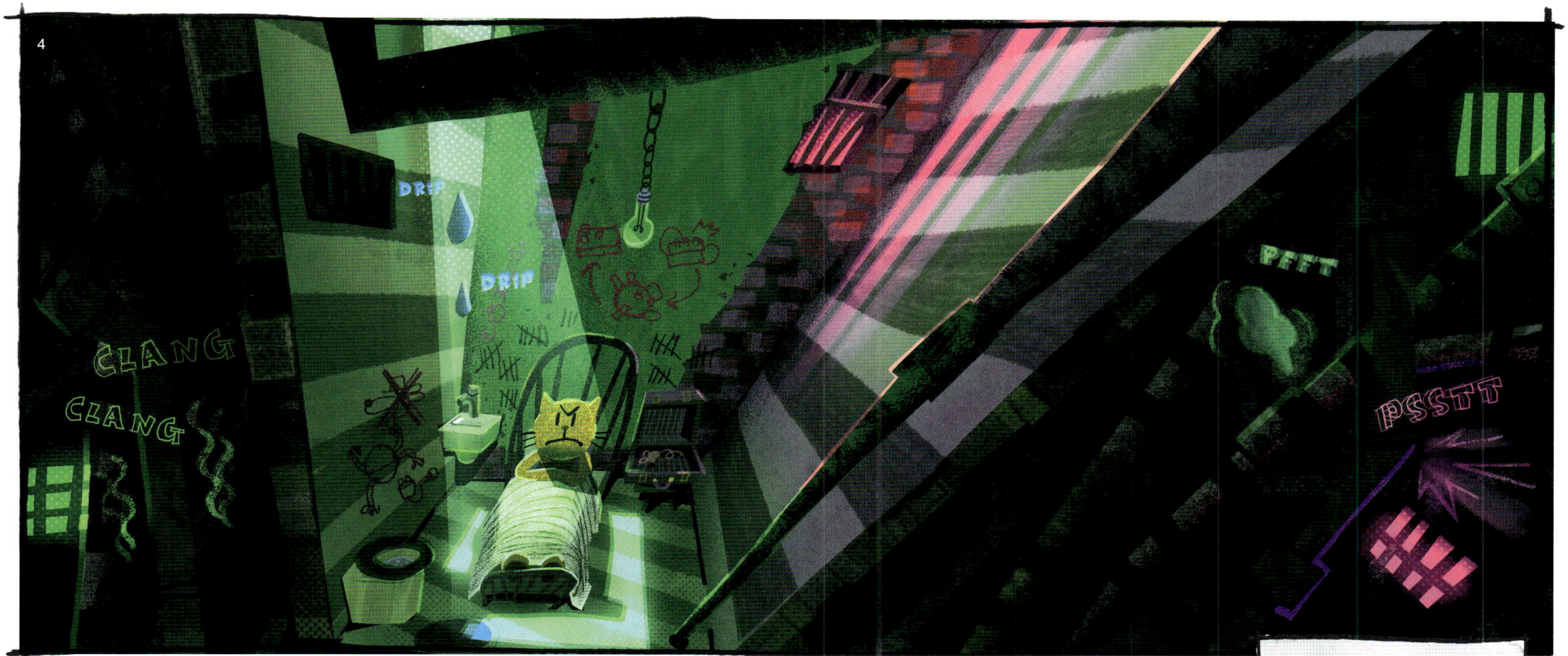

5

1, 3–5: Katy Wu; 2: Nate Wragg

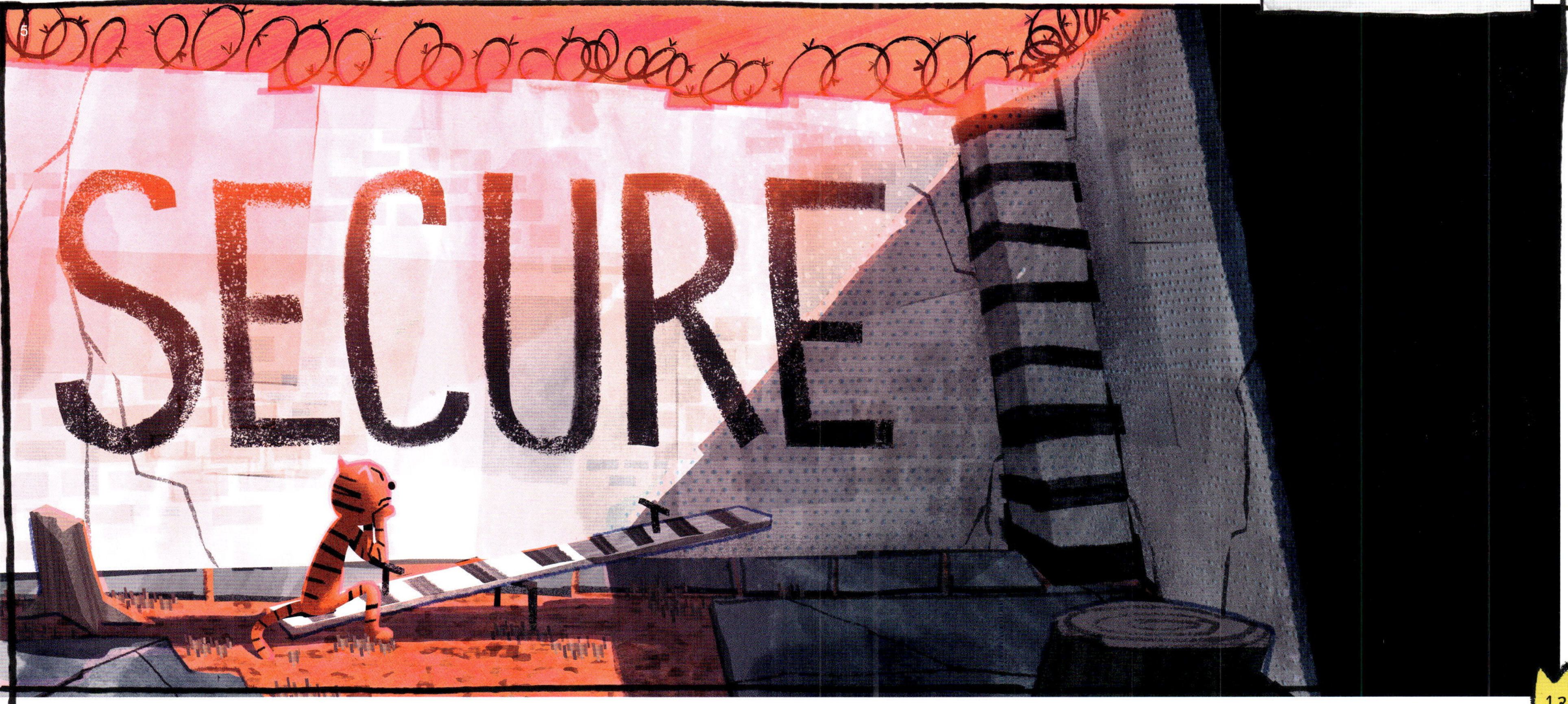

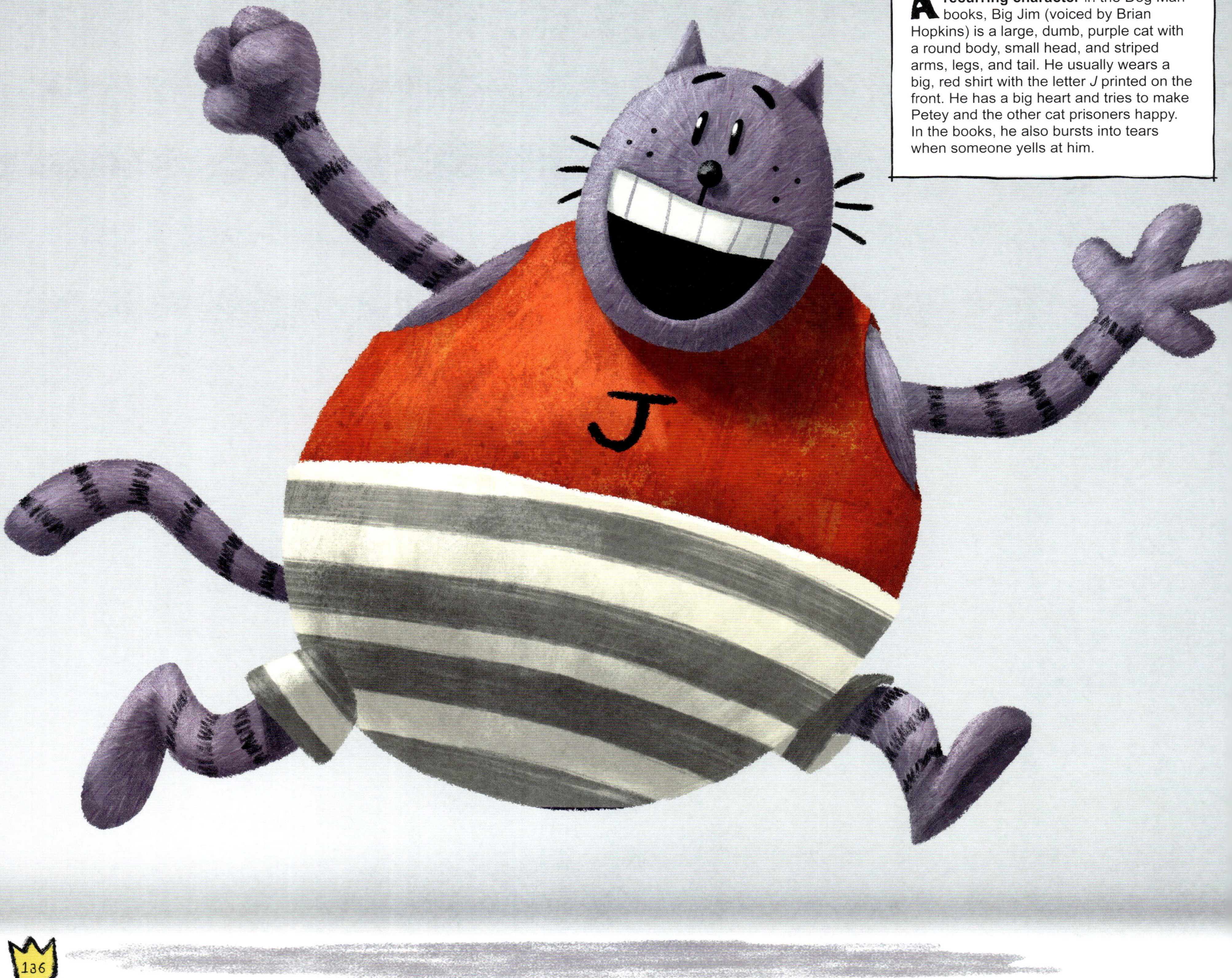

1

Big Jim

A recurring character in the Dog Man books, Big Jim (voiced by Brian Hopkins) is a large, dumb, purple cat with a round body, small head, and striped arms, legs, and tail. He usually wears a big, red shirt with the letter *J* printed on the front. He has a big heart and tries to make Petey and the other cat prisoners happy. In the books, he also bursts into tears when someone yells at him.

2

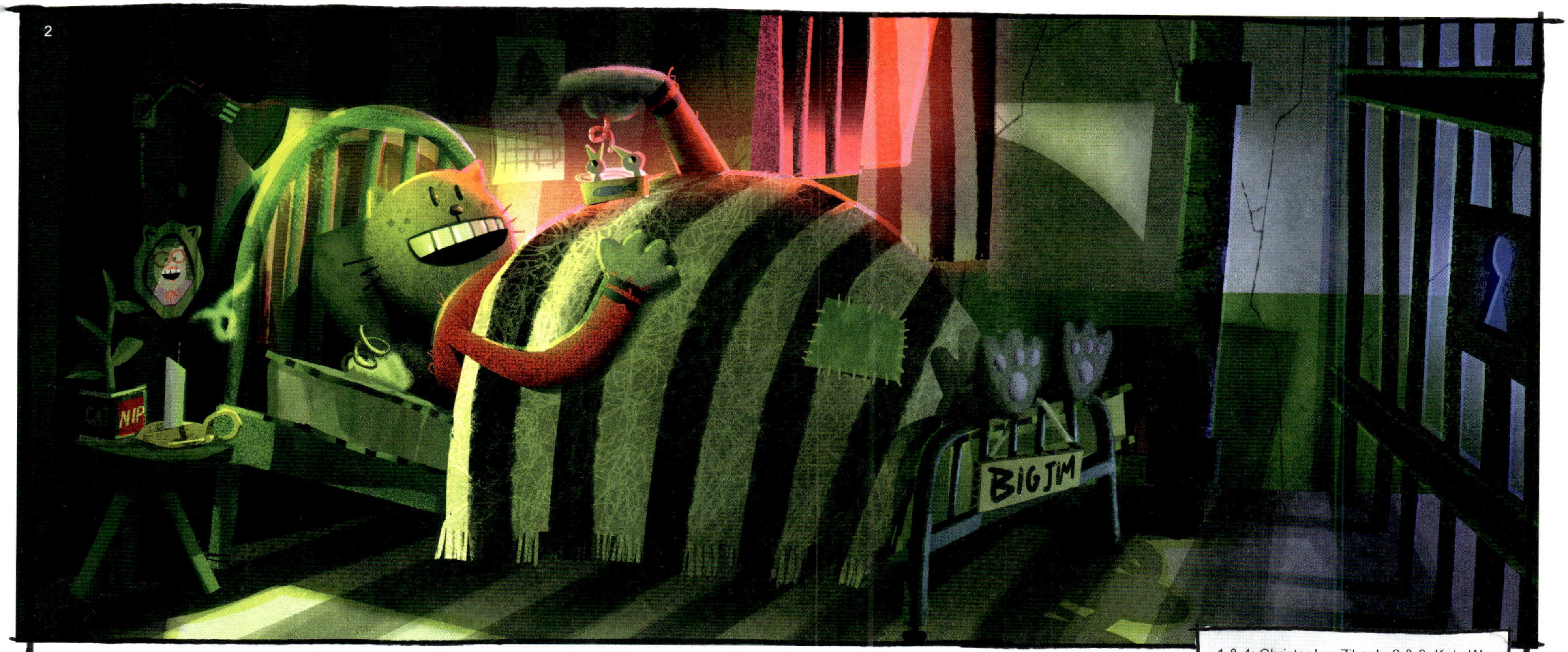

3

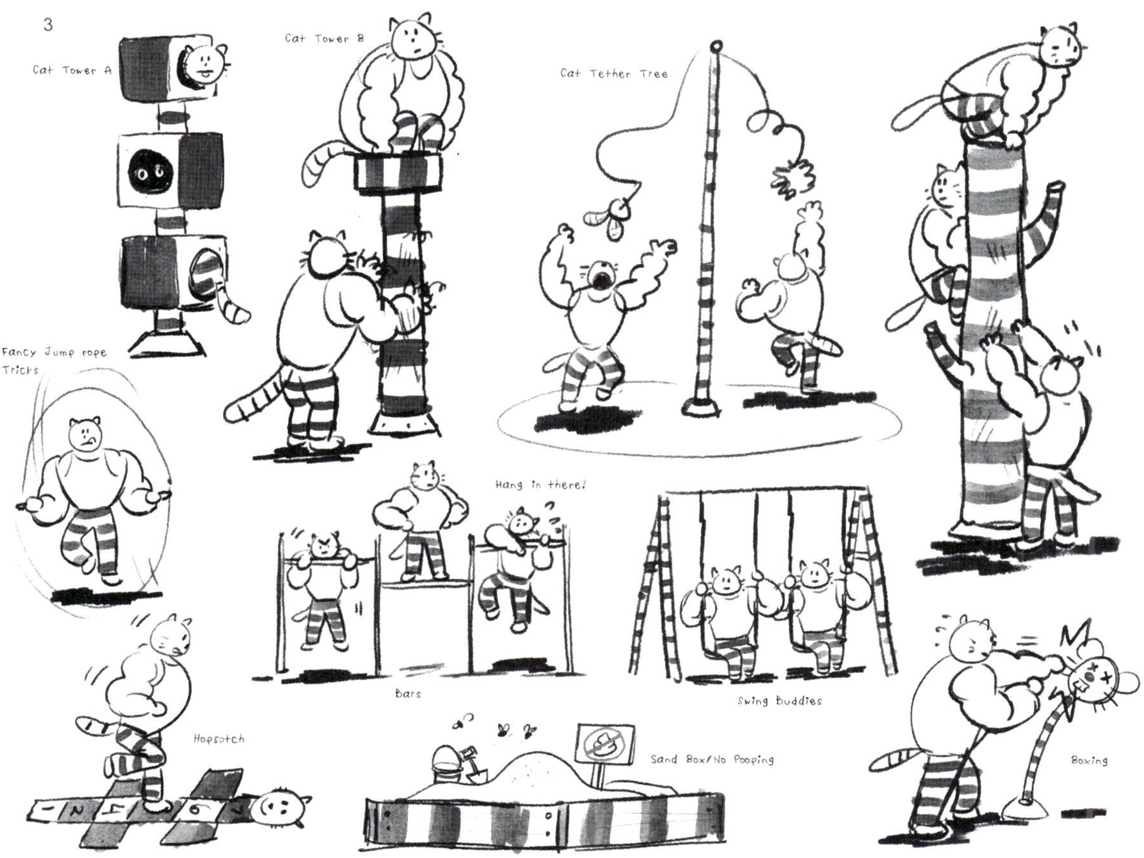

1 & 4: Christopher Zibach; 2 & 3: Katy Wu

4

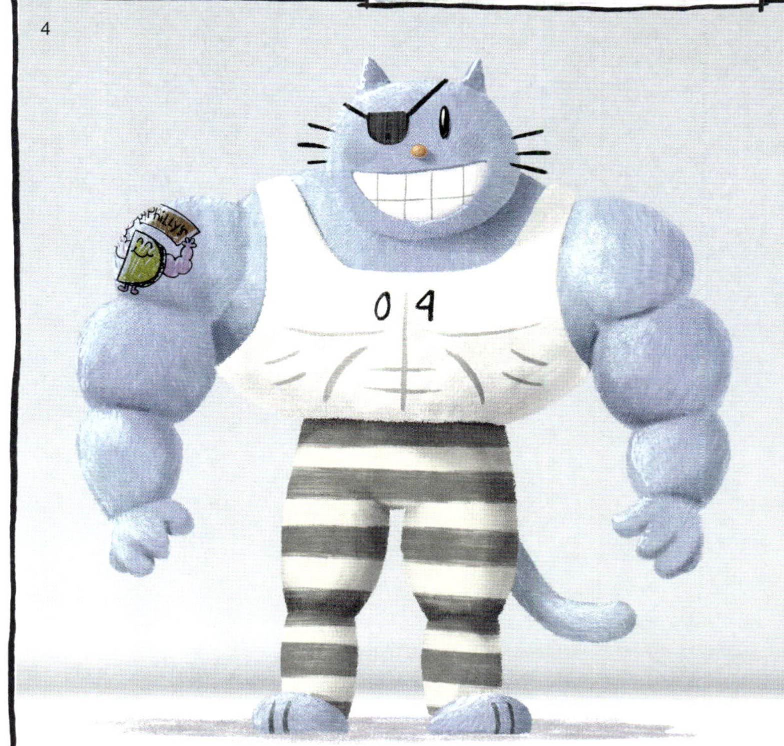

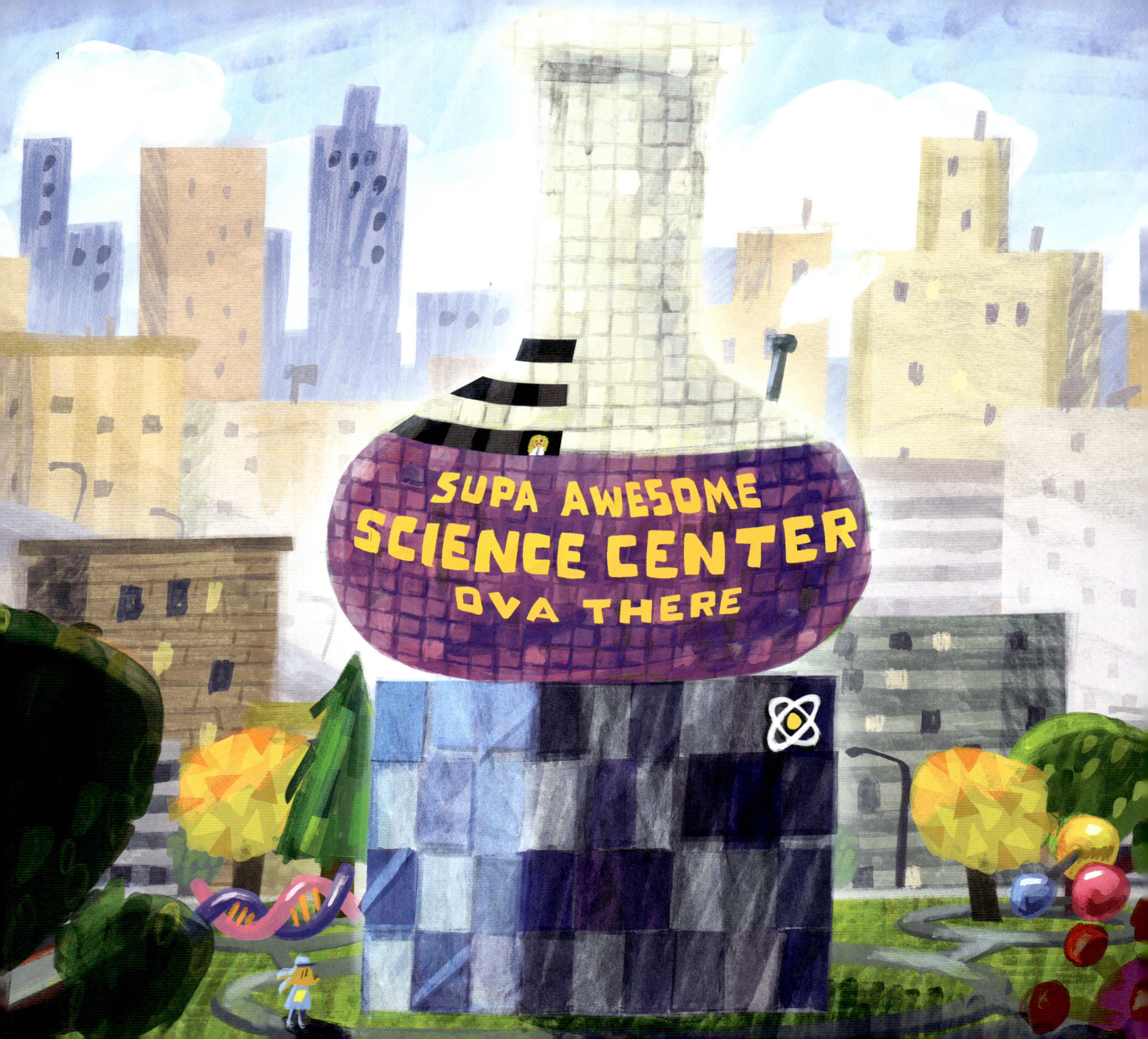
SUPA AWESOME
SCIENCE CENTER
OVA THERE

2

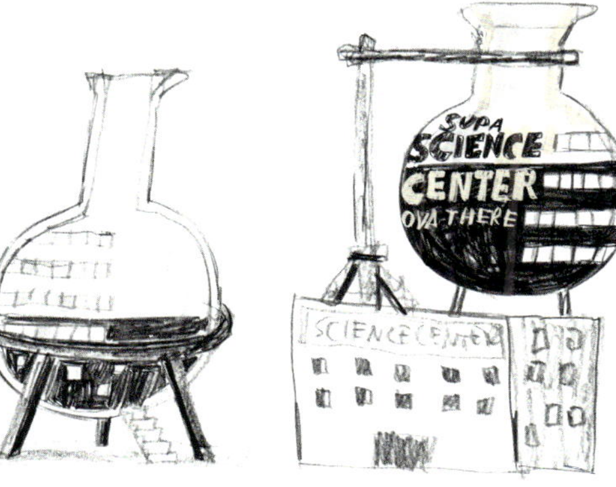

Supa Awesome Science Center Ova There

First introduced in the book *A Tale of Two Kitties*, the Supa Awesome Science Center Ova There is exactly the kind of generic building a young kid would imagine scientists conducting experiments in and sharing their inventions with the public. "It's our take on what people in the 1970s thought the future was going to look like," explains production designer Nate Wragg. "It's the most modern building in town. There are lots of clean lines, as well as some really dopey colors. You can describe it as retro-modern. Basically, it's a big glass square that has a giant tile beaker with the name 'Supa Awesome Science Center Ova There,' just like in the books, but it's even sillier in its silhouette and tone."

As art director Christopher Zibach points out, "The funny thing about it is that it's not totally a museum, and it's not a place where you go to buy 'science stuff.' It's a science center. It's not really for kids because we don't see any kids touring it—it's just a weird lab. We had a lot of fun playing with the notion of sci-fi from the 1970s. It has this retro look about it, and even the most advanced technological tool looks a bit dated."

The Supa Awesome Science Center Ova There is also where the movie's mad scientist lady (voiced by Laraine Newman) tells the press about how her team has rebuilt Flippy with titanium bones and created a Psychokinetic Supa Mecha fish. She's quite proud of a short video her daughter has made about this astonishing achievement. Of course, later on, Petey steals the Mecha fish, and exposure to the Living Spray brings it back to life.

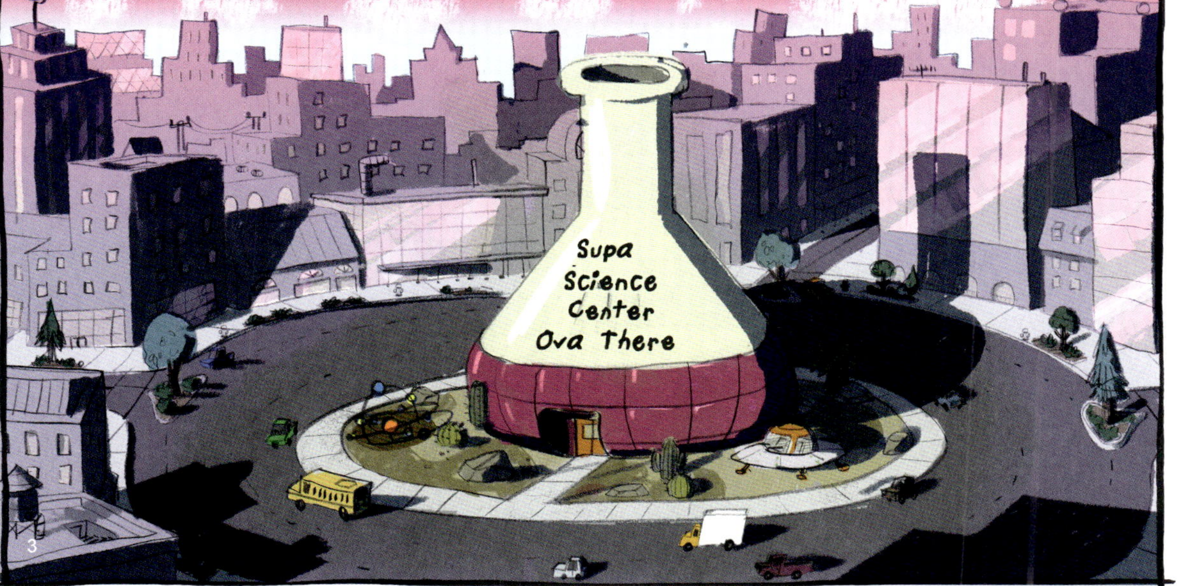

3

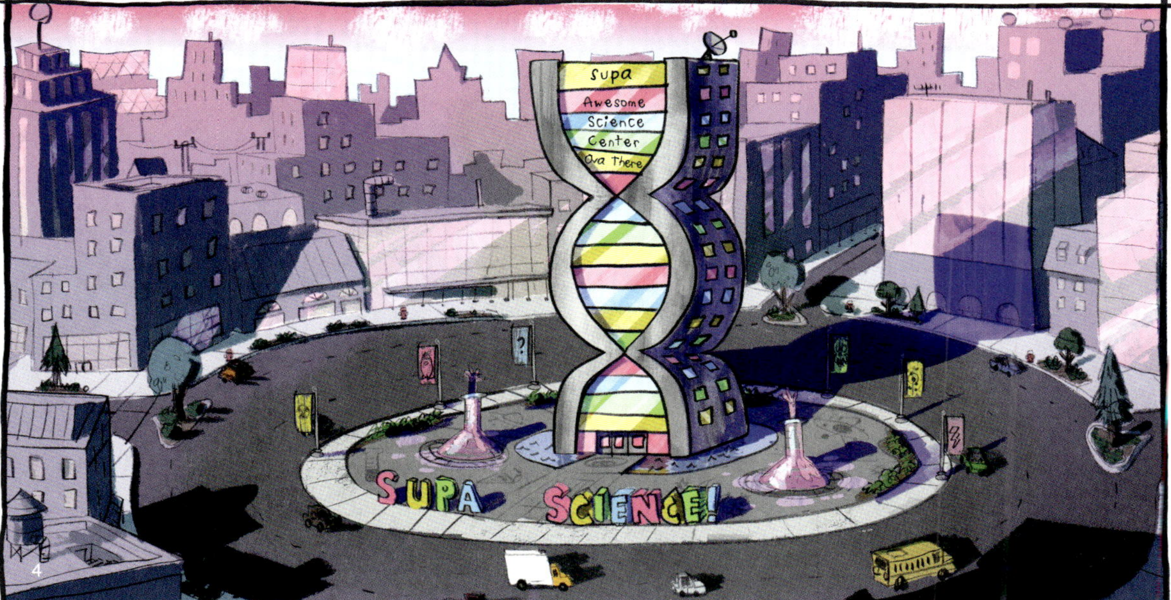

4

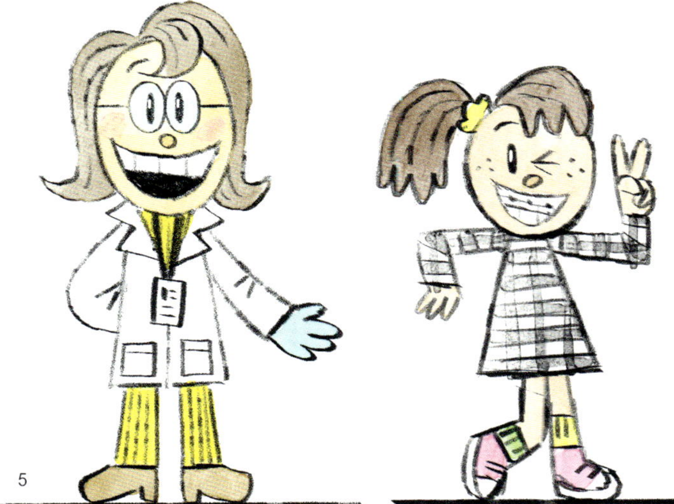

5

1 & 2: Lia Tin; 3 & 4: Christopher Zibach; 5: Nate Wragg

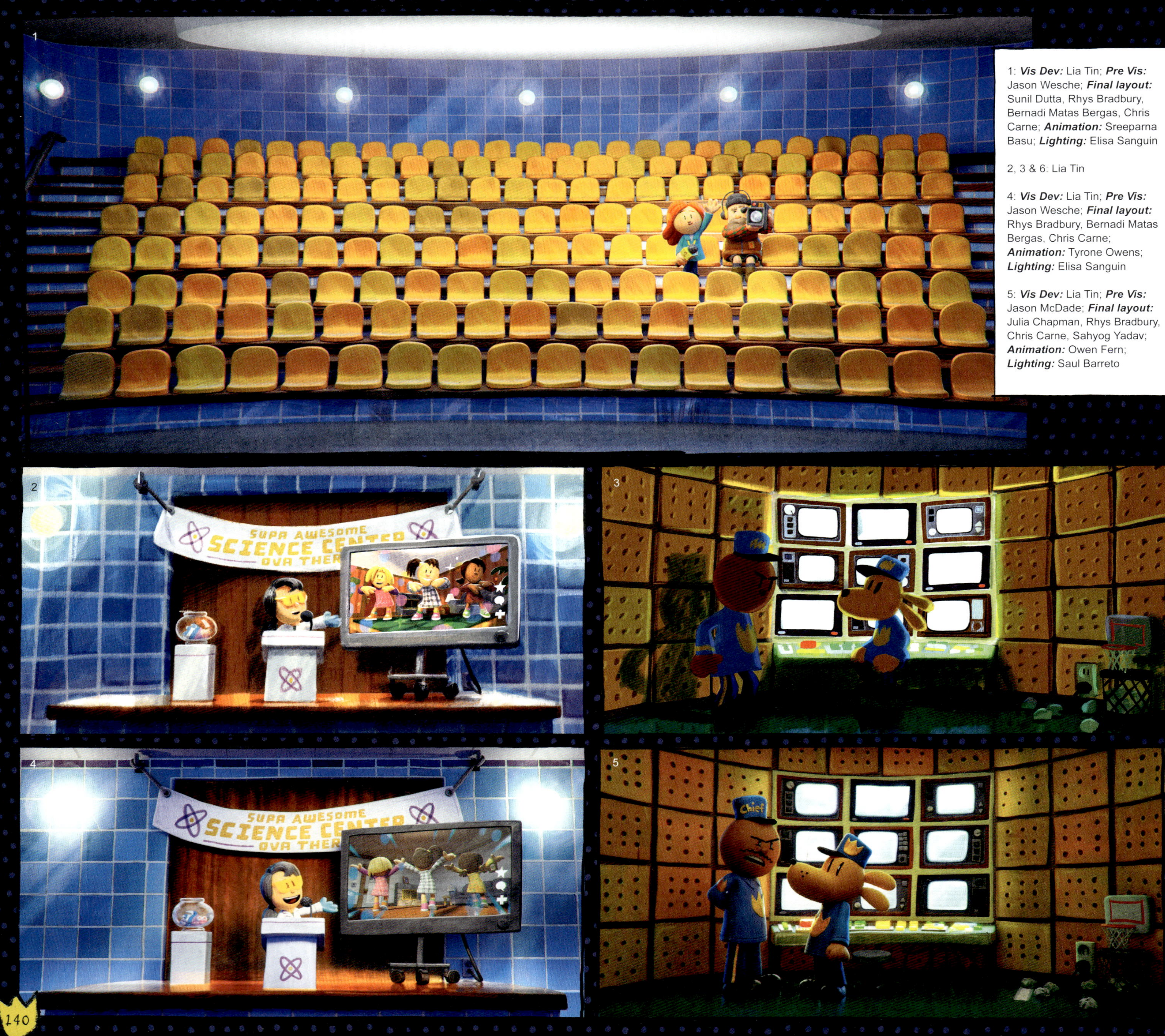

1: ***Vis Dev:*** Lia Tin; ***Pre Vis:*** Jason Wesche; ***Final layout:*** Sunil Dutta, Rhys Bradbury, Bernadi Matas Bergas, Chris Carne; ***Animation:*** Sreeparna Basu; ***Lighting:*** Elisa Sanguin

2, 3 & 6: Lia Tin

4: ***Vis Dev:*** Lia Tin; ***Pre Vis:*** Jason Wesche; ***Final layout:*** Rhys Bradbury, Bernadi Matas Bergas, Chris Carne; ***Animation:*** Tyrone Owens; ***Lighting:*** Elisa Sanguin

5: ***Vis Dev:*** Lia Tin; ***Pre Vis:*** Jason McDade; ***Final layout:*** Julia Chapman, Rhys Bradbury, Chris Carne, Sahyog Yadav; ***Animation:*** Owen Fern; ***Lighting:*** Saul Barreto

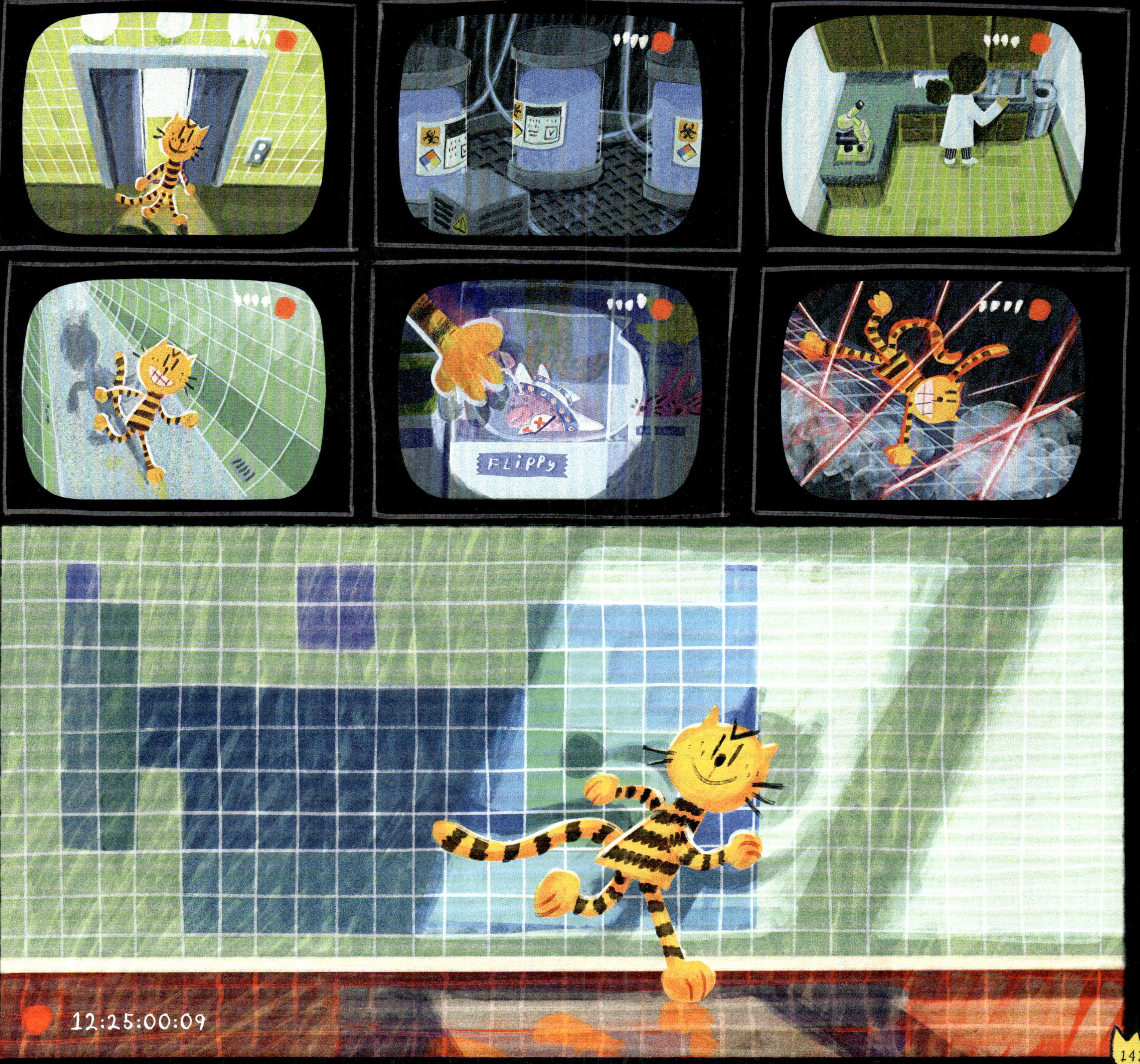
FLIPPY
12:25:00:09

The Living Spray Factory

First introduced in *A Tale of Two Kitties*, The Living Spray Factory is where Flippy is brought back to life after he punctures the gas tank. The escaped gas also turns the building itself into a living monster and brings the other buildings to life, resulting in entertaining insanity and mayhem. Janet and Rocco are the two clueless employees at the factory whose negligence results in Flippy the Fish being exposed to Living Spray and coming back to life. “They really don’t understand how serious it could be if something in the factory malfunctions,” explains production designer Nate Wragg. “They’re kind of dopey and playing jokes on each other. Of course, then the Living Spray gets out and starts bringing everything to life. They provide some comic relief before the factory starts to melt down and things spin out of control.”

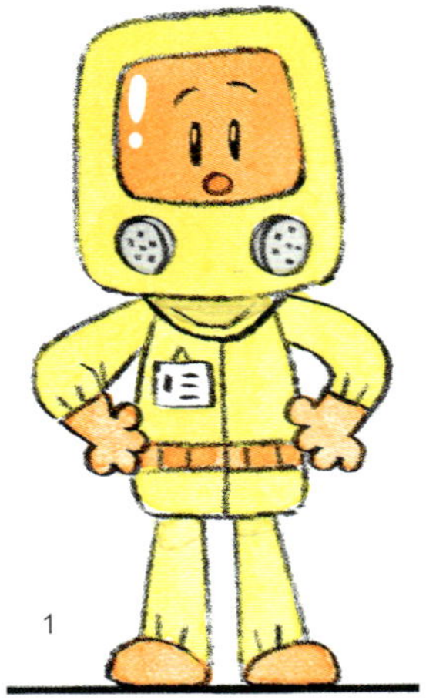

1

1 & 2: Nate Wragg; 3–5: Vahe Yefremian; 6 & Overleaf: Sébastien Piquet

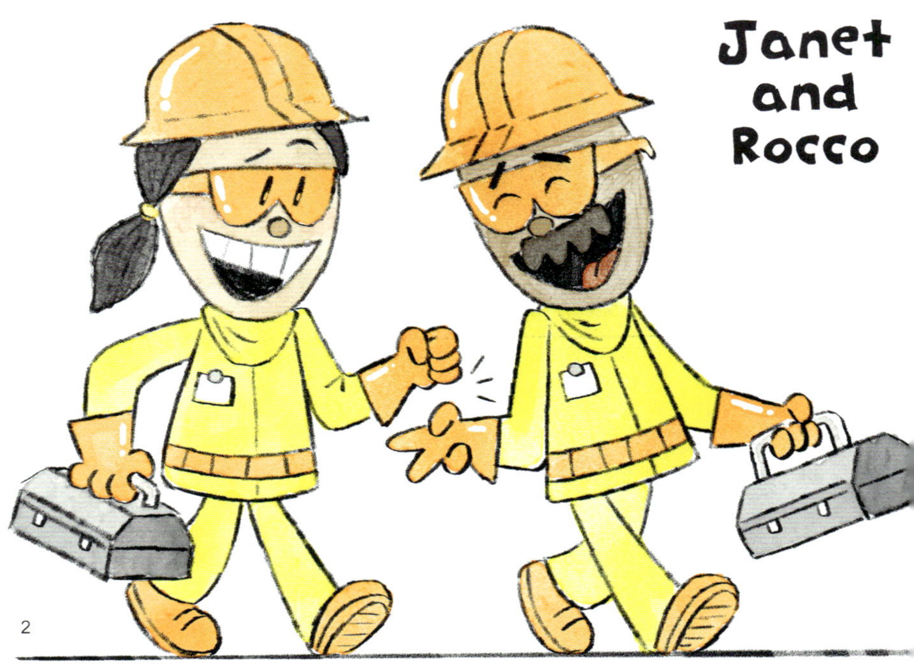

2

3

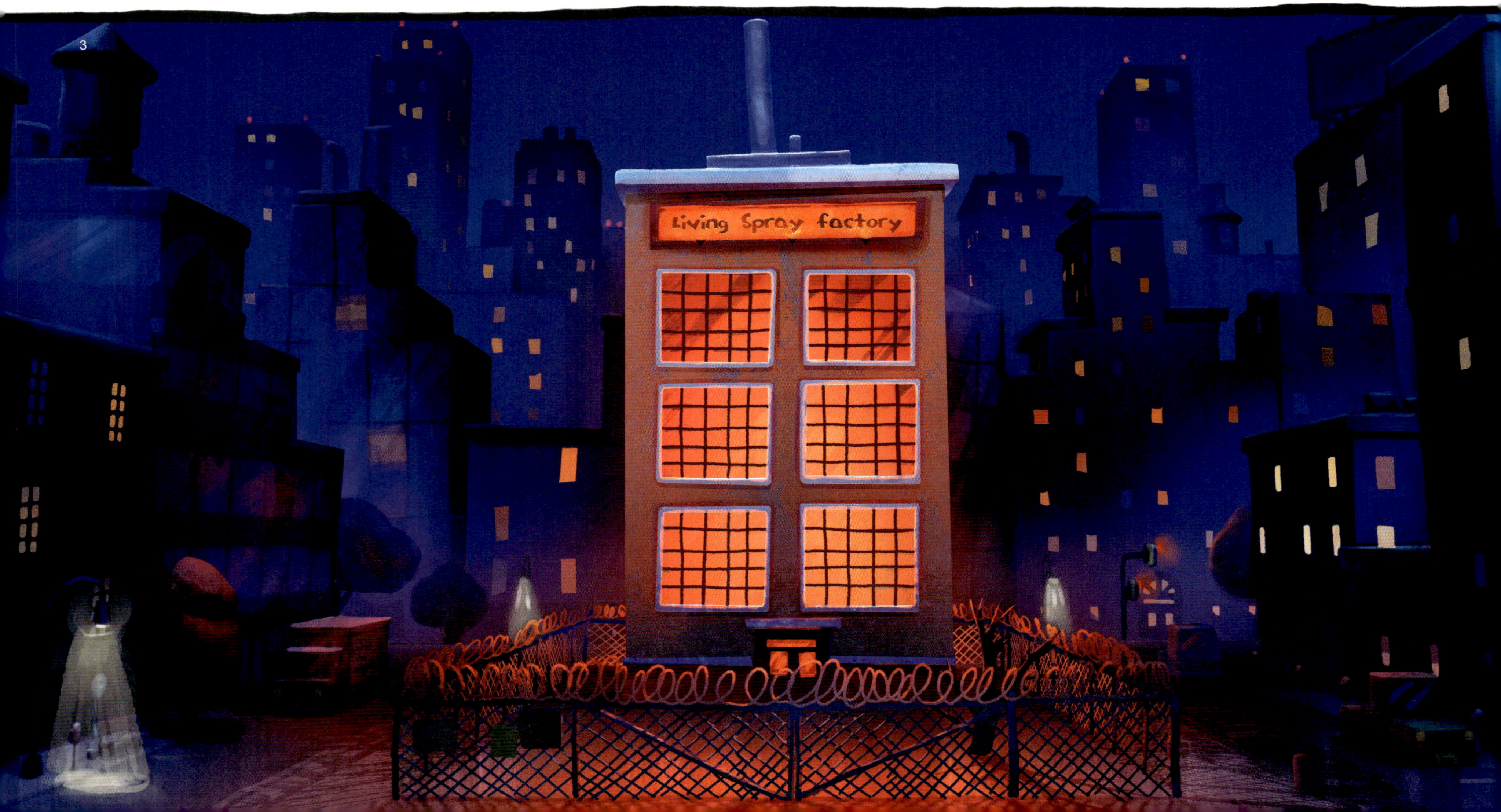

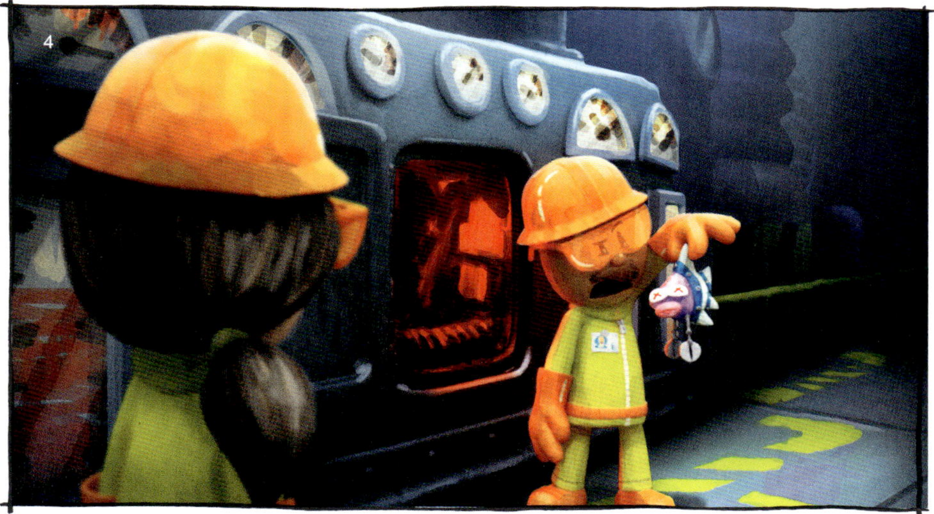
4

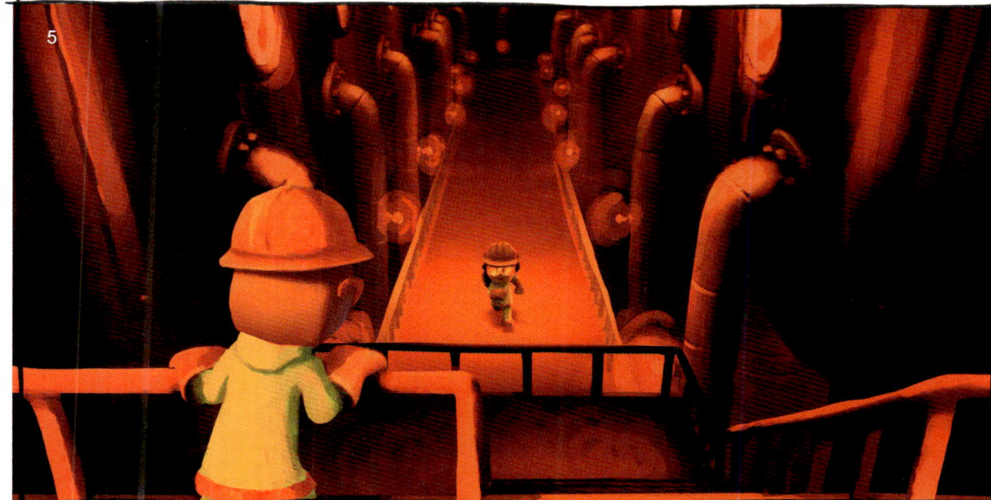
5

6
DANGER
RUN
Panic!
BURNT
HOT

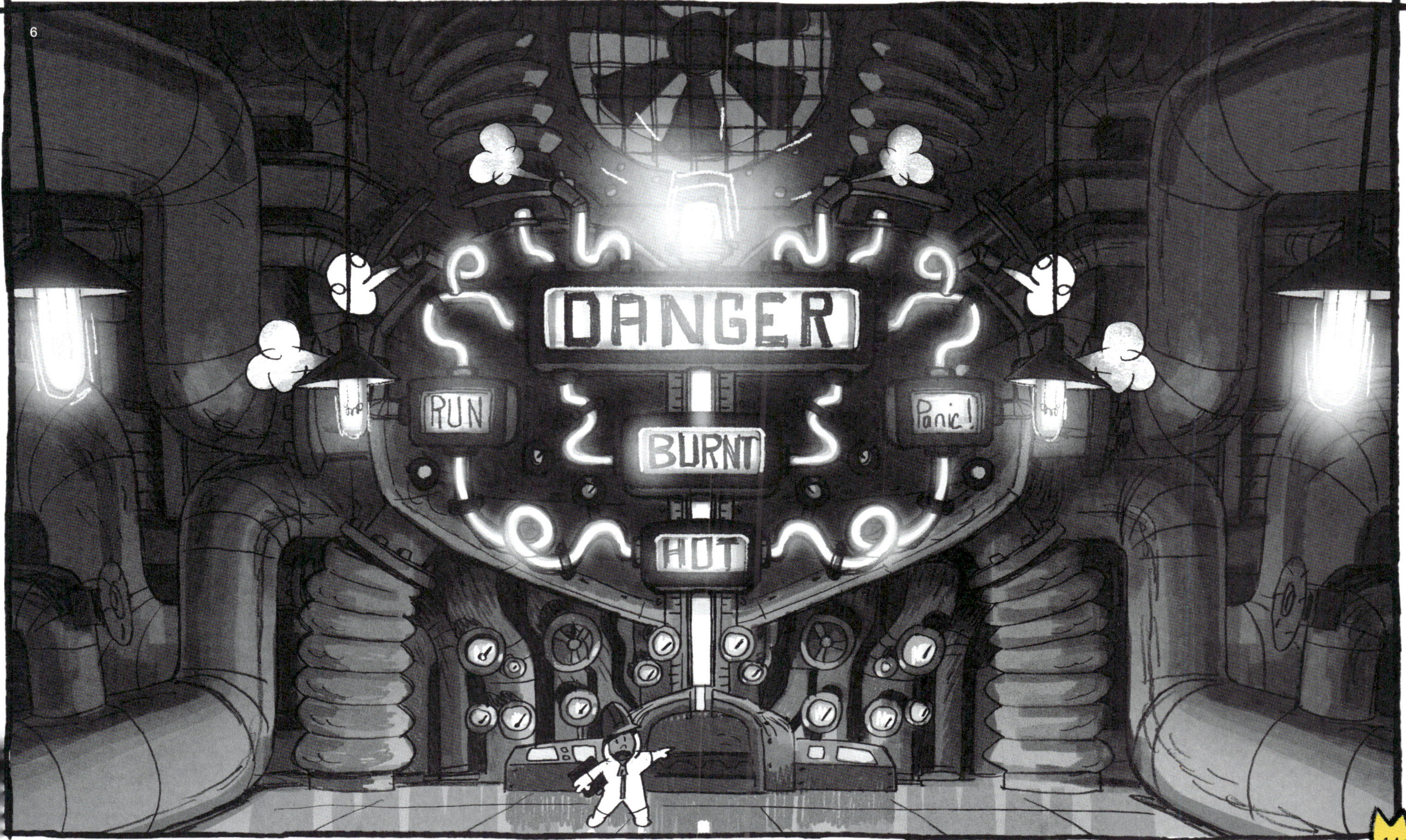

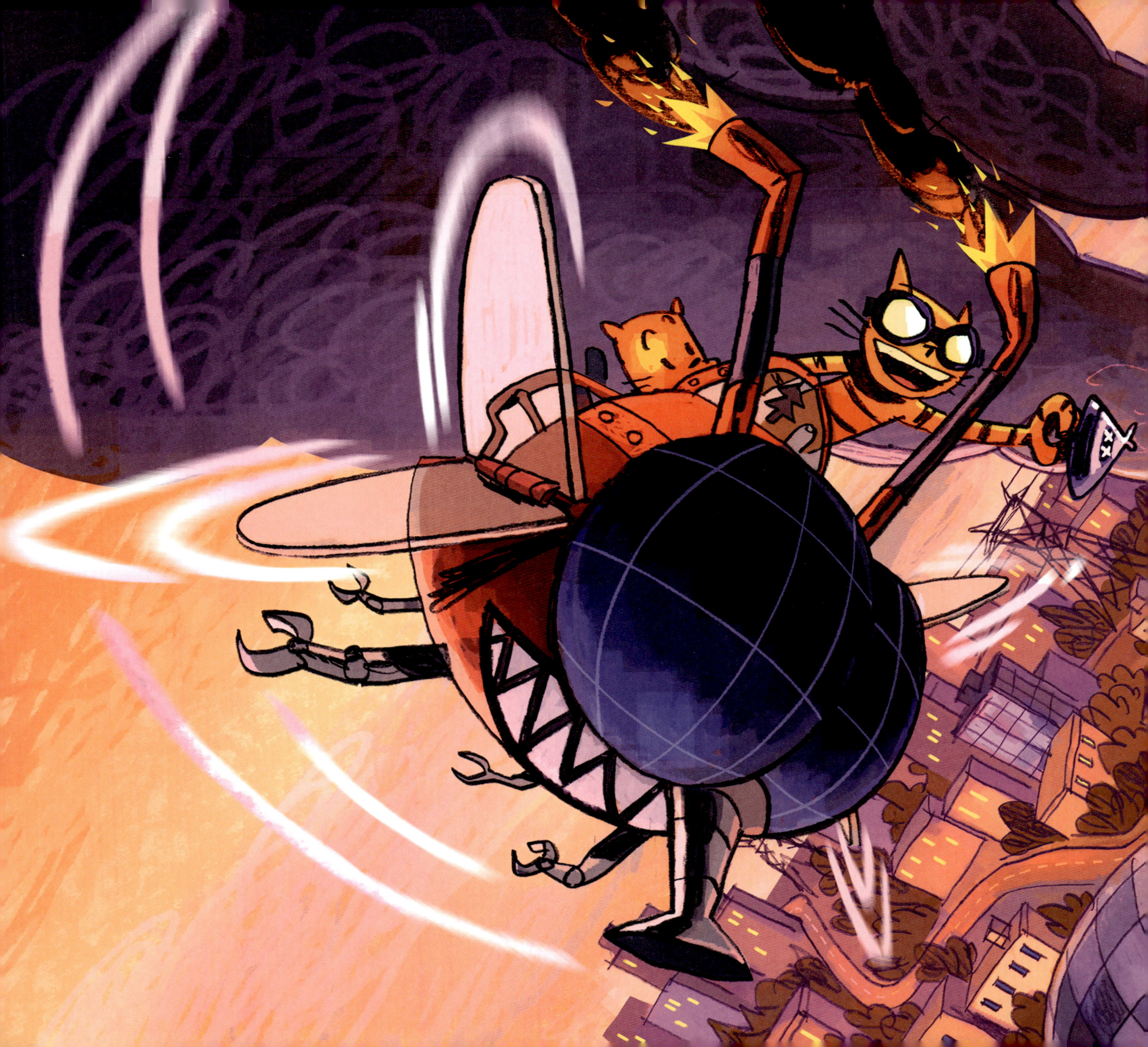

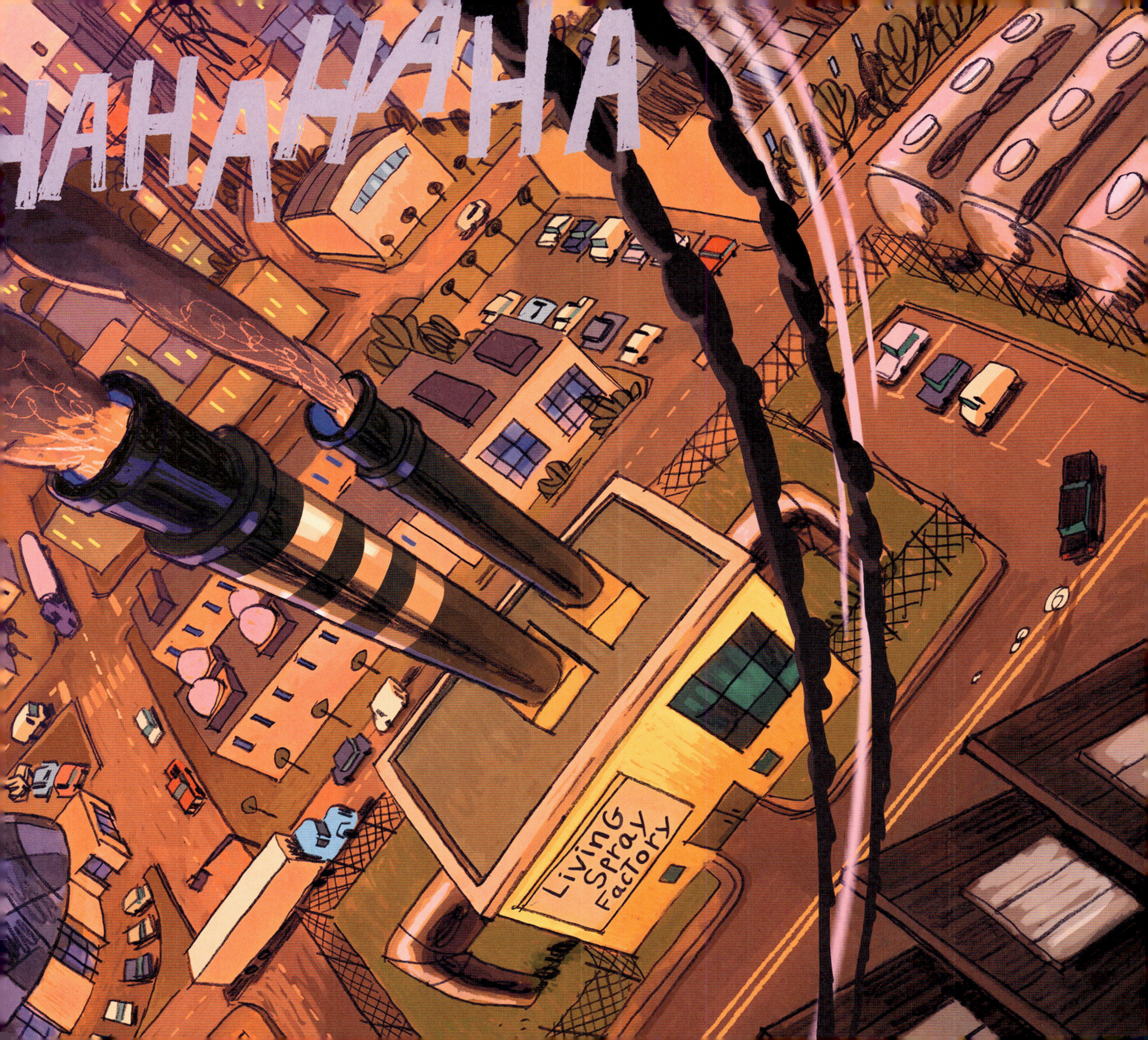
HAHAHAHAHA
Living Spray Factory

The Living Spray Factory Monster

In the third act of the movie, when The Living Spray Factory comes to life and becomes a monster, the unhinged plot turn gave the artists and animators the opportunity to create hilarious transformations. "The building itself kind of looks the same, but it develops strong arms from its sides and grows legs, and googly eyes pop up on its 'face' as well," says production designer Nate Wragg.

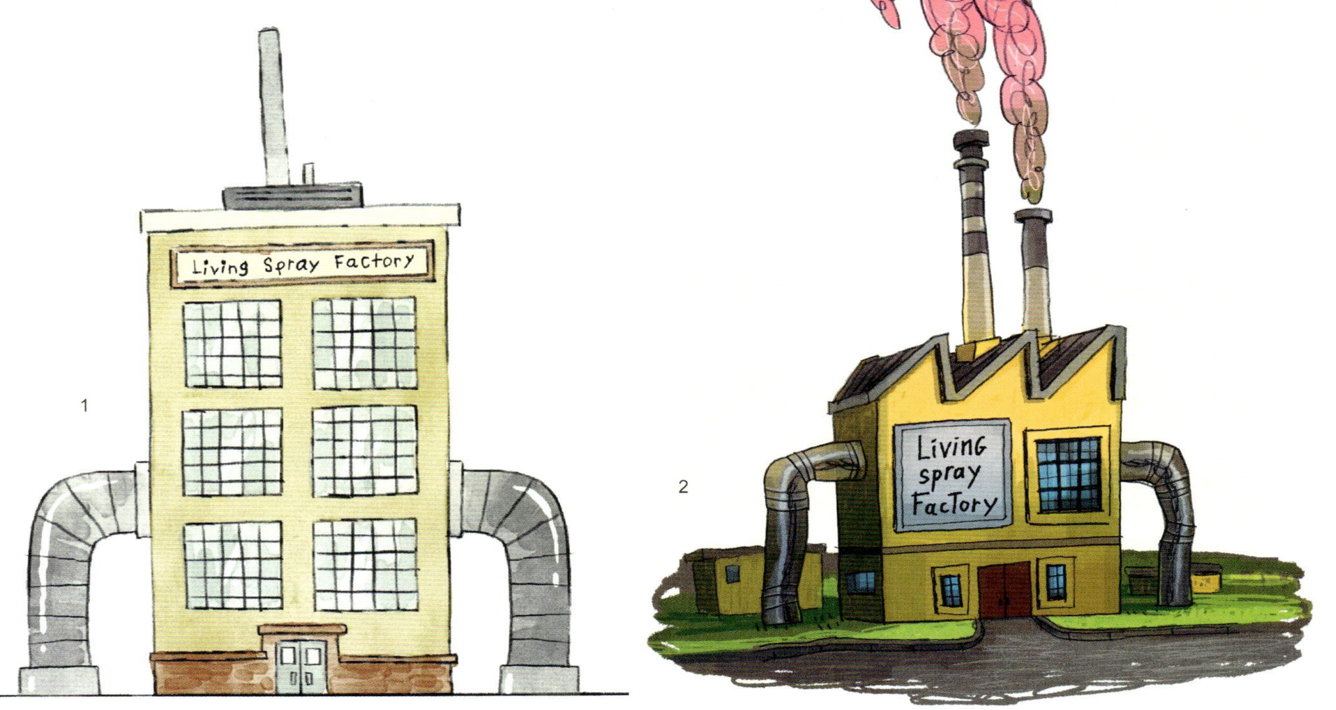

3

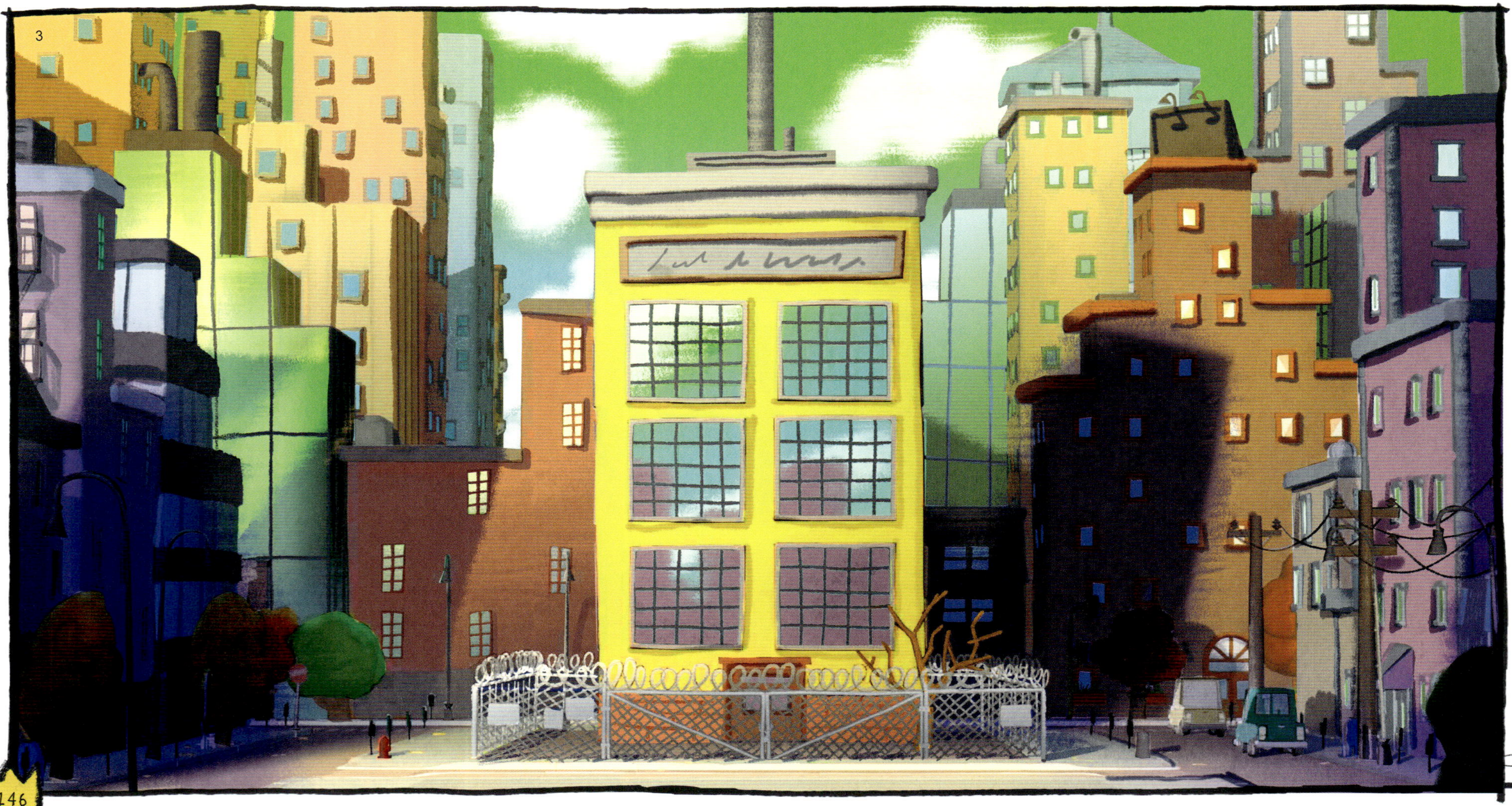

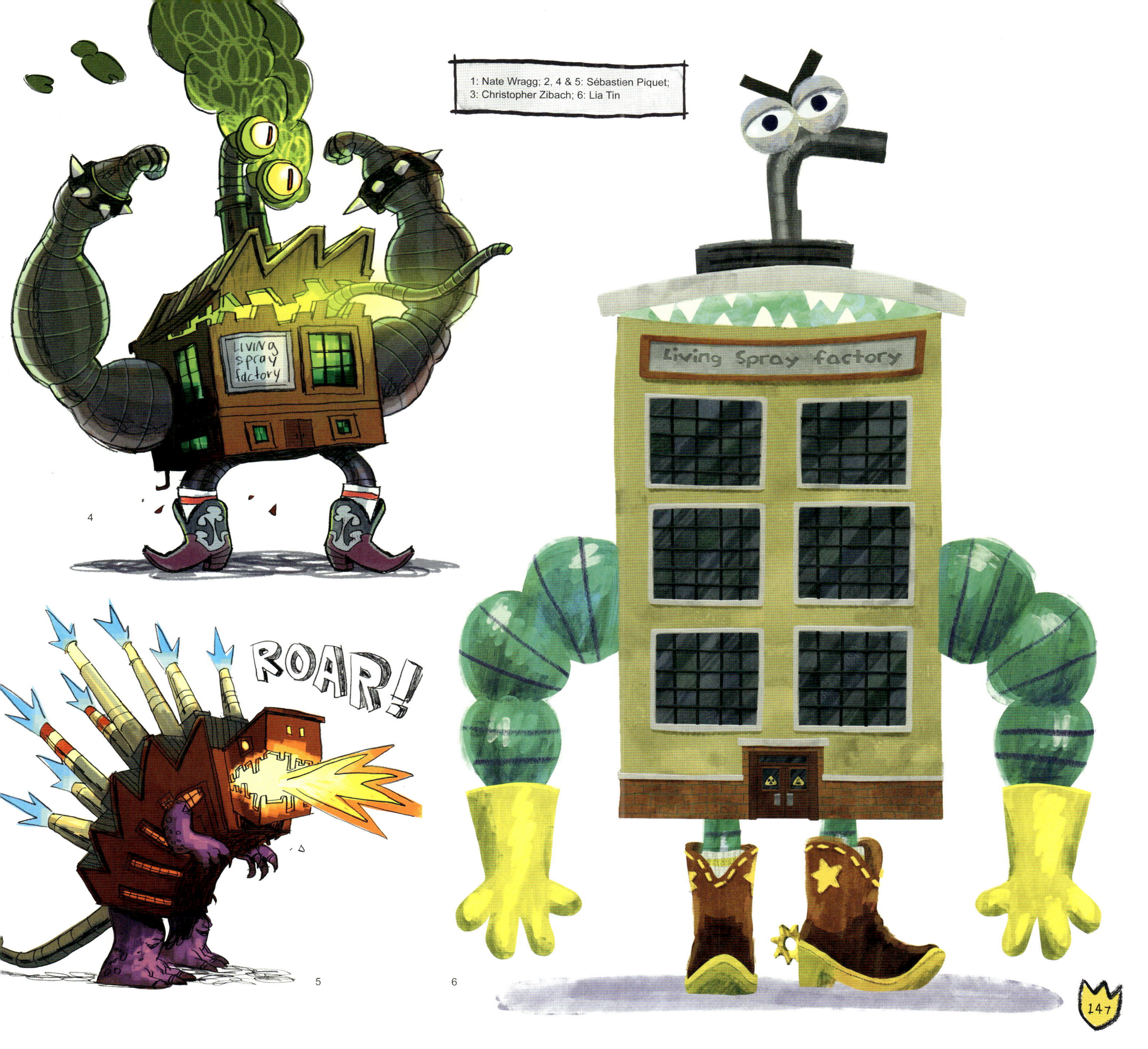

1: Nate Wragg; 2, 4 & 5: Sébastien Piquet;
3: Christopher Zibach; 6: Lia Tin

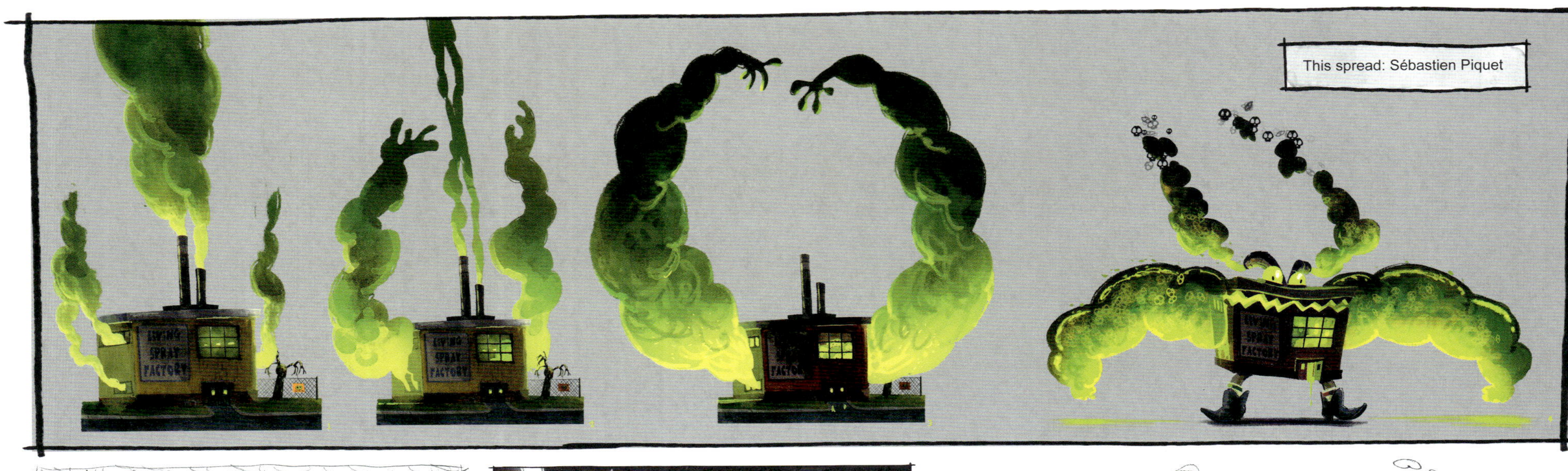

This spread: Sébastien Piquet

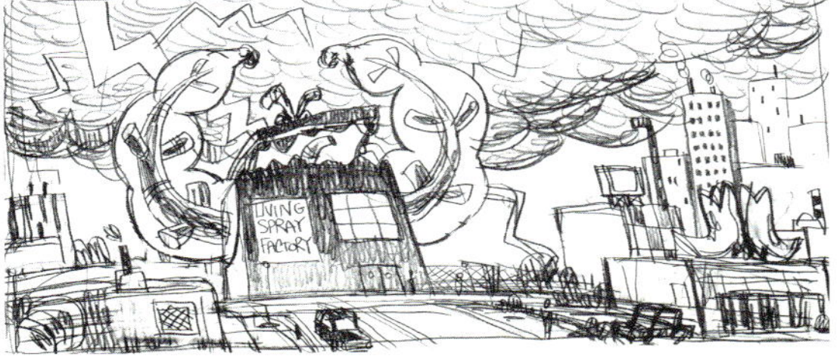

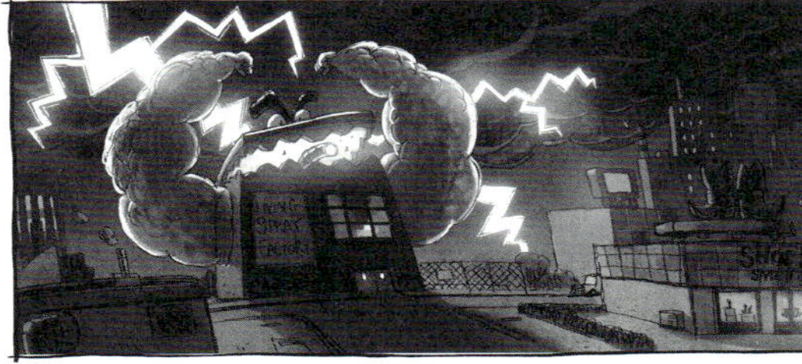

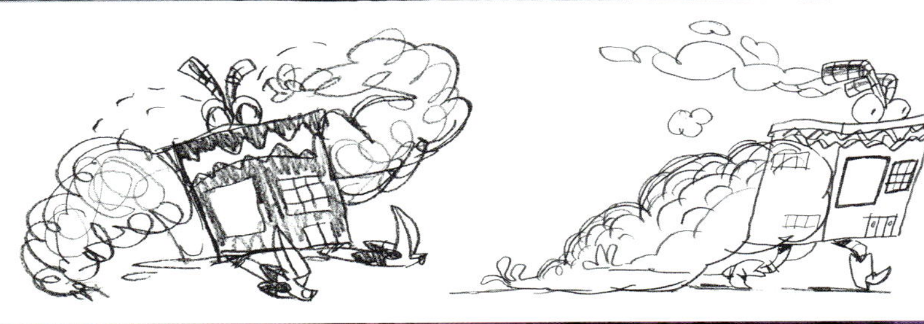

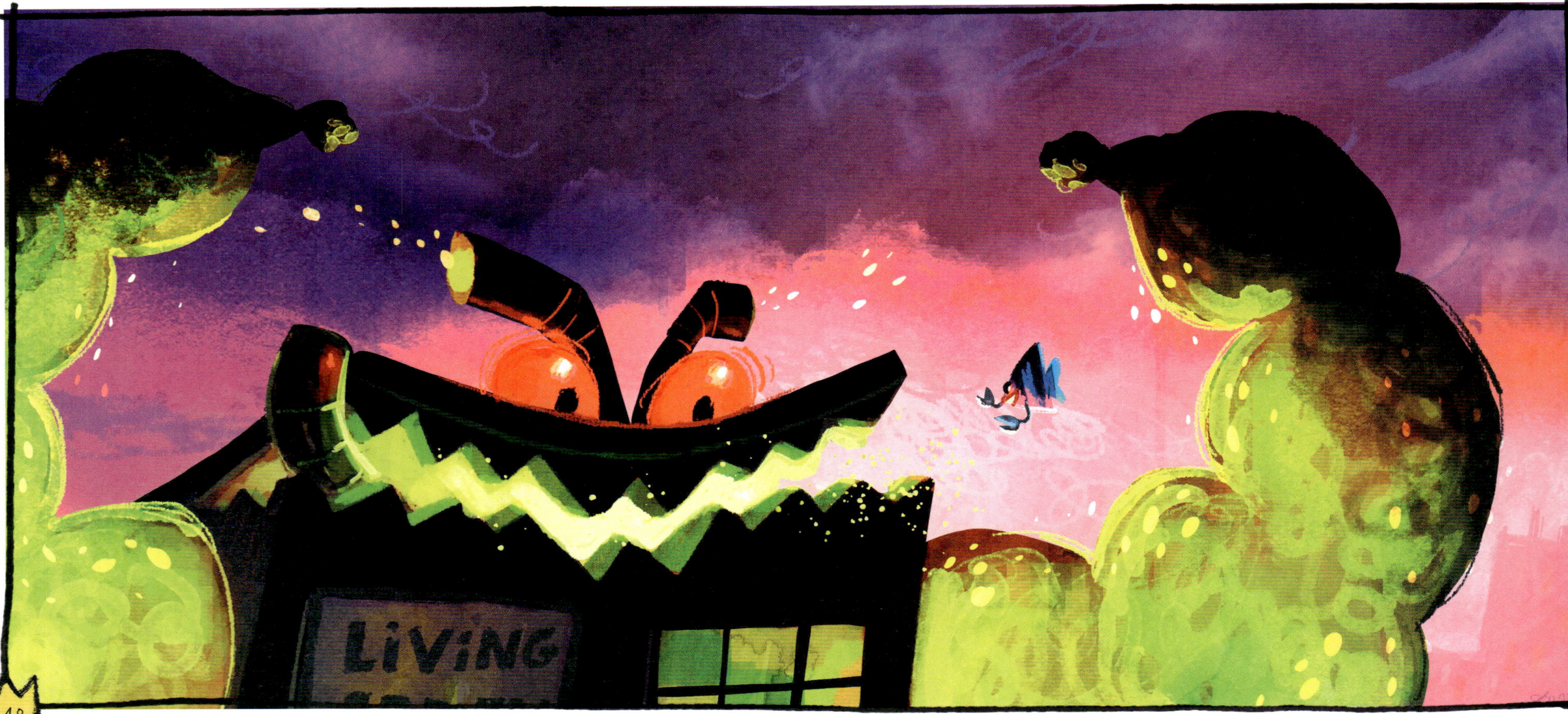

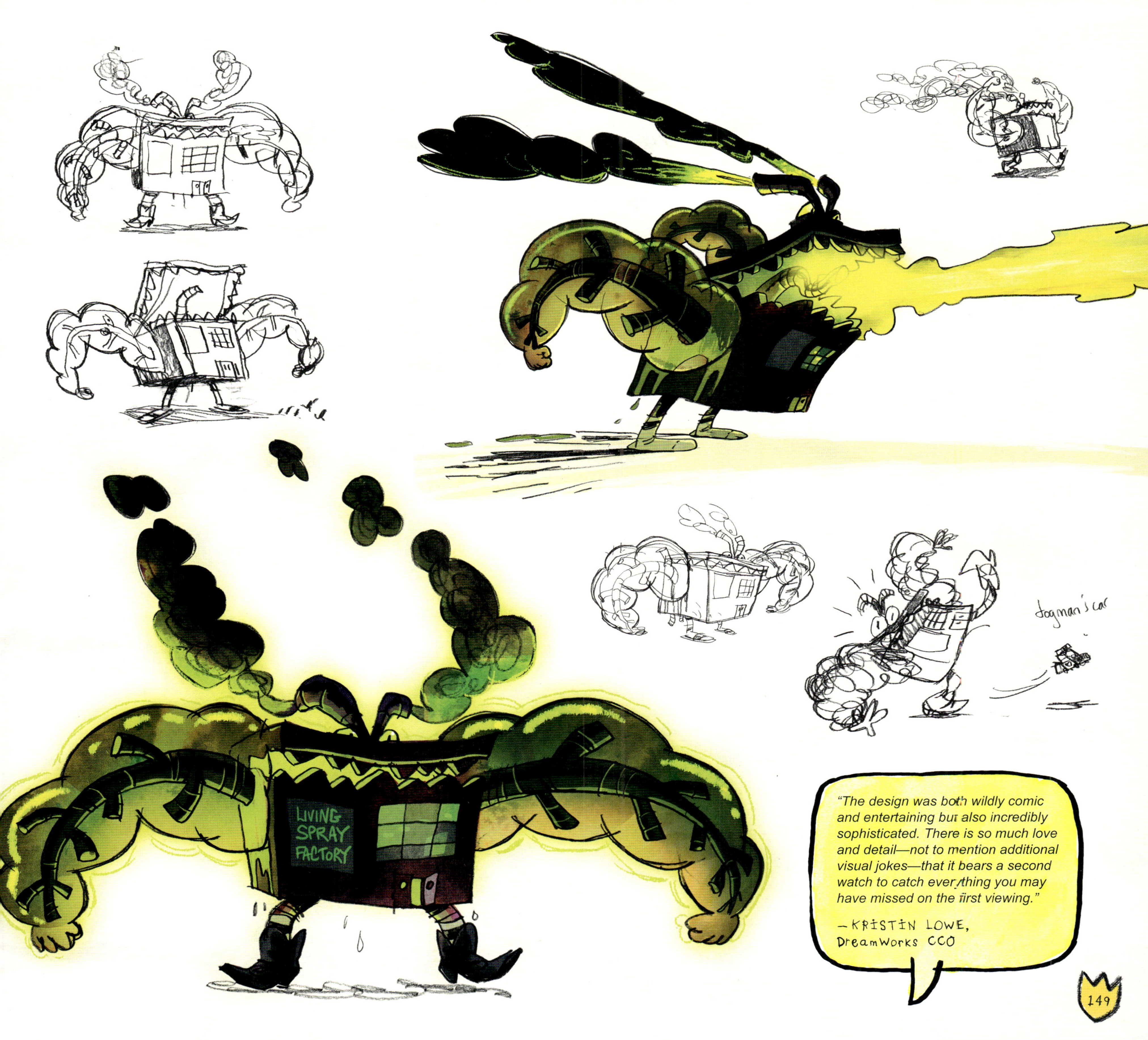
dogman's car
LIVING SPRAY FACTORY
"The design was both wildly comic and entertaining but also incredibly sophisticated. There is so much love and detail—not to mention additional visual jokes—that it bears a second watch to catch everything you may have missed on the first viewing."
—KRISTIN LOWE, DreamWorks CCO

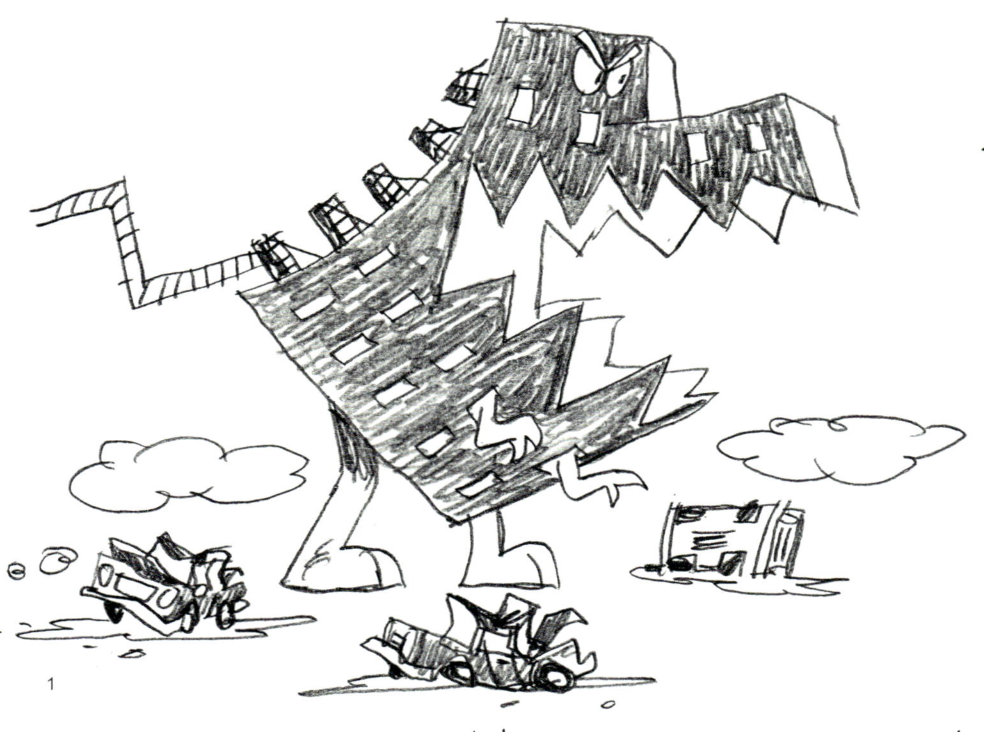

1

Monster buildings

"We have a lot of fun** playing with the camera language as the film progresses," says Scott Cullen, director of cinematography and layout. "The camera also comes alive as the buildings are exposed to the Living Spray gas. We started out the movie flatly, but as the buildings start their big fight, the camera really goes wild. We use a lot of low, dramatic angles, and everything opens up like a true action movie."

Art director Christopher Zibach adds, "I think fans will enjoy this sequence's moments of anime-inspired heightened action, which utilizes stylized backgrounds with extreme lighting to play up a joke as the buildings become living monsters. We introduce a vehicle called The Squirrel Shooter 2000, which begins the very long domino effect that results in bigger monsters and higher stakes. First, you have Dog Man versus The Squirrel Shooter 2000, then The Squirrel Shooter 2000 versus The Living Spray Factory, then The Mecha Mail Man against The Squirrel Shooter 2000 against The Living Spray Factory, etc. The fight and the world keep expanding."

Zibach says he and his team were constantly trying to up the ante in this larger-than-life sequence. "We were trying to figure out which choices would be more dramatic: *Should we play it like a classic western in the heat of the sun, or should we stage it against stormy weather with thunder and lightning?*" he recalls. "Our goal was to elevate a scene that is already insane without getting in the way of the action and what was originally envisioned in the books and the script. It was a fun problem to have!"

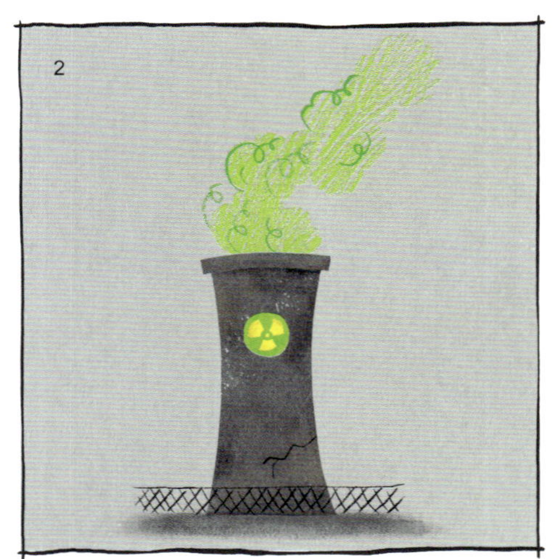

2

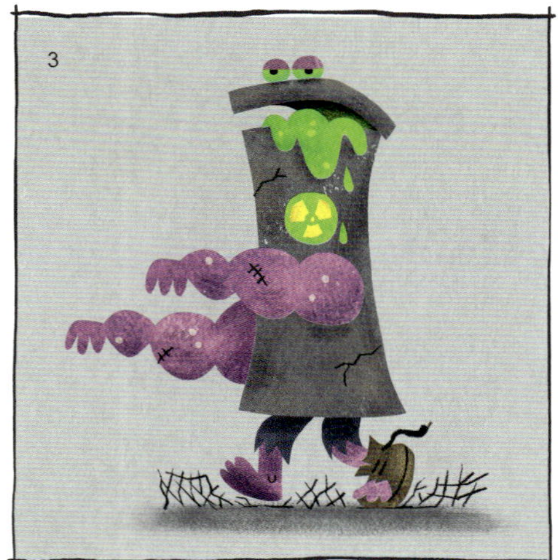

3

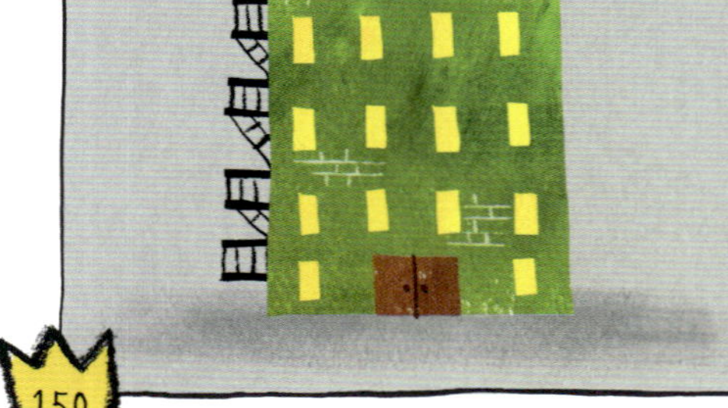

4

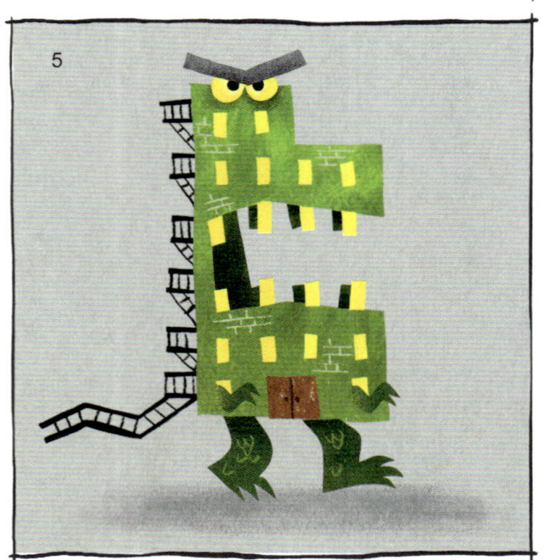

5

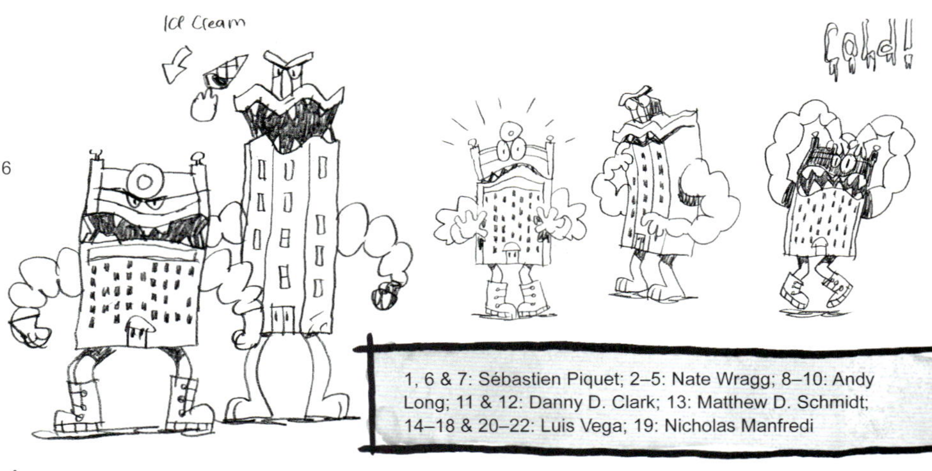

6

1, 6 & 7: Sébastien Piquet; 2–5: Nate Wragg; 8–10: Andy Long; 11 & 12: Danny D. Clark; 13: Matthew D. Schmidt; 14–18 & 20–22: Luis Vega; 19: Nicholas Manfredi

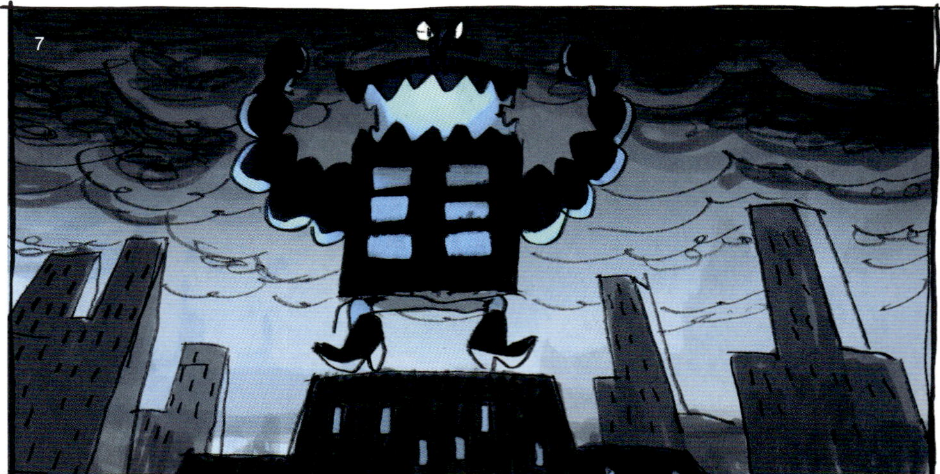

7

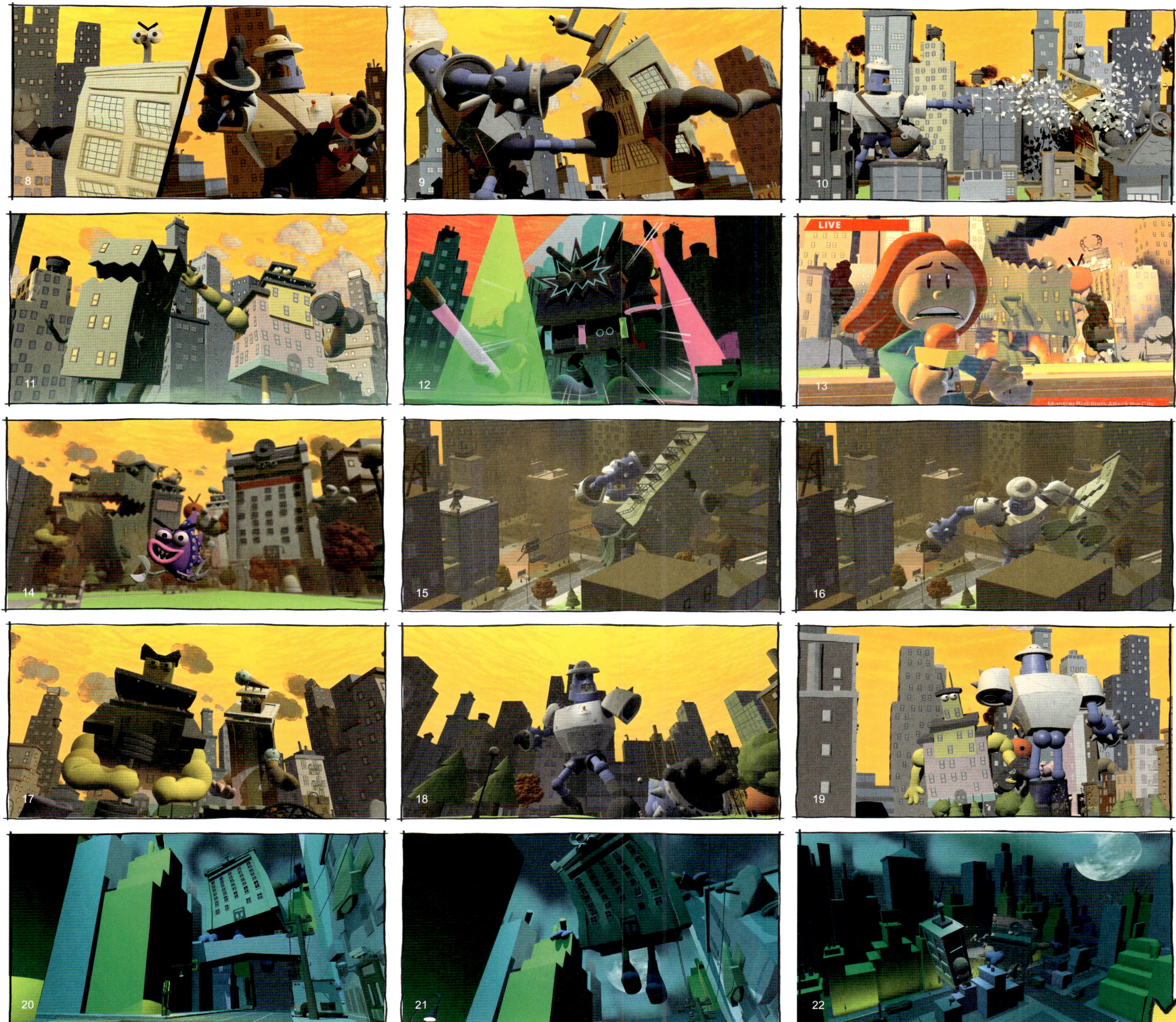
8
9
10
11
12
LIVE
13
14
15
16
17
18
19
20
21
22

1–7 & Overleaf: Nate Wragg; 8 & 9: Sébastien Piquet;

10–13: ***Modeling:*** Sarah von Fersen, Marta Macedo; ***Animation:*** Mark Spokes; ***Rigging:*** Alessandro Boschian-Pest, Xavier Roca Crespo, Joan Valdivielso, Élia Garcia Amores, Roger Bosque, Asier Lizaso Zelaia

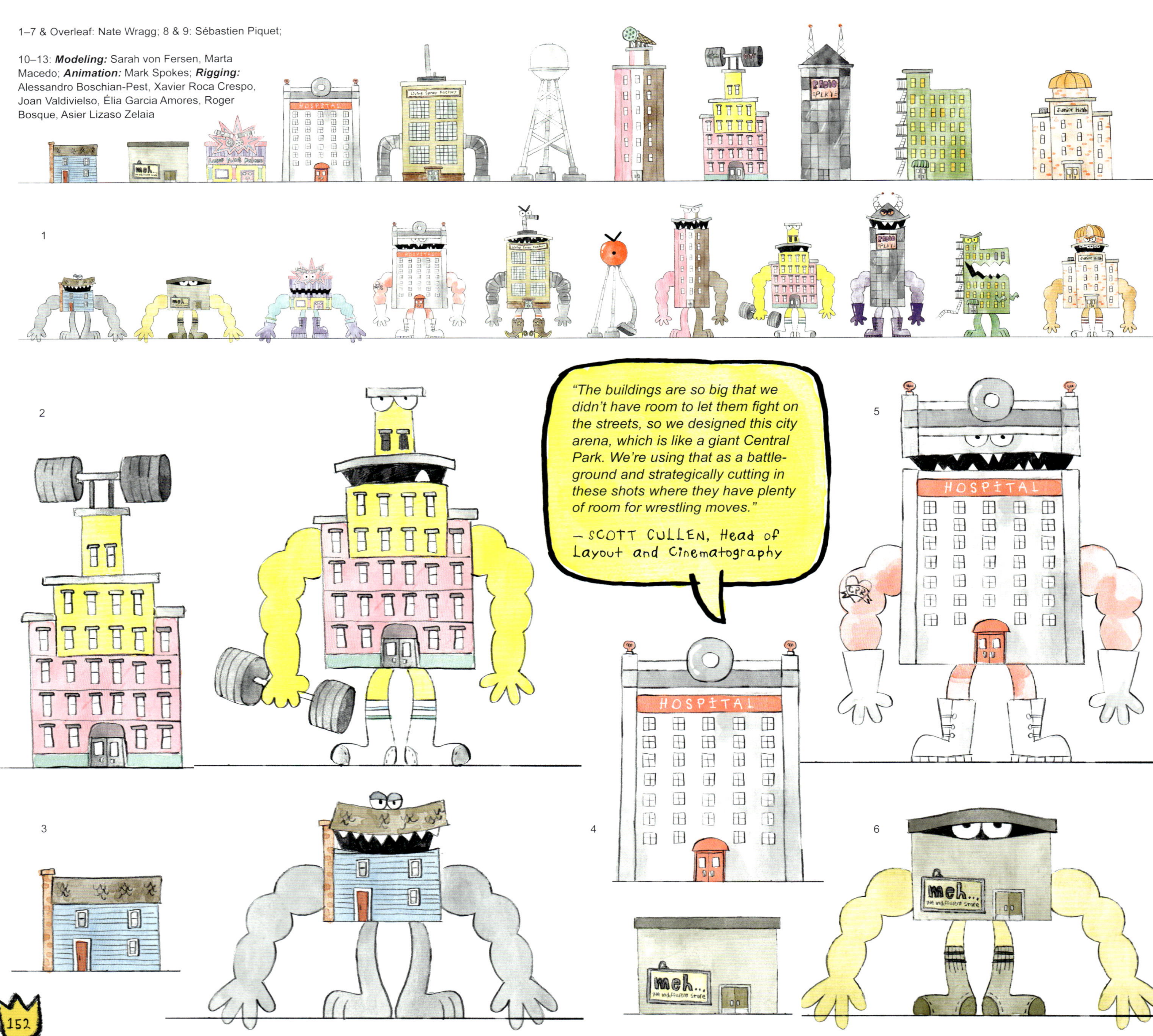

7

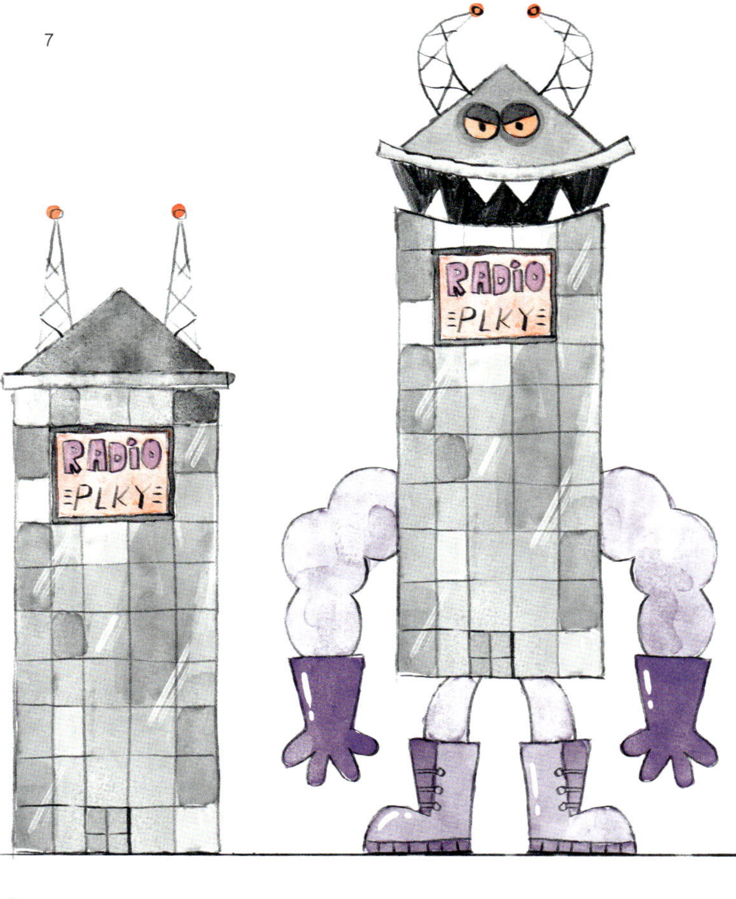

8

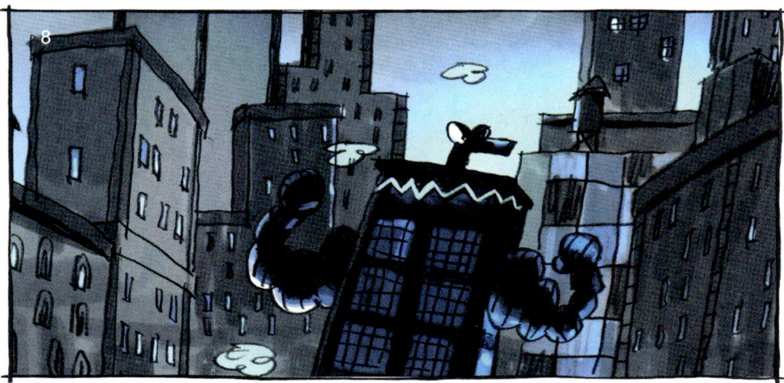

9

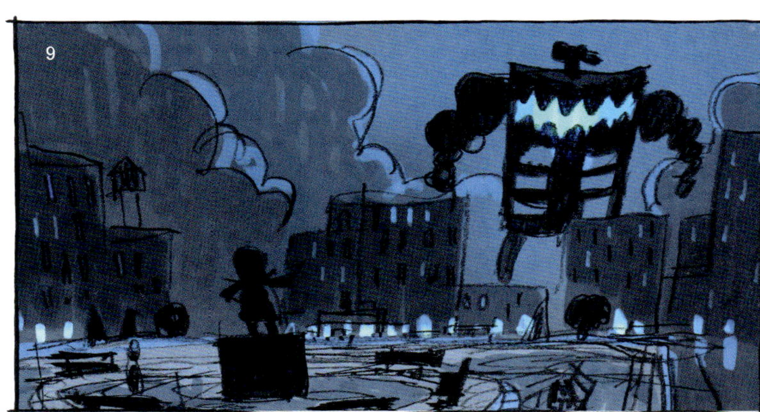

10

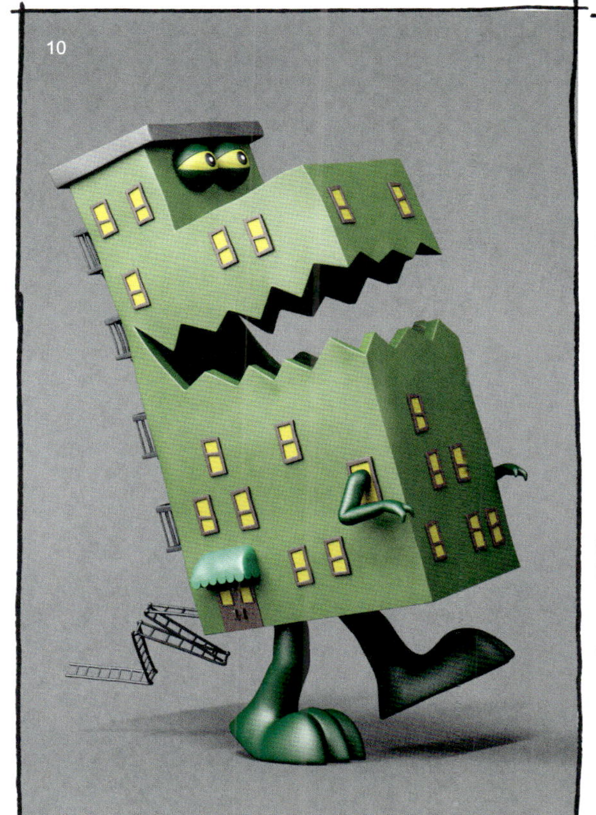

11

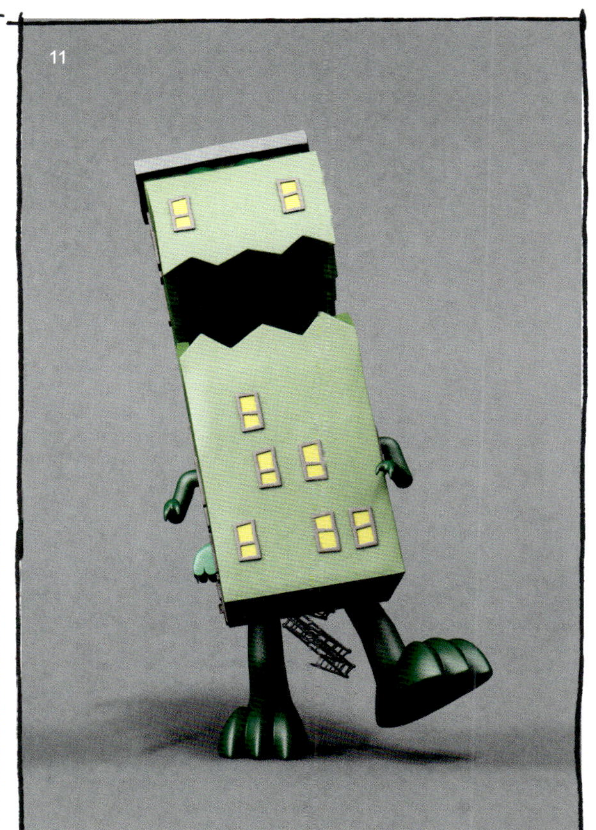

12

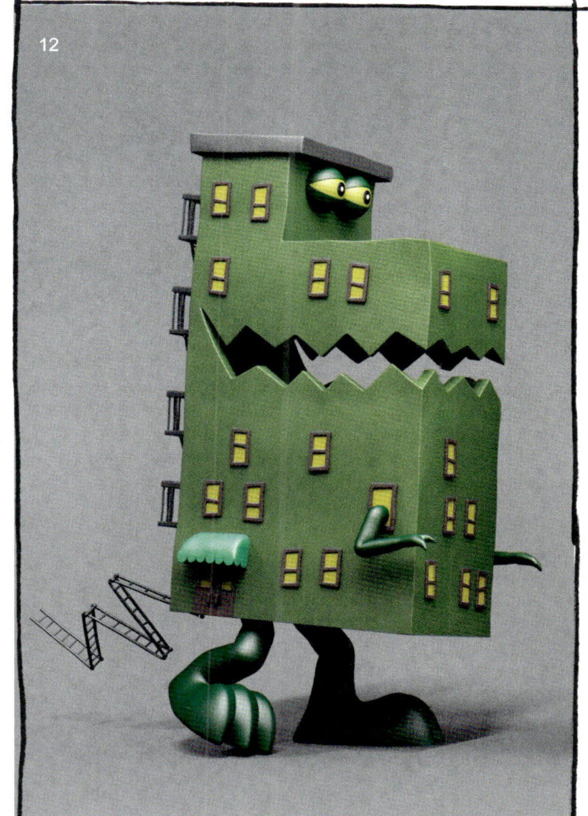

13

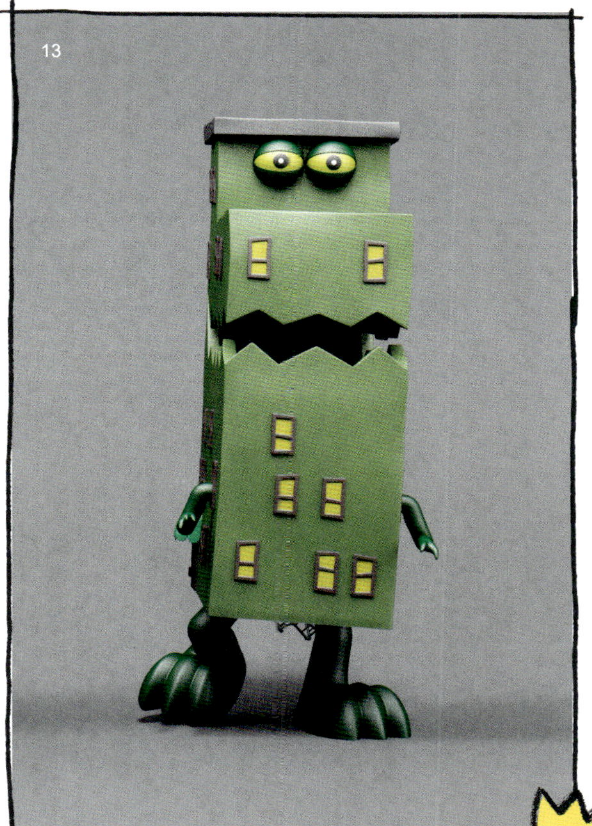

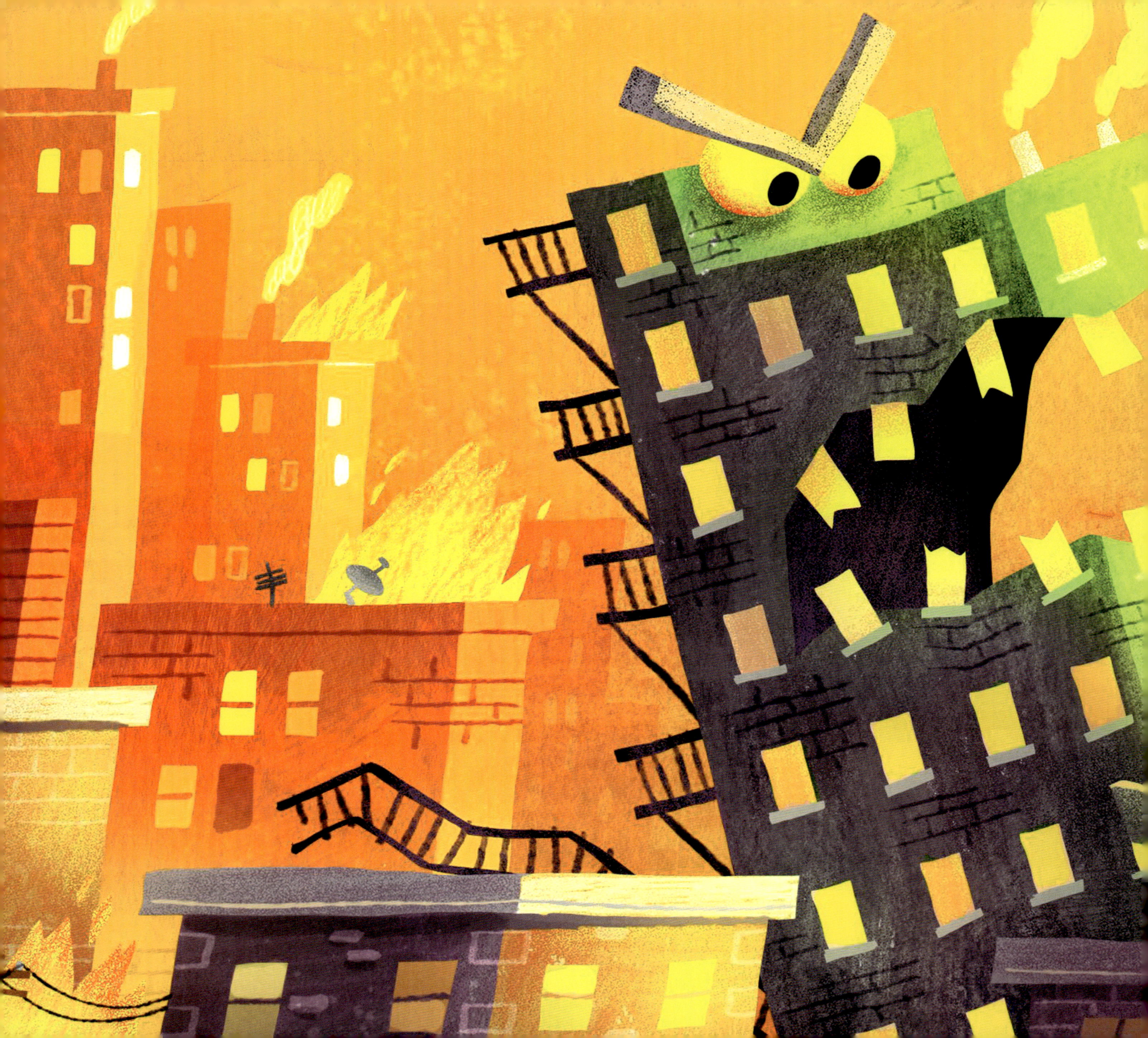

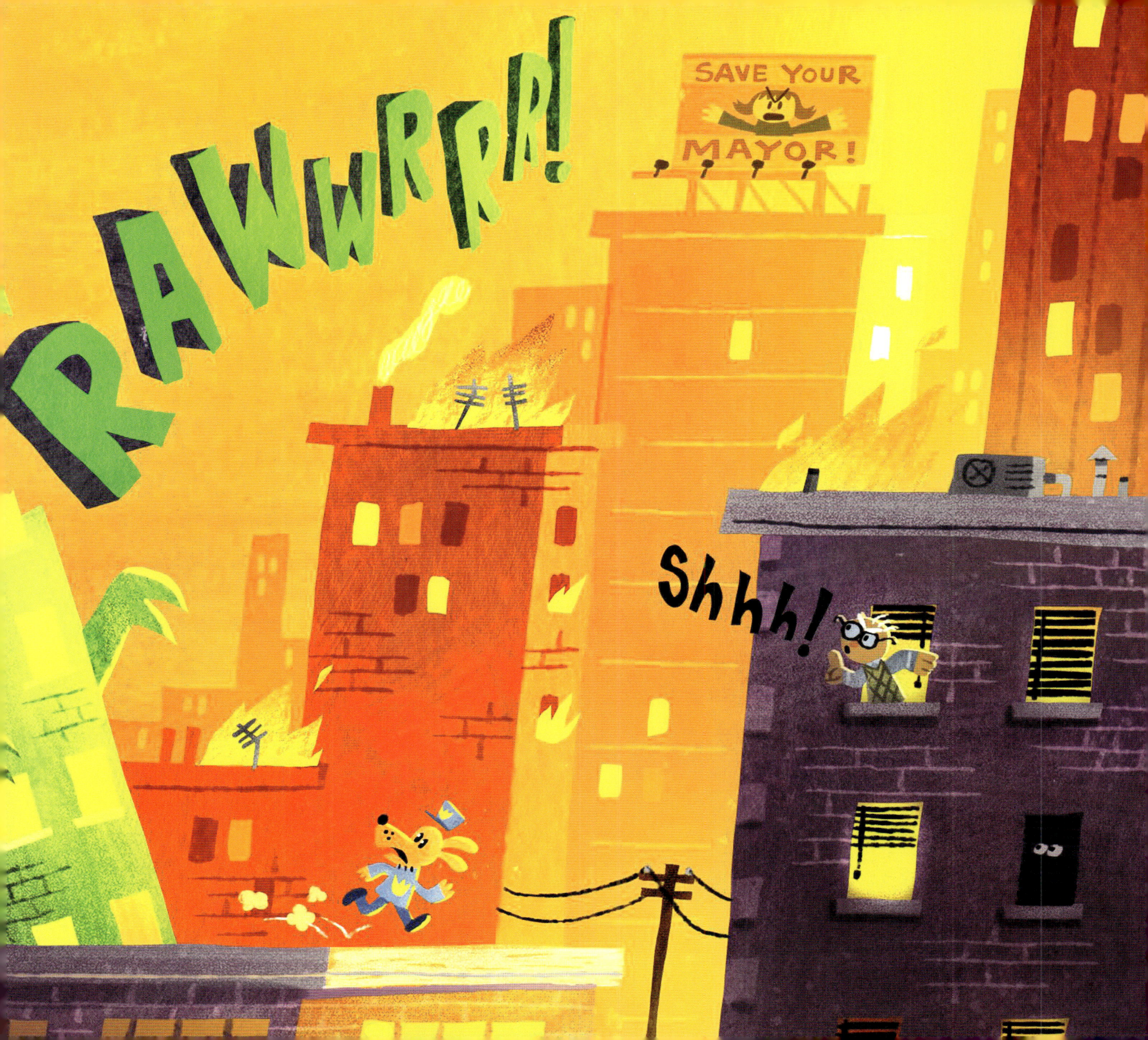
RAWWRRR!
SAVE YOUR MAYOR!
Shhh!

The Mecha Mail Man

After The Living Spray Factory turns into a monster, Petey comes up with the not-so-great idea of building something to defeat it, and Dog Man believes that the scariest thing in the world is a mailman. So, of course, Petey decides to build a giant robotic mailman. “It’s a totally absurd and ridiculous idea, but it all makes sense in this world,” says production designer Nate Wragg. “We created this mecha mailman to be like a giant-super-robot-type creature. Basically, it takes the classic third-act good versus evil fight and filters it through the lens of a silly Godzilla movie or the Stay-Puft Marshmallow Man from *Ghostbusters*.”

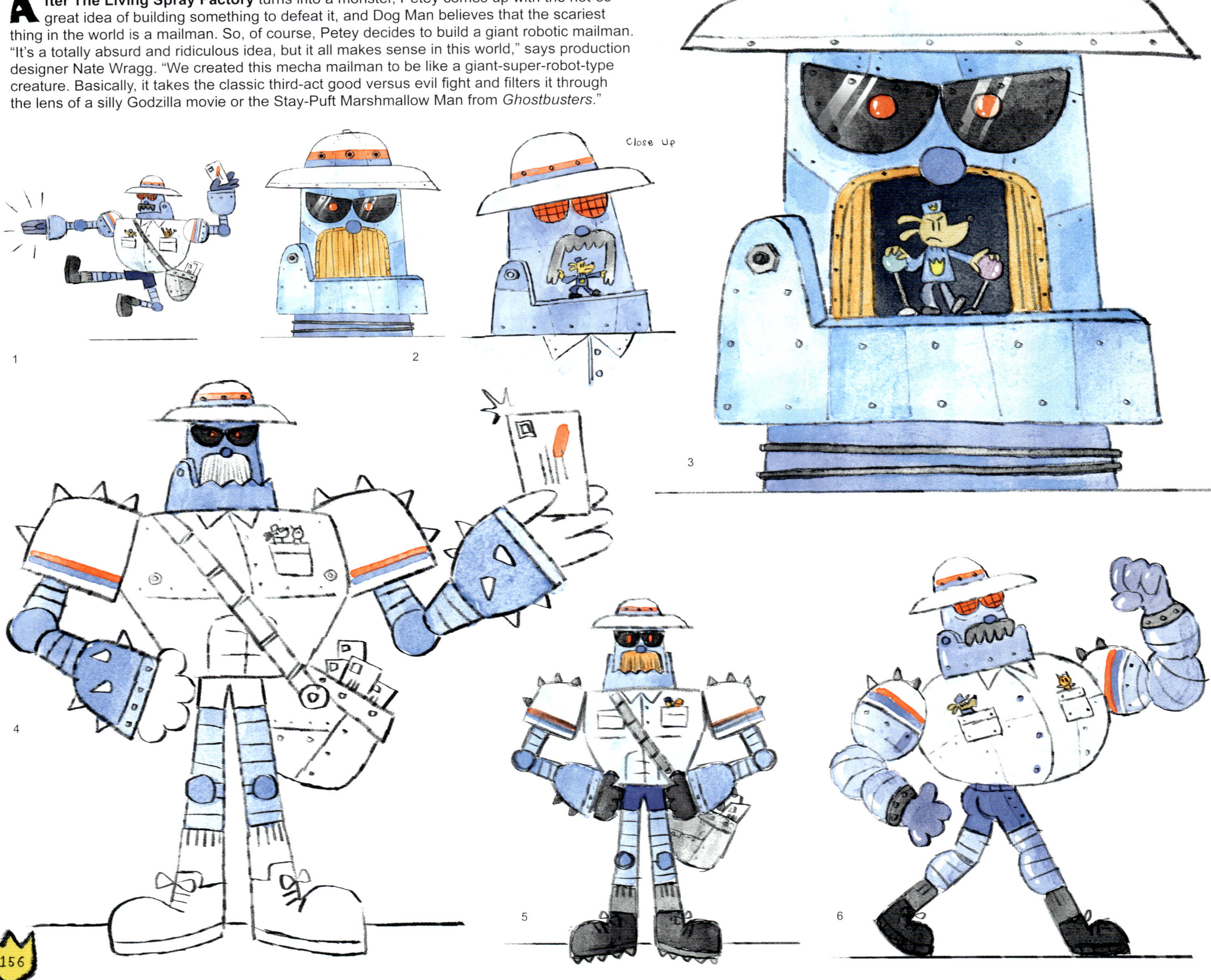

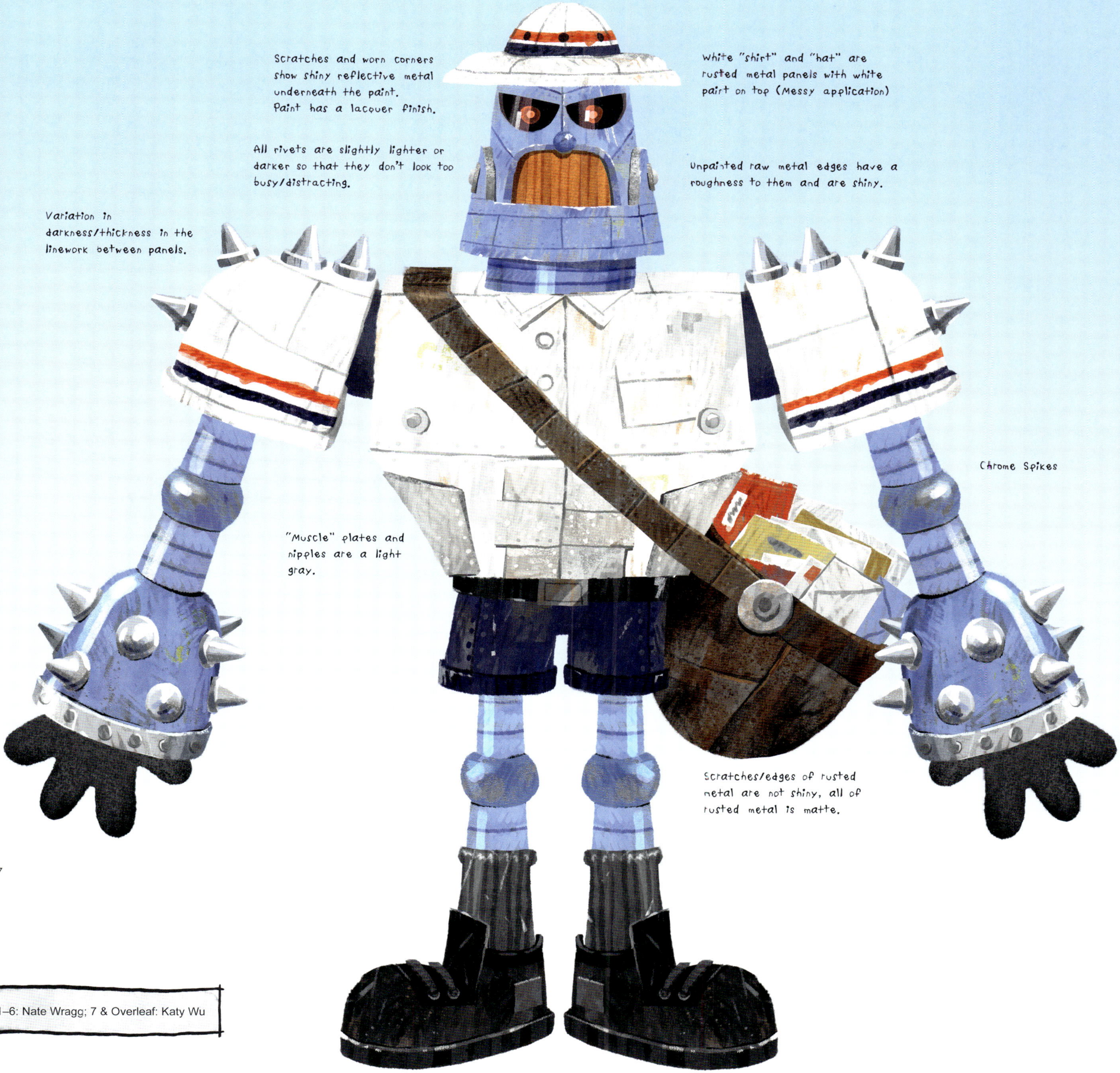

Scratches and worn corners show shiny reflective metal underneath the paint. Paint has a lacquer finish.

White "shirt" and "hat" are rusted metal panels with white paint on top (Messy application)

All rivets are slightly lighter or darker so that they don't look too busy/distracting.

Unpainted raw metal edges have a roughness to them and are shiny.

Variation in darkness/thickness in the linework between panels.

Chrome Spikes

"Muscle" plates and nipples are a light gray.

Scratches/edges of rusted metal are not shiny, all of rusted metal is matte.

7

1–6: Nate Wragg; 7 & Overleaf: Katy Wu

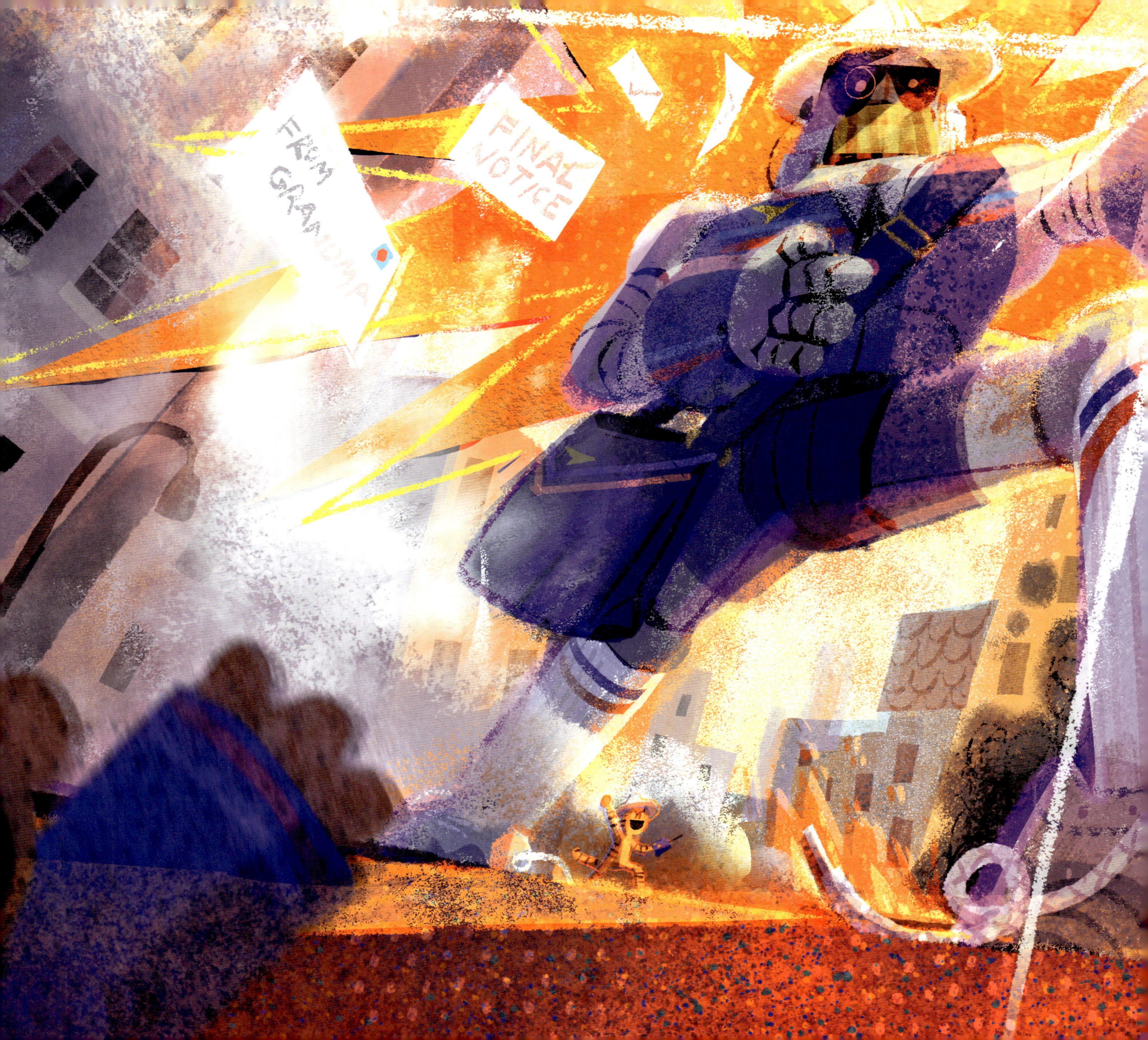
FROM GRANDMA
FINAL NOTICE

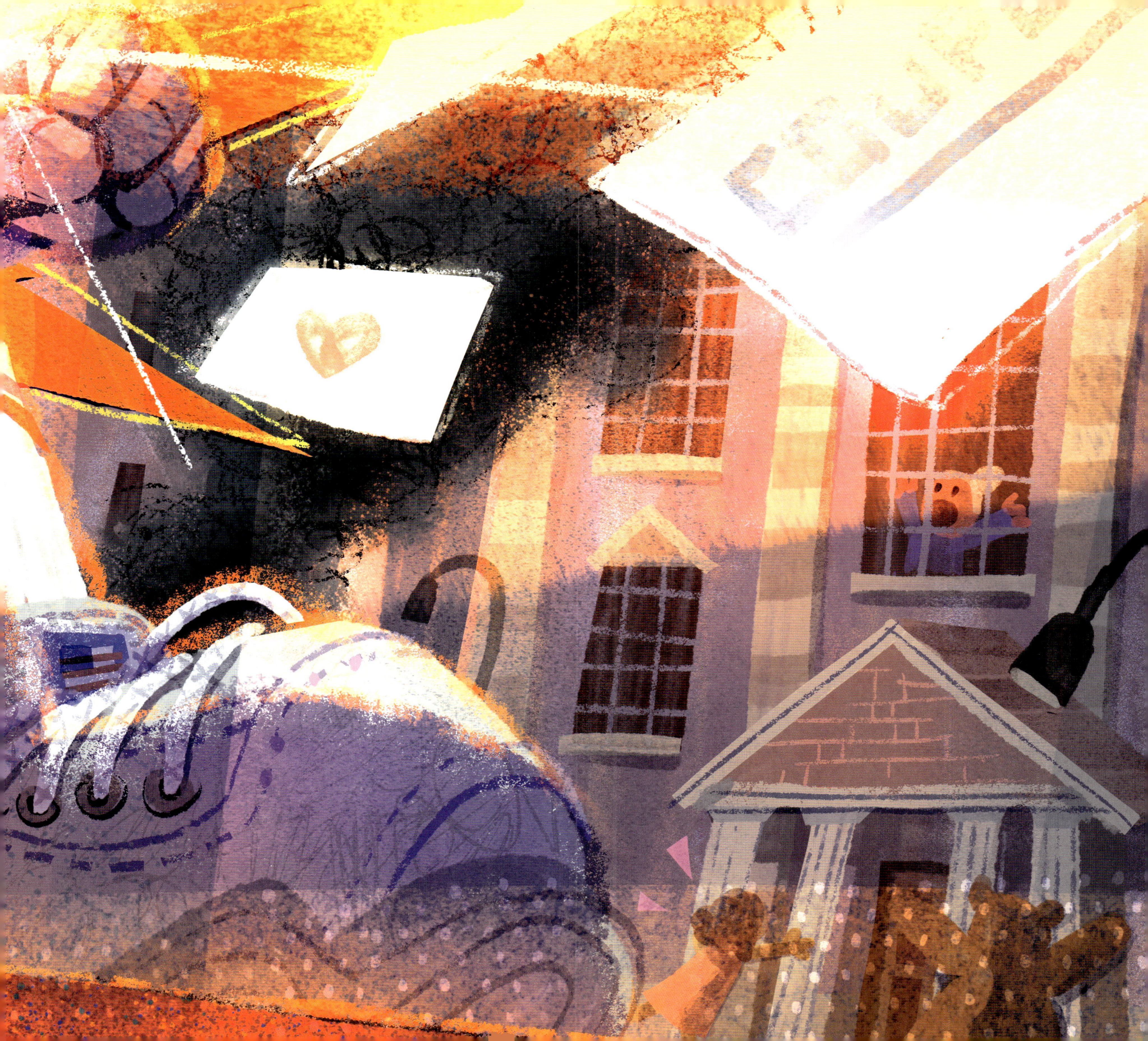

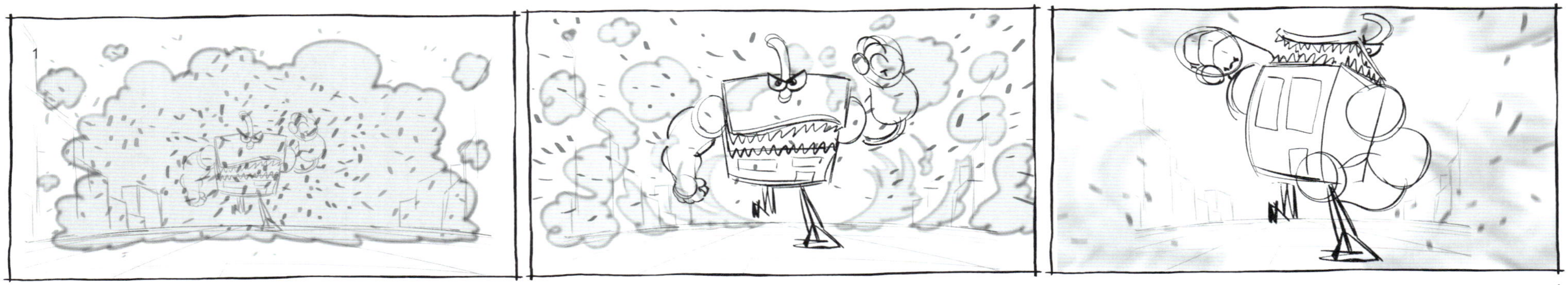

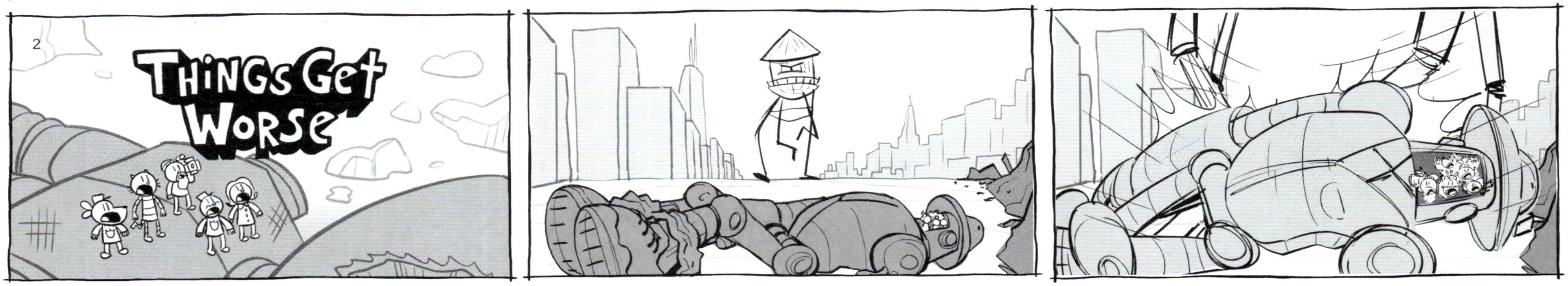

1

2

THINGS GET WORSE

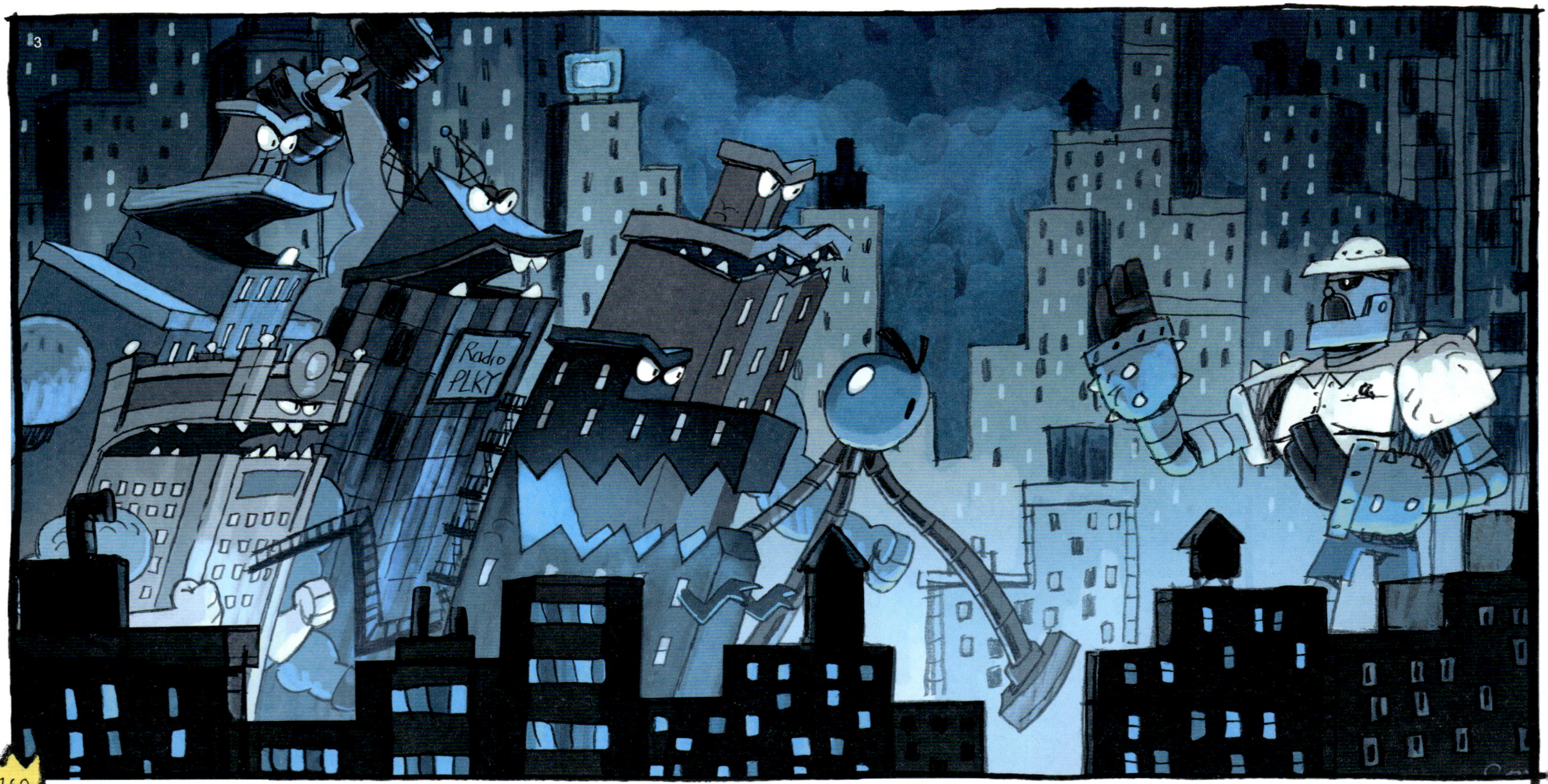

3

Radio PLKY

4

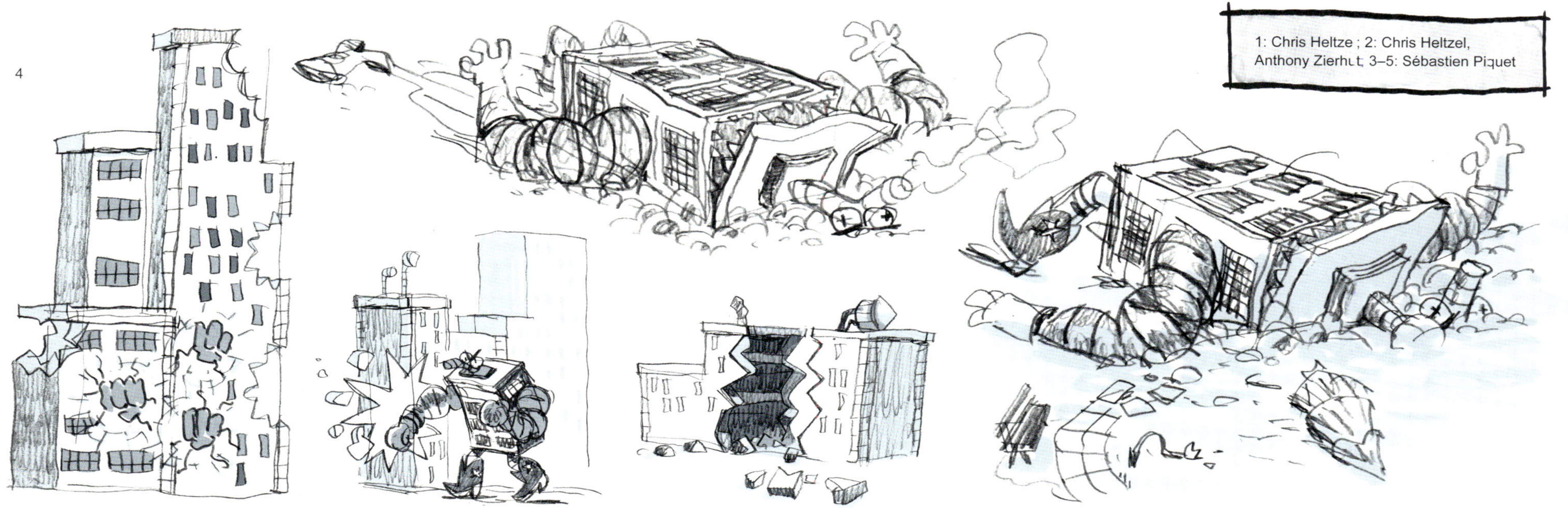

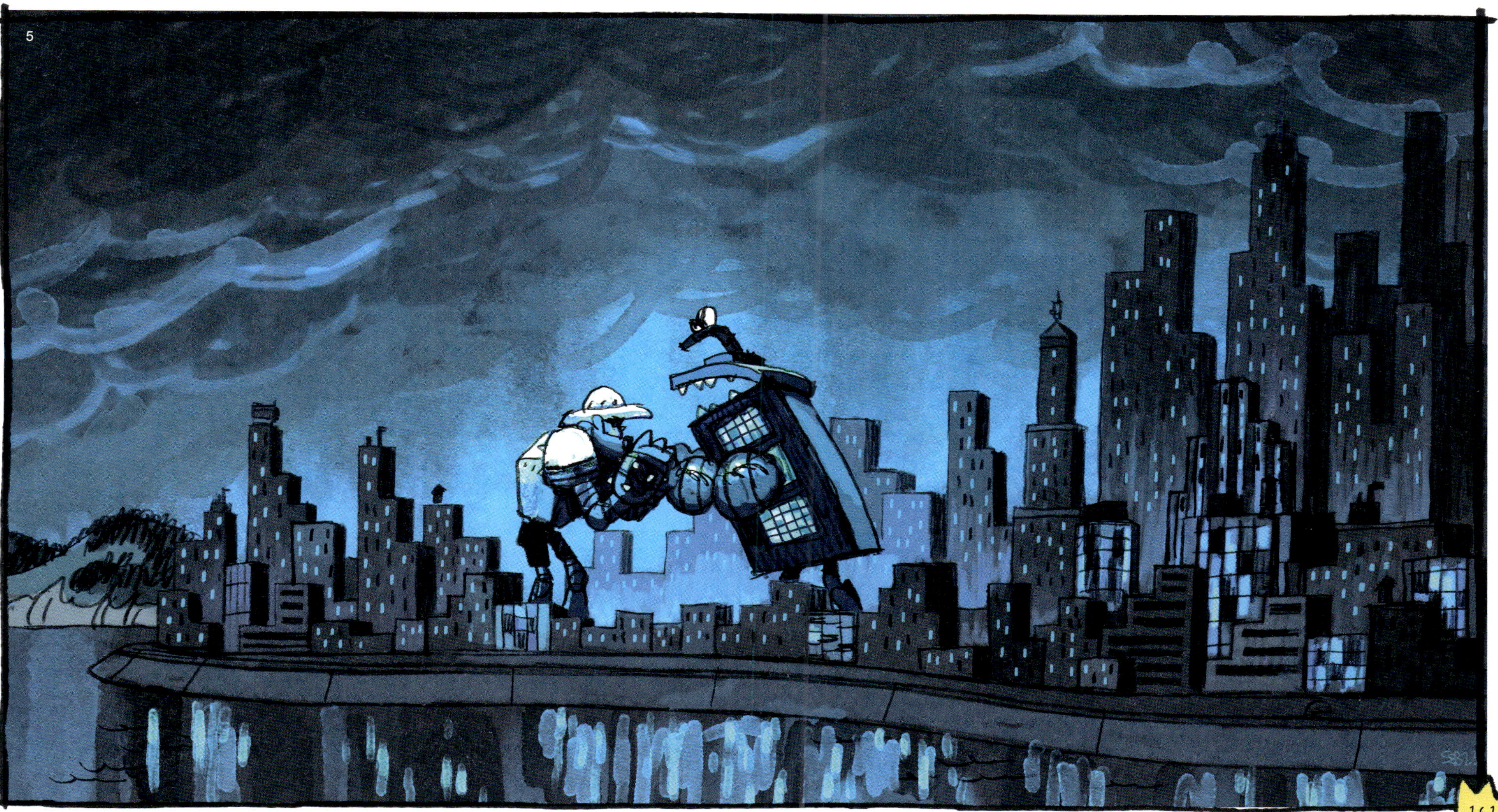

1: Chris Heltze ; 2: Chris Heltzel, Anthony Zierhut; 3–5: Sébastien Piquet

5

The finale

One of the jokes included in the third-act set piece is that as dastardly Flippy is looking for ways to get rid of Petey and 80-HD, he wants to pick the most dramatic option possible. He first sees the tar pits but rejects them as "too slow and boring." For a split second, he considers using fireworks from the Explosives and Things Store but decides against it because that option is "too fast and pedestrian." But his eyes widen when he notices the volcano. The notion of having a volcano right outside of the OhKay City suburbs fits in perfectly with the rest of the amusing absurdities of the Pilkey universe.

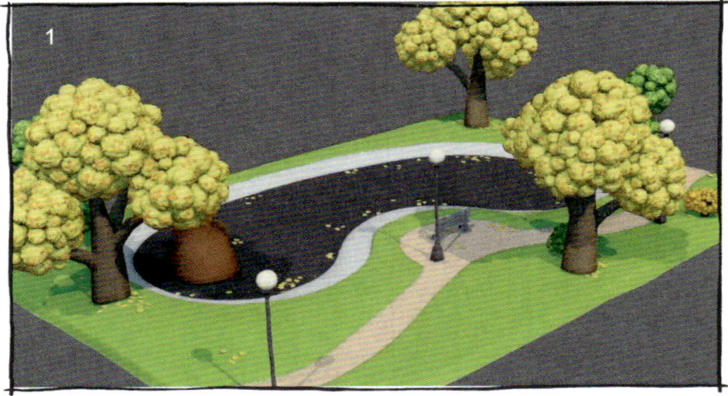

1

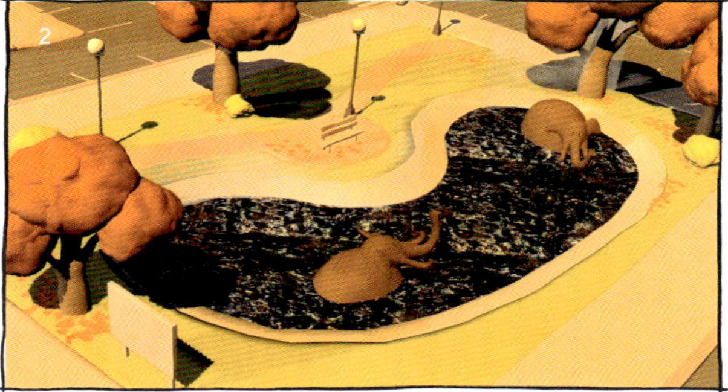

2

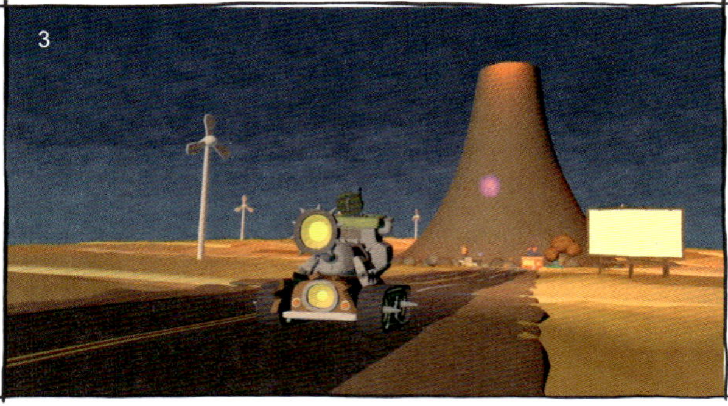

3

4

1: Fran Lara; 2 & 3: Zac Cavaliero; 4: Christopher Zibach

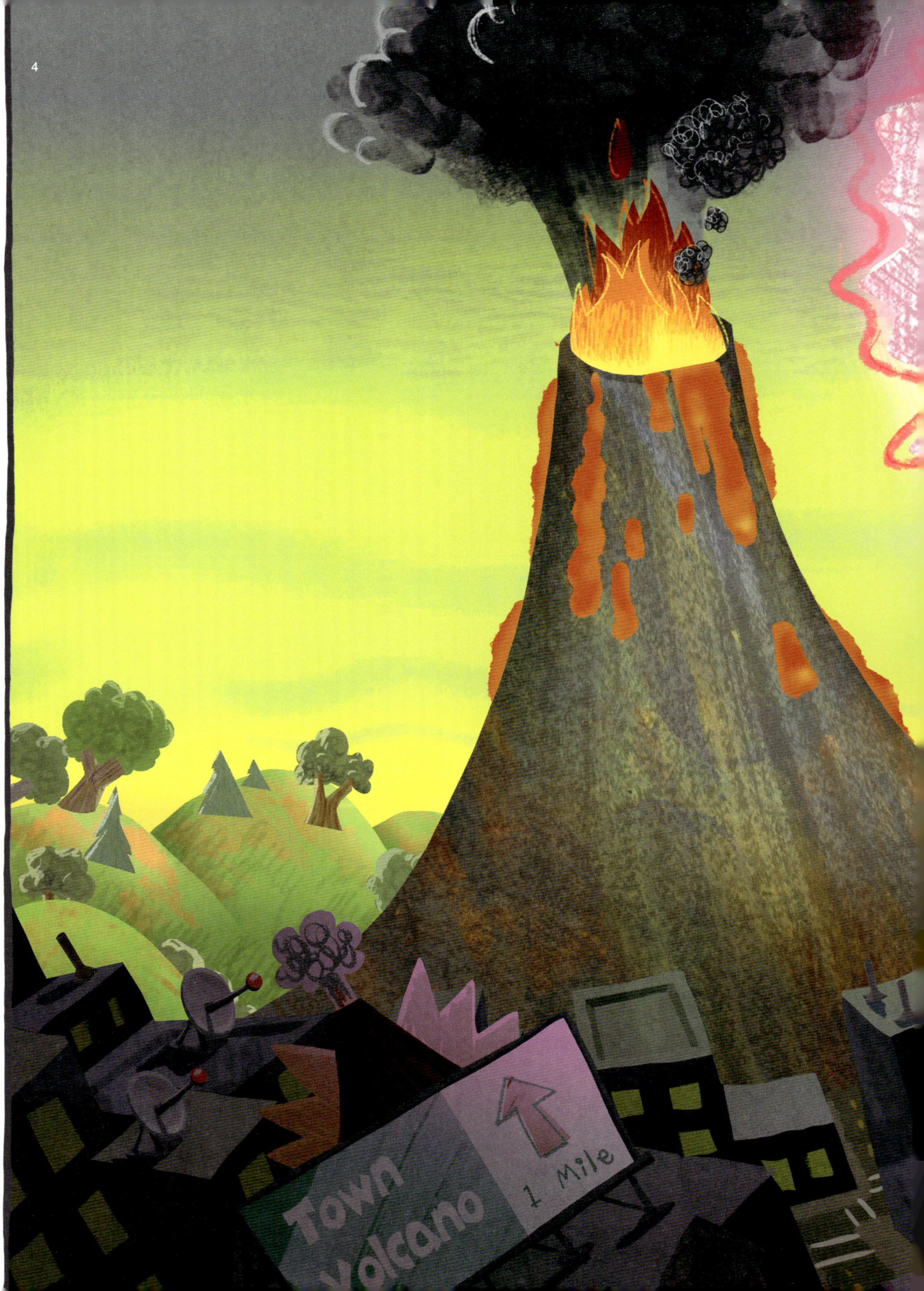

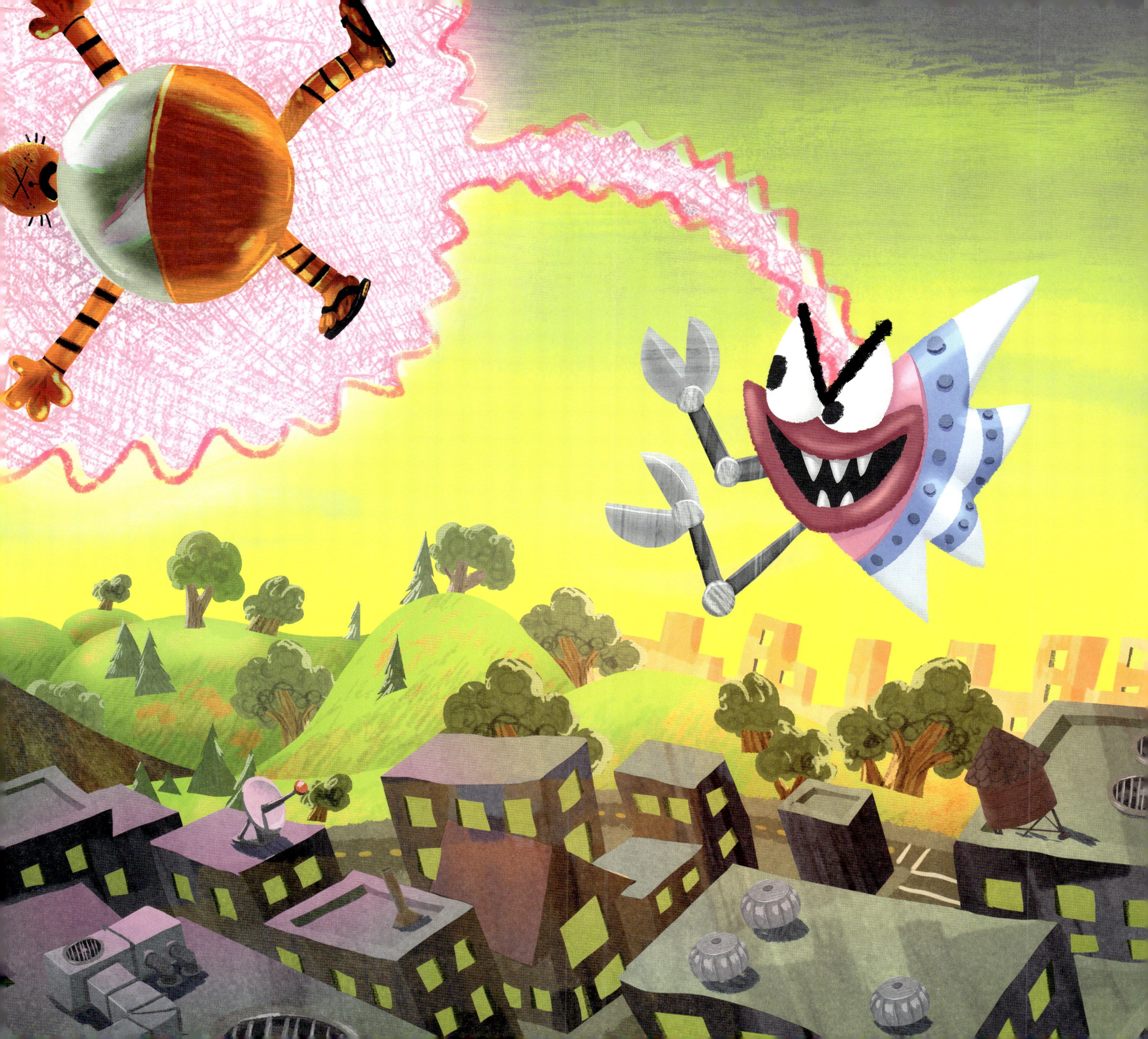

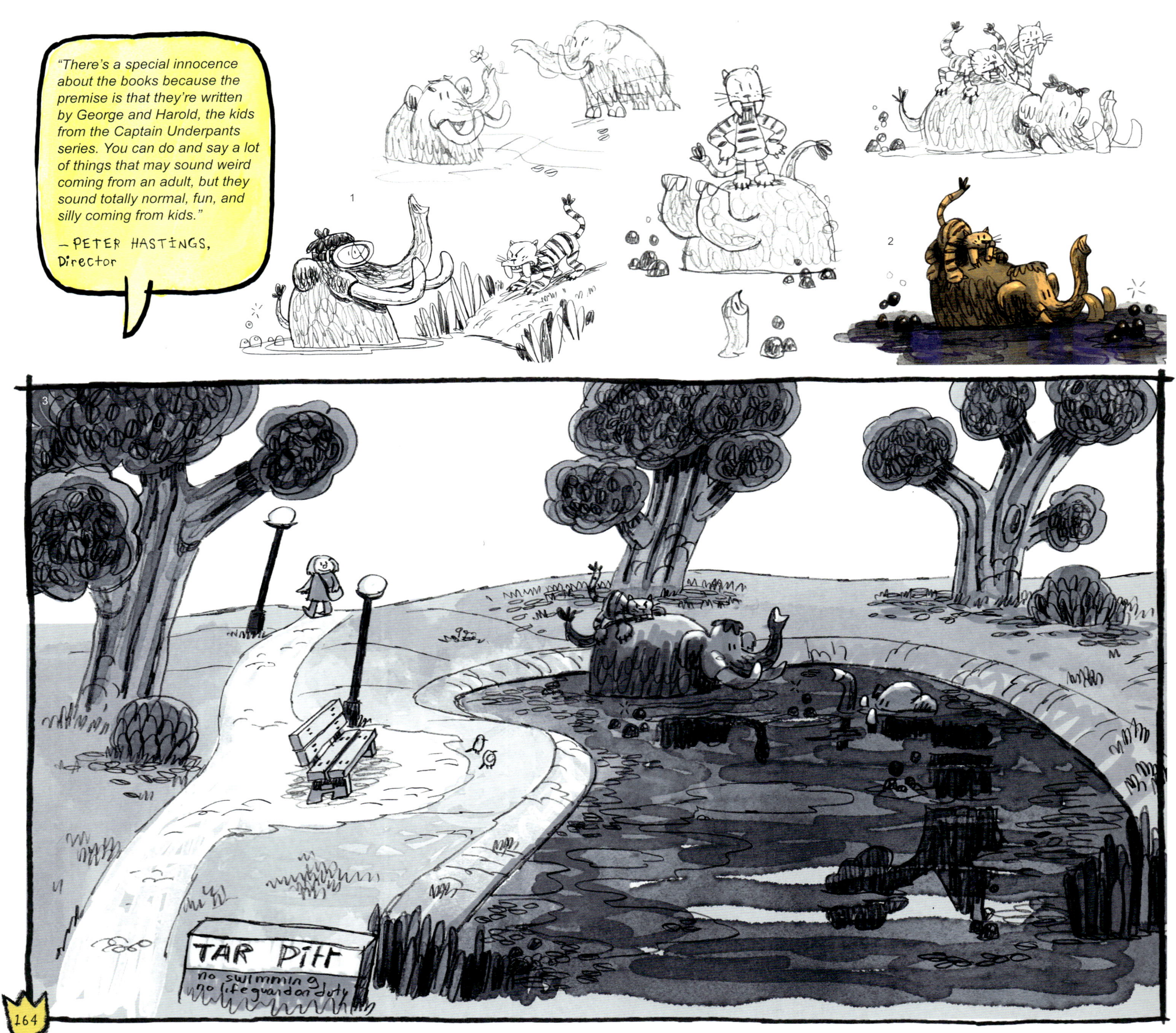
"There's a special innocence about the books because the premise is that they're written by George and Harold, the kids from the Captain Underpants series. You can do and say a lot of things that may sound weird coming from an adult, but they sound totally normal, fun, and silly coming from kids."
—PETER HASTINGS, Director
1
2
3
TAR PITT
no swimming
no lifeguard on duty

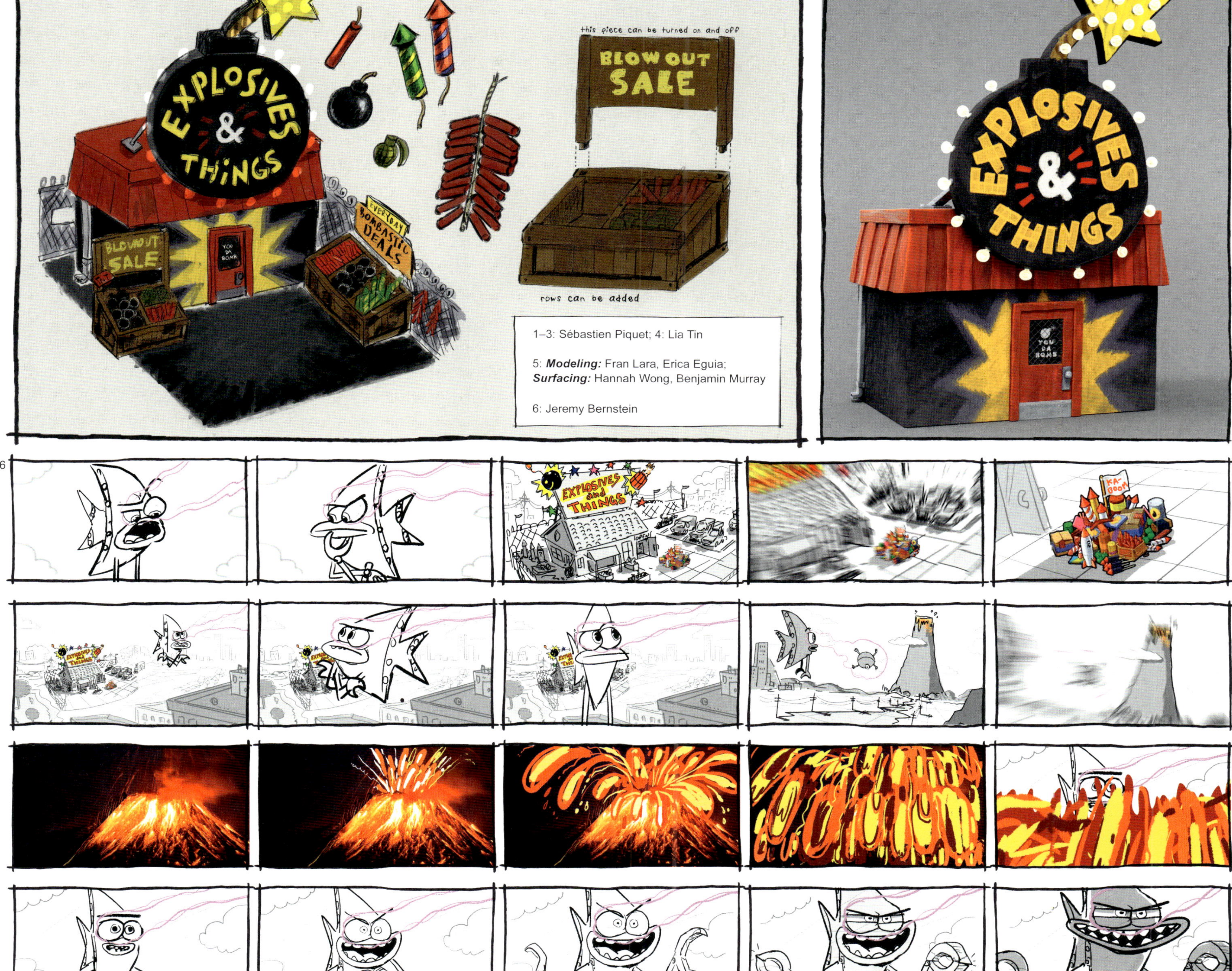

1–3: Sébastien Piquet; 4: Lia Tin

5: ***Modeling:*** Fran Lara, Erica Eguia; ***Surfacing:*** Hannah Wong, Benjamin Murray

6: Jeremy Bernstein

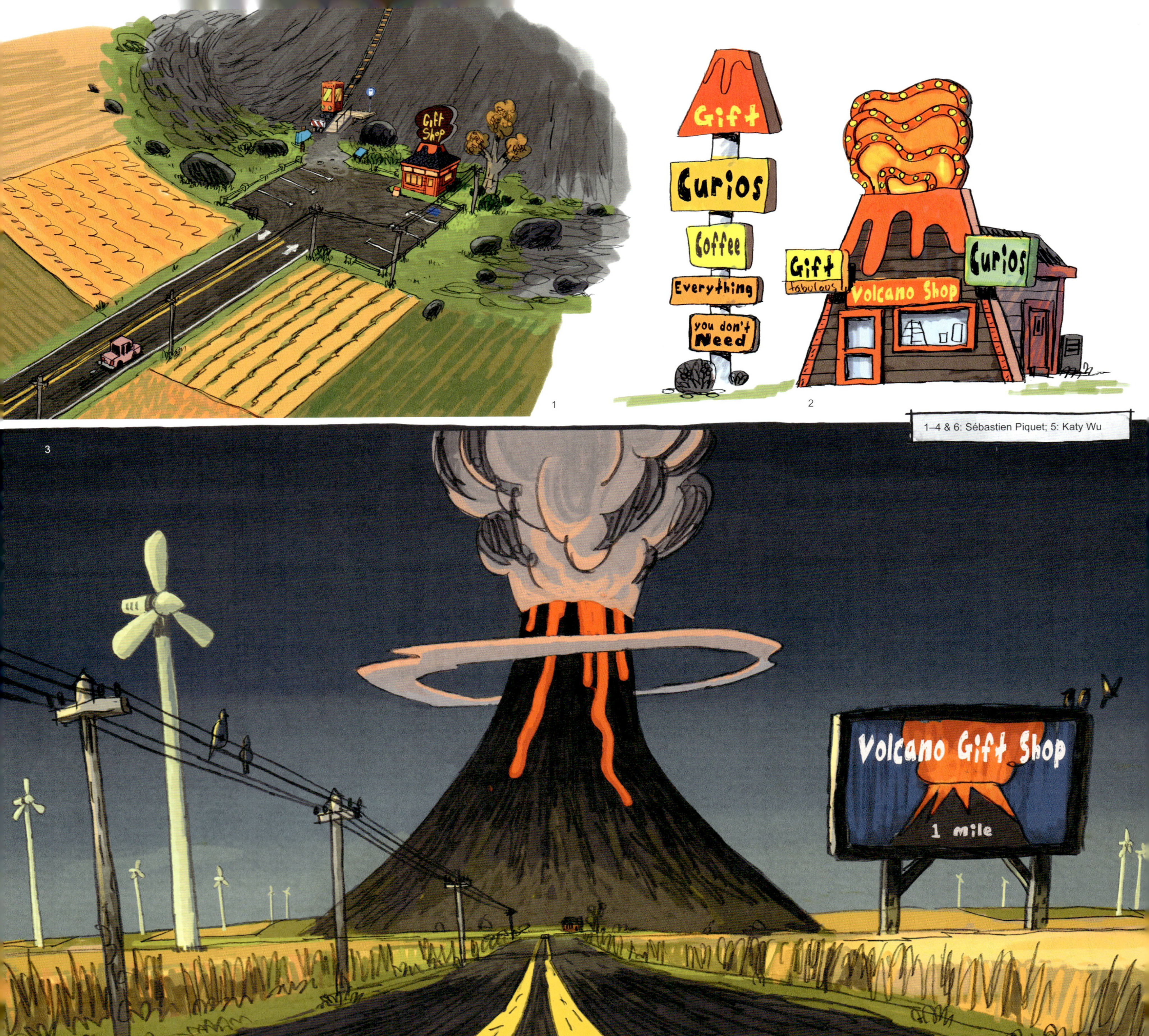

1
2
3
1–4 & 6: Sébastien Piquet; 5: Katy Wu

4

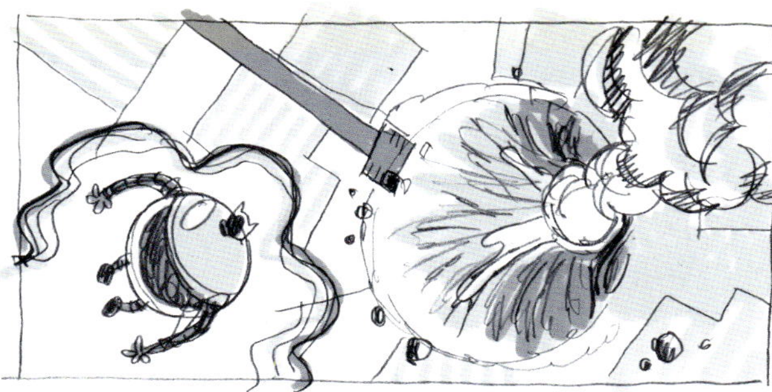

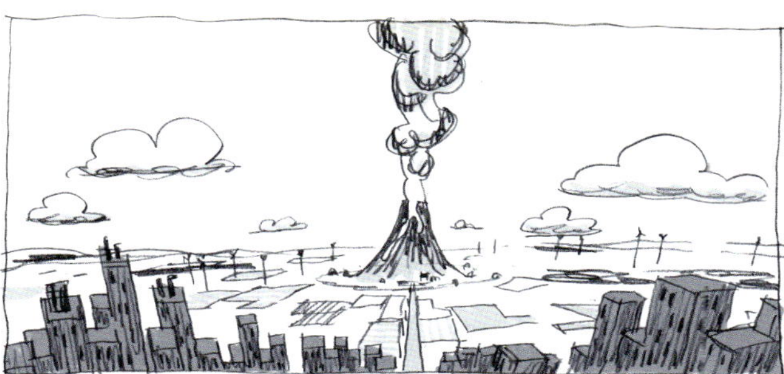

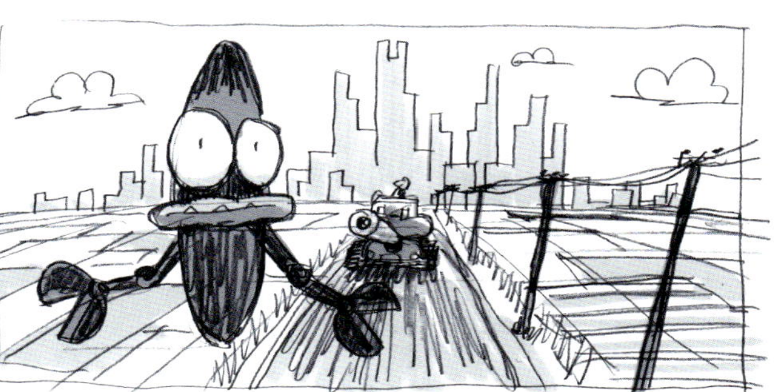

5

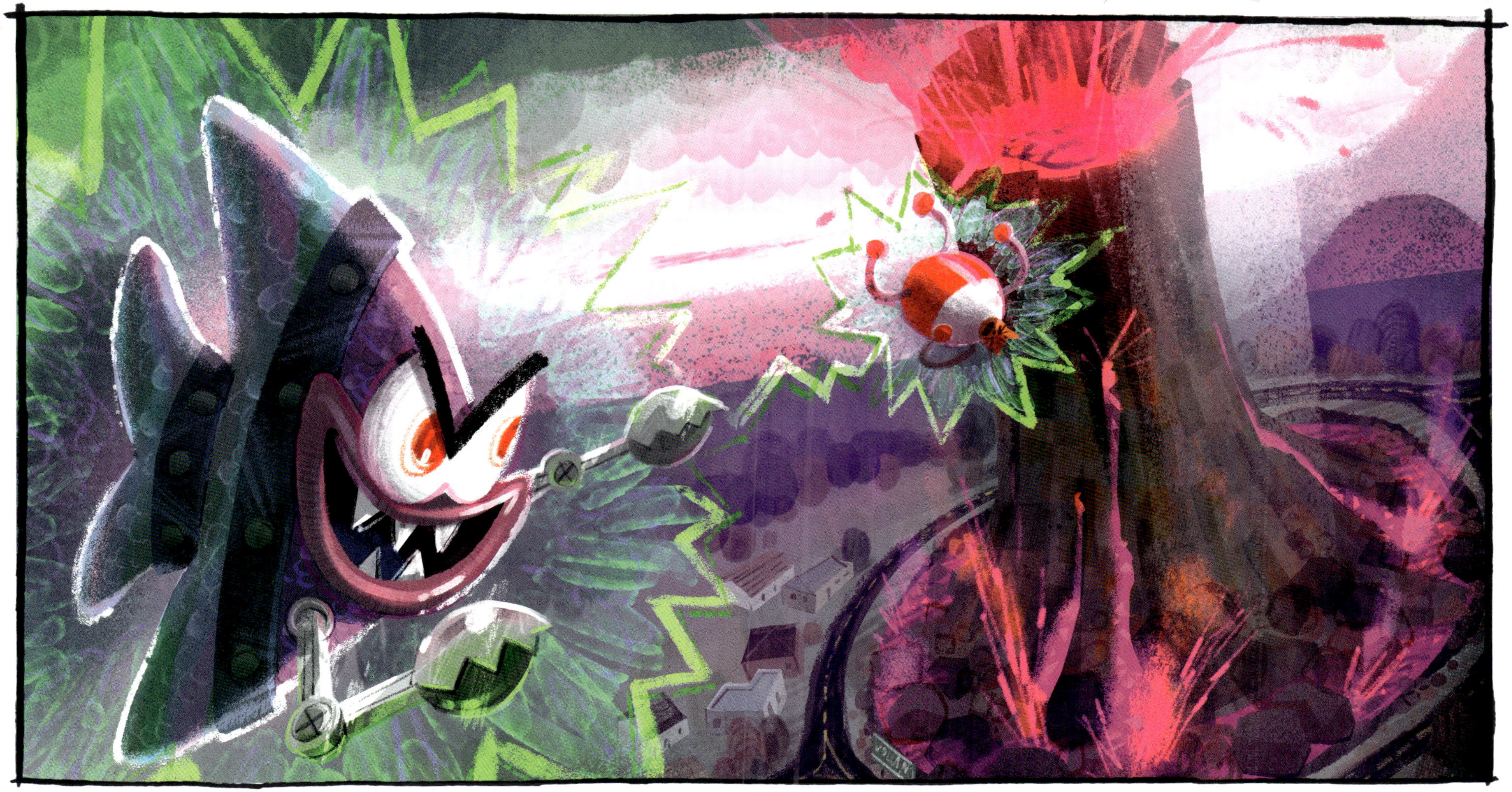

6

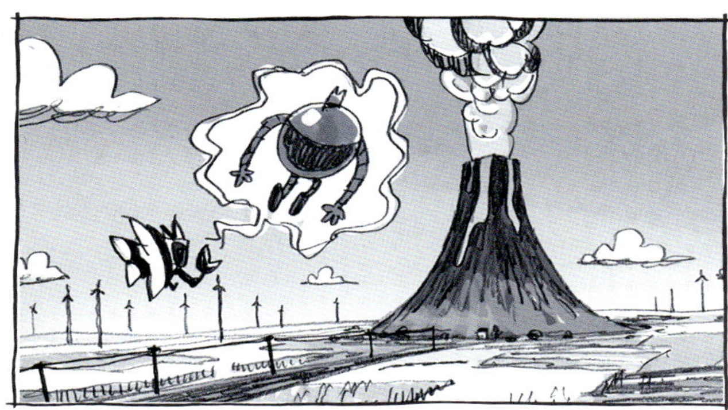

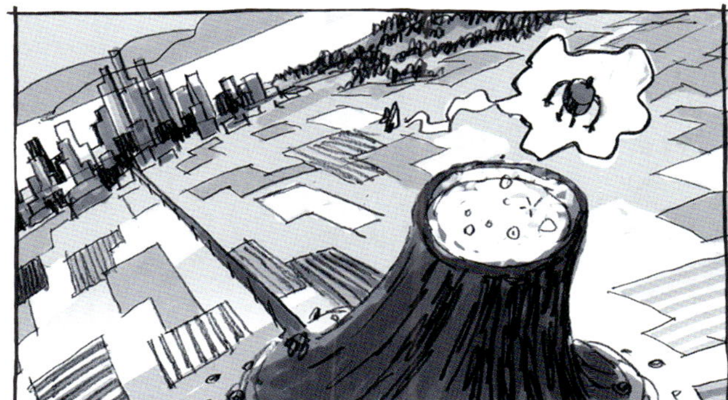

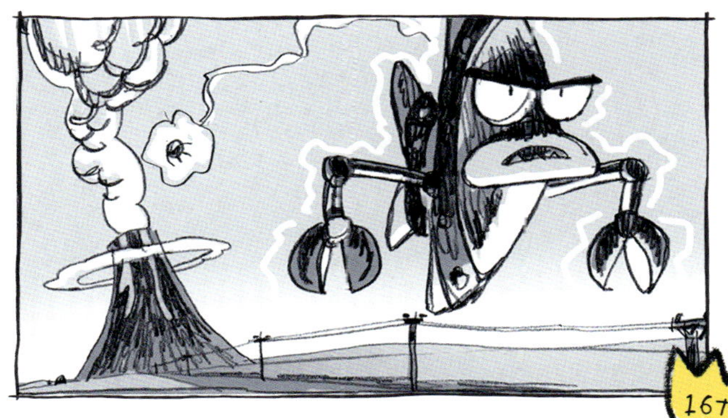

Conclusion: Every Dog Man Has His Day

"**Dog Man is a lot like me** because he jumps into situations with the best of intentions," says *Dog Man* creator Dav Pilkey in a promotional video made by the books' publisher, Scholastic. "He often messes things up—whether he's absent minded, distracted, or too overly enthusiastic. But fortunately, if your heart is in the right place, like Dog Man's heart is, usually things work out for the best."

The great news for fans of Pilkey's charming character and his world is that everyone at DreamWorks Animation who set out to adapt his book series into an animated movie had their hearts in the right place too. Fortunately, there were no evil cats or psychokinetic fish to wreak havoc on the project. As director Peter Hastings concludes, "We hope this special collection of art created for the movie and the insights of the team reflect the unmatched love and passion everyone shared for Dog Man and his adventures.

"I love the fact that the movie has these subtle messages about creativity, compassion, and generosity. There's a scene toward the end of the movie where Petey tells Li'l Petey, 'The world has a lot of problems, but it could never be a horrible place because you are in it.' Our movie is silly and funny, but I love the fact that it also sends out a very important and emotional message into the world."

1

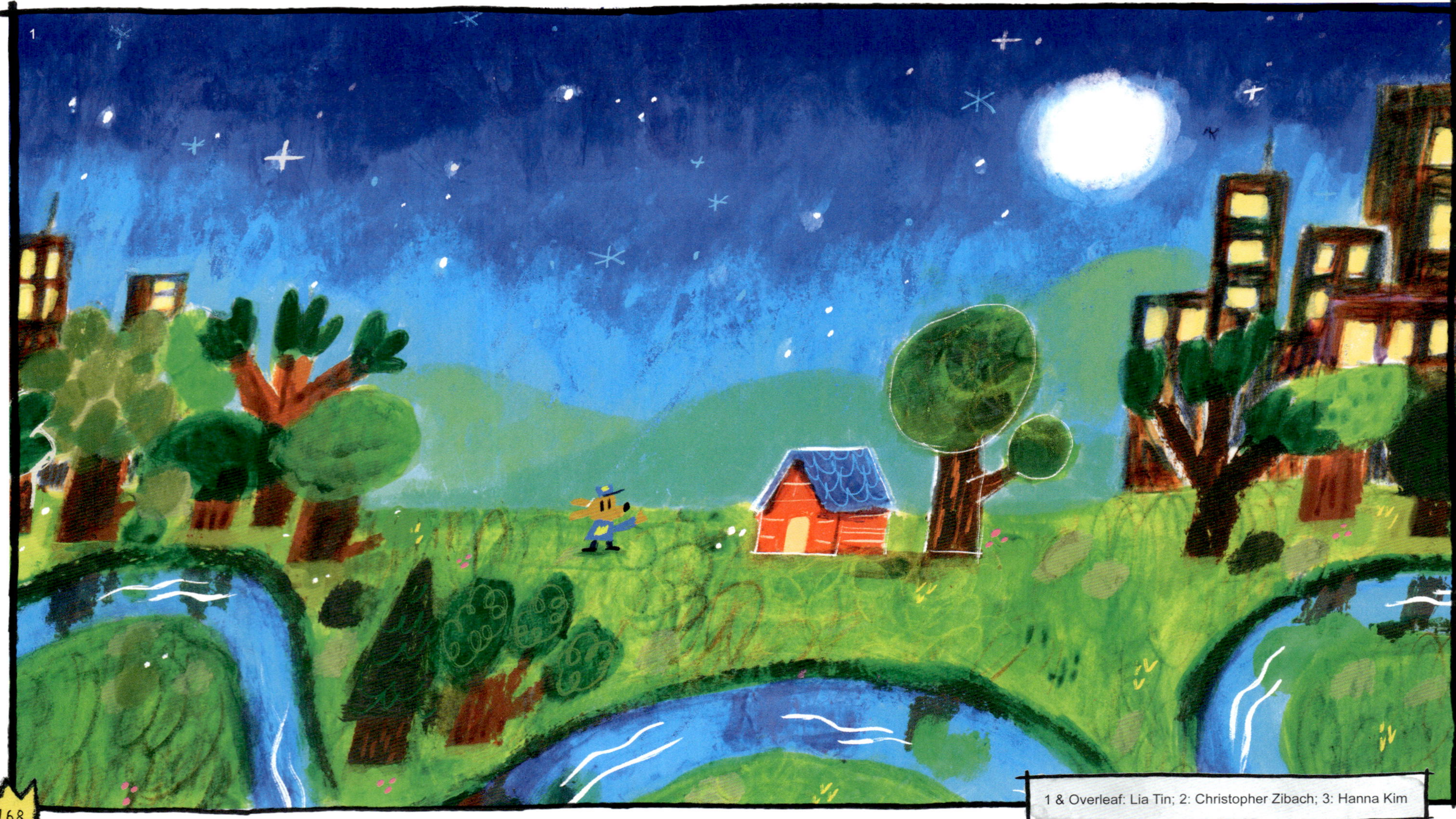

1 & Overleaf: Lia Tin; 2: Christopher Zibach; 3: Hanna Kim

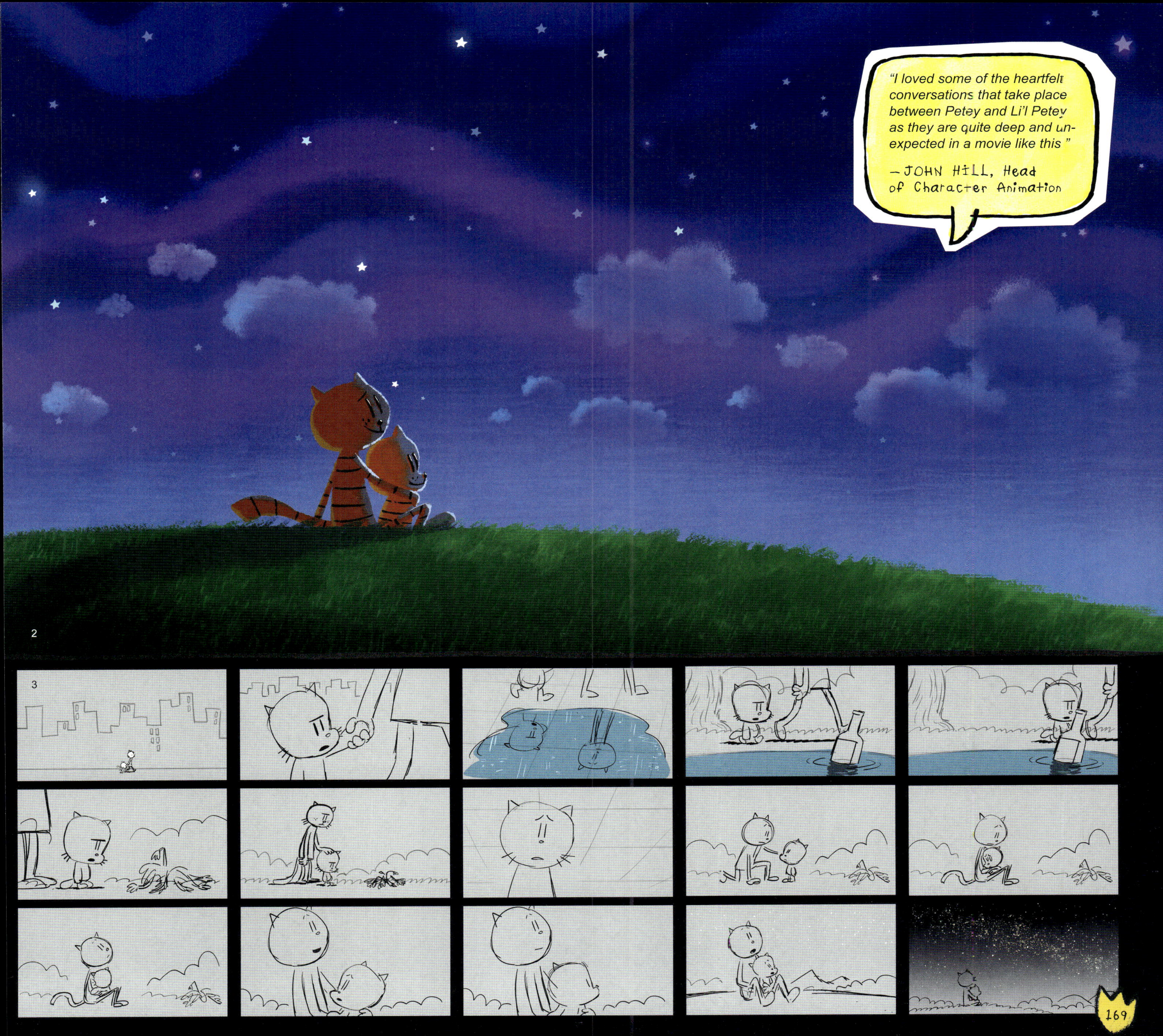
"I loved some of the heartfelt conversations that take place between Petey and Li'l Petey as they are quite deep and unexpected in a movie like this."
—JOHN HILL, Head of Character Animation

2

3

Afterword by Peter Hastings

"Wow. So great!" As the director of the *Dog Man* movie, I think I said this in every single art review that we did from the early visual development all the way through lighting (the last step). It was a privilege and a pleasure to work with a small but mighty team of artists under the direction of production designer Nate Wragg and art director Christopher Zibach, as well as head of story Anthony Zierhut, head of layout Scott Cullen, head of animation John Hill, editor Brian "Hoppy" Hopkins, and our friends at Jellyfish Pictures. I didn't really tell them what to do; I told them what the idea was and what I wanted it to feel like—and they ran with it. And in understanding the tone, everyone was able to apply their own style and personality to their work and have it all fit together.

The style of Dav Pilkey's Dog Man books—under the premise that they are created by two ten-year-olds—is simple and charming in a way that adds to both the comedy and emotion. So the approach was not to "reimagine" the style but to expand on it—to keep the simplicity of the characters and the charm in crooked lines and visible brushstrokes—but also bring a production sophistication, like reflections of metal and surfaces, to the picture. Early on we referred to this approach "high-end handmade."

And now it's so nice to see all this work together, the development of the look, and the tremendous output of these talented artists and proudly be able to look through this book and say, "Wow. So great!"

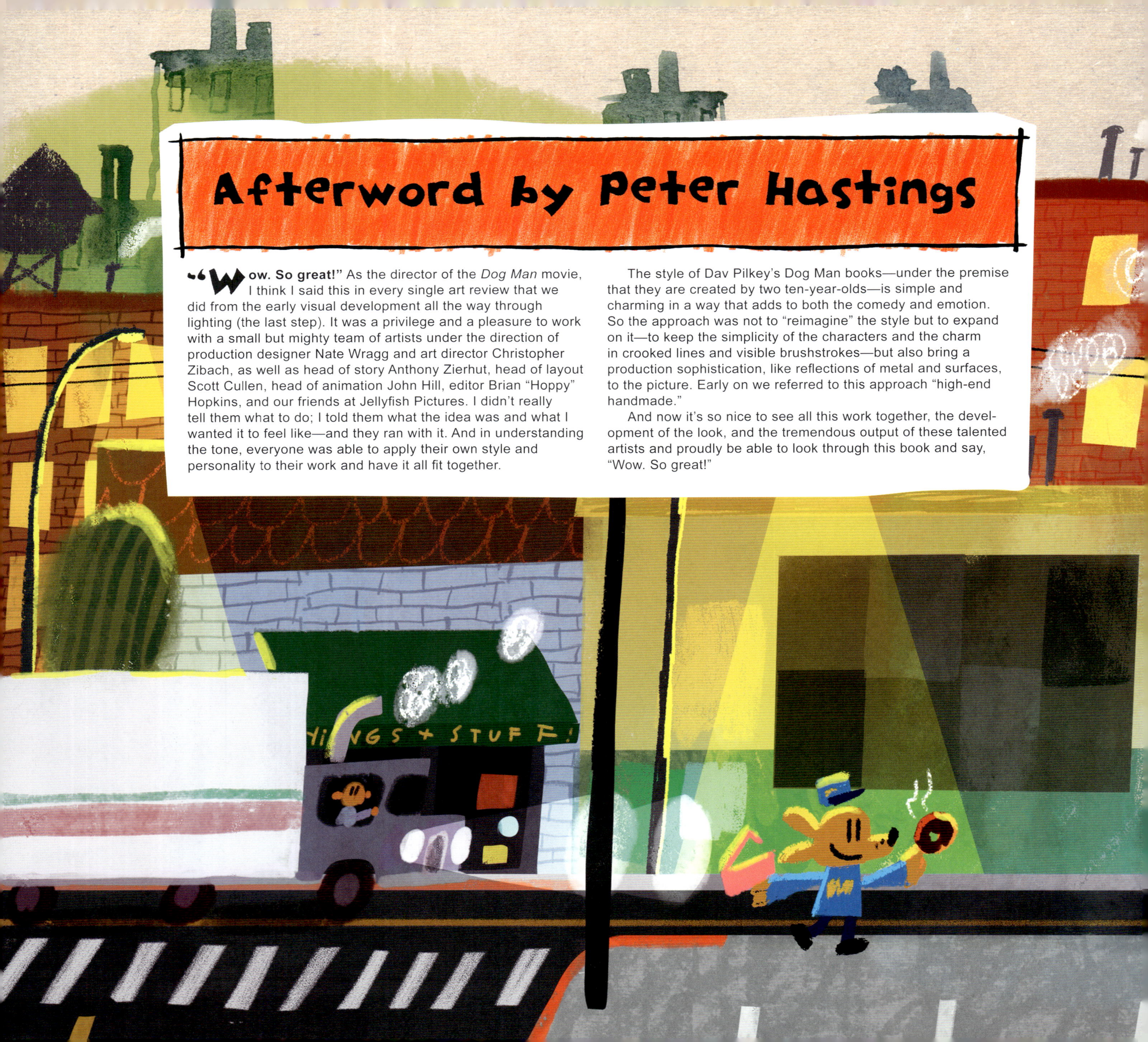

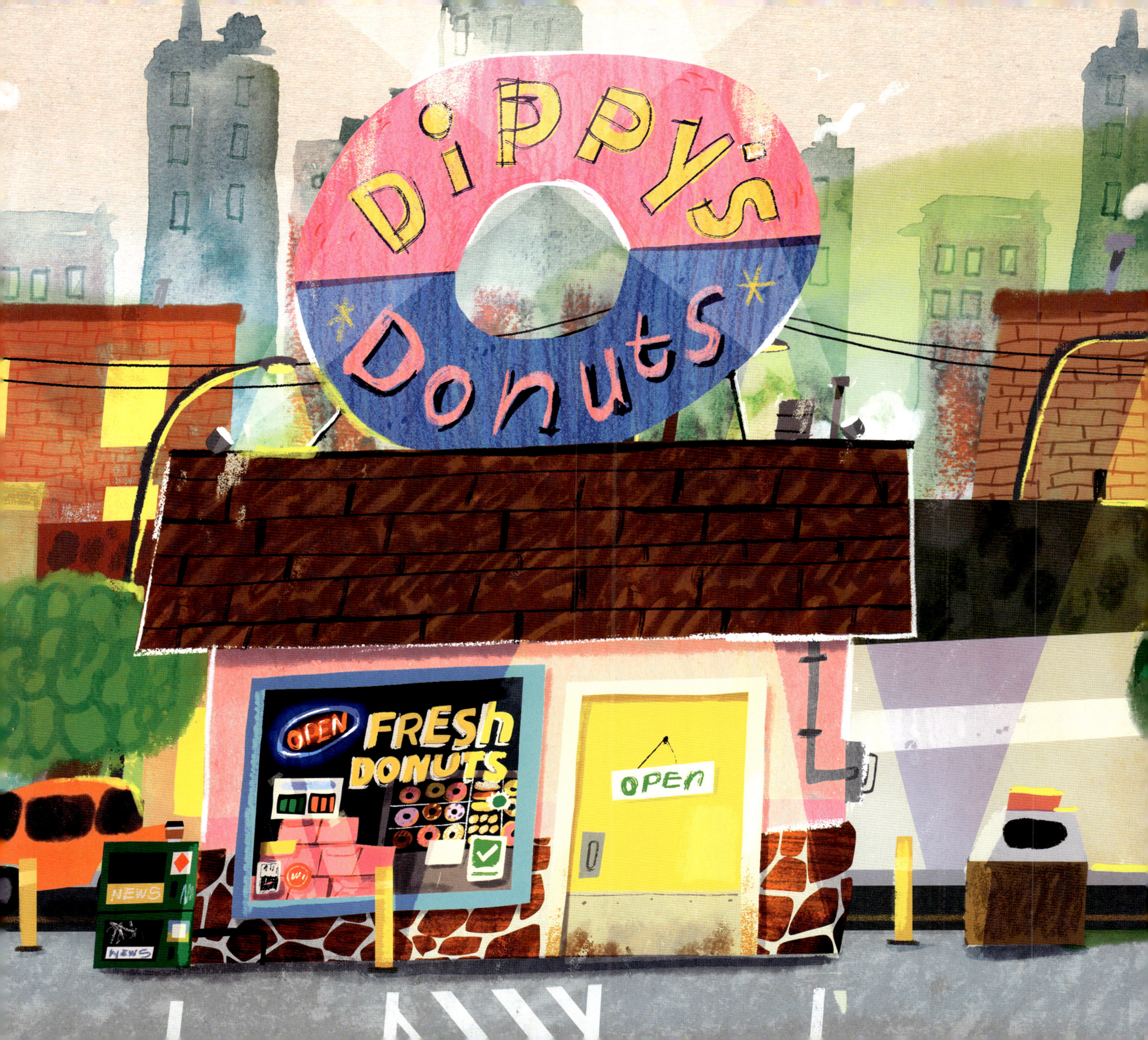
Dippy's
Donuts
OPEN
FRESh
DONUTS
OPEN
NEWS
NEWS

Da Supa Crew

DREAMWORKS ANIMATION
Sayah Amburgey
Kristina Anderson
Leda Annest
Taylor Aseere
David Badgerow
Marianne Bell
Jeremy Bernstein
Theophile Bondoux
Tom Bruno
Juan Pablo Bugarin
Katie Canadas
Nadiehzda Cardona
Zac Cavaliero
Yung-Lo Chang
Danny D. Clark
Shabrayia Cleaver
Shayna Cohen
Robert E. Crawford
Scott Cullen
Camryn Del Vecchio
Laura C. Denton
Mark Edwards
Cassandra Fanning
Karen Foster
Kitty Fung
Jorge Garcia
Mark Gillins
Zachary Gold
Juan Gonzalez
David Guo
Peter Hastings
Chris Heltzel
Felipe A. Hernández Jr.
John Hill
Brian “Hoppy” Hopkins
Alexander Hunt
Robert Huth
Brian Jefcoat
Karen Jeffers
Daria Khil
Hanna Kim
Amy Sun Kwa
Maarten Lemmens
Jillian Brooke Levy
David Lisbe
Matt Loman
Andy Long
Nick Lormand
Nicholas Manfredi
Bianca Margiotta
Noé Martínez
Kevin McCann
Jason McDade
Patrick McQuade
Justin Monnier
Josie Neylan
Ryan Noftall
Ellery Ortiz
Sébastien Piquet
Kaitlin Pollock
Reece Porter
Richard Ramazinski
Adam Rosette
Huong Lan Ross
Matthew D. Schmidt
Paul Schoeni
Carder Scholin
Aubin Schuler
Stan Seo
Randy Spahr
Daniel Tal
Marceline Tanguay
Lia Tin
Kathy Tran
Stephanie Ugo
Baptiste Van Opstal
Luis Vega
John Venzon
Samantha Wade
Brian Ward
Jason Wesche
Nate Wragg
Katy Wu
Vahe Yefremian
Christopher Zibach
Anthony Zierhut

JELLYFISH PICTURES
Hayley Adams
Joel Airebamen
Alex Alabadi
Shadia Ali
Makayla Anderson
Aymeric Arnaud
Rosie Ashforth
Alessandra Aucello
Paul Baaske
Arran Baker
Felix Balbas
Cédric Balet
Bianca Florina Bancila
Saul Barreto
Sreeparna Basu
Marion Bayard
Valentin Beaumont
Holly Bensley
Bernadi Matas Bergas
Elinor Bergman
Carina Bichler
Matthew Bilton
Tim Birks
Louise Blackwell
Roberta Bononi
Josué Borges Expósito
Emma Spruce Boronat
Alessandro Boschian-Pest
Roger Bosque
Benny Bovone
Joshua Luigi Bowen
James Boyle
Rhys Bradbury
Benjamin Brown
Nathan Brown
Kahu Burrows
Darren Byford
Chris Callow
Angel Cano
Anh Cao
Chris Carne
Ana Caro
Sam Derek Cassidy
Karen Castillo
Julia Chapman
Benjamin Cheong
Lucía Álvarez Cisneros
Rémi Colcombe
Stanley Cornwell
Richard Counsell
Adam Cracknell
Stephanie Croall
Emmanuel Cutillas
Virginia Daniele
Federica Darsie
Lucy Davies
Dale Davis
Alberto de la Guía Marín
Maddalena Delvecchio
Helen Dixon
Luke Dodd
Luca Doran
Dylan Duffy
Antoine Dupriez
Maxwell Durham
Oz Durose
Clélia Durris
Sunil Dutta
Maria Eduarda Mariano

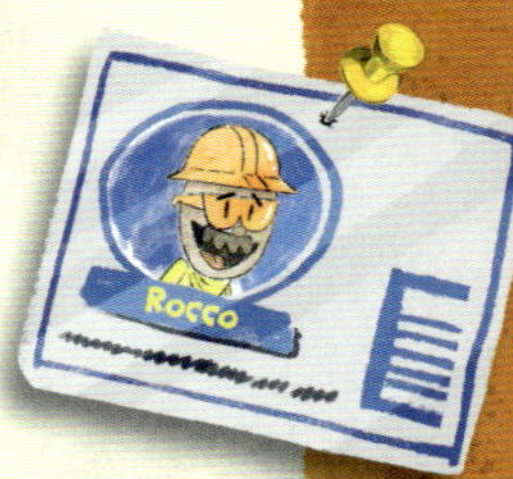

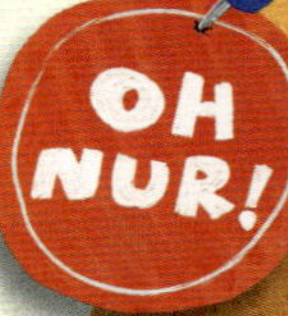

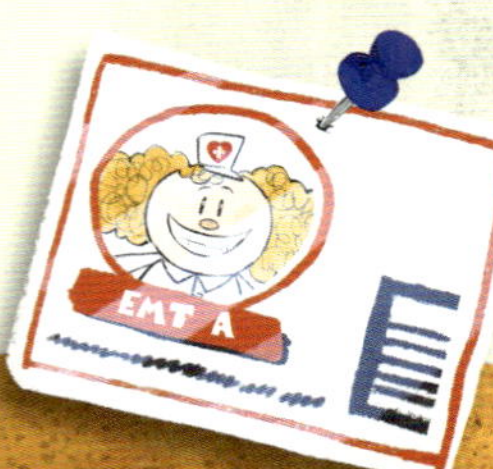

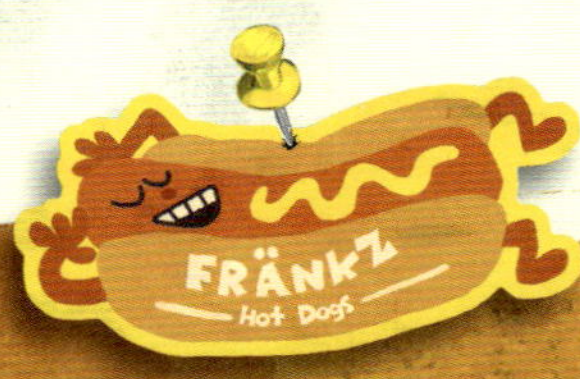

This spread: Christopher Zibach

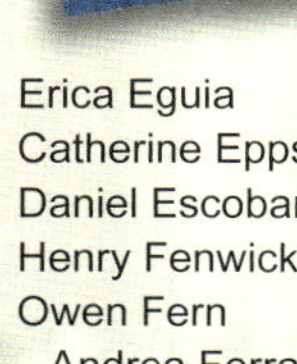

Erica Eguia
Catherine Epps
Daniel Escobar
Henry Fenwick
Owen Fern
Andrea Ferrara
Francesco Ferraro
Skye Fisher
Nathan Fitzpatrick
Poppy Flett
Louis Flores
Katie Rose Foster
Lilian Fu
Jaime Fuerte
Farzana Gafoor
Yaniv Garber
Èlia Garcia Amores
Jessica Garment
Lukas Gecas
Nicholas Georgeou
Tim Gibson
Paula C. Gödecke
Raúl Gómez Díez
Celia Blazquez Gomez
Bruno Got
Giles Greenhalgh
Fabio Gubetti
Ethan Guerin
Karis Handy
Peter Hargan
Keira Harrell
Callum Harwood
Sean Hedman
Teresa Hernández
Claire Louise Hodges
Ricky Honmong
Imogen Horn
James Hughes
Tamara Kalisilira
Abhishek Karmakar
Berkay Kasin

Raphael Kennedy
Jon Kiefert
Michael Klim
Aziz Koçanaoğulları
Diana Kontrimaviciute
Thomas Kristensen
Victorine L'écu
Daniele La Mura
India Alice Lane
Zoe Arabella Lane
Fran Lara
Gautier Laudren
Matthew Lee
Ada Leung
Laura Leveque
Greta Levickyte
Rachel Lewis
Yu Rong Lin
Natalie Llewellyn
Mike Lockett
Suzanne Lokker
Luis Galindo Lopez
Daniel Lotter
Joao Lourenco
Kelly Lowe
Stefania Luise
Alex Luna
Marta Macedo
Simon Maddocks
Aceysele Madorran Armas
Beverly Maguire
Haidi Marburger
Poppy Marlow
Sabrina Martins
Gaël Matchabelli
Rory McGrath
Alfonso Badia Melis
Chrissy Metge
Maria Vilaseca Miguel
Divyasa Mishra
Frank Morales

Julia Fortin Moreau
Marion Morgante
Anne Moth
Benjamin Murray
Ryan Narvaez
Matei Neagoe Focsa
Samir Necib
Will Newis
Liam Offord
John Ogden
Daniel Olah
Daniela de Osma Arreciado
Tyrone Owens
Ben Ozeri
Christopher Page
Tom Pastorello
Leopoldine Perdrix
Dennis Petkov
Paul Phippen
Davide Pieropan
Alex Pilalis
Andrea Pinchera
Samuel Pinhorne
Arnaud Pitois
Siobhan Platten
Paweł Pohnke
Emma Porter
Katie Prentice
Arnold Pryada
Zac Rae
Chloe Randall
John Ray
Sara Rebuli
James Robinson
Xavier Roca Crespo
Noel Rodriguez
Brenda Ximena Roldan Romero
Eleonore Rolewski
David Rollinson
Sergio Roque Guevara
Julia Sadler
Chester Sampson

Elisa Sanguin
Paola Santoro
Natalie Scott
Shaun Scott
Romain Bivar Segurado
Jordan Sewell
Katie Shacklady
Azmae Shahzad
Paul Singh
Jared Smith
Bebe Solabis
Salvatore Sorvillo
Andy Spilsted
Mark Spokes
Daniel Stenhouse
Jason Stewart-Richardson
Anthony Tang
Marcus Taylor
Alex Thorn
Emma Townsend
Jamie Tremelling
Andrea Trovato
Heather Truman
Barbara Tucci
Sandeep Tuladhar
Joan Valdivielso
Thomas Vaughan
Sarah von Fersen
Callum Walters
Lucy Ward
Sam Webster
Owen Williams
Hannah Wong
Ayush Yadav
Sahyog Yadav
Mert Yildiz
Summer Young
Athanasios Zagkliveris
Daniele Zannone
Asier Lizaso Zelaia

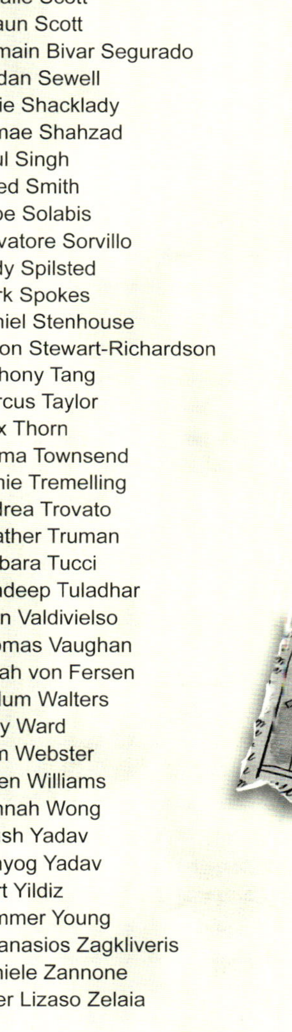

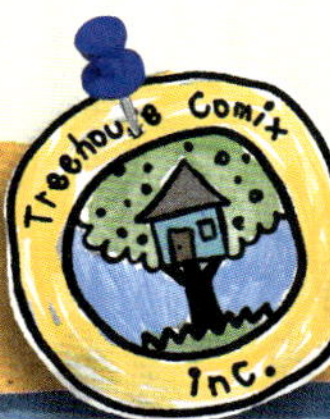

DreamWorks Animation would like to express a deep gratitude to the entire crew of *Dog Man*, who poured love into every frame of this beautiful movie and every piece of art on these pages.

This book would not have been possible without the outstanding leadership team and creative contributions of Margie Cohn, Kristin Lowe, Chris Kuser, Karen Foster, Peter Hastings, Dav Pilkey, Nate Wragg, Christopher Zibach, Bianca Olivencia, Laura Denton, Jill Levy, Kristina Anderson, Adria Munnerlyn, Stephanie Kent, Courtenay Palaski, Jerry Schmitz, Nayiri Nazarian, Michael Vollman, Alyssa Cardenas, Joey DeMers, Ramin Zahed, and Scott Seiffert.

Our appreciation also extends to the great Cameron + Company team of Chris Gruener, Jan Hughes, Krista Keplinger, and Iain R. Morris.

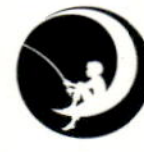

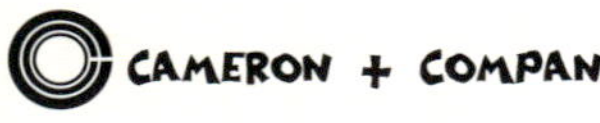

an imprint of ABRAMS

CREATIVE DIRECTOR & DESIGNER:
Iain R. Morris
MANAGING EDITOR: Jan Hughes
EDITORIAL ASSISTANT: Krista Keplinger

Library of Congress Control Number: 2023949947

ISBN: 978-1-4197-7628-1

10 9 8 7 6 5 4 3 2

Printed and bound in Canada

This spread: Katy Wu; Overleaf: Lia Tin

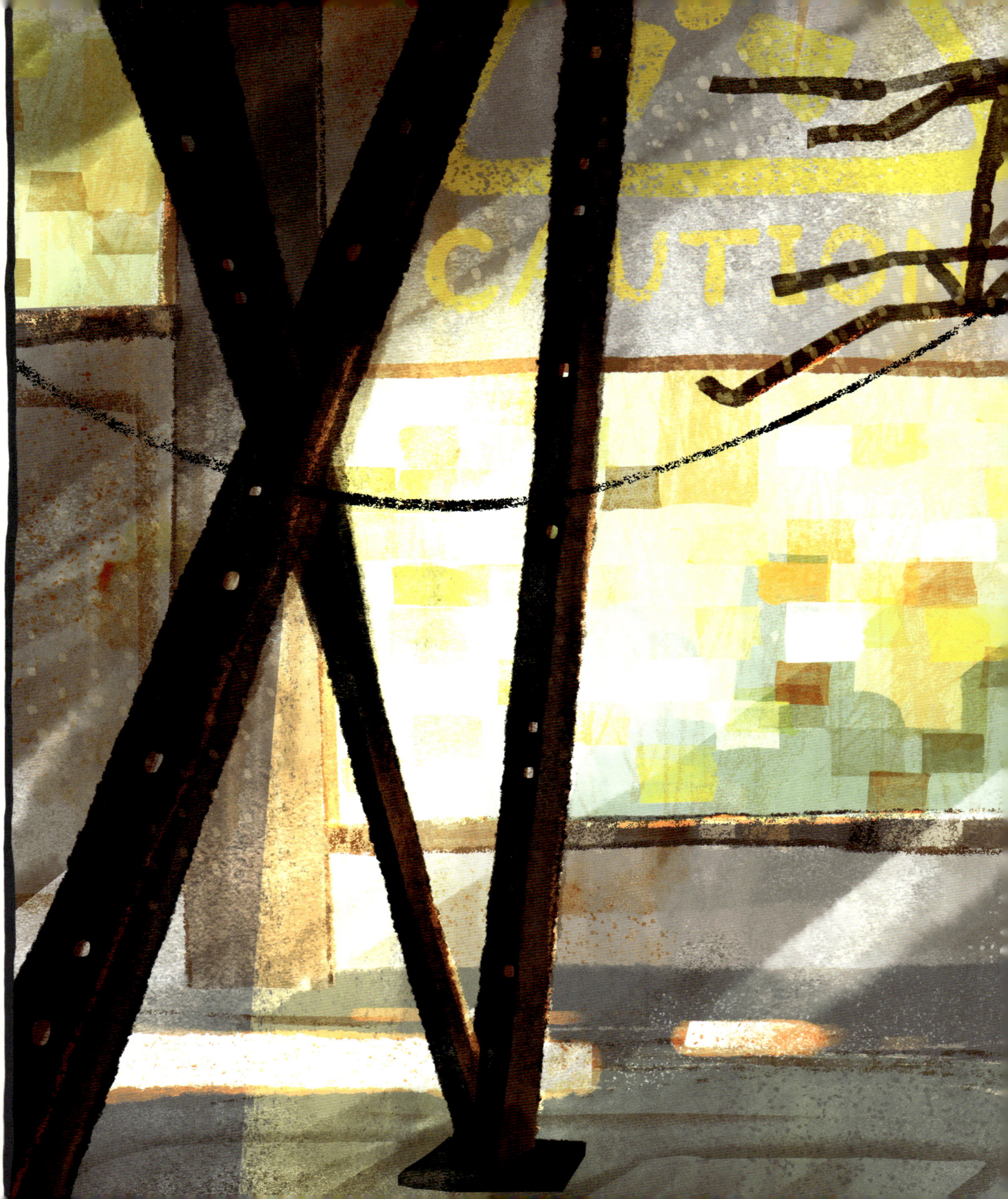

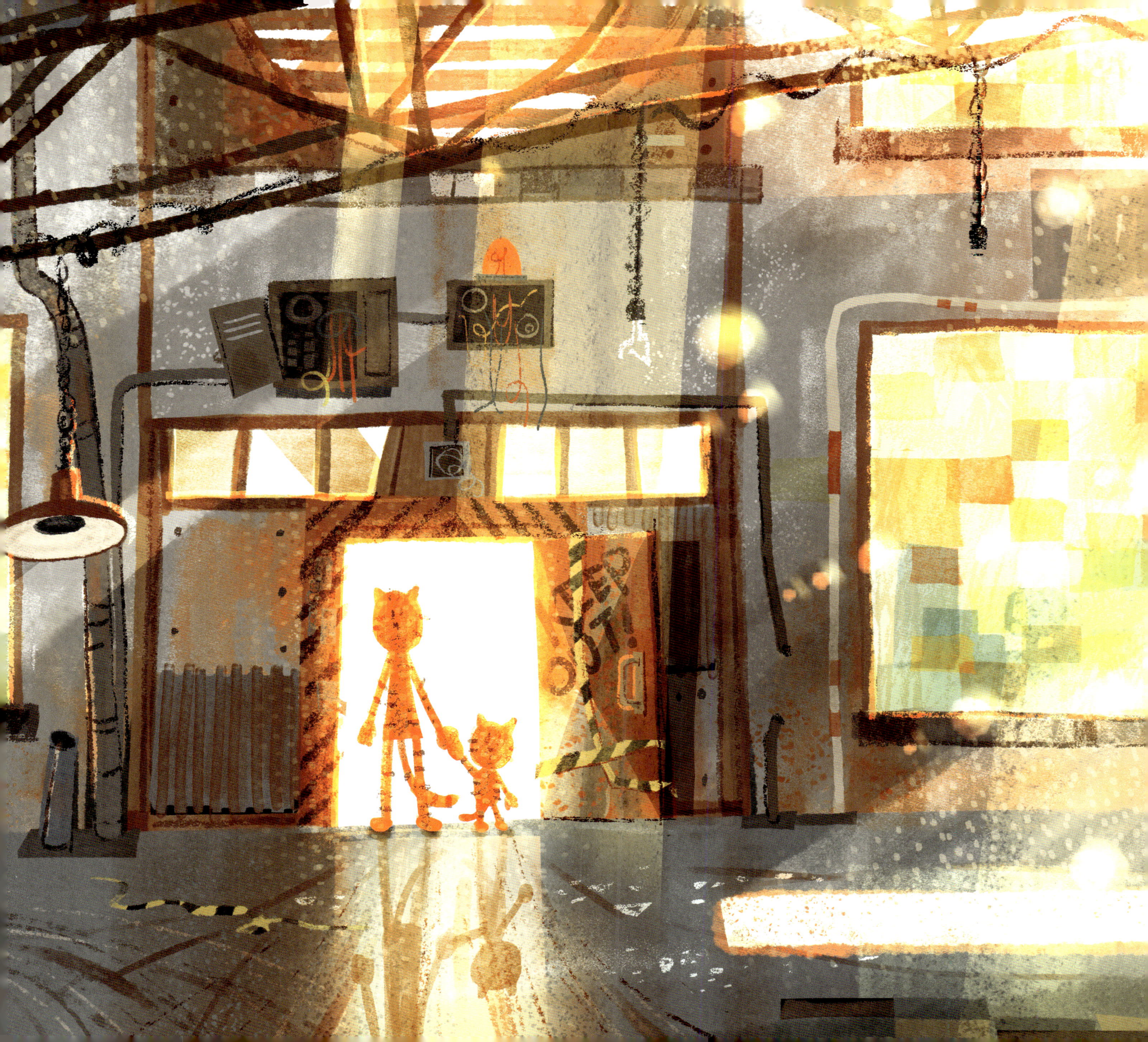
OUT!

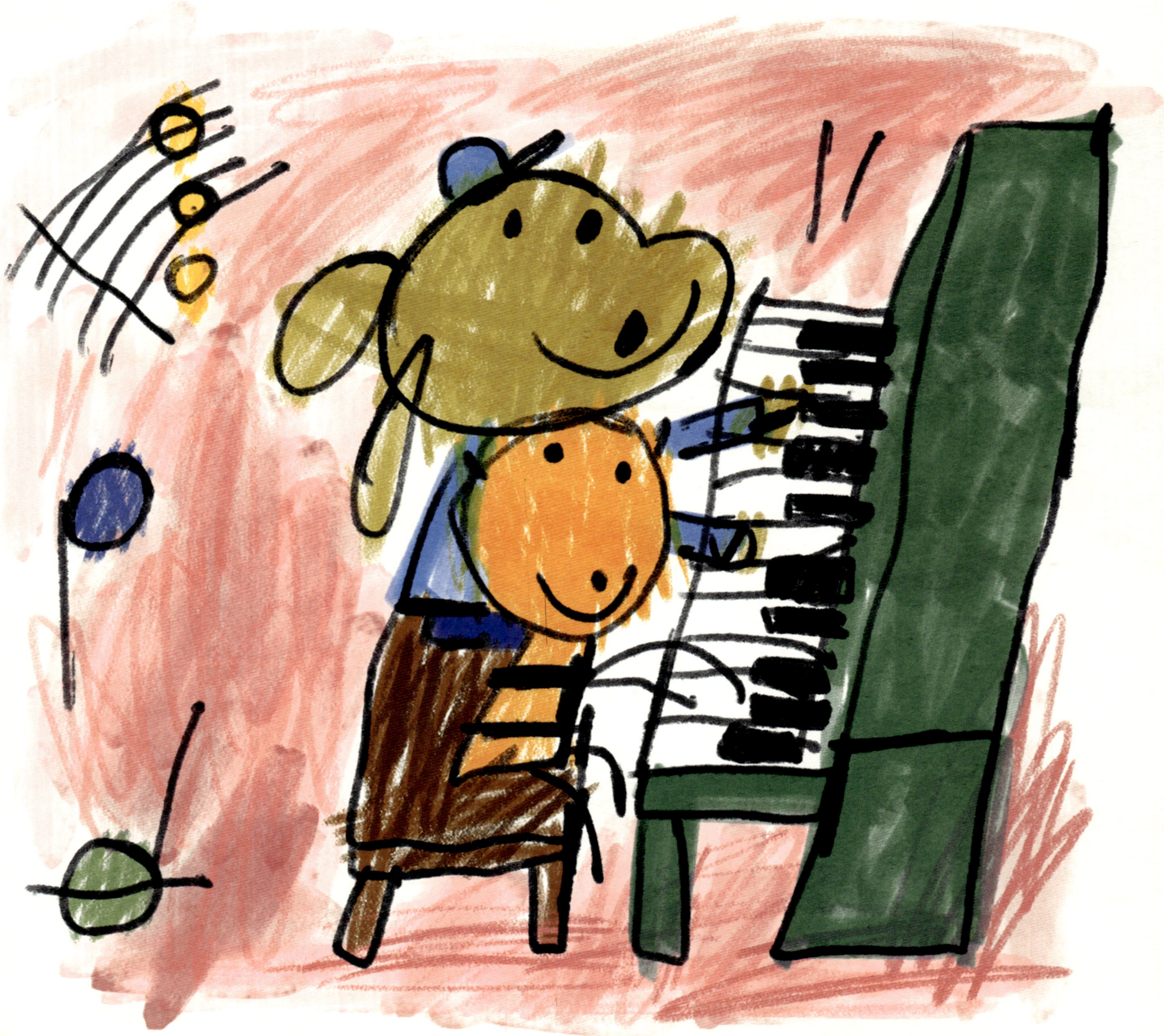

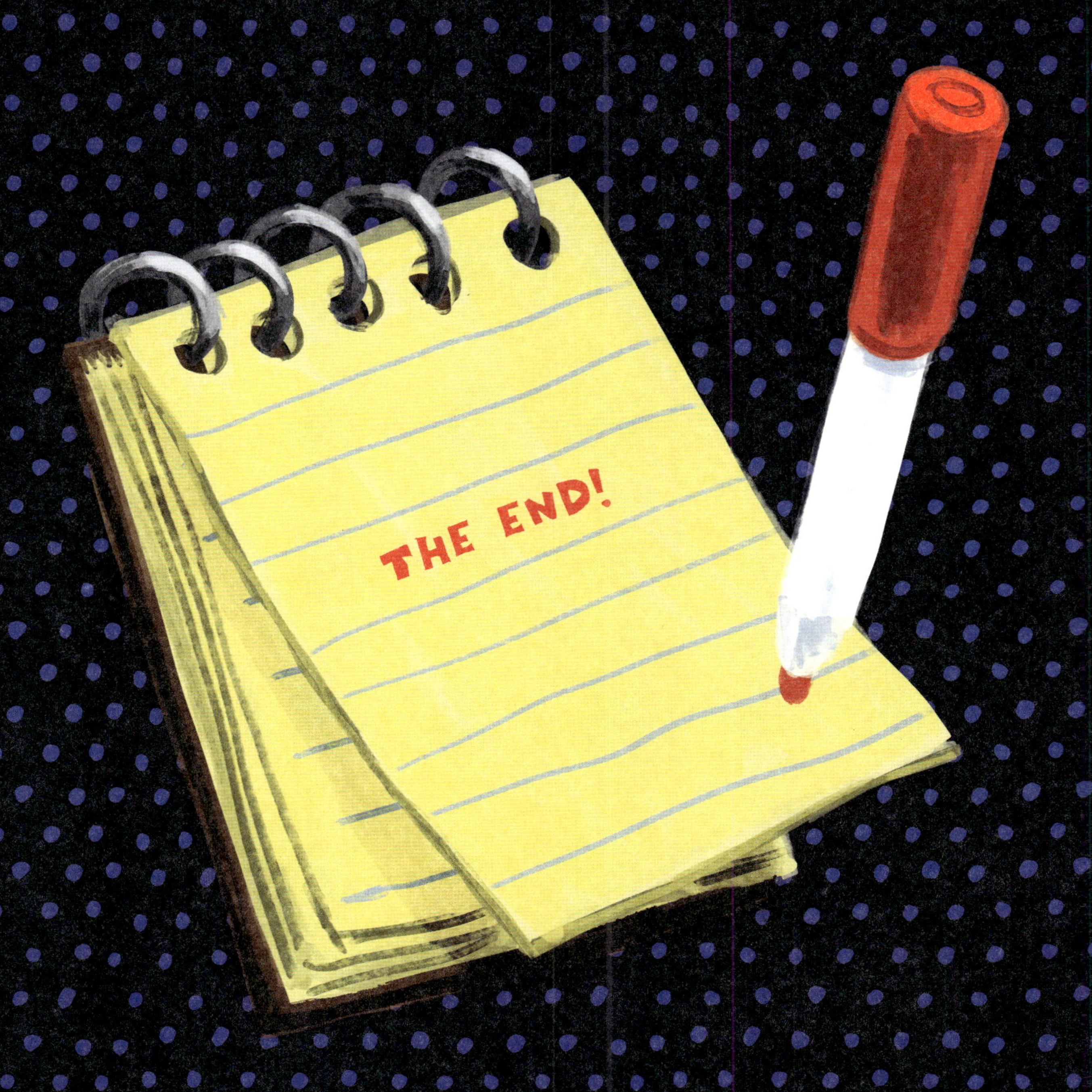
THE END!

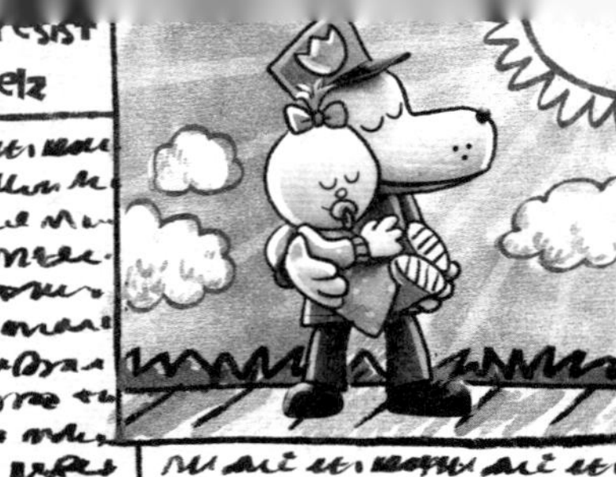

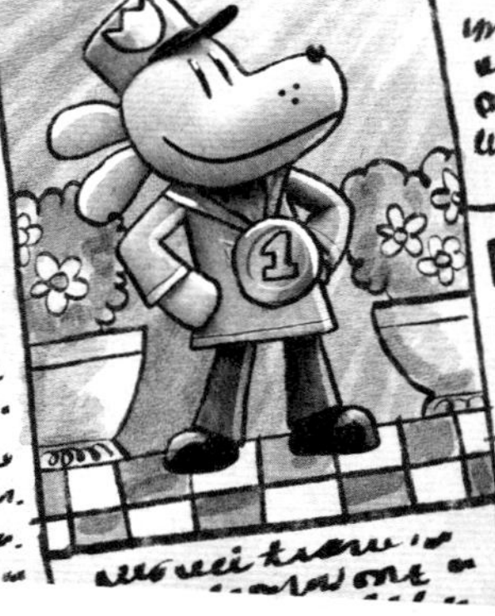

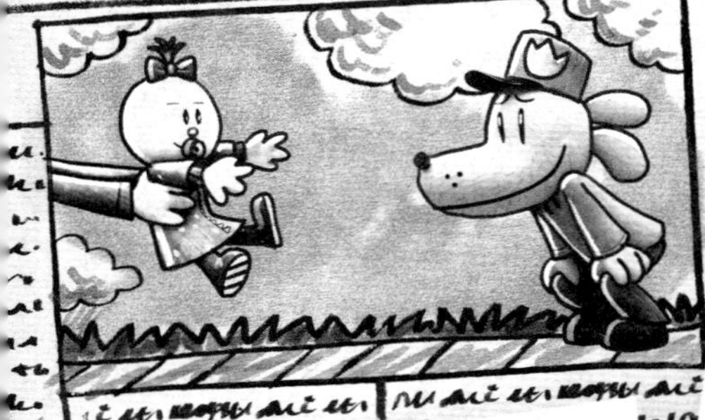

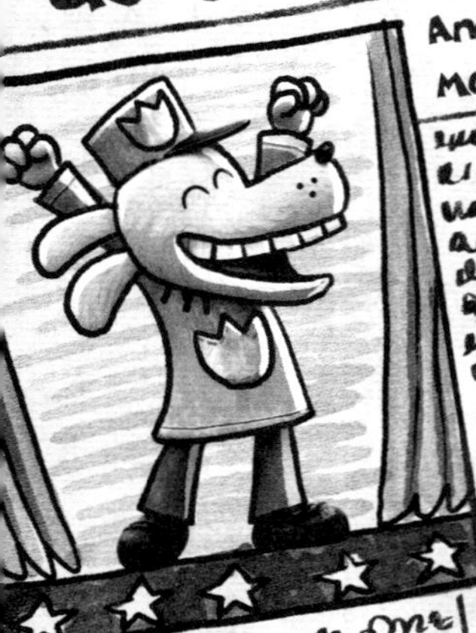

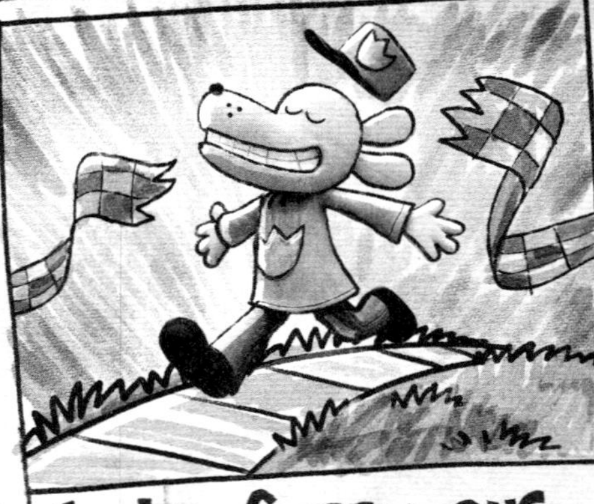

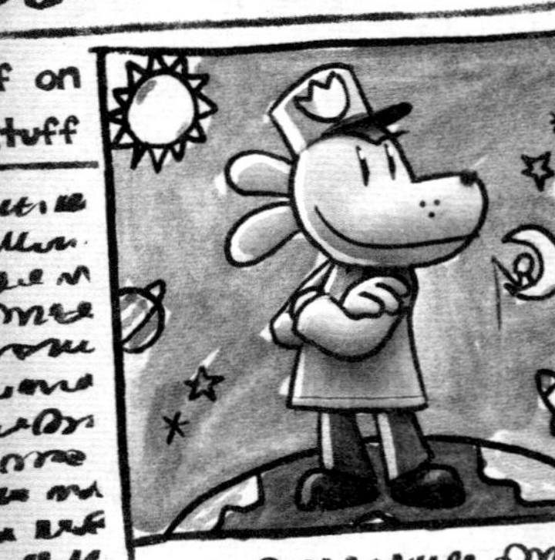

OHKAY CITY

ANOTHERDAY 11, 2024

DA TIMES

DOG+MAN=SUPER HERO

Who doesn't love dog man?

Sarah Hatoff
World's greatest reporter

What is up Dog!?? No Seriously!?

EVEN MORE?

Bagel actually Donut

Chapter 3

Page ?!★

DA TIMES

OG NABS SECOND 1ST

MAN DOG STILL WINNING

IS THIS TOO MUCH SHOW BOATING!?

Bugs...More Legs Than Humans

ANOTHERDAY 11, 2024

DA TIMES

ERZ TRUST DOG MAN

ANOTHERDAY 11, 2024

DA TIMES

ST PLACE IS THE ONLY PLAC

mpetition es up!?

OHKAY CITY

CHIE

Dog man unstopp

ANOTHERDAY 11, 2024

TIMES

does it again!?

Another Dog Man Story.

Early Real Bummer

CANINE UNIT

officials non plussed.

Cats furry-ous

ANOTHERDAY 11, 2024

DA TIMES

OBAL DOG MAN DAY

ff on stuff

Car Goes Vroom!

DAD'

OHKAY

VILLAIN